Organizational Auditing and Assurance in the Digital Age

Rui Pedro Marques
University of Aveiro, Portugal

Carlos Santos
University of Aveiro, Portugal

Helena Inácio
University of Aveiro, Portugal

A volume in the Advances in Finance, Accounting, and Economics (AFAE) Book Series

IGI Global
DISSEMINATOR OF KNOWLEDGE

Published in the United States of America by
IGI Global
Business Science Reference (an imprint of IGI Global)
701 E. Chocolate Avenue
Hershey PA, USA 17033
Tel: 717-533-8845
Fax: 717-533-8661
E-mail: cust@igi-global.com
Web site: http://www.igi-global.com

Library of Congress Cataloging-in-Publication Data

Names: Marques, Rui Pedro Figueiredo, editor. | Santos, Carlos, 1953- editor. | Inacio, Helena, 1966- editor.
Title: Organizational auditing and assurance in the digital age / Rui Pedro Marques, Carlos Santos, and Helena Inacio, editors.
Description: Hershey, PA : Business Science Reference, [2019]
Identifiers: LCCN 2018024609| ISBN 9781522573562 (hardcover) | ISBN 9781522573579 (ebook)
Subjects: LCSH: Auditing, Internal. | Information technology--Auditing.
Classification: LCC HF5668.25 .O74 2019 | DDC 657/.458--dc23 LC record available at https://lccn.loc.gov/2018024609

This book is published in the IGI Global book series Advances in Finance, Accounting, and Economics (AFAE) (ISSN: 2327-5677; eISSN: 2327-5685)

British Cataloguing in Publication Data
A Cataloguing in Publication record for this book is available from the British Library.

Advances in Finance, Accounting, and Economics (AFAE) Book Series

Ahmed Driouchi
Al Akhawayn University, Morocco

ISSN:2327-5677
EISSN:2327-5685

Mission

In our changing economic and business environment, it is important to consider the financial changes occurring internationally as well as within individual organizations and business environments. Understanding these changes as well as the factors that influence them is crucial in preparing for our financial future and ensuring economic sustainability and growth.

The **Advances in Finance, Accounting, and Economics (AFAE)** book series aims to publish comprehensive and informative titles in all areas of economics and economic theory, finance, and accounting to assist in advancing the available knowledge and providing for further research development in these dynamic fields.

Coverage

- Managerial Accounting
- Economics of Innovation and Knowledge
- Economics of Migration and Spatial Mobility
- E-finance
- Ethics in Accounting and Finance
- Risk Analysis and Management
- Field Research
- Fiscal Policy
- Economic Theory
- Economics of Agriculture and Biotechnology

IGI Global is currently accepting manuscripts for publication within this series. To submit a proposal for a volume in this series, please contact our Acquisition Editors at Acquisitions@igi-global.com or visit: http://www.igi-global.com/publish/.

The Advances in Finance, Accounting, and Economics (AFAE) Book Series (ISSN 2327-5677) is published by IGI Global, 701 E. Chocolate Avenue, Hershey, PA 17033-1240, USA, www.igi-global.com. This series is composed of titles available for purchase individually; each title is edited to be contextually exclusive from any other title within the series. For pricing and ordering information please visit http://www.igi-global.com/book-series/advances-finance-accounting-economics/73685. Postmaster: Send all address changes to above address.

Titles in this Series

For a list of additional titles in this series, please visit: www.igi-global.com/book-series

Planning and Analyzing Foreign Direct Investment Projects Emerging Research and Opportunities
Halil Sarıaslan (Başkent University, Turkey)
Business Science Reference • copyright 2019 • 338pp • H/C (ISBN: 9781522576969) • US $215.00 (our price)

Maintaining Financial Stability in Times of Risk and Uncertainty
Abhishek Behl (Indian Institute of Technology Bombay, India) and Sushma Nayak (Symbiosis International University (Deemed), India)
Business Science Reference • copyright 2019 • 377pp • H/C (ISBN: 9781522572084) • US $265.00 (our price)

Global Trends of Modernization in Budgeting and Finance
Denis Ushakov (Suan Sunandha Rajabhat University, Thailand)
Business Science Reference • copyright 2019 • 354pp • H/C (ISBN: 9781522577607) • US $215.00 (our price)

Corporate Insolvency Law and Bankruptcy Reforms in the Global Economy
Amit Kashyap (Nirma University, India)
Business Science Reference • copyright 2019 • 261pp • H/C (ISBN: 9781522555414) • US $185.00 (our price)

Time Bank as a Complementary Economic System Emerging Research and Opportunities
Lukas Valek (University of Hradec Kralove, Czech Republic) and Vladimir Bures (University of Hradec Kralove, Czech Republic)
Business Science Reference • copyright 2019 • 208pp • H/C (ISBN: 9781522569749) • US $175.00 (our price)

Economic Dynamics of Global Energy Geopolitics
Ahmet Salih Ikiz (Muğla Sıtkı Koçman University, Turkey)
Engineering Science Reference • copyright 2019 • 305pp • H/C (ISBN: 9781522542032) • US $195.00 (our price)

Co-Manufacturing and New Economic Paradigms
Giulio Focardi (Osun WES, Italy) and Lorenza Salati (Osun WES, Italy)
Business Science Reference • copyright 2019 • 217pp • H/C (ISBN: 9781522570899) • US $185.00 (our price)

Handbook of Research on Microfinancial Impacts on Women Empowerment, Poverty, and Inequality
Ramesh Chandra Das (Katwa College, India)
Business Science Reference • copyright 2019 • 452pp • H/C (ISBN: 9781522552406) • US $275.00 (our price)

IGI Global
DISSEMINATOR OF KNOWLEDGE

701 East Chocolate Avenue, Hershey, PA 17033, USA
Tel: 717-533-8845 x100 • Fax: 717-533-8661
E-Mail: cust@igi-global.com • www.igi-global.com

Kátia Lemos, *Polytechnic Institute of Cávado and Ave, Portugal*
Antonio Minguillón-Roy, *Audit Office of the Community of Valencia, Spain*
Radiah Othman, *Massey University, New Zealand*
David Ortiz-Rodríguez, *University of Granada, Spain*
Rui Robalo, *School of Management and Technology of Santarém, Portugal*
Nedal Sawan, *Liverpool Business School, UK*
Miguel Mira da Silva, *Instituto Superior Técnico, Portugal*

Table of Contents

Section 2
Impact of Technological Development on the Audit Function

Section 3
Fraud and Forensic Audit

Detailed Table of Contents

The main purpose of this chapter is to analyze the relationship between internal and external audit and its effect on external audit fees, through a questionnaire addressed to the external auditors of Portugal and Spain. It obtained 131 answers for Portugal and 149 answers for Spain. According to the results, the competencies and characteristics of internal auditors, as well as the type of activities performed by them and the communication between internal and external auditors, have a significant influence on the decision of using the internal audit work. However, the Portuguese external auditors do not consider this influence to be so significant that it affects the number of substantive tests, the quality of external audit, and external audit fees. However, for Spanish auditors using internal audits decreases the planned hours, the number of control and substantive tests, and improves external audit quality, but does not reflect in the fees to be charged to the client.

The purpose of this chapter is to analyze the effect that corporate governance measures have in external audit fees in two countries where this matter is not much developed: Portugal and Spain. The analysis includes a sample of 39 listed companies on the Portuguese Stock Exchange and 104 listed companies on the Spanish Stock Exchanges for the years 2013 to 2015 using an OLS regression model. For the Spanish sample, the results show that the capital hold by the Board of Directors influence negatively external audit fees. The results are in accordance with the supplier perspective which states that better corporate governance practices decrease the control risk and, consequently, audit fees. On the other hand, the Board of Directors' diligence also affected external audit fees but positively, that is, the greater the number of meetings the greater the demand for an audit with quality which result in higher fees charged (demand perspective). For the Portuguese sample it can be observed that corporate governance characteristics do not affect external audit fees.

The audit expectation gap (AEG) is present in society and, while there, will encourage discrediting the auditors. Given the seriousness of this situation, several solutions have been pointed out, one of which is to promote audit education. The aim of this chapter is to verify if adult education, taught at the Polytechnic Institute of Cávado and Ave (IPCA), reduces the AEG, considering the perceptions of its students about the role assigned to the auditors and the degree of success of the auditors in certain situations. The application of a questionnaire allowed to conclude that, as the literature review showed, audit education changes the perceptions of IPCA students about the role and degree of success of the auditors, generally reducing the AEG.

Based on the premise that the quality of the audit is related to the quality of the financial reporting, the purpose of this chapter is to verify if the audit is a determining factor in derivative financial instruments disclosures. However, the academic literature has revealed that audit quality is influenced by a number of factors, such as gender, experience, and auditor's fees, as well as the type of audit firm (Big4 or not Big4). In order to achieve the proposed objective, a disclosure index was prepared, based on the requirements of the International Accounting Standards Board (IASB), applied to companies listed on Euronext Lisbon, excluding the sports corporations. The results revealed that the level of disclosure is influenced by the size of the audited company and by the auditor's gender, being greater in the larger companies and in the companies audited by a male auditor.

Standards are applicable to any kind of activity and could be defined, in a general way, as an activity aiming to apply an ordered system to repetitive functions that take place in the context of industry, technology, science, and economy. Auditing is deeply connected to the implementation of any standard, and this chapter aims to do its connection. Standardization can stimulate international comparability eliminating obstacles arising from some different national practices in accounting and in auditing using IFRS and ISA, in risk analysis using ERM or ISO 31000, in people's safety, in the product or in the environment. A case study about ISO 31000 in a municipality where IFRS and ISA are followed and ISO 9001, 14001, 18000 are a reality will frame this issue. ISO 26000 about corporate social responsibility will be the new future challenge.

Section 2
Impact of Technological Development on the Audit Function

Mobile cloud computing is a concept that has been gaining popularity, resulting from the synergistic integration of cloud computing and mobile computing with the goal of minimizing some of the limitations inherent in mobile computing (bandwidth, storage, autonomy, etc.) and giving greater plasticity to the services of the cloud computing providers. This new paradigm of computation has similar limitations to those associated with the paradigms that are at its origin. Therefore, it is essential that the research carried out in this area is concerned about understanding its impact on audit processes, which aim to verify and evaluate the mechanisms of the internal control system implemented to minimize threats to integrity, confidentiality, and availability of the information assets (data and/or information) stored on these platforms. Based on a literature review, this chapter aims to list a set of challenges associated with the adoption of mobile cloud computing within the scope of organizational auditing.

Massive usage of internet and digital devices make it easier accessing the desired information. In the past, auditing was a periodic, reactive approach, but this must change. Today, volume, velocity, variety, veracity, and value of the information, which are the main criteria of big data, are crucial. Decision makers demand timely, true, and reliable information. This need has affected every sector including auditing. For this reason, the continuous auditing system comes to debate in the big data era. The main aim of this chapter is to shed light on how traditional auditing transformed into the continuous auditing and where big data stands in this transformation. It is concluded that even though many obstacles arise, continuous auditing systems and harvesting big data benefits are crucial to gain a competitive advantage. Also, using big data analytics and continuous auditing system together, management and shareholders gain detailed information about the company's present situation and future direction.

Organizations face a challenge on the emerging technology-enabled businesses to prevent fraud and mitigate risks. Information technology (IT) advancements also provided the possibility of ongoing risk assessment and ongoing control assessment on the growing data volume in the digital age. Although organizations perceive the benefits of continuous auditing (CA) and continuous monitoring (CM), its adoption is low. Some barriers limit CA and CM adoption along with common challenges that organizations must face during implementation. This chapter provides a systematic literature review to promote CA and CM by presenting the main challenges in implementations and general guidance to overcome the identified challenges.

The purpose of this chapter is to investigate the role of audit activities and auditors in Industry 4.0. The preferred methodological approach in the study is a general analysis of auditing in Industry 4.0 in the form of a literature review. According to the purpose of the study, the effect and role of auditing big data, the internet of things, the cloud, artificial intelligence, and other components in Industry 4.0 are investigated. Furthermore, auditing activities that can be implemented in Industry 4.0 are presented as suggestions in the study. The study explains the role of auditing as a whole in Industry 4.0 as a consequence of examining audit activities for each component in Industry 4.0.

The auditing software is an essential tool to the auditor, being a mechanism that helps to achieve auditing goals to obtain efficiency, quality, and to increase reliability on data analysis and evidence collection. The auditing software can be proprietary software or free and open source software. The purpose of this chapter is to understand which factors affect open source software adoption. To achieve these goals, a survey aimed at financial auditors was carried through, and 64 complete answers were collected. Results indicate that the most used software is the proprietary software and that 43% of the respondents belong to the first stage of open source software assimilation. Additionally, it was verified that the external environment is the macro factor, which positively affects the adoption of open source software in auditing.

Preface

ABOUT THE SUBJECT

Auditing is constantly and quickly changing due to the regulatory harmonization, the continuous evolution of information and communication technologies, and other issues, which means that it needs to adapt accordingly. In this context, if these issues are not adequately addressed by auditing, there will be a decrease in the auditing effectiveness and efficiency, leading to a greater dissatisfaction among users, and therefore contributing to the increase in the audit expectation gap. Thus, there are several auditing challenges to be addressed: the standards to be applied; the auditing process and report; the respective techniques, tools and procedures used; the control mechanisms; the monitoring; among others.

In the last decade we have been witnessing a major concern regarding auditing, in particular in what regards the confidence of the capital markets. In addition, organizations, such as IFAC, have been requesting studies from academics to assess certain changes that need to be made to standards, as was the case of the latest amendments to the content of the report that came into force from 2016. Hence, it is crucial for academics to discuss the various challenges that auditing is facing, providing appropriate ways to ensure auditing efficiency and quality.

This publication intends to gather investigations and empirical researches on the challenges and developments in the auditing field to ensure the auditing quality despite the continuous changes on IT and market requirements (supervisors, shareholders, stakeholders, among others). Furthermore, this publication also intends to fill a gap in the areas related to the use of information technologies and systems to support auditing, to the internal control and to fraud detection.

The editors realize that a specific and rigorous publication is needed to make known the outcomes of several researches and innovative practical cases developed in these areas, whether they are theoretical chapters, empirical works, case studies or literature reviews. The impacts of the information systems and the technologies which support them on the disclosure of the organizations' financial statements have increasingly been felt, particularly regarding the publicly listed organizations, as the stakeholders should always have information properly assessed and validated in real time. The use of information systems on auditing and the assurance services are research areas whose goal is to evaluate and validate the control mechanisms, providing effective management of the risk associated to the organizational transactions, mitigating the risk and assigning a more reliable and accurate character to the execution of business transactions and processes.

OBJECTIVES

The editors hope that this book may contribute to discuss auditing challenges, to identify opportunities and to present solutions and case studies. By doing so, we believe that this discussion is important and has an impact on the academic world, on supervisors, and on other professionals, as all of them expect that auditing may provide increasingly quality service and business compliance.

Furthermore, it may contribute to the leverage of the use of information technology and systems on auditing and the assurance services as crucial areas so that the financial statements of organizations can be disclosed with guarantee of accuracy and transparency (accountability).

In addition, the editors believe that the book may be useful for academics, researchers and practitioners, especially those to whom the issues of auditing in general may concern, including those who have interest in information systems applied to this area. Moreover, it intends to get the attention of higher education students who are studying these topics. Also, it may be an outstanding publication to internal and external auditors, assurance providers, as well as managers and risk managers, and other professionals with interest in this subject.

This book aims to achieve the following main objectives:

- Discuss and disseminate recent audit development, being useful to entities, regulators and researchers;
- Review the auditing processes in view of enhancing quality and benefiting from information technologies;
- Analyze and discuss the new information technologies issues and their effects on the auditing processes in order to help the auditing professionals to be aware of their risks and advantages;
- Disseminate methodologies that would allow entities to implement practices to prevent and detect fraud;

ORGANIZATION OF THE BOOK

This book is made up of sixteen chapters, divided into three sections, as follows:

- Section 1, "Audit function," is composed of five chapters on various aspects that influence the audit function, namely the relationship between internal and external auditing, corporate governance, audit expectation gap, and the auditor's role in disclosure.
- Section 2, "Impact of Technological Development on the Audit Function," is composed of six chapters that discuss different news issues related to information technologies that have an impact on the audit function.
- Section 3, "Fraud and Forensic Audit," is the last five chapters that are related to fraud and presenting different approaches to detect and prevent it.

Each section is divided as follows.

Section 1:

- **Chapter 1: The Influence of Internal Audit on External Audit: Evidence From Portugal and Spain:** The main purpose of this study is to analyze the relationship between internal and external audit and its effect on external audit fees, through a questionnaire addressed to the external auditors in Portugal and Spain.
- **Chapter 2: Corporate Governance Characteristics and Audit Fees: Evidence From Portugal and Spain:** The purpose of this paper is to analyze the effect that corporate governance measures have on external audit fees in two countries where this matter is not very developed: Portugal and Spain.
- **Chapter 3: Audit Education in the Polytechnic Institute of Cávado and Ave and the Audit Expectation Gap:** The aim of this chapter is to verify whether adult education, at the Polytechnic Institute of Cávado and Ave (IPCA), reduces the audit expectation gap, considering the perceptions of its students about the role assigned to auditors and their degree of success in certain situations.
- **Chapter 4: The Auditor as a Determining Factor on Derivative Financial Instrument Disclosures:** Based on the premise that the quality of the audit is related to the quality of the financial reporting, the purpose of this chapter is to verify whether the audit is a determining factor in derivative financial instruments disclosures.
- **Chapter 5: ISO Standards and Audit: A Case Study About ISO 31000:** Auditing is deeply connected to the implementation of any standard and this paper aims to do its connection exemplifying with a ISO 31000 case study in a municipality.

Section 2:

- **Chapter 6: An Overview on Mobile Cloud Computing: Impact on the Auditing Process:** Based on a literature review, this chapter aims to list a set of challenges associated with the adoption of mobile cloud computing within the scope of organizational auditing.
- **Chapter 7: The Transformation of Auditing From Traditional to Continuous Auditing in the Era of Big Data:** The main aim of this chapter is to shed light on how traditional auditing turned into the continuous auditing and on the positioning of big data in this transformation.
- **Chapter 8: Addressing Continuous Auditing Challenges in the Digital Age: A Literature Review:** This study provides a systematic literature review to promote continuous auditing and continuous monitoring by presenting the main challenges in implementations and general guidance to overcome the identified challenges.
- **Chapter 9: Emerging Auditing Perspectives in the Age of the Fourth Industrial Revolution:** The purpose of this study is to investigate the role of audit activities and auditors in Industry 4.0 based on a literature review.
- **Chapter 10: Open Source Software in Financial Auditing:** The purpose of this chapter is to understand which factors affect open source software adoption.
- **Chapter 11: Transparency in Latin American and Caribbean Supreme Auditing Institutions:** This chapter analyzes whether Latin American and Caribbean Supreme Auditing Institutions are using the Internet as a means to enhance transparency and interaction with stakeholders.

Section 3:

- **Chapter 12: To Monitor and Detect Suspicious Transactions in a Financial Transaction System Through Database Forensic Audit and Rule-Based Outlier Detection Model:** The objective of this research work is to monitor database transactions and provide information accountability to databases.
- **Chapter 13: Forensic Auditing Tools in Detecting Financial Statements' Irregularities: Benford's Law and Beneish Model in the Case of Toshiba:** This chapter illustrates a three-stage analytical procedure to examine and detect the likelihood of financial statements manipulation and to identify the accounts that were manipulated by Toshiba.
- **Chapter 14: Internal Control System in Cooperative Society:** This study aims to examine the relationship between the effectiveness of internal control systems and the likelihood of fraud occurrence by focusing on the control environment, risk assessment and monitoring activities of co-operative societies in Malaysia.
- **Chapter 15: Internal Audit Structure and Fraud Risk Assessment from a Regulatory Perspective: An Insight Into Turkish Financial Services Sector:** This chapter aims to depict the role of internal audit in Turkish capital markets by comparing the internal audit structure and its role in detecting fraud in financial institutions and developing a framework for assessing fraud risk in intermediary institutions.
- **Chapter 16: External vs. Internal Auditors in Prevention and Detection of Fraud: The Perception of Portuguese Tax Auditors:** This study aims to analyze, from the perspective of tax inspectors, the appreciation of the collaboration between external and internal auditors for the prevention and detection of fraud in organizations.

Rui Pedro Marques
University of Aveiro, Portugal

Carlos Santos
University of Aveiro, Portugal

Helena Inácio
University of Aveiro, Portugal

Acknowledgment

The editors would like to acknowledge the help of all the people involved in this project and, more specifically, the authors and reviewers who took part in the review process. Their effort was an excellent and relevant contribution to this publication process. Without their support, this book would not have become a reality.

First, the editors would like to thank each of the chapters' authors who contributed with their time and expertise to this book.

Second, the editors wish to acknowledge the excellent and valuable work of the Editorial Advisory Board members regarding the improvement of quality, coherence, and content presentation of chapters which ensured the highest accuracy in the double-blinded review process. Most of the authors also served as referees; we highly appreciate their double task.

Rui Pedro Marques
University of Aveiro, Portugal

Carlos Santos
University of Aveiro, Portugal

Helena Inácio
University of Aveiro, Portugal

Section 1
Audit Function

Chapter 1
The Influence of Internal Audit on External Audit: Evidence From Portugal and Spain

Ana Silva
University of Aveiro, Portugal

Helena Inácio
https://orcid.org/0000-0003-1281-2156
University of Aveiro, Portugal

Elisabete Vieira
https://orcid.org/0000-0003-3593-368X
University of Aveiro, Portugal

ABSTRACT

The main purpose of this chapter is to analyze the relationship between internal and external audit and its effect on external audit fees, through a questionnaire addressed to the external auditors of Portugal and Spain. It obtained 131 answers for Portugal and 149 answers for Spain. According to the results, the competencies and characteristics of internal auditors, as well as the type of activities performed by them and the communication between internal and external auditors, have a significant influence on the decision of using the internal audit work. However, the Portuguese external auditors do not consider this influence to be so significant that it affects the number of substantive tests, the quality of external audit, and external audit fees. However, for Spanish auditors using internal audits decreases the planned hours, the number of control and substantive tests, and improves external audit quality, but does not reflect in the fees to be charged to the client.

DOI: 10.4018/978-1-5225-7356-2.ch001

INTRODUCTION

Internal audit carries out important functions within an organization, ranging from the verification of control procedures to the evaluation of subjects related to external audit. The work developed by the internal audit can be used by the external audit since *the well-defined interface between internal and external audits ensures a better coverage of the audit universe, improves the risk oriented focus of audited activities, avoids redundant audit activities and saves costs* (European Confederation of Institutes of Internal Audit, 2007). External auditors must, however, make an appropriate assessment of the internal audit' work to enable them to decide whether or not to use that work and, if they choose to do so, also define the level of confidence to be placed in that work, thereby preserving their independence. In accordance with this, The International Standard Audit 610, §11, establishes that in order to be able to use the work performed by internal auditors, external auditors must evaluate it and perform procedures with the purpose of determining their level of adequacy.

Internal and external auditors have different strengths that combine to increase the effectiveness of external audit (Wood, 2004). The combination of these two types of audits may, in fact, allow an improvement in the effectiveness of external audit, although it is necessary that the external auditor perceive (after appropriate evaluations) that the internal audit´s department is credible, competent, objective, properly qualified and that there is a good coordination between external and internal auditors, which is not always easy.

In this context, the main purpose of this study is to analyze the relationship between internal and external audit, identifying the characteristics that the external auditors consider more relevant in the decision of using the internal audit' work. It is also important to verify whether the use of internal audit affects the performance of the external auditor with respect to the time spent, the number of tests applied, the quality and, consequently, the cost of external audit. Hence, it was prepared a questionnaire for the external auditors of Peninsula Iberian. The relation between internal and external audit has not been much developed in Portugal and Spain and considering that these two countries have a strongly related economic and cultural history, thereby it is relevant and interesting to analyze these countries and verify if the external auditors have different perceptions.

This study is organized as follows. Section two presents the literature review and formulates research hypotheses. The third section presents the methodology, describing the sample, the models and variables. In the fourth section the results are presented and analyzed. Finally, conclusions, limitations and suggestions for future research are presented.

LITERATURE REVIEW AND RESEARCH HYPOTHESES

Activities Developed by Internal Audit

The type of activities developed by internal audit is an important issue in the decision and extension of the use of its work, since there are matters that become more important than others for the work of external auditors.

By analyzing the Hong Kong' market, Ho and Hutchinson (2010) found that the reliance that external auditors place on the work of internal audit is related to the time that internal audit spends on activities that decrease the risk of material misstatement on financial statements and the gathering of evidence by the external auditors. The authors found that the effort spent by internal auditors on the analysis of financial statements and on matters related to external audit, system development and maintenance, fraud investigation, operational efficiency and effectiveness review including internal controls decrease the effort of external auditors during the audit and, consequently, their fees. In turn, Pestrascu and Tieanu (2014) demonstrated the benefits of internal audit' fight against fraud, and Goodwin and Seow (2002) found that external audit preferably uses internal audit as a mechanism for detecting weaknesses in procedures for controlling and preventing fraud.

In this context, the following research hypothesis was formulated:

H_1: The type of activities developed by internal audit influences the use of internal audit' work by external auditors.

Internal Audit' Characteristics

Several characteristics have been discussed in the literature as essential in the decision of the level of confidence that the external audit places on internal audit' work, particularly the competence, size, objectivity, and due professional care of internal audit.

Internal Audit' Competency and Size

The skills and qualifications of internal auditors make their work reliable. The more competent and qualified the internal auditors, the greater their performance and consequently, the quality of their work. In this context, external auditors assess the extent in which internal auditors have the necessary qualifications, with regard to their training and experience, to make the decision of using their work.

The study of Lee and Park (2016) in South Korea, shows that the existence of internal auditors with high accounting and legal experience can decrease external audit' hours. In Malaysia, several studies show the importance that external auditors attribute to the experience (Zain, Zaman & Mohamed, 2015) and the training program of internal auditors that certifies their competence (Haron, Chambers, Ramsi and Ismail 2004), contributing these characteristics, as well as the certification of internal auditors in accounting and audit, to decrease external audit' fees (Mohamed, Zain, Subramaniam and Yusoff, 2012). However, internal auditors' skills in information technology did not contribute to a decrease in external audit cost (Mohamed et al, 2012). On the contrary, Ho and Hutchinson (2010) found no relationship between audit fees and internal auditors' qualifications.

The literature has also highlighted the importance of internal audit department' size and the resources available, to the efficiency and effectiveness of internal audit. Internal audit' departments with more human, technological and financial resources are able to competently extend their work to the most diverse areas. The credibility of internal audit is, therefore, closely dependent of management because even if management does not involve or does not attempt to involve internal audit in its issues, it is important to show concern about investing in the internal audit' department and directs a part of company 'resources to make it properly qualified.

Al-Twaijry, Brierley and Gwilliam (2004) concluded through a study in Saudi Arabia that there is no propensity by external auditors to use the internal audit work. This low level of confidence in the work of internal auditors and the low level of collaboration between these two types of auditors is mainly related to the small number of properly qualified internal auditors and the small size of internal audit departments, because of the limitation to the scope and extent of the functions/duties performed by internal auditors. According to the authors, companies should undertake more resources to establish competent and independent audit departments so that external auditors can rely on the work of the internal audit' team. Zain et. al (2015) also found that the greater the size of internal audit, the greater the contribution of internal audit to external audit. Goodwin and Kent (2006) confirmed that firms with a larger internal audit department, measured by the number of employees in that department, have a greater need for monitoring and a greater requirement for external audit. Likewise, the study of Ho and Hutchinson (2010) shows that external audit' rates are lower when internal audit departments are larger. However, Gerrard, Houghton and Woodliff (1994) measured internal audit by the number of staff working in the internal audit department and found no significant relationship between this factor and external audit fees.

Based on the results obtained in the studies mentioned above, the following research hypothesis was formulated:

H_2: The skills and characteristics of internal audit influence the use of internal audit' work by external auditors.

Internal Audit' Objectivity

The objectivity of internal audit provides the assurance that it is not restricted to any limitations, impositions or any kind of constraints that may limit the scope of its work.

Several factors have been identified as very important in the external auditors' assessment of the objectivity of internal auditors, in particular the autonomy to implement the necessary internal procedures and their independence of the other departments of the company, pointed by Suwaidan and Qasim (2010), and the mandatory reporting to the audit committee, analyzed by Abbass and Aleqab (2013). Abbass and Aleqab (2013) analyzed the relationship between internal audit objectivity and external audit fees. The authors found a negative and significant relationship between these criteria and audit fees, specifically the support for internal auditors by top management, non-existence of internal audit management constraints / impositions and the mandatory report by internal auditors to the Audit Committee.

Regarding the relationship between the Audit Committee and internal audit, the literature argues that when this connection is high, external audit places a greater confidence in internal auditors' work (Munro & Stewart, 2011). The audit committee' responsibility to appoint and remove the director of the internal audit department was also considered as one of the most important factors in the external auditors' assessment of internal audit' quality (Al-Twaijry, 2017). Following these discussions, Jiang, André and Richard (2017) showed that internal audit' quality is negatively associated with the supremacy of the Chief Executive Officer and positively associated with the Audit Committee' diligence.

Given the above results, the following research hypothesis was formulated:

$H_{3:}$ Internal audit' objectivity influences the use of internal audit work by external auditors.

Internal Audit' Due Professional Care

The internal audit' due professional care is closely associated to the way in which internal auditors perform their work. External auditors assess internal audit' work and have more or less confidence depending on how internal auditors do their work through a proper planning and supervision of their activities, supporting documentation and sufficient evidence gathering. When external auditors perceive a poor quality of the work performed by internal auditors, the confidence in their work decreases significantly (Desai, Roberts, Srivasta, 2010).

Suwaidan and Qasim (2010) have shown that the external audit' decision of relying on the work performed by the internal auditor is dependent of the existence, in the internal audit department, of an efficient documentation system, of an annual audit plan covering several areas, of other control systems verification, and of the use of the company's accounting system. According to Abbass and Aleqab (2013) other criteria such as the efficiency of the internal audit planning and supervision, the adequacy of the supporting documentation of internal auditor' work and sufficiency of the evidence obtained by the internal auditors, have proved to be extremely important in determining the due professional care of internal auditor and, consequently, external audit fees.

Haron et. al., (2004) found that the satisfactory performance of follow-up procedures for deficiencies in the company system and the methods and procedures observed in previous audits that demonstrate the work performed by the internal auditors were considered as the most important factors in the evaluation of internal auditors by the external ones.

Based on the literature review the present research hypothesis was formulated:

H_4: The due professional care of internal auditors influences the use of internal audit work by external auditors.

Communication Between Internal and External Auditors

The issue of communication and coordination between internal and external auditors is also very important to the analysis of the relationship between internal and external audit. An inadequate coordination between external and internal auditors may result in a duplication of work, leading to an increase in external audit fees, without a correspondingly increasing on audit' effectiveness (Wood, 2004).

According to literature there are several obstacles to the communication between the two types of auditors, specifically: distortion or omission of information requested, external auditors' perception of the lack of internal auditors credibility, propensity of not listening each other, external auditors' resistance to the changes / improvements / innovations proposed by internal auditors, and the insufficient accounting skills of the internal auditors that require cooperation between both auditors (Golen, 2008). The lack of feedback and trust, physical distance in communication, resistance to changes, and prejudgment are others obstacles that have also been referenced as the main barriers on the communication between external and internal auditors (Paino, Razali and Jabar, 2015).

Felix, Gramling and Maletta (2001) did not verify, however, that the coordination between internal and external auditors has a significant relevance for the contribution of internal audit to external audit.

However, as the inherent risk is greater, this importance increases. On the other hand, the availability shown by internal auditors as well as the free access to their documentation is very advantageous for external audit. Felix et. al., (2001) concluded that the greater the availability of internal auditors to assist external auditors during the external audit, the greater the contribution to external audit, and the importance of this availability decreases as the inherent risk increases. Ho and Hutchinson (2010) have also verified that external audit fees are lower when they have unlimited access to internal auditors' work papers.

The following research hypothesis was formulated:

H_5: The communication between internal and external auditors influences the use of internal audit work by external auditors.

Internal Audit' Contribution

On the Work Performed by External Audit

Internal audit can become a very useful tool for external audit since, by choosing to use the work developed during the year by internal auditors, the external auditor can make a good use of their knowledge about the company audited, and decrease the performance of certain audit procedures, as well as the time spent.

Internal auditors have a better understanding of the business, procedures and policies of the audited company (Schneider, 2009), and can provide audit evidence for various balance sheet accounts or classes of transactions and for the operational effectiveness of audit control policies and procedures (Whittington and Winters, 1990). Thus, by relying on the work of internal audit, external auditors can avoid duplication of certain audit procedures (Schneider, 2009) and even replace the performance of certain substantive tests (Ho and Hutchinson, 2010).

The literature has also shown that the use of internal audit' work not only decreases the time spent with external audit but also increases its quality. Lee and Park (2016) analyzed the South Korean market and found that the number of hours spent by the external audit is positively associated with the proportion of internal auditors over the total number of employees of the audited company. According to the authors, these results suggest that *the greater the availability of internal auditors, the greater their contribution will be to the financial statement audit, resulting in greater audit efficiency* (p.1). By analyzing the U.S.A market, Pizzini, Lin and Ziegenfuss (2015) found that the higher the quality of internal audit, the smaller the external audits delay. According to the authors, these results suggest that companies with an external audit quality function present a lower control risk. The authors also found that "competence and fieldwork quality are consistently associated with significant reductions in audit delay" (p.27).

Based on the literature review, the following hypotheses of investigation were formulated:

H_6: Internal audit is advantageous for external audit.
H_7: The use of the internal audit work influences the planned external audit hours.
H_8: The use of the internal audit work influences the amount of control tests performed by the external auditors.
H_9: The use of the internal audit work influences the amount of substantive tests performed by the external auditors.
H_{10}: The use of internal audit work influences the quality of external audit.

On External Audit Cost

The effect of internal audit on the cost of external audit has also been much debated by literature, although the results are not consensual. Some authors verified that internal and external audits complement each other, that is, there is a greater requirement of an external audit with quality, since there is a need of information with a high level of reliability. On the other hand, other authors have verified that internal audit and external audit are substitute of each other, allowing the external auditor to incur in a less effort, which is reflected in a reduction on external audit fees.

Several studies found a positive relationship between the existence of an internal audit department in audited companies and the fees of external auditors, specially Walker and Casterella (2000), in U.S.A, Hay, Knechel and Ling (2008), in New Zealand, and Singh and Newby (2010) in Australia. According to Singh and Newby (2010) these results show that companies use internal audit to increase their monitoring system. Anderson and Zéghal (1994), through a study in Canada, verified the existence of a significant and positive relationship between the costs incurred by the company audited with internal audit activities and external audit fees in large companies. In Australia, Goodwin and Kent (2006) found that companies that incur in a higher cost with external audit fees have an internal audit (measured by the number of audit department' employees) with higher quality.

On the contrary, studies such as Felix et al. (2001), Mohamed et al. (2012), Zain et. al., (2015), Abbass and Aleqab (2013), found that the greater the contribution given by internal audit to the external one, the lower the cost incurred with external audit fees. According to Felix et al. (2001), the client can influence this contribution by providing an increase in the quality of internal audit, in the availability of management, and by facilitating communication / coordination between external and internal auditors. Razek (2014) elaborated an extension of the work of Abbass and Aleqab (2013) using a different methodology: the questionnaire method addressed only to external auditors. The author concluded that a reduction on the audit program, procedures, and tests caused by the confidence on internal auditor' work can lead to a decrease in the time, effort, and consequently, in the cost of external audit. Some authors also verified this reduction in the cost of external audit through the use of internal auditors as assistants. Abbot, Parker and Peters (2012) and Prawitt, Sharp and Wood (2011) found that the cost of external audit is lower, the longer the time spent by internal audit in the direct assistance to external auditors. Prawitt et. al (2011), also concluded that this reduction does not occur for the total time spent with the work previously developed by internal audit.

There are also several studies that did not find any relationship between internal audit and external audit fees, in particular the studies of Gist (1992), Gerrard et al. (1994), Suwaidan and Qasim (2010), Saidin (2014). In the U.S.A, O 'Keefe, Simunic and Stein (1994) found that the external auditor' confidence in the internal control of the audited company does not affect the hours spent during the external audit and, consequently, external audit fees. Saidin (2014) performed a questionnaire to internal and external auditors, through the competent authorities in England, and compared the perceptions of both types of auditors regarding the reliability of the external auditor in internal audit work. The author concluded that, for both internal and external auditors, the confidence on internal auditor' work does not affect external audit fees. However, internal auditors realize that the confidence in their work decreases the work of external auditors, while external auditors do not have that perception.

The following research hypothesis was performed:

H_{11}: The use of internal audit work influences audit fees.

METHODOLOGY

Collection and Processing of Data

In order to perform the present study, a questionnaire was addressed to the *Revisores Oficiais Contas* and to the *Censores Jurados de Cuentas* that are the Statutory Auditors, respectively of Portugal and Spain. A list of Spanish (2 332 auditors) and Portuguese active auditors (1 375 auditors) was collected at the beginning of 2017 through the official website of the Institute of Accounting and Audit (ICAC) and the official website of the Order of Chartered Accountants (OROC), and a link by e-mail with the respective questionnaire (three-way) was sent between February and March of 2017. The questionnaire is divided into two parts, a first part allowing the analyses of the characteristics of the respondents' auditors, and a second part that allows testing the formulated hypotheses.

This questionnaire is based on the studies of Abbass and Aleqab (2013) and Razek (2014), both from Egypt, also introducing questions related with the type of activities performed by internal audit and with the relationship between these two types of auditors. We used these studies as the basis because the methodology chosen by these authors is very similar to what we intended to do in this study. The questionnaire was tested by a group of auditors before being sent to the Portuguese and Spanish external auditors.

The collected data were processed through the SPSS statistical program.

Regarding Portugal, the questionnaire was sent by e-mail to the 1 375 auditors, of which 21 were not active and were returned, so we obtained a sample of 1 356 auditors. We obtained 143 responses from Portugal, which represents a response rate of nearly 10%. In Spain, the questionnaire was only sent to 1 774 external auditors, since the electronic address was only available to these auditors. However, 92 of these e-mails were not active and have been returned, resulting in a sample of 1 682. We obtained 168 responses from Spain, which also resulted in a response rate around 10%. Thus, we obtained a response rate below the one obtained by Abbass and Aleqab (2013) that had a response rate of 20.5%, but closer to the 12,7% obtained by Felix et al. (2001). It was also considered invalid 6 answers from Portugal and 19 answers from Spain because they were incompletely answers.

The final sample corresponds to 137 answers from Portugal and 149 answers from Spain, which represents a total of 286 answers, as it can be shown in table 1. We verified, however, that some auditors answered the questionnaire, choosing not to answer certain questions which were considered as non-responses and, therefore, removed to test the hypotheses.

The table 2 shows the correspondence between the research hypotheses of the present study and the questions that allow them to be validated as they appear in appendix I (questionnaire).

Hypothesis 1 and Hypothesis 2 are tested by Q 1.1 and Q 1.2 where we presented, respectively, a list of different activities performed by internal audit and a list of different skills and characteristics of

Table 1. Description of the sample

Description	Portugal	Spain	Totals
Initial Sample	143	168	311
Invalid answers	6	19	25
Totals	**137**	**149**	**286**

Table 2. Correspondence between the investigation hypotheses and the questionnaire submitted auditors

Research Hypotheses to Test	Issues to Validate the Research Hypotheses
H_1: The type of activities developed by internal audit influences the use of internal audit' work by external auditors.	Q 1.1
H_2: The skills and characteristics of internal audit influence the use of internal audit' work by external auditors	Q 1.2
H_3: Internal audit' objectivity influences the use of internal audit work by external auditors.	Q 1.3
H_4: The due professional care of internal auditors influences the use of internal audit work by external auditors.	Q 1.4
H_5: The communication between internal and external auditors influences the use of internal audit work by external auditors	Q 1.5
$H_{6:}$ Internal audit is advantageous for external audit.	Q 2
H_7: The use of the internal audit work influences the planned external audit hours.	Q 3a
H_8: The use of the internal audit work influences the amount of control tests performed by the external auditors.	Q 3b
$H_{9:}$ The use of the internal audit work influences the amount of substantive tests performed by the external auditors.	Q 3c
$H_{.10}$: The use of internal audit work influences the quality of external audit.	Q 3d
H_{11}: The use of internal audit work influences audit fees.	Q 3e

The variables used to test the research hypotheses H_1 to H_5 were measured using the likert scale, where 1 = unimportant, 2 = less important, 3 = moderate, 4 = important, and 5 = very important.

internal audit and we asked the external auditors to give punctuation to each one of them about their importance for external audit.

Hypothesis 3 and 4 are tested by Q 1.3 and Q, 1.4, respectively. We presented in each of these questions important characteristics that define respectively the objectivity and the due professional care of internal auditors and we asked the external auditors to also give a punctuation of its importance.

Hypothesis 5 is tested with Q 1.5 where we showed a list of important issues for the good communication between internal and external auditors and asked them to also give an importance punctuation.

Hypothesis 6 is tested through Q 2 where external auditors are inquired about if they consider, or not, internal audit advantageous for external audit. They only can answer yes or no.

Hypothesis 7, 8, 9, 10 and 11 are tested through Q 3a, Q 3b, Q 3c, Q 3d and Q 3e. We asked external auditors to answer if they consider that internal audit work can increase, maintain or decrease the external audit tasks listed.

The Kolmogorov-Smirnov test, which is considered the most adequate to test the Normality of the variables (Maroco, 2010), was used to decide which tests were adequate to test these hypotheses. The Normality test showed that the variables do not have normal distribution, one of the conditions of parametric tests application. Thus, to test these hypotheses of investigation it was necessary to choose the non-parametric tests.

To test H_6 to H_{11}, because there are involved dichotomous variables, we used the binomial test, in order to compare the proportions of the classes of these variables. The variables used to test H_7, H_8, H_9, $H_{10,}$ and H_{11} have three different classes (decrease, increase and maintain), so the use of the cut-off option was adequate. With this option, the auditors' responses were grouped into 2 groups: the group that considers internal audit to influence external audit, increasing or decreasing the planned hours, control tests, substantive tests, quality of external audit and external audit fees, and the group that considers that internal audit has no influence on external audit. A 50% proportion was used in the binomial test, that is, this influence will only be verified for a percentage of external auditors significantly higher than 50%.

The research hypotheses will be tested using a type III error probability (α) of 0.10.

Sample' Characterization

The first part of the questionnaire consists of questions related to the auditors' activity, their audit experience, and experience with companies that have internal audit department, allowing the characterization of the sample as shown in table 3.

Table 3 shows that most of the Portuguese interviewed auditors perform their activity as members of a society of statutory auditors (56%) while the Spanish auditors inquired are divided between the exercise of their activity individually (49%) and as members of an audit firm (48%). Regarding the experience presented, the majority of external auditors, both Portuguese (83%) and Spanish (86%), have a professional experience of more than 10 years.

Respondents' answers also show that the percentage of companies that they currently audit with an internal audit department is very small. Most Portuguese external auditors (64%) and almost half of the Spanish ones (44%) do not currently audit companies with internal audit departments. Thus, our sample combines the opinions of the auditors with experience in working with internal auditors and those who do not have it, but who have their own perception resulting from their professional experience.

PRESENTATION AND DISCUSSION OF RESULTS

Internal Audit' Activities

In order to evaluate the extent to which the type of activities performed by internal audit influences the external auditors decision about the utilization of internal audit' work (H1), it was made a descriptive statistical analysis (table 4) and then the Kruskal-Wallis non-parametric test was applied, followed by the multiple comparison of orders as described in Maroco (2010).

Table 3. Characterization of the sample

Auditor' Activity	Portugal	Spain	Experience	Portugal	Spain	Auditing Companies With Internal Audit	Portugal	Spain
As an individual	27%	49%	Less than 5 years	7%	6%	No one	44%	64%
As a partner of an audit company	56%	48%	Between 5 and 10 years	10%	8%	Less than 50%	50%	36%
Under contract of audit services with an audit company	17%	3%	More than 10 years	83%	86%	More than 50%	5%	0%
						Every companies	1%	0%
Totals	**100%**	**100%**		**100%**	**100%**		**100%**	**100%**

Table 4. Descriptive statistics for H_1

	Activities Performed by Internal Audit	Portugal			Spain		
		N	Mean	Median	N	Mean	Median
1	Evaluation of the internal control procedures of the company	134	4,18	4	124	4,06	4
2	Fraud detection and prevention	133	4,17	4	121	4,03	4
3	Evaluation in accordance with the law of company' policies and procedures	133	4,01	4	123	3,93	4
4	Risk management	132	3,91	4	121	3,95	4
5	Review of operating activities	133	3,77	4	122	3,99	4
6	Subjects related to corporate governance	133	3,56	4	121	3,44	4
7	Review of financial information and subjects related to external audit	133	3,23	4	124	3,90	4

The statistical analysis shows that for both, Portugal and Spain, the evaluation of the company' internal control procedures and the detection and prevention of fraud are considered as the most important internal audit activities for external auditor' work. On the contrary, the review of financial information and subjects related to external audit and activities related to corporate governance are the least important activities for the external auditors of these two countries.

The results of the non-parametric test show that the type of activity developed has a statistically significant effect on external auditors' decision, since the degree of importance that they attribute to the different activities performed by internal audit are statistically different for Portugal (X2 kw (6) = 80,480, p = 0.000) and for Spain (X2 kw (6) = 31,655, p = 0.000). According to the multiple comparisons of the orders, the review of financial information, the subjects related to external audit, and the activities related to corporate governance stand out significantly from all the other activities. These activities are the ones with the lowest levels of importance, so it can be concluded for the non-rejection of H_1 for both Portugal and Spain.

These results are consistent with those of Petrascu and Tieanu (2014) and Goodwin and Seow (2002) who place greater emphasis and importance on internal audit as an instrument for detecting weaknesses in the company' internal control and fraud prevention.

Internal Audit' Characteristics and Competences

In order to test H2, a descriptive statistical analysis of the data was also performed (table 5), and then the Kruskal-Wallis non-parametric test was applied, followed by the multiple comparison of orders as described in Maroco (2010).

As it can be verified through table 5, external auditors give more importance to academic background, professional experience, computer techniques, and appropriate policies for hiring and training, and less importance to internal audit department size and certification of internal auditors. The type of skills and characteristics developed have a statistically significant effect on external auditors' decision, since the degree of importance attributed to them by external auditors is statistically different for Portugal (X2 kw (5) = 33,641, p = 0,000) and for Spain (X2 kw (5) = 68,023, p = 0.000).

Table 5. Descriptive statistics for H_2

	Internal audit' Characteristics and Competences	Portugal			Spain		
		N	Mean	Median	N	Mean	Median
1	Internal auditors have the appropriate academic background	125	3,70	4	116	3,63	4
2	Internal auditors have adequate / relevant professional experience	123	3,67	4	116	3,53	4
3	Level of use of computer techniques by internal auditors	124	3,49	4	115	3,50	4
4	Appropriate policies for hiring and training internal auditors	122	3,42	4	116	3,21	3
5	Internal auditors are certified	125	3,21	3	116	2,87	3
6	Internal audit department' size	123	3,11	3	114	2,66	3

We conclude by not rejecting H_2 for both countries.

Several authors also emphasized the importance of the experience and professional training of internal auditors as important factors that influence external auditors to trust in their work (Lee and Park, 2016, Zin 2005, Haron et al.)

Internal Audit' Objectivity

Table 6 shows the importance that the external auditors attribute to the different factors that allow evaluating internal audit' objectivity.

As shown in table 6, the lack of constraints on the performance of internal audit functions imposed by management and the requirement that internal auditors have to report to the Audit Committee or other equivalent body were considered as the most important elements in characterization of objectivity by the Portuguese and Spanish external auditors.

To test H_3, we consider that internal audit' objectivity influences the use of internal audit work by external auditors if the median is significantly higher than 3 (value classified as moderate importance). So, we used the Wilcoxon test, the non-parametric test that equals the t-test of comparison of the means. We do not use the T-test (comparison of means) because of the sample' characteristics, mentioned before.

The results show that the median is significantly higher than 3 (p-value = 0.000), for each of the elements that compose objectivity, for Portugal and Spain. Consequently, we do not reject H_3.

Table 6. Descriptive Statistics for H_3

	Objectivity	Portugal			Spain		
		N	Mean	Median	N	Mean	Median
1	No constraints / limitations on the performance of internal audit functions imposed by management	125	4,06	4	113	3,73	4
2	Obligation of internal auditors to report to the Audit Committee or other equivalent body	126	3,97	4	115	3,79	4
3	Lack of conflicting responsibilities by internal auditors	126	3,92	4	114	3,61	4
4	Management performance in accordance with internal audit recommendations	126	3,87	4	114	3,66	4

These results are in accordance with the literature that has pointed the objectivity as one of the determining factors of the decision of using internal audit work by the external one. As in the studies of Munro and Stewart (2007), Al-Twaijry (2017), Abbass and Aleqab (2013), this study also shows that the role of management and the obligation of reporting to the Audit Committee have a great influence on the external auditor' evaluation of the internal auditor' objectivity.

Internal Audit' Due Professional Care

Table 7 shows the importance that external auditors attribute to the different factors that allow evaluating the due professional care of internal audit.

The descriptive statistics presented in table 7 show that an appropriate planning, supervision and documentation of the activities performed by internal audit were considered by the Portuguese and Spanish external auditors as the most important elements characterizing the due professional care of internal auditors.

In order to test H_4, we also consider that the due professional care of internal audit influences the use of internal audit work by external auditors if the median is significantly higher than 3 (value classified as moderate importance). To do so, we also used the Wilcoxon test. The results show that the median is significantly higher than 3 (p-value = 0.000) for each of the elements that compose the due professional care, as presented in table 7, so we do not reject H_4 for both Portugal and Spain.

The due professional care is important in that it allows external auditors to determine the quality of the work developed by the internal audit, so the results obtained are in agreement with several authors (Abbass and Aleqab, 2013; Desai et al, 2010).

Communication Between Internal and External Auditors

The importance given by external auditors to the communication with internal auditors is presented in table 8.

The descriptive statistics (table 8) show that the communication of relevant subjects by internal auditors to the external ones and the access by external auditors to internal audit' work papers were considered by the Portuguese and Spanish external auditors as the most important elements in the communication between internal and external auditors.

In order to test H_5, we consider that the communication between internal and external auditors influences the use of internal audit' work by external auditors if the median is significantly higher than 3

Table 7. Descriptive statistics for H_4

	Due Professional Care	Portugal			Spain		
		N	Mean	Median	N	Mean	Median
1	Appropriate planning and supervision of the activities performed by the internal audit	124	3,90	4	113	3,73	4
2	Appropriate documentation of the activities performed by the internal audit	125	3,91	4	114	3,77	4
3	Existence of appropriate audit manuals / work papers	124	3,78	4	113	3,53	4
4	Sufficiency and adequacy of the audit evidence collected	123	3,74	4	114	3,57	4

Table 8. Descriptive statistics for H_5

	Communication Between Internal and External Auditors	Portugal			Spain		
		N	Mean	Median	N	Mean	Median
1	Communication by the internal auditors to external auditors of relevant subjects	129	4,02	4	114	3,80	4
2	External auditors have access to internal audit' work papers	130	3,91	4	114	3,78	4
3	Frequency of meetings between internal and external auditors	129	3,57	4	113	3,45	4
4	Coordination between internal and external audit	130	3,61	4	112	3,68	4

(value classified as moderate importance). With the application of the Wilcoxon test, we verified that the median is significantly higher than 3 (p-value = 0,000) for each of the elements mentioned in table 8, so we do not reject H_5 for both Portugal and Spain.

The lack of communication between internal and external auditors has been pointed in the literature as a major obstacle to the use of internal audit work by external audit. Thus, the greater the availability of internal auditors, in communication and in giving access to their documentation, the greater the external audit confidence in their work (Félix et al., 2001; Ho and Hutchinson, 2010).

Advantages of Internal Audit

In order to evaluate whether external auditors consider internal audit to be advantageous (H6), we performed a descriptive statistical analysis (table 9) followed by the binomial test.

As can be seen in table 9, only 1% and 4% of the Portuguese and Spanish external auditors, respectively, do not consider internal audit to be advantageous for external audit.

The results obtained with the binomial test indicate that the proportion of external auditors who consider internal audit to be advantageous is significantly higher than 50% (p-value = 0.000), so we do not reject H_6. It can be concluded that almost all the Portuguese (99%) and Spanish (96%) external auditors' respondents consider that the internal audit presents potentialities that should be taken advantage of. Several authors have highlighted these potentialities, such as increasing the quality of external audit (Lee and Park, 2016), decreasing the performance of various types of procedures and tests (Ho and Hutchinson, 2010), reduction in time (Pizzini, 2015) and cost of external audit (Abbot et al., 2012).

Table 9. Descriptive statistic for H_6

Internal Audit Is Advantageous	Portugal	%	Spain	%	Totals	%
Yes	135	99%	130	96%	265	97%
No	2	1%	6	4%	8	3%
Totals	**137**	**100%**	**136**	**100%**	**273**	**100%**

Planned Hours

Table 10 presents the descriptive statistics for H_7.

As it can be seen from table 10, 58% of Portuguese auditors and 72% of the Spanish auditors consider that internal audit influences the planned hours of the external one, with the majority, 57% and 70% respectively, perceiving that this effect decrease the planned hours.

The binomial test allows us to conclude that the proportion of auditors who consider internal audit to influence the planned hours of external audit is significantly higher than 50% for both Portugal (p-value = 0.087) and for Spain (p-value = 0,000). These results are in accordance with those of Lee and Park (2016) and Pizzini *et.* al (2015).

Control Tests

The statistical analysis of the effect that the use of internal audit work has on the control tests is presented in table 11.

According to table 11, 58% and 64%, respectively, of the Portuguese and Spanish external auditors consider that the use of internal auditor's work influences the number of control tests to be applied. For both countries this influence is reflected mainly in a reduction of the control tests.

The results of the binomial test for H_8 allow us to conclude that the majority of Portuguese (p-value = 0.071) and Spanish auditors (p = 0.002) consider that internal audit has a significant effect on external auditors' control tests. We do not reject H_8 either for Portugal or Spain. Schneider (2009) and Razek (2014) also showed that the use of internal audit can decrease various types of audit procedures and tests.

Table 10. Descriptive statistics for H_7

Planned Hours	Portugal	%	Spain	%	Totals	%
Decreasing	78	57%	93	70%	171	64%
Increasing	1	1%	3	2%	4	1%
Maintain	58	42%	36	27%	94	35%
Totals	**137**	**100%**	**132**	**100%**	**269**	**100%**

Table 11. Descriptive statistics for H_8

Control Tests	Portugal	%	Spain	%	Totals	%
Decreasing	72	53%	79	60%	151	57%
Increasing	7	5%	5	4%	12	4%
Maintain	57	42%	47	36%	104	39%
Totals	**136**	**100%**	**131**	**100%**	**267**	**100%**

Substantive Tests

Table 12 presents the descriptive statistical analysis of the effect that the use of internal audit work have on substantive tests.

According with the presented data, in Spain, the majority of the auditors surveyed (65%) consider that internal audit influences the amount of substantive tests to be applied, and this influence is mainly reflected in a reduction of substantive tests. However, in Portugal, less than 50% of the external auditors consider that this influence exists.

The performance of the binomial test allows us to conclude that most of the Spanish auditors consider that internal audit influences the amount of substantive tests to be applied by external auditors (p-value = 0.001). On the contrary, the Portuguese auditors do not have this perception. We, therefore, reject H_9 for Portugal but not for Spain. The results are very different for Portugal and Spain. While Spanish auditors, like on the study of Ho and Hutchinson (2010), consider that the use of internal auditors' work influences the performance of substantive tests, Portuguese auditors do not have this perception.

Internal Audit' Quality

Regarding the influence of internal audit on external audit quality, we also performed a descriptive statistical analysis, presented in table 13, followed by the binomial test.

The data presented in table 13 means that 52% of the Portuguese external auditors consider that the external audit quality does not change with the use of internal audit work. In Spain, 60% of the auditors consider that internal audit influences the quality of internal audit, and this influence results mainly, in an improvement in the quality of external audit (55%).

The performance of the binomial test allows us to conclude that the proportion of external auditors that considers that internal audit influence the external one is significantly higher than 50% (p value =

Table 12. Descriptive statistics for H_9

Substantive Tests	Portugal	%	Spain	%	Totals	%
Decreasing	61	45%	84	64%	145	54%
Increasing	2	1%	1	1%	3	1%
Maintain	73	54%	47	35%	120	45%
Totals	**136**	**100%**	**132**	**100%**	**268**	**100%**

Table 13. Descriptive statistics for H_{10}

Internal Audit Quality	Portugal	%	Spain	%	Totals	%
Decreasing	3	2%	7	5%	10	4%
Increasing	63	46%	72	55%	135	50%
Maintain	71	52%	53	40%	124	46%
Totals	**137**	**100%**	**132**	**100%**	**269**	**100%**

0.029). Because of this, we reject H_{10} for Portugal but not for Spain. Although the Portuguese auditors do not perceive an increase on the quality of external audit through the use of internal audit' work, the Spanish auditors have this perception, similar to Lee and Park (2016).

External Audit Fees

Finally, in order to understand the effect that the use of internal audit' work have on external audit fees, we perform a descriptive statistical analysis, presented in table 14, followed by the application of the binomial test to test H_{11}.

According to the data shown in table 14, it can be seen that for 30% and 41% of Portuguese and Spanish auditors, respectively, the internal audit influence the fees charged by the external audit, mainly reflected in a reduction of the fees charged.

The results of the binomial test show that the percentages referred above are significantly lower than 50% for Portugal (p-value = 0.000) and Spain (p-value = 0.000), so we reject H_{11} for both countries. Despite the advantages that internal audit have, they are not reflected in the cost of the external audit. Gist (1992), Gerrard et al. (1994), Suwaidan and Qasim (2010), Saidin (2014), among others, also found no significantly relationship between external audit fees and internal audit.

Summary Results

Table 15 presents a summary of the results of the hypotheses validation for Portugal and Spain.

As it can be seen from table 15 the results show that the main differences between external auditors from Portugal and Spain are basically in the perception about the extent of substantive tests and the audit quality. For Spanish external auditors the internal audit work allows a decrease in the substantive tests applied and an increase in audit quality. On the contrary, Portuguese auditors have the perception that this influence doesn't exist.

CONCLUSION

The results of this study allow us to conclude that the type of activities, such as competencies, characteristics, objectivity and professional due care of internal audit, as well as the communication between internal and external auditors, have a significant influence in the decision of using the internal audit work by the external auditors. We also note that the Portuguese external auditors, as well as the Spanish ones, consider that internal auditing is advantageous.

Table 14. Descriptive statistics for H_{11}

External Audit Fees	Portugal	%	Spain	%	Totals	%
Decreasing	36	26%	48	37%	84	31%
Increasing	4	3%	5	4%	9	3%
Maintain	96	71%	78	59%	174	65%
Totals	**136**	**100%**	**131**	**100%**	**267**	**100%**

Table 15. Results of the hypotheses validation regarding the relationship between the internal and external audit for Portugal and Spain

Research Hypotheses	Portugal	Spain
H_1: The type of activities developed by internal audit influences the use of internal audit' work by external auditors.	Not rejected	Not rejected
H_2: The skills and characteristics of internal audit influence the use of internal audit' work by external auditors	Not rejected	Not rejected
H_3: Internal audit' objectivity influences the use of internal audit work by external auditors.	Not rejected	Not rejected
H_4: The due professional care of internal auditors influences the use of internal audit work by external auditors.	Not rejected	Not rejected
H_5: The communication between internal and external auditors influences the use of internal audit work by external auditors	Not rejected	Not rejected
$H_{6:}$ Internal audit is advantageous for external audit.	Not rejected	Not rejected
H_7: The use of the internal audit work influences the planned external audit hours.	Not rejected	Not rejected
H_8: The use of the internal audit work influences the amount of control tests performed by the external auditors.	Not rejected	Not rejected
$H_{9:}$ The use of the internal audit work influences the amount of substantive tests performed by the external auditors.	Rejected	Not rejected
H_{10}: The use of internal audit work influences the quality of external audit.	Rejected	Not rejected
H_{11}: The use of internal audit work influences audit fees.	Rejected	Rejected

However, when we consider the direct effect of internal audit work on external audit work, we find that the Portuguese external auditors do not consider this effect to be so significant that it influences the number of substantive tests, the quality of the external audit and, finally, external audit fees. The perception of the Spanish external auditors, however, is different. For the Spanish external auditors, using the work of the internal auditor decreases the planned hours, the number of control and substantive tests to be applied and improve the quality of the external audit, but it isn't reflected in the fees to be charged to the client.

The difference in results may be related to the importance that both external auditors attribute to the internal audit and to the attitude that they decide to follow when facing this type of advantages offered by the internal audit. Both the Portuguese and Spanish auditors considered the internal audit to be very advantageous. However, the Portuguese external auditors seem to choose to take advantage of these characteristics and capabilities mainly in relation to the assessment of the company's internal control and the detection of possible fraud, thus reducing the control tests they carry out and the planned hours, but in a way that does not affect the substantive tests applied and audit quality. Following this perspective, the Portuguese external auditors prefer to opt for a neutral stance in which internal audit is advantageous, but then there is no direct passage of this advantage to external audit fees. On the other hand, the Spanish external auditors seem to take a greater advantage of the potential offered by external auditing, i.e they take advantage of these potentialities in a deeper way, not only in terms of evaluating internal company control and fraud detection, but also in the way they perform their work in terms of planned hours and external audit quality. However, with no influence on the fees charged. It is important to point out that the results obtained may simply result from the sample characteristics, i.e the percentage of Spanish external auditors that have clients without an internal audit department (64%) is significantly higher than the Portuguese ones (44%), which could mean that the Portuguese external auditors are closer to the Portuguese reality and can give more concrete answers.

In terms of limitations, the use of the questionnaire as a research method is in itself a limitation of the present study. On the other hand, the existence of few companies with an internal audit department makes the results obtained more directed to the external auditors' perception and not to a direct reality.

As a future suggestion, the preparation of a questionnaire addressed to the external and internal auditors of each of the companies listed on the Portuguese and Spanish stock exchanges would make it possible to verify the variation on the fees of each of these companies. This type of study would make it possible to perceive the characteristics of the internal audit departments of these companies (if they exist) in terms of size, qualification, technology, type of activities developed, procedures used, among other aspects. However, it would also be more difficult to obtain answers since it would include two different questionnaires and would require each of the respondents (internal audit department of the audited company and corresponding external auditor) to reply. It would also be interesting to study the effect of outsourced internal audit work on the external audit quality and consequently on the external auditors' fees as well as the effect of the direct assistance of internal auditors to external auditors.

REFERENCES

Abbass, D. A., & Aleqab, M. M. (2013). Internal Auditors ' Characteristics and Audit Fees : Evidence from Egyptian Firms. *International Business Research*, *6*(4), 67–80. doi:10.5539/ibr.v6n4p67

Abbot, A., Parker, S., & Peters, G. (2012). Audit Fee Reductions from Internal Audit-Provided Assistance: The Incremental Impact of Internal Audit Characteristics. *Contemporary Accounting Research*, *29*(1), 94–118. doi:10.1111/j.1911-3846.2011.01072.x

Al-Twaijry, A. (2017). Internal Audit Quality Evaluation and Reliance Decision: External Auditors' Perception. *International Journal of Economics & Management Sciences*, *6*(5).

Al-Twaijry, A., Brierley, J., & Gwilliam, D. (2004). An examination of the relationship between internal and external audit in the Saudi Arabian corporate sector. *Managerial Auditing Journal, 19*(7), 924–944.

Anderson, T., & Zéghal, D. (1994). The Pricing of Audit Services: Further Evidence From the Canadian Market. *Accounting and Business Research*, *24*(95), 195–207. doi:10.1080/00014788.1994.9729479

Desai, V., Roberts, R. & Srivastava, R. (2010). An Analytical Model for External Auditor Evaluation of the Internal Audit Function Using Belief Functions. *Contemporary Accounting Research, 27*(2), 346. doi:10.1111/j.1911-3846.2010.01023_4.x

European Confederation of Institutes of Internal Auditing. (2007). *The role of internal audit in corporate governance in Europe : current status, necessary improvements, future tasks.* Berlin: Erich Schmidt Verlag.

Felix, W. L. J. Jr, Gramling, A. A., & Maletta, M. J. (2001). The Contribution of Internal Audit as a Determinant of External Audit Fees and Factors Influencing This Contribution. *Journal of Accounting Research*, *39*(3), 513–534. doi:10.1111/1475-679X.00026

Gerrard, I., Houghton, K., & Woodliff, D. (1994). Audit Fees: The Effects of Auditee, Auditor and Industry Differences. *Managerial Auditing Journal*, *9*(7), 3–11. doi:10.1108/02686909410067534

Gist, W. E. (1992). Explaining Variability in External Audit Fees. *Accounting and Business Research, 23*(89), 79–84. doi:10.1080/00014788.1992.9729863

Golen, S. (2008). Communication Barriers Between Internal and External Auditors. *ABEA Journal, 27*(Fall), 35–43.

Goodwin, J., & Seow, J. (2002). The Influence of Corporate Governance Mechanisms on the quality of financial reporting and Auditing: Perceptions of auditors and directors in Singapor. *Accounting and Finance, 42*(3), 195–223. doi:10.1111/1467-629X.t01-1-00074

Goodwin-Stewart, J., & Kent, P. (2006). Relation between external audit fees, audit committee characteristics and internal audit. *Accounting and Finance, 46*(3), 387–404. doi:10.1111/j.1467-629X.2006.00174.x

Haron, H., Chambers, A., Ramsi, R., & Ismail, I. (2004). The reliance of external auditors on internal auditors. *Managerial Auditing Journal, 19*(9), 1148–1159. doi:10.1108/02686900410562795

Hay, D., Knechel, W. R., & Ling, H. (2008). Evidence on the Impact of Internal Control and Corporate Governance on Audit Fees. *International Journal of Auditing, 12*(1), 9–24. doi:10.1111/j.1099-1123.2008.00367.x

Ho, S., & Hutchinson, M. (2010). Internal audit department characteristics/activities and audit fees: Some evidence from Hong Kong firms. *Journal of International Accounting, Auditing & Taxation, 19*(2), 121–136. doi:10.1016/j.intaccaudtax.2010.07.004

International Federation of Accountants. (2010). ISA 610: Using the Work of External Auditors. In Handbook of International Quality Control, Auditing, Review, Other Assurances, and Related Services Pronouncements. Author.

Jiang, L., André, P., & Richard, C. (2017). An international study of internal audit function quality. *Accounting and Business Research, 19*(9), 264–298. doi:10.1080/00014788.2017.1357461

Lee, H.-Y., & Park, H.-Y. (2016). Characteristics of the internal audit and external audit hours: Evidence from S. Korea. *Managerial Auditing Journal, 31*(6/7), 629–654. doi:10.1108/MAJ-05-2015-1193

Marôco, J. (2010). Análise Estatistica com o SPSS Statistics (6th ed.). Pêro Pinheiro. Report Number Análise e Gestão de Informação, Lda.

Mohamed, Z., Zain, M. M., Subramaniam, N., Fadzilah, W., & Yusoff, W. (2012). Internal Audit Attributes and External Audit ' s Reliance on Internal Audit. *Implications for Audit Fees, 285*, 268–285. doi:10.1111/j.1099-1123.2012.00450.x

Munro, L., & Stewart, J. (2011). External auditors' reliance on internal auditing: Further evidence. *Managerial Auditing Journal, 26*(6), 461–481. doi:10.1108/02686901111142530

O'Keefe, T. B., Simunic, D., & Stein, M. T. (1994). The Production of Audit Services: Evidence from a Major Public Accounting Firm. *Journal of Accounting Research, 32*(2), 241–261. doi:10.2307/2491284

Paino, H., Razali, F., & Jabar, F. (2015). The Influence of External Auditor's Working Style, Communication Barriers and Enterprise Risk Management toward Reliance on Internal Auditor's Work. *Procedia Economics and Finance, 28*(April), 151–155. doi:10.1016/S2212-5671(15)01094-1

Petrascu, D., & Tieanu, A. (2014). The Role of Internal Audit in Fraud Prevention and Detection. *Procedia Economics and Finance, 16*(May), 489–497. doi:10.1016/S2212-5671(14)00829-6

Pizzini, M., Lin, S., & Ziegenfuss, D. E. (2015). The Impact of Internal Audit Function Quality and Contribution on Audit Delay. *Auditing, 34*(1), 25–58. doi:10.2308/ajpt-50848

Prawitt, D. F., Sharp, N. Y., & Wood, D. A. (2011). Reconciling Archival and Experimental Research. *Does Internal Audit Contribution Affect the External Audit Fee, 23*(2), 187–206. doi:10.2308/bria-10065

Razek, M. A. (2014). The Association between Internal Auditing Function Quality and External Audit Costs- Evidence from Egypt. *Research Journal of Finance and Accounting, 5*(20), 104–110.

Saidin, S. Z. (2014). Does reliance on internal auditors ' work reduced the external audit cost and external audit work? *Procedia: Social and Behavioral Sciences, 164*(August), 641–646. doi:10.1016/j.sbspro.2014.11.158

Schneider, A. (2009). The Nature, Impact and Facilitation of External Auditor Reliance on Internal Auditing. *Academy of Accounting and Financial Studies Journal, 13*(4), 41–53.

Singh, H., & Newby, R. (2010). Internal audit and audit fees: Further evidence. *Managerial Auditing Journal, 25*(4), 309–327. doi:10.1108/02686901011034153

Suwaidan, M. S., & Qasim, A. (2010). External auditors' reliance on internal auditors and its impact on audit fees: An empirical investigation. *Managerial Auditing Journal, 25*(6), 509–525. doi:10.1108/02686901011054845

Walker, P. L., & Casterella, J. R. (2000). The Role of Auditee Profitability in Pricing New Audit Engagements. *Auditing, 19*(1), 157–167. doi:10.2308/aud.2000.19.1.157

Whittington, A., & Winters, J. (1990). Considering the Work of an Internal Auditor. *The CPA Journal, 60*(4), 28–34.

Wood, D. A. (2004). *Increasing Value Through Internal and External Auditor Coordination*. The Institute of Internal Auditors Research Foundation.

Zain, M. M., Zaman, M., & Mohamed, Z. (2015). The Effect of Internal Audit Function Quality and Internal Audit Contribution to External Audit on Audit Fees. *The International Journal of Accounting, 19*(3), 134–147. doi:10.1111/ijau.12043

KEY TERMS AND DEFINITIONS

Audit Fees: The price paid by a company for an external audit that will certificate its financial statements.

Censores Jurados de Cuentas: Responsible for the review of the financial statements of the companies and therefore, for the legal certification of account in Spain.

Control Tests: Audit procedures used by the auditor to test the effectiveness of the control system of the audited company.

Corporate Governance: Is a system of practices, processes, and rules by which companies are governed and controlled, in order to protect the stakeholders' interests.

Internal Audit: According to The Institute of Internals Auditors, internal auditing is an independent, objective assurance and consulting activity designed to add value and improve an organization's operations. It helps an organization accomplish its objectives by bringing a systematic, disciplined approach to evaluate and improve the effectiveness of risk management, control, and governance processes.

Revisores Oficiais Contas: The responsible for the review of the financial statements of the companies and therefore, for the legal certification of account in Portugal.

Substantive Tests: Audit procedures used by the auditor to obtain sufficient and substantial evidence about the transactions of the audited company and providing an opinion basis about certain facts.

APPENDIX: QUESTIONNAIRE

This questionnaire is part of a Thesis of the Doctoral Program in Accounting, from the University of Aveiro and the University of Minho and aims to analyze the relationship between the internal audit and external audit' fees. The data obtained will only be used for this study its confidentiality is guaranteed.

1. Do you perform your auditor's activity:
    a. As an individual
    b. As a partner of an audit company
    c. Under contract of audit services with an audit company
2. How many years do you perform your auditor's activity?
    a. Less than 5 years
    b. Between 5 and 10 years
    c. More than 10 years
3. Do the companies you audit have an internal audit department?
    a. No one
    b. Less than 25% of the clients' companies
    c. Between 25% and 50% of the clients' companies
    d. Between 50% and 75% of the clients' companies
    e. More than 75% of the clients' companies
    f. Every companies
4. Considering the existence of an internal audit in a client company, indicate (in table 16) the degree of importance that you attribute to the external audit process, to each of the factors associated with the following aspects, considering a scale of 1 to 5 in which 1-does not have importance and 5-very important.
5. From your point of view, the use of internal audit work by external auditing is advantageous?
    a. Yes
    b. No
6. For each of the following items, indicate (in Table 17) whether the work performed by the internal audit allows the external auditor to:
7. Do you want to receive a summary of the results obtained with this work?
    a. Yes
    b. No

If you had indicated yes in the previous answer, please enter your email address.

Table 16.

1.1. Activities Performed by Internal Audit	1	2	3	4	5
a) Evaluation of the internal control procedures of the company					
b) Review of financial information and subjects related to external audit					
c) Review of operating activities					
d) Evaluation in accordance with the law of company' policies and procedures					
e) Risk management					
f) Subjects related to corporate governance					
g) Fraud detection and prevention					
h) Others. Which?					
1.2. Internal Audit' Characteristics and Competences					
a) Internal auditors have the appropriate academic background					
b) Internal auditors have adequate / relevant professional experience					
c) Level of use of computer techniques by internal auditors					
d) Appropriate policies for hiring and training internal auditors					
e) Internal auditors are certified					
f) Internal audit department' size					
g) Others. Which?					
1.3. Objectivity					
a) No constraints / limitations on the performance of internal audit functions imposed by management					
b) Obligation of internal auditors to report to the Audit Committee or other equivalent body					
c) Lack of conflicting responsibilities by internal auditors					
d) Management performance in accordance with internal audit recommendations					
e) Others. Which?					
1.4. Due Professional Care					
a) Appropriate planning and supervision of the activities performed by the internal audit					
b) Appropriate documentation of the activities performed by the internal audit					
c) Existence of appropriate audit manuals / work papers					
d) Sufficiency and adequacy of the audit evidence collected					
e) Others. Which?					
1.5. Communication Between Internal and External Auditors					
a) Communication by the internal auditors to external auditors of relevant subjects					
b) External auditors have access to internal audit' work papers					
c) Frequency of meetings between internal and external auditors					
d) Coordination between internal and external audit					
e) Others. Which?					

Table 17.

	Decrease	Maintain	Increase
Planning hours			
Quantity of control tests			
Quantity of substantive testes			
External audit quality			
eExternal audit fees			

Chapter 2
Corporate Governance Characteristics and Audit Fees:
Evidence From Portugal and Spain

Ana Silva
University of Aveiro, Portugal

Helena Inácio
https://orcid.org/0000-0003-1281-2156
University of Aveiro, Portugal

Elisabete Vieira
https://orcid.org/0000-0003-3593-368X
University of Aveiro, Portugal

ABSTRACT

The purpose of this chapter is to analyze the effect that corporate governance measures have in external audit fees in two countries where this matter is not much developed: Portugal and Spain. The analysis includes a sample of 39 listed companies on the Portuguese Stock Exchange and 104 listed companies on the Spanish Stock Exchanges for the years 2013 to 2015 using an OLS regression model. For the Spanish sample, the results show that the capital hold by the Board of Directors influence negatively external audit fees. The results are in accordance with the supplier perspective which states that better corporate governance practices decrease the control risk and, consequently, audit fees. On the other hand, the Board of Directors' diligence also affected external audit fees but positively, that is, the greater the number of meetings the greater the demand for an audit with quality which result in higher fees charged (demand perspective). For the Portuguese sample it can be observed that corporate governance characteristics do not affect external audit fees.

DOI: 10.4018/978-1-5225-7356-2.ch002

INTRODUCTION

The profession of auditing as an activity whose main function is to contribute to the reliability of information is experiencing a strong pressure on its ethical position, independence and quality. Audit fees can jeopardize the auditor's independence to the extent that if they are set high they can lead to evidence of corruption between client and auditor, but if too low it can also be indicative that the auditor did not take the necessary efforts to issue a proper opinion.

In general, external audit fees are defined considering three important aspects: client characteristics, auditor characteristics and corporate governance characteristics (Kikhia, 2014). With the various financial scandals that resulted in a global economic instability, the importance of corporate governance in the business world has substantial increased.

The implementation of the Sarbanes-Oxley Act (SOX), considered as the most extreme change in securities market laws in the U.S.A (Calder, 2008) has promoted the importance of corporate governance with the creation of a set of practices and measures of auditing, supervision and control. This study aims, therefore, to focus on the relationship between characteristics of corporate governance and external audit fees, given the relevance and interest that these two themes have in the current world, in Portugal and Spain. These two countries that form the Iberian Peninsula have a strongly related economic and cultural history, having also joined the European Union on the same date. In addition, Portugal and Spain have particular corporate governance' characteristics and the subject audit fees have not been much studied in these countries which makes important to understand its behavior by comparing results. Besides that in Portugal the liberalization of audit services was made with the elimination in 2005 of the table setting the minimum fees based on the size standards of the audited company. So the perception about this matter is very limited for Portugal which makes this study more interesting.

In fact, most of the studies that have focused on the relationship between corporate governance mechanisms and audit fees present an Anglo-Saxon corporate governance model, such as the US, UK and Australia, which are characterized by strong legal protection and transparency in the dissemination of information.

Unlike the Anglo-Saxon countries, listed companies in Portugal and Spain are characterized by a concentrated shareholder structure. In Spain, this concentrated structure creates conflicts of interest between majority and minority shareholders (Castells, Sanz, & Chiner, 2013). The reduction of agency costs caused by the separation of ownership and management is due to the high presence of controlling shareholders (majority) in the Board of Directors (Cristobal, Ucieda, & Navallas, 2011). Also "the ownership in Portuguese listed firms is highly concentrated. This feature can influence the earnings management activity, because it is highly concentrated in determining the nature of the agency problem in Portuguese firms "(Alves, 2012, p.59).

The importance of the Audit Committee has also stood out as the codes of good governance have undergone updates, reinforcing their role as supervisory body. It is important, however, to point out that this code is voluntary and not mandatory "unlike in countries such as the UK, where these recommendations constitute, in effect, 'strong guidance' (Sánchez, Frias-Aceituno, & Garcia, 2012).

In Portugal, the structure of administration and supervision is more complex than in Spain since the Commercial Companies Code (CSC) allows companies to opt for the Latin, Anglo-Saxon or Germanic (dualist) model considering what is best for them. Thus, according to CSC: the management and supervision of the company may be structured in one of three ways: a) Board of Directors and Supervisory

Board b) Board of Directors, comprising an Audit Committee, and Statutory Auditor; c) Executive Board of Directors, General and Supervisory Board and Statutory Auditor.

The analysis of corporate governance of a company involves the verification of a whole set of boards and commitees, practices and measures. In this study, we will emphasis mainly on the characteristics of the Supervisory Board and the Board of Directors as corporate governance measures that will allow us to analyze the relationship between it and external audit fees. This choice was due to the importance that these mechanisms have in corporate governance, as it will be explained in section two.

This study is organized as follows. Section two presents the literature review and formulates the research hypotheses. The third section highlights the methodology, describing the sample, the models and the variables. In the fourth section the results are presented and analyzed. Finally, conclusions, limitations and suggestions for future research are presented.

BACKGROUND

Corporate Governance: Framework

With the various financial scandals that have created global economic instability, the concept of corporate governance has gained increasing importance in the business world.

The implementation of the Sarbanes – Oxley Act (SOX) considered as the most extreme change in securities laws in the U.S. (Calder, 2008) promoted this concept by creating a set of measures and mechanisms for auditing, oversight and control. This regeneration on corporate governance allows to avoid intolerable activities and increase the transparency of how companies behave (Ghafran & O' Sullivan, 2017).

So, in general, corporate governance can be defined as "a set of relationships between a company's management, its board, its shareholders and other stakeholders. Corporate governance also provides the structure through which the objectives of the company are set, and the means of attaining those objectives and monitoring performance are determined…The presence of an effective corporate governance system, within an individual company and across an economy as a whole, helps to provide a degree of confidence that is necessary for the proper functioning of a market economy. As a result, the cost of capital is lower and firms are encouraged to use resources more efficiently, thereby underpinning growth" (Organization for Economic Co-operation and Development, 2004, p. 11).

The relationship between corporate governance' characteristics and audit fees has been very controversial because the literature holds two distinct perspectives: the demand perspective and the supplier perspective.

According to the demand perspective, i.e. the public, the relationship between audit fees and corporate governance practices is positive, that is, companies with more efficient and effective corporate governance practices and measures will lead to a greater demand for an audit with quality that is reflected in a greater auditor effort and, consequently, in higher audit fees. According to Farooq, Kazim, Usman and Latif (2018) from this point of view audit fees will be greater to ensure trustworthiness and legitimacy of accounting statements.

The supplier perspective, i.e. the auditor that provides a service, shows a negative relationship between audit fees and corporate governance practices. According to this perspective, better corporate governance practices will decrease the control risk of the company, which will allow the auditor, keeping audit quality, to reduce the number of substantive tests to a certain level, which will result in a reduction in the fees charged. Farooq et. al (2018) also found that companies can moderate agency costs by improving audit committee's as external auditors consider companies with high audit committee' quality less risky and because of that charge less audit fees.

According to Hines, Masli, Mauldin, and Peters (2015) these relationships become complicated since a demanding Audit Committee is seen by the auditors as a strong internal control measure, however commissions with this type of requirement also seek for demanding audits. On the other hand, "*company Boards often purchase additional or higher quality auditing services (outside or internal) to effect better corporate governance, which in turn influences how auditors audit*" (Griffin, Lont, & Sun, 2008, p. 19).

Griffin et al. (2008) developed a study in the U.S.A that covers the passage to the Sarbanes-Oxley Act and reflects these two theories. On the one hand, the authors found that, in fact, companies with better corporate governance practices such as independent Audit Committees and Board of Directors and with a greater need for audit quality pay higher fees. According to the authors, this happens because external audit constitutes itself a corporate governance measure. On the other hand, they verified that better corporate governance practices lead to a reduction in audit risk and, consequently, in audit fees. Griffin et al. (2008) concluded that auditing affects the relationship between audit risk and corporate governance, because itself constitutes a governance measure, and not because its influence.

Figure 1 shows a summary of these two perspectives in accordance with literature.

Corporate Governance: Mechanisms and Measures

Analyzing the literature of corporate governance it can be observed that mainly four mechanisms have been considered as being important factors to the introduction of good corporate governance practices: the internal audit, the external audit, the Supervisory Board, where usually the Audit Committee is referred and the Board of Directors. In this study, we have chosen to relate the audit fees with the Board of Directors and with the Supervisory Board. Most of the studies that analyze the relationship between audit fees and corporate governance are usually devoted essentially to these two organizations (Carcello, Hermanson, Neal and Riley, 2002; Conheady, McIlkenny, Opong, & Pignatel, 2015; Farooq, et al. 2018; Ghafran & O' Sulivan, 2017; Kikhia, 2014).

Figure 1. Relationship between corporate governance and external audit fees
Source: Own Elaboration

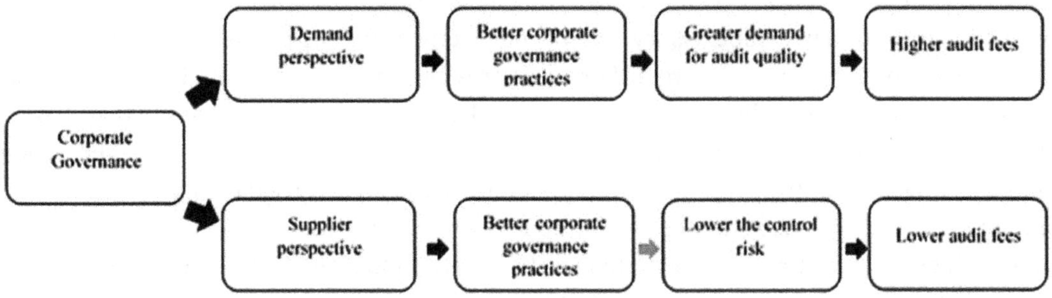

Board of Directors

We chose the Board of Directors to be analyzed in this study as a mechanism of Corporate Governance for many reasons. First of all, the role of the Board is very deeper because, as pointed by Rioux (2012), the strongest values of the organization are established by the Board of Directors. Second, as it can be seen by literature, its efficiency is an important factor in determining audit quality and, therefore, external audit fees. Audit quality is associated with the Board of Directors, not only because the Board is responsible for the auditors' selection decision but also because the auditor will incur in a greater effort if perceive a greater demand for audit quality from the Board (Carcello et. al., 2002). Corporate governance emerges as a mechanism that protects shareholders' interests and decrease agency costs. Therefore, the ability of the Board of Directors to achieve its duties, monitoring executive directors and protect shareholders' interests is particularly important (Conheady et. al,, 2015). A well-defined corporate governance structure helps ensure that managers will fairly report the financial condition and operating performance of the company and acted in accordance with shareholders' interests (Lin & Hwang, 2010). In this sense, Board of Directors and its designated committees are primarily responsible for management oversight (Lin & Hwang, 2010). The OECD (2004) also pointed that the integrity of the corporation's accounting and financial reporting systems, which includes the external audit, should be guarantee by the Board of Directors.

Some authors (Carcello et. al, 2002; Kikhia, 2014) argued that the characteristics of the Board of Directors may affect the relationship between the Audit Committee' characteristics and audit fees. Carcello et al. (2002) did not find a significant relationship between Audit Committee' characteristics and audit fees by including in the same model characteristics of the Board of Directors. The authors found, however, that a more independent, diligent and specialized Board of Directors requires a greater security and quality of external audit, in order to protect their reputation, avoid legal responsibilities and promote shareholders' interests. Kikhia (2014) also analyzed the relationship between audit fees and Audit Committee and the characteristics of the Board of Directors. The author verified that the Board' characteristics are positively related with audit fees but regarding the Audit Committee' characteristics only the independence is significantly associated. The next points analyze the following characteristics of the Board of Directors: independence, diligence, size, and the capital hold by the Board in the audited company. Given the difficulty in obtaining information from corporate governance reports about the specialization of the Board of Directors, we have chosen to exclude this characteristic from our investigation.

Board of Directors' Independence

A Board of Directors is independent when its members do not exercise executive functions in the company and therefore play a supervisory role of management free of any pressure and professional / personal interest. An independent Board of Directors provides more transparent disclosures, which will require more effort from the audit team and, consequently, more audit fees (Kikhia, 2014). On the other hand, there is also the question of their reputation, as independent members are concerned about their own personal exposure requiring a deeper audit to minimize the risk aroused by management. Executive directors are concerned about audit cost while non-executive directors show a greater concern about audit quality since they are more concentrated on the control, identification and correction of mistakes made, intentionally, or not, by management (O 'Sullivan, 2000). According to Hay, Knechel and Ling

(2008), in order to avoid acts that could bring undesirable obligations and damage their status, outsiders directors will require better corporate governance practices and external audit. Beasley (1996) also found that companies with fraudulent financial statements had a lower proportion of independent members on the Board of Directors when compared to companies that did not present fraudulent financial statements.

Some authors have concluded that a more independent Board of Directors influences positively external audit fees (Abbott, Parker, Peters, & Raghunandan, 2003; Al-Najjar, 2018; Bliss, 2011; Carcello et al., 2002; Knechel & Willekens, 2006; Kikhia, 2014; Yatim, Kent, & Clarkson, 2006). O'Sullivan (2000) also found that the proportion of non-executive directors on the Board of Directors influences positively the external audit fees since they use the audit function as a complement to their monitoring.

Based on the literature review, it was developed the following research hypothesis:

H_1: There is a significant relationship between the Independence of the Board of Directors and external audit fees.

Board of Directors' Diligence

The diligence of the Board of Directors is related to the care on its performance. Thus, determining its activity is important to verify whether we are facing a more or less active Board, which influences, or not, the auditors' behavior and, consequently, their fees.

Although some studies such as Yatim et al. (2006) have not found a significant relationship between the diligence of the Board of Directors and audit fees, the literature has generally found that this relationship is positive (Abbott et al., 2003; Carcello et al.,2002; Stewart & Kent, 2006; Krishnan & Visvanathan, 2009; Zaman, Hudaib & Haniffa, 2011). Xie, Davidson and DaDalt (2003) also found that the level of discretionary accruals is lower when the Board meets more frequently. According to the authors, active Boards are able to perform their monitoring role more efficiently and address important issues such as earnings management. According to Conger, Finegold and Lawler (1998), assessing the suitability of the time available for group meetings and the efficient use of that time to deliberate on important issues is essential on a Board of Directors.

In this context, the following hypothesis was formulated:

H_2: There is a significant relationship between the diligence of the Board of Directors and external audit fees.

Board of Directors' Size

The literature has also given importance to the Board of Directors' size, although it is not consensual. On the one hand, some studies did not find significant relationships between the Board of Directors' size and audit fees (Knechel & Willekens, 2006; Yatim et al., 2006). On the other hand, some studies found that this relationship is positive. According to Kikhia (2014), the probability of fraud on the financial statements increases with a greater number of members. Therefore, a high number of members on the Board of Directors is perceived by auditors to be more risky and, consequently, they charge higher fees (Bliss, 2011). On a different perspective Al-Najar (2018) pointed that the positive relation between Board' size and audit fees is due to the fact that companies with large Boards are more likely to require an audit report with more quality putting more pressure in that.

The following hypothesis was formulated:

H_3: There is a significant relationship between the size of the Board of Directors and external audit fees.

Capital Hold by the Board of Directors

The separation between ownership and control, that occurs when the owner delegates certain decision-making powers to managers, makes the owners incur in agency costs. These costs are intended to discourage/decrease the risk that management will act for its own benefit and against shareholders' interests. This is the basis of agency theory, which argues that when managers have access to information that is different from the one that shareholders have access, they can act in their own interest and in detriment of shareholders' interests (Jermias & Gani, 2014, p.135). In order to mitigate the conflicts that result from the separation between shareholders and managers, shareholders (i) attribute incentives to management, (ii) incur in costs for monitoring management activities and iii) in costs that prevent management from engaging in activities that damage them or that protect them in harmful situations (Jensen & Meckling, 1976).

When managers are also shareholders, the risk of management engaging in timely activities is lower (Jensen & Meckling, 1976), so this separation of interests is smaller. Thus, the more significant the proportion of capital hold by managers the lower the risk of fraud and manipulation of results, which leads to a lower effort by auditors and, consequently, in lower audit fees.

According to O'Sullivan (2000), the auditor doesn´t need to perform additional tests during the audit when managers hold a significant percentage of the capital since they have less incentives to change the information issued to shareholders. O'Sullivan (2000) found that the higher the percentage of capital hold by executive directors the lower the demand for a deeper audit and, consequently, the lower the amount of audit fees. Mitra, Hossain, and Deis (2007) also verified that the higher the proportion of capital hold by managers, the lower the agency problems as well as the risk premium and /or the effort spent by auditor, which result in lower audit fees. However, Oktorina and Wedari (2015) found a positive relationship between the percentage of managers who became owners and audit fees. These results are in accordance with the demand perspective, that is, there is a greater motivation by managers to produce financial information with quality when they own the capital of the company they manage. According to the authors, managers look for this quality in auditing so that investors have confidence in the accounting information reported and, consequently, in their work.

Some studies have also analyzed the relationship between ownership structure and external audit fees, in particularly whether the fact that the ownership structure is more or less concentrated on a person or a group affect audit fees and what type of group or person holds that capital. Desender, Aguilera, Crespi, and García-Cestona (2013) found a significant positive relationship between the proportion of non-executive Board members over the total members of the Board and external audit fees for listed companies on the Paris and on the Madrid Stock Exchanges. The authors also found that when the President also performs the role of CEO, both non-executive directors and the external auditor face more constraints in the pursuit and execution of a deeper audit. However, when the ownership structure is concentrated these relationships are insignificant. The authors considered companies with a concentrated ownership structure the ones holding at least 20% per person, family group or company. Desender et al. (2013) argued that the composition of the Board of Directors is intrinsically linked to its main objective, that is, it composition will be more disperse or concentrated if the Board's main concern is to monitor the management or to ensure the success of the company through its capacity and experience. Hence, there is a greater monitoring and demand for audit quality when the ownership structure is dispersed, as shareholders seek a greater protection of their interests, while if the structure is concentrated the shareholders have already a greater influence on the Board of Directors and have a easily access to information (Desender et al., 2013).

Khan, Hossain and Siddiqui (2011) analyzed the relationship between external audit fees and the type of "group" that holds the company's capital in Bangladesh, an economy with a strong concentration of family businesses. The authors found a significant negative relationship between audit fees when company capital is dominated by sponsors (family owners) and by institutional investors. According to Khan et al. (2011) the market in emerging economies is not so efficient, so the demand for audit quality in companies where capital is concentrated in families or in an individual will be lower.

The following hypothesis was, therefore, formulated:

H_4: There is a significant relationship between the capital hold by the Board of Directors and external audit fees.

Supervisory Board

When analyzing audit fees, we must not forget the importance of the Supervisory Board for many motives. The Supervisory Board is an independent board of the company whose objectives are, among others, supervise company's management, prepare and disclose financial information, supervise external audit and ensure its quality. In Spain, the company's Supervisory Board is the Audit Committee as is required by Spanish law, however, in Portugal, the Supervisory Board can take three different forms: The Statutory Audit Board, the Audit Committee and the General and Supervisory Board. The Audit Committee is the one that is most used in the universe of companies worldwide and because of this, when it comes to corporate governance issues the literature highlights mainly the figure of the Audit Committee as a Supervisory Board.

With the various financial scandals that have shaken the world economy, the role of the Audit Committee as a corporate governance mechanism has received special attention (Krishnan & Visvanathan, 2009). The Audit Committee plays a relevant role in the quality of external audit services as it can collaborate with the Board of Directors in the decision of selecting the external auditor and review the audit plan and the proposed fees, besides that, by assuming an attitude of audit quality requirement the auditor can perform the auditing with a superior quality (Carcello et al., 2002).

However, the mere presence of the Audit Committee does not mean that it is efficient and because of that most authors are concerned with the effect that the Audit Committee' characteristics have on external audit fees. Regarding this, Abbott et al. (2003) stated that the characteristics of the Audit Committee are the ones that determine the efficiency in which their tasks are performed. In turn, Knechel and Willekens (2006) verified that the existence of an Audit Committee influences itself audit fees.

Audit Committee characteristics have been much debated in the literature. For example, Zaman et al. (2011) found a positive relationship between the effectiveness of the Audit Committee and audit fees through the UK FTSE-350, which covers large and small UK companies. This effectiveness was measured by a composite variable, which determines that Audit Committee is effective when it is simultaneously independent, specialized, diligent and has a minimum size (at least three members). However, when analyzing the relationship between these characteristics and audit fees independently, the authors found that the specialization of the Audit Committee is not a relevant characteristic in the determination of audit fees.

Other studies considered different aspects in their analysis about Audit Committee quality. Engel, Hayes, and Wang (2010) found that the attribution of high compensations for the Audit Committee leads to a higher quality on its performance and, consequently, to an increase on audit quality and audit fees. In turn, Ittonen, Miettinen, and Sami (2010) analyzed the presence of women in the Audit Committee, concluding that this presence allows to increase Audit Committee' effectiveness and decrease the need for security provided by the auditing and audit fees (by affecting the assessment of risk by external auditors). In a more recent study, Karim, Robin, and Suh (2015) analyzed the relationship between audit fees and the Audit Committee' overlap (number of directors who are both members of the Audit Committee and the Compensation Committee). Karim et al. (2015) found that this relationship is negative, stating that the presence of members in both commissions discourages monitoring.

The most debated characteristics of the Supervisory Board by literature are independence, specialization and diligence. The specialization of the Supervisory Board is associated with the experience and knowledge of its members, however, this information is difficult to obtain in Corporate Governance' reports, especially in the case of the listed companies in Spain. Because of this reason we decided to exclude this characteristic from our study and to analyze only the independence and diligence of the Supervisory Board.

Supervisory Board Independence

The independence of the Supervisory Board members is very important as they must be impartial in their assessment and on the pressure they place on audit quality. The more independent the Supervisory Board, the more focused and concentrated it will be to ensure the transparency and reliability of financial information and, consequently, the external audit quality. Owens-Jackson, Robinson and Shelton (2009) verified that in companies with totally independent audit committees, the probability of financial statements fraud is lower when there is a greater number of meetings hold by the Audit Committee and a higher ownership concentration. Klein (2002) also found a significant and negative relationship between abnormal accruals and the independence of the Audit Committee and Board of Directors. According to Zaman et al. (2011), Audit Committee is more able to exert pressure on management for a greater audit quality when its members are all non-executive.

The literature has not been consensual on this matter. On the one hand, some studies did not find a significant relationship between Audit Committee' independence and audit fees (Stewart & Kent, 2006; Krishnan & Visvanathan, 2009; Yatim et al., 2006); on the other hand, there are also authors that have found a positive and significant relationship between Audit Committee' independence and external audit fees (Abbott et al., 2003; Kikhia, 2014; Vafeas & Waegelein, 2007; Zaman et al., 2011).

In this context, the following hypothesis was formulated:

H_5: There is a significant relationship between the Supervisory Board' independence and external audit fees.

Supervisory Board' Diligence

The diligence of the Supervisory Board is related with the work developed by itself. Therefore, due to insufficient data, the literature has analyzed this characteristic through its meetings frequency. The number of meetings hold by the Supervisory Board indicates whether we are dealing with a more or less active and dedicated Board focused on the matters that concern it. According to Zaman et al. (2011) "For an audit committee to be effective, it must be active" (p.171). It is through these meetings that the Audit Committee debates and informs itself about the accounting and control issues, transmitting the "image" that the Audit Committee remain active (McMullen & Raghunandan, 1996).

Some authors did not find a significant relationship between external audit fees and the frequency that an Audit Committee meets (Abbott et al., 2003; Kikhia, 2014) which could mean that the number of meetings hold by the Audit Committee does not prove by itself that the Committee is diligent. However, in general, literature has found a positive and significant relationship between the frequency Audit Committee meets and audit fees (Al-Najjar, 2018; Stewart & Kent, 2006; Krishnan & Visvanathan, 2009; Oktorina & Wedari, 2015; Yatim et al., 2006; Zaman et al., 2011). An active Audit Committee requires greater effort and quality from the external audit (Krishnan & Visvanathan, 2009).

We, formulated, therefore, the following research hypothesis:

H_6: There is a significant relationship between the diligence of the Supervisory Board and external audit fees.

METHODOLOGY

Variables and Model

The study aims to analyze the effect that certain characteristics of corporate governance have on audit fees, so the dependent variable to consider corresponds to the amount of audit fees (FEE). The introduction of a dichotomous variable to control the country made it possible to verify that the factors analyzed influence in a different way the audit fees for listed companies in Portugal and Spain. Thus, it became necessary to separate the study into two models, so we consider as dependent variables, respectively for Portugal and Spain:

- **External Audit Fees for Listed Companies in Portugal (FEEPORT):** Correspond to the natural logarithm of the external audit fees for listed companies on the Euronext Lisbon Stock Exchange;
- **External Audit Fees for Listed Companies in Spain (FEESPAIN):** Correspond to the natural logarithm of the external audit fees for listed companies on the Valencia, Madrid, Bilbao and Barcelona Stock Exchange.

In order to test the hypotheses formulated, we consider the following independent variables:

- **Board of Directors' Independence (BDIN):** The literature has measured this variable by the percentage (proportion) of non-executive directors (Carcello et al., 2002, Stewart & Kent, 2006; Yatim et al., 2006) and the percentage (proportion) of independent directors (Abbott et al. 2003; Bliss, 2011; Kikhia, 2014) on the Board. For our study we consider the percentage of independent directors since they are members who are not associated with any interest group of the company and because of that are more suitable to issue unbiased opinions.
- **Board of Directors' Diligence (BDDL):** It has been measured by the number of annual meetings hold by the Board (Carcello et al., 2002, Stewart & Kent, 2006, Krishnan & Visvanathan, 2009), so we chose this measure;
- **Board of Directors' Size (BDS):** It is measured by the total number of members who belongs to the Board (Bliss, 2011);
- **Capital hold by the Board of Directors (CHBD):** O'Sullivan (2000) analyzed the relationship between the percentage of capital hold by executive directors and the percentage of capital hold by non-executive directors and external audit fees. In turn, Desender et al. (2013) used the percentage of capital hold by non-executive members of the Board. In this study, we chose to measure Board of Directors shareholding by the total percentage that the Board holds on the company's capital in order to perceive the influence that shareholders who are also members of the Board have in audit performance, and, consequently, in audit cost;
- **Supervisory Board independence (SBI)**: We used the percentage of independent members that belongs to the Supervisory Board (Kikhia, 2014; Zaman et al., 2011);
- **Supervisory Board Diligence (SBD):** We used the number of annual meetings hold by this organism (Stewart & Kent, 2006; Krishnan & Visvanathan, 2009, Oktorina & Wedari, 2015, Yatim et al., 2006; Zaman et al., 2011).

As control variables, we used the audited company' size (SIZE), measured by the natural logarithm of the client's total assets, the complexity of the audited company (COMPL), measured by the natural logarithm of the number of subsidiaries of the client, the audited company (BIG4), measured by a dummy variable that indicates if the company is, or not, a big four audit firm and the audited company risk (RISK), measured by the quick ratio. These factors have been identified as important factors for the determination of audit fees (Al-Harshani, 2008; Campa, 2013; Fleischer & Goettsche, 2012; Kimeli, 2016; Palmrose, 1996; Simunic, 1980; UlHaq & Leghari, 2015; Urhoghide & Izedonmi, 2015). Thus, it is expected that companies with a greater size and complexity pay higher audit fees and that the big four firms charge higher fees as well. On the other hand, it is expected a negative relationship between liquidity and audit fees as the lower the liquidity the greater the risk and, consequently, the audit fees.

Considering that Portuguese companies can choose between three types of Supervisory Boards, it is important to verify whether the adoption of different supervising structures affects, or not, audit fees. Through figure 2 it can be observed that 74% of the listed companies on the Portuguese Stock Exchange (corresponding to 28 companies) have chosen the Statutory Audit Board as a Supervisory Board, 23% of the companies (corresponding to 9 companies) opted for the Audit Committee and 3% of companies (corresponding to 1 company) opted for the General and Supervisory Board. The General and Supervisory Board was chosen by only 1 company (which is an insignificant number) so we decided to introduce,

Figure 2. Supervisory board assumed by listed companies on the Portuguese stock exchange

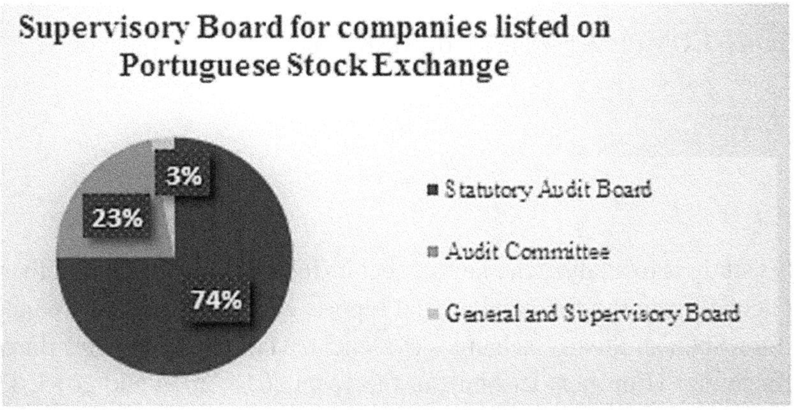

only for the Portuguese model, a dummy variable that controls whether, or not, the company has assumed as Supervisory Board the Audit Committee (AC). For the Spanish model, this variable is not necessary since all companies have as Supervisory Board the Audit Committee.

Table 1 shows a summary of all the variables introduced in the formulated models.

In order to analyze the determinants of audit fees for Portugal and Spain, we have tested our hypotheses using the least squares regression (OLS). The research models to be tested are as follows:

$$FEEPORT = \beta_0 + \beta_1 BDIN + \beta_2 BDDL + \beta_3 BDS + \beta_4 CHBD + \beta_5 SBI$$

$$+ \beta_6 SBD + \beta_7 SIZE + \beta_8 COMPL + \beta_9 BIG4 + \beta_{10} RISK + \beta_{11} AC + \varepsilon \quad (1)$$

Table 1. Variable's description

Variables	Measures	Expected Effect
FEEPORT	The natural logarithm of the external audit fee in Portugal	
FEESPAIN	The natural logarithm of the external audit fee in Spain	
BDIN	Percentage of independent members of the Board of Directors	?
BDDL	Number of annual meetings hold by the Board of Directors	?
BDS	Total number of members of the Board of Directors	?
CHBD	Percentage of capital hold by the Board of Directors	?
SBI	Percentage of independent members of the Supervisory Board	?
SBD	Number of annual meetings hold by the Supervisory Board	?
SIZE	The natural logarithm of the client' total assets	+
COMPL	The natural logarithm of the number of subsidiaries of the client	+
BIG4	Dummy variable: 1= The audit firm is a BIG 4; 0= otherwise	+
RISK	Liquidity ratio: (Current assets – Inventories) / Current liabilities	-
AC	Dummy variable: 1= The Audit Committee is the Supervisory Organism of the audited company; 0=otherwise	?

$$FEESPAIN= \beta_0 + \beta_1 BDIN+ \beta_2 BDDL +\beta_3 BDS+ \beta_4 CHBD + \beta_5 SBI$$

$$+ \beta_6 SBD + \beta_7 SIZE + \beta_8 COMPL + \beta_9 BIG4 + \beta_{10} RISK + \varepsilon \quad (2)$$

where ε is the error term.

Sample

The objective of this study is to analyze the factors that influence audit fees in the Iberian Peninsula. As such, data were collected from the financial annual reports and corporate governance reports of listed companies on the four Spanish Stock Exchanges (Valencia, Madrid, Bilbao and Barcelona) and on the Portuguese Stock Exchange (Euronext Lisbon) for the years 2013, 2014 and 2015. These reports were obtained through the official websites of the Securities Market Commission of Portugal[1] and Spain[2]. From the initial sample of the listed companies we excluded the ones which we couldn´t obtain the necessary data to test the formulated hypotheses and also the companies that were not listed on the stock exchange during 2 years of the period under review We also excluded companies providing financial services, since these companies have very specific characteristics and a degree of financial leverage that can bias the results (Fuentes & Pucheta-Martínez, 2009), resulting in a final sample of 142 companies, of which 38 are Portuguese and 104 Spanish, as shown in table 2. It is important to point out that despite the small sample size, especially in the Portuguese case, it results from an initial sample that represents all companies listed on the stock exchange markets analyzed. The final sample, after the necessary eliminations explained, translates, respectively for Portugal and Spain, 74% and 59% of the total companies and 83% and 68% of the non-financial ones.

PRESENTATION AND RESULTS DISCUSSION

Descriptive Statistics: Listed Companies in Portugal

Table 3 shows the information about audit fees and total assets of the listed companies on the Portuguese Stock Exchange by sectors.

Table 2. Sample's description

Companies With Securities Exchange	Portugal	Spain
Initial Sample:	51	175
Filters:		
Insufficiency of data	-8	-34
Companies that are not listed on the stock exchange during 2 years of the period under review	0	-14
Financial services	-5	-23
Final Sample	38	104
Total Sample	142	

Table 3. Classification of listed companies on the Portuguese stock exchange by sector

Sector	Number of Companies	External Audit Fees	Total Assets
Agriculture, fishing, livestock, forestry, mining, hunting	0	-	-
Industry, construction, electricity, gas and water supply	7	1 174 127.00 €	68 564 872 615.58 €
Trade and services	31	6 408 460,44 €	88 338 660 249,05 €
Total	**38**	**7 582 587,44 €**	**156 903 532 864,63 €**

Most of the companies are dedicated to the third sector (trade and services) and the remaining companies belong to the secondary sector (industry, construction, electricity, gas and water supply). During the analysis period of the present study, the listed companies in Portugal spent a total of 7 583 million euros in external audit fees and reported a total assets amount of 156 904 billion euros.

The descriptive statistics for the Portuguese model is reported in table 4.

From the analysis presented in table 4 it can be seen that, on average, 19% of the members of the Board of Directors are independent (BDIN) and that the Board meets about 12 times per year (BDDL). It can be also observed that the Board' size of the Portuguese listed companies (BDS) corresponds, on average, to 9 directors, ranging between a minimum of 3 directors and a maximum of 22 directors. The members of the Board also hold about 18% of the capital of the audited company (CHBD). Regarding the Supervisory Board, on average, 93% of its members are independents (SBI) and meets about 7 times per year (SBD), meeting at a lower frequency when compared with the Board of Directors. Table 4 also shows that 84% of the companies are audited by big four companies (BIG4) and the liquidity (RISK) of the audited companies is, on average, reasonable. Finally, it should be noted that only 23% of the audited companies have the Audit Committee as their Supervisory Body.

Table 4. Descriptive statistics for listed companies on the Portuguese stock exchange

Variables	Mean	Median	Minimum	Maximum	Standard Deviation (SD)
FEEPORT	10,51	10,59	6,91	14,02	1,15
BDIN	0,19	0,20	0,00	0,60	0,17
BDDL	12,30	11,00	1,00	59,00	7,55
BDS	8,71	8,00	3,00	22,00	4,33
CHBD	0,18	0,01	0,00	0,80	0,27
SBI	0,93	1,00	0,50	1,00	0,13
SBD	6,52	5,00	0,00	17,00	3,60
SIZE	19,80	19,56	16,59	23,83	1,47
COMPL	2,69	2,71	0,00	6,02	1,61
BIG4	0,84	1,00	0,00	1,00	0,37
RISK	3,16	0,60	0,02	97,82	12,42
AC	0,23	0,00	0,00	1,00	0,42

Table 5. Classification of listed companies on the Spanish stock exchange by sector

Sector	Number of Companies	Audit Fees	Total Assets
Agriculture, fishing, livestock, forestry, mining, hunting	2	324 322,16 €	1 303 427 374,06 €
Industry construction, electricity, gas and water supply	36	25 947 049,06 €	210 812 139 974,27 €
Trade and services	66	62 831 915,28 €	831 239 229 150,41 €
Total	**104**	**89 103 286,50 €**	**1 043 354 796 498,74 €**

Descriptive Statistics: Listed Companies in Spain

The business classification of the listed companies on the Spanish Stock Exchanges is presented in table 5.

As it can be seen in table 5, only 2 companies belong to the primary sector, 36 to the secondary sector and most of the companies to the tertiary sector. During the years 2013 to 2015 the listed companies on the Spanish Stock Exchanges were charged in a total of 89 103 million euros related to external audit fees and reported a total amount of assets of 1 043 billion euros.

The descriptive analysis of the data obtained for the listed companies in Spain is presented in table 6.

According to table 6, on average, 37% of the members of the Board of Directors are independent (BDIN) and meets 10 times per year (BDDL). It can also be noted that, on average, the Board's size of the listed companies in Spain (BDS) corresponds to 10 directors, ranging between a minimum of 1 director and a maximum of 21 directors. Besides that, the members of the Board hold, about 25% of the capital of the audited company (CHBD). Regarding the Supervisory Board, on average, 58% of its members are independent (SBI) and meets 6 times per year (SBD) which means that they are meeting at a lower frequency than the Board of Directors. The descriptive analysis show that 88% of the listed companies on the Spanish Stock Exchanges are audited by the big four firms (BIG4) and the liquidity (RISK) of the audited companies is reasonable.

Table 6. Descriptive statistics for listed companies on the Spanish stock exchanges

Variables	Mean	Median	Minimum	Maximum	Standard Deviation (SD)
FEESPAIN	11,52	11,46	7,75	15,52	1,40
BDIN	0,37	0,33	0,00	1,00	0,18
BDDL	10,26	10,00	0,00	45,00	4,77
BDS	9,85	10,00	1,00	21,00	3,69
CHBD	0,25	0,19	0,00	1,00	0,25
SBI	0,58	0,67	0,00	1,00	0,25
SBD	6,36	6,00	0,00	16,00	2,89
SIZE	19,91	19,97	11,77	25,18	2,24
COMPL	3,12	2,86	0,00	7,14	1,59
BIG4	0,88	1,00	0,00	1,00	0,32
RISK	1,98	0,89	0,00	60,14	5,38

Regression Analysis Results: Listed Companies in Portugal

Table 7 presents the correlation matrix of the independent and control variables.

Through the correlation matrix, it can be observed that the strongest correlations are between the SIZE and BDS variables, with a correlation of 0,55 and between the AC and SBI variable, with a correlation of -0,53. However, the collinearity test was performed and the results did not reveal any problem of this type. The heteroscedasticity (White's test) and the normality of the residuals tests also revealed no concern with the dispersion of the data and the distribution of the error.

Table 8 shows the results obtained for listed companies on the Portuguese Stock Exchange using the pooled OLS model, as it was verified to be more adequate than the fixed effects model and the random effects model. The adjusted R^2 obtained with the pooled OLS model is higher than the other models mentioned, which means that this model is the most explanatory of the external audit fees.

The adjusted R^2 indicates that the model explains almost 30% of the external audit fees. Regarding the control variables, the results show that only the audited company's size (SIZE) and complexity (COMPL) affects audit fees (at 1% level). The remaining control variables as well as the experimental variables have no influence on audit fees. Similar to Hassan and Naser (2013), Thi and Hong (2017), Palmrose (1986), Urhoghide and Izedonmi (2015), among others, we also found in Portugal a positive relationships between the size of the audited company and the external auditors' fees. On the other hand, unlike Carcello et al. (2002), Stewart and Kent (2006), Zaman et al. (2011), Desender et al. (2013) there were no significant relationships between the corporate governance mechanisms and the external auditors' fees. This low explanatory power of the model may indicate that in Portugal, although the minimum fees' table has not been mandatory since 2005, auditors continue to be heavily influenced by its base' construction factor: the size. These results can also indicate that there are other factors, which have not been studied, that may in fact influence Portuguese' audit fees or may simply result from the small size of the sample.

As can be seen from table 9 the results do not support any research hypothesis for the Portuguese model.

Table 7. Correlation matrix for listed companies on the Portuguese stock exchange

Variables	BDIM	BDDL	BDS	CHBD	SBI	SBD	SIZE	COMPL	BIG4	RISK	AC
BDIN	1,00	-0,21	0,36	-0,18	-0,12	0,34	0,32	0,28	-0,04	0,03	-0,41
BDDL		1,00	0,01	-0,07	-0,11	0,38	0,08	0,09	-0,15	-0,10	-0,12
BDS			1,00	-0,26	-0,04	0,42	0,55	0,18	-0,01	-0,14	-0,37
CHBD				1,00	0,12	-0,28	-0,29	-0,11	-0,14	-0,05	-0,13
SBI					1,00	-0,42	-0,11	-0,03	-0,17	0,03	-0,53
SBD						1,00	0,43	0,04	0,09	-0,04	-0,45
SIZE							1,00	0,41	0,23	0,04	0,18
COMPL								1,00	-0,05	0,12	0,10
BIG4									1,00	0,07	0,06
RISK										1,00	-0,03
AC											1,00

Table 8. Results for the Portuguese model

Variables	Coefficient	T-Statistic	P Value
CONST	4,02	2,20	0,00***
BDIN	0,95	1,42	0,18
BDDL	0,02	1,46	0,17
BDS	0,02	0,46	0,60
CHBD	−0,31	−0,86	0,35
SBI	1,13	1,25	0,26
SBD	0,06	1,47	0,16
SIZE	0,26	2,87	0,01***
COMPL	−0,19	−2,84	0,01***
BIG4	−0,31	−1,15	0,23
RISK	0,00	0,08	0,51
SAB	−0,43	1,40	0,21
Mean dependent variable: 10,51			
S.D. dependent variable: 1,15			
Sum squared residuals: 93,25			
S.E. of regression: 0,96			
Adjusted R-squared (R^2): 0,30			
F(11, 24): 5,48			
P Value (F): 0,00			

Notes: ***Significant at $p < 0.01$, **Significant at $0.01 < p < 0.05$, *Significant at $0.05 < p < 0.10$

Table 9. Summary of the research hypotheses for the Portuguese model

Hypothesis	Description	Support Evidence
Hypothesis 1	There is a significant relationship between the independence of the Board of Directors and external audit fees.	No
Hypothesis 2	There is a significant relationship between the diligence of the Board of Directors and external audit fees.	No
Hypothesis 3	There is a significant relationship between the size of the Board of Directors and external audit fees.	No
Hypothesis 4	There is a significant relationship between the capital hold by the Board of Directors and external audit fees.	No
Hypothesis 5	There is a significant relationship between the independence of the Supervisory Board and external audit fees.	No
Hypothesis 6	There is a significant relationship between the diligence of the Supervisory Board and external audit fees.	No

Regression Analysis Results: Listed Companies in Spain

The correlation matrix of the independent and control variables for listed companies on the Spanish Stock Exchange is presented in table 10.

The results show that the strongest correlations were found between SBI and BDIN variables, with a correlation of 0,61, SIZE and BDS variables, with a correlation of 0,67 and between the variables COMPL and SIZE, with a correlation of 0,68. However, the collinearity test was performed and the results did not reveal any problem. The heteroscedasticity tests (White's test) and on the residuals normality also showed no concern about the dispersion of the data and the distribution of the error.

The regression model for listed companies on the Spanish Stock Exchanges was introduced in the gretl program, using the Pooled OLS for the same reasons presented for the Portuguese model. The results obtained are indicated in table 11.

The adjusted R^2 indicates that the Spanish model explains 66% of the external audit fees. As expected, the control variables for size (SIZE), complexity (COMPL) and for audit firms (BIG4), are positively related to audit fees. The control variable for the risk (RISK) indicates that the lower the liquidity the higher the amount of audit fees to be charged, that is, the lower the liquidity, the greater the audited company risk and the higher the audit fees. These results are in line with those of Campa (2013), Fleischer and Goettsche (2012), Kimeli (2016), UlHaq and Leghari (2015), Urhoghide and Izedonmi (2015).

Regarding the experimental variables, the results allow us to conclude that only the Board of Directors' diligence (BDDL), with a significance of 10%, and the percentage of capital hold by the Board of Directors (CHBD), with a significance of 1%, are significantly related to the external audit fees. These results indicate that the greater the diligence of the Board of Directors, measured by the number of annual meetings hold by the Board, the greater the demand for an audit with quality, which leads to an increase on audit price and are in accordance with the results of Carcello et al. (2002), Stewart and Kent (2006), Zaman et al. (2011). On the other hand, the greater the percentage of capital hold by the Board of Directors, the greater the influence of shareholders on the Board and the greater the access to information (Desender et al., 2013). There is, therefore, a less concern with management monitoring and audit demanding since the Board of Directors are themselves shareholders and they already do this monitoring resulting in a lower demand for auditor effort and, consequently, in lower audit fees.

Table 10. Correlation matrix for listed companies on the Spanish stock exchanges

	BDIN	BDDL	BDS	CHBD	SBI	SBD	SIZE	COMPL	BIG4	RISK
BDIN	1,00	0,01	-0,05	-0,20	0,61	0,12	0,11	0,10	0,01	0,20
BDDL		1,00	0,04	-0,22	0,10	0,42	0,15	0,20	0,07	-0,06
BDS			1,00	-0,10	-0,01	0,34	0,67	0,48	0,39	-0,10
CHBD				1,00	0,01	-0,14	-0,12	-0,06	-0,06	0,00
SBI					1,00	0,16	0,04	0,04	0,01	0,07
SBD						1,00	0,42	0,35	0,22	-0,01
SIZE							1,00	0,68	0,37	-0,15
COMPL								1,00	0,27	-0,14
BIG4									1,00	-0,16
RISK										1,00

Table 11. Results for the Spanish model

Variables	Coefficient	T-Statistic	P Value
CONST	3,34	5,78	0,000 ***
BDIN	0,14	0,41	0,68
BDDL	0,02	1,69	0,09*
BDS	0	-0,41	0,68
CHBD	-0,75	-3,77	0,00***
SBI	-0,08	-0,35	0,73
SBD	0,03	1,28	0,2
SIZE	0,36	10,05	0,00 ***
COMPL	0,12	2,97	0,00***
BIG4	0,67	4,23	0,00 ***
RISK	-0,03	-3,55	0,00***
Mean dependent variable: 11,51			
S.D. dependent variable: 1,39			
Sum squared residuals: 193,44			
S.E. of regression: 0,81			
Adjusted R-squared (R^2): 0,66			
F(10, 102): 60,44			
P Value (F): 0,00			

Notes: ***Significant at $p < 0.01$, **Significant at $0.01 < p < 0.05$, *Significant at $0.05 < p < 0.10$.

Another important conclusion is that the Supervisory Board of the audited companies is not important in determining audit quality (SBI and SBD variables) and, consequently, external audit fees for listed companies in Spain. This result is in line with Carcello et al. (2002) that verified in their study that Audit Committee' characteristics were not important in determining external audit fees when the Board of Directors' characteristics are presented in the model. In the same sense Kikhia (2014) found that only Audit Committee independence was significantly associated with audit fees. These results reflect the influence of the Board of Directors on the way in which the auditing will be conducted and, consequently, on the external audit fees. However, the Board of Directors independence (BDIN) and the Board of Directors' size (BDS) were not significant in determining audit fees.

Finally, table 12 indicates that the results only supports the research hypotheses 2 and 4.

CONCLUSION

This study analyzed the effect of corporate governance' mechanisms on audit fees for listed companies on the Portuguese Stock Exchange (Euronext Lisbon), and on the four Spanish Stock Exchanges (Bilbao, Valencia, Barcelona and Madrid), for the years 2013 to 2015.

The results are very different for Portugal and Spain. In general terms, the characteristics of corporate governance influence audit fees in Spain but not in Portugal.

Table 12. Summary of the research hypotheses for the Spanish model

Hypothesis	Description	Support Evidence
Hypothesis 1	There is a significant relationship between the independence of the Board of Directors and external audit fees.	No
Hypothesis 2	There is a significant relationship between the diligence of the Board of Directors and external audit fees.	**Yes**
Hypothesis 3	There is a significant relationship between the size of the Board of Directors and external audit fees.	No
Hypothesis 4	There is a significant relationship between the capital hold by the Board of Directors and external audit fees.	**Yes**
Hypothesis 5	There is a significant relationship between the independence of the Supervisory Board and external audit fees.	No
Hypothesis 6	There is a significant relationship between the diligence of the Supervisory Board and external audit fees.	No

For Portugal, the results show that the characteristics of the Board of Directors and Supervisory Body analyzed in the present study have no influence on audit fees.

For Spain, the results indicate that the characteristics of the Supervisory Board, in particular its independence and diligence, do not have a significant effect on audit fees. On the opposite, the Board of Directors is an important organism in determining audit fees. The percentage of capital hold by the Board of Directors is negatively and significantly related to audit fees. These results indicate that the higher the capital hold by the Board of Directors the greater the monitoring performed by them and the lower the demand for external audit quality. The audit cost to be borne by the audited company will be, therefore, lower. On the other hand, the Board of Directors' diligence is positively and significantly associated with audit fees. These results show that a greater number of meetings leads to a greater demand for audit quality that result in higher audit fees.

The results between these two countries could indicate that in Portugal external auditors still have as reference the minimum fees based on the size and complexity of audited companies which were in for until 2005.

The limitations of the present study are mainly related to the sample because the Portuguese sample is smaller when compared with the Spanish one. This happens because we only used the companies listed on the Portuguese and Spanish Stock Exchanges which limits the sample. However, including other companies could be very difficult because some information as the amount of audit fees are not required to disclose for companies that are not listed.

Regarding future research, if the companies disclose these kind of information it would be very interested to expand the samples. In addition it would be interesting to explore the relationship of audit fees with other corporate governance measures such as internal audit and the capital's structure of the audited company (whether it is more concentrated or dispersed and the type of group or person holding the capital of the audited company).

REFERENCES

Abbott, L. J., Parker, S., Peters, G. F., & Raghunandan, K. (2003). The Association between Audit Committee Characteristics and Audit Fees. *Auditing*, *22*(2), 17–32. doi:10.2308/aud.2003.22.2.17

Al-Harshani, M. O. (2008). The pricing of audit services: Evidence from Kuwait. *Managerial Auditing Journal*, *23*(7), 685–696. doi:10.1108/02686900810890643

Al-Najjar, B. (2018). Corporate governance and audit features: SMEs evidence. *Journal of Small Business and Enterprise Development*, *25*(1), 163–179. doi:10.1108/JSBED-08-2017-0243

Alves, S. (2012). Ownership Structure and Earnings Management: Evidence from Portugal. *Australasian Accounting Business and Finance*, *6*(1), 57–74.

Beasley, M. S. (1996). An Empirical Analysis of the Relation Between the Board of Director Composition and Financial Statement Fraud. *The Accounting Review*, *71*(4), 443–465.

Bliss, M. A. (2011). Does CEO Duality Constrain Board Independence? Some Evidence From Audit Pricing. *Accounting and Finance*, *51*(2), 361–380. doi:10.1111/j.1467-629X.2010.00360.x

Calder, A. (2008). *Governo das sociedades: A Pratical Guide to the Legal Frameworks and International Codes of Practice*. London: Kogan Page Limited.

Campa, D. (2013). Big 4 fee premium" and audit quality: Latest evidence from UK listed companies. *Managerial Auditing Journal*, *28*(8), 680–707. doi:10.1108/MAJ-11-2012-0784

Carcello, J. V., Hermanson, D. R., Neal, T. L., & Riley, R. A. Jr. (2002). Board Characteristics and Audit Fees. *Contemporary Accounting Research*, *19*(3), 365–384. doi:10.1506/CHWK-GMQ0-MLKE-K03V

Castells, A. R., Sanz, F. L., & Chiner, N. L. (2013). Corporate Boards in Spain. In P. Davies, K. J. Hopt, R. Nowak, & G. Van Solinge (Eds.), *Corporate Boards in Law and Practice: A Comparative Analysis in Europe* (pp. 549–616). New York: Oxford University Press. doi:10.1093/acprof:oso/9780198705154.003.0008

Código das Sociedades Comerciais (CSC), Decreto-Lei n.o 262/1986 de 2 de Setembro da Assembleia da Républica. Diário da República: I série, No 201 (1986).

Conger, J. A., Finegold, D., & Lawler, E. E. (1998). Appraising Boardroom performance. *Harvard Business Review*, *76*(1), 136–148. PMID:10176916

Conheady, B., McIlkenny, P., Opong, K. K., & Pignatel, I. (2015). Board effectiveness and firm performance of Canadian listed firms. *The British Accounting Review*, *47*(3), 290–303. doi:10.1016/j.bar.2014.02.002

Cristobal, E. de las H., Ucieda, J. L., & Navallas, B. (2011). Law, Corporate Governance, and Accounting: European Perspectives. New York: Routledge.

Desender, K. A., Aguilera, R. V., Crespi, R., & García-Cestona, M. (2013). When Does Ownership Matter? Board Characteristics and Behavior. *Strategic Management Journal*, *34*(7), 823–842. doi:10.1002mj.2046

Engel, E., Hayes, R. M., & Wang, X. (2010). Audit Committee Compensation and the Demand for Monitoring of the Financial Reporting Process. *Journal of Accounting and Economics*, *49*(1-2), 136–154. doi:10.1016/j.jacceco.2009.08.001

Farooq, M., Kazim, I., Usman, M., & Latif, I. (2018). Corporate Governance and Audit Fees: Evidence from a Developing Country. *Pakistan Journal of Commerce and Social Sciences*, *12*(1), 94–110.

Fleischer, R., & Goettsche, M. (2012). Size effects and audit pricing: Evidence from Germany. *Journal of International Accounting, Auditing & Taxation*, *21*(2), 156–168. doi:10.1016/j.intaccaudtax.2012.07.005

Fuentes, C. De, & Pucheta-Martínez, M. C. (2009). Auditor independence, joint determination of audit and non-audit fees and the incidence of qualified audit reports. *Revista Latinoamericana de Administración*, *43*(2), 63–92.

Ghafran, C., & O' Sullivan, N. (2017). The impact of audit committee expertise on audit quality: Evidence from UK audit fees. *The British Accounting Review*, *49*(6), 578–593. doi:10.1016/j.bar.2017.09.008

Griffin, P., Lont, D. H., & Sun, Y. (2008). Corporate Governance and Audit Fees: Evidence of Countervailing Relations. *Journal of Contemporary Accounting & Economics*, *4*(1), 18–49. doi:10.1016/S1815-5669(10)70028-X

Hay, D., Knechel, W., & Ling, H. (n.d.). Evidence on the Impact of Internal Control and Corporate Governance on Audit Fees. *International Journal of Auditing*, (12), 9–24.

Hines, C. S., Masli, A., Mauldin, E. G., & Peters, G. F. (2015). Board Risk Committees and Audit Pricing. *Auditing*, *34*(4), 59–84. doi:10.2308/ajpt-51035

Ittonen, K., Miettinen, J., & Sami, V. (2010). Does Female Representation on Audit Committees Affect Audit Fees? Quarterly Journal of Finance and Accounting. *Quarterly Journal of Finance and Accounting*, *49*(3-4), 113.

Jensen, M. C., & Meckling, W. H. (1976). Theory of the firm : Managerial behavior, agency Costs and ownership structure. *Journal of Financial Economics*, *3*(4), 305–360. doi:10.1016/0304-405X(76)90026-X

Jermias, J., & Gani, L. (2014). The impact of board capital and board characteristics on firm performance. *The British Accounting Review*, *46*(2), 135–153. doi:10.1016/j.bar.2013.12.001

Karim, K., Robin, A., & Suh, S. (2015). Board Structure and Audit Committee Monitoring: Effects of Audit Committee Monitoring Incentives and Board Entrenchment on Audit Fees. *Journal of Accounting, Auditing & Finance*, *31*(2), 249–276. doi:10.1177/0148558X15583412

Khan, A. R., Hossain, D. M., & Siddiqui, J. (2011). Corporate ownership concentration and audit fees: The case of an emerging economy. *Advances in Accounting*, *27*(1), 125–131. doi:10.1016/j.adiac.2011.04.007

Kikhia, H. Y. (2014). Board Characteristics, Audit Committee Characteristics, and Audit Fees: Evidence from Jordan. *International Business Research*, *7*(12), 98–111. doi:10.5539/ibr.v7n12p98

Kimeli, E. K. (2016). Determinants of Audit Fees Pricing : Evidence from Nairobi Securities Exchange (NSE). *International Journal of Research in Business Studies and Management*, *3*(1), 23–35.

Klein, A. (2002). Audit committee, board of director characteristics, and earnings management. *Journal of Accounting and Economics*, *33*(3), 375–400. doi:10.1016/S0165-4101(02)00059-9

Knechel, W. R., & Willekens, M. (2006). The Role of Risk Management and Governance in Determining Audit Demand. *Journal of Business Finance & Accounting*, *33*(9-10), 1344–1367. doi:10.1111/j.1468-5957.2006.01238.x

Krishnan, G., & Visvanathan, G. (2009). Do Auditors Price Audit Committee's Expertise? The Case of Accounting versus Nonaccounting Financial Experts. *Auditing*, *28*(1), 241–261. doi:10.2308/aud.2009.28.1.241

Lin, W. & Hwang I. (2010). Audit Quality, Corporate Governance, and Earnings Management: A Meta-Analysis. *International Journal of Auditing, 14*, 57-77. doi:10.1111/j.1099-1123.2009.00403.x

McMullen, D. A., & Raghunandan, K. (1996). Enhancing Audit Committee Effectiveness. *Journal of Accountancy*, *182*(2), 79–81. doi:10.1016/S0165-4101(02)00059-9

Mitra, S., Hossain, M., & Deis, D. R. (2007). The empirical relationship between ownership characteristics and audit fees. *Review of Quantitative Finance and Accounting*, *28*(3), 257–285. doi:10.100711156-006-0014-7

O'Sullivan, N. (2000). The Impact of Board Composition and Ownership on Audit Quality: Evidence From Large Uk Companies. *The British Accounting Review*, *32*(4), 397–414. doi:10.1006/bare.2000.0139

Oktorina, M., & Wedari, L. K. (2015). An Empirical Investigation on Ownership Characteristics, Activities of the Audit Committee, and Audit Fees in Listed companies on Indonesia Stock Exchange. *Applied Finance and Accounting*, *1*(1), 20–29. doi:10.11114/afa.v1i1.639

Organisation for Economic Co-operation and Development. (2004). *OECD Principles of Corporate Governance*. Paris: OECD.

Owens-Jackson, L. A., Robinson, D., & Shelton, S. W. (2009). The Association Between Audit Committee Characteristics, the Contracting Process and Fraudulent Financial Reporting. *American Journal of Business*, *24*(1), 57–66. doi:10.1108/19355181200900005

Palmrose, Z.-V. (1986). Audit Fees and Auditor Size: Further Evidence. *Journal of Accounting Research*, *24*(1), 97–110. doi:10.2307/2490806

Rioux, G. (2012). Board Directors and Corporate Social Responsibility. In S. Boubaker & D. K. Nguyen (Eds.), New York: Palgrave Macmillan.

Sánchez, I.-M. G., Frias-Aceituno, J. V., & Garcia-Rubio, R. (2012). Determining Factors of Audit Committee Attributes: Evidence from Spain. *International Journal of Auditing*, *16*(2), 184–213. doi:10.1111/j.1099-1123.2012.00451.x

Simunic, D. A. (1980). The Pricing of Audit Services: Theory and Evidence. *Journal of Accounting Research*, *18*(1), 161. doi:10.2307/2490397

Stewart, J., & Kent, P. (2006). Relation between external audit fees, audit committee characteristics and internal audit. *Accounting and Finance*, *46*(3), 387–404. doi:10.1111/j.1467-629X.2006.00174.x

Thi, N., & Hong, P. (2017). The Determinants of Audit Fees for Companies in Vietnam. *Journal of Economic Development, 19*(2), 68–88.

Ul Haq, A., & Leghari, M. K. (2015). Determinants of Audit Fee in Pakistan. *Research Journal of Finance and Accounting, 6*(9), 176–189.

Urhoghide, R. O., & Izedonmi, F. O. (2015). An Empirical Investigation of Audit Fee Determinants in Nigeria. *International Journal of Business and Social Research, 5*(8), 48–58.

Vafeas, N., & Waegelein, J. F. (2007). The association between audit committees, compensation incentives, and corporate audit fees. *Review of Quantitative Finance and Accounting, 28*(3), 241–255. doi:10.100711156-006-0012-9

Xie, B., Davidson, W. N. III, & DaDalt, P. J. (2003). Earnings management and corporate governance: The role of the board and the audit committee. *Journal of Corporate Finance, 9*(3), 295–316. doi:10.1016/S0929-1199(02)00006-8

Yatim, P., Kent, P., & Clarkson, P. (2006). Governance structures, ethnicity, and audit fees of Malaysian listed firms. *Managerial Auditing Journal, 21*(7), 757–782. doi:10.1108/02686900610680530

Zaman, M., Hudaib, M., & Haniffa, R. (2011). Corporate Governance Quality, Audit Fees and Non-Audit Services Fees. *Journal of Business Finance & Accounting, 38*(1-2), 165–197. doi:10.1111/j.1468-5957.2010.02224.x

KEY TERMS AND DEFINITIONS

Agency Theory: A supposition that explains the problems that can exist between principals (shareholders) and the agents (managers) resulting from the different goals among them.

Audit Fees: The price paid by a company for an external audit that will certificate its financial statements.

Big Four Firms: The biggest four companies that offers services in audit, taxation, management consulting and other related services: Deloitte, Pricewaterhousecoopers, Ernst & Young, and KPMG.

Corporate Governance: Is a system of practices, processes and rules by which companies are governed and controlled, in order to protect the stakeholder's interests.

Discretionary Accruals: The accruals that do not result from the normal course of business activity, also known as abnormal accruals.

Earnings Management: Is a practice that involves a set of accountings decisions by management in order to obtain profitable advantageous of it.

Supervisory Board: An independent Board which main goal is providing an independent review of the financial reporting process, internal controls and external audit.

ENDNOTES

1 http://www.cmvm.pt/pt/Pages/home.aspx

2 https://www.cnmv.es/portal/home.aspx

Chapter 3
Audit Education in the Polytechnic Institute of Cávado and Ave and the Audit Expectation Gap

Sara Serra
Polytechnic Institute of Cávado and Ave, Portugal

Patrícia Gomes
https://orcid.org/0000-0002-7587-2028
Polytechnic Institute of Cávado and Ave, Portugal

Cristiana Silva
Polytechnic Institute of Cávado and Ave, Portugal

ABSTRACT

The audit expectation gap (AEG) is present in society and, while there, will encourage discrediting the auditors. Given the seriousness of this situation, several solutions have been pointed out, one of which is to promote audit education. The aim of this chapter is to verify if adult education, taught at the Polytechnic Institute of Cávado and Ave (IPCA), reduces the AEG, considering the perceptions of its students about the role assigned to the auditors and the degree of success of the auditors in certain situations. The application of a questionnaire allowed to conclude that, as the literature review showed, audit education changes the perceptions of IPCA students about the role and degree of success of the auditors, generally reducing the AEG.

DOI: 10.4018/978-1-5225-7356-2.ch003

INTRODUCTION

The AEG has become an important issue for everyone because of the financial scandals and bankruptcies of enterprises. This situation has led to a crisis of public trust and raised concerns about the relationship between auditor and client (Wolf, Tackett, & Claypool, 1999). According to Almeida (2005), the AEG has been affecting audit professionals for several years, creating a critical and litigious environment, promoted by the courts, politicians, the press, and society in general, that hinders responsibilities and performance. Therefore, the AEG is due to the uncertainty associated with the objective, value, nature, and effect of an audit. As such, according to Otalor and Okafor (2013), the greater the AEG, the greater the negative impact on the financial statements of the entities.

It is therefore urgent to identify solutions to minimize the problem of the AEG. Audit education is one of the solutions pointed out because, according to Pierce and Kilcommins (1996) and Lee et al. (2008), this improves the knowledge and understanding of the auditor's role and responsibilities. Moreover, Okafor and Otalor (2013) and Devi and Devi (2014) argued that a lack of education about audit standards and audit practices is the main reason for the AEG. Thus, the importance of the effect of audit education on the AEG, which has already been investigated by several authors (Ali, Heang, Mohamad, & Ojo, 2008; Almeida, & Colomina, 2009; Bailey, Bylinski, & Shields, 1983; Enes, 2013; Epstein, & Geiger, 1994; Fadzly, & Ahmad, 2004; Ferguson, Richardson, & Wines, 2000; Gramling, Schatzberg, & Wallace, 1996; Idowu, & Oluwatoyin, 2014; Ihendinihu, & Robert, 2014; Kose, & Erdogan, 2015; Lee, Azham, & Kandasamy, 2008; Madsen, 2013; Monroe, & Woodliff, 1993; Pierce, & Kilcommins, 1996; Rehana, 2010).

Following this research line, the objective of this paper is to verify whether audit education as taught at the IPCA reduces the AEG, considering the students' perception of the role assigned to the auditors and the degree of success of the auditors in certain situations. Although it is not the aim of this research, it is also expected that its results will allow the identification of the subjects that students are not yet aware of and, therefore, to highlight the programmatic contents of education in financial auditing that should be improved.

In order to measure the students' perception of the role assigned to auditors, as well as the degree of success of the auditors in certain situations, a questionnaire was elaborated based on Enes (2013), Ferguson et al. (2000), and Gramling et al. (1996). The questionnaire was applied to two distinct groups of IPCA students: (1) students who had obtained audit training in the course and (2) students who had not obtained audit education in the course.

The analysis of the data reveals that audit education has an impact on the AEG, reducing it in all situations except the auditor's role regarding the internal control system, management, and continuity of the audited entity. Even after audit education, students continue to believe that the auditor is responsible for ensuring that the internal control system is well implemented, that the company is managed efficiently, and that its continuity is not in doubt. This denotes the problem of students' lack of knowledge.

This study also allows us to conclude that audit education increased the students' confidence in the work of the auditor, since they considered that, in the course of their work, auditors are successful in finding solutions to detected problems, complying with laws and regulations, as well as preventing and detecting the occurrence of errors and irregularities.

In addition to this introduction, this study contemplates a theoretical framework on the AEG and the importance of audit education for its reduction. This is followed by the case study, where the research methodology is presented, as well as the analysis and interpretation of the results. The study ends with the conclusion and respective solutions and recommendations, as well as future research directions.

THE AUDIT EXPECTATION GAP

As mentioned by Liggio (1974), the AEG results from the difference between the performance idealized by the auditors and that idealized by the users of financial information, but this can be motivated by several factors. According to the study by Almeida and Colomina (2009) carried out in Portugal, and that by Masoud (2017b) carried out in Libya, the AEG is due not only to the lack of adequate standards and the inadequate performance of the auditors but also to the differences in reasonableness related to society and the organization. According to Adeyemi and Olowookere (2011) and Almeida (2012), the factor that most influences audit dissatisfaction is the auditor's inadequate performance.

In South Africa, Gloeck and Jager (1993) concluded that the AEG is due to the auditor's lack of independence and objectivity, uncertainties about the auditor's role, and dissatisfaction with the audit. In addition to these aspects, Bailey, Bylinski and Shields. (1977), Humphrey, Moizer, & Turley (1993), and Almeida (2012) pointed out that the AEG is essentially motivated by the stakeholders' perceptions about the role and success of the auditor in the detection of errors and fraud, as well as the detection of illegal acts. According to Low, Foo and Koh (1988), stakeholders understand the audit as a seal of accuracy on the company's financial statements and expect auditors to provide an absolute guarantee (Enofe, Mgbane, Aronmwan, & Ogbeide, 2013). Incidentally, Salehi (2016) stated that stakeholders expect the auditor to ensure that financial statements are free of errors and fraud and that entities are managed efficiently and in accordance with the law.

McEnroe and Martens (2001), Dixon, Woodhead, & Soliman (2006), and Madsen (2013) also pointed out as the cause of the AEG the auditors' responsibility to detect and prevent fraud, monitor the audited entities' internal control systems, and prepare financial statements.

In New Zealand, Cameron (1993) analysed the relationship between auditors and audited companies through the opinions of accountants. The author concluded that stakeholders expect auditors to provide accounting advisory services, be proactive, identify problems, and advise on the development of the business.

Importance of Audit Education to the Audit Expectation Gap

Following the literature review cited, it is concluded that the AEG exists and is present in society. Thus, the need arises to eliminate the AEG or at least reduce it. Humphrey (1997) hoped that the problem estates' over time, but the constant scandals of fraud and bankruptcy of audited companies make this problem difficult to solve.

Auditors' responses to the AEG can be described as either defensive or constructive (Sweeney, 1997; Gay, Schelluch, & Baines, 1998). A constructive response defends the extension of the scope and function of the audit. The defensive response emphasizes the need to educate the public about the role and functions of the auditor. Therefore, Godsell (1991), Almeida (2005), Lee et al. (2008), Heliodoro (2009), and Kose and Erdogan (2015) stated that audit education is essential for users of audit services. Monroe and Woodliff (1993), Epstein and Geiger (1994), Gramling et al. (1996), Pierce and Kilcommins (1996), Ferguson et al. (2000), Shaikh and Talha (2003), and Enes (2013) reported that users' knowledge of financial information about auditing has a direct influence on the AEG. Thus, audit education may play an important role in solving this problem.

In Australia, Monroe and Woodliff (1993) analysed the effect of audit education on the AEG. They concluded that students' opinions changed considerably after receiving audit education. Thus, after receiving audit education, students now considered the most credible audited financial information, and the belief that audit reports conveyed messages about the future prospects of the audited entity declined, reducing the AEG.

Epstein and Geiger (1994) also performed a study on the subject in the United States. After analysing two groups of investors, they concluded that investors with education in the areas of accounting, finance, and investment analysis do not expect audit reports to convey an absolute level of security to financial statements.

Pierce and Kilcommins (1996) indicated in their study in Ireland that there is a significant reduction in the misunderstanding of auditing standards as students obtain audit education. Thus, the authors concluded that audit education can be an effective approach to reduce the AEG.

Gramling et al. (1996) carried out a study with students in higher education courses related to auditing in North American universities and with auditors, allowing comparison of the perspectives of finalist students and auditors. The authors compared the students' perception of the audit at the end of the education with the auditors' perception and concluded that, in some areas, the AEG was reduced.

Ferguson et al. (2000) made a comparison between the perspectives of Canadian and Australian students in the course of their academic education, students who trained with auditors, and auditors themselves. They concluded that audit education is a determining factor in the reduction of the AEG, but that this reduction is considerably higher when the students have a more practical contact with these subjects, bringing their perception about the role of the audit to that of the auditors.

Enes (2013) concluded that audit education does not completely reduce the AEG but has a positive impact on students' perception that the main role of auditors is not to focus on the prevention and detection of errors, fraud, and illicit acts that, according to Almeida (2012), would be the causes for the existence of the AEG in Portugal.

Fadzly and Ahmad (2004) studied the existence of the AEG in Malaysia by surveying auditors and stakeholders (bankers, investors, and brokers). The major differences were related to the auditor's responsibilities in fraud detection and prevention, preparation of financial statements and accounting records, and internal control. Using reading material as an audit teaching method, the results indicated that after reading the material, there were no significant differences between the auditors and the stakeholders, who were interviewed before and after obtaining the education.

Also in Malaysia, Ali et al. (2008) conducted research to verify whether there were significant differences in the perceptions of accounting students before and after performing an audit internship. In this study, the results are not conclusive, since the audit internship did not reveal anything unequivocal about the audit.

Rehana (2010) also investigated the role of audit education in the AEG, in Bangladesh. The author concluded that audit education improved knowledge about the auditor's responsibilities, audit reliability, and utility of audited information. That is, the author concluded that audit education significantly reduces the AEG.

In Nigeria, Ihendinihu and Robert (2014) investigated the extent to which public confidence about the outcome of the audit process can be improved by audit education. The authors concluded that audit education has a significant effect on the AEG.

Also in Nigeria, Idowu and Oluwatoyin (2014) found that audit education reduced the AEG. After education, students became more aware of the auditor's responsibilities and the role of the company's management in preparing the company's financial statements. These results were consistent with those obtained by Masoud (2017a) in Jordan and by Kumari, Dissabandara, & Ajward (2018) in Sri Lanka.

The study Elad (2017) conducted in Sweden also showed that audit education reduced the AEG with regard to the responsibilities of the auditor in preparing a company's financial statements and in the selection of audit procedures. However, audit education had no impact on perceptions of the auditors' responsibilities for detecting fraud or on the credibility of the audit and reliability of the financial statements.

In Turkey, Koşe and Erdogan (2015) revealed that more experienced users have less unreasonable expectations regarding the auditor's responsibilities. Similarly, when the level of education increases, the AEG decreases.

Considering that the mentioned studies show that audit education contributes to reducing the AEG by altering the perceptions of stakeholders about the role of the auditor and the degree of success of the auditors resulting from the audit, we defined the following hypotheses of investigation:

Hypothesis One: Students have different perceptions about the role of auditors before and after receiving audit education.

Hypothesis Two: Students have different perceptions about auditors' success in certain situations before and after receiving audit education.

CASE STUDY

Methodology

The objective of this research is to verify whether audit education reduces the AEG. Starting from the basic research problem, this study aims to explore how audit education changes students' perceptions of (1) the role assigned to the auditors and (2) auditors' degree of success in certain situations. The fulfilment of the aforementioned objective will provide empirical evidence on the effect of audit education on the change of the perception of the stakeholders but will also show the limitations of this research and potential points to improve.

In order to measure the students' perceptions of the role assigned to auditors as well as the auditors' degree of success in certain situations, the questionnaire method was applied to two distinct groups of IPCA students: (1) students who obtained audit education in the course and (2) students who did not obtain audit education in the course. This data collection technique fits better considering the objectives of the study that it was used in similar prior researches such as Gramling et al. (1996), Ferguson et al. (2000), and Enes (2013).

The questionnaire was adapted from Enes (2013), whose questionnaire, in turn, was based on that of Ferguson et al. (2000), who in turn supported their research on Gramling et al. (1996), which allows validation of the statements formulated and ensures their consistency. The questionnaire applied is composed of six groups of statements. However, considering the purpose of this study, two groups of statements were considered in the analysis: (1) statements about the students' perceptions about the role of auditors (see table 1) and (2) statements related to perceptions regarding auditors' success in relation to certain activities (see table 3). In total, there are 41 statements. A 7-point Likert scale was used, where 1 means "total disagreement" and 7 means "total agreement" (1 = Strongly disagree; 2 = Moderately disagree; 3 = Partially disagree; 4 = Neither agree nor disagree; 5 = Partially agree; 6 = Moderately agree; 7 = Totally agree).

It should also be noted that the questionnaires were distributed face-to-face in the classrooms of the courses involved in the research during the months of May and June of 2016.

The data obtained through the questionnaires were processed through SPSS Statistics software (version 23). It is assumed that the sample is representative of the population, that is, that students who answered the questionnaire represent all students of the IPCA School of Management who have, or lack, audit education.

In order to analyse the internal consistency of the data, Cronbach's alpha test was used, which is the most used indicator to evaluate the reliability and consistency of data, especially when using a Likert scale in a survey. Through the analysis of this indicator, it is concluded that the data are reliable, since Cronbach's alpha has a value of 0.733. According to Serra (2013), the results of this test, when the indicators are positively related, vary between 0 and 1. The reliability of these indicators is proven when Cronbach's alpha has a value higher than 0.8 or, in exploratory investigations, between 0.6 and 0.7.

To test the hypotheses formulated in this study, an analysis of the statistical significance of the two groups of students' responses was carried out. To evaluate the statistical significance of the differences in the responses, the T-test was applied to two independent samples, as was done in the studies of Ferguson et al. (2000) and Enes (2013). In rejecting the null hypothesis, we confirm the research hypothesis that the students have different perceptions about the role and success of auditors before and after receiving audit education.

To calculate the test statistic, we considered the assumption of equality of variances of the two samples, each sample corresponding to each of the groups analysed. Therefore, according to Enes (2013), an F-Test was carried out, which allowed us to test the equality of variances, that is, $\sigma_{G1}^2 = \sigma_{G2}^2$. If the sigma value is less than or equal to 0.05, the variances are different in the two groups. Conversely, if the sigma is greater than 0.05, we do not reject the null hypothesis and assume that the variances are equal.

Sample

Two groups of students enrolled in the academic year 2015/2016 were selected: The first group (G1) is composed by students who had not yet obtained an education in auditing, and the second group (G2) is composed by students who had obtained an education in auditing. The first group included the IPCA students in the second year of the course in Accounting and the course in Banking and Insurance Management, both day and post-work regimes. In the second group were students in the courses for the third year of the Degree in Accounting and the Degree in Banking and Insurance Management, also in the day and post-work regimes.

Therefore, the population consisted of the number of students enrolled in the courses, and the sample selected was composed of the students who were interviewed and were in the class in which the questionnaire was distributed. A response rate of 51.20% was obtained: Of the 334 students enrolled, 171 completed the questionnaire.

ANALYSIS AND INTERPRETATION OF DATA

In this section, we analyse and interpret the data about students' perception of the audit, as well as the influence of education in auditing, with a univariate analysis of the data, followed by a bivariate analysis.

Students' Perceptions About the Auditor's Role

The descriptive analysis of students' perceptions about the auditor's role is presented in table 1 and is based on nine statements. In all statements, a mean of responses greater than 4 was obtained on a 7-point scale. This shows that, on average, students agreed with all statements about the auditor's role. However, there was a tendency to increase the level of agreement on all issues among students with auditing education, with the exception of statement 7, that "the company is managed efficiently". This means that audit education has altered the perception of IPCA students regarding the auditor's role.

Concerning statement 1 ("*Auditors must ensure that the financial statement is in conformity with the conceptual framework*"), the overall average response was 5.61. The answer most often given by G1 students was "neither agree nor disagree" (27.5%) and by G2 was "totally agree" (40.2%). At first, the students were hesitant to agree with this statement, but after audit education, their doubts were eliminated, and students mostly agreed with this statement. This demonstrates that audit education altered students' perception, helping to elucidate the stakeholders' overall objectives for the independent auditor and the conduct of an audit in accordance with international standards on auditing: "the purpose of the audit is to express an opinion on whether the financial statements are prepared, in all material respects, in accordance with an applicable financial reporting framework." This was also confirmed by the T-test result (see table 2).

Contrary to what has been observed in this study, the intensity of concordance decreased in the studies of Ferguson et al. (2000) and Enes (2013) after students received audit education. In the study by Gramling et al. (1996), the means of the answers remained unchanged in the value of 6.37.

This trend was also noted in statement 2 ("*Auditors must ensure that the financial statements do not contain material misstatements resulting from intentional acts*") and statement 3 ("*Auditors must ensure that the financial statements do not contain material misstatements of errors*"), demonstrating once again that audit education changed the students' perceptions and reduced the AEG because, according to paragraph 5 of ISA 200, "Overall objectives of the independent auditor and the conduct of an audit in accordance with international standards on auditing", the international auditing standards require the auditor to obtain reasonable assurance about whether the financial statements as a whole are free from material misstatement, whether due to fraud, understood as intentional acts, or error. This finding was also confirmed by the application of the T-test, the result presented in table 2.

In addition, Enes (2013) concluded that audit education had a positive impact on students' perception of the role of auditors in the prevention and detection of errors, fraud, and illicit acts, which, according

Table 1. Descriptive analysis: Perceptions about the auditor's role

Statements	Group	Frequency (%)							Measures of Central Tendency and Dispersion		
		1	2	3	4	5	6	7	Mean	Median	Standard Deviation
1. Auditors must ensure that the FS is in conformity with the conceptual framework.	G1	1.4	0	4.3	27.5	23.2	23.2	20.3	5.2174	5	1.30462
	G2	0	0	3.9	11.8	17.6	26.5	40.2	5.8725	6	1.18298
	Total	0.6	0	4.1	18.1	19.9	25.1	32.2	5.6082	6	1.27129
2. Auditors must ensure that the FS does not contain material misstatements resulting from intentional acts.	G1	1.4	0	5.8	33.3	23.2	18.8	17.4	5.0290	5	1.30577
	G2	0	1.0	2.0	20.6	20.6	15.7	40.2	5.6863	6	1.29722
	Total	0.6	0.6	3.5	25.7	21.6	17.0	31.0	5.4211	5	1.33655
3. Auditors must ensure that the FS does not contain material misstatements resulting from errors.	G1	1.4	0	7.2	31.9	20.3	23.2	15.9	5.0290	5	1.31698
	G2	1.0	0	3.9	21.6	18.6	20.6	34.3	5.5588	6	1.34660
	Total	1.2	0	5.3	25.7	19.3	21.6	26.9	5.3450	5	1.35613
4. Auditors must ensure that the FS presents a true and fair view of the company.	G1	2.9	1.4	7.2	15.9	13.0	27.5	31.9	5.4493	6	1.55806
	G2	0	0	4.9	10.8	11.8	21.6	51.0	6.0294	7	1.23044
	Total	1.2	0,6	5.8	12.9	12.3	24.0	43.3	5.7953	6	1.39713
5. Auditors must ensure that the company has the responsibility to prepare the FS.	G1	0	0	5.8	26.1	20.3	29.0	18.8	5.2899	6	1.55806
	G2	0	1.0	2.9	11.8	28.4	20.6	35.3	5.7059	6	1.20714
	Total	0	0.6	4.1	17.5	25.1	24.0	28.7	5.5380	6	1.22355
6. Auditors must ensure that the internal control system is well implemented.	G1	0	1.4	8.7	37.7	23.2	15.9	13.0	4.8261	5	1.23618
	G2	1.0	0	1.0	21.6	21.6	28.4	26.5	5.5392	6	1.21600
	Total	0.6	0,6	4.1	28.1	22.2	23.4	21.1	5.2515	5	1.26999
7. Auditors must ensure that the company is managed efficiently.	G1	1.4	2.9	8.7	23.2	24.6	31.9	7.2	4.9130	5	1.30315
	G2	1.0	0	3.9	19.6	22.5	28.4	24.5	5.4608	6	1.25605
	Total	1.2	1.2	5.8	21.1	23.4	29.8	17.5	5.2398	5	1.29970
8. Auditors must ensure that regulators are informed of any irregularity committed by the company.	G1	1.4	1.4	7.2	29.0	26.1	20.3	14.5	4.9565	5	1.32215
	G2	0	2.9	2.9	11.8	24.5	31.4	26.5	5.5784	6	1.24627
	Total	0.6	2.3	4.7	18.7	25.1	26.9	21.6	5.3275	5	1.30983
9. The auditor must ensure that the continuity of the company is not in doubt.	G1	1.4	2.9	8.7	34.8	20.3	17.4	14.5	4.7971	5	1.38882
	G2	0	3,9	1.0	20.6	25.5	25.5	23.5	5.3824	5	1.29005
	Total	0.6	3.5	4.1	26.3	23.4	22.2	19.9	5.1462	5	1.35765

Legend: FS = Financial statement

to Humphrey et al. (1993), Baron, Johnson, Searfoss and Smith (1977), McEnroe and Martens (2001), Dixon et al. (2006), Almeida (2012), and Madsen (2013), would be one of the main causes of the AEG.

In statement 4 ("*Auditors must ensure that the financial statements present a true and fair view of the company*"), both groups' most often chosen answer was "strongly agree". Nevertheless, as in the study by Gramling et al. (1996), there was an increase in the level of agreement after audit education. This demonstrates, once again, the influence of audit education on altering students' perceptions and reducing the AEG. In fact, in accordance with Article 45 (2) (i) of the Statute of the Order of Statutory Auditors and paragraph 3 of ISA 200, "Overall objectives of the independent auditor and the conduct of an audit in accordance with international standards on auditing", the auditor must give an opinion on whether the financial statements are appropriately presented, in all material respects, or give a true and proper picture according to the conceptual framework. It should be noted that this result is contrary to the studies of Ferguson et al. (2000) and Enes (2013).

Concerning statement 5 ("*Auditors must ensure that the company has the responsibility to produce the financial statements*"), the overall average response was 5.54. After audit education, the students changed their perception and agreed more with the presented question. This means that there was a reduction of the AEG, since according to paragraph 13 (j) of the ISA 200, "Overall objectives of the independent auditor and the conduct of an audit in accordance with international standards on auditing", management is responsible for preparing financial statements in accordance with the applicable financial reporting framework. The level of significance presented in table 2 also allows us to prove the independence of the samples. These results coincide with those of Fadzly and Ahmad (2004) and Elad (2017).

In statement 6 ("*Auditors must ensure that the internal control system is well implemented*"), the overall mean response was 5.25, which was higher in G2 than in G1. The change in students' perceptions is also evident in table 2. Incidentally, this is the statement where the differences are statistically most significant. This result was not expected because the auditor does not have the function of ensuring that the internal control system is well implemented. In fact, in the course of the audit, the auditor assesses the internal control system, but only to identify the risks of material misstatement. In addition, the report on the findings and recommendations about the internal control system is made known only to the entity's management. For these reasons, Gramling et al. (1996), Ferguson et al. (2000), Fadzly and Ahmad (2004), and Enes (2013) revealed that, after audit education, the tendency to agree with this statement was reduced.

The results of the univariate analysis of statement 7 ("*Auditors must ensure that the company is managed efficiently*"), presented in table 1, reveal students' different perceptions after audit education through a higher average and median in G2 and consequently an increase in the AEG, since according to Article 44 (5) of the Statute of the Order of Statutory Auditors, the audit does not include a guarantee as to the efficiency or effectiveness with which the board of directors conducted the activities of the audited entity. This was also found by Gramling et al. (1996). In contrast, Enes (2013) and Ferguson et al. (2000) revealed a reduction in the level of agreement by students who had already received audit education, that is, a reduction of the AEG. Although the univariate analysis revealed the students' different perceptions before and after obtaining audit education, the results of the T-test, presented in table 2, did not reveal a statistically significant difference between the groups.

In statement 8 ("*Auditors must ensure that the regulators are informed of any irregularity committed by the company*"), an overall average response of 5.33 was found. However, the average of the answers was higher in G2, proving that the audit education altered the students' perceptions and reduced the AEG, since this duty of communication is imposed by articles 79 and 81 of the Statute of the Order of Statutory Auditors. These results were also obtained by Enes (2013) and Gramling et al. (1996). Ferguson et al. (2000), although in this aspect evidencing an increase in the AEG, revealed statistically significant differences in students' perceptions, as occurs in the present study, whose level of significance is found in table 2.

Statement 9 ("*Auditor must ensure that the continuity of the company is not in doubt.*") presents an overall average of 5.15. However, the level of agreement with the statement was higher after audit education, like in the study of Gramling et al. (1996), but unlike in the studies by Monroe and Woodliff (1993), Ferguson et al. (2000), and Enes (2013). The change in perceptions is also evident in table 2.

However, in this case, audit education increased the AEG, since according to paragraph 5 of Article 44 of the Statute of the Order of Statutory Auditors, the audit does not include a guarantee as to the future viability of the audited entity. However, Article 45 (2) (f) of the Statute of the Order of Statutory Auditors states, "the statutory certification of accounts must be in writing and shall include a statement of any material uncertainties relating to events or conditions which may give rise to doubts the entity's ability to continue with its activities." Furthermore, according to Article 45 (3) of the Statute of the Order of Statutory Auditors, "statutory certification of accounts of public interest entities also includes the elements provided for in Article 10 of Regulation (EU) No 537/2014 of the European Parliament and of the Council of 16 April 2014". Among these elements is giving an opinion on the economic and financial viability of the entity.

ISA 570, "Going Concern", was changed in 2016 for this reason, and this is up to the auditor responsible for assessing whether the principle of continuity was properly used by the management body in the preparation of financial statements and to check whether there are materially relevant uncertainties that impede the continuity of the company.

Table 2 presents the results of the Levene test and the T-test. The Levene test reveals the existence of different variances only for statement 4, since it is unique in that the value of "Sig" is below the level of significance (0.05). As such, in this case, we will consider the value of the T-test presented for the equal

Table 2. Levene test and T-test result: Perception about the auditor's role

Statements		Levene Test for Equality of Variances		T-Test for Equality of Means			
		F	Sig.	T	Gl	Sig. (Two-Tailed)	Mean Difference
1.	Equal variances assumed	1.115	.293	-3.408	169	.001	-.65516
	Equal variances not assumed			-3.344	136.292	.001	-.65516
2.	Equal variances assumed	1.004	.318	-3.242	169	.001	-.65729
	Equal variances not assumed			-3.238	145.457	.001	-.65729
3.	Equal variances assumed	.726	.395	-2.547	169	.012	-.52984
	Equal variances not assumed			-2.558	148.267	.012	-.52984
4.	Equal variances assumed	6.188	.014	-2.713	169	.007	-.58014
	Equal variances not assumed			-2.594	122.769	.011	-.58014
5.	Equal variances assumed	.052	.702	-2.206	169	.036	-.40153
	Equal variances not assumed			-2.204	143.419	.038	-.40153
6.	Equal variances assumed	.017	.819	-3.737	169	.000	-.71313
	Equal variances not assumed			-3.725	144.479	.000	-.71313
7.	Equal variances assumed	.042	.838	-2.756	169	.950	.03197
	Equal variances not assumed			-2.736	74.132	.958	.03197
8.	Equal variances assumed	.033	.856	-3.312	169	.002	-.62191
	Equal variances not assumed			-3.088	140.207	.002	-.62191
9.	Equal variances assumed	.303	.583	-2.822	169	.005	-.58525
	Equal variances not assumed			-2.782	138.727	.006	-.58525

non-assumed variances, which is -2.594. In all other cases, the value of the T-test to be considered is what is presented in the same assumed variances. The analysis of T-test significance levels shows that in all cases except statement 7, there were statistically significant differences. This allows us to validate H1 and affirm that students have different perceptions about the role and responsibilities of auditors before and after receiving audit education.

Students' Perception of the Degree of Auditors' Success

In this part of the paper, we intend to analyse students' perceptions regarding some desirable attributes in auditors that contribute to the success of the audit. Table 3 presents the descriptive statistics of the obtained data.

Analysing the results, it is verified that, in both groups, there is agreement, since in all the statements, the averages are above 4. It is emphasized that there is an increase in the average level of agreement after the audit education, as occurred previously in the perception of the auditor's role.

Statement 1 ("In the course of their work, auditors are successful in finding solutions to the problems detected") presents an average response of 5.32. As in the studies by Gramling et al. (1996), Ferguson et al. (2000), and Enes (2013), students attributed a higher value to this attribute of auditors after obtaining audit education. Cameron (1993) also concluded that stakeholders expect auditors to identify problems and advise on the development of the business.

Table 3. Descriptive analysis: Students' perception of the degree of auditors' success

Statements	Group	Frequency (%)							Measures of Central Tendency and Dispersion		
		1	2	3	4	5	6	7	Mean	Median	Standard Deviation
1. In the course of their work, auditors are successful in finding solutions to the problems detected.	G1	2.9	2.9	4.3	27.5	23.2	26.1	13.0	4.9565	5	1.40832
	G2	0	0	2.0	20.6	23.5	26.5	27.5	5.5686	6	1.15621
	Total	1.2	1.2	2.9	23.4	23.4	26.3	21.6	5.3216	5	1.2549
2. In the course of their work, auditors are successful in preventing the occurrence of errors and irregularities.	G1	1.4	0	2.9	23.2	21.7	34.8	15.9	5.3188	6	1.21864
	G2	0	0	1.0	13.7	21.6	26.5	37.3	5.8529	6	1.10263
	Total	0.6	0	1.8	17.5	21.6	29.8	28.7	5.6374	6	1.17704
3. In the course of their work, auditors are successful in detecting errors and irregularities.	G1	1.4	0	4.3	21.7	18.8	29.0	24.6	5.4203	6	1.32183
	G2	0	0	0	9.8	19.6	30.4	40.2	6.0098	6	0.99995
	Total	0.6	0	1.8	14.6	19.3	29.8	33.9	5.7719	6	1.17349
4. In the course of their work, auditors are successful in complying with laws and regulations.	G1	1.4	0	7.2	15.9	18.8	24.6	31.9	5.5217	6	1.39967
	G2	0	0	2.9	12.7	21.6	19.6	43.1	5.8725	6	1.19132
	Total	0.6	0	4.7	14.0	20.5	21.6	38.6	5.7310	6	1.28710
5. In the course of their work, auditors succeed in acting independently without regard to self-interest.	G1	5.8	4.3	4.3	27.5	15.9	11.6	30.4	5.0000	6	1.77400
	G2	0	1.0	2.9	11.8	19.6	16.7	48.0	5.9216	6	1.25616
	Total	2.3	2.3	3.5	18.1	18.1	14.6	40.9	5.5497	6	1.54981

The changes in students' perceptions were also confirmed by the level of significance resulting from the T-test (see table 4). Indeed, while solving problems is not the purpose of the audit, the resulting audit recommendations help the entity to solve many deficiencies. Moreover, according to Dias (2006), all the suggestions and references mentioned in the audit report are valuable elements to support the entity's strategic decisions and to help it fulfil its mission and achieve its objectives.

Both groups strongly agreed with statement 2 ("In the course of their work, auditors are successful in preventing the occurrence of errors and irregularities"). However, unlike in studies by Gramling et al. (1996), Ferguson et al. (2000), and Enes (2013), after receiving audit education, students agreed more with the statement. The prevention of errors and irregularities is the responsibility of the audited entity, through the implementation of an adequate internal control system. However, as evidenced by Kinney and Martin (1994), Navarro and Martínez (2004), and Monterrey and Sánchez (2007), the imminence of the audit and the resulting output increases employees' fear of irregularities. In addition, each audit results in a report identifying internal control weaknesses and respective recommendations. Based on all this, it is concluded that students have come to rely more on the work of auditors, as their main function is to verify that statements have material misstatements resulting from errors and irregularities. In fact, Monroe and Woodliff (1993) showed that, after receiving audit education, students began to consider audited financial information more credible.

In statement 3 ("In the course of their work, auditors can detect errors and irregularities"). Similarly, Gramling et al. (1996) also demonstrated the level of agreement among students who obtained audit education. However, Enes (2013) and Ferguson et al. (2000) found the reverse. This result, in addition to evidencing a change of perceptions about the background of the audit in relation to the area, reveals the importance of the audit work in most areas of knowledge.

To statement 4 ("In the course of their work, auditors are successful in complying with laws and regulations"), the most common answer by the students was "totally agree". Nevertheless, as in the studies by Ferguson et al. (2000) and Enes (2013), the level of agreement on this issue increased after students received audit education. In fact, according to Humphrey et al. (1993), García, Humphrey, Moizer, & Turley (1993), and Duréndez (2003), the audit gives more security to stakeholders regarding compliance with accounting and legal standards. However, the T-test result, shown in Table 4, reveals that the differences between the groups are not statistically significant, as was also the case with Gramling et al. (1996), Ferguson et al. (2000), and Enes (2013).

Statement 5 ("In the course of their work, auditors succeed in acting independently without regard to self-interest.") follows the tendency of previous answers. The increase in agreement intensity after audit education is also found in the studies of Ferguson et al. (2000) and Gramling et al. (1996). The bivariate analysis (see table 4) reveals that this is the item where audit education caused the greatest influence on students' perceptions. This result reveals a great advance in the reduction of the AEG because, as the study of Gloeck and Jager (1993) revealed, the AEG is due to the perceived lack of independence and objectivity of the auditors. Villacorta (2006) stated that if the auditor is not independent, then his or her opinion will be no more reliable than the financial statements prepared by the entity. This means that auditors are only in a position to properly serve stakeholders if they maintain a position of independence. Being aware of this situation, the audit professional bodies have issued various audit standards to promote independence, and the Sarbanes Oxley Act is one of the pioneers.

The results of the Levene test, presented in Table 4, reveal equal variances in statements 1, 2, and 4 and different variances in statements 3 and 5. As such, in statements 3 and 5, the T-test values presented

Table 4. Levene test and T-test result: Perception of auditors' degree of success

Statements		Levene Test for Equality of Variances		T-Test for Equality of Means			
		F	Sig.	T	Gl	Sig. (Two-Tailed)	Mean Difference
1.	Equal variances assumed	.592	.443	-3.107	169	.002	-.61211
	Equal variances not assumed			-2.992	126.448	.003	-.61211
2.	Equal variances assumed	.643	.424	-2.978	169	.003	-.53410
	Equal variances not assumed			-2.921	136.075	.004	-.53410
3.	Equal variances assumed	10.153	.002	-3.316	169	.001	-.58951
	Equal variances not assumed			-3.145	118.849	.002	-.58951
4.	Equal variances assumed	2.275	.133	-1.759	169	.080	-.35081
	Equal variances not assumed			-1.706	129.965	.090	-.35081
5.	Equal variances assumed	9.191	.003	-3.978	169	.000	-.92157
	Equal variances not assumed			-3.729	113.185	.000	-.92157

are for the equal non-assumed variances. In all other cases, the value of the T-test to be considered is what is presented in the same assumed variances. Considering the levels of significance from the T-test, it can be affirmed that statistically significant differences were obtained in all statements except statement 4. Therefore, H2 is validated, proving that the students had different perceptions about the degree of auditors' success in certain situations before and after receiving audit education.

SOLUTIONS AND RECOMMENDATIONS

From the above, it is concluded that, despite the reduction of the AEG through audit education, there is scope to improve the quality of audit education. As such, it is critical that stakeholders who need financial information to make their decisions obtain audit education, especially on audit standards and the audit process, because this is the only way they will understand the auditor's role, as well as the degree of success of their work.

FUTURE RESEARCH DIRECTIONS

For future research, it would be interesting to add to the groups of this investigation two other groups: students with professional audit experience and auditors. In this way, the results could be compared with the global research of Ferguson et al. (2000), which analysed the perceptions of students without professional audit experience before and after audit education, students with professional audit experience, and auditors. It would also be interesting to extend this study to other areas of the country and to other interested groups, such as audit teachers.

CONCLUSION

The AEG raises serious concerns, as not only the work but also the social responsibility of the auditor is concerned. This puts at risk the credibility that auditors provide to financial statements and affects the function of financial markets.

The AEG is motivated primarily by the fact that society does not understand the role of the auditor. The users of the financial information believe that auditors must give their opinions on certain matters that are not included in audit reports and must also increase their responsibilities, particularly in relation to fraud.

The several studies carried out have indicated ways to minimize the AEG. One of the solutions mentioned is audit education. In line with this solution, this study intended to show the effect of audit education on the AEG, namely, the IPCA students' perceptions about the role and degree of auditors' success. The study was carried out based on a questionnaire based on the studies of Gramling et al. (1996), Ferguson et al. (2000), and Enes (2013).

Analysis of the data showed that, in fact, audit education has an impact on the AEG. It was proved that audit education altered students' perceptions regarding the role and degree of auditors' success, since 12 statistically significant differences were obtained among the 14 total statements on this matter. Given the statistically significant differences in most of the statements, it is concluded that the research hypotheses formulated (Hypothesis One: Students have different perceptions about the role of auditors before and after receiving audit education; Hypothesis Two: Students have different perceptions about the success of auditors in certain situations before and after receiving audit education) have been validated, as in the studies of Gramling et al. (1996), Ferguson et al. (2000), and Enes (2013).

In most situations, audit education contributed to the reduction of the AEG. Contrary to what might be expected, even after obtaining audit education, students continued to believe that the auditor should ensure that the internal control system is well implemented, that the company is managed efficiently, and that the company's continuity is not in doubt. Regarding this aspect, even if the new model of the audit report requires the auditor to pronounce on this aspect, it will never guarantee the economic and financial viability of the entity, since this document will only mention that the auditor is not aware of any material uncertainties related to events or conditions that could raise significant doubts about the entity's ability to continue its activities.

This study also concluded that education in auditing increased the students' confidence in auditors' work and, essentially, in their usefulness, since they considered that, in the course of their work, auditors are successful in finding solutions to problems encountered, comply with laws and regulations, and prevent and detect the occurrence of errors and irregularities. Students also considered that, in the course of their work, auditors successfully act independently without regard to their own interest. This is a very important finding given that independence is one of the most important characteristics of the auditor, essentially because, as stated in paragraph 3 of ISA 200, "Overall objectives of the independent auditor and the conduct of an audit in accordance with international standards on auditing", the purpose of an audit is to increase the degree of confidence of financial statements' users.

The main limitation of this article is the size and diversity of the sample. Another of the limitations found was a large number of neutral answers: That is, a large percentage of the students "neither agreed nor disagreed" with several statements. This made it more difficult to determine the students' views on each issue.

The main contribution of this study is the presentation of the effect of the Financial Audit education on the students of the Degree in Banking and Insurance Management and Degree in Accounting of the IPCA, since there has never been a study on this subject in this institution of higher education. The results of this research will also allow us to identify the programmatic contents of audit education that should be improved.

REFERENCES

Adeyemi, S., & Olowookere, J. (2011). Stakeholders' perception of audit performance gap in Nigeria. *International Journal of Accounting and Financial Reporting*, *1*(1), 152–172. doi:10.5296/ijafr.v1i1.808

Ali, A., Heang, L., Mohamad, R., & Ojo, M. (2008). Internship and audit expectation gap among undergraduate students in Universiti Utara Malaysia. *Journal of Financial Reporting & Accounting*, *6*(1), 55–74. doi:10.1108/19852510880000635

Almeida, B. (2005). *Auditoria e sociedade: diferenças de expetativas*. Lisboa: Publisher Team.

Almeida, B. (2012). The Portuguese expectation gap: Empirical evidence. *Business and Management Review*, *2*(10), 28–46.

Almeida, B., & Colomina, C. (2009). Evidencia de las diferencias de expectativas en auditoria en mercados bursátiles de reducida dimensión: El caso portugués. *Revista Universo Contábil*, *5*(1), 100–114.

Bailey, K., Bylinski, J., & Shields, M. (1983). Effects of audit report wording changes on the perceived message. *Journal of Accounting Research*, *21*(2), 355–370. doi:10.2307/2490779

Baron, C., Johnson, D., Searfoss, D., & Smith, C. (1977). Uncovering corporate irregularities: Are we closing the expectation gap? *Journal of Accountancy*, *144*(4), 56–66.

Cameron, A. (1993). Do chartered accountants live up to small business expectation? *Accountants Journal*, *72*, 76–78.

Devi, A., & Devi, S. (2014). Audit expectation gap between auditors and users of financial statements. *European Journal of Business and Management*, *6*(14), 75–82.

Dias, A. (2006). *A Auditoria e a Tomada de Decisão*. Paper presented at the XI Congresso Internacional de Contabilidade e Auditoria, Coimbra.

Dixon, R., Woodhead, A., & Soliman, M. (2006). An investigation of the expectation gap in Egypt. *Managerial Auditing Journal*, *21*(3), 293–302. doi:10.1108/02686900610653026

Duréndez, A. (2003). The usefulness of the audit report in investment and financing decisions. *Managerial Auditing Journal*, *18*(6/7), 549–559. doi:10.1108/02686900310482687

Elad, F. (2017). *The Impact of Audit Education on the Audit Expectation Gap Evidence from Civilekonom Students in Sweden* (Business Administration Master's Thesis). Karlstand University, Karlstad.

Enes, E. (2013). *A educação como contributo para a redução das diferenças de expectativas em auditoria: o caso Português* (Unpublished Master's Thesis). Instituto Politécnico de Tomar, Tomar.

Enofe, A., Mgbane, C., Aronmwan, E., & Ogbeide, I. (2013). Audit reasonableness expectation gap: Users' perception in Nigeria. *International Journal of Business and Social Research, 3*(3), 154–163.

Epstein, M., & Geiger, M. (1994). Investor views of audit assurance: Recent evidence of the expectation gap. *Journal of Accountancy, 177*(1), 60–66.

Fadzly, M., & Ahmad, Z. (2004). Audit expectation gap: The case of Malaysia. *Managerial Auditing Journal, 19*(7), 897–915. doi:10.1108/02686900410549420

Ferguson, C., Richardson, G., & Wines, G. (2000). Audit education and training: The effect of formal studies and work experience. *Accounting Horizons, 14*(2), 137–167. doi:10.2308/acch.2000.14.2.137

García, M., Humphrey, C., Moizer, P., & Turley, S. (1993). Auditing expectations and performance in Spain and Britain: A comparative analysis. *The International Journal of Accounting, 28*(4), 281–307.

Gay, G., Schelluch, P., & Baines, A. (1998). Perceptions of messages conveyed by review and audit reports. *Accounting, Auditing & Accountability Journal, 11*(4), 472.494.

Gloeck, J., & Jager, H. (1993). *The focus point of the audit expectation gap in the Republic of South Africa.* Working paper, School of Accountancy, University of Pretoria.

Godsell, D. (1991). Auditors' legal liability and the expectation gap. *Australian Accountant, 61*(1), 22–28.

Gramling, A., Schatzberg, J., & Wallace, W. (1996). The role of undergraduate auditing coursework in reducing the expectation gap. *Issues in Accounting Education, 11*(1), 131–161.

Heliodoro, P. (2009). Expectation gap em auditoria. XIV *Encuentro AECA Innovación y responsabilidade: desafíos y soluciones.*

Humphrey, C. (1997). Debating audit expectations. *Current Issues in Auditing, 3*, 3–30.

Humphrey, C., Moizer, P., & Turley, S. (1993). The audit expectation gap in Britain: An empirical investigation. *Accounting and Business Research, 23*(1), 395–411. doi:10.1080/00014788.1993.9729907

Idowu, A., & Oluwatoyin, A. (2014). Impact of auditing education on audit expectation gap in Nigeria. *International Journal of Academic Research in Accounting. Finance and Management Sciences, 4*(3), 109–116.

IFAC. (2009). *International Standard on Auditing 200: Overall objectives of the independent auditor and the conduct of an audit in accordance with international standards on auditing*. New York: International Federation of Accountants.

IFAC. (2016). *International Standard on Auditing 570: Going Concern.* New York: International Federation of Accountants.

Ihendinihu, J., & Robert, S. (2014). Role of audit education in minimizing audit expectation gap (AEG) in Nigeria. *International Journal of Business and Management, 9*(2), 203–211. doi:10.5539/ijbm.v9n2p203

Kinney, W., & Martin, R. (1994). Does Auditing Reduce Bias in Financial Reporting? A Review of Audit-Related Adjustment Studies. *Auditing, 13*, 149–156.

Kose, Y., & Erdogan, S. (2015). The audit expectation gap in Turkey. *Journal of Accounting & Finance*, 193-214.

Kumari, J., Dissabandara, D., & Ajward, A. (2018). The Audit Expectations Gap and the Role of Audit Education: Evidence from Sri Lanka. *Vidyodaya Journal of Management*, *3*(1), 1–26. doi:10.31357/vjm.v3i1.3386

Lee, T., Azham, M., & Kandasamy, S. (2008). Towards reducing the audit expectation gap: Possible mission? *Accounting Today*, *21*(2), 18–22.

Liggio, C. (1974). The expectation gap: The accountant's Waterloo. *Journal of Contemporary Business*, *3*(3), 27–44.

Low, A., Foo, S., & Koh, H. (1988). The expectation gap between financial analysts and auditors – some empirical evidence. *Singapore Accountant*, *4*, 10–13.

Madsen, P. (2013). *Commercial loan officers and the audit expectation gap* (Master's thesis). Uppsala Universitet Department of Business Studies.

Masoud, N. (2017a). Audit expectation gap among undergraduate accounting at Jordanian Universities. *Journal of Private Equity*, *20*(2), 73–89. doi:10.3905/jpe.2017.20.2.073

Masoud, N. (2017b). An empirical study of audit expectation-performance gap: The case of Libya. *Research in International Business and Finance*, *41*, 1–15. doi:10.1016/j.ribaf.2017.04.012

McEnroe, J., & Martens, S. (2001). Auditors' and investors' perceptions of the expectation gap. *Accounting Horizons*, *15*(4), 345–358. doi:10.2308/acch.2001.15.4.345

Monroe, G., & Woodliff, D. (1993). The effect of education on the audit expectation gap. *Accounting and Finance*, *33*(1), 61–78. doi:10.1111/j.1467-629X.1993.tb00195.x

Monroe, G., & Woodliff, D. (1994). An empirical investigation of the audit expectation gap: Australian evidence. *Accounting and Finance*, *34*(1), 47–74. doi:10.1111/j.1467-629X.1994.tb00262.x

Monterry, J., & Sánchez, A. (2007). Rotación y dependencia económica de los auditores: Sus efectos sobre la calidad del resultado en las compañías cotizadas españolas. *Investigacion Economica*, *XXXI*(1), 119–159.

Navarro, J., & Martínez, I. (2004). Manipulación contable y calidad del auditor: Un estudio empírico de la realidad española. *Revista Española de Financiación y Contabilidad*, *33*(123), 1025–1061.

Okafor, C., & Otalor, J. (2013). Narrowing the expectation gap in auditing: The role of the auditing profession. *Research Journal of Finance and Accounting*, *4*(2), 43–52.

OROC. (2016). *Estatuto dos Revisores Oficiais de Contas*. Lisboa: Ordem dos Revisores Oficiais de Contas.

Otalor, J., & Okafor, C. (2013). Imperatives of bridging the audit expectation gap and enhancing the credibility of corporate financial information. *International Journal of Business and Social Research*, *3*(5), 125–138.

Pierce, B., & Kilcommins, M. (1996). The audit expectation gap: the role of auditing education. *Dublin City University Business School Research Papers,* (13), 1995-1996.

Rehana, F. (2010). *An empirical study on audit expectation gap: role of auditing education on Bangladesh.* Stamford University Bangladesh.

Salehi, M. (2016). Quantifying Audit Expectation Gap: A new approach to Measuring Expectation Gap. *Zagreb International Review of Economics & Business, 19*(1), 25–44. doi:10.1515/zireb-2016-0002

Serra, S. (2013). *A relevância do relatório de auditoria para os investidores institucionais, analistas financeiros e analistas de crédito* (Unpublished doctoral dissertation). Universidade do Minho, Braga.

Shaikh, J., & Talha, M. (2003). Credibility and expectation gap in reporting on uncertainties. *Managerial Auditing Journal, 18*(6/7), 517–529. doi:10.1108/02686900310482650

Sweeney, B. (1997). Bridging the expectations gap – on shaky foundations. *Accountancy Ireland, 29,* 18–20.

Wolf, F., Tackett, J., & Claypool, G. (1999). Audit disaster futures: Antidotes for the expectation gap? *Managerial Auditing Journal, 14*(9), 468–478. doi:10.1108/02686909910301556

ADDITIONAL READING

Chandler, R., Edwards, J., & Anderson, M. (1993). Changing perceptions of the role of the company auditor: 1840-1940. *Accounting and Business Research, 23*(92), 443–459. doi:10.1080/00014788.1993.9729890

IFAC. (2009). *International Standard on Auditing 240: the auditor's responsibilities relating to fraud in an audit of financial statements.* New York: International Federation of Accountants.

Low, A. (1980). The auditors' detection responsibility: Is there an expectation gap? *Journal of Accountancy, 150,* 65–70.

Lowe, D. (1994). The expectation gap in the legal system: Perception differences between auditors and judges. *Journal of Applied Business Research, 10*(3), 39–44. doi:10.19030/jabr.v10i3.5922

Mansur, H., & Tangl, A. (2018). How to Bridge the Audit Expectation Gap?. *Journal of Social Sciences (COES&RJ-JSS), 7*(2), 61-73.

Salehi, M. (2011). Audit expectation gap: Concept, nature and trace. *African Journal of Business Management, 5*(21), 8376–8392. doi:10.5897/AJBM11.963

Salehi, M., & Rostami, V. (2009). Audit expectation gap: International evidences. *International Journal of Academic Research, 1*(1), 140–146.

Sikka, P., Puxty, A., Wilmot, H., & Cooper, C. (1998). The impossibility of eliminating the expectation gap: Some theory and evidence. *Critical Perspectives on Accounting, 9*(3), 299–330. doi:10.1006/cpac.1997.0159

KEY TERMS AND DEFINITIONS

Audit: The review process of the financial demonstrations conducted by an independent auditor, which includes planning, execution, and opinion issues.

Audit Expectation Gap: The difference between the performance idealized by the auditors and the performance idealized by the users of the financial information.

Auditor: A qualified and independent professional, whose main role is to carry out audits of financial statements in order to express an opinion about their reliability.

Financial Statements: All the accounting documents prepared by the entity, comprising the balance sheet, income statement, statement of changes in financial position, statement of cash flows, and annexed notes.

Fraud: An intentional act of falsifying accounts for an illicit and improper advantage.

Independence: The ability to perform a pressure-free audit with all necessary procedures to obtain sufficient and appropriate evidence and issue an unbiased opinion on the financial statements.

Material Misstatement: A significant difference between the amount that was reported and the amount that should be reported in accordance with the applicable financial reporting framework.

Chapter 4
The Auditor as a Determining Factor on Derivative Financial Instrument Disclosures

Kátia Lemos
Instituto Politécnico do Cávado e do Ave, Portugal

Sara Serra
Instituto Politécnico do Cávado e do Ave, Portugal

Amidel Barros
Instituto Politécnico do Cávado e do Ave, Portugal

ABSTRACT

Based on the premise that the quality of the audit is related to the quality of the financial reporting, the purpose of this chapter is to verify if the audit is a determining factor in derivative financial instruments disclosures. However, the academic literature has revealed that audit quality is influenced by a number of factors, such as gender, experience, and auditor's fees, as well as the type of audit firm (Big4 or not Big4). In order to achieve the proposed objective, a disclosure index was prepared, based on the requirements of the International Accounting Standards Board (IASB), applied to companies listed on Euronext Lisbon, excluding the sports corporations. The results revealed that the level of disclosure is influenced by the size of the audited company and by the auditor's gender, being greater in the larger companies and in the companies audited by a male auditor.

INTRODUCTION

The disclosure of information about derivative transactions and risks incurred in contracting these instruments has been the subject of some debate at an international level. These instruments are associated with financial disasters and their complexity has raised worries among stakeholders, who are eager to understand how companies operate in derivatives markets and the associated risks. Given the above, the accounting standard bodies have tried to improve the quality of information disclosed, in order to ensure comparability at national and international levels.

DOI: 10.4018/978-1-5225-7356-2.ch004

According to Rijwani and Rajpurohit (2017), the audit has an important role in the financial reporting process because it provides assurance about its credibility. A study by Nwanyanwu (2017) revealed a statistically significant positive and strong relationship between audit quality and financial reporting. According to this author, audit practices aim to ensure that financial statements reveal relevant and reliable information to members of an organization and to the public. According to Baffa (2017), the role of an audit is to improve the quality of financial statements, since quality reporting reduces the problems of information asymmetry. Similarly, the studies of Ogundana, Ojeka, Ojua and Nwaze (2017), Gebrayel, Jarrar, Salloum and Lefebvre (2018), and Tambingon, Yadiati and Kewo (2018) revealed that the audit – in these cases, internal – has a significant effect on the quality of financial information on risk assessment.

According to Fukukawa and Kim (2017), because auditors are concerned about the quality of their audit, they try to influence disclosure practices. Because the management body has a discretionary power over the disclosure of financial information, auditors can obtain a competitive advantage by providing useful advice to the management body regarding the information to be disclosed, and the extent and type of disclosure that is appropriate. Also, Barako, Hancock and Izan (2006) argue that while it is the responsibility of the management body to prepare the financial report, an auditor can significantly influence the amount of information disclosed.

Regardless of whether it is an internal or external audit, it is undeniable the role of this supervisory mechanism on the quality of financial information. Based on this premise and the assumptions of agency theory, it is assumed that the external audit – called a statutory audit when imposed by law or auditing the accounts when exercised voluntarily in Portugal – will be a determining factor in the disclosure of financial derivative instruments. Moreover, Peters, Abbott and Parker (2001) argue that the quality of the auditor may be negatively associated with the level of disclosure because firms can legitimize themselves by compensating for the disclosure of reduced information through auditor quality. According to agency theory, managers are incentivized to hire quality auditors in order to make their disclosures credible and avoid the costs of non-disclosure (Peters et al., 2001). These authors obtained empirical evidence of a negative association between the level of voluntary disclosure about commodity derivatives and the level of expertise of the auditor.

Based on this premise and the assumptions of agency theory, it is assumed that auditing will be a determining factor in the disclosure of derivative instruments. However, the academic literature has revealed that the audit process and its consequent quality can be influenced by numerous factors, such as gender and professional experience of the auditor, as well as the fees received by the audit service and even the type of firm where the auditor carries out their function (Big 4 or not Big 4). Therefore, the purpose of this study is to verify if the auditor is a determining factor in derivative financial instrument disclosures.

This research has an innovative character because, although there are studies about the determinants of derivative instrument disclosures, there is no study that analyses in isolation the influence of the auditor in the level of disclosure.

The next section of this chapter sets out the background to our research. Subsequently, the hypotheses of the investigation are defined. The remaining sections describe the research design and method, and report the content analysis results. Finally, we present solutions and recommendations, future research directions, and the main conclusions.

BACKGROUND

Any literature review and empirical study should be supported by theories that help to explain the theoretical foundations used, research instruments developed, and data interpretation. Given the central objective of this study, which is to assess whether the auditor is a determining factor in derivative financial instrument disclosures, it seems important to us to first address agency theory.

According to Jensen and Meckling (1976), the agency relationship is defined as a contract by which one or more persons (principal) hire another person (agent) to provide a particular service, which involves the delegation of some decision-making to the agent. If the two parts of the contract are utility-maximizing, there is reason to believe that the agent will not always act in the best interest of the principal.

According to Hansmann and Kraakman (2004), agency conflicts may involve different actors, such as:

- **Owners and Managers:** In this situation, the challenge is to ensure that the manager (agent) will act in the interests of the owners (principal);
- **Majority Shareholders (Agents) and Minority Shareholders (Principal):** Here, the challenge is to ensure that majority shareholders do not appropriate wealth to the detriment of minority shareholders; and
- **The Company and All Parties With Whom It Establishes Contractual Relationships, Such as Creditors, Employees, and Their Customers:** In this regard, the challenge is to ensure that the company will not act opportunistically to the detriment of these stakeholders.

Independent of the stakeholders, the basis of this theory is the assumption of the existence of a conflict of interests because, although the principal and the agent are subordinated to a contract, they have different objectives and attitudes regarding risk; as rational beings, they want to satisfy their own interests (monetary and non-monetary) and maximize their wealth (Jensen & Meckling, 1976; Eisenhardt, 1989; Deutsch, 2005). This leads to agency costs. Jensen and Meckling (1976) define agency costs as the sum of the costs incurred by the principal to monitor the agent, the costs incurred by the agent to ensure compliance with the contract, and the residual costs resulting from the possibility that the agent does not always act in the principal's interests.

In a restricted view, agency costs can be analysed from the perspective of conflicts between capital holders and managers. The existence of a separation between ownership and management (i.e., when the owners of capital do not act as managers) leads to the establishment of a contract with the manager, who acts as the owners' agent. From another perspective, there are agency costs in the relationship between the company and its creditors. Control mechanisms are established and contractual clauses are defined which seek to reduce existing conflicts of interest, and encourage managers to act in the interests of owners of capital or creditors.

Auditing is an example of one of these control mechanisms. Piot (2001) mentions that the audit acquires technical legitimacy by reducing agency costs. Watts and Zimmerman (1978) also claim that the audit was not developed as a result of legal requirements, but rather to reduce agency costs and conflicts of interest between the agent and the principal. This opinion is shared by Wilson and Francis (1988), Chan and Walter (1996), Chen, Su and Zhao (2000), Hay and Davis (2004), and Fan and Wong (2005). Also, Kuntari, Chariri and Nurdhiana (2017) argue that the role of the audit is to reduce the asymmetry of accounting information.

Given the above, Fernando, Elder and Abdel-Meguid (2010) consider that one of the main functions of the audit is to ensure the best use of resources entrusted to the agent by the principal because, as Sikka, Filling and Liew (2009) explain, auditors are able to mediate uncertainty and construct an objective report of matters related to the entity's business, allowing stakeholders to adequately manage the risks. Therefore, Jensen and Meckling (1976) conclude that the audit dilutes the adverse effects of the separation of ownership and control.

In addition, disclosure of information plays an important role in reducing agency costs, because it ensures the reduction of existing information asymmetries, both between the holders of capital and managers, and between the company and its creditors and potential investors. In this line, Eisenhardt (1989) affirms that information asymmetry can be reduced by the installation of information channels which report on the behaviour of the agent and the results of their work. In this regard, Almeida and Almeida (2011) state that the formal or informal contracts established between the principal and the agent impose objectives and information to be provided.

When accountability is placed in the context of agency control, the function of the measure is essential, making reporting documents essential. Similarly, Evans (2003) mentions that financial reporting is the means by which agents show accountability to principals. Thus, financial statements are assumed to be a primary mechanism for the monitoring of the agents' performance.

Because financial information is a way to monitor managers, they will be interested in disclosing additional information to the market (Depoers, 2000) as a way to positively affect the stock price, which can reward them with higher salaries.

Aggarwal and Simkins (2004) obtained empirical evidence of the influence of management and agency costs, as well as political and strategic costs, in the decision to disclose information about derivative instruments.

RESEARCH HYPOTHESES

In order to assess the influence of the auditor in the level of derivative financial instrument disclosures, a set of research hypotheses was formulated, which relate the level of disclosure to some variables associated with the auditor, as follows.

Auditor's Gender

According to Ittonen, Vähämaa and Vähämaa (2013), behavioural differences between women and men may have important implications for audit quality and financial reporting. According to Costa, Serra and Gomes (2013), the auditor's gender has a significant influence on the way information is collected and processed, as well as on the risk profile, because female auditors are more risk-averse than male auditors (Breesch & Branson, 2009).

The results of the study by Breesch and Branson (2009) indicate that female auditors found more potential distortions than male auditors. Therefore, Hardies, Breesch and Branson (2016) assert that the quality of the audit is greater when it is performed by female auditors.

Given the results obtained by these authors, it is expected that the level of derivative disclosures is dependent on the auditor's gender. Therefore, the following investigation hypothesis can be defined:

Hypothesis One: The level of derivative instrument disclosures by listed companies is lower in companies audited by male auditors.

Auditor's Experience

According to Dunn and Mayhew (2004), Gul, Fung and Jaggi (2009), and Chiang and Lin (2012), the level of experience, knowledge, and expertise of auditors affects the audit quality. The greater the auditor's experience, the more ability they will have to select and apply auditing techniques and procedures. Thus, it is expected that the auditor will have a greater capacity to detect errors and irregularities in the entity's accounting information (Palmrose, 1986; O'Keefe, King, & Gaver, 1994; Craswell, Francis, & Taylor, 1995; Hogan & Jeter, 1999; Taylor, 2000; Gómez, 2003; Chiang & Lin, 2012; Reheul, Van Caneghem, Van den Bogaerd, & Verbruggen, 2017). Therefore, the auditor's experience increases the quality of the services provided and, consequently, the audit quality. Libby and Frederick (1990), Cahan and Sun (2015), Zarefar and Zarefar (2016), Kuntari et al. (2017), and Chi, Myers, Omer and Xie (2017) revealed that the auditor's experience has a significant positive effect on the audit quality.

Given the above, it is expected that the level of derivative instrument disclosures will depend on the auditor's experience. As such, the following research hypothesis can be defined:

Hypothesis Two: The level of derivative instrument disclosures by listed companies is higher in companies audited by more experienced auditors.

Auditor's Fees

Another factor that may affect the audit quality is the amount of fees received by the auditor. More money spent on the audit should result in more effort made in the audit, which can lead to a higher audit quality perception and more reliable financial statements. Therefore, studies by Novie (2013), Babatolu, Aigienohuwa and Uniamikogbo (2016), Kuntari et al. (2017), and Abdul-Rahman, Benjamin and Olayinka (2017) revealed that the fees received by the auditor have a significant positive effect on the audit quality.

Considering the results obtained by the cited authors and based on studies by Adznan and Nelson (2014), whose empirical study evidenced a relationship between the level of auditors' fees and the level of derivative instrument disclosures, the hypothesis of investigation three is defined in the following terms:

Hypothesis Three: The level of derivative financial instrument disclosures by listed companies is higher in companies audited by auditors with higher fees.

Type of Audit Firm (Big4 or not Big4)

Audit firms are concerned with the market's perception of its quality and with the consequences that may result from auditing companies which do not disclose all the recommended information. Thus, more reputable audit firms are more likely to advise their clients to disclose the recommended information (Chalmers & Godfrey, 2004). According to the empirical studies of DeFond (1992), Khrisnan and Khrisnan (1996), Rollins and Bremser (1997), Sucher, Moizer and Zarova (1999), García, Garrido, Vico, Moizer and Humphrey (1999), Ferguson and Stokes (2002), and Moctezuma (2017), the most reputable auditors belong to multinational companies; i.e., the Big 4.

Empirical studies by Shockley and Holt (1983), Francis and Stokes (1986), Keasey, Watson and Wynarczk (1988), Menon and Williams (1994), Chan and Walter (1996), Reynolds and Francis (2000), Gómez (2003), Aronmwan, Ashafoke and Mgbame (2013), Pham, Duong, Pham and Ho (2017), Jiang, Wang and Wang (2018), and Asthana, Kalelkar and Raman (2018) revealed that multinational audit firms provide a higher audit quality. This is due not only to reputation but to the fact that multinational audit firms are more likely to have more technical competence, given their structure, size, and solidity; they also tend to have more specialized and trained employees (Colbert & Murray, 1998). In addition, they have more financial resources, which allow them to acquire superior technology. In fact, according to Bamber, Bamber and Schoderbeck (1993), the auditor's judgment is affected by the technological level of the audit firm in which they are inserted.

Based on previous assumptions, the empirical studies of Ali, Ahmed and Henry (2004), Chalmers and Godfrey (2004), Hassan, Percy and Stewart (2006), Lopes and Rodrigues (2007), Lemos (2011), Hassan, Salleh, Yatim and Rahman (2012), and Birt, Rankin and Song (2013) revealed a positive association between the level of derivative disclosures and the fact that the auditor belongs to a Big 4. The following research hypothesis is therefore defined:

Hypothesis Four: The level of derivative disclosures by listed companies is greater in companies audited by Big 4 auditors.

Considering the literature review and the results obtained by other authors, the following research hypotheses were also considered for control purposes, which relate characteristics of the audited companies to the level of derivative disclosure.

Size

The existence of an association between the level of disclosure and the size of the company has been proven by several empirical studies (e.g., Watts & Zimmerman, 1978).

Large companies tend to incur lower information processing costs and higher political costs which encourage them to disclose more information. On the other hand, larger firms are subject to greater scrutiny, which leads them to increase compliance with disclosure requirements in response to institutional pressures and in an attempt to avoid threats to their legitimacy.

A number of authors have argued that there is an association between the level of derivative financial instrument disclosure and the size of the firm (Chalmers & Godfrey, 2004; Mir Fernández, Moreno, & Olmeda, 2006; Hassan et al., 2006; Lopes & Rodrigues, 2007; Lemos, Rodrigues, & Rodríguez Ariza, 2009; Lemos, 2011; Mapurunga, Ponte, Coelho, & Meneses, 2011). Thus, Hypothesis Five is defined in the following terms:

Hypothesis Five: The level of derivative financial instrument disclosures by listed companies is greater in larger companies.

Leverage

Companies with higher levels of leverage tend to avoid the adoption of accounting methods that would reduce reported results or increase the volatility of results (Dhaliwal, 1980). It is therefore likely that these companies will tend to conceal transactions in derivatives markets, not only because of the risks associated with these transactions, but also because of the 'bad reputation' these instruments have acquired as a result of various news stories disclosed by the media about losses incurred in derivative transactions.

However, agency theory suggests a high association between the level of leverage and the level of disclosure (Jensen & Meckling, 1976), because in heavily leveraged companies there is greater pressure from creditors to provide more detailed information about their activity.

On the other hand, according to signalling theory, disclosure reduces the existing asymmetries between companies and their potential creditors, thus reducing financing costs (Sengupta, 1998).

Mir Fernández et al. (2006) and Hassan et al. (2006) also obtained empirical evidence of a positive association between the index of disclosure about derivative instruments and the level of leverage. Taking into account the results obtained by these authors, the following research hypothesis is defined:

Hypothesis Six: The level of derivative instrument disclosures by listed companies will be higher in companies with higher levels of leverage.

RESEARCH METHODOLOGY

The population of this study is composed of the companies listed on Euronext Lisbon because they are considered to be the ones that, together with financial companies, use derivative instruments most frequently and those with a more demanding reporting level. However, sports corporations were excluded, because their reporting period differs from the rest.

To study the disclosed information, we used the technique of content analysis, coding the information collected into attributes or categories, and we used, as a source of data collection, the consolidated annual reports and accounts of the companies studied, referring to the accounting period 2016.

With regard to the object of the study, several authors have used a content analysis technique, using annual reports to measure and identify the determinants of disclosure of derivative instruments (Chalmers & Godfrey, 2004; Hassan et al., 2006; Aggarwal & Simkins, 2004; Peters et al., 2001; Mir Fernández et al., 2006; Lopes & Rodrigues, 2007; Lemos et al., 2009; Lemos, 2011; Mapurunga et al., 2011; Adzan & Nelson, 2014).

To identify the determinants of disclosure and to assess the influence of the auditor, a multiple linear regression model will be used, considering the variables identified in the research hypotheses previously presented.

Dependent Variable: Disclosure Index (DI)

In order to measure the level of disclosure of derivative instruments, a disclosure index (DI) was prepared based on the requirements contained in the IASB standards. Since the companies under study are companies listed on Euronext Lisbon, the disclosure index is based on the disclosure requirements contained in the IASB standards, because these companies have been obliged to adopt these standards since 2005. On the other hand, taking into consideration the subject of the study, we based our disclosure index on IFRS 7 financial instruments (i.e., disclosures) because it is this standard that defines which disclosures should be made by the entities that transact financial instruments.

Subsequently, the consolidated annual reports and accounts of listed companies were collected for the year 2016. For that purpose, electronic documents relating to the entities and of the Securities Market Commission were consulted. In addition, all accounting documents were analysed, including the chairman's letter, management report, corporate governance report, financial statements, and related appendices and audit reports.

In order to measure the level of derivative financial instrument disclosure, in accordance with the IASB standards, we adopted the same methodology as used by Mir Fernández et al. (2006) and Lopes and Rodrigues (2007); we constructed a disclosure index (DI) based on the IASB's IFRS 7. Although the new IFRS 9 relating to financial instruments, which replaces International Accounting Standards 32 and 39, and IFRS 7, is already approved, it is mandatory only from January 2018 onwards; thus, considering the period under analysis, we used IFRS 7, which was still mandatory in 2016.

The use of indexes to measure the level of disclosure has been widely used in the literature. Regarding the object of study of this paper, studies such as Chalmers (2001), Yong, Chalmers and Faff (2005), Morais and Fialho (2008), Darus and Taylor (2009), Peters et al. (2001), Chalmers and Godfrey (2004), Mir Fernández et al. (2006), Hassan et al. (2006), Lopes and Rodrigues (2007), Lemos et al. (2009), Lemos (2011), and Adzan and Nelson (2014) used an index to measure companies' levels of derivative transaction disclosures.

The index contains a total of 38 items (described in Table 13 at Appendix I), which are classified into five main categories, namely:

1. Accounting policies (six items);
2. Specific information on risks (eight items);
3. Operations that do not qualify for hedging purposes (two items);
4. Hedging (18 items), divided into the following subcategories:
    a. General information (five items);
    b. Cash flow hedges (seven items);
    c. Fair value hedges (two items);
    d. Net investments in foreign entities hedges (four items);
5. Fair value (four items).

Determination of the Disclosure Index Value

In the analysis of the reports and accounts of the companies included in the sample, we verified whether each of the items constituting the DI was disclosed or not, giving each of them a weighting of 0 or 1, according to the following criteria:

0 – the item was not disclosed;
1 – the item was disclosed.

Thus, the value of the index for each of the companies was obtained by the quotient between the total items disclosed by the company under analysis and the sum of the total of the items which make up the disclosure index, according to the following formula (see Table 1).

The index value varies between 0 and 1, and the higher the value of the DI, the higher the level of the disclosure presented.

Table 1. Disclosure index determination formula

$$DI_{it} = \sum_{j=i}^{e} e_j / e$$	
Where:	
DIit	Disclosure index of company i, at time t;
e_j	Disclosure element under analysis: Dichotomous variable, which assumes the value 0, if element j is not disclosed, and value 1, if element j is disclosed
e	Maximum number of elements analyzed

The DI is an unweighted index; that is, it is assumed that all items considered have the same level of importance for the various users of financial statements. The use of weighting factors would imply a prior study of the importance attributed by the various users of financial information to each of the considered elements and, consequently, the results obtained would always be biased by subjective factors.

On the other hand, it should be noted that the fact that the undisclosed items are not distinguished from non-applicable items may affect the results obtained. Many of the items not disclosed by the companies may be related to operations that were not carried out and, therefore, non-disclosure does not mean a lack of compliance with the standards. However, since it is impossible to control (given the lack of information presented) if the non-disclosure of an item is due to non-compliance with the standard or its non-application, the classification was given as undisclosed.

Independent Variables

The independent variables were derived from the previously formulated research hypotheses and were obtained through the analysis of annual reports. If it was not possible to obtain the required information, the item was considered to be undisclosed and was statistically treated as a missing value.

The formulas which determined the independent variables are shown in Table 2, with an indication of the associations predicted for each variable.

Characterization of the Sample

The sample used in this study consists of companies listed on Euronext Lisbon on April 20, 2018, excluding sports companies and another entity for which it was not possible to obtain the annual report for the year 2016. Thus, the sample is made up of 44 companies, which are concentrated in the Lisbon and Tejo Valley area or to the north of that region, as shown in Table 3.

The group of companies analysed was divided into the different industry sectors, as shown in Table 4.

Table 4 shows that the sector with the greatest weight is the consumer services sector, followed by the industry sector and, thirdly, gas, oil, and energy, and finance. It should be noted that financial companies that trade in derivative instruments not only in their own name but also on behalf of their customers account for 13.6% of the total of the sampled companies.

Table 2. Independent variables

Variable	Determination Formula	Expected Association With DI	Hypothesis
Auditor's gender (GenAud)	Dummy Variable: 0 - the auditor is female 1 - the auditor is male	Negative	H1
Professional experience of the auditor (ExpAud)	Dummy Variable: 0 - the auditor has less than 10 years of professional experience 1 - the auditor has more than 10 years of professional experience	Positive	H2
Fees received by the auditor (LogFees)	Logarithm of the amount of fees received by the auditor	Positive	H3
Auditor belong to a Big 4 (Big4)	Dummy Variable: 0 - the auditor does not belong to a Big 4 1 - the auditor belongs to a Big 4	Positive	H4
Size (LogAsset)	Logarithm of total assets	Positive	H5
Leverage (Lev)	Total liabilities / total equity x 100	Positive	H6

Table 3. Characterization of the sample according to geographical location

Location	Frequency	Percent
North	14	31.8
Center	2	4.5
Lisboa and Tejo Valley	28	63.6
Alentejo	0	0
Algarve	0	0
Açores	0	0
Madeira	0	0
Total	44	100.0

Table 4. Characterization of the sample according to the industry sector

Industry Sector	Frequency	Percent
Gas, Oil Energy	6	13.6
Basic Materials	1	2.3
Industry	10	22.7
Consumer goods	3	6.8
Consumer Services	11	25.0
Telecommunications	4	9.1
Financial	6	13.6
Technology	3	6.8
Total	44	100.0

RESEARCH RESULTS

Descriptive Analysis

At this point, we performed a descriptive analysis of the dependent variables, characterizing the sample considering the variables under study. Thus, as can be seen in Table 5, the average value of the asset logarithm stands at 8.92, the average value of the logarithm of the fees is 5.49, and the level of leverage is 37,743%.

Concerning the dichotomous variables, as shown by the analysis presented in Table 6, only one company had a female auditor, only nine auditors had less than 10 years of professional experience, and only six companies did not use one of the four largest audit firms to carry out their auditing. It can be concluded, therefore, that the market is very homogeneous regarding the choice of the type of external auditor.

Concerning the disclosure of information on derivative instruments, it appears that only four of the 44 companies did not disclose any type of derivative information (as shown in Table 7).

Regarding the disclosure index, Table 8 shows that DI has an average value of 49.32%, with a maximum value of 92%, which indicates that Portuguese companies are concerned about compliance with the disclosure requirements contained in the applicable standards, yet do not disclose all the information required.

Table 5. Descriptive statistics: Quantitative variables

	LogAsset	LogFees	Lev
N	44	44	44
Mean	8.9215	5.4951	37743%
Standard deviation	.90692	.63433	55448%
Minimum	7.26	4.38	-120109%
Maximum	10.85	6.85	233764%

Table 6. Descriptive statistics: Dichotomous variables

		N	%
GenAud	Female	1	2.3
	Male	43	97.7
	Total	44	100.0
ExpAud	Less than 10 years	8	18.2
	More than 10 years	36	81.8
	Total	44	100.0
Big4	Not Big 4	6	13.6
	Big 4	38	86.4
	Total	44	100.0

Table 7. Number of disclosing and non-disclosing companies

	N	%
Yes	4	9.1
No	40	90.9
Total	44	100.0

Table 8. Descriptive statistics - disclosure index

	ID
N	44
Mean	.4932
Standard deviation	.339048
Minimum	.00
Maximum	.92

Multivariate Analysis

In order to verify the relationship between the independent variables and the dependent variable (DI), a multiple linear regression model was developed, in agreement with the hypotheses formulated, which is expressed as shown in Table 9.

The stepwise method was used in the estimation of the regression model. According to Pestana and Gageiro (2003, p. 614), "whenever the stepwise procedure enters a new variable in the model, we analyze the significance of each variable X, eliminating variables that do not have the capacity for meaningful explanation. It is repeated until the variables not introduced in the model are not capable of meaningful explanation and when all those in the model have it." Consequently, the results shown in Tables 10, 11, and 12 were obtained:

Table 10 presents a summary of the model, indicating that only two explanatory variables – the size of the company and the gender of the auditor – are considered (as can be seen in Table 12).

The first variable entered into the model is the size of the company, which explains 45.4% (value of R square in Table 10) of the DI, and the second variable entered into the model is the gender of the auditor, which increases the explanatory power of the DI to 51.9% (R square).

Table 9. Multiple linear regression model

$$DI_{it} = \alpha_0 + \beta_1 GenAud_{it} + \beta_2 ExpAud_{it} + \beta_3 LogFees_t + \beta_4 Big4_{it} + \beta_5 LogAsset_{it} + \beta_6 Lev_{it} + \varepsilon i_{it}$$

DIit: Value of the disclosure index for company i at time t
GenAud: Gender of the auditor
ExpAud: Auditor's professional experience
LogFees: Logarithm of auditor's fees
Big4 - Auditor belonging to a Big4
LogAsset: Company size, measured by the logarithm of total assets
Lev: Level of leverage

Table 10. Model summary

Model Summary[c]					
Model	**R**	**R Square**	**Adjusted R Square**	**Std. Error of the Estimate**	**Durbin-Watson**
1	.674[a]	.454	.441	.24699	
2	.720[b]	.519	.495	.23484	2.015

a. Predictors: (Constant), Asset
b. Predictors: (Constant), Asset, GenAud
c. Dependent Variable: DI

Table 11. Anova

ANOVA[a]						
Model		**Sum of Squares**	**df**	**Mean Square**	**F**	**Sig.**
1	Regression	2.134	1	2.134	34.988	.000[b]
	Residual	2.562	42	.061		
	Total	4.696	43			
2	Regression	2.435	2	1.218	22.078	.000[c]
	Residual	2.261	41	.055		
	Total	4.696	43			

a. Dependent Variable: DI
b. Predictors: (Constant), Asset
c. Predictors: (Constant), Asset, GenAud

Table 12. Coefficients

Coefficients[a]								
Model		**Unstandardized Coefficients**	**Standardized Coefficients**	**Beta**	**t**	**Sig.**	**Collinearity Statistics**	
		B	Std. Error				Tolerance	VIF
1	(Constant)	-1.698	.372		-4.561	.000		
	Asset	.246	.042	.674	5.915	.000	1.000	1.000
2	(Constant)	-2.269	.430		-5.275	.000		
	Asset	.249	.040	.683	6.296	.000	.999	1.001
	GenAud	.555	.238	.253	2.336	.024	.999	1.001

a. Dependent Variable: ID

According to the sign of the unstandardized coefficients (see Table 12), we can verify that there is a positive association between the level of disclosure and the size of the company, and the fact that the auditor is male. It is then possible to validate Hypothesis 5, but it is not possible to validate Hypothesis 1 because a negative association was expected for the condition of the auditor being male; however, a positive association was obtained.

The level of significance of the *t* test (as shown in Table 12) allows us to confirm the existence of a linear relationship between the explanatory variables and the dependent variable; thus, we can conclude that the DI will be greater in larger audited companies and with a male auditor. The level of significance of the *F* test (presented in Table 11) allows us to validate the models in global terms and to conclude that they are adequate to describe the relationship between explanatory variables and the dependent variable.

Contrary to what was expected, the remaining variables did not obtain statistically significant results and, therefore, it is not possible to validate the remaining hypotheses formulated. In fact, the sample is quite homogeneous in relation to the study variables related to the auditor because, of the 44 companies analysed, only six did not choose one of the four largest audit firms and only eight have one auditor with less than 10 years of professional experience, which justifies the results obtained.

Chalmers and Godfrey (2004), Mir Fernández et al. (2006), Hassan et al. (2006), Lopes and Rodrigues (2007), Lemos et al. (2009), Lemos (2011), and Mapurunga et al. (2011) also obtained empirical evidence of the association between the disclosure index on derivatives and the size of the company.

The results obtained are contrary to the results obtained by Breesch and Branson (2009) which pointed to a higher level of quality of the disclosed information if the auditor were female. However, it should be pointed out that, of the total of the companies analysed only one of the companies had a female auditor and that company did not present any disclosure on derivative transactions, which justifies the result obtained.

On the other hand, the results obtained in this study are not consistent with the results obtained by:

- Libby and Frederick (1990), Cahan and Sun (2015), Zarefar and Zarefar (2016), Kuntari et al. (2017), and Chi et al. (2017), which revealed that the auditor's experience had a significant positive effect on the quality of the audit;
- Novie (2013), Babatolu et al. (2016), Kuntari et al. (2017), and Abdul-Rahman et al. (2017), which revealed that the fees received by the auditor had a significant positive effect on the audit quality, and those by Adznan and Nelson (2014), which demonstrated a relationship between the auditor's fee level and the level of derivative financial instrument disclosures;
- Chalmers and Godfrey (2004), Hassan et al. (2006), Lopes and Rodrigues (2007), Lemos (2011), Hassan et al. (2012), which revealed a positive association between the level of derivative disclosures and the fact that the auditor belongs to a Big 4; and
- Mir Fernández et al. (2006) and Hassan et al. (2006), which included empirical evidence of a positive association between the disclosure index on derivative instruments and the level of leverage.

SOLUTIONS AND RECOMMENDATIONS

The study concluded that the level of disclosure on derivative instruments presented by listed companies in Portuguese capital market is still incipient since there is an average disclosure of around 50% of the items required by applicable accounting standards. As such, the authors believe it is important to encourage companies to increase the disclosure levels presented, in order to respond to the information needs of the different users of financial statements and to ensure compliance with the requirements of IFRS 7. The auditor can play a key role in this process, exercising influence with its clients to properly disclose all the required information.

However, it should be noted that, according to the adopted methodology, it was not possible to verify whether the failure to comply with a certain item is due to the fact that it does not apply to the analyzed entity or if it is effectively a failure to disclose the required information. For this reason, the results obtained may be influenced by this effect, the reason why not always the lack of disclosure could be understood as noncompliance with the applicable standards. In this sense, it would be important to seek this confirmation from the respective entities, so it is proposed for future investigation to carry out a questionnaire to the companies analyzed, which allows crossing results with the analysis of annual reports, in order to confirm the levels of disclosure obtained.

FUTURE RESEARCH DIRECTIONS

In addition to the limitation identified in the previous paragraph, this study presents, as another limitation, the focus on listed companies and the analysis of annual reports for a single accounting period. It was concluded that the Portuguese capital market is very homogeneous with respect to the characteristics of the external auditor, so the results obtained do not show different levels of disclosure depending on the type of auditor.

In view of the above, it is suggested that future research extend the sample to other Portuguese companies not listed on a regulated market, which use derivative instruments and have different external auditors. On the other hand, it is also suggested that future studies extend the period of analysis to verify the evolution of the level of disclosure and to determine if there are significant changes in the type of auditor over time.

Also, taking into account the adoption of IFRS 9 (which replaces IFRS 7) since January 2018 onwards, we suggest that the creation of a new index of disclosure based on this new standard, which would be applied to the annual reports referring to the accounting periods from 2018 onwards, would verify any changes in the adopted disclosure policies and the influence of the auditor in these changes.

CONCLUSION

Based on the premise that the quality of the audit is related to the quality of financial reporting, the objective of this study is to verify if the auditor is a determining factor in disclosures about derivative financial instruments. However, academic literature has revealed that audit quality is influenced by a number of factors, such as gender and auditor experience, as well as the fees received by the audit service provided and the type of audit firm where the auditor performs their function (Big4 or not Big4).

In order to achieve the proposed objective, a disclosure index was constructed, taking into account the requirements of the IASB's IFRS 7, and applied to companies listed on Euronext Lisbon.

The results showed an average disclosure level of around 50%, revealing that companies do not disclose all the information required by the IASB standards and that the disclosure level is greater in larger audited companies and in companies audited by a male auditor.

Contrary to expectations, it was not possible to prove the existence of any association between the disclosure index and the other characteristics associated with the auditor; i.e., the level of derivative financial instrument disclosure is not influenced by the auditor's experience, the fees received by the auditor, nor by the type of audit firm where the auditor performs their duties. This is due to the homogeneity of the sample because the companies listed on Euronext Lisbon are audited mainly by male auditors with more than 10 years of experience and who belong to Big4 companies.

REFERENCES

Abdul-Rahman, O., Benjamin, A., & Olayinka, O. (2017). Effect of audit fees on audit quality: Evidence from cement manufacturing companies in Nigeria. *European Journal of Accounting. Auditing and Finance Research*, *5*(1), 6–17.

Adznan, S., & Nelson, S. (2014). Financial instruments disclosure practices: Evidence from Malaysian listed firms. *Procedia: Social and Behavioral Sciences*, *164*, 62–67. doi:10.1016/j.sbspro.2014.11.051

Aggarwal, R., & Simkins, B. (2004). Evidence on voluntary disclosures of derivatives usage by large US companies. *Journal of Derivatives Accounting*, *1*(1), 61–81. doi:10.1142/S0219868104000063

Ali, J., Ahmed, M., & Henry, K. (2004). Disclosure compliance with national accounting standards by listed companies in South Asia. *Accounting and Business Research*, *34*(3), 183–199. doi:10.1080/00014788.2004.9729963

Almeida, B., & Almeida, J. (2011). En torno a las teorías justificativas de la auditoría. *Partida Doble*, *228*, 55–66.

Aronmwan, E., Ashafoke, T., & Mgbame, C. (2013). Audit firm reputation and audit quality. *European Journal of Business and Management*, *5*(7), 66–75.

Asthana, S., Kalelkar, R., & Raman, K. (2018). Unintended consequences of Big 4 auditor office-level industry specialization. *International Journal of Accounting, Auditing, and Performance Evaluation*, *14*(2-3), 254–289. doi:10.1504/IJAAPE.2018.091066

Babatolu, A., Aigienohuwa, O., & Uniamikogbo, E. (2016). Auditor's independence and audit quality: A study of selected deposit money banks in Nigeria. *International Journal of Finance and Accounting*, *5*(1), 13–21.

Baffa, A. (2017). The differential effect of auditor type on the value relevance of earnings and book values: Evidence from listed firms in Nigeria. *European Journal of Multidisciplinary Studies*, *6*(1), 187–204. doi:10.26417/ejms.v6i1.p187-204

Bamber, E., Bamber, L., & Schoderbeck, M. (1993). Audit structure and other determinants of audit report lag: An empirical analysis. *Auditing*, *12*(1), 1–23.

Barako, D., Hancock, P., & Izan, H. (2006). Factors influencing voluntary corporate disclosure by Kenyan companies. *Corporate Governance*, *14*(2), 107–125. doi:10.1111/j.1467-8683.2006.00491.x

Birt, J., Rankin, M., & Song, C. (2013). Derivatives use and financial instrument disclosure in the extractives industry. *Accounting and Finance*, *53*(1), 55–83. doi:10.1111/acfi.12001

Breesch, D., & Branson, J. (2009). The effects of auditor gender on audit quality. *The IUP Journal of Accounting Research & Audit Practices*, *8*(3-4), 78–107.

Cahan, S., & Sun, J. (2015). The effect of audit experience on audit fees and audit quality. *Journal of Accounting, Auditing & Finance*, *30*(1), 78–100. doi:10.1177/0148558X14544503

Chalmers, K., & Godfrey, J. (2004). Reputation costs: The impetus for voluntary derivative financial instrument reporting. *Accounting, Organizations and Society*, *29*(2), 95–125. doi:10.1016/S0361-3682(02)00034-X

Chan, Y., & Walter, T. (1996). Qualified audit reports and costly contracting. *Asia Pacific Journal of Management*, *13*(1), 37–63. doi:10.1007/BF01739681

Chen, C., Su, X., Zhao, R., & Kong, C. U. H. (2000). An emerging market's reaction to initial modified audit opinions: Evidence for the Shanghai Stock Exchange. *Contemporary Accounting Research*, *17*(3), 429–455. doi:10.1506/GCJP-5599-QUWB-G86D

Chi, W., Myers, L., Omer, T., & Xie, H. (2017). The effects of audit partner pre-client and client-specific experience on audit quality and on perceptions of audit quality. *Review of Accounting Studies*, *22*(1), 361–391. doi:10.100711142-016-9376-9

Chiang, H., & Lin, S. (2012). Auditor's industry specialization and disclosure quality of IAS No. 39 -Related accounts. *Journal of Applied Finance & Banking*, *2*(2), 59–98.

Colbert, G., & Murray, D. (1998). The association between auditor quality and auditor size: An analysis of small CPA firms. *Journal of Accounting, Auditing & Finance*, *13*(2), 135–150. doi:10.1177/0148558X9801300203

Costa, R., Serra, S., & Gomes, P. (2013). Fatores determinantes da opinião do auditor: estudo empírico das empresas portuguesas, *Proceedings of XIV Congresso Internacional de Contabilidade e Auditoria*.

Craswell, A., Francis, J., & Taylor, S. (1995). Auditor brand name reputations and industry specializations. *Journal of Accounting and Economics*, *20*(3), 297–322. doi:10.1016/0165-4101(95)00403-3

Darus, F., & Taylor, D. (2009). Influences of proprietary and political costs on voluntary disclosure relating to financial instruments before and after mandatory requirements. *Corporate Ownership and Control*, *6*(4), 391–406. doi:10.22495/cocv6i4c3p5

DeFond, M. (1992). The association between changes in client firm agency costs and auditor switching. *Auditing*, *11*(1), 16–31.

Depoers, F. (2000). A cost-benefit study of voluntary disclosure: Some empirical evidence from French listed companies. *European Accounting Review*, *9*(2), 245–263. doi:10.1080/09638180050129891

Deutsch, Y. (2005). The impact of board composition on firms' critical decisions: A meta-analytic review. *Journal of Management*, *31*(3), 424–444. doi:10.1177/0149206304272185

Dhaliwal, D. S. (1980). The effect of firm's capital structure on the choice of accounting methods. *The Accounting Review*, *LV*(1), 78–84.

Dunn, K., & Mayhew, B. (2004). Audit firm industry specialization and client disclosure quality. *Review of Accounting Studies*, *9*(1), 35–58. doi:10.1023/B:RAST.0000013628.49401.69

Eisenhardt, K. (1989). Agency theory: An assessment and review. *Academy of Management Review*, *14*(1), 57–74. doi:10.5465/amr.1989.4279003

Evans, L. (2003). Auditing and audit firms in Germany before 1931. *The Accounting Historians Journal*, *30*(2), 29–65. doi:10.2308/0148-4184.30.2.29

Fan, J., & Wong, T. (2005). Do external auditors perform a corporate governance role in emerging markets? Evidence from East Asia. *Journal of Accounting Research*, *43*(1), 35–72. doi:10.1111/j.1475-679x.2004.00162.x

Ferguson, A., Stokes, D., & Technology, U. (2002). Brand name audit pricing, industry specialization, and leadership premiums post-Big 8 and Big 6 Mergers. *Contemporary Accounting Research*, *19*(1), 77–110. doi:10.1506/VF1T-VRT0-5LB3-766M

Fernando, G., Elder, R., & Abdel-Meguid, A. (2010). Audit quality attributes, client size, and cost of equity capital. *Review of Accounting and Finance*, *9*(4), 363–381. doi:10.1108/14757701011094571

Francis, J., & Stokes, D. (1986). Audit prices, product differentiation and scale economies: Further evidence from the Australian market. *Journal of Accounting Research*, *24*(2), 383–393. doi:10.2307/2491141

Francis, J., & Wilson, E. (1988). Auditor changes: A joint test of theories relating to agency costs and auditor differentiation. *The Accounting Review*, *13*(4), 663–707.

Fukukawa, H., & Kim, H. (2017). Effects of audit partners on clients' business risk disclosure. *Accounting and Business Research*, *47*(7), 780–809. doi:10.1080/00014788.2017.1299619

García, M., Garrido, P., Vico, A., Moizer, P., & Humphrey, C. (1999). La calidad del servicio de auditoría: Los auditores vistos por sus clientes. *Revista Española de Financiación y Contabilidad*, *28*(102), 1005–1041.

Gebrayel, E., Jarrar, H., Salloum, C., & Lefebvre, Q. (2018). Effective association between audit committees and the internal audit function and its impact on financial reporting quality: Empirical evidence from Omani listed firms. *International Journal of Auditing*, *22*(1), 1–17.

Gómez, N. (2003). *El Informe de auditoría y su efecto sobre la decisión del cambio de Auditor. Premio de Investigación Contable José Mª Fernández Pirla*. XI Edición, Instituto de Contabilidad y Auditoría de Cuentas.

Gul, F., Fung, S., & Jaggi, B. (2009). Earnings quality: Some evidence on the role of auditor tenure and auditors' industry expertise. *Journal of Accounting and Economics*, *47*(3), 265–287. doi:10.1016/j.jacceco.2009.03.001

Hansmann, H., & Kraakman, R. (2004). *Agency problems and legal strategies*. Center for Law, Economics and Public Policy, Research paper no. 301.

Hardies, K., Breesch, D., & Branson, J. (2016). Do (fe)male auditors impair audit quality? Evidence from going-concern opinions. *European Accounting Review*, *25*(1), 7–34. doi:10.1080/09638180.2014.921445

Hassan, M., Percy, M., & Stewart, J. (2006). The transparency of derivative disclosures by Australian firms in the extractive industry. *Corporate. Ownership and Control*, *4*(2), 257–270.

Hassan, M., Salleh, N., Yatim, P., & Rahman, M. (2012). Risk management committee and financial instrument disclosure. *Asian Journal of Accounting and Governance*, *3*(1), 13–28. doi:10.17576/ajag-2012-3-6512

Hay, D., & Davis, D. (2004). The voluntary choice of an audit of any level of quality. *Auditing*, *23*(September), 37–53. doi:10.2308/aud.2004.23.2.37

Hogan, C., & Jeter, D. (1999). Industry specialization by auditors. *Auditing*, *18*(1), 1–17. doi:10.2308/aud.1999.18.1.1

Ittonen, K., Vähämaa, E., & Vähämaa, S. (2013). Female auditors and accruals quality. *Accounting Horizons*, *27*(2), 205–228. doi:10.2308/acch-50400

Jensen, M., & Meckling, W. (1976). Theory of the firm: Managerial behavior, agency costs, and ownership structure. *Journal of Financial Economics*, *3*(4), 305–360. doi:10.1016/0304-405X(76)90026-X

Jiang, J., Wang, I., & Wang, K. (2018). *Big N auditors and audit quality: New evidence from quasi-experiments*. The Accounting Review. In-Press.

Keasey, K., Watson, R., & Wynarczk, P. (1988). The small company audit qualifications: A preliminary investigation. *Accounting and Business Research*, *18*(72), 323–333. doi:10.1080/00014788.1988.9729379

Krishnan, J., & Krishnan, J. (1996). The role of economic trade-offs in the audit opinion decision: An empirical analysis. *Journal of Accounting, Auditing & Finance*, *4*(4), 565–586. doi:10.1177/0148558X9601100403

Kuntari, Y., Chariri, A., & Nurdhiana, N. (2017). The effect of auditor ethics, auditor experience, audit fees and auditor motivation on audit quality. *Sriwijaya International Journal of Dynamic Economics and Business*, *1*(2), 203–218. doi:10.29259ijdeb.v1i2.203-218

Lemos, K. (2011). *Contabilidade de instrumentos derivados. Estudo da informação divulgada pelas empresas portuguesas* (Unpublished doctoral dissertation). Facultad de Ciencias Económicas y Empresariales, Universidad de Santiago de Compostela.

Lemos, K., Rodrigues, L., & Rodríguez Ariza, L. (2009). Determinantes do nível de divulgação de informação sobre instrumentos derivados. Evidência empírica no mercado de capitais português. *Tékhne – Revista de Estudos Politécnicos, 7*(12), 145-175.

Libby, R., & Frederick, D. (1990). Experience and the ability to explain audit findings. *Journal of Accounting Research*, *28*(2), 348–367. doi:10.2307/2491154

Lopes, P., & Rodrigues, L. (2007). Accounting for financial instruments: An analysis of the determinants of disclosure in the Portuguese stock exchange. *The International Journal of Accounting*, *42*(1), 25–56. doi:10.1016/j.intacc.2006.12.002

Mapurunga, P., Ponte, V., Coelho, A., & Meneses, A. (2011). Determinantes do nível de *disclosure* de instrumentos financeiros derivativos em firmas brasileiras. *Revista Contabilidade e Finanças. USP São Paulo, 22*(57), 263–278.

Menon, K., & Williams, J. (1994). The use of audit committees for monitoring. *Journal of Accounting and Public Policy, 13*(2), 121–139. doi:10.1016/0278-4254(94)90016-7

Mir Fernández, C., Moreno, D., & Olmeda, I. (2006). *Determinantes de la Revelación de Información sobre derivados financieros en el mercado Español*. Paper presented at the I Jornada de Investigación de la REFC, Madrid.

Moctezuma, J. (2017). Why the Big 4 are leaders in the audit market? A literature review. *Archives of Business Research, 5*(12), 227–244.

Morais, A., & Fialho, A. (2008). Do harmonized accounting standards lead to harmonized accounting practices? An empirical study of IAS 39 measurement requirements in some European Union countries. *Australian Accounting Review, 46*(18), 225–235.

Novie, S. (2013). An empirical analysis of auditor independence and audit fees on audit quality. *International Journal of Management and Business, 3*(3), 82–87.

Nwanyanwu, L. (2017). Audit quality practices and financial reporting in Nigeria. *International Journal of Academic Research in Accounting. Finance and Management Sciences, 7*(2), 145–155.

O'Keefe, T., King, R., & Gaver, K. (1994). Audit fees, industry specialization, and compliance with GAAS reporting standards. *Auditing, 13*(2), 41–55.

Ogundana, O., Ojeka, S., Ojua, M., & Nwaze, C. (2017). Quality of accounting information and internal audit characteristics in Nigeria. *Journal of Modern Accounting and Auditing, 13*(8), 333–344.

Palmrose, Z. (1986). Audit fees and auditor size: Further evidence. *Journal of Accounting Research, 24*(1), 97–110. doi:10.2307/2490806

Pestana, M., & Gageiro, J. (2003). *Análise de dados para Ciências Sociais – a complementaridade do SPSS*. Lisboa: Edições Sílabo.

Peters, G., Abbott, L., & Parker, S. (2001). *Voluntary disclosures and auditor specialization: the case of commodity derivative disclosures*. Paper presented at the Western Regional Accounting Association Meeting, San Jose, CA.

Pham, N., Duong, H., Pham, T., & Ho, N. (2017). Audit firm size, audit fee, audit reputation and audit quality: The case of listed companies in Vietnam. *Asian Journal of Finance & Accounting, 9*(1), 429–447. doi:10.5296/ajfa.v9i1.10074

Piot, C. (2001). Agency costs and audit quality: Evidence from France. *European Accounting Review, 10*(3), 461–499. doi:10.1080/713764630

Reheul, A., Van Caneghem, T., Van den Bogaerd, M., & Verbruggen, S. (2017). Auditor gender, experience and reporting in nonprofit organizations. *Managerial Auditing Journal, 32*(6), 550–577. doi:10.1108/MAJ-01-2016-1296

Reynolds, J., & Francis, J. (2001). Does size matter? The influence of large clients on office-level auditor reporting decisions. *Journal of Accounting and Economics*, *30*(3), 375–400. doi:10.1016/S0165-4101(01)00010-6

Rijwani, P., & Rajpurohit, P. (2017). Assessment of audit quality: An investigation into proxies. *Asian Journal of Management*, *8*(2), 262–266. doi:10.5958/2321-5763.2017.00040.3

Rollins, T., & Bremser, W. (1997). The SEC's enforcement actions against auditors: An auditor reputation and institutional theory perspective. *Critical Perspectives on Accounting*, *8*(3), 191–206. doi:10.1006/cpac.1996.0106

Sengupta, P. (1998). Corporate disclosure quality and the cost of debt. *The Accounting Review*, *73*(4), 459–474.

Shockley, R., & Holt, R. (1983). A behavioral investigation of supplier differentiation in the market for audit services. *Journal of Accounting Research*, *21*(2), 545–564. doi:10.2307/2490790

Sikka, P., Filling, S., & Liew, P. (2009). The audit crunch: Reforming auditing. *Managerial Auditing Journal*, *24*(2), 135–155. doi:10.1108/02686900910924554

Sucher, P., Moizer, P., & Zarova, M. (1999). The images of the Big Six audit firms in the Czech Republic. *European Accounting Review*, *8*(3), 499–521. doi:10.1080/096381899335916

Tambingon, H., Yadiati, W., & Kewo, C. (2018). Determinant factors influencing the quality of financial reporting local government in Indonesia. *International Journal of Economics and Financial Issues*, *8*(2), 262–268.

Taylor, M., & Carolina, U. S. (2000). The effects of industry specialization on auditors' inherent risk assessments and confidence judgments. *Contemporary Accounting Research*, *17*(4), 693–712. doi:10.1506/3LDH-AV52-0F4W-H4BB

Watts, R., & Zimmerman, J. (1978). Towards a positive theory of the determination of accounting standards. *The Accounting Review*, *53*(1), 112–134.

Yong, H., Chalmers, K., & Faff, R. (2005). Asia Pacific banks' derivative and risk management disclosures. *Asian Review of Accounting*, *13*(1), 15–44. doi:10.1108/eb060781

Zarefar, A., & Zarefar, A. (2016). The influence of ethics, experience, and competency toward the quality of auditing with professional auditor skepticism as a moderating variable. *Procedia: Social and Behavioral Sciences*, *219*, 828–832. doi:10.1016/j.sbspro.2016.05.074

ADDITIONAL READING

Ahmed, K., & Courtis, J. K. (1999). Associations between corporate characteristics and disclosure levels in annual reports: A meta-analysis. *The British Accounting Review*, *31*(1), 35–61. doi:10.1006/bare.1998.0082

Baeten, X., Balkin, D., & Berghe, L. (2011). Beyond agency theory: A three-paradigm approach to executive compensation. *The IUP Journal of Corporate Governance*, *X*(4), 7–36.

Bekiaris, M., & Tasios, S. (2012). Auditor's perceptions of financial reporting quality: The case of Greece. *International Journal of Accounting and Financial Reporting*, *2*(1), 57–74. doi:10.5296/ijafr.v2i1.1286

Carcello, J., Hermanson, R., & McGrath, N. (1992). Audit quality attributes: The perceptions of audit partners, preparers, and financial statement users. *Auditing*, *11*(1), 1–15.

Chavent, M., Ding, Y., Fu, L., Stolowy, H., & Wang, H. (2005). *Disclosure and determinants studies: an extension using the divisive clustering method (DIV). Working-paper*. France: University of Bordeaux.

Cohen, S., & Kaimenakis, N. (2011). Assessing quality of financial reporting through audit reports: The case of Greek municipalities. *Global Business and Economics Review*, *13*(3-4), 187–203. doi:10.1504/GBER.2011.041848

DeAngelo, L. (1981b). Auditor size and audit quality. *Journal of Accounting and Economics*, *3*(3), 183–199. doi:10.1016/0165-4101(81)90002-1

Marston, C., & Shrives, P. (1991). The use of disclosure indices in accounting research: A review article. *The British Accounting Review*, *23*(3), 195–210. doi:10.1016/0890-8389(91)90080-L

KEY TERMS AND DEFINITIONS

Audit: Review of the financial statements, carried out by an external auditor, with the purpose of issuing an audit report, which includes the opinion on the audited financial statements.

Auditor: Qualified and independent professional, whose main role is to carry out audits of financial statements, with the purpose of expressing an opinion about their reliability.

Derivative Instrument: A forward contract that focuses on an underlying asset (which may be a commodity, a price index, an interest rate, an exchange rate, etc.), the settlement price of which is determined on the date of hiring, which allows the settlement of the contract to be made through the physical delivery of the underlying asset or by the simple financial settlement of the difference between the fixed price and the price of the asset in the spot market, with an initial investment that is nil or extremely low.

Disclosure Index: Indicator of the extent of the disclosure presented by a certain company, relative to certain information, measured by the sum of the items disclosed on the total items considered.

Hedging: Using derivative instruments for the purpose of hedging risk in other current operations of the company.

Quality of the Audit: The ability to perform the audit with knowledge, technical ability, and independence, that is, ability to detect and disclose material misstatements.

APPENDIX

Table 13. Index of disclosure on derivative instruments, in accordance with IASB's standards (ID)

	ACCOUNTING POLICIES
1	Risk management policy, including hedging policy
2	Objectives of holding or contracting derivatives
3	Accounting policies and methods used
4	Information on the guarantees committed by hiring derivatives
5	Internal control procedures followed by the company in the supervision of derivatives
6	Identification of transacted derivative instruments
	SPECIFIC RISK INFORMATION
7	Segregation by risk categories
8	Risk management objectives, policies and procedures
9	Methods used to measure risk
10	Maximum exposure to credit risk
11	Sensitivity analysis for each type of risk
12	Face value, notional value
13	Analysis of contractual maturity
14	Information on the counterparty of derivatives
	OPERATIONS THAT DO NOT QUALIFY AS HEDGE
15	Accounting method
16	Gains or losses obtained during the year
	HEDGING
17	Description of each type of hedge
18	Accounting method
19	Description of financial instruments designated as hedging instruments
20	Fair values of the hedging instruments at the reporting date
21	Nature of risks covered
	Cash Flow Hedges
22	Periods in which cash flows are expected to occur
23	The period in which operations are expected to affect gains and losses
24	Description of forecasted transactions for which hedge accounting has previously been used but which are no longer expected to occur
25	Amount carried in equity during the period/gains realized during the year
26	The amount that was removed from equity and included in gains and losses during the period
27	The amount that was removed from equity during the period and included in the initial costs or another carrying amount of a non-financial asset or non-financial liability, the acquisition or occurrence of which is a forecasted and highly probable hedged transaction
28	The ineffectiveness recognized in results from the cash flow hedges

continued on following page

Table 13. Continued

	Fair Value Hedges
29	Gains or losses of hedges at fair value over the hedging instrument;
30	Gains or losses of hedges at fair value over the hedged item, attributable to the hedged risk;
	Hedging of Net Investments in Foreign Entities
31	Amount carried in equity during the period attributable to the hedging instrument
32	Amount carried in equity during the period attributable to the hedged item
33	The amount that was removed from equity and included in the profit or losses accounts during the period
34	The ineffectiveness recognized in profit or losses accounts from the hedges of net investments in foreign entities
	FAIR VALUE
35	Fair value
36	Methods and techniques used to determine the fair value
37	Assumptions applied in the determination of fair values
38	Average fair value during the year

Chapter 5
ISO Standards and Audit: A Case Study About ISO 31000

Alcina Sena Portugal Dias
Instituto Politécnico do Porto, Portugal

Madalena Maria Ribeiro Magalhaes
Instituto Politécnico do Porto, Portugal

ABSTRACT

Standards are applicable to any kind of activity and could be defined, in a general way, as an activity aiming to apply an ordered system to repetitive functions that take place in the context of industry, technology, science, and economy. Auditing is deeply connected to the implementation of any standard, and this chapter aims to do its connection. Standardization can stimulate international comparability eliminating obstacles arising from some different national practices in accounting and in auditing using IFRS and ISA, in risk analysis using ERM or ISO 31000, in people's safety, in the product or in the environment. A case study about ISO 31000 in a municipality where IFRS and ISA are followed and ISO 9001, 14001, 18000 are a reality will frame this issue. ISO 26000 about corporate social responsibility will be the new future challenge.

INTRODUCTION

This chapter aims to make the connection between the audit function and the applicable standards. Audit consists of an activity of analysis, inspection and verification carried out about any subject, with the purpose of issuing an opinion about its veracity, transparency and accuracy according to a reference or a benchmark of performance. These benchmark tools, often called standards, may be related either to accounting, auditing, risk, safety or to the quality of the product, the environment and the social responsibility of the organization. After considering each of them – IFRS, ISA, ERM and ISO standards 9001,14001,18000, 31000, 26000 – a brief description of the respective audit process associated will be considered. Finally, so as to frame this issue, a case study about ISO 31000 in a municipality of the District of Porto – that has already implemented most of these standards –will be displayed.

DOI: 10.4018/978-1-5225-7356-2.ch005

BACKGROUND

Over the last few years, an acceleration of the process of standardization concerning business management has taken place in an economic context characterized by a marked process of globalization and economic integration of markets. Under this scope of analysis, many studies have been undertaken considering the role of standards that are, in many cases, non-tariff barriers to international trade relationships.

As various authors have emphasized, while tariff barriers are becoming lower and lower, non-tariff barriers (i.e., technical standards and regulations affecting the requirements for products, services and, indirectly, production processes) are acquiring increasing importance (Blanco & Bustos, 2004). In short, the importance of international trade in the global economy has grown dramatically over the last two decades, but while tariffs and quantitative restrictions on trade have been lowered or eliminated, barriers of a different nature have had an increasingly restrictive effect on trade, especially in the case of a broad range of technical standards (Dias, 2014; Giovannucci & Ponte, 2005; Henson & Loader, 2001).

Standardization has been crucial for the development of the industrial society (Blind, 2004). At its origins, in the early 20th century, standardization was introduced in order to curb an uneconomical divergence of components, parts and supplies and to foster their interchangeability so as to facilitate mass production and the repair and maintenance of products and services.

However, standardization has gone further than this and comes to be applied to the very management processes and systems by which products and services are produced (Antonelli, 1999; Brunson & Jacobsson, 2000; Dias, 2014; Heras, 2006). Standards-based management is a research field that has received considerable attention in recent years, due to the great success experienced by management standards all over the world. Therefore, it is important to review the different approaches of the study of standardization in a management context, in order to try to synthesize and, thus, improve the academic knowledge about these interesting management tools, within the interest of the various different stakeholders involved (e.g., managers, consultants, policy makers and researchers). It is well known from the perspective of the executives of organizations that all these standards need an accurate plan of audit in order to test their fulfillment. This way, audit must be considered as a proactive and adaptive issue of analysis and assurance that should make part of the management of any organization.

The auditing function concerning financial statements is developed according to ISA (International Standards on Audit). This audit process has the aim of analyzing the organization accounting transactions that must fulfil IFRS (International Financial Reporting Standards) (issued by IASB – International Accounting Standards Board – United Kingdom). These standards have the purpose of creating the global harmonization and comparability of the financial statements once they are applied worldwide. These standards start with ISA 200 – Overall Objectives of the Independent Auditor and the Conduct of an Audit in Accordance with International Standards on Auditing, and end with ISA 810 – Engagements to Report on Summary Financial Statements covering the most relevant aspects of the audit process. Nowadays they are a compulsory tool to be used by auditors along the development of the work on the organizations' financial statements.

Many articles have been written about the early application of IFRS. Some organizations were not very interested in implementing these standards. It is interesting to note that there are very different opinions. Hans, Edward, Martin, and Cheng (2015), in Germany, decided to measure the impact that the early implementation of these standards would have on the quality of management reports. They took as reference previous studies that measured the accounting quality through the management of the results, the timely recognition of losses and the relevance of value. While the literature showed that IFRS add to the improvement of accounting quality, these authors considered that these improvements were confined to companies that had incentives for their adoption. In this way, this study showed that companies that resist the adoption of IFRS have closer links with banks and internal shareholders, which are consistent with lower incentives for the use of more comprehensive accounting standards. The authors concluded from the evidence gathered that they could not infer about changes in the quality of accounting around the voluntary adoption of the early implementation of IFRS. With similar conclusions, another study (Lourenço & Castelo Branco, 2015), which analyzed of a set of 67 articles published in accounting journals that integrate the Social Sciences Citation Index (SSCI), published between 2000 and 2013, refers a positive effect on the quality of information, capital markets, analysts' predictability, comparability and use of information as consequences of the implementation of IFRS. However, this effect is also related to other factors, such as the characteristics of both countries and companies. In short, they result from factors such as the country's socio-cultural framework. The authors conclude that rule-sharing is not by itself sufficient to create a common business language; only with management incentives and institutional factors playing an important role in framing the characteristics of financial reporting can it be really achieved.

Consistent with and under the scope of these ideas, Mukhlisin and Antonio (2018) considered the accounting standards' development in the United Kingdom and Indonesia according to a different path and history. The results of their study confirm the importance of the legal foundation, as well as political and social differences of both countries, as factors and reasons that explain a unique development and results.

However, regardless of getting an advantage with their implementation, IFRS and IAS (International Accounting Standards) are a global reality. What is important is the comparability and harmonization of financial information – the great motive inherent in these standards. This analysis and inspection of what is done in the accounting is carried out by the audit, whose process activity development is also ruled by standards.

ISA: International Standards on Audit

Independent Audit aims to increase the degree of confidence of the users who receive the financial statements (as per ISA 200 stating the general objectives of the independent auditor and the conduct of an Audit in Accordance with the International Standards on Auditing). This is achieved through an opinion expressed by the auditor on whether the financial statements are prepared, in all material respects, in accordance with the applicable financial reporting framework. The Independent Audit is characterized as an important type of assurance service. To execute audit firm inspections, the work paper files of audit firms that audit companies listed on US-based exchanges for review, use a risk-based approach (Cheng & Flasher, 2018). This is to guarantee that the work of auditors is good and faithful.

Besides this and according to the definition of assurance services of AICPA (American Institute of Certified Public Accountants), assurance services are independent professional services that improve the quality of information for the users' decision-making.

However and according to Boynton, Johnson, and Kell (2003), assurance services and audit services have different meanings because audit highlights information that affects accounting statements, and assurance services cover a wide range of information used for decision making and are not restricted to the financial statements.

It is well known that assurance services can cover financial and non-financial information, isolated in a process or system, direct or indirect, external or internal. The audit process will be achieved according to ISA (issued by IAASB – International Auditing and Assurance Standards Board /IFAC – International Federation of Accountants – United States of America).As a curiosity and just considering the above mentioned issues, it may be stated that the mix of these standards – being at the same time from Europe and from the USA – with a different global positioning of their issuing bodies contribute to the so-called global financial harmonization.

Boolaky and Soobaroyen's (2017) study about the ISA implementation and the advantages that may follow uses the neo-institutional perspective, and seeks, for the first time, to investigate empirically the determinants of the adoption of ISA and the commitment to harmonization on a cross-national basis (89 countries). The results show that the protection of minority interests, law enforcement, creditor and borrower rights, foreign aid, the prevalence of foreign ownership, educational level, and particular forms of political system (level of democracy), prevailing in a country, are observed as significant predictors. The degree of commitment to the adoption and harmonization of ISA's statistical analysis shows that coercive, mimetic and normative pressure have a significant impact on their adoption in relation to economic factors (led by efficiency). The findings of the study reveal that the current efforts of IFAC and other international agencies are directed to the use of ISA and should encompass a broad range of institutional, rather than economic factors. These are, in fact, relevant reasons in the development of audit policies around the world. It is well considered by all the stakeholders that, for an effective achievement of audit functions, the support of management and the implementation of the auditor's opinion play the most important role (Mihret & Yismaw, 2007). It seems that the power established in the organization is something quite relevant that must be fitted to each organization depending on the activity, placement and socio-cultural environment. Yet, it is the combination and consideration of all these variables that can explain the assurance that is expected from the audit on the financial statements. If one of them fails, it becomes a risk factor.

ERM: Enterprise Risk Management

When considering an organization, a perspective of risk management must be encompassed. It is important to identify some of the tools available for the organizations, namely ERM (Enterprise Risk Management), whose last review is from 2017. ERM considers the life of organizations just like a process where one gets as inputs the core values of the company, translated in its Mission and Vision. A a set of risk procedures should be implemented in order to comply with the mission and vision, so that an enhanced performance may be the final outcome of ERM. So, Enterprise Risk Management (COSO, 2017) is a tool – a benchmark, a standard – that, if correctly implemented in the organization, will contribute to a better performance.

As mentioned before and according to Figure 1, the inputs of this process are a clear definition of the organization's Mission and Vision. The former has to do with the development of the organization's activity and the latter has to do with its future placement in the market. The core values are related to the history tradition, beliefs and stories connected to the organization, that is, its cultural aspects, which is a real innovation of ERM 2017 when compared to the previous Cube COSO.

The operational process consists of identifying the following aspects related to the organization's business strategy and objectives:

Figure 1. ERM 2017
Source: 2017-COSO-ERM-Integrating-with-Strategy-and-Performance-Executive-Summary.pdf

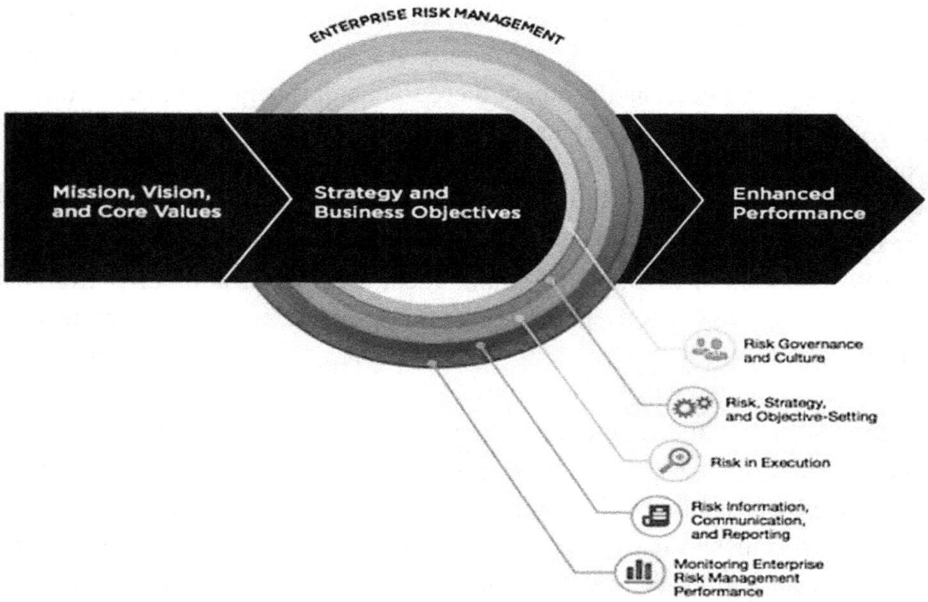

- Risk Governance and Culture, that is, how the organization identifies the risk and the relevance of the organization's culture in terms of risk;
- Risk Strategy and Objective Setting has to do with the guidelines defined to identify risk situations;
- Risk in Execution has to do with the implementation of the risk;
- Risk Information, Communication and Reporting means how and to whom the risk environment is communicated;
- Monitoring Enterprise Risk Management Performance, that is, the ways found in order to test the risk in the organizations.

This new COSO (2017) assumes that if these procedures are undertaken in order to match the organization's Mission and Vision, the attainment of the organization's goals will be reached and an enhanced performance will be displayed.

An interesting study, quite similar to the one developed along this chapter, was carried out in a municipality in Finland (Vinnari & Skærbæk, 2014), having as purpose the analysis of the implementation of risk management as a tool for internal audit activities. The authors found that risk management, rather than reducing uncertainty, created unexpected uncertainties that would otherwise not have emerged. These include uncertainties relating to legal aspects of risk management solutions, in particular the issue concerning which types of documents are considered legally valid; uncertainties relating to the definition and operationalization of risk management; and uncertainties relating to the resources available for expanding risk management. More generally, such uncertainties relate to the professional identities and responsibilities of operational managers as defined by the framing devices.

The connection between audit and ERM is strong. In order to identify the areas and the issues that may reveal a risk in a company, it is necessary to investigate, to check and to conclude about the risky events that may occur along a dynamic operational process of any kind of organization. And this process is made up of enquiries, testing and defining goals to be attained expressed in KPI (Key Performance Indicators).

ISO Standards (ISO 31000; ISO 9001; ISO14001; ISO18001; ISO 26000)

ISO 31000

Furthermore, besides ERM, and still regarding risk management, ISO 31000 (Figure 2) can also be implemented. This standard's last revision occurred in March 2018.

It should be noted that companies that used to work with ISO 9001 prefer ISO 31000 because the language is objective and direct, in the same way and approach as ISO 9001..

In terms of input, communication and consultation is considered about risk position in the organization, defining a framework and then assessing the risk in three distinct phases: identification, analysis, and evaluation. Finally, there is the risk treatment. An output called monitoring and review ends the process. Yet, this is an iterative process leading to continuous improvement, which means that after monitoring and reviewing, there is a return to the first phase by communication and consultation because the non-conformities must be disclosed and treated.

An application of ISO 31000 was considered by Oliveira, Marins, Rocha, and Salomon (2017) regarding the supply chain. The authors posit that breaks and interruptions in supply chains can cause huge financial losses and damage the companies' reputation. Thus, Supply Chain Risk Management (SCRM) is considered to involve a multi-step process analysis. However, researchers differ on the number and content of these steps. The objective of this study was to analyze the applicability of ISO 31000 as a systematic procedure for SCRM. And, if so, how the standard can be implemented in the context of SCRM,

Figure 2. Risk management and the ISO 31000 standard
Source: ISO 31000 – risk management – flowchart

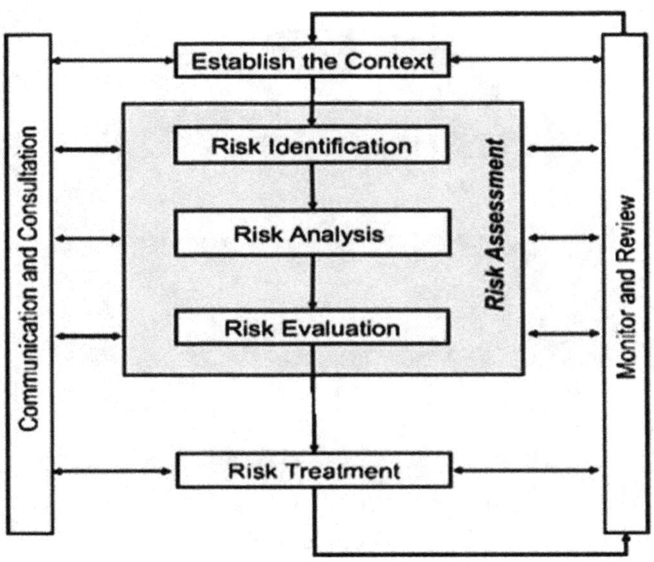

with a structure and in a specific company. Through the literature review, the risk management steps proposed by SCRM surveys were compared and harmonized. In addition, a way has been developed to identify and prioritize the risk assessment tools and techniques in ISO 31000: 2009 that should integrate a procedure for SCRM, based on the Analytic Hierarchy Process (AHP), exemplified in a car industry supply chain. Based on the results of the research (Dias, 2017), the authors concluded that ISO 31000 can be used in a beneficial way as a standardized method to execute SCRM, provided that the tools and techniques are selected according to the needs of the company and the characteristics of the business.

As to the relation of audit to ISO 31000, it may be stated that its implementation is based on audit. After its implementation, the monitoring is a kind of audit that must be achieved within the working process of the organization.

ISO 9001

ISO 9001, in its 2015 version, is the standard that organizations must apply to have their product or service certified and, in this way, through their sales, have associated a guarantee, to and from the transaction, in the global market. In schematic terms its composition is as depicted in Figure 3.

The main items to be considered for the implementation of ISO 9001 are shown in Table 1.

Studies about the "quality" factor show that the quality process can add to a change in the structure of organizations (Deming, 1989; Dias, 2014; Heras, Dick, & Casadesús, 2002; Hyvönen, 2007). The way hierarchy is established or positioned can be altered to better serve the purposes of quality and, ultimately, the management goals embodied in the organization's mission. It is common knowledge that any organization, to work efficiently and effectively, needs to have leadership (Dias, 2009; Mintzberg, 1987; Zahirul, 2003), but this too is now changing. It is the good leadership that will make the organization's mission-oriented objectives guided by strategies (Dias & Lima, 2010; Drucker, 1986; Kaplan & Norton,

Figure 3. ISO 9001
Source: ISO 9001 diagram

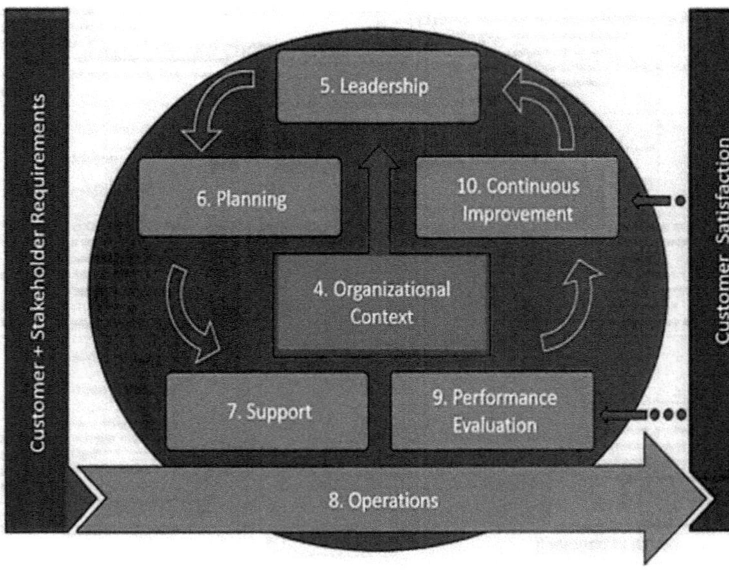

Table 1. Crucial items from ISO 9001

1 Organization Context: interested parts in the Quality Management System
2 Leadership: distribution of power within the organization
3 Planning: the way the organization sees and plans its future business
4 Support: operational structure towards organization "core business"
5 Operations: process related to the product or service
6 Performance Evaluation: prevailing schedule in the organization
7 Continuous Improvement: KPI definition for the Quality Management System and follow up associated

1992; Oakland & Tanner, 2007; Ortiz, Benito, & Galende, 2006) that can and should be understood through cultural factors (Schein, 1999).

The global market impels the organizations to look at ISO 9001 as a challenge. The universities were entities studied in Malaysia. Basir, Davies, and Douglas (2017), based on the literature review and considering only the academic culture, classified according to four elements – academic freedom, individualism, professionalism and collegiality –, carried out two case studies in Malaysian universities, which were ISO 9001 certified for five years. At the time of this research, these two were the only universities that had certification for the entire organization (most organizations obtain certification only for specific departments). The results showed that academic freedom, individualism and collegiality worked against the maintenance of ISO 9001, while professionalism influenced the maintenance of ISO 9001 both positively and negatively. The opposites of individualism (teamwork) and collegiality supported the maintenance of ISO 9001 in one case.

A Quality Management System is the result of ISO 9001implementation (Dias, 2010) and can be responsible for the company's sustainability. For this the company must achieve a previous audit so as to evaluate the degree of compliance of the areas/sectors to be included within the scope of certification. Then some actions and performance indicators will be settled to sustain it.

Subsequently, an audit plan will be designed to be in force since the moment ISO 9001 is granted to the company and it will be working out along the life of the standard (evidencing and presenting non conformities and trying to solve them). This audit function performance is described in the very ISO 9001 contents and is a compulsory figure to be followed.

ISO 14001

Any entity that wishes to use ISO 14001 regarding the environment should already have an ISO 9001 (Dias, 2013) because it is almost compulsory and its implementation procedures are quite similar and complementary, but the environmental focus is the ultimate goal. Typically, the most polluting sectors (such as pulp, chemicals, petroleum and civil construction, among others) will be most interested in meeting this standard in order to show compliance with the environment and all the other stakeholders. In terms of the diagram, it is possible to identify ISO 14001 as shown in Figure 4.

As can be noted in this standard, as in all the others, the responsibility of management and the environment policy defined by the organization to meet the environmental directives (usually European directives for Europe) are the main issues. Planning is associated to the company's environment approach. The monitoring phase and actions include corrective measures whenever results come out of the plan. From

Figure 4. Diagram of ISO 14001
Source: ISO 14001 flowchart

the implementation of this standard a lot has been developed academically. A recent study by Murmura, Liberatore, Bravi, and Casolani (2018) states that, over the last decades, the adoption of Environmental Management Systems, as structures for the integration of corporate environmental protection policies and programs, has become a growing practice among national and multinational companies around the world. The study carried out by the authors is an empirical survey conducted among Italian companies certified with the ISO 14001 Environmental Management System (EMS) and the European System of Eco-Management and Audit (EMAS). The objective was to identify the types of companies that have implemented an EMS standard, to examine the motivations that led them to introduce it, to identify perceived benefits and barriers and to assess the differences and similarities between these two systems. The research was carried out through a questionnaire sent to 1,657 certified organizations, of which 190 participated. The analysis of variance; the chi-test ($\chi 2$ test) and the Pearson's correlation were used to frame the items of motivations, benefits and barriers. The survey results show that EMAS certification appears to be strictly related to ISO 14001; in fact, most companies operating in the international markets have both standards. In addition, especially the larger companies have embarked on certification when compared to the smaller ones, because they are almost "pushed" to certification for different reasons. Time was also considered a relevant discriminant factor. Regarding the analysis of perceived benefits and barriers, there was an important correlation similarity between ISO 14001 and EMAS. The research made an added contribution to the importance of good environmental management.

The connection of this standard to audit follows the assumptions described for ISO 9001, that is to say, the audit is a function needed in order to guarantee the granting and maintenance of this certification.

ISO 18001

People who work in an organization should be secured from any harm that can happen in the working environment. For this objective OHSAS (18001:2007) must be referred and they deal with a management system that helps an organization to control the work risks and improve performance. The main issues of its implementation are depicted in Figure 5.

The requisites to implement the Norm consist of the definition of the legal framework of the organization and its workers and then a full description of the objectives and the monitoring program associated, as well as the resources available to achieve them. The functions associated with human resources, responsibilities/authorities related to the competence and the training and the awareness of the class are also central. Communication, operational control and measures implemented to deal with emergencies are factors that help to justify performance improvement. The final goal is the continuous improvement and this way the organizations that follow these recommendations of safety and health policy will record a minimized risk. However, it is very important that the human resources of the organization know that they contribute to success and that they are recognized for it.

Usually the Human Resources Department of any company develops some audit procedures in order to test the security and availability of the resources devoted to implementing this standard.

ISO 26000

This standard is intended to help organizations contribute to a sustainable development and to encourage it by going beyond legal compliance, as this is a fundamental duty of any organization and an essential part of its social responsibility. In presenting ISO 26000, it is advisable for an organization to focus on social, environmental, legal, cultural, political and organizational diversity, as well as on differences in economic conditions, consistent with international standards of behavior.

However, for the purpose of the WTO (World Trade Organization)-Marrakesh Agreement, it is not intended to be interpreted as an "international standard", "guideline" or "recommendation", nor is it intended to provide a basis for any presumption or decision of a measure compatible with WTO obligations. The performance of an organization that holds social responsibility can influence, among other things:

Figure 5. ISO 18001
Source: Diagram of ISO 18001

- Competitive advantage and reputation (organization, management, governance, operational practices);
- The ability to attract and retain workers or members, clients and third parties (human rights, labor practices);
- Maintenance of employee morale, commitment and productivity (human rights, labor practices);
- The perception of investors, owners, donors, sponsors and the financial community (customer/stakeholder issues);
- The relationship with companies, government, media, suppliers, peers, clients and the community in general (involvement or development in the community).

In brief, there are seven central issues of social responsibility defined in Figure 6:

Gupta, Briscoe, and Hambrick (2017) researched the position of United States' companies in relation to CSR (Corporate Social Responsibility) and questioned why companies presented different positions towards this issue. Previous research had emphasized the role of external pressures as well as CEO's (Chief Executive Officer) preferences, while little attention had been paid to the possibility that CSR may also derive from the prevailing beliefs of company's political body. The authors introduced the concept of organizational political ideology to explain how the political beliefs of organizational members can shape corporate advancement in CSR. They used a new measure based on the political contributions of corporate employees, evidenced in the Fortune 500, and found that ideology foresees advances in CSR. This effect seems to be stronger when CSR is rare in: (i) the business sector where firms are located; (ii) when firms have high human capital intensity; and (iii) when the CEO has been in the organization for a long time. Another relevant issue addressed by the authors was the reason why companies vary their positions regarding CSR. Previous research suggests that companies get involved in CSR when they are under pressure to do so, or when their CEOs have liberal values. The concept of organizational political ideology was then used and it was concluded that CSR can also result from the values of the largest number of employees. Introducing a new measure of organizational political ideology based on employee donations to the two main political parties in the United States, it has been found that liberal

Figure 6. Social responsibility

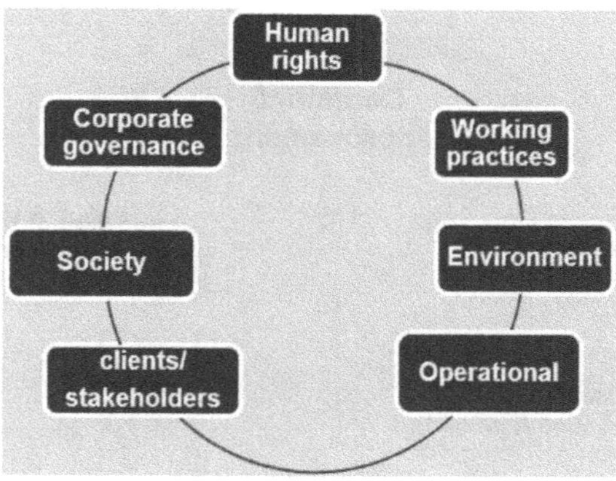

companies are more concerned with CSR than conservative ones, and even more so when other companies belonging to the same branch of industry have weaker CSR records, when the company relies heavily on human resources (thus having many workers) and when the CEO of the company has a long organizational mandate.

From these final ideas of Gupta, Briscoe, and Hambrick (2017), it can be stated that they are in line with the conclusions from a PWC's (PricewaterhouseCoopers) study, dating back to 2012, carried out in Portugal. This study covered different sectors of activity with CSR implemented, such as energy, transport, logistics and real estate construction, which accounted for about 65% of all CSR companies. In a detailed characterization analysis, it may be concluded that companies with a strong and shared leadership, having a large number of workers, and presenting a considerable turnover need to defend their reputation/ brand and are looking for something that sets them apart from the others – the peers – and that is CSR.

After considering the importance of standards and the related function of audit, this chapter will now consider risk management in a Portuguese municipality.

CASE STUDY OF A MUNICIPALITY

This study is under the scope of many other carried out about municipalities and local entities that have somehow inspired it.

As to municipalities, it is important to refer that a great part of Portuguese municipalities are already implementing most of the standards described above.

The District of Porto includes 18 municipalities[1]. Considering the size of the population to be served/ provided, the following municipalities stand out: Maia, Matosinhos, Porto and Vila Nova de Gaia[2].

The municipality of Maia is an entity with autonomous administration of the Portuguese State and is geographically located in the District of Porto (Portugal). The municipality of Maia has implemented ISO 9001, ISO14001and ISO 18001. Furthermore, it is important to mention that this municipality decided to implement in advance some procedures and measures to face the risk, being this fact one of the good reasons that justifies this case study.

As initially mentioned, some studies have revealed interest on municipalities (Félix, 2013) either about the environmental accounting and related reporting procedures or about the importance of internal control as to the usefulness of the information displayed.

Ribeiro, Aibar-Guzmán, Aibar-Guzman, and Monteiro (2016) considered the development of Environmental Accounting and Reporting Practices (EARP) and an index was developed by a set of eight of these entities from the 69 Portuguese local entities included in the considered sample. Three variables were considered in this study as possible factors that drive the development of Environmental Management Practices (EMP) by local entities. They were: size of entity, accounting framework, and degree of development of EMP. Results indicate that the degree of development of EARPs in Portuguese local entities is low. Additionally, accounting regulation and the degree of development of EMPs are explaining factors of the degree of development of EARPs in Portuguese local entities. The information about the environment seems to be relevant but internal control and the usefulness of the financial information obtained for internal decision making is also quite a relevant issue (Nogueira & Jorge, 2017). The authors made a quantitative research, based on a cross-sectional analysis developed in the local government context. Data were collected from a survey addressed to decision makers (politicians and chief officials) in charge of the financial area in all Portuguese municipalities. The response rate was approximately

49%, assuring representativeness. As to the perceived usefulness of financial and budgetary reporting for internal decision making, the results show that the attitudes of municipalities' internal users towards using accrual-based financial reporting for decision making is changing. Additionally, internal decision makers consider financial and budgetary information as being very useful for decision making, and the different types of internal control applicable to that information are referred to as very important. The results also clearly point towards the existence of a significant and positive relationship between internal control (including internal auditing) about financial and budgetary information and its perceived usefulness for municipal decision making (Nogueira & Jorge, 2017). This introduction allows identifying the interest that municipalities have on financial reporting and the transparency and usefulness of its contents.

Objectives

According to literature suggestions and taking into account the needed policy and business requirements for the public sector in Portugal, a case study, based on ISO 31000, was carried out in a Town Hall belonging to Maia, District of Porto, in Portugal. It is well known that municipalities have a quite different organizational environment and positioning as to the hierarchical distribution of functions and related management process (Azevedo, 2014).

As to the Portuguese Public Sector, risk management practices are quite recent. Emerging from paragraph 1 of the United Nations Convention against Corruption, the Prevention Council was created in Portugal in 2008 [3].The objective was to have a formal institution coordinating the anti-corruption model. Until that date only agencies acting on a repressive scope of analysis were provided (Central Directorate for Investigation of Corruption and Economic and Financial Crime – Judicial Police and the Central Investigation Department and Criminal Action – Attorney General's Office).

Since then, the Corruption Prevention Council has been working closely with the Court of Accounting (Tribunal de Contas) and has taken on a leading role in the adoption of new risk management practices, issuing recommendations with a binding and compulsory application.

In order to comply with the guidelines laid down by the Recommendation of July 1, 2015, the Directorate General of Local Authorities prepared and approved the Management Risk Prevention Plan, including the Corruption and Related Offenses, called PPRGCIC, which identifies, in a very exhaustive manner, the different activities developed in an operational environment with potential risk. These should be considered within the internal control measures/mechanisms to be implemented in a municipality in order to prevent/avoid their occurrence.

In this context, the project described in the present chapter is based on the integrated Risk Management Model for the Portuguese Public Sector. The overall objective (see Table 2) is to design an integrated risk management model encompassing.

Table 2. Aims of the case study

To check the existence of mechanisms and instruments of Risk Management implemented in the municipality.	Quality Management System – already implemented in the municipality.
To develop a risk management model based on ISO 31000 – Risk Management – integrating it into the Management System based on ISO 9001.	To assess the operationalization of the Risk Management Plan designed for corruption and related infractions and ascertain its contribution to management.

The creation of a risk management model based on the compliance with legal and regulatory requirements is a useful model for municipal management and adaptable to the reality of any of the entities that belong to the Portuguese Public Sector. This study aims to contribute to the continuous improvement of the management system of the organization, placing it above the peers' level (Dias, 2017; Magalhães & Dias, 2017)[4].

Identification of the Organization: The Municipality of Maia

The Portuguese supreme law (Constituição da República Portuguesa), in Article 235, establishes that the democratic organization of the Portuguese State includes the existence of local authorities. Local authorities are collective persons of population and territory with representative bodies, elected by direct and secret universal suffrage, which aim at the pursuit of their own interests, common and specific to the populations (Almeida, 2000; Amaral, 2007).

The municipality of Maia is part of the group of local authorities, which includes the City Council (executive body), composed of the President, Vice-President and Councilors, and the Municipal Assembly (deliberative body), which includes the members representing the respective political parties and the Presidents of the county's parishes. It is headquartered in the city of Maia, located in the District of Porto, and is one of the 18 municipalities that make up the Metropolitan Area of Porto. Over the last thirty years, this municipality, has become one of the most important poles of attraction in the north of the country being responsible for more than 100,000 inhabitants.

Aware of the importance of meeting the collective and individual needs of the local public, the municipality of Maia has directed its strategy to reaching high levels of quality of life of the M*aiatos* citizens. They highlight the guidelines for total certification for Quality and partial certification for the environment; the international projection and entrepreneurship and the bet on youth, sports, culture, environment, education and social support.

As to Risk Management, the municipality of Maia complies strictly with the recommendations of the Corruption Prevention Council. Yet, as the authors verified by conducting this case study, the process exists in the organization, but needs consolidation.

However, the specificities of municipal management and the fact that their action results from the interface between the organization and the population implies a greater concern in identifying the risks that may jeopardize their tasks (Rocha, 1997). There are numerous risks to be taken into account, such as the fact that all public entities are subject to the primacy of legality and exist in the light of political cycles; do not have as their main objective the attainment of profit; are entities governed by public law, but also practice acts of private law (purchase, sale); their Top Management responds in some cases to electors and in others cases to ministerial tutelage (Carvalho, 2013). In addition, it should not be forgotten that there is also the risk of continuity, since the municipalities are mostly dependent on transfers from the State Budget (Moura, 2011). At the same time, the risk of corruption is inherent. According to a study on criminal sociology coordinated by Luís de Sousa in 2010, entitled "A corrupção participada em Portugal 2004-2008" (Participated corruption in Portugal 2004-2008), 345 of the 838 lawsuits analyzed during the 2004-2008 period were related to local government authorities and municipal enterprises (Cruz & Sousa, 2014).

Methodology

According to the proposed objectives, a case study of an exploratory and descriptive nature was developed.

Scientific research seeks to attain a reliable solution to a given problem through a logical procedure. Thus, it relies on an orderly and systematic logic of data collection and interpretation (Quivy & Campenhoudt, 2005).

Literature presents different perspectives regarding methodological options (what to do) and the design of information collection tools (how to do it), ascertaining them according to the objectives and the research questions and considering the available resources and even the position of the researcher him/herself (Monteiro, 2012).

In this sense, this case study was selected because one of the researchers has a professional link to this municipality. As mentioned, a case study of an exploratory and descriptive nature was developed, on a qualitative approach based on indirect observation, through the use of the documentary research technique and direct observation through the interview techniques.

The documentary research consisted of gathering and analyzing the documentary sources (documents generated within and across the organization) that consisted of the consideration of:

1. Risk Management practices existing in the organization;
2. Dynamics of the Organization Management System;
3. Implementation and monitoring of the Risk Management Plan.

As to the internal documentary sources consulted, they were the following: The Organization Macrostructure; the Management Report; the Management Policy; Review by Management; Management Guide; Internal Control Standard; Risk Management Plan and Implementation Report.

It was considered appropriate, for the objectives of this case study, to carry out semi-structured interviews, under previously studied specific objectives. The interviewees were chosen according to the organizational hierarchy (mainly quality managers, related staff and top management), their position in the municipality and the level of knowledge about the organization's Management System. The contents of the interview guide were displayed beforehand to the interviewees and consisted of the following main issues: (i) involvement of the workers in the anti-corruption plan; (ii) relation of the internal audit department to this anti-corruption plan; (iii) identification of the main risks considered; (iv) strategy to be used to face the risks; (v) report about the execution of the measures defined to prevent the risks and respective KPI. Content analysis and documentary analysis were the methods used for the analysis of the collected information, so as to allow for data triangulation. Thus, a content analysis grid was used, in which the interviewees' perceptions were characterized in an individualized way. Each issue asked to the interviewees corresponded to each study objective. After performing this content analysis, data was compared to the previously referenced document sources.

At this moment it is important to put forward the formulated assertions that rule this project (Table 3).

Risk Management

The Integrated Risk Management Model for the Portuguese Public Sector is based on the consideration of ISO 31000 – Risk Management – Principles and Guidelines for the management practices of the organization. The municipality of Maia has already been quality certified by ISO 9001 – Quality Man-

Table 3. Assertions

The existence and contribution of Risk Management practices for the municipal management.	The contribution of the Internal Audit for the management of the risks of the organization.
Integration of ISO 31000 – Risk Management – in the Quality Management Systems.	The effectiveness of the Risk Management Plan as an instrument to support the management of the municipality.

agement Systems (updated 2015). This last version provides a new approach for a Risk-Based Thinking, which converges and announces a facilitator for the integration of the ISO 31000 within organization management practices. Thus, the risk model to be constructed has the objectives shown in Table 4.

Since the municipality of Maia has clearly defined guidelines and strategic objectives, it is important to try to identify the risks that may affect their fulfilment. Therefore, a Risk Management Policy must be formally created. This will contribute to the consolidation of the risk management practices already instituted and, consequently, to the improvement of the Organization Management System. In this context, the elaboration of a Manual of Risk Management became a reality, having a main role in the implementation and maintenance of the process. It will allow to standardize concepts, to institute in the organization the adequate practices for managing the risks and, consequently, to keep a systematic follow-up. It also considers all stakeholders in the process and contributes to the transparency of the organization's risk management.

In short, the content of the Manual is shown in Table 5.

So, the Risk Management scope of analysis within all the processes of the municipality will include different paths:

Table 4. Objectives of the risk model

To be oriented for the implementation of the process of Risk Management.	To integrate the risk culture into the organization's culture.
To establish a structured and systematic risk management.	To contribute to improving the organization's image and reputation.

Table 5. Risk management manual

Manual
Applicable legal and regulatory imperatives and risk management procedures.
Concept of risk, description of level of risks and synthesis of the control and reporting systems that integrate and support the process.
Responsible people and their interaction in the process.
Procedures to be followed in the evaluation of the risks and periodicity of execution.
Criteria considered in the implementation of measures to mitigate risks and responsibilities in this area.
Graduation methodologies and quantification of risks (inherent and residual risk).
Methods of monitoring, responsible persons and periodicity. Measures to be implemented when risk limits are exceeded.
Model of risk report to be prepared.
Parameters to follow in the evaluation of the risk management process.

- Identification of the risks taking into account the strategic objectives;
- Detailed characterization of the organization: vision, mission and strategic objectives; articulation of the Internal Audit and Risk Management process; organizational macro-structure and data on human and financial resources;
- Presentation of the methodology underlying the plan and the report;
- Introduction of data analysis concerning the execution of the plan (partial and global results of the management of the organizational risks);
- Insertion of a chapter for final considerations (inquiries regarding recommendations issued by the Corruption Prevention Council or changes to the International Organization for Standardization referential);
- Adequacy of the schedules and annexes attached to the plan and report (identification of processes and objectives, articulation between strategic guidelines and objectives of each process, identification of risk factors, expected dates for carrying out risk management actions and evaluation of effectiveness).

In addition to the preparation of this Manual, the Risk Execution Plan was also developed. To attain it, some complementary supports were carried out:

1. A Checklist for the Independent Evaluation of the Risk Management Process;
2. A Risk Management Implementation Schedule;
3. A Communication Report.

The Manual is closely linked to the Risk Management Plan and to the Implementation Report. It establishes the methodology to be followed by the management of the organization as to the risks and, in this sense, the Plan and the Report are the tools that will shape this methodology.

As can be seen from the contents of ISO 31000 previously described in this chapter (Figure 2), this standard is fully used in this case. From establishing the context within the municipality until the moment of assessing the risk and treating it, all the phases were considered and the guidelines and procedures were implemented. For the integration of these documents in the organization's Management System (that is depending on ISO 9001) it was suggested to implement the following actions:

ACTION 1: Adapt all the processes to the new approach of Risk Based Thinking, including strategic and change management. This approach is, in fact, one of the most important changes in ISO 9001. Being present in practically all the requirements of this conceptual structure, it alerts to the necessity of establishing a cause-effect thought. So, municipal management should be developed taking into account the risks, their causes and their impact (both positive and negative) on all projects, programs and organizational plans.

ACTION 2: Quarterly monitoring of actions defined for the treatment of risks. The organization has an internal event registration system. Under a logic of continuous improvement and embedded in this recording scheme, all the actions to be implemented, responsible parties, execution dates of the actions undertaken and the evaluation of their effectiveness are identified. This internal event recording system should include risk management strategies in order to direct the organization towards possible changes to the risk profile and to the definition of measures to be implemented when the risk limits are exceeded.

ACTION 3: Integration in the annual review of the organizational performance information concerning the risk management activity and its analysis by the top management. The municipality maintains an annual cycle of revision of the organization system. Monitoring the evolution of the risk management strategies' implementation may be a valid indicator of process performance.

Internal Audit Process

The Risk Management process should be kept along with the approaches established in the organization (under PDCA Plan-Do-Check-Act Cycle, Process Approach and Risk Based Thinking) and according to the organization's strategy. For the implementation of this model, the municipality will consider an analysis of the risks related to the already established processes, and whenever there are expected changes the provision of services should be used.

On the other hand, all steps concerning planning the actions needed to treat the risks and considering the usual factors and their impact will take place. This task will take into account not only the rate of risk implementation but also the evaluation of the actions undertaken about the risks, which shall be disclosed to all stakeholders, once they are relevant for the Quality Management System. As concerns the role of Internal Audit within the process, and taking into account that the new paradigm is based on a vision focused on management risks, the Internal Audit is closely related to Risk Management and to Internal Control. When internal auditors assess Internal Control, they question whether the controls are appropriate to the risks identified by the organization. Controls exist because there are risks, and the risks exist because the organization has goals. As to the Internal Audit, the municipality of Maia considers that this is an important tool for top management to be involved.

Nonetheless, reflection on two aspects was considered quite beneficial:

- The first concerns the formal consideration of "risk" in the planning and implementation of Internal Audits. Since the audit work is based on sampling, and it is well known that auditors cannot focus on all areas of the organizations, some criteria and some faithful samples must be previously defined. If the focus lays upon the mostly risky areas, it is essential that planning continues to have a number of reflections about the critical processes, top management, internal service requests, macrostructure changes, legal, regulatory or regulatory changes and available resources.
- The second is the periodic performance of an independent evaluation of the Risk Management process. This evaluation should be developed according to the organization's specific characteristics, and this could happen within the scope of analysis of internal audits and/or verifications carried out by the Management System. Assuming it as a credibility factor, the independent evaluation about risk management process of the organization should have as main objective to provide security on the effectiveness of Risk Management activities in the municipality.

Thus, these guidelines are most important to frame this issue, as shown in Figure 7.

At this moment, the project is completely designed and some final comments about it may be put forward.

Figure 7. Guidelines for the evaluation of risk management

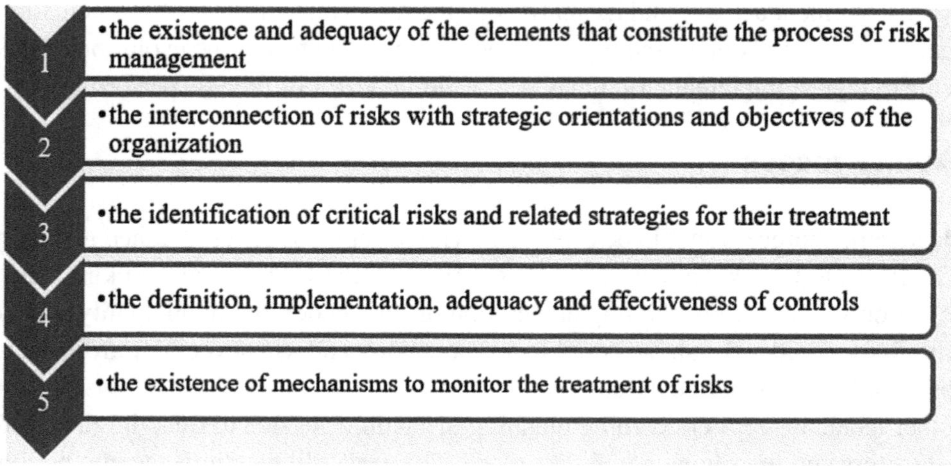

CONCLUSION

From this short travel around standards it can be observed that they are quite important in the management of any organization. They represent some accrued value and account for a lot to the top management when the company has a good market-share to defend, relevant business numbers, significant assets and a large number of workers. This study started considering the importance of using IFRS and ISA as to the financial statements of any company. Additionally, some other ISO standards were considered. As to the internal environment of any organization, a particular attention was driven to Risk Management placed under two versions: ERM and ISO 31000. A case study about the implementation of ISO 31000 was carried out in the Portuguese municipality of Maia, from which the following main ideas may be drawn:

1. The improvement opportunities suggested by the Integrated Risk Management Model for thePortuguese Public Sector are numerous. The positive view of risk in the organization's culture may be highlighted. It seems that, if well seized, risk may also become an opportunity.
2. In addition to the organization's context, other internal information became crucial, such as monitoring stakeholders' expectations and objectives, thus enabling satisfaction assessment results, audit results, nonconformities and opportunities for improvement.
3. It is also important to emphasize the implementation of the Residual Risk Graduation practice: the quantification and graduation of the remaining risk, the one that is left after the implementation of the mitigation measures, allows to assess the levels of the exceeding risk and, consequently, a decision making about it.
4. Internal Audit considers risk in its planning, which is also important, since it directs the activity towards the critical areas.
5. Another important issue is that, by defining KPI (consequent to the Quality Management System), the organization can regularly monitor the achievement of objectives and, consequently, do a direct planning. The redesign and integration of the Risk Management Plan and the Implementation of the Report into the Organization Management System is crucial to get evidence about process compliance.

6. Finally, the organization can report about the risk decisions in the Management Report and in the Management Review Minutes.

The consolidation of the Risk Management process established in the Municipality of Maia proves to be an added value for the organization's management. Managing the risk can be named as a competitive advantage (Magalhães & Dias, 2017; Dias, 2017). A favorable corporate culture characterized by a clear involvement of top management across the whole process was fundamental. This is a very positive stance, inasmuch that the options and decisions about issues related to Risk Management in the Portuguese Public Sector may, very frequently, involve political options that stand somehow beyond the scope of the sole organization. As to this particular case study, it may be stated that its study and development is applicable either to the private or to the public sector.

From the whole study, it may be concluded that all standards from the ISO family (such as the 9001, 18001 and 14001 standards) considered are important for the process of any kind of organization. Finally, and as a tone of the top ISO 26000 was mentioned, meaning that only some companies can address it because CSR is a top positioning of companies in the market.

As a limitation of this study, the authors assume the absence of the calculation of the added value of the ISO 31000 implementation (it is still too early to measure it). Furthermore, the consideration of only one municipality is somehow a short sample. As future research paths, this study could be replicated in other municipalities or in some entrepreneurial sectors from industry or services and it would be quite interesting to record the different outcomes.

REFERENCES

Almeida, J. R. (2000). *Contabilidade de custos para autarquias locais* [Cost accounting for local authorities]. Porto: Vida Económica – Editorial.

Amaral, D. F. (2007). *Curso de Direito Administrativo* [Course of Administrative Law] (3rd ed.). Coimbra: Almedina.

Antonelli, C. (1999). *Localized technological change and the evolution of standards as economic institutions*. Oxford, UK: Oxford University Press. doi:10.1093/0198296045.003.0005

Azevedo, S. R. C. (2014). Auditoria aos municípios estudo de caso – uma aplicação à Área Metropolitana do Porto [Audit to municipalities case study – an application to the Metropolitan Area of Porto]. Master's work project. Porto: Instituto Superior de Contabilidade e Administração do Porto do Politécnico do Porto.

Basir, S. A., Davies, J., Douglas, J., & Douglas, A. (2017). The influence of academic culture on quality management system ISO 9001 maintenance within Malaysian universities. *Journal of Higher Education Policy and Management*, *39*(3), 320–340. doi:10.1080/1360080X.2017.1298199

Blanco, H., & Bustos, B. (2004). *Normalización y comercio sustentable en Sudamérica* [Standardization and sustainable trade in South America]. Santiago de Chile: RIDES.

Blind, K. (2004). *The economics of standards: Theory, evidence, policy*. Edward Elgar Publishing.

Boolaky, P. K., & Soobaroyen, T. (2017). Adoption of International Standards on Auditing (ISA): Do institutional factors matter? *International Journal of Auditing, 1*(21), 59–81. doi:10.1111/ijau.12081

Boynton, W. C., Johnson, R. N., & Kell, W. G. (2003). *Modern auditing* (7th ed.). New York: John Willey & Sons Inc.

Brunsson, N., & Jacobsson, B. (2000). The contemporary expansion of standardization. In N. Brunsson & B. Jacobsson (Eds.), *A world of standards* (pp. 1–17). Oxford, UK: Oxford University Press.

Carvalho, R. (2013). Auditoria da Administração Pública – Factores de risco mais comuns na Administração Pública [Audit of Public Administration – Most common risk factors in Public Administration]. Visual Projection, Master's in Auditing, Edition 2013-2015. Porto: Instituto Superior de Contabilidade e Administração do Porto do Politécnico do Porto.

Cheng, C., & Flasher, R. (2018). Two short case studies in staff auditor and student ethical decision making. *Issues in Accounting Education, 33*(1), 45–52. doi:10.2308/iace-51881

Committee of Sponsoring Organizations of the Treadway Commission. (2017). *Enterprise risk management integrating with strategy and performance.* Available at https://www.coso.org/Documents/2017-COSO-ERM-Integrating-with-Strategy-and-Performance-Executive-Summary.pdf

Cruz, N. F., & Sousa, L. (2014). *Local integrity system assessment Portugal.* Lisboa: TIAC.

De Sousa, L. (2010). *A corrupção participada em Portugal 2004-2008. Resultados globais de uma pesquisa em curso.* Lisboa: PGR/DCIAP and CIES-ISCTE.

Deming, W. (1989). *Calidad, productividad y competitividad. La salida de la crisis* [Quality, productivity and competitiveness. The way out of the crisis]. Madrid: Díaz de Santos.

Dias, A. (2009). Quality management systems for global business as a competitive advantage. Journal Many faces of Innovation – from literature synthesis to empirical studies, 78-103.

Dias, A. (2010). Quality management systems for globally competing. *Revista de Gestão e Sustentabilidade – Portuguese Review of Management and Sustainability, 1*, 79-96.

Dias, A. (2013). *Diffusion and efficiency of ISO standards within the European Union: A qualitative and quantitative analysis in Portuguese organizations* (PhD Thesis). Proquest LLC UMI 3570823.

Dias, A. (2014). *Diffusion and efficiency of ISO 9000 standards in EU.* Lambert Academic Publishers.

Dias, A. (2017). A more effective audit after COSO ERM 2017 or after ISO 31000:2009? *Perspectiva Empresarial, 4*(2), 73–82. doi:10.16967/rpe.v4n2a7

Dias, A., & Lima, L. (2010). Quality systems for global business as a competitive advantage. In T. Riihelä & M. Mattila (Eds.), *Many faces of Innovation – from literature synthesis to empirical studies* (pp. 78–103). Hyvinkaa, Finland: Laurea University of Applied Sciences.

Drucker, P. (1986). *Managing for results.* New York: Harper & Row.

Félix, S. A. L. (2013). Uma análise sistémica da auditoria interna nos municípios em Portugal [A systemic analysis of internal auditing in municipalities in Portugal]. Master's work project. Coimbra: Instituto Superior de Contabilidade e Administração de Coimbra do Politécnico de Coimbra.

Giovannucci, D., & Ponte, S. (2005). Standards as a new form of social contract? Sustainability initiatives in the coffee industry. *Food Policy*, *30*(3), 284–301. doi:10.1016/j.foodpol.2005.05.007

Gupta, A., Briscoe, F., & Hambrick, D. C. (2017). Red, blue, and purple firms: Organizational political ideology and corporate social responsibility. *Strategic Management Journal*, *38*(5), 1018–1040. doi:10.1002mj.2550

Hans, C., Edward, L., Martin, W., & Cheng, Z. (2015). Incentives or standards: What determines accounting quality changes around IFRS adoption? *Journal of European Accounting Review*, *24*(01), 31–61. do i:10.1080/09638180.2015.1009144

Henson, S., & Loader, R. (2001). Barriers to agricultural exports from developing countries: The role of sanitary and phytosanitary requirements. *World Development*, *29*(1), 85–102. doi:10.1016/S0305-750X(00)00085-1

Heras, I. (Coord.). (2006). ISO 9000, ISO 14001 y otros estándares de gestión: Pasado, presente y futuro [ISO 9000, ISO 14001 and other management standards: Past, present and future]. Madrid: Editorial Civitas.

Heras, I., Dick, G., & Casadesús, M. (2002). ISO 9000 registration's impact on sales and profitability. A longitudinal analysis of performance before and after accreditation. *International Journal of Quality & Reliability Management*, *19*(6), 774–791. doi:10.1108/02656710210429618

Hyvönen, J. (2007). Strategy, performance, measurement techniques and information technology of the firm and their links to organizational performance. *Management Accounting Research*, *18*(3), 343–366. doi:10.1016/j.mar.2007.02.001

Kaplan, R., & Norton, D. (1992). The balanced scorecard – Measures that drive performance. *Harvard Business Review*, *70*(1), 71–79.

Lourenço, I. M. E. C., & Castelo Branco, M. E. M. A. D. (2015). Principais consequências da adoção das IFRS: Análise da literatura existente e sugestões para investigação futura [Main consequences of adopting IFRS: Analysis of existing literature and suggestions for future research]. *Revista Contabilidade & Finanças*, *26*(68), 126–139.

Magalhães, M., & Dias, A. (2017). Modelo integrado de gestão do risco para o sector público português. Estudo de caso – O município da Maia [Integrated risk management model for the Portuguese public sector. Case study – The municipality of Maia]. Master's work project. Porto: Instituto Superior de Contabilidade e Administração do Politécnico do Porto.

Mihret, D. G., & Yismaw, A. W. (2007). Internal audit effectiveness: An Ethiopian public sector case study. *Managerial Auditing Journal*, *22*(5), 470–484. doi:10.1108/02686900710750757

Mintzberg, H. (1987). The strategy concept II: Another look at why organizations need strategies. *California Management Review*, *30*(1), 25–32. doi:10.2307/41165264

Monteiro, S. C. (2012). *Percursos de excelência académica no ensino superior: Estudo em alunos de engenharia em Portugal* [Courses of academic excellence in higher education: Study in engineering students in Portugal] (PhD Thesis). Braga: Escola de Psicologia da Universidade do Minho.

Moura, N. J. (2011). Procedimentos de auditoria a adoptar na revisão legal das contas dos municípios: enquadramento teórico e aplicação prática. *Revista Revisores & Auditores, Ordem dos Revisores Oficiais de Contas, 52*, 22-34.

Mukhlisin, M., & Antonio, M. S. (2018). Meta-analysis on direction of accounting standards for islamic financial institutions: Case studies in United Kingdom and Indonesia. *Al-Iqtishad: Jurnal Ilmu Ekonomi Syariah, 10*(1), 231–254. doi:10.15408/aiq.v10i1.5676

Murmura, F., Liberatore, L., Bravi, L., & Casolani, N. (2018). Evaluation of Italian companies' perception about ISO 14001 and Eco Management and Audit Scheme III: Motivations, benefits and barriers. *Journal of Cleaner Production, 174*, 691–700. doi:10.1016/j.jclepro.2017.10.337

Nogueira, S. P. S., & Jorge, S. M. F. (2017). The perceived usefulness of financial information for decision making in Portuguese municipalities: The importance of internal control. *Journal of Applied Accounting Research, 18*(1), 116–136. doi:10.1108/JAAR-05-2014-0052

Oakland, J., & Tanner, S. (2007). A new framework for managing change: Total Quality Management & business excellence. *Journal of Quality & Reliability Management, 18*(1-2), 1-19.

Oliveira, U. R., Marins, F. A. S., Rocha, H. M., & Salomon, V. A. P. (2017). The ISO 31000 standard in supply chain risk management. *Journal of Cleaner Production, 151*, 616–633. doi:10.1016/j.jclepro.2017.03.054

Ortiz, J., Benito, J., & Galende, J. (2006). Total quality management as a forerunner of business innovation capability. *Technovation, 26*(10), 1170–1185. doi:10.1016/j.technovation.2005.09.008

Quivy, R., & Campenhout, L. V. (2005). *Manual de investigação em ciências sociais* [Manual of research in social sciences] (4th ed.). Lisboa: Gradiva.

Ribeiro, V. P., Aibar-Guzmán, C., Aibar-Guzman, B., & Monteiro, S. M. (2016). Determinants of environmental accounting and reporting practices in Portuguese local entities. *Corporate Communications, 21*(3), 352–370. doi:10.1108/CCIJ-11-2015-0071

Rocha, J. A. O. (1997). Esboço dum modelo de análise dos municípios. *Cadernos de Estudos Municipais, 8*, 1–25.

Schein, E. (1999). *The corporate culture survival guide. Sense and nonsense about culture change* (1st ed.). San Francisco: Jossey-Bass.

Vinnari, E., & Skærbæk, P. (2014). The uncertainties of risk management. *Accounting, Auditing & Accountability Journal, 27*(3), 489–526. doi:10.1108/AAAJ-09-2012-1106

Zahirul, H. (2003). Total Quality Management and the balanced scorecard approach: A critical analysis of their potential relationships and directions for research. *Critical Perspectives on Accounting, 14*(5), 553–566. doi:10.1016/S1045-2354(02)00160-0

KEY TERMS AND DEFINITIONS

Audit: An analysis, an inspection, and verification of any issue done according to a reference. Audit development process may concern different scopes of application – from a financial to a nonfinancial scope of application.

Enterprise Risk Management (ERM): A management tool related to the prevention and mitigation of Risk. ERM is a kind of risk approach applicable to a top down process of management pertaining to any company. ERM makes part of the mission, vision, and strategy of the organization and is considered across the hierarchy established in the organization.

Implementation of ISO 31000: Depends on the culture of the organization mainly on a risk perspective allocated to the top management. The process will start with the definition of risk and its scope of analysis, the associated prevention and mitigation plan and at last the risk execution. All these steps need to be connected to the top of the organization´s hierarchy. Risk procedures are needed.

International Financial Reporting Standards: References established by International Accounting Standards Board (UK), as to the accounting register, to be in force worldwide. Their application aims to get the Global Financial Harmonization. If all the countries use these standards to register their transactions the consequent financial statements will be comparable.

International Standards on Audit: References established by International Federation of Accountants (USA) so that the financial audit achieved worldwide, follow them. If the audit to be developed upon the financial statements of the organizations follow the same procedures across the world, the auditor´s opinion will be recognized by the global market.

ISO 31000: Reference established by International Organization for Standardization that deals with risk management. The definition, scope analysis, identification, and mitigation plan related to the risk context, in any organization, will be considered. ISO 31000 is easier to be implemented in organizations that have previously adopted an ISO 9001.

Maia (Municipality): The municipality of Maia is headquartered in the city of Maia, located in the District of Porto, Portugal. It is one of the 18 municipalities that make up the Metropolitan Area of Porto which, in a whole, represents 2040 Km2 and 1,8 million people. The population related to Maia municipality management is more than 100,000 inhabitants.

Standards: A reference or a benchmark used for any type of activity. Financial and nonfinancial management should use them. From World Trade Organizations we know that the global market transaction has to comply with TBT agreement – Technical Barriers to Trade. So there are lot of applicable standards to products and services. Only the ones considering the financial management of an organization will be considered.

ENDNOTES

1 Porto District: Amarante; Baião; Felgueiras; Gondomar; Lousada; Maia; Marco de Canaveses; Matosinhos: Paços Ferreira; Paredes; Penafiel; Porto; Póvoa de Varzim; Santo Tirso; Trofa; Valongo; Vila do Conde; Vila Nova de Gaia.

2 Source: Direção Geral das Autarquias Locais – Data from August 13, 2018.

3 the United Nations Convention includes Portugal since December, 11 2003, as from the date of signature, and since September 28, 2007, as from the date of ratification).

4 A deep and recognized feeling for the help, knowledge transmission and team spirit granted by Rita Daniela Oliveira de Sousa, who is part of the Top Management of this Municipality, must be put forward.

Section 2

Impact of Technological Development on the Audit Function

Chapter 6
An Overview on Mobile Cloud Computing:
Impact on the Auditing Process

Carlos Santos
https://orcid.org/0000-0001-9728-8538
University of Aveiro, Portugal

Helena Inácio
https://orcid.org/0000-0003-1281-2156
University of Aveiro, Portugal

Rui Pedro Marques
https://orcid.org/0000-0001-8449-0526
University of Aveiro, Portugal & University of Minho, Portugal

ABSTRACT

Mobile cloud computing is a concept that has been gaining popularity, resulting from the synergistic integration of cloud computing and mobile computing with the goal of minimizing some of the limitations inherent in mobile computing (bandwidth, storage, autonomy, etc.) and giving greater plasticity to the services of the cloud computing providers. This new paradigm of computation has similar limitations to those associated with the paradigms that are at its origin. Therefore, it is essential that the research carried out in this area is concerned about understanding its impact on audit processes, which aim to verify and evaluate the mechanisms of the internal control system implemented to minimize threats to integrity, confidentiality, and availability of the information assets (data and/or information) stored on these platforms. Based on a literature review, this chapter aims to list a set of challenges associated with the adoption of mobile cloud computing within the scope of organizational auditing.

DOI: 10.4018/978-1-5225-7356-2.ch006

INTRODUCTION

The integration of cloud computing with mobile computing has given rise to a new paradigm in the use of information and communication technologies (ICT) and of mobile applications (apps). This new paradigm, mobile cloud computing, has facilitated ubiquitous access to a wide range of ICT resources, yet it does pose several challenges that need to be adequately addressed for the security of owners, of information assets in the cloud, and of app users.

In the coming years, this new concept may continue to grow, with all the risks associated with it, as in all projects involving the use of ICT in organizations (Hatefi & Fasanghari, 2016). According to Hatefi and Fasanghari (2016), most organizations seek to define their strategy and objectives, taking into account the potential risks posed by the adoption of new ICTs associated with the storage of informational assets in the cloud, considering that these risks have a strong impact in the daily routines of any organization.

The information and communication technology (ICT) industry is in the midst of a shift that takes place once every 20-25 years to a new technology platform for growth and innovation. International Data Corporation (IDC) calls it the 3rd Platform, built on mobile devices and apps, cloud services, mobile broadband networks, big data analytics, and social technologies. These paradigm shifts are intertwined and rapidly impacting organizations around the world. In fact, from 2013 through 2020, IDC believes that 90% of IT industry growth will be driven by 3rd Platform technologies that, today, represent just 22% of ICT spending (Crook & Hopkins, 2013, p. 2).

The growing adoption of this new computational paradigm, which has taken place in the various organizational areas, especially the administrative and financial area, particularly in the accounting sector, is due to several reasons, namely the reduction of costs associated with the ICT management and the large-scale consolidation and optimization of the use of hardware and software resources (Wyslocka & Jelonek, 2015). According to Chou (Chou, 2015), this paradigm is highly complex, taking into consideration the convergence of several technological dimensions that pose enormous challenges regarding the protection and security of the information assets and that make the auditors' task difficult.

The auditability of information assets, when stored and processed according to the new paradigm of mobile cloud computing, must be ensured, allowing auditors to perform a correct risk assessment so that they can then implement the mechanisms necessary to mitigate risks. In order to develop an adequate understanding of this new technology and to rigorously advise organizations on the most relevant risks and control mechanisms, the role of internal auditors is crucial (Elefterie & Badea, 2016).

The mobile cloud computing in the cloud, providing scalability, mobility and reduced maintenance costs, has had a very positive role in the development of various types of business, with more organizations adopting these technologies as an integral part of the infrastructure that supports their operational activities, with a significant impact on accounting information systems. Considering that these systems are responsible for the processing and storage of sensitive and confidential information assets, the adoption of those technologies requires a rigorous analysis regarding the security of information assets and the use of apps (Brandas, Megan, & Didraga, 2015; Duncan & Whittington, 2016).

The security analysis of the information assets and of the use of apps can benefit from the research that has been or will be done in the field of cloud computing and of mobile computing, focused on the practices of the audit process. This action is fully justified now, when the research is reaching good levels in this area and the environmental context presents risk levels which can be harmful to organizations

(Duncan & Whittington, 2016). We should bear in mind that cloud computing and mobile computing provide rapid updating cycles with an increasing rate of adoption of critical apps, thus requiring these technologies to be highly reliable.

In order to achieve high levels of reliability, information assets should be auditable and subject to auditing processes. We should not forget that continuous auditing can provide a high level of security and reliability for organizations that use it. However, the methodologies to develop an efficient continuous audit in these new platforms are still embryonic, and it is necessary to increase the research work in these areas (Roshan, Prashanth, & Vineet, 2017).

This chapter, in addition to this section, which introduces it, is structured as follows: it has a section that presents the methodology used in the elaboration of this chapter and its relevance for the development of knowledge on the adoption of new paradigms for the use of new ICT and their impact on the management of organizations; another section looks at the particularities of cloud computing as a paradigm of ICT use; a third section describes the impact of mobile computing on organizations and also another section which describes the impact of mobile cloud computing on the audit process and consequently on ensuring auditability of information assets. Finally, a synthesis of the main conclusions of this exploratory study is made.

METHODOLOGY

The impact of mobile cloud computing in organizations, particularly with regard to the audit process, has not been properly consolidated yet. Thus, the authors of this chapter understood that it is opportune to develop an exploratory study that allows to establish goals for future investigations in this area, very important for society, in general, and for organizations, in particular.

This exploratory study, similar to other studies (Al-zoubi, 2017; Brandas *et al.*, 2015; Gupta & Shakya, 2015; Pazowski & Pastuszak, 2013; Rashdi, Dick, & Storey, 2016), was developed based on a literature review in which the keywords were cloud computing, mobile computing and organizational auditing. In essence, three bibliographic sources were used: scientific papers; professional papers and technical reports. As aforementioned, this literature review focused on cloud computing, mobile computing and organizational auditing, and the following resources were consulted: Google Scholar; b-on; Scielo and SSRN. In the first analysis, 202 bibliographic elements were collected, which turned out to be 51 after analysis to their abstracts. These were then analyzed in more detail and cited in this chapter.

CLOUD COMPUTING

Cloud computing has become a platform of great potential for organizations, both public and private, at their various levels. We can highlight, in particular, the administrative and financial area, emphasizing the importance in the overall performance of accounting. We should not forget that accounting was one of the first organizational areas to be treated as a true information system. Thus, the accountants should be aware of the evolution of this technological platform, which offers several advantages, such as: accessibility to data, where space and time barriers cease to exist, and a strong reduction in operating costs, considering that these are shared by multiple users. These benefits will have a strong impact on the accountants' performance but will give rise to new risks which the professionals need to be prepared for and implement appropriate mechanisms to mitigate them (Corkern, Kimmel, & Morehead, 2015).

The adoption of cloud computing by organizations presupposes, on their part, availability, as previously mentioned, to deal with new risks and also to migrate their information systems and technologies to a third party entity. The assumption of this availability involves costs that must be evaluated and faced with the benefits that may result from the shift paradigm. Cloud computing, from the perspective of shared services, can offer advantages associated with economies of scale (Pazowski & Pastuszak, 2013).

Due to the degree of user maturity in the use of cloud computing, the provision of these services is typically grouped into three large groups, as depicted in Figure 1 (Pazowski & Pastuszak, 2013):

- SaaS (software as a service) - in this offer, the service provider makes available applications which are accessed by the users through the internet, usually using a browser;
- PaaS (platform as a service), which consists of offering the hosting service and implementation of hardware and software to provide applications;
- IaaS (infrastructure as a service), which consists of the provision of a server infrastructure which allows the user to use various resources, namely storage

The decision on which category of services to be contracted depends not only on the degree of maturity of the organization, which contracts the services, but also on their willingness to be able to do it without considerable loss of control over information assets by delegating custody to a third party entity. The control that the organization has over its information assets, when outsourced, varies according to the type of service contracted, see Table 1, adapted from (Pazowski & Pastuszak, 2013) and TechTarget. The green cells correspond to the elements whose control is the information assets owner's responsibility, the cells with no color indicate that this responsibility is the service provider's. This table clearly shows that the adoption of cloud computing is associated with a considerable loss of control responsibility.

According to Rasheed (Rasheed, 2014), for many organizations one of the barriers to the adoption of cloud computing is related to security aspects. This barrier is one of the challenges that auditors face in the perspective of the auditability of information assets being ensured when using cloud computing, and thus minimizing the risks of adopting this paradigm by many organizations.

Figure 1. Typical grouping of services offered by cloud computing
(Carlin & Curran, 2011)

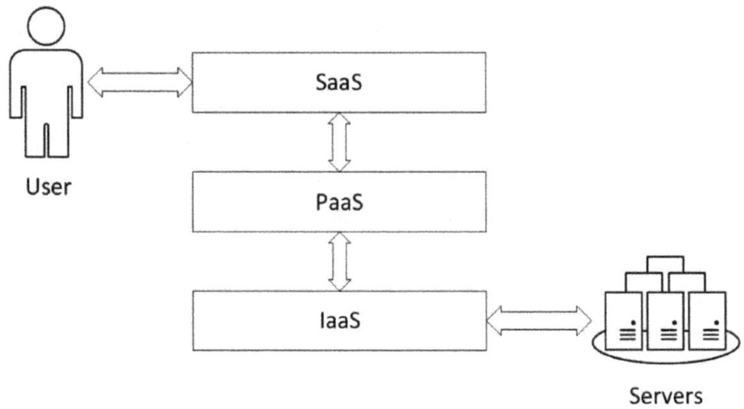

Table 1. Sharing of control over information assets when transferred to a third party entity

Local Infrastructure	IaaS	PaaS	SaaS
Data	Data	Data	Data
Aplications	Aplications	Aplications	Aplications
Runtime	Runtime	Runtime	Runtime
Middleware	Middleware	Middleware	Middleware
Operating System	Operating System	Operating System	Operating System
Virtualization	Virtualization	Virtualization	Virtualization
Servers	Servers	Servers	Servers
Storage	Storage	Storage	Storage
Network	Network	Network	Network

The adoption of the paradigm of cloud computing, a trend that is becoming widespread, has a strong impact on organizations, particularly regarding the risks that organizations should be available to take, implementing mechanisms that can minimize their impacts. These risks include: the loss of control over the information assets and part of the internal control system (procedures related to the storage); interruptions in the provision of services (Mehri, Khakzadi, & Shamsi, 2016; Rashdi *et al.*, 2016; Reads, 2015).

For these reasons two aspects of greater relevance in the computing paradigm in the cloud can be identified. The first aspect, which organizations that adopt cloud computing cannot ignore, is related to the migration of their data to a platform whose control does not depend on the organization that owns the data. This requires that appropriate security policies are agreed between the service user (organization) and the service provider (cloud computing service provider). The second aspect is related to ensuring continuity of the service in the event of a system failure that jeopardizes its operation. Also, in this case, the non-existence of full organizational control over information assets requires that appropriate security policies are negotiated between the user and the service provider (Kinkela, 2012).

There are other issues related to the security of the main assets of any organization, their data and the information which can be obtained from it and disclosed to the stakeholders, namely the possibility of being threatened by intruders that through the network can obtain unauthorized access to those assets or being misused by the cloud computing service provider. These issues, which stem essentially from organizations' lack of control over their information assets, are one of the reasons that have some reservations when organizations need to decide whether to migrate to cloud computing. These security issues have posed new challenges for accounting and auditing professionals, especially those that are more related to protecting integrity, confidentiality and availability of information assets, and maintaining digital evidence to ensure their auditability (Rezarta & Muça, 2014).

These challenges have inhibited the adoption of cloud computing by organizations. The adoption of this computational paradigm requires that organizations carefully analyze all possible service providers and evaluate the level of security offered by each of them. This is very relevant considering that when organizations migrate their information assets to a third party entity, they no longer have full control over them. (Kavya & Lobo, 2017).

The security weaknesses associated with cloud computing introduce new challenges in the context of the audit process. According to Yang and Jia (Yang & Jia, 2014), these challenges require an independent auditing service to identify and validate integrity, confidentiality, and availability of information assets when they are migrated to a cloud computing platform managed by a third party entity.

Schmidt *et al.* (Schmidt, Wood, & Grabski, 2016), considering that cloud computing is a critical area for organizational auditing, sought to assess its impact on the role of the auditor and audit procedures, concluding that the paradigm shift for cloud computing is not sufficiently mature yet regarding the risks involved, and therefore, studies should continue in order to acquire this knowledge and thus provide the necessary confidence to organizations which adopt this paradigm.

The increase of popularity in cloud computing has not diminished the need to implement measures that ensure the protection and privacy of information assets (Chou, 2015). The nature of cloud computing, of remote connectivity, is a reason for thinking about new ways of auditing these new computing environments.

According to Carlin and Curran (Carlin & Curran, 2011), it is necessary to think and develop new security techniques and adjust the older security techniques and adapted to different paradigms in order to be able to work in cloud computing. The existing security technologies are not good for cloud computing because this new paradigm introduces new approaches to access and use the computing resources.

Regardless of security aspects, cloud computing offers significant developments related to the progressive computing power and the updating of the distribution of information assets and data storage resources. The cloud computing services store information assets on the platform and ensure that they are distributed to their users. As previously stated, the storage of information assets in the cloud is related to issues of integrity, confidentiality, availability, and access by unauthorized users. Thus, these assets must be auditable and subject to an audit process that ensures that information assets are properly stored and processed in the cloud (Geeta, Raghavendra, Buyya, & Venugopal, 2018).

Yang and Jia (Yang & Jia, 2012) have conducted a study where one can verify that cloud computing as a data storage service introduces new security challenges because data owners (organizations) have different identities and interests. Therefore, an independent audit service is needed to ensure that the organizational assets (data/information) are properly stored in the cloud.

Another critical issue related to security aspects in cloud computing is the processing of confidential data done outside organizations. The storage of these data needs additional care because they ignore the physical, logical and personnel controls. The retention of sensitive data must meet a specific set of regulatory standards, so the cloud computing service provider must be prepared and certified to ensure the requirements necessary to deal, in all its aspects, with sensitive data (Neto, 2011; Srinivasan & Raja, 2014).

Therefore, cloud computing has several vulnerabilities, some of which have high potential to become risks that need research and development of control mechanisms specifically designed to constitute the internal control system of this new paradigm of computing.

MOBILE COMPUTING

In recent years we have been witnessing a huge and successfully unprecedented expansion of all kinds of mobile devices. Apps are constantly evolving, challenging the imagination of users and developers and delivering innovative features. However, many abuses of information assets in mobile computing have been reported (Xia, Gong, Lyu, Qi, & Liu, 2015). In response to these abuses, Xia *et al.* (2015) propose an app called AppAudit to efficiently and effectively check and evaluate apps in real time.

Mobile computing, looking at how mobile devices have access to information assets stored in the cloud, presents new challenges inherent in mobile computing: low bandwidth and limited mobility and storage capacity (Fernando, Loke, & Rahayu, 2013).

The mobile devices enable any employee in an organization to perform their duties when and where they want, leveraging the ubiquity of these devices, and developing fieldwork with the various front-office stakeholders. However, these devices need to have a back office with data / information and organizational processes that are constantly updated and available. A mobile device can virtually house an entire company in the same way as a physical hosting space for organizations (Archer *et al.*, 2012).

Mobile computing, while offering a high degree of accessibility to its users, regardless of the day and time, is particularly oriented to certain organizational activities, such as e-commerce. In a similar way, apps are diversifying their relationship with other organizational activities and transforming the client-company relationship taking this relationship to new levels of demand and posing new challenges. The integration that has been occurring between cloud computing and mobile computing is opening up new business possibilities with lower costs and high benefits for both parties (Carlin & Curran, 2011).

The synergistic use of cloud computing and mobile computing have applicability in various domains of society, especially business. The business applicability of mobile cloud computing has a huge impact on organizations, in particular on aspects in which the protection of information assets must be guaranteed, namely on their integrity, confidentiality and availability (Rahimi, Ren, Liu, Vasilakos, & Venkatasubramanian, 2014).

Mobile cloud computing is a convergent technology composed of three fundamental heterogeneous technologies: mobile computing; cloud computing and networking. The integration of these highly heterogeneous technologies makes the mobile cloud computing concept complex, which can impact the success of its implementation (Sanaei, Abolfazli, Gani, & Buyya, 2013).

The app developers are those who make the new computing platforms (the reconfigurable base of compatible components where companies and users can manage the available computing resources) valuable to their users. There are platforms oriented to different purposes that respond differently to different needs of their users. The development of the platforms should also take into account the response that their infrastructures should provide, not only with regard to the obligations of cloud computing service providers but also concerning the rights of their users (Bresnahan & Greenstein, 2014).

As discussed in previous paragraphs, mobile computing and cloud computing pose new challenges. The authors of this chapter have identified gaps in the research that has been carried out to respond to the various challenges posed by these new computational paradigms, regarding solutions that ensure auditability of the information assets when housed in these new computational platforms. The answer to these challenges may be the study and development of new control mechanisms that allow the implementation of new audit processes aligned with the needs of these new paradigms.

IMPACT OF MOBILE CLOUD COMPUTING ON THE AUDITING PROCESS

Being accounting an essential component of the framework which supports any organizational activity, it is critical to verify and evaluate the impact of cloud computing and mobile computing (mobile cloud computing) on organizational activities, particularly on accounting and auditing (Dimitriu & Matei, 2014).

Still according to Dimitriu and Matei (2014), the development and implementation of new technologies, the organizations, and therefore the administrative and financial department, particularly with regard to accounting, are generally influenced by: business digitization; intense potential created by the Internet; implications of Big Data; and increasing importance attributed to the identification of patterns in the set of information assets. In this context, cloud computing paved the way for the creation of new business models. Thus, the impact of cloud computing is currently undisputed and will provide the basis for future changes in the economic field.

Mehri *et al.* (2016) developed a study in which they realized that if the user does not have the time, feasibility or resources to verify and evaluate the conditions in which the information assets are stored, they can delegate this task to an external auditor, thus this makes the storage of information assets in the cloud publicly auditable. To safely delegate this task to an external auditor, there must be assurance that the audit process does not bring new vulnerabilities to integrity, confidentiality, and availability of the organization's information assets.

The auditing process of information assets performed by external auditors in cloud computing is an area of emerging research that has received increasing attention in recent years (Sookhak, Talebian, Ahmed, Gani, & Khan, 2014). The evolution of ICT and the rapid growth of the digital economy have introduced significant changes to the methods and tools used in the audit process. Large organizations have been investing in the development and implementation of audit processes, with a view to enabling them to check and evaluate their internal control systems on an ongoing basis, thereby increasing the efficiency, effectiveness and coverage of audits carried out on information assets.

Cloud computing opens a new era in information technology, delivering various sharable services with high plasticity and scalability, making a significant contribution to enabling users to reduce the investments made in their own information technology infrastructure. With this new computational paradigm, users of cloud computing services physically lose direct control over their information assets, which makes their security assurance one of the main concerns when migrating information systems to this new paradigm (Liu, Chen, Member, Yang, & Zhang, 2014).

There is no easy solution to protect the organizations' infrastructure, processes, and information assets, which are essential to the development of their business. These elements and the implementation of an adequate internal control system require time, effort and planning. Incorporating good security practices into an appropriate combination of organizational policies, deployed technologies, and security configurations can provide an environment that can minimize the risk of attacks against organizational infrastructure viewed in a holistic manner (Salazar, 2015).

Cloud computing enables organizations to remotely store their information assets and leverage high-quality apps with no local storage capacity, benefiting from the security of cloud computing. This security refers to a vast set of policies and control mechanisms deployed to protect information assets from attempts to breach their integrity, confidentiality, and availability. However, it should be borne in mind that cloud computing services are subject to frequent updates, and existing certifications may be questioned if they are not subject to similar updating or renewal processes. Roshan *et al.* (2017) concluded in their study that the business processes of any organization should be continuously audited. Most of the existing methodologies do not apply to auditing processes carried out by external auditors. Therefore, an architecture and a conceptual process were proposed which should be implemented to discuss the benefits and challenges that should be used to disseminate the concept of continuous auditing in services offered by mobile cloud computing.

Therefore, we can conclude that the security of information assets has become a critical problem for organizations and it has prevented this new information-asset-hosting service paradigm from being widely adopted by most organizations. One of the major concerns related to information asset security is ensuring integrity, confidentiality, and availability of the information assets transferred to a third party entity that provides cloud computing services (Luo, Xu, Huang, Wang, & Fu, 2018).

From what we said previously, we can see that there are some consequences, with significant impact, which result from the adoption of mobile cloud computing by organizations. Some of these consequences can be seen as having a positive impact: ease of use; cost reduction; reliability; etc., while others can be seen as having a negative impact: loss of security; infrastructure sharing; etc. We can conclude that despite the benefits that cloud computing offers, it is also subject of both internal and external threats, like any other information technology infrastructure, which depending on the organization's appetite for risk-taking, can be accepted or mitigated.

Regarding the security of information assets transferred to a provider of cloud computing services, we should not forget that there may be lack of honesty and the possibility of information assets being discarded if they are not accessed or rarely accessed for reasons related to saving storage space or to maintain fewer replicas than the established in the contractual terms. Thus, the owners of the information assets should be convinced that they are properly stored and managed and that they meet all the regulatory standards of the contracted cloud computing service. In order to ensure the existence and continuity of these requirements there should exist audit procedures on the type of contracted service and on the hosting of information assets (Ren, Shen, Wang, Han, & Lee, 2015).

Understandably, ensuring the security of any type of cloud computing service, especially with respect to integrity, confidentiality, and availability of information assets, is a highly challenging task. To address these security issues, a number of control mechanisms have been proposed which should be periodically or continuously verified and evaluated by external auditors to ensure their integrity, confidentiality, and availability for the security of organizations using mobile cloud computing (Razaque & Rizvi, 2017).

The reliability of information assets transferred to a third party entity is not always achieved due to the loss of physical control and ownership over information assets. As a result, many researchers have focused their efforts on minimizing this type of threat to the security of outsourced information assets by proposing remote data auditing techniques as a new concept that allows the development of audit processes of the information assets hosted in the cloud (Sookhak *et al.*, 2015). In the same vein, Garg and Bawa (Garg & Bawa, 2017) developed a study in which they found that to ensure that outsourced information assets are secure and are not possibly tampered with, the entity responsible for providing the computing cloud service should allow the owner of the information assets to periodically audit their integrity, confidentiality and availability.

The current trends are presented considering that the processing and hosting of information assets is done with the aim of maintaining a high level of relationship between the provider of cloud computing services and the owner of the information assets and the users of these services, the processing in the cloud and the inclusion of mobile devices as access terminals to the information assets (Rus, 2015).

Kumar (2016) concluded that with the development of cloud computing service offerings over the last decade, outsourcing information assets regarding cloud computing is a trend to be considered by organizations, and no effort should be spared to implement best practices regarding the maintenance and massive management of information assets. However, as the outsourced hosting in the cloud will never be completely reliable, efforts must also be made to improve the security mechanisms associated with cloud computing, while focusing on the development and implementation of appropriate auditing processes.

Figure 2. Audit process using or not an external auditor
(Wei & Yang, 2017)

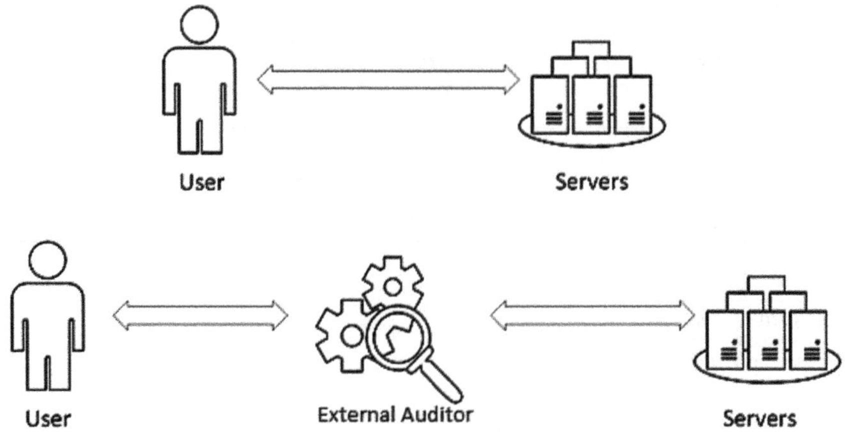

Thus, at the level of the financial audit, the auditor must carry out a set of procedures in order to evaluate the reliability of the information contained in the financial statements. These procedures may be of three types: risk assessment procedures (carried out to assess the risk of material misstatements), control tests (to assess the effectiveness of internal control) and substantive procedures (to assess the assertions contained in financial statements). According to the International Standards on Auditing (ISA) 330, §8 (International Federation of Accountants, 2016), the performance of control tests is conditioned to the auditor's expectation that the internal control is adequate, as if it is not an internal control there is no need to check whether it is working effectively or inadequately; or to situations in which insufficient substantive procedures are considered. This last situation, according to §A24 of the same standard (IFAC, 2016, p. 359), "*this may occur when in the entity conducts its business using IT and in the documentation of transactions is produced or maintained, other than through the IT system*". Thus, traditionally, the performance of control tests depends on the adequacy of internal control while substantive procedures should always be performed since they are the ones that effectively test the content of the financial statements on which the auditor's opinion is focused. From this we can conclude that in normal situations the audit strategy regarding the accomplishment of the different types of procedures can be schematized as in Figure 3.

When we are faced with the dependence on the reliance of the information technology used, control testing becomes mandatory. This dependence is referred to in the standard as documentation produced and maintained only through information technology and it is, therefore, necessary to validate the controls that ensure that the information is true and that it was not changed. In the case of mobile cloud computing, as we seen before, there is a loss of control over stored data, and data reliability is also involved, and it is therefore vital for the financial auditor to verify internal controls. Thus, the financial audit approach to be applied through interpretation of §8 of ISA 330 will involve the carrying out of control tests, and substantive procedures will be performed if there is confidence in the key controls and in greater depth and number in proportion to the potential material misstatement of the financial statements, as depicted in Figure 4.

Figure 3. Strategy for applying audit procedures to a financial audit in a traditional environment (Inácio, 2014)

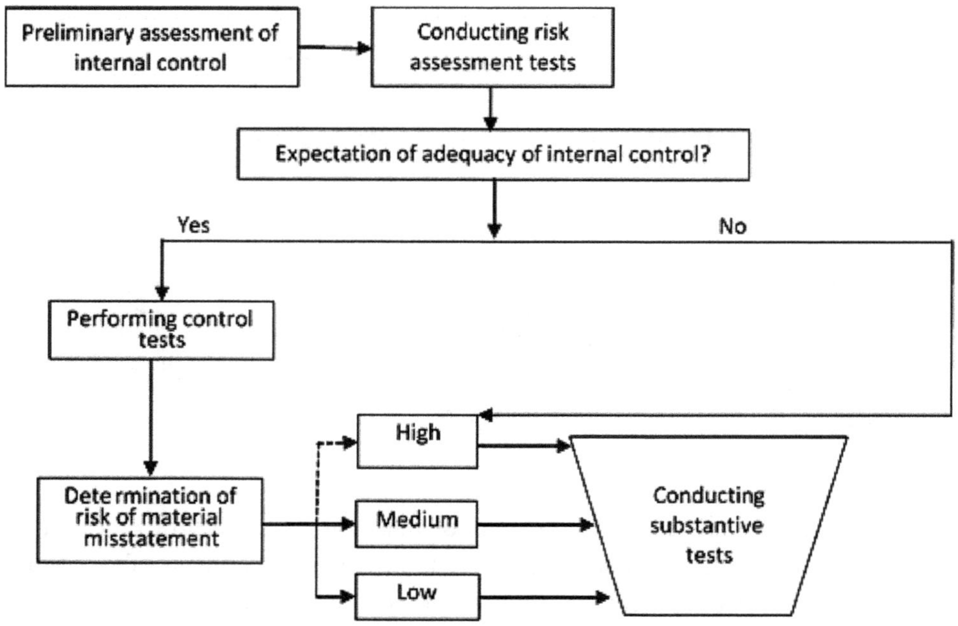

Figure 4. Strategy for applying financial audit procedures in the case of mobile cloud computing

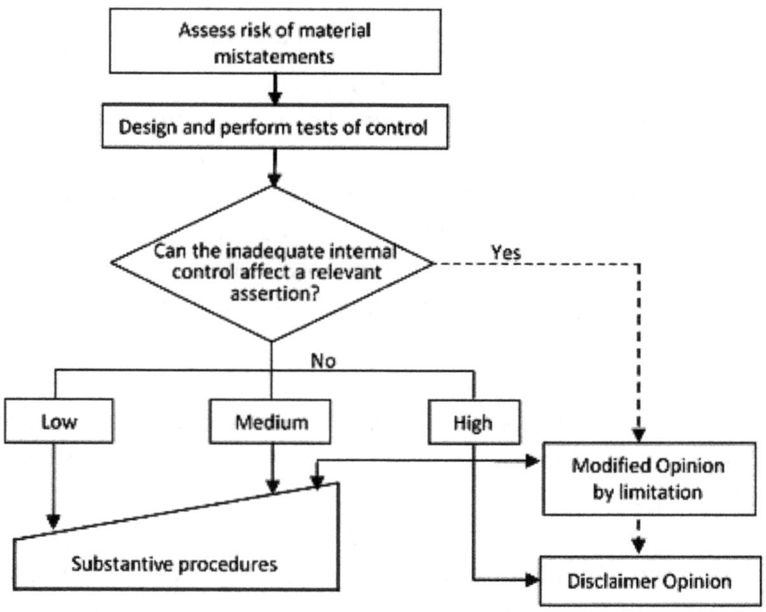

As can be seen in Figure 4, the audit approach in the case of using mobile cloud computing requires the mandatory testing of control tests still to be relied upon to obtain confidence in the key controls so that an unqualified opinion on the financial statements can be effectively made. Clearly there is a reinforcement of the importance of control over the monitoring of data reliability.

CONCLUSION

According to Özdoğan (Özdoğan, 2017), the future certified accountants should focus on improving their skills with regard to the technological innovation that has been taking place in organizations and which has an impact on their profession. In particular, attention should be paid to the rapid transformation of organizations with the emergence of new laws and regulatory procedures. These technicians may be responsible for managing the compliance process of organizations with the impact that this will have on the management of organizations. Similarly, auditors cannot remain indifferent to these changes. These new developments will certainly bring new challenges to cloud computing services and mobile computing, and should therefore be addressed, discussed and properly analyzed. When there are changes in technology used by organizations, security policies and procedures should be reviewed to ensure integrity, confidentiality, and availability of information assets (Kumar, Raj, & Jelciana, 2018).

In light of the above, it is extremely important to adopt a new legal framework for the protection of information assets and to develop uniform standards to regulate their hosting and processing in order to ensure security of the provision of services by this new platform (Wyslocka & Jelonek, 2015).

The long experience associated with organizational auditing fails to address the various types of problems and conflicts of interest, and it does not make clear the understanding and interpretation of the audit role, either, and hence the need to consider some of the most relevant issues that organizations currently face with globalization and also with the dematerialization of business processes. We should keep in mind that information is now as valuable to companies as money, and deserves serious thought and the appropriate action for their protection (Duncan & Whittington, 2016).

In organizational computing (local infrastructure), information assets are stored using resources of the organization itself and are entirely under the control of the organization. In cloud computing services, information assets are stored under the custody of a third party entity outside the organization's premises. Therefore, cloud computing must implement additional security procedures and measures in addition to traditional security checks and assessments to ensure that information assets are secure and that the possibility of security breaches of information assets due to security vulnerabilities is minimized (Kumar *et al.*, 2018).

Regarding the need organizations have today to reduce their physical size in terms of building and office space, globalization makes it easier for the property to be located anywhere without compromising the quality of its management, regardless of its location. For this reason, organizations allow employees and other interested parties to use apps that are supported on computers or other mobile devices in order to access information assets, regardless of their location, as long as they have access to the Internet (Al-zoubi, 2017).

In the coming years the mobile cloud computing paradigm will become common and will be used in the vast majority of organizations as the use of this technology becomes safer and less expensive and more options are available. We have already seen that the adoption of cloud computing across the organization presents many new challenges to the audit process, both in the context of internal and operational auditing, namely internal control, and in the scope of the financial audit. The adoption of mobile cloud computing should allow to deal with and be able to solve the enormous investments made by organizations in the infrastructures of existing information technologies (Elefterie & Badea, 2016).

This change, as will be clear, will have enormous impacts on organizations. James (James, 2013) has no doubt that the use of ICT, regardless of its degree of innovation, has a profound impact on several professional classes, namely audit professionals. On the other hand, Lins, Teigeler, and Sunyaev (2016) developed a study arguing that continuous auditing performed by external auditors is necessary to ensure that the services offered by cloud computing remain reliable and secure.

Given that the accounting information system processes and stores a number of sensitive information assets, adoption of cloud computing requires rigorous analysis of the information assets and security offered by the use of apps to access such information assets *(Brandas et al.*, 2015).

REFERENCES

Al Rashdi, Z., Dick, M., & Storey, I. (2016). *A Conceptual Framework for Accountability in Cloud Computing Service Provision*. Pearson. Retrieved from http://arxiv.org/abs/1606.03540

Archer, J., Boehme, A., Cullinance, D., Puhlmann, N., Kurz, P., & Reavis, J. (2012, December). Security Guidance for Critical Areas of Mobile Computing. *Cloud Security Alliance*, 1–60. doi:10.1017/CBO9781107415324.004

Brandas, C., Megan, O., & Didraga, O. (2015). Global Perspectives on Accounting Information Systems: Mobile and Cloud Approach. *Procedia Economics and Finance*, *20*(15), 88–93. doi:10.1016/S2212-5671(15)00051-9

Bresnahan, T., & Greenstein, S. (2014). Mobile Computing: The Next Platform Rivalry. *The American Economic Review*, *104*(5), 475–480. doi:10.1257/aer.104.5.475

Carlin, S., & Curran, K. (2011). Cloud Computing Security. *International Journal of Ambient Computing and Intelligence*, *3*(1), 14–19. doi:10.4018/jaci.2011010102

Chou, D. C. (2015). Cloud computing risk and audit issues. *Computer Standards & Interfaces*, *42*, 137–142. doi:10.1016/j.csi.2015.06.005

Corkern, S. M., Kimmel, S. B., & Morehead, B. (2015). Accountants Need To Be Prepared For The Big Question : Should I Move To The Cloud? *International Journal of Management & Information Systems*, *19*(1), 13–20.

Crook, S. K., & Hopkins, S. (2013). *SAP Enterprise Mobility: Bringing a Cohesive Approach to a Complex Market*. Academic Press.

Dimitriu, O., & Matei, M. (2014). A New Paradigm for Accounting through Cloud Computing. *Procedia Economics and Finance*, *15*(14), 840–846. doi:10.1016/S2212-5671(14)00541-3

Duncan, B., & Whittington, M. (2016). Enhancing Cloud Security and Privacy: The Cloud Audit Problem. *Cloud Computing 2016: The Seventh International Conference on Cloud Computing, GRIDs, and Virtualization*, 119–124.

Elefterie, L., & Badea, G. (2016). The impact of information technology on the audit process. *Economics, Management and Financial Markets, 11*(1), 303–309. Retrieved from http://www.addletonacademicpublishers.com/economics-management-and-financial-markets

Fernando, N., Loke, S. W., & Rahayu, W. (2013). Mobile cloud computing: A survey. *Future Generation Computer Systems, 29*(1), 84–106. doi:10.1016/j.future.2012.05.023

Garg, N., & Bawa, S. (2017). RITS-MHT: Relative indexed and time stamped Merkle hash tree based data auditing protocol for cloud computing. *Journal of Network and Computer Applications, 84*, 1–13. doi:10.1016/j.jnca.2017.02.005

Geeta, C. M., Raghavendra, S., Buyya, R., & Venugopal, K. R. (2018). Data Auditing and Security in Cloud Computing : Issues, Challenges and Future Directions. *International Journal of Computer, 28*(1), 8–57.

Gupta, A., & Shakya, S. (2015). Information System Audit. *Cloud Computing Security and Challenges, 4*(11), 48–56.

Hatefi, M., & Fasanghari, M. (2016). A DEA-Based Approach for Information Technology Risk Assessment through Risk Information Technology Framework. *The International Arab Journal of Information Technology, 13*(1), 51–58.

IFAC. (2016). ISA 330: The auditor's responses to assessed Risks. In *Handbook of International Quality Control, Auditing, Review, Other Assurance, and Related Services Pronouncements* (pp. 347–369). New York: International Federation of Accountants.

Inácio, H. (2014). *Controlo Interno - Enquadramento teórico e aplicação prática.* Escolar Editora.

James, O. A. (2013). The Impact of Information and Communication Technology on Internal Control's Prevention and Detection of Fraud. *Ph.D Thesis, 3*(13), 1738–1752.

Kavya, A., & Lobo, P. (2017). An Analysis of Security Issues and Solutions in Cloud Computing. *International Journal ofEmerging Research in Management &Technology, 6*(6), 279–285. doi:10.9790/0661-1902046772

Kinkela, K. (2012). Practical and ethical considerations on the use of cloud computing in accounting. *Journal of Finance and Accountancy*, 1–10.

Kumar, P. R., Raj, P. H., & Jelciana, P. (2018). Exploring Data Security Issues and Solutions in Cloud Computing. *Procedia Computer Science, 125*(2009), 691–697. doi:10.1016/j.procs.2017.12.089

Kumar S, K. (2016). Secure Auditing and Deduplication of Data on Cloud. *International Journal of Engineering Sciences & Research Technology, 5*, 289–292.

Lins, S., Teigeler, H., & Sunyaev, A. (2016). Towards A Bright Future: Enhancing Diffusion of Continuous Cloud Service Auditing by Third Parties. *Twenty-Fourth European Conference on Information Systems (ECIS)*, 1–17. Retrieved from https://www.researchgate.net/profile/Sebastian_Lins/publication/301287731_TOWARDS_A_BRIGHT_FUTURE_ENHANCING_DIFFUSION_OF_CONTINUOUS_CLOUD_SERVICE_AUDITING_BY_THIRD_PARTIES/links/570f93d308aec95f0614c528.pdf

Liu, C., Chen, J., Member, S., Yang, L. T., & Zhang, X. (2014). *Authorized Public Auditing of Dynamic Big Data Storage on Cloud with Efficient Verifiable Fine-Grained Updates*. Academic Press.

Luo, Y., Xu, M., Huang, K., Wang, D., & Fu, S. (2018). Efficient auditing for shared data in the cloud with secure user revocation and computations outsourcing. *Computers & Security*, *73*, 492–506. doi:10.1016/j.cose.2017.12.004

Mehri, F., Khakzadi, M., & Shamsi, M. (2016). *A Survey of Third-party Audit for Data Storage Security in Cloud Computing*. Academic Press.

Neto, P. (2011). Demystifying Cloud Computing. In *Proceeding of Doctoral Symposium on Informatics Engineering* (*Vol. 24*, pp. 16–21). Academic Press. 10.1007/978-1-84996-241-4

Özdoğan, B. (2017). *The Future of Accounting Profession in an Era of Start-Ups*. Accounting and Corporate Reporting - Today and Tomorrow. doi:10.5772/intechopen.69264

Pazowski, P., & Pastuszak, Z. (2013). Cloud Computing: A Case Study for the New Idea of the IS/IT Implementation. *Management, Knowledge and Learning International Conference 2013*, 855–862. Retrieved from http://www.toknowpress.net/ISBN/978-961-6914-02-4/papers/ML13-332.pdf

Rahimi, M. R., Ren, J., Liu, C. H., Vasilakos, A. V., & Venkatasubramanian, N. (2014). Mobile cloud computing: A survey, state of art and future directions. *Mobile Networks and Applications*, *19*(2), 133–143. doi:10.100711036-013-0477-4

Rasheed, H. (2014). Data and infrastructure security auditing in cloud computing environments. *International Journal of Information Management*, *34*(3), 364–368. doi:10.1016/j.ijinfomgt.2013.11.002

Razaque, A., & Rizvi, S. S. (2017). Privacy preserving model: A new scheme for auditing cloud stakeholders. *Journal of Cloud Computing*, *6*(1), 1–17. doi:10.118613677-017-0076-1

Reads, C. (2015). *Financial Audit in Cloud Computing: State of the Art Review*. Academic Press.

Ren, Y., Shen, J., Wang, J., Han, J., & Lee, S. (2015). Mutual verifiable provable data auditing in public cloud storage. *Journal of Internet Technology*, *16*(2), 317–323. doi:10.6138/JIT.2015.16.2.20140918

Rezarta, S., & Muça, E. (2014). An analysis of cloud computing and its role in accounting industry in Albania. *Journal of Information Systems & Operations Management*, 1–12. Retrieved from http://ezproxy.aut.ac.nz/login?url=http://search.proquest.com/docview/1646125309?accountid=8440

Roshan, A. H. V., Prashanth, B., & Vineet, K. N. (2017). *Creating Secure Clouds by Continuous Auditing*. Academic Press.

Rus, I. (2015). Technologies and Methods for Auditing Databases. *Procedia Economics and Finance, 26*(15), 991–999. doi:10.1016/S2212-5671(15)00921-1

Salazar, D. (2015). *Cloud Security Framework Audit Methods.* The SANS Institute.

Sanaei, Z., Abolfazli, S., Gani, A., & Buyya, R. (2013). Heterogeneity in Mobile Cloud Computing:Taxonomy and Open Challenges. *IEEE Communications Surveys and Tutorials*, 1–24. doi:10.1109/SURV.2013.050113.00090

Schmidt, P. J., Wood, J. T., & Grabski, S. V. (2016). Business in the Cloud: Research Questions on Governance, Audit, and Assurance. *Journal of Information Systems, 30*(3), 173–189. doi:10.2308/isys-51494

Sookhak, M., Gani, A., Talebian, H., Akhunzada, A., Khan, S. U., Buyya, R., & Zomaya, A. Y. (2015). Remote Data Auditing in Cloud Computing Environments: A Survey, Taxonomy, and Open Issues. *ACM Computing Surveys, 47*(4), 65:1--65:34. doi:10.1145/2764465

Sookhak, M., Talebian, H., Ahmed, E., Gani, A., & Khan, M. K. (2014). A review on remote data auditing in single cloud server: Taxonomy and open issues. *Journal of Network and Computer Applications, 43*, 121–141. doi:10.1016/j.jnca.2014.04.011

Srinivasan, S., & Raja, K. (2014). Dynamic Group Audit Control Mechanism for Cloud Computing Using k-means Inter-Batch Cluster Method Dynamic Group Audit Control Mechanism for Cloud Computing Using k- means Inter-Batch Cluster. *International Journal of Applied Engineering Research, 9*, 16821–16835.

Wei, Z., & Yang, W. (2017). Research on building of cloud accounting financial sharing management model based on analysis in the era of big data. *Revista de la Facultad de Ingeniería, 32*(14), 34–40.

Wyslocka, E., & Jelonek, D. (2015). *Accounting in the Cloud Computing*. Academic Press.

Xia, M., Gong, L., Lyu, Y., Qi, Z., & Liu, X. (2015). Effective real-time android application auditing. *Proceedings - IEEE Symposium on Security and Privacy,* 899–914. 10.1109/SP.2015.60

Yang, K., & Jia, X. (2012). Data storage auditing service in cloud computing: Challenges, methods and opportunities. *World Wide Web (Bussum), 15*(4), 409–428. doi:10.100711280-011-0138-0

Yang, K., & Jia, X. (2014). An Efficient and Secure Dynamic Auditing Protocol for Data Storage in Cloud Computing. *IEEE Transactions on Parallel and Distributed Systems, I*(9), 2–5. doi:10.1109/ICS.2016.137

KEY TERMS AND DEFINITIONS

Audit Process: A set of actions and procedures to monitor and control the activities at an organization.

Auditability of Information Assets: The auditability promotes confidence in the information, allowing it to be analyzed methodically (quality of being audited).

Mobile Cloud Computing: Concept which has been gaining popularity, resulting from the synergistic integration of cloud computing and mobile computing.

Information Assets: An identifiable collection of data recognized as having value for the purpose of enabling an organization to perform its business processes.

Internal Control System: Consists of a set of rules, procedures and organizational structures to ensure that operations comply with all existing laws and regulatory procedures.

Laws and Regulatory Procedures: An effort to bring legislation in compliance with the enterprise model.

Mobile Application: Application software designed to run on a mobile device, such as a smartphone or tablet computer.

Mobile Computing: Mobile computing is the set of IT technologies (products and services) that enable end users to gain access to computation, information, and related resources when they are in movement.

Chapter 7
The Transformation of Auditing From Traditional to Continuous Auditing in the Era of Big Data

Adem Çabuk
Uludağ University, Turkey

Alp Aytaç
Uludağ University, Turkey

ABSTRACT

Massive usage of internet and digital devices make it easier accessing the desired information. In the past, auditing was a periodic, reactive approach, but this must change. Today, volume, velocity, variety, veracity, and value of the information, which are the main criteria of big data, are crucial. Decision makers demand timely, true, and reliable information. This need has affected every sector including auditing. For this reason, the continuous auditing system comes to debate in the big data era. The main aim of this chapter is to shed light on how traditional auditing transformed into the continuous auditing and where big data stands in this transformation. It is concluded that even though many obstacles arise, continuous auditing systems and harvesting big data benefits are crucial to gain a competitive advantage. Also, using big data analytics and continuous auditing system together, management and shareholders gain detailed information about the company's present situation and future direction.

INTRODUCTION

Economic development of one country relies heavily on companies. Decision makers, whether they are major or small investors, demand true, timely and reliable information about their possible investment. Auditing provides this kind of information to decision makers. Auditing approach has started to change since the 20th century from traditional to continuous. With the auditing approach change, the volume of information changed as well. Today's information is voluminous and variable it is impossible to catch up. This era is called 'Big Data'. In the era of Big data, decision makers, whether they are managers of a company or president of a country, demand true, timely and reliable information. In this era, big data and continuous auditing system interaction are key in the name of providing this kind of information.

DOI: 10.4018/978-1-5225-7356-2.ch007

In the literature, big data and continuous auditing are researched severely by practitioners and academicians separately. However, not many study focus on the interaction of both. In this study, the authors make an exploratory study and try to give a detailed examination of big data and continuous auditing development and their relationship.

This chapter organized as follows: In the second section, aim and methodology of the chapter are mentioned. Immediately after, the theoretical framework of traditional to continuous auditing, continuous auditing, and big data is mentioned. After that, the relationship between big data and continuous auditing is discussed based on related literature. This chapter is concluded with future research directions and conclusion.

MAIN FOCUS OF THE CHAPTER

The Aim of the Study

The main of this chapter is to shed light on how traditional auditing transformed into the continuous auditing and where big data stands in this transformation based on related literature.

Methodology

In this chapter, the authors used an archival method. In Chiu, Liu, & Vasarhelyi (2014) study, they shed light on extant continuous auditing research and reveals its longitudinal development by reviewing, summarizing, and cross-comparing research characteristics of 118 relevant continuous auditing studies. The three main research methods identified in the CA literature are: analytical, archival, and experimental/behavioral. They define archival study as studies utilize sources from secondary records. In Brown, Wong, & Baldwin (2007) study they divided the research streams into five categories: demand factors, theory, and guidance, enabling technologies, applications, and impacts. The authors use theory and guidance from secondary sources to shed light on the transformation of auditing, how big data accelerate this transformation and the relationship between big data and continuous auditing.

THEORETICAL FRAMEWORK

From Traditional to Continuous Auditing

Massive usage of internet and digital devices make it easier to access the desired information. In the digitalization and globalization era, decision makers demand timely, true and reliable information. This pace has both positive and negative impacts. On the positive side, being able to reach the desired information anywhere and anytime. On the negative side, information noise, biased information and useless information are all over the place. Accurate, reliable and timely information is crucial for everyone. In the context of business, this kind of information is crucial for management, employees, and stakeholders who make decisions based on gathered information. To accomplish this task, auditing holds a very important position.

Auditing is the accumulation and evaluation of evidence about information to determine and report on the degree of correspondence between the information and established criteria (Arens, Elder, & Beasley, 2012, p. 4) The objectives of any audit are to identify the vulnerability of the system where it exists, evaluate internal controls, and verify implementation (Koch, 1981, p. 29). A traditional audit is a reactive approach which means it is executed after the year-end and on an annual basis. If anomalies occur during the year, it could be detected only after the auditing process. However, today's tough and instantly changing economic conditions cannot tolerate this time difference. Due to this reason, continuous auditing (CA) concept has emerged. When examining the literature, Canadian Institute of Chartered Accountants/American Institute of Certified Public Accountants' (CICA/AICPA) definition is generally used. CICA/AICPA (1999) defines CA as a methodology for issuing audit reports simultaneously with, or a short period after, the occurrence of the relevant events.

From the beginning of the 20th century, traditional audit started to evolve into the continuous audit. Frequency, approach, procedures, work, and role of the auditors, nature, timing, extent, testing, and reporting of auditing started to change. In this context, how traditional audit evolves into a continuous audit can be seen from the table 1.

As seen from the table, traditional auditing is periodic and reactive, and this is the main reason why traditional auditing is not sufficient enough to meet decision makers' needs in today's circumstances. Decision-makers want more frequent and reactive approach. Therefore continuous auditing is the ideal one. Also, in traditional auditing system testing is performed by humans, whereas in the continuous auditing system data modeling and data analytics are used for monitoring and testing. In this case, auditors can spend more time on risky areas. In Lombardi, Bloch, & Vasarhelyi (2014) study the expert's indicated that audits have changed from periodic to continuous, covering a much higher percentage of company data and monitoring of business processes. As a result of increased audit automation, auditors can now spend more time reviewing analyses and interpreting results rather than performing tasks. Audit auto-

Table 1. Traditional auditing vs. continuous auditing methodology

Traditional Auditing	Continuous Auditing
1. Frequency: Periodic	1. Frequency: Continuous or more frequent
2. Approach: Reactive	2. Approach: Proactive
3. Procedures: Manual	3. Procedures: Automated
4. Work and role of auditors • Bulk of the work performed is centered around labor and time intensive audit procedures • Independent roles of the internal and external auditor	4. Work and role of auditors • Bulk of the work performed is centered around handling exceptions and audit procedures requiring human judgment • External auditor role becomes certifier of the continuous auditing system
5. Nature, timing and extent: • Testing consist of analytical and review procedures and substantive details testing (nature) • Controls testing and detailed testing occur independently (timing) • Sampling in testing (extent)	5. Nature, timing and extent: • Testing consist of continuous controls monitoring and continuous data assurance (nature) • Controls monitoring and detailed testing occur simultaneously (timing) • Whole population is considered in testing(extent)
6. Testing: Humans perform testing	6. Testing: Data modelling and data analytics are used for monitoring and testing
7. Reporting: Periodic	7. Reporting: Continuous or more frequent

Source: (Chan & Vasarhelyi, 2011)

mation tools evaluate inherent risks for a particular audit, so the auditor can spend more time reviewing and interpreting analyses (rather than performing tests) and determining the desired course of action.

As CA performs frequent or real-time monitoring on the entity's existing control system and compares certain controls with the auditor's expectations, a problematic event (i.e., a critical business risk that is not identified by the entity's risk management process) may be immediately observed and evaluated, and, if necessary, trigger a system alarm which automatically informs the management for further investigation(Sun, Alles, & Vasarhelyi, 2015, p. 176).

With the CA system, almost %100 of transactions can be audited because CA is more frequent, reactive, covers a broad area, use data modeling and data analytics. In the next section, detailed information about the continuous auditing system will be given.

Continuous Auditing System

Continuous auditing system holds an important position in the name of providing timely, true and reliable information. In the literature, there is a consensus on what CA is. According to CICA-AICPA report (1999), continuous auditing is defined as a methodology for issuing audit reports simultaneously with, or a short period after, the occurrence of the relevant events by CICA/AICPA 1999 report. One of the ways to gain a competitive advantage in implementing the CA system.

Continuous auditing system is frequently examined with various variables from different kind of aspects such as technical infrastructure, organizational factors, applied and proposed models.

On the technical infrastructure studies mainly focus on online system implementation (Kogan, Sudit, & Vasarhelyi, 1999), information technology structure (Brown et al., 2007), enterprise resources planning (ERP) structure (Alles, Kogan, & Vasarhelyi, 2004; Kuhn & Sutton, 2010) and factors influencing the use computer-related programs (Janvrin, Bierstaker, & Lowe, 2009). Apart from technical infrastructure, Pathak, Chaouch, & Sriram (2005) focus on the economic feasibility of CA system.

Some studies focus on organizational factors such as management support, employee knowledge, government interference, acceptance, adoption and impact of CA system by internal auditors and functional and dysfunctional effects of this system (Hunton, Mauldin, & Wheeler, 2008; A Kiesow, Schomaker, & Thomas, 2016; Rikhardsson & Dull, 2016; Sun et al., 2015; Vasarhelyi, Alles, Kuenkaikaew, & Littley, 2012).

Continuous auditing system gets its power from computer-assisted programs. These programs automatize existing procedures, and if there are anomalies occur, the systems send reports to the person in charge. In the literature, like Du & Roohani (2007) and Santos, Sousa, Ferreira, & Tribolet (2008) proposed a continuous auditing model. Also, some programs such as Continuous Intermittent Solution (Koch, 1981), Embedded Audit Modules (Flowerday & Von Solms, 2005; Groomer & Murthy, 1989) and Continuous Process Auditing System (Halper, Snively, & Vasarhelyi, 1992; Vasarhelyi, Halper, & Ezawa, 1991) is used by academicians.

Many criteria affect continuous auditing. First of all, culture is vital in the continuous auditing system. Management and employees' embrace this system and auditing should become a corporate culture.

Habits are stable whereas the conditions we are in are changing enormously. Companies that do not follow the current trends are destined to disappear. When talking about current trends not just mentioning technical infrastructure, but also management and employees' skill set as well. Ca system requires technical knowledge about how to use computer-assisted programs, how to interpret its result and to report it to related parties. Due to this fact, management and employees' have to adapt themselves to instantly changing conditions.

Internal control system and continuous auditing system have a close relationship. Especially, internal auditors make great use of the CA system. Internal auditor independence is vital. Even though internal auditors are the employee's in companies, they should independently collect data and report it to the person in charge. In this process, effectively using the CA system brings many advantages to internal auditors and therefore to the companies as well.

Continuous auditing system made it possible for companies and auditors to audit transactions simultaneously with or shortly after. Because of this, they can audit almost %100 of the transactions. When examining, all transactions, quality and timing of the information will increase and that increase decreases the fraudulent financial reporting. Advanced auditing tools made it possible to audit %100 of transactions whereas number and source of the data have also been increasing. Data is flowing from every channel, and it is not as easy to obtain and store such a mass data. This development has brought the literature 'Big Data' notion.

In the next section general information, literature review and how big data interacts with continuous auditing system will be explained.

Big Data

The invention of the internet and world wide web (www) makes everyone to access the information they want instantly. In the past, all the information are stored in print. For example, when doing homework, people went to libraries and looked at books and encyclopedias. If people want to look at pictures, they print them. But now, nearly everything stored in digital format.

In the third century BC, the Library of Alexandria was believed to house of the sum of human knowledge. Today, there is enough information in the world to give every person alive 320 times as much of it as historians think was stored in Alexandria's entire collection- an estimated 1.200 exabytes' worth. If all this information were placed on CDs and they were stacked up, the CDs would form five separate piles that would all reach to the moon (Cukier & Mayer-Schoenberger, 2014, p. 28). This huge information has brought 'Big Data' to debate. In the literature, there is consensus on big data definition. Just like Capriotti (2014), most studies define big data as the generation of data has started to outpace the processing capabilities of the typical technology tools and as a result, computer engineers and scientists started calling it "big data."

In the past decision makers and auditors are using and analyzing structured information like financial data. But now, with the big data revolution, information are both structured and unstructured.

Big Data can exist as large structured data (e.g., data that fit into a defined schema, such as relational data), semi-structured data (e.g., data that are tagged with XML), unstructured data (e.g., text and video), and multi-structured data (e.g., integrated data of different types and structural levels). Unstructured data represent the largest proportion of existing data and the greatest opportunity for exploiting Big Data (Moffitt & Vasarhelyi, 2013, p. 5).

Like many systems, big data includes some criteria as well. In the literature, there is no agreement on what these are. For example, Gandomi & Haider (2015) use 3V's of big data, and according to them, volume refers to the magnitude of data, variety refers to the structural heterogeneity in a dataset, and velocity refers to the rate at which data are generated and the speed at which it should be analyzed and acted upon. In Zhang, Yang, & Appelbaum (2015) study they add veracity to the big data criteria. In line with Zhang, Yang, & Appelbaum (2015), Gepp, Linnenluecke, O'Neill, & Smith (2018) also use 4V's of big data criteria. In addition, Fosso Wamba, Akter, Edwards, Chopin, & Gnanzou (2015) define 'big data' as a holistic approach to manage, process and analyze 5 Vs (i.e., volume, variety, velocity, veracity, and value) in order to create actionable insights for sustained value delivery, measuring performance and establishing competitive advantages. In this chapter, the authors use, Fosso Wamba, Akter, Edwards, Chopin, & Gnanzou (2015) big data features. The authors agreed that volume, variety, velocity, and veracity are crucial factors but the value is the centerpiece of these criteria.

The term 'Big Data' has been affecting the world. People are accessing an unprecedented volume of information at an unprecedented time. This pace affects business, decision makers and the accounting profession. According to McAfee & Brynjolfsson (2012) because of big data, managers can measure, and hence know, radically more about their businesses, and directly translate that knowledge into improved decision making and performance. And they gave an example that by using Big Data on the airline industry gaps eliminated between estimated and actual arrival times.

Big data's usage in business is limitless. For example, Walmart used it to improve supermarket performance, CERN used it to solve universe mystery, Netflix used it to offer the programs customers want, APIXIO used it to transform Public Health sector, Facebook used it to understand their customers, Royal Scotland Bank used it to individualize customer services, LinkedIn used it to increase the visibility on social media, ACXIOM used it to improve marketing etc. The accounting profession is affecting big data usage as well. As mentioned before, decision makers want timely, true and reliable information and big data provide timely information. But is this information is true and reliable? Auditors hold an important position to give a satisfying answer to this question. Therefore, big data revolution has great impacts on auditing and accounting. Information that someone might think is useless could be an important feature with the big data. According to McAfee & Brynjolfsson (2012) the big data movement, like analytics before it, seeks to glean intelligence from data and translate that into a business advantage.

Big Data will have increasingly important implications for accounting, even as new types of data become accessible. The video, audio, and textual information made available via Big Data can provide for improved managerial accounting, financial accounting, and financial reporting practices. In managerial accounting, Big Data will contribute to the development and evolution of effective management control systems and budgeting processes (Warren, Moffitt, & Byrnes, 2015, p. 397). Using big data in accounting bring my advantages to the profession. Pros of using big data in accounting and auditing can be seen from Table 3.

Big Data will play an important role in auditing because it complements traditional evidence with sufficient, reliable, and relevant information. Big Data will be used to decrease auditors' dependency on client data and provide an independent benchmark to evaluate internal audit evidence. The change in the auditing environment brought about by Big Data gives auditors unique opportunities to build up first-mover advantage and achieve economies of scale (Yoon, Hoogduin, & Zhang, 2015, p. 436). As auditors gain greater access to data and audit procedures that can be performed by a computerized tool, the role of the audit will become more like a master control plan, which includes greater automated controls and greater timeliness. Analytics are part of the equation. As more work is performed automatically, auditors will have the opportunity to focus more honing their judgment to the client's environment (Vasarhelyi, Warren, Teeter, & Titera, 2014, p. 36). Auditors should seek to verify transactions not with just an invoice and receipt, but with multi-modal evidence that a transaction took place. Photo, video, GPS location, and other metadata could accompany transaction data (Moffitt & Vasarhelyi, 2013, p. 17). Big data will be used to correlate log data and identify malicious activity in real time, allowing companies to react quickly, rather than after the event (Press, 2013, p. 4). Companies can also monitor employee telephone calls, emails, and in-office behaviors. Furthermore, companies can track what employees do with company resources away from the office including vehicles, cell phones, and P-Cards. Big Data could convert MCSs into comprehensive monitoring and control systems (CMCSs) (Warren et al., 2015, pp. 400–401). Auditors will likewise benefit from radio frequency identification use. If an entire inventory can be counted and located automatically, then sampling and spot testing will become supplements to, rather than substitutes for, full population tests (Krahel & Titera, 2015, p. 412).

Big data offers a different kind of information to decision makers. In addition to financial data, non-financial data plays an important role in the decision-making process. In Table 3, where to use financial data can be seen.

As can be seen from the tables, using big data in audits has many benefits. But, as always, it is not easy to receive benefits. Like many other techniques, big data has some obstacles as well.

Table 2. Pros of incorporating big data into audits

Potential Advantages	Comments
Strong predictive power, which is a powerful tool for setting expectations for financial statement auditor.	Events/transactions included in Big Data can predate accounting transactions by days, weeks months, and even years. For example, knowing someone is pregnant (by analyzing sales of pregnancy test kits) enables prediction of a permanent change in purchase patterns.
Rich data sources to identify potential fraudulent activities.	Difficult for fraudster to change all upstream non-financial transactions to cover up financial statement fraud. For example, trade based money laundering can be detected by comparing invoices with the actual weight of shipping containers. Some potentially valuable data may be unavailable due to privacy considerations.
Analyzing all data increases probability of discovering red flags, "smoking guns," and suspicious outliers.	Fraud represents a very small percentage of transactions and could be easily not included in the small samples auditors traditionally select.
Developing more predictive models of going concern, using leading indicators of sales and costs.	Going concern issues are not a major part of the audit of most well established businesses in normal circumstances and there is no limit to the resources that auditors will devote to its estimation.

Source: (Alles & Gray, 2015)

Table 3. Summary of big data benefits

Area/Domain	Big Data Can Assist in Addressing
Audio	Asset security/surveillance, employee productivity, individual characteristics such as integrity, mood, deception, etc.
Video and Image	Nonverbal communications, manufacturing process productivity, asset security/surveillance, employee productivity, object recognition
Text	Fraud, customer satisfaction, sentiment, employee satisfaction
Managerial Accounting	Management control systems, budgeting, manufacturing process issues, employee productivity, customer satisfaction
Financial Accounting	Asset valuation, accounting record completeness and accuracy, accounting estimates, reporting transparency, fair value accounting issues, convergence of accounting standards, evolution of accounting standards, audit efficiency and effectiveness

Source: (Warren et al., 2015)

In the era of Big Data, data can easily be associated with other data. Once some sensitive data are leaked, they can propagate with high velocity and connect to a large amount of related data. Thus, Big Data confidentiality becomes even more urgent and important to preserve brand image and secure competitive advantage (Zhang et al., 2015, p. 474). Through experience in audit engagements, training and development of auditors and, most recently, as a vendor of data analysis tools, the practitioner has observed that internal and external auditors struggle with the use of data analytics in their audits for a number of reasons. These reasons include difficulty in acquiring appropriate data, a lack of trained staff, reluctance to invest, not knowing where to start, uncertain benefits and costs of the audit, and concerns about ''false positives.''(Wang & Cuthbertson, 2015, pp. 155–156). The use of Big Data involves extracting information for analysis from an extremely larger population of data from multiple nonfinancial sources that auditors are not accustomed to having to collect and analyze during the conduct of an audit Data analytic tools used to analyze Big Data give auditors the ability to incorporate and use both structured (e.g., general ledger or transaction data) and unstructured (e.g., email communications, Wi-Fi sensors, electronic tags, free-text fields in databases) data to identify potential transactional anomalies (e.g., unauthorized disbursements), patterns of behavior (e.g., split payments to bypass transaction limit), and trends (e.g., increased fraudulent transactions before a big holiday). Nonetheless, even in the Big Data environment limitations exist that cannot be overcome with advanced tools alone. Decisions made based on information derived from Big Data still involve interpretation and judgment (Brown-Liburd, Issa, & Lombardi, 2015, pp. 453–454). According to Yoon et al. (2015) critical challenges for applicability of big data, including integration with traditional audit evidence, information transfer issues, and information privacy protection.

Increasing usage of big data and advanced auditing tools have made auditors to change their skill sets. In the era of continuous auditing system and big data, auditors must have proper knowledge about business analytics, data mining, how to interpret the text, audio, and images, what kind of tools should be used to spend more time on critical areas and how to eliminate false positives, etc. According to Braun & Davis (2003) to be able to execute continuous auditing, it seems clear that auditors will not only have to increase their conceptual abilities in defining the techniques that are the foundation of the continuous auditing process but also their technical skills in implementing these techniques.

Unfortunately, auditors are failed to keep up this pace. In Appelbaum, Kogan, & Vasarhelyi (2017) study, they sort the factors that auditors' lack of competencies in the big data and continuous auditing era, which are;

- Accounting faculties tend not to be prepared to teach analytics.
- There is a widespread general feeling that students are not receptive to learning analytics (however, the feeling is not pervasive—there are some anecdotal reports to the contrary).
- The accounting curriculum is too full to add more IT, statistics, and modeling.
- As the CPA exam does not include these topics, there is little motivation by students for their addition to the curriculum of study.
- Firms will tend/or already have hired specialist groups from non-accounting backgrounds.
- Practitioners are also not prepared and their internal audit practices have not caught up properly with these issues.

Based on the literature, it can be seen that many obstacles arise from adopting big data into auditing. But no benefits can be achieved without consequences. If auditors and companies can keep up with this pace and adopt today's situations, there is a win-win situation for companies, auditors, and shareholders.

Continuous auditing system and big data have a lot in common, and they complement each other. Via CA system, %100 of transactions can be audited and through big data %100 information can be generated. In the next section, the relationship between big data and continuous auditing will be mentioned.

RELATIONSHIP BETWEEN BIG DATA AND CONTINUOUS AUDITING SYSTEM

Big Data revolution and continuous auditing have affected auditors deeply. This transformation made auditors leave their comfort zone. In the past, auditors mainly use a sampling method to give a general description of companies' financial statements. Now, shareholders and managers want timely information because of rapidly changing information. On one side, managers use timely information but on the other side, auditors audit this timely information after the transactions occurred. But now, this must change. To eliminate this difference, auditors must also audit transactions simultaneously with or shortly after the transactions occurred. Only by doing this, auditors can give reliable information to the shareholders. Continuous auditing system helps auditors and managers to eliminate this time difference. With the help of CA, auditors instantly check transactions whether they include fraudulent activities and give insurance to the decision makers. In this context, big data come into the play. Advanced auditing tools and obtaining detailed information both structured and unstructured, give auditors and decision makers an advantage to deeply analyze information.

In the literature, many different kinds of data analytics techniques can be used such as, clustering, data mining, artificial neural network, sentiment analysis, natural language processing, machine learning, regression, visualization, predictive modeling, time series analysis, local outlier factor, social network analysis, etc. By using data analytics techniques and continuous auditing together, companies will be able to get the results that gives them competitive advantage effectively. According to Singh, Best, Bojilov, & Blunt (2014) opportunity for CA/CM exists in the area of process mining of large amounts of structured and unstructured data, namely ''Big Data'' and with the growth and ''explosion'' of social media and machine-generated data, there appears to be a growing need to perform analytics on this unstructured data combined with existing ERP system-generated data. According to Liddy (2014), in the future, using high powered analytics, auditors will have the capacity to examine 100 percent of a client's transactions and they will be able to sort, filter and analyze tens of thousands or millions of transactions to identify anomalies, making it easier to focus in on areas of potential concern and drill down on those items that may have the highest risks.

To effectively run continuous auditing, it is important to use appropriate data analytics techniques. In the literature, many studies focus on different kind of data analytic techniques and how these techniques affect companies in the auditing process.

Chen, Wang, & Chen (2007) use local outlier factor (LOF) values to measure the outlying behavior among peer groups to gauge the financial performance of companies.

Koskivaara & Back (2007) proposed an artificial neural network analysis (ANNA) based decision support system for analytical procedures in the continuous auditing environment. A system like ANNA can be used either predicting the yearly account values or, even more specifically, for modeling the dynamics of the account values on a monthly basis. ANNA could serve a continuous monitoring and controlling purpose as follows: It could automatically give, for example, a monthly report of those accounts which follow the trend and two conventional analytical review methods. Furthermore, it could raise the alarm to those accounts that occasionally either start or stop following the trend (Koskivaara & Back, 2007, p. 43).

Thiprungsri & Vasarhelyi (2011) focus on how cluster analysis is used in the auditing for anomaly detection in a major US insurance company. According to them, cluster analysis may flag transactions not identified via other methodologies, and while universal detection is never guaranteed, flagged transactions demonstrate suspicious characteristics worth investigating.

Debreceny & Gray (2011) investigated the Enron's public released E-mail by using data mining technique. According to them, e-mails are likely to contain exchanges of information that can provide evidence and context for matters that are of interest to auditors. They add that an area for future development is in continuous auditing and continuous monitoring of e-mails.

Kiesow, Zarvic, & Thomas (2014) study showed the correlation between continuous auditing and big data criteria. In the continuous auditing, computer-assisted audit tools are commonly used. According to Kiesow et al. (2014), Test data are data, which is created by the auditor and processed within the client's system. Considering the dimension Volume, Test Data can be used to test the load capacity of programs, i.e., to what extent is the program able to process large data sets. The dimension Veracity could be addressed through the examination of the completeness and accuracy of programs. Privacy aspects could be addressed by simulating personal data and examine their processing considering data leaks. Velocity is not covered by using Test Data, since the continuous input of data in the AIS cannot be tested by a single Test Data set.

According to Tysiac (2015) the power of data analytics could make it possible for external financial statement auditors to improve audits by testing complete sets of data, aiding risk assessment through the identification of anomalies and trends, perhaps even through comparison to industry data, pointing auditors toward items they need to investigate further and to provide audit evidence through comprehensive analysis of organizations' general ledger system. Tysiac (2015) also added that auditors should use Big Data and perform deeper analytics and audit procedures should be continuous.

Medinets, Gross, & Brennan (2015) made a case study at Siemens about developing continuous assurance. In their case, vice president of controls management said that 'Exceptions in the data pool are like fish in the lake. Just because they are there doesn't mean you will catch any.' According to them, continuously assessing 100 percent of data attributes (validity, authorization, completeness, valuation, time period and disclosure) for exceptions gives far greater assurance that the data represents the company's underlying economic position that periodic sampling ever could.

Another case study is done by Laslett & Hardy (2015). Laslett and Hardy's study is about implementing continuous auditing and continuous monitoring in MetCash which operates in four market areas: food, grocery, liquor and automotive. In this case study, MetCash made an application called 'The Leave Continuous Monitoring Routine'. This app detects if any staff member who has not logged in for two or more business days is identified and the exception is cross-matched to the human resources leave records. This app could be much useful if MetCash uses social media as well. If an employee does not sign up in the system, the system may detect whether an employee is on leave or not from the employee's social media accountants.

Lins, Schneider, & Sunyaev (2016) focus on cloud service certifications and its need for continuous auditing. Cloud service customers can benefit when CA is performed. Typically, cloud environments are characterized by a lack of control since cloud customers cedes governance to cloud service providers. Especially when storing data in the cloud, customers fear that data could be compromised or leaked since they are lacking transparency about how and where data is stored and processed. CA can counteract this lack of control by increasing transparency regarding operations of providers. Through an increased transparency, CA ultimately tries to increase trustworthiness of customers in cloud services (Lins et al., 2016, p. 12).

Big Data and continuous auditing system have changed the auditing profession dramatically. With the continuous auditing system, audit reports have changed from periodic, extent of auditing has changed from sampling to whole population and auditing approach has changed from reactive to a proactive approach. The proactive approach gives decision-makers the ability to take actions before they occur. Companies may gain a competitive advantage; shareholders may get more profit and decision makers to get true, timely and reliable information in the proactive approach. In this transformation, volume, variety, velocity, veracity, and value which are the main criteria of big data holds a key position. In the continuous auditing approach whole population is considered and this whole population comes from the big data. Big data offers both structured (e.g., general ledger or transaction data) and unstructured (e.g., email communications, Wi-Fi sensors, electronic tags, free-text fields in databases) information. Merging structured information with unstructured one gives management and shareholders detailed point of view about companies' present situation and future direction. To achieve this, information comes from big data has to be continuously audit. Only by doing this, the ore of big data can be processed.

FUTURE RESEARCH DIRECTIONS

In this chapter, an exploratory study was made based on related literature. The authors tried to give detailed information about how traditional auditing has been changed to continuous auditing and where big data stands in this transformation. In future studies, it is recommended that a case study could be done to show the interaction of continuous auditing and big data in practice. Also, what kind of unstructured information is used among auditors in the auditing process. Also, whether sectorial differences exist with the application of CA and big data can be investigated.

CONCLUSION

Using big data is not an easy task. It has obstacles that must be overcome to gain full benefits from it. Something is clear: Big Data has radically changed the business environment. Related parties must adopt this change to survive in the tough economic environment. If auditors are failed to keep up this pace, they might lose their jobs to data scientist. If managers are failed as well, someone will be found who can adopt.

In this chapter, there are some limitations. Only using English based references is a limitation in this chapter. The authors think that, in other languages, there are studies that contribute to the development of big data and continuous auditing relationship. Also, unable to make an empirical study is another limitation. By merging big data and continuous auditing theory to the practice is an excellent way to generalize outcomes.

Based on the literature, it can be said that traditional auditing leaves its place to the continuous auditing. However, the CA system cannot survive on its own. It must be feed with big data. Big data may provide such information that this information does not have a meaning when used alone but can collectively make it possible to see the whole thing easily. Cukier & Mayer-Schoenberger (2014) mentioned the term 'datafication'. In today's circumstances, data-intense decision are the forefront and holds an important position. Widely usage of internet, instantly accessing the information, technological development, using advanced analytic tools make every data important, and it is crucial to correlate this voluminous information. Companies that harvest this information and instantly audit this information have a good chance to gain a competitive advantage. Like Capriotti (2014) said, the future of auditing is here now, and big data is leading the way.

REFERENCES

Alles, M. G., & Gray, G. L. (2015). *The Pros and Cons of Using Big Data in Auditing: a Synthesis of the Literature and a Research Agenda*. Academic Press.

Alles, M. G., Kogan, A., & Vasarhelyi, M. A. (2004). Reply Restoring auditor credibility: Tertiary monitoring and logging of continuous assurance systems. *International Journal of Accounting Information Systems*, *5*(2), 211–212. doi:10.1016/j.accinf.2004.02.008

Appelbaum, D., Kogan, A., & Vasarhelyi, M. A. (2017). Big Data and Analytics in the Modern Audit Engagement: Research Needs. *Auditing*, *36*(4), 1–27. doi:10.2308/ajpt-51684

Arens, A. A., Elder, R. J., & Beasley, M. S. (2012). *Auditing and Assurance Servies: An Integrated Approach* (14th ed.). Pearson Prentice Hall.

Braun, R. L., & Davis, H. E. (2003). Computer-assisted audit tools and techniques: Analysis and perspectives. *Managerial Auditing Journal*, *18*(9), 725–731. doi:10.1108/02686900310500488

Brown, C. E., Wong, J. A., & Baldwin, A. A. (2007). A Review and Analysis of the Existing Research Streams in Continuous Auditing. *Journal of Emerging Technologies in Accounting*, *4*(1), 1–28. doi:10.2308/jeta.2007.4.1.1

Brown-Liburd, H., Issa, H., & Lombardi, D. (2015). Behavioral implications of big data's impact on audit judgment and decision making and future research directions. *Accounting Horizons*, *29*(2), 451–468. doi:10.2308/acch-51023

Capriotti, R. J. (2014). Big Data Bringing Big Changes to Accounting. *Pennsylvania CPA Journal*, 1–3.

Chan, D. Y., & Vasarhelyi, M. A. (2011). Innovation and practice of continuous auditing. *International Journal of Accounting Information Systems*, *12*(2), 152–160. doi:10.1016/j.accinf.2011.01.001

Chen, M. C., Wang, R. J., & Chen, A. P. (2007). An empirical study for the detection of corporate financial anomaly using outlier mining techniques. *2007 International Conference on Convergence Information Technology, ICCIT 2007*, 612–617. 10.1109/ICCIT.2007.237

Chiu, V., Liu, Q., & Vasarhelyi, M. A. (2014). The development and intellectual structure of continuous auditing research. *Journal of Accounting Literature*, *33*(1–2), 37–57. doi:10.1016/j.acclit.2014.08.001

Cukier, K., & Mayer-Schoenberger, V. (2014). The Rise of Big Data. *Foreign Affairs*, *92*(3), 28–40.

Debreceny, R. S., & Gray, G. L. (2011). Data Mining of Electronic Mail and Auditing: A Research Agenda. *Journal of Information Systems*, *25*(2), 195–226. doi:10.2308/isys-10167

Du, H., & Roohani, S. (2007). Meeting Challenges and Expectations of Continuous Auditing in the Context of Independent Audits of Financial Statements. *International Journal of Auditing*, *11*(2), 133–146. doi:10.1111/j.1099-1123.2007.00359.x

Flowerday, S., & Von Solms, R. (2005). Continuous auditing: Verifying information integrity and providing assurances for financial reports. *Computer Fraud & Security*, *2005*(7), 12–16. doi:10.1016/S1361-3723(05)70232-3

Fosso Wamba, S., Akter, S., Edwards, A., Chopin, G., & Gnanzou, D. (2015). How "big data" can make big impact: Findings from a systematic review and a longitudinal case study. *International Journal of Production Economics*, *165*, 234–246. doi:10.1016/j.ijpe.2014.12.031

Gandomi, A., & Haider, M. (2015). Beyond the hype: Big data concepts, methods, and analytics. *International Journal of Information Management*, *35*(2), 137–144. doi:10.1016/j.ijinfomgt.2014.10.007

Gepp, A., Linnenluecke, M. K., O'Neill, T. J., & Smith, T. (2018). Big Data TECHNIQUES in Auditing RESEARCH AND PRACTICE: current trends and future opportunities. *Journal of Accounting Literature*, 1–42.

Groomer, S. M., & Murthy, U. S. (1989). Continuous Auditing of Database Applications: An Embedded Audit Module Approach. *Journal of Information Systems*.

Halper, F., Snively, J., & Vasarhelyi, M. (1992). The Continuous Process Audit System: Knowledge Acquisition and Representation. *Edpacs*, 1-13.

Hunton, J. E., Mauldin, E. G., & Wheeler, P. R. (2008). Potential functional and dysfunctional effects of continuous monitoring. *The Accounting Review*, *83*(6), 1551–1569. doi:10.2308/accr.2008.83.6.1551

Janvrin, D., Bierstaker, J. L., & Lowe, D. J. (2009). An Investigation of Factors Influencing the Use of Computer-Related Audit Procedures. *Journal of Information Systems*, *23*(1), 97–118. doi:10.2308/jis.2009.23.1.97

Kiesow, A., Schomaker, T., & Thomas, O. (2016). Transferring Continuous Auditing to the Digital Age – The Knowledge Base after Three Decades of Research. *Twenty-Fourth European Conference on Information Systems (ECIS)*, 1–18.

Kiesow, A., Zarvic, N., & Thomas, O. (2014). Continuous Auditing in Big Data Computing Environments: Towards an Integrated Audit Approach by Using CAATTs. *Management of Complex IT-Systems and Applications (MITA) - INFORMATIK, P-232*, 901–912.

Koch, H. S. (1981). Online Computer Auditing through Continuous and Intermittent Simulation. *Management Information Systems Quarterly, 5*(1), 29–41. doi:10.2307/249156

Kogan, A., Sudit, E. F., & Vasarhelyi, M. A. (1999). Continuous Online Auditing: A Program of Research. *Journal of Information Systems, 13*(2), 87–103. doi:10.2308/jis.1999.13.2.87

Koskivaara, E., & Back, B. (2007). Artificial Neural Network Assistant (ANNA) for Continuous Auditing and Monitoring of Financial Data. *Journal of Emerging Technologies in Accounting, 4*(1), 29–45. doi:10.2308/jeta.2007.4.1.29

Krahel, J. P., & Titera, W. R. (2015). Consequences of big data and formalization on accounting and auditing standards. *Accounting Horizons, 29*(2), 409–422. doi:10.2308/acch-51065

Kuhn, J. R. Jr, & Sutton, S. G. (2010). Continuous Auditing in ERP System Environments: The Current State and Future Directions. *Journal of Information Systems, 24*(1), 91–112. doi:10.2308/jis.2010.24.1.91

Laslett, G., & Hardy, C. C. (2015). Case Study B. *Audit Analytics*, 157-168.

Liddy, J. P. (2014). The Future of Audit. *Forbes*, 1–3.

Lins, S., Schneider, S., & Sunyaev, A. (2016). *Trust is Good, Control is Better: Creating Secure Clouds by Continuous Auditing. IEEE Transactions on Cloud Computing.*

Lombardi, D. R., Bloch, R., & Vasarhelyi, M. A. (2014). The Future of Audit. *Journal of Information Systems and Technology Management, 11*(1), 21–32. doi:10.4301/S1807-17752014000100002

McAfee, A., & Brynjolfsson, E. (2012). Big data: The Management Revolution. *Harvard Business Review, 90*(10), 61–67. PMID:23074865

Medinets, A.F., Gross, J.A., Brennan, G. (2015). Case Study A. *Audit Analytics*, 147-156.

Moffitt, K. C., & Vasarhelyi, M. A. (2013). AIS in an Age of Big Data. *Journal of Information Systems, 27*(2), 1–19. doi:10.2308/isys-10372

Pathak, J., Chaouch, B., & Sriram, R. S. (2005). Minimizing cost of continuous audit: Counting and time dependent strategies. *Journal of Accounting and Public Policy, 24*(1), 61–75. doi:10.1016/j.jaccpubpol.2004.12.004

Press, G. (2013). $16.1 Billion Big Data Market Predictions From IDC And IIA. *Forbes.*

Rikhardsson, P., & Dull, R. (2016). An exploratory study of the adoption, application and impacts of continuous auditing technologies in small businesses. *International Journal of Accounting Information Systems, 20*, 26–37. doi:10.1016/j.accinf.2016.01.003

Santos, C., Sousa, P., Ferreira, C., & Tribolet, J. (2008). Conceptual Model for Continuous Organizational Auditing with Real Time Analysis and Modern Control Theory+. *Journal of Emerging Technologies in Accounting*, *5*(1), 37–63. doi:10.2308/jeta.2008.5.1.37

Singh, K., Best, P. J., Bojilov, M., & Blunt, C. (2014). Continuous Auditing and Continuous Monitoring in ERP Environments: Case Studies of Application Implementations. *Journal of Information Systems*, *28*(1), 287–310. doi:10.2308/isys-50679

Sun, T., Alles, M., & Vasarhelyi, M. A. (2015). Adopting continuous auditing : A cross-sectional comparison between China and the United States (Kaynakçasına ileride bakmayı UNUTMA!!!). *Managerial Auditing Journal*, *30*(2), 176–204. doi:10.1108/MAJ-08-2014-1080

Thiprungsri, S., & Vasarhelyi, M. (2011). Cluster analysis for anomaly detection in accounting. *The International Journal of Digital Accounting Research*, *11*, 69–84.

Tysiac, K. (2015). Data analytics helps auditors gain deep insight. *Journal of Accountancy*, *219*(4), 52.

Vasarhelyi, M. A., Alles, M., Kuenkaikaew, S., & Littley, J. (2012). The acceptance and adoption of continuous auditing by internal auditors: A micro analysis. *International Journal of Accounting Information Systems*, *13*(3), 267–281. doi:10.1016/j.accinf.2012.06.011

Vasarhelyi, M. A., Halper, F. B., & Ezawa, K. J. (1991). The Continuous Process Audit System: a UNIX-based auditing tool. *EDP Auditor Journal*, 85-91.

Vasarhelyi, M. A., Warren, J. D., Teeter, R. A., & Titera, W. R. (2014). Embracing the Automated Audit. *Journal of Accountancy*, *217*(4), 34–37.

Wang, T., & Cuthbertson, R. (2015). Eight Issues on Audit Data Analytics We Would Like Researched. *Journal of Information Systems*, *29*(1), 155–162. doi:10.2308/isys-50955

Warren, J. D. Jr, Moffitt, K. C., & Byrnes, P. (2015). How big data will change accounting. *Accounting Horizons*, *29*(2), 397–407. doi:10.2308/acch-51069

Yoon, K., Hoogduin, L., & Zhang, L. (2015). Big data as complementary audit evidence. *Accounting Horizons*, *29*(2), 431–438. doi:10.2308/acch-51076

Zhang, J., Yang, X., & Appelbaum, D. (2015). Toward effective big data analysis in continuous auditing. *Accounting Horizons*, *29*(2), 469–476. doi:10.2308/acch-51070

KEY TERMS AND DEFINITIONS

Archival Study: Studies utilize sources from secondary records.

Auditing: Accumulation and evaluation of evidence about information to determine and report on the degree of correspondence between the information and established criteria.

Big Data: The generation of data has started to outpace the processing capabilities of the typical technology tools.

Continuous Auditing: A methodology for issuing audit reports simultaneously with, or a short period after, the occurrence of the relevant events.

Datafication: A modern technological trend turning many aspects of our life into computerized data and transforming this information into new forms of value.

Structured Data: Data that fit into a defined schema, such as relational data.

Unstructured Data: Information that either does not have a pre-defined data model or is not organized in a pre-defined manner.

Chapter 8
Addressing Continuous Auditing Challenges in the Digital Age:
A Literature Review

Hugo Miguel Cipriano
Instituto Universitário de Lisboa, Portugal

Ruben Pereira
Instituto Universitário de Lisboa, Portugal

Rafael Almeida
Universidade de Lisboa, Portugal

Miguel MIra da Silva
Universidade de Lisboa, Portugal

ABSTRACT

Organizations face a challenge on the emerging technology-enabled businesses to prevent fraud and mitigate risks. Information technology (IT) advancements also provided the possibility of ongoing risk assessment and ongoing control assessment on the growing data volume in the digital age. Although organizations perceive the benefits of continuous auditing (CA) and continuous monitoring (CM), its adoption is low. Some barriers limit CA and CM adoption along with common challenges that organizations must face during implementation. This chapter provides a systematic literature review to promote CA and CM by presenting the main challenges in implementations and general guidance to overcome the identified challenges.

DOI: 10.4018/978-1-5225-7356-2.ch008

INTRODUCTION

Currently, organizations are completely dependent on information technology (IT) and information systems (IS) to deliver value to their customers and reach higher performance levels (Jacobson, 2009). Moreover, organizations are now facing times of digital revolution. Throughout the last two decades, IT/IS evolved at an exponential rate leading to a digital transformation in several industries and businesses (Bharati et al., 2009; Law & Ngai, 2005). Such digital transformation era seems to be a reality that organizations must embrace. However, organizations must also be aware of the outcoming risks and properly control them.

When technology develops faster than regulations, there is a higher risk of scandals and fraud which may lead to financial and reputational losses. Significant corporate and accounting scandals led to the implementation specific regulations such as Sarbanes-Oxley (SOX) act in 2002. To comply with such regulations' requirements organizations implemented internal controls to mitigate risks and consequently reducing fraud. In 2011 the Association of Certified Fraud Examiners (ACFE) estimated that organizations lose 5% of their revenues to fraud (Association of Certified Fraud Examiners, 2018). Even facing numerous compliance obligations (Protiviti, 2013) organizations fraud is increasing(KPMG, 2013).

We are facing times where IT/IS are being used by organizations to help them collect more and more information to support decision making (Power, Sharda, & Burstein, 2015). However, decision making has an associated risk, and as the volume of information grows, the ability to deal with it decreases (KPMG, 2013). A study conducted by PwC demonstrated that its respondents expected internal audit to be a *trusted advisor* (PwC, 2014). Internal audit reliance is increasing yet their budgets are decreasing (Protiviti, 2012; PwC, 2012). To do more with less, internal audit urges to increase its productivity.

Nowadays, organizational IS are capable of processing and logging huge amounts of transactions, however, manually finding wrong actions among these is costly and wouldn't guarantee the needed assurance additionally data generation is growing at an exponential rate (Singh, Best, Bojilov, & Blunt, 2014). This increases the chances of not noticing a problem within time of corrective action.

IT advancements also provided the possibility of new auditing and internal control approaches. Continuous Auditing (CA) and Continuous Monitoring (CM) provide the ability to verify 100% of the data based on a determined ruleset, shorten audit cycles while providing near real-time alerts on unexpected situations allowing faster responses to unusual situations to prevent or mitigate impacts. It is believed that only 0.5% of the world's generated data is analyzed and thus, there is plentiful of potential insights given by the remaining data (Gantz & Reinsel, 2012).

Continuous assurance, CA and CM are three commonly used terms to describe this thematic. Most authors define frontiers between these related terms(M. G. Alles, Kogan, & Vasarhelyi, 2008; David Coderre, 2015; Deloitte, 2010; Gonzalez, Sharma, & Galletta, 2012; M. A. Vasarhelyi, Alles, Kuenkaikaew, & Littley, 2012; M. Vasarhelyi, Vasarhelyi, Alles, & Kogan, 2004). Others state that there is no difference between CA and CM except who is responsible for each part (Marks, 2009).

Moreover, concerning the upcoming audit reform in the European Union, as well as the propositions of the digital age, one predicts increasing demand for high-quality audit results in real-time and once more thrust in CA research (Kiesow, Schomaker, & Thomas, 2016).

Most organizations believe that adopting CA/CM is useful (M. G. Alles, Riccio, Vasarhelyi, & Tostes, 2006). This is supported by KPMG survey in 2012 stating that the respondents understand the benefits. Respondents believe that CA brings assurance (89% of the respondents), facilitate real-time assurance

(81% of the respondents) and 90% of the respondents believe that CM identifies business process improvements (KPMG, 2012). The benefits of implementing CA/CM are perceived by most organizations but hard to quantify (van Hillo & Weigand, 2016).

Another survey taken by PricewaterhouseCoopers (2006) stated that 50% of the respondents have some CA/CM process which improved from the previous survey in 2005 with 35%. In 2009 a joint survey was conducted by The Institute of Internal Auditors (IIA) and ACL, a software technology company that provides GRC software, concluded that 36% of the respondents had adopted CA/CM and 39% are planning on adopting (Baker, 2009). In 2012 KPMG's survey only 9% of the respondents have implemented CA/CM on their organization, yet 83% have considered implementing it (KPMG, 2012). Based on these survey results across the years no conclusions can be taken as there seems to be an adoption reduction which is contrary to the growing rate of CA/CM academic research (Marques & Santos, 2017).

This proves that organizations are not only aware of CA/CM benefits, but they are also working and evolving new CA/CM processes and techniques. However, with the exponential growth of IT and IS organizations face challenging times ahead. More insights about CA/CM evolution, as well as main challenges and possible solutions to be applied, must be explored.

Organizations continue to increase its reliance on IT which potentiates not only value but also risks. Internal auditors struggle to deal with massive data volume while management expects them not only to provide assurance but also be a *trusted advisor*. CA/CM provides efficiency and productivity gains while performing value-based audits. Although most organizations identify the benefits of CA/CM they strive to quantify them which may lead to low adoption.

Therefore, the authors propose to perform a literature review on the CA/CM field based on the concept-centric approach proposed by Webster and Watson (Webster & Watson, 2002). This research intends to provide answers to the research questions present at Table 1.

The remaining document is organized as following: next section describes how the literature review was conducted and details the identified CA and CM implementation challenges; as well as on how to deal with and/or overcome the identified challenges; then the authors present future research directions and provide final conclusions.

Literature Review

A literature review was conducted between February 2018 and May 2018 on key terms such as *continuous auditing*, *continuous monitoring*, *audit automation*, *audit data mart*, *CAATs* and *audit analytics* which resulted in the collection of relevant articles from IEEEXplore, Scimago Journal & Country Rank, Google Scholar and Science Direct. Additionally, the authors have also looked on reports provided by major consultancy agencies and auditing associations.

Table 1. Research questions

Research Question (RQ)	Description
RQ1	Which are the main challenges organizations may have to deal with during CA/CM implementation?
RQ2	How can organizations overcome the identified challenges?

Then the authors conducted a backward references search followed by compiling the references contained in the previously identified articles. The references identified on the backward reference search were filtered by the number of times they have been referenced in the first step resulting in a final list of relevant articles. All the articles were carefully analyzed in order to elicit the most relevant information regarding the scope of this research.

To increase the scientific rigor of this research, the authors follow the concept-centric approach proposed by Webster and Watson (Webster & Watson, 2002) to maximize the relevance of the proposed conclusions.

CA and CM Implementation Challenges

This section details the main CA and CM implementation challenges that organizations can face. As previously stated, the authors followed the concept-centric approach. Therefore, Table 2 has the list challenges found among the literature as well as all the studies supporting them.

Justifying the Costs

One of the CA/CM potential benefits is reducing the cost of assessing while providing assurance over the adequacy of internal controls (David Coderre, 2015). According to KPMG's study, *organizations find it difficult to quantify the benefits of CA/CM which are needed to justify the business case for its implementation* (KPMG, 2012). Typically, in risk management initiatives, costs are more evident than the benefits (Deloitte, 2010). *Nobody ever gets credits for fixing problems that never happened* says Repenning and Terman (Repenning & Sterman, 2002), and risk management is mostly about mitigating problems that never happened but might happen.

Due to the nature of CA/CM its process implementation requires a significant and multi-year investment. These costs can be broken down into IT resources, such as hardware, software and IT employees; training, as stated on the Proficiency Challenge, and, not so easily seen, business understand efforts which requires effort from auditors and business itself (Anderson & Chambers, 2006).

Conversely, lowering the costs by reducing the effort needed to achieve results isn't the key factor on the CA/CM adoption. Gonzalez et al study indicates that the most important factor for CA/CM adoption is the performance expectancy (Gonzalez et al., 2012), this is also support by (M. A. Vasarhelyi et al., 2012) stating that costs aren't a barrier for adopting CA/CM say the internal audit department managers (M. A. Vasarhelyi et al., 2012). The main reason to adopt CA/CM is to augment performance. Auditors see CA/CM as a tool that helps them achieving performance gains on their tasks, such as increasing productivity, accomplishing tasks quicker and improving organization's financial position (Gonzalez et al., 2012), or freeing their time by allowing the computer to do repetitive tasks (M. A. Vasarhelyi et al., 2012).

Business and Audit Cooperation

In a traditional audit procedure, auditors and management are adversarial. In order to CA/CM flourish, the relationship between auditors and business managers need to develop. Continuous monitoring is a management process that assesses the efficacy internal controls. There is an inverse relationship between CM and CA. In areas where management has not implemented CM, auditors should increase their efforts

Table 2. Continuous auditing and continuous monitoring implementation challenges

#	Challenge	Sources
C1	Justifying the costs	(Anderson & Chambers, 2006; David Coderre, 2015; Deloitte, 2010; Gonzalez et al., 2012; Catherine Anne Hardy & Laslett, 2015; KPMG, 2012; Repenning & Sterman, 2002; van Hillo & Weigand, 2016; M. A. Vasarhelyi et al., 2012)
C2	Business and Audit Cooperation	(M. G. Alles et al., 2008; David Coderre, 2015; Deloitte, 2010; Catherine Anne Hardy & Laslett, 2015; Marks, 2009; van Hillo & Weigand, 2016; M. A. Vasarhelyi et al., 2012; M. Vasarhelyi et al., 2004)
C3	Proficiency	(M. Alles, Brennan, Kogan, & Vasarhelyi, 2006; Byrnes, Criste, Stewart, & Vasarhelyi, 2015; David Coderre, 2015; Flowerday, Blundell, & Von Solms, 2006; C A Hardy, 2015; Catherine Anne Hardy & Laslett, 2015; Kiesow et al., 2016; KPMG, 2012; Rezaee, Sharbatoghlie, Elam, & McMickle, 2002; Sharbatoghlie, Professor, Sepehri, & Professor, 2015; The Institute of Internal Auditors, 2017; van Hillo & Weigand, 2016; M. A. Vasarhelyi et al., 2012; M. Vasarhelyi et al., 2004)
C4	Managing Change	(M. Alles et al., 2006; M. G. Alles et al., 2008; David Coderre, 2015; C A Hardy, 2015; Catherine Anne Hardy & Laslett, 2015; Kiesow et al., 2016; Medinets, Gross, & Brennan, 2015; M. A. Vasarhelyi et al., 2012; M. Vasarhelyi et al., 2004)
C5	Data Access	(M. Alles et al., 2006; M. G. Alles et al., 2008; David Coderre, 2015; C A Hardy, 2015; Catherine Anne Hardy & Laslett, 2015; Laslett & Hardy, 2015; Rezaee et al., 2002; M. A. Vasarhelyi et al., 2012; M. Vasarhelyi et al., 2004)
C6	Data Reliability	(M. Alles et al., 2006; David Coderre, 2015; Flowerday et al., 2006; C A Hardy, 2015; Kiesow et al., 2016; Koskivaara, 2006; Rezaee et al., 2002; van Hillo & Weigand, 2016; M. A. Vasarhelyi et al., 2012; M. Vasarhelyi et al., 2004)
C7	Security	(M. Alles et al., 2006; M. G. Alles et al., 2008; David Coderre, 2015; Flowerday et al., 2006; Catherine Anne Hardy & Laslett, 2015; Kiesow et al., 2016; Koskivaara, 2006; Kuhn & Sutton, 2010; Lins, Thiebes, Schneider, & Sunyaev, 2015; Raja & Ramakrishnan, 2017; Rezaee et al., 2002; Singh et al., 2014; van Hillo & Weigand, 2016; M. A. Vasarhelyi et al., 2012; M. Vasarhelyi et al., 2004)
C8	Scalability	(M. Alles et al., 2006; David Coderre, 2015; C A Hardy, 2015; Catherine Anne Hardy & Laslett, 2015; Kress, 2016; Raja & Ramakrishnan, 2017; Rezaee et al., 2002; van Hillo & Weigand, 2016; M. Vasarhelyi et al., 2004)
C9	Script Adaptation	(M. Alles et al., 2006; David Coderre, 2015; C A Hardy, 2015; Catherine Anne Hardy & Laslett, 2015; Kuhn & Sutton, 2010; M. A. Vasarhelyi et al., 2012; M. Vasarhelyi et al., 2004)
C10	Exception Handling	(M. Alles et al., 2006; Byrnes, Criste, et al., 2015; David Coderre, 2015; Flowerday et al., 2006; C A Hardy, 2015; Catherine Anne Hardy & Laslett, 2015; Kuhn & Sutton, 2010; Laslett & Hardy, 2015; Raja & Ramakrishnan, 2017; Rezaee et al., 2002; van Hillo & Weigand, 2016; M. A. Vasarhelyi et al., 2012; M. Vasarhelyi et al., 2004)

on CA. If CM is being applied in business processes auditors should focus their effort determining the effectiveness and adequacy of the current CM process (David Coderre, 2015).

The objective of CA is to provide assurance while CM enables business process controls improvement (Deloitte, 2010; van Hillo & Weigand, 2016; M. Vasarhelyi et al., 2004). Nonetheless, both CA and CM rely on an ongoing analysis of data and can run on the same layer to collectively provide assurance and business support (M. G. Alles et al., 2008).

Based on Vasarhelyi's proposed audit maturity model the full continuous audit stage states that audit and business share infrastructures and monitoring systems. The goal is having the internal audit department generating an audit report and monitor results and business management receiving a summary of the results (Catherine Anne Hardy & Laslett, 2015; M. A. Vasarhelyi et al., 2012). Even though business managers have access to the monitoring systems, most of the times they never explore it to its full potential (Catherine Anne Hardy & Laslett, 2015; M. A. Vasarhelyi et al., 2012).

Proficiency

According to IIA's Standard 1210 *Internal auditors must possess the knowledge, skills, and other competencies needed to perform their individual responsibilities. The internal audit activity collectively must possess or obtain the knowledge, skills, and other competencies needed to perform its responsibilities* (The Institute of Internal Auditors, 2017). CA/CM brings a new agile paradigm, audit-by-exception (M. Alles et al., 2006; M. G. Alles et al., 2008; David Coderre, 2015; Flowerday et al., 2006; Catherine Anne Hardy & Laslett, 2015; KPMG, 2012; Sharbatoghlie et al., 2015; van Hillo & Weigand, 2016; M. A. Vasarhelyi et al., 2012; M. Vasarhelyi et al., 2004). This approach requires a different type of knowledge and different skill set compared with the most traditional curriculum for auditors is accounting and thus they lack the necessary skills to manage CA/CM (Byrnes, Ames, & Vasarhelyi, 2015; Rezaee et al., 2002).

Along with audit skills, technical skills are needed to deal with specific software tools, such as ACL and IDEA which are Computer assisted audit techniques (CAATs) tools. Moreover, developing routines for these types of software tools requires programming knowledge (Byrnes, Ames, et al., 2015; Catherine Anne Hardy & Laslett, 2015; M. A. Vasarhelyi et al., 2012).

Appropriate training is required to integrate different sources of data, understanding the data fields, understanding how the data is being updated on the data sources and validating the data (David Coderre, 2015).

Asking new and complex questions about the business to gain deeper insights requires not only analytics knowledge but also having the need of an interested analytics person or someone who is interested in developing that specific domain (Catherine Anne Hardy & Laslett, 2015).

Nonetheless, communication is vital to participate in multi-stakeholder interactions and effectively report insights on large volumes of data utilizing data visualization techniques (Catherine Anne Hardy & Laslett, 2015).

Along with these, additional business knowledge is required to understand the business systems and how they support the business itself (David Coderre, 2015).

Managing Change

CA is a new paradigm that exploits IT advancements to automate auditing procedures and minimize the lag between an event and the assurance of that event enabling ongoing risk and control assessments. This is achieved by using IS like ERP, data analysis, CAATs and business intelligence software (David Coderre, 2015; M. A. Vasarhelyi et al., 2012). Given this, CA/CM involves a reengineer of the auditing process to make it as much automated as possible (M. Alles et al., 2006; M. G. Alles et al., 2008; Kiesow et al., 2016; M. A. Vasarhelyi et al., 2012; M. Vasarhelyi et al., 2004). CA will revolutionize how evidences are gathered, how often audits are performed, how audits are conducted and the effort needed by internal auditors (David Coderre, 2015).

Traditionally, audit techniques depend on sampling data and providing a retrospective assessment. On the other hand, CA/CM creates an agile approach that handles exceptions on a timely manner (Catherine Anne Hardy & Laslett, 2015). This allows auditors to examine business processes from an analytical point of view enabling deeper insights as well as offering business advice to become the *trusted advisor* business managers expect (C A Hardy, 2015).

Data Access

One of the reasons why traditional audit methodology consists in testing sampled data is the difficulty and the cost of accessing data (M. G. Alles et al., 2008). Even though it is easier to access data nowadays, data access is still troublesome for auditors (M. A. Vasarhelyi et al., 2012).

Traditionally, auditors captured data during the audit process. The goal is to automate this procedure by creating an automation that accesses multiple systems and loads its data into an audit data warehouse (C A Hardy, 2015; Rezaee et al., 2002).

Interviewees reported that internal auditors do not have direct access to the data. In some companies, they need approval from the data owner or management before gaining access and, even then, the access is time-limited. Normally, data extraction is done by the IT division according to the auditors' request (Catherine Anne Hardy & Laslett, 2015; M. A. Vasarhelyi et al., 2012).

Data Reliability

Data reliability can be defined based on the following principles: integrity, security, availability, and maintainability (Koskivaara, 2006). A system that isn't secure isn't reliable (Flowerday et al., 2006). This is applicable to both organizations' systems and the audit data warehouse itself (Rezaee et al., 2002).

The reliability of business systems and transactional data is crucial for internal control, financial report integrity and business efficiency (David Coderre, 2015; M. A. Vasarhelyi et al., 2012). Therefore assuring data reliability on an audit data warehouse is also crucial (Kiesow et al., 2016) to enable internal audit the ability to base their conclusions on accurate, reliable (Flowerday et al., 2006) and timely data (van Hillo & Weigand, 2016), provide business empirical insights on risk and performance, creating value added audits (C A Hardy, 2015) and assure the effectiveness of the continuous auditing system (M. Alles et al., 2006).

Grounded on the previous statements, data reliability from legacy and modern systems, in different formats (C A Hardy, 2015), physical and logical data fragmentation, millions of daily transactions and the lack of enterprise-level data integrity across different systems emerges as a serious challenge (Rezaee et al., 2002). Modern systems such as ERPs provide in-built automated controls which increases its reliability, as opposed to legacy systems which suffer from a large number of integrity issues (M. Alles et al., 2006). However, data-level assurance is one of the most intricate and difficult problems that will face the real-time economy (M. Vasarhelyi et al., 2004).

Security

Access to the CA/CM system should be limited to auditors, business managers and corporate security officers (Rezaee et al., 2002). This security level should assess privacy regulations, and maintain privacy and security standards, such as the Directive 2013/0027 (COD), which aims to establish a high common level of network and information security in the EU (Kiesow et al., 2016), identical to its system sources or even exceed (David Coderre, 2015).

CA/CM can be based on three system architectures. Traditionally Embedded Audit Modules (EAM) were a viable approach to augment auditing and consisted in a module built into an application designed to gather and test audit-related data in real-time (M. Alles et al., 2006; M. G. Alles et al., 2008; Flowerday et al., 2006; Kiesow et al., 2016; Kuhn & Sutton, 2010; Lins et al., 2015; Rezaee et al., 2002; Singh et al., 2014; van Hillo & Weigand, 2016; M. Vasarhelyi et al., 2004), which reduces the need of large queries to detect such exception among multiple transactions at the cost affecting business performance or with the possibility of being manipulated by application administrators (M. Alles et al., 2006). EAM doesn't need any additional security management as it its audit module is embedded on the source system.

EAM Ghosting is a different approach that benefits from the advantages of EAM while functioning outside the application. This approach consists in mirroring the application to a different physical server mitigating the risk of affecting live production servers (Kuhn & Sutton, 2010), yet requiring additionally security measures.

Monitoring Control Layer (MCL) is the most recent approach (M. Vasarhelyi et al., 2004) and is defined as an independent external module which consists in extracting transforming and loading process (ETL), with data from multiple sources accessing it with read-only privileges (M. Alles et al., 2006; Rezaee et al., 2002), into centralized database (Raja & Ramakrishnan, 2017), generally a data warehouse or data marts (Flowerday et al., 2006; Kiesow et al., 2016; Kuhn & Sutton, 2010), to provide the ability of storing large amounts of data(Catherine Anne Hardy & Laslett, 2015). One of the benefits of MCL is being manipulation-free by the enterprise personnel. Conversely, MCL can't work in real-time thus it can miss suspicious transactions (M. Alles et al., 2006).

As MCL uses an independent and external module thus a secure and controlled system is needed to protect sensitive data (David Coderre, 2015; Catherine Anne Hardy & Laslett, 2015; Kiesow et al., 2016) and prevent unauthorized access (Koskivaara, 2006).

Scalability

One of the recognized benefits of CA/CM is the ability to test transactions on a much larger scale more frequently (C A Hardy, 2015). Analytics software empowers auditors to cover an entire universe of data, thus increasing the probability of finding errors (David Coderre, 2015; van Hillo & Weigand, 2016), and focus on high-risk business by identifying trends and predicting risks (David Coderre, 2015; C A Hardy, 2015; Kress, 2016). IT progress also enabled the cost reduction of transaction costs, information problems and increasing the scope in all business areas (Rezaee et al., 2002).

Being an iterative process, a CA/CM implementation should reside on a scalable system enabling the increasing volume of data extraction and test execution (M. Alles et al., 2006; Catherine Anne Hardy & Laslett, 2015; Rezaee et al., 2002). With the increase of technology enabled business, multiple systems coexist in an organization and may vary in technology (Rezaee et al., 2002).

Script Adaptation

After loading the data into a data warehouse or data marts, scripts can be used to automatically test all transactions, instead of a manual periodic review (Gonzalez et al., 2012; Raja & Ramakrishnan, 2017; M. A. Vasarhelyi et al., 2012) reducing auditing time by examining data faster and efficiently as well as reducing errors induced by manual procedures (M. Alles et al., 2006; Rezaee et al., 2002). These tests identify exceptions or anomalous transactions and confirm the correctness of transactions against a predefined set of rules (C A Hardy, 2015) resulting in exception reports. The goal of the tests is to verify transactions against business rules, norms that must be followed (David Coderre, 2015) such as

SOX (M. A. Vasarhelyi et al., 2012), internal control rules to validate their effectiveness (Rezaee et al., 2002; M. A. Vasarhelyi et al., 2012) or previously defined, observed or expected benchmarks (M. Alles et al., 2006).

Certain vendors on this subject offer pre-written script packages (David Coderre, 2015; M. A. Vasarhelyi et al., 2012), however due to the uniqueness of business rules that each organization follows, these could not be universally applied (Catherine Anne Hardy & Laslett, 2015) and were found problematic (C A Hardy, 2015) as there is a tradeoff between flexibility and complexity like any off-the-shelf product (M. Alles et al., 2006).

A large number of false positives is expected initially (Kuhn & Sutton, 2010), due to wrong parameter of sensitivity, i.e. low tolerance (M. Alles et al., 2006), depth of analysis or simply data interpretation errors (David Coderre, 2015), as business rules require considerable business experience (M. Alles et al., 2006; C A Hardy, 2015; Catherine Anne Hardy & Laslett, 2015) and possible highly skilled resources (M. Vasarhelyi et al., 2004). Leaving the parameter sensitivity too loosely can result in missing relevant exceptions (Kuhn & Sutton, 2010).

Exception Handling

Data analytics is the core of CA/CM, and can be defined as discovering valuable information from the data. This is achieved by using analytics techniques such as analyzing patterns to discover anomalies, identifying relationships among different data that aren't apparently connected, creating models to explain the historical data to furtherly identify deviations (Byrnes, Criste, et al., 2015).

To take advantage of CA/CM, exception handling is crucial to solve the problem within an acceptable time-frame and prevent a larger impact (M. Alles et al., 2006; van Hillo & Weigand, 2016). Tests identify exceptions or anomalous transactions (David Coderre, 2015; C A Hardy, 2015; Rezaee et al., 2002; M. A. Vasarhelyi et al., 2012) and these results must be reported, investigated and actions must be taken (Catherine Anne Hardy & Laslett, 2015). As previously mentioned, these results can lead to a massive number of exceptions, it is necessary that these exceptions are handled properly. This can be achieved by creating alarm systems that notify business management and internal auditors accordingly to its type (M. Alles et al., 2006; Raja & Ramakrishnan, 2017; M. A. Vasarhelyi et al., 2012; M. Vasarhelyi et al., 2004) with the help of data visualization techniques (David Coderre, 2015; Catherine Anne Hardy & Laslett, 2015), allowing further investigation, the so called audit by exception (Catherine Anne Hardy & Laslett, 2015; M. A. Vasarhelyi et al., 2012; M. Vasarhelyi et al., 2004). However it is important that alarm floods do not overwhelm the attention span of the auditor (M. Alles et al., 2006).

CA and CM Solutions and Recommendations

Justifying the Costs

Obtaining the continuous support from board and senior management is vital (David Coderre, 2015). CA/CM should be tackled from a Bottom-Up perspective and recognized as an iterative process engaging multiple stakeholders (Catherine Anne Hardy & Laslett, 2015). The collaboration with the first and second lines of defense is essential to provide results and managing expectations to continue with the never-ending process (David Coderre, 2015).

Automating controls can replace the amount of manual controls needed, and by doing so, the risk of an error is reduced as well as the costs of a corrective response. This exempts resources from problem solving activities, as problems reduce, enabling these resources to be optimized in value-adding activities (David Coderre, 2015; van Hillo & Weigand, 2016).

Considering technologies and capabilities on the organization's IT portfolio helps reducing costs (David Coderre, 2015).

Business and Audit Cooperation

Cooperation between audit and business managers is critical to develop business knowledge and transform internal audit into a *trusted advisor* to reveal insights from analytics (Catherine Anne Hardy & Laslett, 2015). However, the overlap between assurance and management is the biggest issue yet the biggest opportunity on CA/CM (M. G. Alles et al., 2008). At glance, the only difference between CA and CM is *who is doing it* (M. G. Alles et al., 2008; Marks, 2009), but even though they look similar, they differ (van Hillo & Weigand, 2016).

Proficiency

To tackle this challenge skills and knowledge must be built to make use and take advantage of CA/CM (David Coderre, 2015).

One approach is described as having each person assigned to a specific domain creating knowledge on that specific subject (C A Hardy, 2015; M. A. Vasarhelyi et al., 2012) . These people should be interested on that domain to develop specific skills. Retaining these capabilities is a hard task, as people tend to be trained and leave after two or three years(M. A. Vasarhelyi et al., 2012). It is advised to share the knowledge among each person to mitigate the loss of knowledge if leaves the organization as others are still able to carry out the task (M. A. Vasarhelyi et al., 2012).

A different approach can be taken as well. Auditors can rotate in and out from the internal audit department to various business departments with the cost of affecting internal audit operation and long term internal audit staff's breadth of knowledge and skill (M. A. Vasarhelyi et al., 2012).

Nonetheless, IT proficiency is transversal to every business and needs to be augmented to participate in the CA/CM process, more specifically, reviewing key data fields, the ability to create metadata, assessing the completeness and accuracy of the information and perform integrity tests to ensure data reliability (David Coderre, 2015) therefore resources with audit, IT skills and interest in analytics are preferable (Catherine Anne Hardy & Laslett, 2015; Sharbatoghlie et al., 2015). To coup with this, specific soft skills for instance, willingness to change, flexibility and teamwork are also enablers to the success of a CA/CM implementation (Kiesow et al., 2016).

Managing Change

To successfully tackle change, a strong leadership is required along with a specific change management plan. It should be approached in segmented phases prioritizing the most relevant business systems first. The following key steps should be considered when implementing CA (David Coderre, 2015):

1. A CA strategy should be well-established which involves coordination with first and second lines of defense, the establishment of priorities, gaining management support and adapting the audit plan to include CA.
2. Routines for data access should be developed along with the development of technical and analytical skills to assess the reliability of the source systems and prepare the data.
3. Determine key controls and evaluate its adequacy and effectiveness and design analytics to measure risk
4. Develop a repeatable process and align with CM to adapt the initially established strategy.

Focusing on quick-wins, by choosing a specific area with well-defined business rules facilitates anomaly detection while minimizing false-positives due to the objectivity of the defined rules, enables a faster recognition of CA/CM potential (Medinets et al., 2015).

Data Access

Like any other project, the continuous auditing and continuous monitoring projects require support from management, especially in the areas of access to data and implementation of audit-aid technology. To implement CA/CM it is necessary to acquire data from multiple systems, modern and legacy, in multiple formats while guaranteeing its completeness and integrity (M. G. Alles et al., 2008; David Coderre, 2015; C A Hardy, 2015; Rezaee et al., 2002; M. Vasarhelyi et al., 2004). Furthermore, talking with business system owners can facilitate the data access method and schedule (David Coderre, 2015). It is easier to access data on ERP systems, like SAP, due to the availability of specific tools to access it such as ACL Direct Link™ and Caseware SmartExporter for ACL and IDEA respectively (Laslett & Hardy, 2015).

Data Reliability

Ensuring reliability should be the goal for internal audit and senior management (David Coderre, 2015). Not only CA/CM benefits from the reliability of its source systems, CA/CM also contributes to the reliability of those source systems (M. Vasarhelyi et al., 2004) by auditing all the transactions inside organizations (Rezaee et al., 2002).

Data should be extracted automatically to ensure the preservation of its integrity and security (M. A. Vasarhelyi et al., 2012). After the extraction, numerous tests should be carried out before analysis to ensure its integrity (M. Alles et al., 2006; Kiesow et al., 2016) such as edit checks and comparisons with other sources (David Coderre, 2015). Data from modern systems and systems under IT general controls is more reliable than data from legacy and end-user developed applications (M. Alles et al., 2006; David Coderre, 2015). The level of validation may vary based on the reliability of the source system, higher reliability source systems need lower level of validation and vice-versa (David Coderre, 2015). Additionally, the more management monitors their information systems' controls effectiveness, the higher its reliability is.

To support a large CA/CM implementation, a robust relational database is advised (M. Alles et al., 2006), such as an audit warehouse or multiple data marts (Rezaee et al., 2002). This requires detailed metadata to manage large volumes of data with increasing complexity (M. Alles et al., 2006) along with data warehousing methodology investigation to ensure the data reliability of the data warehouse and/or data marts (Rezaee et al., 2002).

Security

Data should be automatically extracted to guarantee data integrity and security (M. A. Vasarhelyi et al., 2012). After the extraction of the data, tests are conducted and exceptions identified. These exceptions should be retained, while the remaining data shouldn't as the retention of sensitive data in a database carries additional security and confidential risks (M. Alles et al., 2006) besides increasing storage costs. Compression techniques can be used to provide storage space reduction, augment data security and improve database performance (Raja & Ramakrishnan, 2017).

Test exceptions can be reported in multiple ways, as detailed on the Exception Handling Challenge, therefore the way they are transmitted should also be secured (Flowerday et al., 2006). Some results might need an external communication and consequently security must also be assured through secured communication channels such as VPNs, web-enabled agents or Web Services (Flowerday et al., 2006).

Scalability

Implementing a scalable audit data warehouse enables a wider coverage of audit by extracting relevant data from multiple business systems into a single repository. Instead of a data warehouse, data marts can be used. These are *smaller data warehouses* that only focus on one specific business integrating data from a limited number of systems (Rezaee et al., 2002).

This approach enables the ability to discover relationships between multiple systems or business areas using analytics that otherwise wouldn't be possible as embedded audit models aren't built to communicate with each other among different systems and creating this feature would be cost prohibitive (David Coderre, 2015; Rezaee et al., 2002).

The process, as described above on the Security Challenge, consists on the ETL process. The information is collected from the production systems, through source tables and then transformed through a data standardization process (Raja & Ramakrishnan, 2017; Rezaee et al., 2002). Different sources might store common data, such as date, in different formats, therefore it is vital to develop transformation mechanisms to assure data standardization relating multiple tables from different sources. This can be achieved either in the source applications or in the data mart and the decision should be taken considering the cost implications on each. Appending, renaming, labeling or sorting data before importing it into the audit data warehouse are some of the possible data transformation methods and should be done considering business rules (Rezaee et al., 2002). Afterwards, data exploration tools and CAATs access the audit data warehouse. Data analysis such as data exploration, correlation, regression analysis, data summarization and statistical modeling capability provide business empirical insights on risk and performance, creating value added audits (C A Hardy, 2015). Audit tests are predefined rule-based analytics that can monitor internal controls (C A Hardy, 2015; Rezaee et al., 2002; M. A. Vasarhelyi et al., 2012). These tests result in exception that should be further analyzed and the architecture should be able to manage not only the growing number but also the results (Catherine Anne Hardy & Laslett, 2015).

Compression techniques can be used to ease escalation providing storage space and time reduction, thus improving capacity and performance (Raja & Ramakrishnan, 2017).

The CA/CM process should be fully automated thus tools used among the process need to be able to communicate with each other ensuring the extraction, audit tests, analysis and reporting. To achieve this automation level further application development might be needed to handle multifaceted data requirements (Rezaee et al., 2002).

Organizations and the world around them are constantly evolving thus CA/CM implementations will need constant updates in order to scale and maintain their capability (M. Vasarhelyi et al., 2004).

Script Adaptation

It is vital to prioritize the cooperation of business managers, owners of the business experience, and internal auditors as they must work together, on this critical learning process, redesigning and tweaking scripts to reduce errors and irregularities (C A Hardy, 2015; Catherine Anne Hardy & Laslett, 2015). This learning process might be costly to business manager as it will impact their work activities but will benefit auditors by developing enough business knowledge to enable the use of analytics and contribute to be seen as a *trusted advisor* (C A Hardy, 2015). The design of tests must also consider dynamic conditions and adapt accordingly to improve their accuracy however they should ignore pathologic conditions (M. Vasarhelyi et al., 2004).

Exception Handling

CA requires a reengineer of the audit process since it impacts how data is acquired, what tests are executed and how the reporting is made (M. A. Vasarhelyi et al., 2012).

Exceptions should be given weighting to prioritize specific exceptions by grading them, for instance by risk, to have a manageable result set (M. G. Alles et al., 2006; Flowerday et al., 2006; C A Hardy, 2015; Laslett & Hardy, 2015). Siemens implementation graded from 0 to 4 the severity of an exception, with 4 consisting in a critical failure, and even though there was no difficulty assigning a 0 or a 4, the intermediate scores were controversial (M. Alles et al., 2006). Even though there isn't a definitive solution for false positives, they can be lowered using techniques such as shutting down alert systems on specific time periods relevant to the analyzed process, such as month-end and year-end for accounting information (Kuhn & Sutton, 2010), more advanced techniques, such as statistical learning, to identify exceptional exceptions which is commonly used by credit card companies to identify potentially fraudulent transactions without overwhelming clients with false alarms (Byrnes, Criste, et al., 2015) .

The channels used for reporting may vary from simply sending results via e-mail, using a shared network folder, workflow (Catherine Anne Hardy & Laslett, 2015), dashboards or other data visualization techniques even though it is suggested that sensitive data should not be sent via e-mail, preferably it should be stored on a secured database or presented through a web-based platform (David Coderre, 2015). Having a workflow management system for exceptions allows traceability on the actions needed to solve the identified exceptions (Catherine Anne Hardy & Laslett, 2015). Like traditional audit, recommendations can be suggested to solve the identified problems (David Coderre, 2015).

FUTURE RESEARCH DIRECTIONS

Future work may pass by a deep investigation of each challenge or respective solution along with a practical application. Given the scarce amount of empirical work found among the literature, the authors advise future researchers to perform case studies about the challenges and/or solutions presented in this research. Such studies can provide deeper insights about how to deal with the identified challenges, validate the respective identified solutions and give practical examples to furtherly enhance the empirical work on this field of work.

CONCLUSION

This research aimed to explore the challenges organizations may have to deal with during CA/CM implementation as well as possible ways to overcome such challenges and succeed. Therefore, the authors formulated two research questions this study should answer (Table 1).

The first RQ focused on the challenges that organizations can find during CA/CM implementation. At section CA and CM Implementation Challenges the authors provide a list of the most common challenges found in the literature. From the list of challenges, several conclusions can be withdrawn.

- Having human resources with the right skillset to work with this new approach is crucial.
- Reengineering the audit process presents a significant challenge.
- Data access is going to be problematic and time-consuming.
- The trifecta relationship between audit, IT department and business owners is a bureaucratic process.
- Adapting the bundled scripts requires time and resources due to business needs which differ among organizations.

The second RQ intended to explore how can practitioners address and overcome the identified challenges. At section CA and CM Solutions and Recommendations the authors provide a list of some possible ways to overcome the challenges found among the literature. From this list of possible solutions, several conclusions can also be withdrawn.

Audit, IT and analytical are the areas that should be developed. To reduce costs, organization's portfolio should be consulted prior to any acquisitions. The adopted solution must assure scalability, as CA/CM continuous to grow, data reliability and security.

Data handling and false positive handling requires business understanding, so it is advised to create agreements between audit and the business departments. The whole CA/CM implementation takes time and should be treated as an iterative process with phased implementations to manage expectations and achieve the quick wins.

Mega-process areas like Payroll and Procurement are good starting areas as most commercial solutions have automated tests for them and most organizations use Enterprise Resource Planning solutions like SAP.

CA and CM provide an ongoing risk assessment and assurance over the adequacy of internal controls. With the ability to identify possible risks due to analytics the probability of a risk event can be reduced before the impact. Opportunities are also able to be easily discovered. Notifications on exceptions also enable the immediate solution to the identified problems minimizing impact as soon as possible. CA and CM also reduce the compliance costs while providing higher assurance by covering 100% of the transactions. Higher assurance guarantees data reliability and adds business value enabling data-driven decisions and insights.

Undoubtedly CA/CM implementations can improve organizations in many ways, but some barriers affect its adoption. This study contributes to promoting CA and CM implementations by providing general advice, key steps, possible problems and solutions to mitigate these problems.

Grounded on the previous paragraphs the authors state that the proposed RQs were answered. The findings of this research can be useful for both academics and professionals. While academics can use this research as a base to understand possible relevant topics for further investigation, professionals may look to this research as a good source of awareness before any CA/CM implementation project.

REFERENCES

Alles, M., Brennan, G., Kogan, A., & Vasarhelyi, M. A. (2006). Continuous monitoring of business process controls: A pilot implementation of a continuous auditing system at Siemens. *International Journal of Accounting Information Systems*, *7*(2), 137–161. doi:10.1016/j.accinf.2005.10.004

Alles, M. G., Kogan, A., & Vasarhelyi, M. A. (2008). Putting continuous auditing theory into practice: Lessons from two pilot implementations. *Journal of Information Systems*, *22*(2), 195–214. doi:10.2308/jis.2008.22.2.195

Alles, M. G., Riccio, E. L., Vasarhelyi, M. A., & Tostes, F. (2006). Continuous auditing: The USA experience and considerations for its implementation in brazil. *Journal of Information Systems and Technology Management*, *3*(2), 211–224. doi:10.4301/S1807-17752006000200007

Anderson, D., & Chambers, R. (2006). State of the internal audit profession study: Continuous auditing gains momentum. *Pricewaterhouse Coopers*, *30*, 5–12.

Association of Certified Fraud Examiners. (2018). *2018 Report to the Nations: Global study on occupational fraud and abuse*. Association of Certified Fraud Examiners.

Baker, N. (2009). Software trend spotting: Recent IIA survey results show many auditors use software to automate key tasks, though a surprising number have yet to adopt popular tools. *Internal Auditor*, *66*(4), 30–35.

Bharati, P., Lee, I., Chaudhury, A., Qureshi, S., Kamal, M., & Wolcott, P. (2009). Information technology interventions for growth and competitiveness in micro-enterprises. *International Journal of E-Business Research*, *5*(1), 117–140. doi:10.4018/jebr.2009010106

Byrnes, P. E., Ames, B., & Vasarhelyi, M. (2015). The current state of continuous auditing and continuous monitoring. *Audit Analytics and Continuous Audit: Looking Toward the Future*, 53–70.

Byrnes, P. E., Criste, T. R., Stewart, T. R., & Vasarhelyi, M. (2015). Reimagining auditing in a wired world. *Audit Analytics and Continuous Audit: Looking Toward the Future*, 87–103.

David Coderre. (2015). *Global technology audit guide (GTAG) 3: Continuous auditing: coordinating continuous auditing and monitoring to provide continuous assurance* (2nd ed.). The Institute of Internal Auditors.

Deloitte. (2010). *Continuous monitoring and continuous auditing: From idea to implementation*. Retrieved from https://www2.deloitte.com/content/dam/Deloitte/uy/Documents/audit/Monitoreo continuo y auditoria continua.pdf

Flowerday, S., Blundell, A. W., & Von Solms, R. (2006). Continuous auditing technologies and models: A discussion. *Computers & Security*, *25*(5), 325–331. doi:10.1016/j.cose.2006.06.004

Gantz, J., & Reinsel, D. (2012). The digital universe in 2020: Big data, bigger digital shadows, and biggest growth in the far east. *IDC IView: IDC Analyze the Future*, 1–16.

Gonzalez, G. C., Sharma, P. N., & Galletta, D. (2012). Factors influencing the planned adoption of continuous monitoring technology. *Journal of Information Systems*, *26*(2), 53–69. doi:10.2308/isys-50259

Hardy, C. A. (2015). Business analytics and continuous assurance: Theoretical matters, practice issues, and future directions. In *48th Hawaii International Conference on System Sciences (HICSS)* (pp. 4732–4741). IEEE. 10.1109/HICSS.2015.563

Hardy, C. A., & Laslett, G. (2015). Continuous auditing and monitoring in practice: Lessons from Metcash's Business Assurance Group. *Journal of Information Systems*, *29*(2), 183–194. doi:10.2308/isys-50969

Jacobson, D. D. (2009). Revisiting IT governance in the light of institutional theory. In *2009 42nd Hawaii International Conference on System Sciences* (pp. 1–9). IEEE.

Kiesow, A., Schomaker, T., & Thomas, O. (2016). *Transferring continuous auditing to the Digital Age – The Knowledge Base after three decades of research*. Research Papers.

Koskivaara, E. (2006). Integrating analytical procedures into the continuous audit environment. *JISTEM-Journal of Information Systems and Technology Management*, *3*(3), 331–346. doi:10.4301/S1807-17752006000300005

KPMG. (2012). *Continuous auditing and continuous monitoring: The current status and the road ahead*. Retrieved from http://mcr.doingbusiness.ro/uploads/517518efdd1e7CA and CM WEB DE-Survey.pdf

KPMG. (2013). *A survey of fraud, bribery and corruption in Australia & New Zealand 2012*. Retrieved from https://www.kpmg.com/AU/en/IssuesAndInsights/ArticlesPublications/Fraud-Survey/Documents/fraud-bribery-corruption-survey-2012v2.pdf

Kress, R. E. (2016). Transforming the IT audit function: Taking the digital journey. *ISACA*. Retrieved from https://www.isaca.org/Journal/archives/2016/Volume-1/Pages/transforming-the-it-audit-function.aspx

Kuhn, J. R. Jr, & Sutton, S. G. (2010). Continuous auditing in ERP system environments: The current state and future directions. *Journal of Information Systems*, *24*(1), 91–112. doi:10.2308/jis.2010.24.1.91

Laslett, G., & Hardy, C. A. (2015). Implementing continuous auditing and continuous monitoring in metcash: Change, capabilities, and culture. *Audit Analytics and Continuous Audit: Looking Toward the Future*, 157–167.

Law, C., & Ngai, E. (2005). IT business value research: A critical review and research agenda. *International Journal of Enterprise Information Systems*, *1*(3), 35–55. doi:10.4018/jeis.2005070103

Lins, S., Thiebes, S., Schneider, S., & Sunyaev, A. (2015). What is really going on at your cloud service provider? Creating trustworthy certifications by continuous auditing. In *2015 48th Hawaii International Conference on System Sciences* (pp. 5352–5361). IEEE. 10.1109/HICSS.2015.629

Marks, N. (2009). *A Look into the future: The next evolution of internal audit*. Retrieved from https://www.iia.nl/SiteFiles/CRCA Final.pdf

Marques, R. P., & Santos, C. (2017). Research on continuous auditing: A bibliometric analysis. In *2017 12th Iberian Conference on Information Systems and Technologies (CISTI)* (pp. 1–4). IEEE. 10.23919/CISTI.2017.7976048

Medinets, A. F., Gross, J. A., & Brennan, G. (2015). Developing Continuous Assurance at Siemens. *Audit Analytics and Continuous Audit: Looking Toward the Future*, 147–155.

Power, D. J., Sharda, R., & Burstein, F. (2015). Decision support systems. In *Wiley Encyclopedia of Management* (pp. 1–4). Chichester, UK: John Wiley & Sons, Ltd.

Protiviti. (2012). *Top priorities for internal audit in technology | Protiviti - Canada*. Retrieved February 26, 2018, from https://www.protiviti.com/CA-en/insights/top-priorities-internal-audit-technology

Protiviti. (2013). *Executive perspectives on top risks for 2013*. Retrieved from https://www.protiviti.com/sites/default/files/united_states/insights/nc-state-protiviti-survey-top-risks-2013.pdf

PwC. (2012). *A study examining the future of internal auditing and the potential decline of a controls-centric approach*. Retrieved from https://www.pwc.com/sg/en/advisory/assets/publication-internal-audit-2012.pdf

PwC. (2014). *2014 state of the internal audit profession study. Higher performance by design: A blueprint for change*. Retrieved from https://www.iia.nl/SiteFiles/Nieuws/PPPPpwc-state-of-internal-audit-profession-study-2014-03-en.pdf

Raja, J., & Ramakrishnan, M. (2017). Implementing continuous auditing and compression technique in log auditing. In *2016 Eighth International Conference on Advanced Computing (ICoAC)* (pp. 196–200). IEEE. 10.1109/ICoAC.2017.7951769

Repenning, N. P., & Sterman, J. D. (2002). Nobody ever gets credit for fixing problems that never happened: Creating and sustaining process improvement. *IEEE Engineering Management Review*, *30*(4), 64. doi:10.1109/EMR.2002.1167285

Rezaee, Z., Sharbatoghlie, A., Elam, R., & McMickle, P. L. (2002). Continuous auditing: Building automated auditing capability. *Auditing, 21*(1), 147–163. doi:10.2308/aud.2002.21.1.147

Sharbatoghlie, A., Professor, A., Sepehri, M., & Professor, A. (2015). An integrated continuous auditing project management model (CAPM). In *6th International Management Conference* (pp. 1–11). Academic Press.

Singh, K., Best, P. J., Bojilov, M., & Blunt, C. (2014). Continuous auditing and continuous monitoring in ERP environments: Case studies of application implementations. *Journal of Information Systems, 28*(1), 287–310. doi:10.2308/isys-50679

The Institute of Internal Auditors. (2017). *International standards for the professional practice of internal auditing (standards)*. Retrieved from https://na.theiia.org/standards-guidance/Public Documents/IPPF-Standards-2017.pdf

van Hillo, R., & Weigand, H. (2016). Continuous auditing & continuous monitoring: Continuous value? In *2016 IEEE Tenth International Conference on Research Challenges in Information Science (RCIS)* (pp. 1–11). IEEE.

Vasarhelyi, M., Vasarhelyi, M. A., Alles, M. G., & Kogan, A. (2004). Principles of analytic monitoring for continuous assurance. *Journal of Emerging Technologies in Accounting, 1*(1), 1–21. doi:10.2308/jeta.2004.1.1.1

Vasarhelyi, M. A., Alles, M., Kuenkaikaew, S., & Littley, J. (2012). The acceptance and adoption of continuous auditing by internal auditors: A micro analysis. *International Journal of Accounting Information Systems, 13*(3), 267–281. doi:10.1016/j.accinf.2012.06.011

Webster, J., & Watson, R. T. (2002). Analyzing the past to prepare for the future: Writing a literature review. *Management Information Systems Quarterly, 26*(2).

ADDITIONAL READING

Chan, D. Y., & Kogan, A. (2016). Data analytics: Introduction to using analytics in auditing. *Journal of Emerging Technologies in Accounting, 13*(1), 121–140. doi:10.2308/jeta-51463

Chan, D. Y., & Vasarhelyi, M. A. (2018). Innovation and practice of continuous auditing. In Continuous Auditing: Theory and Application (pp. 271-283). Emerald Publishing Limited. doi:10.1108/978-1-78743-413-420181013

Issa, H., Sun, T., & Vasarhelyi, M. A. (2016). Research ideas for artificial intelligence in auditing: The formalization of audit and workforce supplementation. *Journal of Emerging Technologies in Accounting, 13*(2), 1–20. doi:10.2308/jeta-10511

Kokina, J., & Davenport, T. H. (2017). The emergence of artificial intelligence: How automation is changing auditing. *Journal of Emerging Technologies in Accounting, 14*(1), 115–122. doi:10.2308/jeta-51730

Kokina, J., Mancha, R., & Pachamanova, D. (2017). Blockchain: Emergent industry adoption and implications for accounting. *Journal of Emerging Technologies in Accounting*, *14*(2), 91–100. doi:10.2308/jeta-51911

Koskivaara, E., & Back, B. (2007). Artificial neural network assistant (ANNA) for continuous auditing and monitoring of financial data. *Journal of Emerging Technologies in Accounting*, *4*(1), 29–45. doi:10.2308/jeta.2007.4.1.29

Vasarhelyi, M. A., & Halper, F. B. (2018). The continuous audit of online systems. In Continuous Auditing: Theory and Application (pp. 87-104). Emerald Publishing Limited. doi:10.1108/978-1-78743-413-420181004

Weirich, T. R., Tschakert, N., & Kozlowski, S. (2017). Teaching Data Analytics Using ACL. *Journal of Emerging Technologies in Accounting*, *14*(2), 83–89. doi:10.2308/jeta-51895

KEY TERMS AND DEFINITIONS

Analytics: A multidisciplinary field that explores, infers and communicates patterns in data.

Automation: A procedure that can be executed without any human intervention.

Bottom-Up Approach: An approach that starts with subparts to create a large unified part.

Continuous Assurance: The combination of continuous auditing and continuous monitoring.

Continuous Auditing: Technology-enabled automation that enables internal auditors to perform ongoing risk and control assessment.

Continuous Monitoring: Technology-enabled automation that enables management to perform an ongoing control effectiveness assessment.

Data Mart: A subset of a data warehouse that is generally oriented to a specific domain or business.

Data Warehouse: A system used for reporting and data analysis to provide business insight.

Chapter 9
Emerging Auditing Perspectives in the Age of the Fourth Industrial Revolution

Mahmut Sami Ozturk
https://orcid.org/0000-0002-7657-3150
Suleyman Demirel University, Turkey

ABSTRACT

The purpose of this chapter is to investigate the role of audit activities and auditors in Industry 4.0. The preferred methodological approach in the study is a general analysis of auditing in Industry 4.0 in the form of a literature review. According to the purpose of the study, the effect and role of auditing big data, the internet of things, the cloud, artificial intelligence, and other components in Industry 4.0 are investigated. Furthermore, auditing activities that can be implemented in Industry 4.0 are presented as suggestions in the study. The study explains the role of auditing as a whole in Industry 4.0 as a consequence of examining audit activities for each component in Industry 4.0.

INTRODUCTION

The invention of the telegraph at the beginning of the nineteenth century allowed instant orders for products for enterprises and communication among people across the country. Towards the end of the nineteenth century, the invention of the phone made it possible for traders to talk with customers in real time. The rapid spread of the internet in the late twentieth century enabled the marketing of products and services in virtual environments, and the instantaneous transmission of consumer opinions. But the rapid progress of technology brought about various risks. This rapidity of communication has also triggered the rapid spread of fraudulent and incorrect information. The use of advanced technologies in the global world leads to more information being exchanged and spread over a wider area, and more audit practices (Jackson, 2013).

DOI: 10.4018/978-1-5225-7356-2.ch009

There have been four industrial revolutions in history: Industry 1.0, known as "Mechanization," the usage of mechanical systems and the emergence of mechanical production systems between the years of 1760 and 1840; Industry 2.0, known as "Mass Production," the invention and use of electricity between the years of 1870 and 1914; Industry 3.0, known as "Computerization," the integration of information technologies into industry between the years of 1960 and 2000; and Industry 4.0, the fourth industrial revolution.

When historical industrial revolutions are examined in general, it is clear that there has been a shift from mechanical and manual audits to digital audits. In the past, auditing had a highly manual and human-focused structure. Auditors often tried to examine, conceptualize, and audit systems using manual methods. It has been seen that audit methods have had to be changed because manual control processes are insufficient for auditing complex production processes and business activities. Instead of traditional audits, technology-driven instant audits are now being carried out, instant assurance can be obtained as a result of instant audits. Currently, the application of technology-based audit techniques eliminates the problems and negativity of manual control methods. Automatic auditing is rapidly spreading with audit software.

Industry 4.0 is not an unmanned factory. With the increased use of information technology, it is important to create a highly human-focused organization that adds value for all stakeholders. In this structure, there are concepts such as the internet, connected products, machines, people, organizations, and virtualization. With industry 4.0, modern automation systems, data exchange, and production technologies are being used intensively. Audit activities should also keep up with Industry 4.0. Due to technology-driven change in the industry, an audit structure based on automation occurs in enterprises. Technology is a very important part of many controls. With the fourth industrial revolution, auditors are also strongly influenced by automation. Technology is a necessary tool for auditors, as well as enhancing the efficiency and effectiveness of the audit process. Nowadays technology-enabled auditing is spreading rapidly, and due to the use of automatic audit tools, audits are becoming easier, more effective, and more efficient. The use of automation tools in auditing activities may also bring about institutionalization and standardization.

Computer assisted audit tools and techniques (CAATTs) particularly increase audit efficiency and effectiveness (Braun and Davis, 2003). Also, successful adoption of generalized audit software (GAS) by internal auditors would help broaden the development of the technologies in audit activities (Mahzan and Lymer, 2014).

In the Industry 4.0 environment, audit personnel are able to provide digitalized services such as continuous auditing, continuous monitoring, and anomaly detection (Dai and Vasarhelyi, 2016). Continuous auditing is implemented in non-written, real-time accounting systems, and is aimed at assessing whether the presented financial statements reflect the truth. It refers to bringing together audit evidence in the electronic environment (Rezaee et al., 2001).

Industry 4.0 brings production elements such as product, machine, and operator into communication with each other through an open internet network. In this revolution, a new generation of "smart factories" has been established, and this period has become a lifestyle of the production sector. Industrial computerized control systems are beginning to be used in production processes that evolve into a smart factory. Nonetheless, Common Control Systems are becoming widespread in conjunction with Programmable Intelligent Controls. Due to the creation of smart factories in industry 4.0, physical systems are being transferred to cybersystems. Also, objects communicate with each other and with people. As a result, decentralized decisions are made. With blockchain technology and decentralized decisions, audits will no longer be centralized but begin to be implemented in all areas of the organization away from the centralized structure. In this respect, there will be no uncontrolled area, and control mechanisms will be established in all fields of activity.

The research question of the study is how audit activities take shape in the age of Industry 4.0, and the aim of this study is to investigate what changes have taken place in auditing as a result of industrial revolutions and to examine how audit activities can be implemented in Industry 4.0. The methodological approach of the study is a general literature review. According to the aim of the study, a general review of Industry 4.0 was first carried out, then an analysis was undertaken of the main issues that emerged in this new industrial revolution and how the audit activities could be carried out with respect to the main issues in Industry 4.0.

BACKGROUND

When auditing studies conducted in Industry 4.0 area are investigated, specific studies of components of Industry 4.0 draw attention.

For example, when the studies that have been done on big data are examined, the following publications stand out. Da Costa and Dutra (2014) conducted research into financial audits in big data fields. In their study, they examined new methods that could be exposed to the assessment and prevention of risks in the financial statements of the Federal State. They referred to big data and analysis. A publication published by Whitehouse (2014) describes the role of auditing in the era of big data. In a study by Kiesow et al. (2014), the role of continuous auditing in a big data computing environment is analyzed. The report, published by Ernst and Young in 2015, refers to big data and analysis of the auditing process. Jie and Fang (2015) conducted research into online audit-warning technology in the big data environment. Liburd and Vasarhelyi (2015) examine the relationship between big data and audit evidence in an article. In a framework published by the Institute of Internal Auditors (IIA) in 2017 (i), the understanding and auditing of big data is explained.

Continuing Professional Education's (CPE, 2016) study is about the auditing of cloud computing. In this study, the subjects of cloud computing background, security in the cloud, top security risk areas in cloud computing, auditing the cloud, international regulations, and e-discovery are mentioned.

Studies on the auditing of the Internet of Things include the following. Salman (2015) investigates auditors' responsibilities as the Internet of Things advisors, assurance of new risks, and the benefits of auditing. Tabuena (2016) examines the role of the Internet of Things in internal auditing and compliance. In Underwood's (2017) study, Internet of Things provenance, the benefits of auditing, forensics, and safety are researched. Erturan and Ergin (2017) examine the transformation in auditing and the application of the concept of the Internet of Things for the inventory cycle in auditing.

There have been some studies into the use of artificial intelligence in auditing activities. Meservy et al. (1992) applied artificial intelligence to accounting, tax, and auditing services. A study by Issa et al. (2016) raises a series of methodological and evolutionary research questions aiming to study the artificial intelligence-driven transformation of today's world of auditing into the assurance of the future. In another report published by the IIA (ii) (2017), global perspectives and insights are analyzed. The role of artificial intelligence for the profession of internal auditing is mentioned in this publication.

Dai and Vasarhelyi (2016) propose a new definition, giving the name "Audit 4.0" to auditing activities conducted in the Industry 4.0 environment. This article is one of the very rare examples of an audit study on the whole of Industry 4.0.

AUDITING IN DEVELOPING PRODUCTION TECHNOLOGIES

Industry 4.0

Companies need to follow and implement technology closely so that they can continue their operations and survive in a competitive environment (Erturan and Ergin, 2017). Recently, the concept of Industry 4.0, which is often heard throughout the world and was introduced in Germany, has had a profound impact on commercial and social life, while at the same time undergoing important changes that will change all functions of businesses.

The first industrial revolution, which started with the use of machines as production tools in the second half of the eighteenth century, enabled the mechanization of production. With the second industrial revolution, the production capacities of the machines were increased and mass production evolved. The third industrial revolution, which resulted in the use of computer technology and automation at a basic level, enabled the digitization of production. The fourth industrial revolution is defined as the ability of machines to communicate amongst themselves, especially on the internet, and to coordinate intelligent and self-managing production facilities. Industry 4.0 is shaped on the basis of the intelligent production concept (Yazıcı and Düzkaya, 2016).

Like all industrial revolutions, needs and expectations have also created Industry 4.0.

The ability of machines to be coordinated by computers and internet technologies, along with the replacement of human power by machine power, can be described as Industry 4.0 (EBSO, 2015). But Industry 4.0 does not only imply communication with machines. Unlike previous revolutions, it is possible to say that the technological developments interact with each other and move coordinately, and that all scientific fields are affected by improvements (Bulut and Akçacı, 2017).

Industry 4.0 is characterized by three distinct features, as follows (Özsoylu, 2017):

- **Speed:** Industrial developments change very rapidly. Every day a new technological development takes place. These developments always pave the way for better development.
- **Width and Depth:** This rapid development leads not only to the structure of production, but also to profound changes in business, society, and individual living conditions.
- **System Impact:** Industry 4.0 changes the structure of companies, sectors, and even whole countries, and includes a holistic transformation of systems.

The main purpose of the fourth industrial revolution technology, which is rapidly spreading, is to establish factories that are made up of self-managing production processes. This is possible only with the "Cyber-Physical System" and the "Internet of Things." It is also useful to know about the other technologies in Industry 4.0 in order to understand it (EBSO, 2015).

Auditing in Industry 4.0

Today in the Industry 4.0 environment, internal auditors constantly face new and improved technologies. Mobile devices, cloud computing, and social media help the improvement of businesses. It is important to realize that the proper use and management of these applications is difficult, and that they bring their own risks. Therefore, technology expertise has become a necessary qualification for the auditing profession. To obtain assurance in a virtualized environment, auditors should have full knowledge of the technology in Industry 4.0 (Jackson, 2013).

There are basic topics, such as big data, the Internet of Things, the cloud, artificial intelligence and other technologies, in Industry 4.0. The role and impact of auditing on these components will be explored in order to investigate the role of auditing in Industry 4.0. Auditing activities that can be performed in Industry 4.0 will also be offered as a recommendation at the end of this section.

Big Data

Nowadays, data is produced with the help of machines or other devices, and also stored on cloud computing systems. Big data has a very important place in Industry 4.0. Also, according to the German government, big data underpins Industry 4.0 (Pamuk and Soysal, 2018).

Such large quantities of data are stored, analyzed, and then converted into meaningful information through secure systems. For businesses in particular, possible errors are prevented by foresight, and the possibility of their occurrence is evaluated in advance (Siemens, 2018).

Entities such as machines and production tools in the factory, intelligent products, and cloud applications can communicate and interact with each other in an interactive way.

Since large amounts of data are used for analysis of big data systems, audit programs should also include testing steps to ensure the safety, privacy, and quality of the data to be used in the analyses. Since big data sets are intended to address everything about events and situations, data is collected from many different sources. Therefore, audit programs should provide reasonable assurance that data is protected from unauthorized access and can only be viewed by authorized persons. In addition, audit programs should test the quality of the data-entry qualification, the quality of the output, and system reporting. Thus, the quality of key system data and reports can be improved (IIA-i, 2017).

From the perspective of external auditors, an examination of customers who use big data and analytics in their audit contracts to compete in today's business world should take place. The customer's systems are integrated with external data sources such as cloud computing, the Internet of Things, and social media. In addition, many customers use big data with new and complex business analytics approaches. This situation requires auditors to use advanced analytics. In the big data environment, audit experts must move forward with more predictions and have more sophisticated rule-based analytics (Appelbaum et al., 2017).

The board of directors and audit committees can be proactive by conducting early interviews with external auditors about the external auditor's risk assessment process and the scope and use of the data analysis in the audit test (Ernst and Young, 2015).

Internal auditing should take into account the role of big data within organizations as part of risk assessment and audit planning. If risks are important, internal auditing can set an appropriate plan to cover the scope of significant data risks and controls. Internal auditing has the opportunity to train the board of directors on big data initiatives, and emerging risks and challenges, and significant opportunities and benefits. Typically, the internal audit performs audits to encompass big data through multiple audits (IIA-i, 2017).

The creation of appropriate audit solutions to be performed in big data environments is extremely important. Using big data at transaction level increases performance and offers opportunities to increase audit quality. On the other hand, the complexity of analysis and control of accounting data presents a challenge for experts. However, compliance with privacy and security guidelines in a big data environment should be audited. Computer-aided audit tools and techniques are required for audits. In this context, it is recommended to use an Audit Cockpit, which allows the use of managed and monitored techniques together. In this respect, the development of the Auditing Cockpit, which allows the technical reorganization of accounting processes and the insertion of automatic control points into the analysis and processes, will provide significant benefits (Kiesow et al., 2014).

Internal auditors can benefit from big data solutions to support their data analysis in auditing projects. Since data is already purchased, combined, and integrated, an internal audit can derive significant efficiencies by receiving data from a data warehouse or data repository rather than targeting multiple source systems. Big data control programs will vary by organization and usage, and program governance is an important component of big data audit programs. Internal auditors should verify that the objectives of a big data program are in line with entrepreneurial business strategy. In addition, internal auditors should conduct tests to ensure that the big data program provides value and is fully supported by appropriate leadership within the organization. Although the specific technology and level of the suppliers of big data for big data solutions vary from organization to organization, internal auditors should ensure that the confidentiality, integrity, usability, and performance of big data systems are aligned with the needs and requirements of the management (IIA-i, 2017).

Transparency and accountability obtained in real time in business activities where big data is used is an important requirement. From the management point of view, auditing and analytical applications, as well as continuous audits, should be carried out by both internal audit and external audit units in order to ensure that large amounts of data, which is increasingly changing, are analyzed. At this point, the effectiveness, efficiency, and timeliness of audit activities can be increased (Da Costa and Dutra, 2014).

Compared with traditional audits, online audits in big data environments seem to reduce audit risk and work continuously in real time. Audit models with early-warning systems increase the frequency of audits, and remote audit activities become widespread. Embedded audit modules and audit-alert models increase the value of the audit report from integrated data. In addition to using audit-warning models and conducting online audit activities efficiently, there is a need for a team of experienced data analysis personnel and professional analysts who have been extensively trained. Online audits should be designed and optimized according to the specific characteristics and operating conditions of the company to be audited. Therefore, significant investment must be made in people, technology, and financing to create the infrastructure of online audits (Jie and Fang, 2015).

The domains of auditing may be changed by extended and non-traditional data sources (Vasarhelyi et al., 2015). Big data definitely changes business functions and the capability of business processes. Anachronistic business functions can be eliminated, and business processes can be accelerated (Appelbaum et al., 2017).

Regarding big data, automatic validation will limit the need for data integrity and population verification. Auditors should also verify with multiform evidence, not only with invoices and receipts. For example, different metadata such as photos, videos, and GPS location can also be used. Auditors are required to expand existing corporate data, but an obstacle is that new forms of audit evidence bring new risks (Moffitt and Vasarhelyi, 2013). Further obstacles are integration of big data and the traditional audit evidence, information transfer among clients, and information privacy, which should be considered when using big data (Yoon et al., 2015).

The factors that determine how big data usage will progress in audit applications are facilitators and obstacles. The identified auditing standards are the most important facilitator, whereas the greatest potential obstacle is the lack of trained personnel. In brief, there are many fields in which auditors can benefit from big data in both the near future and in the long run. However, against the challenges of the technological requirements of big data, they should learn to live with them rather than succumb to big data (Alles, 2015).

The Internet of Things

The concept of the Internet of Things first emerged in 1999 when Ashton made a presentation to P & G (Ashton, 2009). According to Ashton, the internet is today dependent on information that is provided by people. If this situation changes and computers become more powerful and able to gather information for them, it is thought that the errors, damage and cost caused by people can be reduced.

The concept of the Internet of Things is regarded by a commission created in Europe as the internet of the future. At the same time, the Internet of Things is defined as a self-organizing network that has an identity, a mind, and physical and virtual things (Erturan and Ergin, 2017). IoT is a revolutionary technology that solves problems that arise out of the ordinary, using software applications, daily objects, and internet connectivity (Oral and Çakır, 2017).

Along with the developing technology, the number of smart things and usage areas are increasing day by day, from intelligent phones to intelligent houses, intelligent metros and bus stops, it has a wide range of usage. According to research and advisory firm Gartner Inc., within the scope of the Internet of Things, 26 billion objects will be in service by 2020. Soon, machines will tell us what is going on and what should be bought (Stamford, 2013; Bircan, 2017).

The Internet of Things and cyber-physical systems will be able to communicate in real time with each other, and with people in cooperation. Both internal and cross-organizational services will be provided through the services' internet and be evaluated by users of the value chain. Due to Industry 4.0, the Internet of Things will be implemented in factories and make production environments smarter. In this way, complex products can be produced to the highest quality and in a shorter time. Control systems related to the Internet of Things should be established in uninterrupted continuous processes.

For businesses in all industries across the globe, it is understood that an audit of the Internet of Things system is necessary. Internal audit units should be confident that Internet of Things systems are operating effectively and that the control of risky areas is being carried out. Internal auditors may conduct audit activities on the resilience, security, occupational health and safety, monitoring, and coverage of the Internet of Things. However, auditors should use new auditing methods for specific areas of Internet of Things. By means of audits, businesses can benefit more from the advantages of Internet of Things (Salman, 2015).

The changes and transformations introduced by new technologies to the industry and the increasing number of internally connected vehicles and systems have brought new opportunities, as well as some risks. The internal auditing task, which is the third and final defense line, plays an important role in defining and defending the risks. Internal auditing also plays a vital role in compliance as an element of corporate risk assessments (Tabuena, 2016).

Internal auditors do not have enough information about the Internet of Things, so they should inform the company management about the benefits, advantages, and discrepancy of Internet of Things. Auditors can provide guidance on how to use Internet of Things in sales operations, product distribution functions, and inventory control activities in businesses. In addition, it is possible to conduct research into what kind of benefits can be gained from Internet of Things in other areas of the business in meetings with the management (Salman, 2015).

Big Data and Internet of Things interact with each other: there is a close relationship between the two. Many Internet of Things devices will produce massive amounts of evidence that can be designated big data. And big data can cause bring new challenges for data management (Underwood, 2017). Privacy in Internet of Things is also a significant challenge. To provide transparency and accountability, data protection requirements should apply to significant volumes of data that are produced within Internet of Things (Pasquier et al., 2017).

Cloud

In today's technology, people's need for data storage is increasing day by day. Cloud computing, a system that provides users with access to the internet from anywhere, provides the data-storage service to meet this emerging demand.

The storage of and access to the big data that is an essential part of Industry 4.0 becomes easy by means of cloud computing technology (Bulut, 2017). Cloud computing, big data, and the Internet of Things work together to provide important contributions to the industry.

Organizational practices involving cloud-specific policies, procedures, and standards should be disseminated. These applications should include the design, implementation, testing, and monitoring of distributed services. Audit mechanisms and tools should be applied to ensure the follow-up of organizational practices throughout the system life cycle. Control mechanisms must be established for the location, confidentiality, and security of data. It is necessary to review and assess whether the proposals of cloud providers are in line with the needs of the organizations. The security and privacy controls, as well as processes provided by cloud providers and performance indicators related to risks, should be continuously monitored. Sensitive data should not be placed in the cloud. Cloud providers should effectively use cloud security applications such as access controls, encryption methods, and data processing procedures to assess risks.

The audit areas that can be applied in cloud computing can be listed as follows (CPE, 2016):

- data management
- information security
- safety features
- resilience
- activity management
- compliance
- service security
- application interfaces

Auditing of secure data-storage services in cloud computing ensures a strong cloud storage correctness guarantee. And it simultaneously achieves fast data error localization (Kanchana et al., 2013).

But cloud computing imposes some risk concerns. There are some challenges in the field of cloud computing, such as technological complexity, security risk, the weaknesses and immaturity of cloud, lack of cloud computing audit standards, and contractual issues (Chou, 2015).

Cloud computing is growing very quickly, especially in the sector of service provision, and this is a new situation for security implementation in the cloud (Saxena and Dey, 2016). So, in other words, security management in information technologies is a significant challenge in distributed systems, especially for emerging cloud computing systems. Necessary precautions should be taken to protect data. In security management, a logging architecture can facilitate the monitoring of user data. So, this will be a solution tool for security (Massonet et al., 2011). Due to the lack of control and physical possession over the data, the integrity and security of the data are a matter of major concern. To deal with this problem, a remote data auditing (RDA) technique is generated for cloud storage systems that incurs minimal costs (Sookhak et.al., 2017). Cloud security challenges can be addressed by cloud security audits. To enable simultaneous cloud security audits, a cloud audit policy language is developed and integrated into the audit architecture (Doelitzscher, 2014). Cybersecurity is also a serious challenge in the cloud. Within the framework of cybersecurity, a properly specified audit trail can be an important tool in the fight against cyber-crime (Duncan and Whittington, 2016).

Another obstacle, the gap between the rapid technological evolution and the supporting standards and legislation in terms of assurance, reliance and information security, should be considered in the cloud computing audits (Bendovschi and Ionescu, 2015).

Artificial Intelligence

Each enterprise should establish its own artificial intelligence strategy that can take advantage of the opportunities offered by artificial intelligence. A framework can be established using artificial intelligence practices that can be dealt with in the enterprises under the following six subjects (IIA-ii, 2017):

- **Artificial Intelligence Management:** Artificial Intelligence Management includes the processes, structures and applications that are used to direct, manage, and monitor the artificial intelligence activities of a firm to achieve the objectives of the enterprise.
- **Data Architecture and Infrastructure:** The data architecture and infrastructure of artificial intelligence should be applied to big data. Accessibility to data within this architecture and infrastructure should be established, information security and confidentiality should be ensured, and responsibilities and roles of data owners should be addressed.
- **Data Quality:** The integrity, correctness, and reliability of artificial intelligence algorithms are highly critical. The data to be used in the field of artificial intelligence in business must be well defined and well structured.
- **Measuring the Performance of Artificial Intelligence:** In businesses that use artificial intelligence systems in their activities, how much artificial intelligence applications contribute to the achievement of the objectives of the enterprises should be carefully measured. Therefore, enterprise management should monitor the performance of artificial intelligence activities very well.
- **Human Factor:** Since algorithms are designed by humans, human error and mistakes affect their success. Therefore, in order for the artificial intelligence to achieve the desired results, the human error risks must be considered.

- **Black Box Factor:** The complicated electronic devices that are concealed for internal mechanics users are called the black box. Transparency and comprehensibility are not emphasized, since some of enterprises using artificial intelligence technologies have applied self-learning systems. The black box factor attracts attention in the complexity of artificial intelligence applications.

The use of artificial intelligence-based systems in audits provides many benefits to auditors. Some of those are effectiveness and efficiency, consistency, the creation of a framework for audit areas, improved decision-making processes and communication facilities, improved staff training, the development of specialization, and shorter decision-making periods. There are also some disadvantages in adopting artificial intelligence technologies. For example, the length of the decision-making period as a result of searching for more alternatives, the higher costs of installation, updating and maintenance, the prevention of professional judgment, and the risk that the tools and equipment will be compromised by competitors, as a result of which evidence in a possible court could be challenge for the enterprises (Omoteso, 2012).

Experts who practice in the auditing profession should not be deprived of the necessary information about future digital applications such as artificial intelligence. In order to be prepared for the future digital world, auditors in particular should understand the fundamentals of artificial intelligence, the roles of artificial intelligence in internal auditing, and the risks and opportunities of artificial intelligence. Internal auditors should assess and improve the effectiveness of artificial intelligence-related risk management, control, and management processes in order to overcome the challenges of auditing (IIA-ii, 2017).

Internal audit specialists are experts in identifying and assessing the risks and opportunities for achieving the objectives of an enterprise. Internal auditors can assist the enterprise in exploiting their experience on the positive or negative effect of artificial intelligence in the short, medium and long-term value creation potential of the business (IIA-ii, 2017).

When the results of the studies are compiled, it is seen that artificial intelligence plays a very important role in digital auditing. The results obtained by using artificial intelligence methods are similar to or better than those provided by traditional statistical methods. Artificial intelligence methods have not been used to date in order to address the question of auditor nomination. Artificial neural networks, learning systems, genetic algorithms, fuzzy logic, etc., and artificial intelligence will be used in auditing activities. In particular, process controls and interference of system by failures would be key elements of these audits.

Other Technologies in Industry 4.0

Due to the competitive environment within the industrial production sector, more factories have begun to apply advanced technological tools. Therefore, increasing usage of sensors and networked machines has led to the creation of the high-volume data calles big data (Bagheri et al., 2015). Cyber-physical systems are intelligent systems that are equipped with sensors that collect data about business movements that affect physical processes, and which are constantly linked together in a virtual cloud system by continuously changing data. That is, the cyber part of the system collects data from the physical processes and applies this data to the production processes through computer software (Alçin, 2016). Industry-based production processes allow systems to connect to different networks through various interfaces and communicate with different services. Just as everyone have access to a variety of content using an internet connection on smart phones, or through communication on different platforms with other smart phones in the industry, Industry 4.0 also communicates between Cyber-Physical Worlds to the machines. The best example of this is "Smart Factories" (Ghafory, 2017). Factories are becoming more and more intelligent thanks to technology that is being developed every day. The combination of Industry 4.0 technologies leads to faster and more efficient production. Therefore, lower costs can be obtained by means of them (Arıksoy, 2016). The use of industrial robots dates back to the 1960s. A robot called "Ultimate" was working independently of human intervention for printing at General Motors in 1961. However, robotic technology has developed very rapidly in recent years and now meets many needs in production. As robotic technology evolves, flexibility in production will be ensured, and intelligent production transition will be accelerated. Moreover, the widespread use of intelligent robots will reduce the problems caused by humans, and automation will become more widespread as robots become more intelligent (Özsoylu, 2017). With the 3D printers created by Charles Hull in 1984, 3D objects designed in the virtual environment can be transformed into solid objects. If someone has this technology, required apparatus can be printed, an object can be output from a 3D scanner, a drawn design can be prototyped, and even personalized products can be created. In brief, there is almost no limit to what can be done with 3D printers (Semiz, 2017). Another technology that comes to mind in the context of Industry 4.0 is "Augmented Reality," which can be termed a simulation. This concept initially evokes video games and the entertainment industry, but it is actually used in many areas, from military applications to the health sector, from education to architecture. When viewed industrially, this technology is used at every point in production planning, design, testing, and quality control stages (Siemens, 2018). Augmented reality is the transfer of objects in the virtual world into the real world in three dimensions. Virtual reality and augmented reality are concepts that need to be separated from each other, because virtual reality hides its users in a virtual environment and users cannot see the real world. However, by means of augmented reality, the virtual world and the real world are merged (Koşan, 2014). Simulation is a modeling technique that forms the basis for monitoring the properties of a real system by transferring data belonging to a physical system existing in the real world to a virtual environment. With a successful simulation, probabilities can be previewed in the virtual environment, and preparations can be planned accordingly. For now, simulation is currently used in the engineering and design phases. However, it is expected that simulation will be used in almost every area in the future, and at the same time, it is expected to be used for making quick and correct decisions (Çelen, 2017). System Integration is the process of bringing together several systems and operating them. It must also be able to integrate with many subsystems in order to improve the functionality of the systems. For this reason, systems should be designed to be integrated with other systems at the design stage (EBSO, 2015).

Other technologies in Industry 4.0 will cause auditing to evolve. Continuous auditing will be carried out using CAATTs and GAS in the audit activities in which the robotic technologies will be used in smart factories. 3D printers, simulations, and augmented reality will enable a transition from a traditional audit to a technology-oriented audit.

Necessary attention should be paid to audit activities in other technologies in Industry 4.0. In particular, it must be ensured that technological tools operate effectively and efficiently, and how well these technologies serve the enterprise's goals should be well established.

For the audits to be done, security should be given great importance. Technological tools to fight against cyberattacks and cyber-risks must be well protected. Because of this, cybersecurity audits must be applied consistently. Information technology audits should be applied continuously to prevent damage to these tools and technologies.

FUTURE RESEARCH DIRECTIONS

Audit studies on Industry 4.0 are extremely inadequate in the literature. Therefore, many studies can be made of the auditing of Industry 4.0. Audit studies can be done on each component of Industry 4.0. In addition, it is possible to research the whole of Industry 4.0 auditing.

In industry 4.0, the ethical dimension of auditing should also be integrated over robotics and automation systems. Therefore, ethical components must be trained by encoding the audits performed in the digital environment.

CONCLUSION

Along with successive industrial revolutions, audit activities are also changing and shifting. How auditing activities should be done in the context of industrial revolutions is an important subject to be examined. So, in this study, the role and effect of auditing activities in Industry 4.0 applications was investigated. The role of auditing in each major component of Industry 4.0 was analyzed in the study. Particularly, audit operations of big data, the Internet of Things, cloud computing, and artificial intelligence were investigated. Thus, it is explained how audit activities will be performed entirely in Industry 4.0.

Production in the Industry 4.0 system is likened to a system in which machines serve and share information in real time with products. In smart factories, products and manufacturing machines can communicate with each other via radio-frequency (RFID) labels. Machines can recognize the products through these labels. By means of this system, it is possible to store the information that a product transmits with radio signals in the digital environment from the beginning of production. A cyber-physical system emerges in this way, and because of the importance of this cyber-physical system in Industry 4.0, auditing activities should be applied in the technological part of these systems.

Audit automation can be provided by embedded controls placed in the business segments of organizations, and risk-based audit activities should be carried out in the digital environment. With red flags created in high-risk areas, systems can automatically sound the alarm. Alerts should be sent to authorized units in the electronic environment. In addition to red flags and warnings, it is also very important that these warnings are taken into account and that mistakes are corrected. Therefore, correction processes must be coded separately when the system is defined. In addition to red flags, alarms should be generated in the system for controls in the digital environment, and alarms should be monitored instantaneously.

Continuous audit activities are extremely crucial in the field of Industry 4.0. Due to the usage of technological auditing tools such as CAATTs and GAS, and the application of continuous monitoring and continuous auditing activities, continuous assurance can be obtained in the Industry 4.0 production environment. Thus, the level of reliability and accountability can be increased.

Quality auditing should also be given importance in automatic production activities. In order to produce the goods to the desired quality, the quality targets should be coded into electronic audit tools, and necessary controls and inspections should be performed. Also, the audit of information systems security, big data, and learning systems come into prominence within Industry 4.0.

By means of Industry 4.0, companies store the large amounts of data generated by users, in cloud computing technologies. In the near future, various assumptions can be reached when considering how auditing will evolve. For example, in the future, the independent audit firms that companies select in the virtual environment will audit the companies. Independent auditing firms will be able to instantly view the information that companies upload to cloud computing technologies and conduct instant audits. Thus, auditors will not have to come to the company. That is, companies will be able to select the auditors in the virtual environment, and auditors will be able to audit the companies in the virtual environment. As can be seen, in conjunction with the Industry 4.0, audit activities are changing beyond our wildest dreams.

REFERENCES

Alçın, S. (2016). A new theme for production: Industry 4.0. *Journal of Life Economics*, *2*, 19–30.

Alles, G. A. (2015). Drivers of the use and facilitators and obstacles of the evolution of big data by the audit profession. *Accounting Horizons*, *29*(2), 439–449. doi:10.2308/acch-51067

Appelbaum, D., Kogan, A., & Vasarhelyi, M. A. (2017). Big data and analytics in the modern audit engagement: Research needs. *Auditing*, *36*(4), 1–27. doi:10.2308/ajpt-51684

Arıksoy, G. (2016). *Endüstri 4.0: Akıllı fabrikaların akıllı güvenliği*. Retrieved April 15, 2018, from https://hbrturkiye.com/blog/endustri-4-0-akilli-fabrikalarin-akilli-guvenligi

Ashton, K. (2009). That internet of things. *RFID Journal*. Retrieved April 15, 2018, from http://www.rfidjournal.com/articles/view?4986

Bagheri, B., Yang, S., Kao, H., & Lee, J. (2015). Cyber-physical systems architecture for self-aware machines in industry 4.0 environment. *IFAC-PapersOnLine*, *48*(3), 1622–1627. doi:10.1016/j.ifacol.2015.06.318

Bendovschi, A. C., & Ionescu, B. Ş. (2015). The gap between cloud computing technology and the audit and information security supporting standards and regulations. *Audit Financiar*, *5*(125), 115–121.

Bircan, G. (2017). *Nesnelerin interneti nedir?* Retrieved April 15, 2018, from https://www.voltimum.com.tr/haberler/nesnelerin-interneti-ve-kullanim

Braun, R. L., & Davis, H. E. (2003). Computer-assisted audit tools and techniques: Analysis and perspectives. *Managerial Auditing Journal*, *18*(9), 725–731. doi:10.1108/02686900310500488

Bulut, C. (2017). *Bulut bilişim (cloud computing) nedir?* Retrieved April 15, 2018, from http://www.endustri40.com/bulut-bilisim-cloud-computing-nedir

Bulut, E., & Akçacı, T. (2017). Industry 4.0 and within the scope of innovation indicators analysis of Turkey. *ASSAM International Refereed Journal*, *7*, 50–72.

Çelen, S. (2017). Industry 4.0 and simulation. *International Journal of 3D Printing Technologies and Digital Industry*, *1*, 9-26.

Chou, D. C. (2015). Cloud computing risk and audit issues. *Computer Standards & Interfaces, 42*, 137–142. doi:10.1016/j.csi.2015.06.005

CPE. (2016). *Auditing cloud computing security.* Retrieved April 15, 2018, from http://www.cpeinteractive.com/session/cloud/

Da Costa, G. P. C. & Dutra, T. A. G. L. (2014). Financial audit the era of big data: New possibilities for evaluating and responding to risks in financial statements of the federal government. *Revista do TCU,* 54-61.

Dai, J., & Vasarhelyi, M. A. (2016). Imagineering audit 4.0. *Journal of Emerging Technologies in Accounting, 13*(1), 1–15. doi:10.2308/jeta-10494

Doelitzscher, F. H. (2014). *Security audit compliance for cloud computing* (Doctoral Dissertation). Plymouth University, School of Computing, Communication & Electronics.

Duncan, B., & Whittington, M. (2016). Cloud cyber-security: Empowering the audit trail. *International Journal on Advances in Security, 9*(3&4), 169–183.

EBSO. (2015). *Sanayi 4.0.* Ege Bölgesi Sanayiler Odası Araştırma Müdürlüğü. Retrieved April 15, 2018, from http://www.ebso.org.tr/ebsomedia/documents/sanayi-40_88510761.pdf

Ernst and Young. (2015). Big data and analytics in the audit process. *BoardMatters Quarterly, 9*, 6–9.

Erturan, E. İ., & Ergin, E. (2017). Internet of things in auditing: Inventory cycle. *The Journal of Accounting and Finance, 75*, 13–30.

Ghafory, I. (2017). *Siber-fiziksel sistemler nedir?* Retrieved April 15, 2018, from http://www.endustri40.com/siber-fiziksel-sistemler

IIA. (2017a). *Understanding and auditing big data*, The Institute of Internal Auditors. Retrieved April 15, 2018, from https://www.iia.nl/SiteFiles/Publicaties/GTAG-Understanding-and-Auditing-Big-Data.pdf

IIA. (2017b). *Global perspectives and insights artificial intelligence - considerations for the profession of internal auditing.* The Institute of Internal Auditors. Retrieved April 15, 2018, from https://na.theiia.org/periodicals/Public%20Documents/GPI-Artificial-Intelligence.pdf

Issa, H., Sun, T., & Vasarhelyi, M. A. (2016). Research ideas for artificial intelligence in auditing: The formalization of audit and workforce supplementation. *Journal of Emerging Technologies in Accounting, 13*(2), 1–20. doi:10.2308/jeta-10511

Jackson, R. A. (2013). *Audit in a digital business world: Big data, cloud, mobile, and social media technologies are transforming the business environment as well as the risks.* Retrieved April 15, 2018, from https://www.highbeam.com/doc/1G1-340425202.html

Jie, S., & Fang, Z. (2015). *Research on the technology of on-line audit warning in big data environment.* Paper presented at 5th International Conference on Information Engineering for Mechanics and Materials.

Kanchana, M., Praveen, C., Kumar, M. K., Hussain, S. N., & Kumar, E. P. (2013). Privacy -preserving audit of secure data storage services in cloud computing. *International Journal of Advanced Research in Computer Science and Software Engineering, 3*(5), 901–905.

Kiesow, A., Zarvic, N., & Thomas, O. (2014). Continuous auditing in big data computing environments: Towards an integrated audit approach by using CAATTs. *GI-Jahrestagung,* 901-912.

Koşan, L. (2014). Augmented reality applications in accounting education. *Cukurova University Faculty of Economics and Administrative Sciences, 2*, 37–47.

Liburd, H. B., & Vasarhelyi, M. A. (2015). Big data and audit evidence. *Journal of Emerging Technologies in Accounting, 12*(1), 1–16. doi:10.2308/jeta-10468

Mahzan, N., & Lymer, A. (2014). Examining the adoption of computer-assisted audit tools and techniques: Cases of generalized audit software use by internal auditors. *Managerial Auditing Journal, 29*(4), 327–349. doi:10.1108/MAJ-05-2013-0877

Massonet, P., Naqvi, S., Ponsard, C., Latanicki, J., Rochwerger, B., & Villari, M. (2011, May). *A monitoring and audit logging architecture for data location compliance in federated cloud infrastructures.* Paper presented at 25th IEEE International Symposium on Parallel and Distributed Processing, IPDPS 2011, Anchorage, AK. 10.1109/IPDPS.2011.304

Meservy, R. D., Denna, E. L., & Hansen, J. V. (1992). Application of artificial intelligence to accounting, tax, and audit services: Research at Brigham Young University. *Expert Systems with Applications, 4*(2), 213–218. doi:10.1016/0957-4174(92)90112-6

Moffitt, K. C., & Vasarhelyi, M. A. (2013). AIS in an age of big data. *Journal of Information Systems, 27*(2), 1–19. doi:10.2308/isys-10372

Omoteso, K. (2012). The application of artificial intelligence in auditing: Looking back to the future. *Expert Systems with Applications, 39*(9), 8490–8495. doi:10.1016/j.eswa.2012.01.098

Oral, O., & Çakır, M. (2017). The concept of internet of things (IoT) and creating a sample prototype. *The Journal of Graduate School of Natural and Applied Sciences of Mehmet Akif Ersoy University,* 172-177.

Özsoylu, F. A. (2017). Industry 4.0. *Cukurova University Faculty of Economics and Administrative Sciences, 1*, 41–64.

Pamuk, N. S., & Soysal, M. (2018). A research on new industrial revolution industry 4.0. *Verimlilik Dergisi, 1*, 41–66.

Pasquier, T., Singh, J., Powles, J., Eyers, D., Seltzer, M., & Bacon, J. (2017). *Data provenance to audit compliance with privacy policy in the Internet of Things.* Springer Personal and Ubiquitous Computing. Retrieved April 15, 2018, from https://scholar.harvard.edu/files/tfjmp/files/main.pdf

Rezaee, Z., Elam, R., & Sharbatoghlie, A. (2001). Continuous auditing: The audit of future. *Managerial Auditing Journal, 16*(3), 150–158. doi:10.1108/02686900110385605

Salman, S. (2015). *Auditing the internet of things.* Retrieved April 15, 2018, from https://iaonline.theiia.org/2015/auditing-the-internet-of-things

Saxena, R., & Dey, S. (2016). Cloud audit: A data integrity verification approach for cloud computing. *Procedia Computer Science, 89*, 142–151. doi:10.1016/j.procs.2016.06.024

Semiz, Y. (2017). *3D yazıcı (printer) nedir? nasıl çalışır? neler yapılabilir?* Retrieved April 15, 2018, from http://maker.robotistan.com/3d-yazici-printer/

Siemens. (2018). *Endüstri 4.0 yolunda.* Retrieved April 15, 2018, from http://siemens.e-dergi.com/pubs/Endustri40/Endustri40/#p=13

Sookhak, M., Gani, A., Khan, M. K., & Buyya, R. (2017). Dynamic remote data auditing for securing big data storage in cloud computing. *Information Sciences*, *380*, 101–116. doi:10.1016/j.ins.2015.09.004

Stamford, C. (2013). *Gartner says the internet of things installed base will grow to 26 billion units by 2020.* Retrieved April 15, 2018, from https://www.gartner.com/newsroom/id/2636073

Tabuena, J. (2016). *Internet of things' role in internal audit & compliance.* Retrieved April 15, 2018, from https://www.complianceweek.com/blogs/jose-tabuena/internet-of-things-role-in-internal-audit-compliance#.WvsGVYiFMdU

Underwood, M. (2017). Big data complex event processing for internet of things provenance: Benefits for audit, forensics, and safety. In Cyber-Assurance for the Internet of Things (pp. 209-223). John Wiley & Sons, Inc.

Vasarhelyi, M. A., Kogan, A., & Tuttle, B. M. (2015). Big data in accounting: An overview. *Accounting Horizons*, *29*(2), 381–396. doi:10.2308/acch-51071

Whitehouse, T. (2014). Auditing in the era of big data. *Compliance Week.* Retrieved April 15, 2018, from http://www.acl.com/pdfs/CW_AuditingintheEraofBigData.pdf

Yazıcı, E., & Düzkaya, H. (2016). Endüstri devriminde dördüncü dalga ve eğitim: Türkiye dördüncü dalga endüstri devrimine hazır mı? *Journal of Education and Humanities: Theory and Practice*, *7*(13), 49–88.

Yoon, K., Hoogduin, L., & Zhang, L. (2015). Big data as complementary audit evidence. *Accounting Horizons*, *29*(2), 431–438. doi:10.2308/acch-51076

KEY TERMS AND DEFINITIONS

Artificial Intelligence: An intelligence by which computers or machines behave similarly to humans.

Big Data: The whole of the processable form of high-volume data obtained from different sources.

CAATTs: Technology-supported audit tools and techniques that are used in computer-based audit activities.

Cloud: A technological tool that enables the storage of big data and access to data on the internet.

Continuous Audit: Auditing of the data created by information technologies in an electronic environment and obtaining an instant audit report.

GAS: Technological audit software that provides auditing of information in an electronic environment.

Internet of Things: Communication networks through which physical objects communicate with themselves or other systems.

Quality Audit: A systematic audit process performed by the auditors to obtain quality.

Chapter 10
Open Source Software in Financial Auditing

Tânia Correia
Instituto Politécnico de Coimbra, Portugal

Isabel Pedrosa
Instituto Politécnico de Coimbra, Portugal & Instituto Universitário de Lisboa, Portugal

Carlos J. Costa
Universidade de Lisboa, Portugal

ABSTRACT

The auditing software is an essential tool to the auditor, being a mechanism that helps to achieve auditing goals to obtain efficiency, quality, and to increase reliability on data analysis and evidence collection. The auditing software can be proprietary software or free and open source software. The purpose of this chapter is to understand which factors affect open source software adoption. To achieve these goals, a survey aimed at financial auditors was carried through, and 64 complete answers were collected. Results indicate that the most used software is the proprietary software and that 43% of the respondents belong to the first stage of open source software assimilation. Additionally, it was verified that the external environment is the macro factor, which positively affects the adoption of open source software in auditing.

INTRODUCTION

The use of audit software is relevant support for auditing, by helping the auditor achieve auditing objectives, increase efficiency, quality and reliability in data analysis and on evidence collection. Regarding software adoption, in recent years, several companies worldwide have been gradually making use of part or all the systems in the form of Copyleft. Among them are several large private and public groups, such as Lufthansa, Walmart, Dow Jones, Amazon.com. Also state bodies and institutions such as NASA and the Pentagon, also use free and open source software.

DOI: 10.4018/978-1-5225-7356-2.ch010

As long as free and open source software is considered reliable by the most demanding organizations in the world, it is relevant to analyse if it is used in the context of financial auditing. This chapter's objective is to answer the following questions: 1) Which computer tools are the most used by financial auditors? 2) Are auditors using Free and Open Source Software (FOSS) as a tool to accomplish their tasks? 3) What are the predictive factors that can significantly influence the adoption or rejection in the use of the FOSS for auditing purposes? 4) What are the facilitating and inhibiting factors in the assimilation of FOSS for auditing?

The main contribution of this is to increase the knowledge on the most utilized tools on auditors' daily work, and, mainly, on the free and open source tools for auditing purposes. In addition, authors intend to contribute to a better awareness of the process of adoption and migration to free and open source software for auditing.

The present chapter is composed of this first section, introduction, a section about the Background, then the objectives and methodological approach. The last parts of the chapter are results, solutions, and recommendations, future directions and conclusions.

BACKGROUND

In this section, the main aspect related to free and open source adoption and auditing software are analysed. This section starts with a comparison between free software, open source software and proprietary software. Then, it describes the evolution of free and open source software, the advantages and inhibitors of free and open source software. Then, it analyses the computer-assisted audit Tools/Software for auditing purposes and open source software adoption. The level of assimilation of open source software is also subject of study.

Free Software vs. Open Source Software vs. Proprietary Software

According to the definition of the Free Software Foundation's website - FSF (FSF, 2017), coined by Richard Stallman, Free Software means that users comply with the four freedoms in software usage.

The freedom to run the program as you wish, for any purpose (freedom 0).

The freedom to study how the program works and change it, so it does your computing as you wish (freedom 1). Access to the source code is a precondition for this.

The freedom to redistribute copies so you can help others (freedom 2).

The freedom to distribute copies of your modified versions to others (freedom 3). (FSF, 2017)

When users complain with these four freedoms, the whole community/society has the opportunity to benefit from undertaken changes. Access to the source code is a precondition for this.

Software that complies with these four principles is referred to as Free Software. Copyleft is added to the four freedoms referred to above. And according to the FSF website (FSF, 2017), it is a method that requires all modified versions and extensions of free software to remain free.

According to the Open Source Initiative (OSI), the Open source does not just mean access to the source code (Laurent, 2004). The distribution terms of open-source software must comply with several following criteria. It is expected to free redistribution and supply the source code. Derived works must be distributed according to the same license, and the integrity of the author's source code should be protected. The license must not discriminate against people, groups or endeavour. In what concerns license, it must not be specific to a product, nor restrict other software and must be technology-neutral. While free software emphasizes freedom, Open Source is an approach that more emphasis on software quality. (Raymond, 1999). These two concepts have much in common and are sometimes confused. However, the difference lies fundamentally in the will of the creator for the distribution and redistribution over the characteristics referred to above.

In contrast to the concepts above, proprietary software is software that is made available upon payment of a use license. The creator owns the rights to the software, not allowing the client to sell, query, modify or redistribute the software. This concept is associated with the Copyright that intends to keep the intellectual property private. Throughout this article, when mentioning open source software, free software, and open source software, it is assumed that they will all have the same meaning.

Evolution of Free and Open Source Software

Over time, this theme has been developed, according to its historical milestones presented below. Where its historical landmarks are presented (MUST always put an introductory text linking the various topics that will include in this). There are some associations in the U.S. In 1969, the first version of Unix was created by Ken Thompson, a researcher at Bell Labs. In universities, large computers used this operating system for some time. Universities and research centres distributed free Unix with their open source code. In 1971, Richard Stallman of the Massachusetts Institute of Technology (MIT) inaugurated the Open Source movement, producing several open source programs at the MIT Artificial Intelligence Lab. In 1983, Richard Stallman started the GNU Project and later the Free Software Foundation (Laurent, 2004). In 1991, Linus Torvalds made the Linux source code available via the internet and requested collaboration from other developers to develop it. Cooperation was positive, and in less than two years, Linux had already become a reasonably stable system. In 1999, Raymond published "The Cathedral & the Bazaar: Musings on Linux and open source by an accidental revolutionary," comparing open source development with the owner (Raymond, 1999).

In the Portuguese context, the Linux Caixa Mágica (Trezentos et al., 2007), was a distribution made for schools until the end of high school, giving support from 2000-2010. Ansol (ANSOL, 2018) represents the Portuguese Association for the free and libre software, defending and promoting the four liberties of free software. Free software is named after the four freedom rules, rather than the cost of its license. ESOP (ESOP, 2018) on the other hand is the association of companies open source software; this association has the mission of guaranteeing service quality of the Portuguese open source companies.

The use of free and open source software is essential in some sectors as the public administration in Portugal. Some important decisions were taken, especially in 2011 and 2012. According to the Law 36/2011 of 21 of June, is established the use of open standards in the computer systems of the government. In the 14th November of 2011, the Portuguese Government through the Council of Ministers Resolution no. 46/2011 deliberated the setting up of the "Project Group for Information and Communication Technologies" (PGICT) to rationalize and reduce costs in Public Administration (PA), regarding the management and use of Information Communication and Technology (ICT) Costs ICT . To reach those goals, the PGICT drew the "Global Strategic Plan for Rationalization of ICT in Public Administration (PGETIC)." This strategic plan was organized around five central action axis: (i) Improve governance mechanism; (ii) Cost reduction; (iii) Use ICT to enhance administrative change and modernization; (iv) implementing common ICT solutions and (v) stimulating economic growth. In the context of Axis V, related to economic growth it is proposed the measure 21, called "Open Source Software". The measure 21 Open Source Software has as its main purpose to promote open source software (OSS) in the Public sector. Its purpose is to make available the best OSS practices and solutions. The software contracting should be preceded by technical and economic viability study, using TCO (the total cost of ownership) and compared with FOSS solutions. This measure has as the main purpose increasing the usage of open source. However, it also allows negotiating with software's vendor better conditions for the public organizations.

Advantages and Inhibitors of Free and Open Source Software Usage

The use of open source software has various implications on microeconomics (Aparicio & Costa, 2012), such as cost savings for open source software adopters; increase profits per sale in the market; pricing advantages; flexibility for vendors; rise of the total market size; companies become more independent of the software houses in the long run. Open source software also may have a good impact on the macroeconomic level (Aparicio & Costa, 2012) regarding the balance of payments (BoP) it can improve the imbalances, because of the software licenses and royalties paid to the exterior. Regarding the labour market, it also gives the opportunity to create more employment in the country specialized in open source. According to the literature (e.g., (Aparicio & Costa, 2012; Costa & Aparicio, 2006; Kavanagh, 2004), there are several advantages related to the use of the free and open software. The social cost is low. FOSS increase independence from the suppliers. Initial disbursement tends to be close to zero. Hardware obsolescence is reduced than in proprietary software. FOSS tends to be more robust and safe. FOSS increases the ability to tailor applications and redistribute a modified version. There is abundant and free support from the community. FOSS tends to be very configurable systems and applications.

Literature (Aparicio & Costa, 2012; Kavanagh, 2004) also refers to the inhibitors related to the use of free software. For example, the user interface is not uniform in applications. Installation and configuration may be hard and difficult. Development and support labour may be scarce and difficult to train.

Kavanagh (2004) point out other advantages such as the possibility of sharing the source code and adapt the software to users' needs and software with higher quality when compared to other types, as it has more users. Therefore, software is tested, and errors are found faster and easily. As referred by (Kavanagh, 2004)some people indicate inhibitors in addition to those already mentioned as lack of guarantees and support since free software generally exempts the author from any liability and quality, reputation, and image are viewed there is not a well-known organization behind the software.

Garcia, Santos, Pereira, and Rossi (2010) carried out research with computer specialists, about the use of free software comparing it with the use of proprietary software. They point out that the main advantages are: reducing costs, ease of use, customization, safety and quality, less dependence on third parties, support and maintenance of software. However, they point out that the main unfavourable aspects are the support and maintenance of the programs and emphasized that social category was also low, revealing that the main issue on how users usually try to solve problems with software and try to know it better was not assured.

Aparicio & Costa (2012) mentioned that additional reasons to use Open Source Software are the availability of Open Source Software to individuals, companies and organizations, and the Government and the options to language customization.

Researchers also developed a study focused on local public administration to determine if FOSS is being adopted by the central government (Godinho, 2012) and also local government (Fernandes, 2011) . In what concerns local municipalities Fernandes (2011) concluded that they were used to support the most critical computer systems and to reveal the determining factors to the adoption or rejection of such technology. Fernandes (2011) concluded that 54% of the respondents were already using FOSS and three factors were particularly relevant to predicting the adoption of FOSS: Awareness of success exemplars, Existence of stable infrastructure and Availability of human resources in OSS (Fernandes, 2011).

Among management software as ERP, Enterprise Resource Planning software, despite the number of researchers working on the topic and the use of OSS at Academia, Open Source ERPs still have a low number of organizational users (Costa & Aparicio, 2006, Costa, 2007). Recently, there was an effort to translate and localize ERP software (e.g., (Batista, Costa, & Aparicio, 2013; Lopes & Costa, 2008) and to improve usability (Costa, 2010). Nevertheless, in Portugal, the invoicing system must be certificated by the requirements of Decree nº 363/2010 and this new Decree nº 340/2013. This situation creates barriers to the diffusion of open source software in the context of the corporate finance system.

Computer-Assisted Audit Tools/Software for Auditing Purposes

Computer-assisted Audit Tools, CAATs, are instruments that the auditor possesses to achieve its objectives, as they were defined previously in audit planning. CAATs are essential for streamlining the auditing process through process automation; complex calculations result in analysis and report creation (Pedrosa & Costa, 2012a).

Hunton (2003) state that there are two concepts of computer-assisted audit software: Computer Assisted Audit Tools and Techniques (CAATT) and Computer Assisted Audit Techniques (CAAT). Computer Assisted Audit Tools and Techniques (CAATT) is a concept that encompasses two categories, "Tools" that are software used to improve auditor productivity and data extraction and analysis, and the "Techniques" that adds greater efficiency and effectiveness to audit procedures. Computer Assisted Audit Techniques (CAAT) is a concept that brings together greater efficiency and effectiveness in auditing procedures.

The various regulatory bodies that group audit-related professions (as The Institute of Internal Auditors - IIA, The International Federation of Accountants - IFAC, ISACA and The American Institute of Certified Public Accountants - AICPA) advocate the use of information technologies for auditing. They point a positive contribution of Computer-assisted Audit Techniques to the effectiveness and efficiency of audit procedures (Pedrosa, Costa, & Laureano, 2015). Pedrosa, Costa, & Laureano (2015) define CAATs as "*any mechanized tool for auditing, such as general-purpose auditing applications, auditing support software, utility audit programs, and computer-aided audit techniques*." Their research also points out that several International Standards for Auditing (ISA) recommend the use of CAATs, namely: ISA 230, ISA 240, ISA 320, ISA 330, ISA 505, ISA 520 and ISA 570.

There are three categories of software for the audit process, according to Lanza (1998): 1) Data Extraction and Analysis Programs, 2) Audit management programs and 3) Instrumental utilities.

Data Extraction and Analysis Programs are intended to investigate the contents of tables in databases and generate comparative reports. In this category, it is included in the following software: Active Data, ACL Data Analysis, CaseWare IDEA Analytics, TeamMate Analytics, and SE Audit.

Audit management programs incorporate specific audit functions, such as risk analysis and evaluation, control of procedures and checks, the creation of automated internal control lists and questionnaires to follow up the audit. In this group, the following software may be included: ACL Workpaper Management, MetricStream Audit Management, MKInsight Audit Management, MyWorkpapers, SAP Audit Management, TeamMate Audit Management, Thomson Reuters AutoAudit, SIPTA - Audit Work Papers System, SIAUDI - Internal Audit and IDEAGen Pentana.

Instrumental utilities include all generic, non-audit-specific programs that have the potential to be used in auditing, such as word processors, spreadsheets, and data extractors based on SQL-Structured Query Language. In this category, we highlight the following software: Microsoft Word, Microsoft Excel, Libre Office, and Apache OpenOffice.

Kim, Mannino, & Nieschwietz (2009) proposed a classification on CAATs based on features, as Database queries, Ratio Analysis, Audit Sampling, Digital Analysis, Data Mining: regression/ANOVA, Data Mining: Classification. Pedrosa & Costa (2012b) included a new feature: Working Papers, to group all the software utilized to support and document auditors' procedures.

Open Source Software Adoption

Glynn, Fitzgerald, & Exton (2005)] conducted a study on one of the most important models of open source organizational adoption derived from the theory of innovation adoption. Adoption of open source software that is, identifying the factors that influenced organizations to adopt this risky project and the factors that prevented them from adopting it.

The model comprises four macro factors that are the (1) external environment, (2) organizational context, (3) technological context and, (4) individual factors.

According to Tornatzky, Fleischer, & Chakrabarti (1990), the external environment represents the space where the organization carries out its activity, referring to industry, its competitors, market regulations and relations with governments. Glynn, Fitzgerald, & Exton. (2005) state that open source software is a paradigm shift in software in an organization's business environment, and for this reason, the authors argue for the need to focus on the outside of the organization. It includes factors such as attitude towards risk in the activity sector; the existence of success stories in the adoption of open source software; government or institutional support; the need for transparency, effective management of public funds, security and the existence of purchase agreements with representatives of proprietary software.

The authors of the model identify the organizational context as a factor that describes the characteristics of an organization. This factor has been referred in some studies on adoption of innovation, as, is by Tornatzky, Fleischer, & Chakrabarti (1990) and Fichman (1992) on the need to increase focus beyond an individual level. The following factors are included in this context: size of the organization, the degree of centralization, support from the administration and the availability of resources (such as limited financial resources or the existence of human resources with open source software experience).

Technological context is related to the technologies that the organization has at its disposal. In this component, Glynn, Fitzgerald, & Exton (2005) add factors such as: technological benefits of open source software, the possibility of superior software quality, possible advantages of having access to source code, dissatisfaction with existing software, the ability of open source software to run on old hardware and the existence of a stable and coherent information technology infrastructure backed by proprietary software.

Individual factors Glynn, Fitzgerald, & Exton (2005) also include in their model the individual factors, based on the adoption of open source software implicitly has a strong ideological motivation, which occurs at the individual level. The charisma and leadership of an "OSS Champion" (someone in the organization with wide experience and motivation in the use of open source software, someone that may assist its pears in any difficulty) are factors that may also have a significant influence on the adoption of open source software.

These factors were researched in a large-scale context of the adoption of open source software at Beaumont Hospital, Dublin, Ireland. The factors that make up the model are presented in Figure 1, where factors that assume an increase in the degree of adoption of open source software are referenced with (+), and factors that are contrary (acting as inhibitors) to the adoption of open source software are referenced with (-). They concluded that the major influences in the external environment are the network externality effects and the fact that other organizations were adopting OSS. Concerning organizational factors, the fact that the OSS is free is seen as important and the existence of an OSS Champion.

Level of Assimilation of the Open Source Software

A relevant issue in the context of FOSS's use is the level/stage of OSS Assimilation. The assimilation stage may be viewed as a combined measure of the earliness of initiation of assimilation activities (awareness, interest, evaluation/trial, commitment, limited deployment, and general deployment), and an absence of rejection, stalling, or discontinuance (Meyer & Goes, 1988). Glynn, Fitzgerald, & Exton (2005, p. 230) run their research with the stages and criteria defined by Fichman & Kemerer (1997): Stage 1 – Awareness, Stage 2 – Interest, Stage 4 – Commitment, Stage 5 - Limited Deployment and Stage 6 - General Deployment.

Figure 1. Framework to investigate OSS adoption.
Source: Glynn, Fitzgerald, & Exton (2005, p. 226)

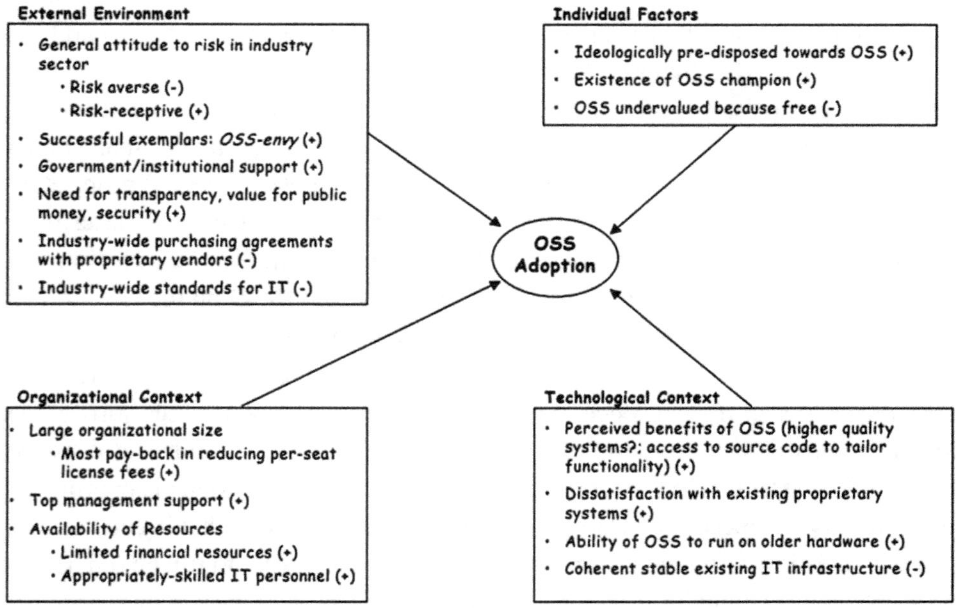

At stage 1 (Awareness), Key decision makers are aware of FOSS. At stage 2 (Interest), the organization is actively committed to learning more about FOSS. At stage 3 (Evaluation and Trial), the organization has acquired specific FOSS products and has initiated an evaluation or trial. At stage 4 (Commitment), the organization has committed to using a specific FOSS product in a significant way or for a production project. At stage 5 (Limited Deployment), the organization has established a program of regular but limited use of the FOSS product. Finally, at stage 6 (General Deployment) the organization is using FOSS product for at least one large and mission-critical system

The stages of assimilation are ordered, from the lower ("1 - Awareness") to the higher ("6 - General Deployment").

OBJECTIVES AND METHODOLOGICAL APPROACH

Research Question and Objectives

Free and Open source software is being used by the most demanding organizations, like American military forces or governments all over the world. Governments, and specifically the Portuguese government issued laws encouraging the usage of open source. But on the other hand, there are also some restrictions resulting from invoice software certification, that creates important barriers to free and open source software diffusion in the context of finance software (invoicing, billing, accounting). On the other hand, while billing, invoicing and accountancy are the first software systems to be implemented in companies, the use of software tools in the context of auditing is far from being an easy task. What happens in the context of financial auditing?

This study's objective is to answer the following questions:

- Which computer tools are the most used by financial auditors?
- Are auditors using Free and Open Source Software as a tool to accomplish their tasks?
- What are the facilitating and inhibiting factors in the assimilation of Free and Open Source Software for auditing?
- What are the predictive factors that can significantly influence the adoption or rejection in the use of the Free and Open Source Software for auditing?

The main contribution of this research is on the knowledge about the most utilized tools on auditors' daily work, and, mainly, on the free and open source tools for auditing purposes. In addition, the authors intend to contribute to a better awareness of the process of adoption and migration to open source software for auditing.

Methodological Approach

To comply with the proposed objectives, it was adopted a positivist and quantitative approach. Supported in the literature was created a questionnaire, focusing the main dimensions related to free and open source adoption.

The questionnaire includes a brief introduction to the research topic, 18 questions, and includes a final space for comments and observations. The respondents have an expected response time of 10 minutes. Respondents were assured that all responses would be confidential, and the results obtained would only be used in the context of this research and publication.

The questionnaire encompasses five areas of information, the characterization of the organization, the set of macro factors previously described (external environment, organizational context, technological context, and individual factors), the level of assimilation of open source software, knowledge and use of audit software.

The data was collected through the previous questionnaire in the online application LimeSurvey. The questionnaire was administered with the collaboration of IPAI, the Portuguese Institute of Internal Audit.

RESULTS, SOLUTIONS, AND RECOMMENDATIONS

In this chapter, the results obtained in the questionnaire will be presented, regarding the characterization of the sample, knowledge, and use of the respondents alluding to software for audit, macro factors influencing the adoption of open source software, and the level of assimilation of open source software that characterizes the organization,

Characterization of the Sample

From the 64 respondents to the questionnaire, 66% are male, with an average age of 38.56 years and the district with the most respondents is Lisbon. Regarding the academic formation, 69% of the respondents are graduates, and 31% are masters. Respondents main currently area of work is accounting (19%), auditing (15%), banking (14%), and government. They predominantly perform functions as internal auditor, external auditor, and auditing director. Their age at present function is, on average, 8.65 years and the average contact time with open source software has been 5.8 years.

Regarding the organizational characterization, which is based on the number of employees employed by the organization and the number of employees directly involved in the audit department, they present high values in the standard deviation, which shows a disparity of values. However, the most common number of employees is 10, with one employee directly involved in the auditing area, which indicates that mostly respondents belong to small organizations.

Knowledge and Use of Respondents Alluding to Audit Software

Based on literature review, respondents were asked if they knew several tools (despite they have never utilized it) and, then, if they use it or not: ActiveData for Excel; ACL Workpaper Management; ACL Data Analytics; CaseWare IDEA Analytics; IDEAGen Pentana; MetricStream Audit Management; Microsoft Excel; MKInsight Audit Management; MyWorkpapers; SAP Audit Management; TeamMate Analytics; TeamMate Audit Management; Thomson Reuters AutoAudit; SIPTA; SiAudit; Libre Office; SE Audit, and OpenOffice. Previous questions were relevant to answer the first objective of this chapter, "*Which computer tools are the most used by financial auditors?*".

Regarding audit software, it was concluded that the best-known software among respondents is Microsoft Excel (87.5%) followed by Caseware IDEA Analytics (45.3%), SAP Audit Management (40.6%), ACL Data Analytics (39.1%), and Open Office (31.3%). Respondents pointed new items as ACD Auditor, Rstudio, SharePoint, MyClient, Caseware Working Papers, and DRAI10. However, there was only one answer to each one of the new listed tools.

Regarding usage, 59 respondents answered the question using a Likert Scale (from 1-Strongly disagree to 7- Strongly agree). Taking the ones who stated that they "Somewhat agree," "Agree" or "Strongly agree," the software that is the most commonly used is Microsoft Excel (86.4%), followed by SAP Audit Management (18.6%) and Caseware IDEA Analytics (16.9%). Concerning Open Source Software, Open Office has 10.2% of respondents saying that they use it on a daily basis. Mostly professionals in the audit area use spreadsheets as the main tool. They often use the proprietary name (Excel) as synonymous of the spreadsheet. But even though, it seems that the proprietary software, like Microsoft Excel which was already mentioned in previous research for financial auditors: there is evidence that Microsoft Excel has about twice the number of users than its competitors ACL, Caseware IDEA, Access (Pedrosa, Laureano, & Costa, 2015).

Macro Influencing Factors in the Adoption of the Open Source Software

In the analysis of the factors influencing the adoption of open source software, the macro factors "external environment" and "technological context" stand out, as they present the most consensual answers, considering that they may significantly influence the adoption of open source software adoption.

In the external environment, it is observed - with the great agreement - that the change from proprietary software to open source software can be problematic due to the absence of maintenance contracts and the lack of knowledge of success stories. These factors are inhibitors of the adoption of open source software, not giving security in this type of applications, because the open source software does not offer the legal comforts that the proprietary software usually grants. The knowledge of other organizations have already opted for this type of software, would contribute to the increase of confidence with this type of solutions, as reported by Glynn, Fitzgerald, & Exton (2005). This Chapter's conclusions on macro influencing factors are listed in Figure 2.

In the technological context, there was greater agreement that the audit department was stabilized and based on proprietary software. In an organization where there are favourable agreements with proprietary software vendors, the implementation of open source software may be more difficult to initiate, resulting in an inhibitor for the adoption of open source software, as mentioned by Glynn, Fitzgerald, & Exton (2005).

Level of Assimilation of Free and Open Source Software That Characterizes the Organization of Respondents

The results obtained from the questionnaire revealed that 43.1% of the respondents defined the level of assimilation of open source software in the organization where they work as "Awareness" assuming that management is aware of the existence of open source software. With roughly 29.3% characterizing their organization with the level of assimilation of open source software of "Interest," attributing that

Figure 2. Conclusions on macro factors on OSS adoption

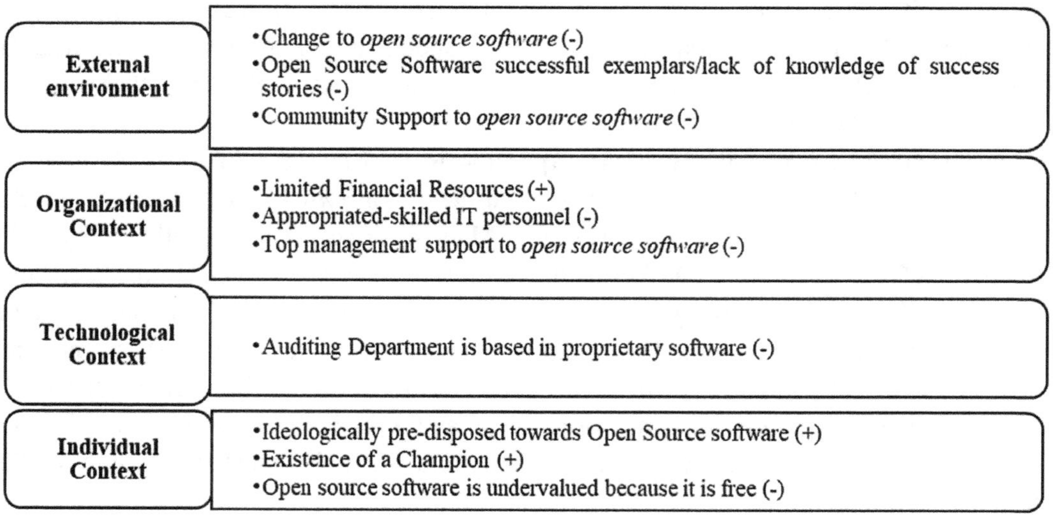

the organization is committed to learning more about open source software. The maximum level of assimilation of open source software "Limited Deployment" and "General Deployment" is 6.9% of the respondents. These results translate the need to try to understand the reasons for auditing professionals not to break the barrier of adopting this type of solution and stay on the first and second stages: awareness and interest.

FUTURE RESEARCH DIRECTIONS

A limitation of the research reported here is the small number of answers. Only 64 respondents answered the questionnaire. A new approach to disseminate the questionnaires to accomplish a higher number of respondents will help to understand if the low numbers related to the use of Free and Open Source Software was connected to the number of internal auditors or if the present conclusions could be generalized to all auditors. In addition, it would be important to understand if the conclusions are coherent to other countries. New research should focus on countries that defined strategies to Free and Open Source Software's use and, then, understand if, among their auditors, the use of Free and Open Source Software is higher than the present ones. It would also be opportune to repeat this study as soon as Millennials are in the labour market: their profile is seen as very distant from the generation that is now in the organizations so, it would be interesting to understand if that also affects their choices between proprietary and open source software. In what concerns Portuguese governments there is an incoherent approach related to the usage of free and open source software. The government issued some measures to increase usage of free and open source software (like the previously referred PGETIC), but on the other hand, the certification of invoicing software almost killed the possibility of disseminating software related to finance. Some challenges, like the impact of Article 13 of the EU directive on copyright may be subject of study in a future research.

CONCLUSION

The main objective of this chapter is to identify which tools are the most used by professionals in the financial auditing area and whether they are using free and open source software as a tool to perform their tasks. In addition, knowing the level of assimilation of free and open source software in the context of auditing, another objective was to recognize the factors that could influence the adoption or rejection of the use of open source software for auditing.

The results were obtained through an online questionnaire and its analysis allowed identifying that the most used software by auditing professionals are spreadsheets software. In this context, the most used is proprietary software Microsoft Excel. There is even the confusion between Excel and spreadsheet. The respondents demonstrated that they also know software such as Caseware IDEA Analytics, SAP Audit Management, ACL Data Analytics, and Open Office. In what concerns open source systems, just a small number of auditors indicated Open Office Si Audit and open Office. It may suggest that these professionals are aware of the existence of open source software as Libre Office, SiAudit and OpenOffice but they chose not to use it.

The level of assimilation of open source software confirms the previous tendency: the respondents characterize the use of Open Source software in the organization where they are working by using the stages of "awareness" and "interest." This demonstrates that the management has knowledge of open source software, and the organization is actively engaged in learning more about this type of application, but they are not yet using it. Moreover, they do not go beyond the "interest" barrier and do not transpose into "experimentation".

From this study, another of this chapter's conclusion is that the macro factors that can influence the use of open source auditing tools by the organizations are the external environment factor and the technological context factor. These factors are related to the lack of knowledge of success cases at the level of assimilation of this type of application, the problem of changing the proprietary software to open source and the audit department is stabilized with proprietary software.

ACKNOWLEDGMENT

We gratefully acknowledge financial support from FCT- Fundação para a Ciencia e Tecnologia (Portugal), national funding through research grant UID/SOC/04521/2013.

The Instituto Português de Auditoria Interna supported this research by disseminating the questionnaires among its members.

REFERENCES

ANSOL. (2018). *ANSOL - Associação Nacional para o Software Livre.* Retrieved June 16, 2018, from https://ansol.org/

Aparicio, M., & Costa, C. J. (2012). Macroeconomics Leverage Trough Open Source. In *Proceedings of the Workshop on Open Source and Design of Communication* (pp. 19–24). Academic Press. 10.1145/2316936.2316941

Batista, M., Costa, C. J., & Aparicio, M. (2013). ERP OS Localization Framework. In *Proceedings of the Workshop on Open Source and Design of Communication* (pp. 1–8). New York: ACM. 10.1145/2503848.2503849

Costa, C. (2007). In C. J. Costa (Ed.), *"ERP Open Source," in Information Technology, Organizations and Teams* (pp. 159–170)., press.itml.org

Costa, C. J. (2010). Testing Usability of ERP Open Source Systems. In *Proceedings of the Workshop on Open Source and Design of Communication* (pp. 25–30). New York: ACM. 10.1145/1936755.1936763

Costa, C. J., & Aparicio, M. (2006). Organizational Tools in the Web: ERP Open Source. In *Proceedings of the IADIS International Conference on WWW/Internet* (pp. 401–408). Academic Press.

ESOP. (2018). *ESOP - Associação de Empresas de Software Open Source Portuguesas.* Retrieved June 1, 2018, from http://www.esop.pt/

Fernandes, N. (2011). *O software open source como suporte à infra-estrutura de TI na administração pública local portuguesa: Factores determinantes na sua adopção - Mestrado em Gestão de Sistemas de informação.* ISCTE-IUL.

Fichman, R. G. (1992). *Information Technology Diffusion: A Review of Empirical Research.* MIT Sloan School of Management.

Fichman, R. G., & Kemerer, C. F. (1997). The Assimilation of Software Process Innovations: An Organizational Learning Perspective. *Management Science, 43*(10), 1345–1363. doi:10.1287/mnsc.43.10.1345

FSF. (2017). *Free software is a matter of liberty, not price — Free Software Foundation — working together for free software.* Retrieved January 21, 2017, from http://www.fsf.org

Garcia, M. N., dos Santos, S., Pereira, R. da S., & Rossi, G. B. (2010). Software livre em relação ao software proprietário: Aspectos favoráveis e desfavoráveis percebidos por especialistas. *Gestão & Regionalidade, 26*(78), 106–120.

Glynn, E., Fitzgerald, B., & Exton, C. (2005). Commercial Adoption of Open Source Software : An Empirical Study. In *2005 International Symposium on Empirical Software Engineering, 2005* (pp. 225–234). Academic Press. 10.1109/ISESE.2005.1541831

Godinho, R. (2012). *O Open Source Software na Administração Pública Central Portuguesa.* ISCTE-IUL.

Hunton, J. E. (2003). Core Concepts of Information Systems Auditing. John Wiley & Sons.

Kavanagh, P. (2004). Open source software: implementation and management. Elsevier.

Kim, H.-J., Mannino, M., & Nieschwietz, R. J. (2009). Information technology acceptance in the internal audit profession: Impact of technology features and complexity. *International Journal of Accounting Information Systems, 10*(4), 214–228. doi:10.1016/j.accinf.2009.09.001

Lanza, P. (1998). La informática en el trabajo de auditoria. *Auditoria Publica, 13*, 93–98.

Laurent, A. M. S. (2004). *Understanding open source and free software licensing: guide to navigating licensing issues in existing & new software.* O'Reilly Media.

Lopes, N. G., & Costa, C. J. (2008). ERP Localization: Exploratory Study in Translation: European and Brazilian Portuguese. In *Proceedings of the 26th Annual ACM International Conference on Design of Communication* (pp. 93–98). New York: ACM. 10.1145/1456536.1456555

Meyer, A., & Goes, J. (1988). Organizational Assimilation of Innovations: A multilevel Contextual Analysis. *Academy of Management Journal, 31*(4), 897–924.

Pedrosa, I., & Costa, C. J. (2012a). Computer Assisted Audit Tools and Techniques in Real World: CAATT's Applications and Approaches in Context. *International Journal of Computer Information Systems and Industrial Management Applications, 4*, 161–168.

Pedrosa, I., & Costa, C. J. (2012b). Financial Auditing and Surveys : how are financial auditors using information technology? An approach using Expert Interviews. In *ISDOC '12 Proceedings of the Workshop on Information Systems and Design of Communication, June 11, 2012, Lisbon, Portugal* (pp. 37–43). Academic Press.

Pedrosa, I., Costa, C. J., & Laureano, R. M. S. (2015). Motivations and limitations on the use of Information Technology on statutory auditors' work: an exploratory study. In CISTI 2015 Proceedings, 2015 (pp. 1132–1137). Aveiro, Portugal: Academic Press.

Pedrosa, I., Laureano, R. M. S., & Costa, C. J. (2015). Motivações dos auditores para o uso das Tecnologias da Informação na sua profissão: aplicação aos Revisores Oficiais de Contas. *Revista Ibérica de Sistemas E Tecologias de Informação, 15*, 101–118.

Raymond, E. S. (1999). *The Cathedral & the Bazaar: Musings on linux and open source by an accidental revolutionary*. O'Reilly Media. doi:10.100712130-999-1026-0

Tornatzky, L. G., Fleischer, M., & Chakrabarti, A. K. (1990). *The processes of technological innovation*. Lexington Books.

Trezentos, P., Dicosmo, R., Laurière, S., Morgado, M., Abecasis, J., Mancinelli, F., & Oliveira, A. (2007). New Generation of Linux Meta-installers. In Research Track of FOSDEM (pp. 1–8). Academic Press.

ADDITIONAL READING

Ahmi, A. (2012). *Adoption of Generalised Audit Software (GAS) by External Auditors in the UK*. London: Brunel University.

Ahmi, A., Saidin, S. Z., & Abdullah, A. (2014). IT Adoption by Internal Auditors in Public Sector: A Conceptual Study. *Procedia: Social and Behavioral Sciences, 164*(August), 591–599. doi:10.1016/j.sbspro.2014.11.151

Aksulu, A., & Wade, M. (2010). A comprehensive review and synthesis of open source research. *Journal of the Association for Information Systems, 11*(11), 576–656. doi:10.17705/1jais.00245

Almeida, N. V., & Pedrosa, I. (2011). Open source data mining tools for audit purposes. In *Proceedings of the 2011 Workshop on Open Source and Design of Communication - OSDOC '11* (pp. 33–34). New York, New York, USA: ACM Press. 10.1145/2016716.2016724

Chau, P., & Tam, K. (1997). Factors Affecting the Adoption of Open Systems: An Exploratory Study. *MIS Quarterly: Management Information Systems, 21*(1), 1–24. doi:10.2307/249740

Holton, C. (2009). Identifying disgruntled employee systems fraud risk through text mining: A simple solution for a multi-billion dollar problem. *Decision Support Systems, 46*(4), 853–864. doi:10.1016/j.dss.2008.11.013

ISACA. (2011). *IT Control Objectives for Cloud Computing: controls and assurance in the cloud.* ISACA.

Laureano, R. M. S., & Pedrosa, I. (2016). A Utilização de Ferramentas Informáticas para a Realização de Tarefas de Verificação: implementação no Microsoft Excel e no CaseWare IDEA. *In CISTI 2016 Proceedings - 11th Iberian Conference on Information Systems and Technologies*, jun 15-18.

Le Grand, C. H. (2013). IT Auditing for Modern Technology Management. *Edpacs, 47*(6), 1–14. doi:10.1080/07366981.2013.795047

Mahzan, N., & Lymer, A. (2014). Examining the adoption of computer-assisted audit tools and techniques: Cases of generalized audit software use by internal auditors. *Managerial Auditing Journal, 29*(4), 327–349. doi:10.1108/MAJ-05-2013-0877

Pedrosa, I. (2015). *Computer-assisted audit tools and techniques use: determinants for individual acceptance.* ISCTE-IUL.

Pedrosa, I., & Costa, C. J. (2014). New trends on CAATTs: what are the Chartered Accountants' new challenges? *In ISDOC '14 Proceedings of the International Conference on Information Systems and Design of Communication*, May 16–17, 2014, Lisbon, Portugal (pp. 138–142).

Pedrosa, I., Costa, C. J., & Laureano, R. M. S. (2015). Use of Information Technology on Statutory auditors' work: new profiles beyond Spreadsheets' users. In CISTI 2015 Proceedings, 2015 (pp. 774–779). Aveiro, Portugal.

Rechtman, Y. (2004). Open-source software implications to CPAs. *The CPA Journal*, (January): 66–69.

KEY TERMS AND DEFINITIONS

Computer-Assisted Audit Tools (CAATs): Any mechanized tool for auditing, such as general-purpose auditing applications, auditing support software, utility audit programs, and computer-aided audit techniques.

Open Source Software: Like in free software, open source software should comply to the four freedoms. But, while free software emphasizes freedom, Open Source is an approach that more emphasis on software quality.

Chapter 11
Transparency in Latin American and Caribbean Supreme Auditing Institutions

David Ortiz-Rodríguez
University of Granada, Spain

Laura Alcaide-Muñoz
University of Granada, Spain

Jesús Mauricio Flórez-Parra
University ECCI, Colombia

Antonio Manuel López-Hernández
University of Granada, Spain

ABSTRACT

One of the objectives of supreme audit institutions (SAIs) is to promote transparency and accountability of the public sector entities. But, at the same time, SAIs must improve their own transparency and accountability. The use of information and communication technologies plays an essential role in making this disclosure. The International Organization of the Supreme Audit Institution (INTOSAI) recognizes that communication is a strategic factor of SAIs. Studies have analyzed information dissemination practices carried out in developed countries. However, SAIs elsewhere, such as the Latin American and Caribbean, have not been the object of research. This chapter analyzes whether these SAIs are using the internet as a means to enhance transparency and interaction with stakeholders. The results indicate that, although in general the institutions analyzed publish the information required by INTOSAI, there is still ample room for improvement, especially regarding interaction with their stakeholders.

DOI: 10.4018/978-1-5225-7356-2.ch011

INTRODUCTION

Advances in information communication technologies (ICTs) have greatly expanded the volume of information available about governments and public administrations (Marland, Lewis, & Flanagan, 2017), and public entities are now disclosing more information than ever about themselves (Wæraas, 2010). As observed in previous research (Krause, Feiock, & Hawkins, 2016; Mol, 2015), the recent financial and economic crisis and public-sector corruption scandals have in many cases spurred this increase in the volume of published information. The quest for social legitimacy seems to impel public entities to define and communicate their differences from other organisations (Brunsson & Sahlin-Anderson, 2000). In this respect, public managers are seeking to respond to citizen demand and thus justify their actions (Neu, Warsame, & Pedwell, 1998; Goodpaster, 1991).

Stakeholder participation in the public sphere must be based on collaboration, in which citizens' opinions, wishes and demands are taken into account (Baur, 2017; Estévez, Fillottrani, Janowski, & Ojo, 2012). However, for this participation to be feasible and beneficial, citizens must have dependable information providing a basis for opinion (Zuiderwijk, Janssen, Zhang, Puron-Cid, & GilGarcia, 2015). In fact, citizens have traditionally been excluded from public management and control processes (Ríos, Benito, & Bastida, 2016), a situation that is particularly acute in less developed countries. As observed by Renzio and Krafchik (2007), transparency is normally weak in countries with high levels of poverty, unnecessary projects, corruption and inefficient services. All of these factors hinder efforts to improve government, consolidate democracy and raise standards of living.

One of the main roles of Supreme Audit Institutions (SAIs) is precisely to ensure the transparency and accountability of public sector entities (INTOSAI, 2009a). However, the SAIs, as public entities responsible for controlling the rest of the public sector, must themselves provide transparency and accountability. For this reason, the International Organization of Supreme Audit Institutions (INTOSAI) has issued a standard (ISSAI 20) for the principles of transparency and accountability (INTOSAI, 2009a) and a code of good practices on transparency (ISSAI 21) (INTOSAI, 2009b), which, among other obligations, requires SAIs to supply information on the results and conclusions of their auditing activity.

Bearing in mind that INTOSAI (2010a) considers communication to be of strategic importance, studies have been conducted to analyse the information published by audit bodies, particularly in developed countries (Garde-Sánchez, Rodríguez-Bolívar, & Alcaide-Muñoz, 2014; González, García, & López, 2013; González, López, & García, 2008; Alcaide-Muñoz, Garde-Sánchez, & Rodríguez-Bolívar, 2013). However, SAIs elsewhere, such as the South America and Caribbean, where participation in INTOSAI is coordinated through the Organization of Latin American and Caribbean Supreme Audit Institutions (OLACEFS), have not been the object of research in this regard. In this paper, the authors examine the level of transparency and accountability of SAIs of the South America and Caribbean, taking into account the peculiarities of this socio-political context. To do so, the authors analyse the websites of these SAIs, comparing the information provided with the criteria and norms set out in ISSAI 20 and 21 to determine the extent to which these institutions apply the ISSAI criteria regarding their own management.

TRANSPARENCY AND ACCOUNTABILITY IN SUPREME AUDITING INSTITUTIONS

In recent years, there has been a climate of uncertainty and mistrust of public institutions, following the exposure of multiple scandals and cases of corruption, and in response to a perceived lack of information (Krause et al., 2016; Tolbert & Mossberger, 2006). Studies of this question (Shin & Eom, 2009; Cuillier & Piotrowski, 2009; Bertot, Jaeger, & Grimes, 2010; Relly, 2012) have concluded that trust in public administrations could be regained via effective mechanisms of transparency, thus increasing credibility in the exercise of their functions, favouring access to information and reinforcing accountability.

SAIs worldwide have taken initiatives to open up these institutions to the public and to improve their transparency and accountability. Thus, to establish the necessary mechanisms to provide this transparency and to ensure public-sector accountability, INTOSAI, through the Declarations of Lima and Mexico, has laid down a series of principles and requirements to guarantee the integrity and professional quality of SAIs and to ensure the provision of reliable, impartial, objective, validated information (International Organization of Supreme Audit Institutions [INTOSAI], 1977, 2007).

SAIs of a general nature perform two main functions (INTOSAI, 2006): on the one hand, they audit the economic-financial activity of the public sector, examining adherence to the principles of legality, efficiency and economy. And at the same time, they carry out a jurisdictional function, to determine the accounting responsibility of those responsible for managing public assets, incomes and disbursements. The main aim of this second function is to protect public funds from misappropriation, from incorrect, incomplete or absence of justification and from other improper causes or behaviours. To achieve these goals, SAIs must remain beyond the control of the executive, thus guaranteeing the accountability of public administrations (INTOSAI, 1977).

In practical terms, this requires the effective, efficient disclosure of relevant information (INTOSAI, 1977). Accordingly, in 2010, INTOSAI issued a Communication Directive setting out communication principles for INTOSAI and its members, to establish and maintain an internal and external communication system providing effective, transparent and reliable communication, which moreover is timely, accessible and promotes the visibility of the SAIs (INTOSAI, 2010a). This strategy, which has been implemented through various action plans and publications since 2005 (González et al., 2008; González et al., 2013), has resulted in two major documents, known as the International Standards of Supreme Audit Institutions (ISSAI): *Principles of Transparency and Accountability* (ISSAI 20) and *Principles of Transparency –Good Practice* (ISSAI 21).

In these documents (INTOSAI, 2010b and 2010c), SAIs are urged to apply to their own case the principles of transparency and accountability. As observed by Garde-Sánchez et al. (2014) and González et al. (2013), ISSAI 20 establishes the principles of transparency and accountability for SAIs to help them become leaders in practices of good governance, while ISSAI 21 describes real-world experiences among SAIs of good practices for each instance of the principles of transparency and accountability addressed in ISSAI 20.

In this regard, the implementation of ICTs, especially the Internet, to promote transparency and accountability plays a fundamental role in the disclosure of public information (Caba-Pérez, Rodríguez-Bolívar, & López-Hernández, 2008; Serrano Cinca, Rueda Tomas, &Portillo Tarragona, 2009; Lim & Lee, 2012; Rodríguez Bolívar, Alcaide Muñoz, & López Hernández, 2013). The use of new technologies enables the SAIs to inform society of their legal competences, their work processes, their activities and their products, making this information readily accessible and transparent, whilst facilitating open communication with the media and other interested parties. In consequence, the SAIs constitute a visible element within the public space (INTOSAI, 2010b).

Previous research has studied transparency and the use of new technologies in public entities, which have mainly focused on fiscal transparency and the dissemination of financial information through the Internet, as well as the possible determining factors (Purón-Cid & Rodríguez-Bolívar, 2018; Cicatiello, De Simone, & Gaeta, 2017; Alcaide, Rodríguez, & López, 2017; Ríos, Benito, & Bastida, 2013). However, the transparency of the SAIs has been poorly analyzed. González et al. (2013) studied the general communication strategy of the SAIs and note the importance of the use of social media and Websites, highlighting the need for implementation and development of these tools in the control institutions.

Alcaide-Muñoz et al. (2013) analyzed the communication practices for the SAIs of the Spanish regions, carrying out a comparison with the INTOSAI proposals. These authors indicate that the Spanish regional SAIs disclosed in their websites an important part of the information established by the ISSAI 20. Thus, the Webs published information about the reports, their conclusions and recommendations and, sometimes, indicators. In terms of design and navigability, websites were basically static, not allowing interaction with stakeholders.

Also, Garde-Sánchez et al. (2014) have analyzed in depth Spanish regional SAIs, and they contrasted the Webs with the INTOSAI principles (2010b and 2010c). These authors highlighted the dissemination of information regarding planning and management of audits over other aspects. Likewise, they pointed out that the design of the websites considers the needs of different stakeholders, but, in their opinion, the main weakness was the lack of interaction with users. It also highlighted that the information is not published on time or not easily manageable.

Thus, it is necessary to continue with the study of the disclosure practices of the SAIs, since it will allow citizens, organizations and researchers to know how the public audit institutions disclose and what the areas could be improved. Thus, the authors believe that a comparative study is necessary, timely and appropriate. In this sense, the study of SAIs in a specific geographic area can be interesting to advance in the knowledge of the transparency practices of these institutions. In this sense, many countries in Latin America have reformed their public accounting systems to increase transparency and improve management (Caba & López, 2007, 2009; Araya Leandro, Caba Pérez, & López Hernández, 2011; Caba Pérez, López Hernández, & Ortiz Rodríguez, 2009). In addition, in recent years the SAIs of these countries have increased their budgets (INTOSAI, 2017). Therefore, an analysis of Latin American area could be of great interested.

EMPIRICAL STUDY

Sample Selection

INTOSAI is composed of seven large regional associations, whose main purpose is to implement the INTOSAI principles in their respective areas. One such association is Organization of Latin American and Caribbean Supreme Audit Institutions (OLACEFS), which comprises the SAIs for the South America and Caribbean countries. Although all these SAIs have previous antecedents, an important part of them were founded between the 20s and 30s of the last century (Table 1), some of them (e.g. Bolivia, Chile, Colombia or Ecuador) as a result of the Kemmerer missions (see Drake, 1989). However, the socio-political events (democratization, market and institutional reforms) present similarities throughout the region, which has meant the rise to a new order (Jordana & Levi-Faur, 2005). In the case of audit institutions, this evolution has led to the fact that almost all SAIs have undergone significant changes in their structure and regulation in the last quarter of the twentieth century and early twenty-first. Most of the SAIs have a unipersonal structure (Auditor General), while in seven of the twenty that has been studied there is a Committee (Table 1).

In October 2009, the Declaration of Asunci6n on Principles of Accountability (Organization of Latin American and Caribbean Supreme Audit Institutions [OLACEFS], 2010) was approved by the delegates of the XIX General Assembly of the OLACEFS, achieving a common vision and providing a greater importance of the SAIs. Nevertheless, despite the important role played by SAIs in the functioning of government agencies and in promoting transparency, little is known about the development of these functions in this geographic area.

The implementation of the same advances is sought to improve the transparency and accountability of OLACEFS members. In this line, in the global survey carried out by INTOSAI, the SAIs that make up of the OLACEFS reported a significant increase in their average budget for the years from 2014 to 2017 (INTOSAI, 2017). According to the audit institutions of this region, SAIs' freedom to obtain timely and unconstrained information is averaged compared to other geographical areas, but *the right to report on audit findings [...] remains a challenge to SAI independence[...], the data show that more SAIs need to exercise their obligation to report on their work as well, particularly SAIs in developing countries* (INTOSAI, 2017, p. 22) and SAIs in Latin American do not present a high level in this point. In addition, only 17% of OLACEFS members have carried out and assessment of their performance (INTOSAI, 2017, p. 28).

Hence, Latin American SAIs are interesting because their current configuration is recent, and they have made important investor efforts in public control. They also face similar contexts, with important institutional reforms. So, it could be very useful to conduct a preliminary investigation to determine the extent to which the organisations that form part of OLACEFS are implementing policies to improve their transparency and accountability to stakeholders, and whether they are using ICTs, and especially the Internet, as a vital element in their information disclosure.

Thus, in this paper, authors review the official websites of the SAIs in this area, examining both their content and the context in which the information disclosure occurs. To achieve this, the authors conducted an information search, finding that of the 22 SAIs that constitute the OLACEFS, 20 have a website available. For Cuba and Republic of the Netherlands Antilles, it was not possible to consult the Websites. Therefore, the sample considered for analysis in the research is composed of 20 SAIs (Table 1).

Research Method

To achieve the stated goals of this empirical study, an analytical model was created to evaluate information disclosure by the SAIs, examining the main aspects of their information content and the context in which this communication took place.

In the first stage of the study, the researchers analysed the information content provided on the websites of the SAIs belonging to the OLACEFS. To this end, the INTOSAI guidelines for improving the transparency and accountability of SAIs (ISSAI 21) were followed. The evaluation model described by Alcaide-Muñoz et al. (2013) was then applied to record the online information disclosure of ten aspects of SAI activity considered in ISSAI 21 (Table 2).

In the second part of the analysis, the researchers reviewed the design, navigability and context of the information disclosure provided, taking into account, in line with previous research in this area (Caba, López y Rodríguez, 2005; Pettersen & Solstad, 2007; Caba et al., 2008; Gallego, Rodríguez, & García, 2011), firstly the design and navigability of the website and then its usability. To classify each of these aspects, following previous practice (Caba et al., 2008; Garde-Sánchez et al., 2014), adopting a binary dichotomous evaluation system (0/1) according to the absence or presence of each aspect on the website (Table 3). This approach was adopted in order to minimise subjectivity in the assessment. When a given aspect was defined by several items, the score assigned was divided evenly (Ho, Tower, & Barako, 2008).

The data were compiled for the authors during April 2018, by viewing all available websites of the OLACEFS SAIs.

Results and Discussion

Table 4 presents the information provided by all the SAIs belonging to OLACEFS, in accordance with the INTOSAI guidelines.

Overall, these SAIs disclose three quarters (77,5%) of the items required by ISSAI 20 and 21. In fact, seven of the ten principles have a rate of diffusion greater than 80%. Thus, all the SAIs in the sample publish full information on legal mandate and include the audit reports on their websites. Similarly, a large majority (90%, all but two SAIs – "Contraloría General del Estado" of Ecuador and "Tribunal de Cuentas" of Uruguay–) use their website to interact with citizens, enabling them, publicly and through a formal mechanism, to present complaints and suggestions related to the audit activity carried out by the SAI. The same level of SAIs (all of them except Paraguay and Venezuela) disclose an annual report about the results, as stipulated in principle 6 of ISSAI 21. Finally, only three ("Contraloría General" of Chile, "Corte de Cuentas" of El Salvador and "Contraloría General de Cuentas" of Guatemala) do not divulge the ethical codes, policies and practices that they apply in their audit processes.

On the contrary, only seven SAIs disclose information about the contracts they conclude in order to carry out their assigned tasks and roles, as stipulated in principle 5 of ISSAI 21. In addition, less than half (45%) publish their conclusions and recommendations resulting from the audits.

Furthermore, the disclosure made by each of the SAIs reveals variability. On the one hand, three SAIs include in the website all the information requested by INTOSAI. These are the SAIs of Bolivia, Nicaragua and Dominican Republic. Similarly, four SAIs report on 9 of the 10 criteria established by ISSAI 21, only failing to provide online information on the contracts they have concluded ("Tribunal de Cuentas" of Brasil, "Contraloría General" of Colombia and "Auditoría Superior de la Federaci6n" of Mexico), or the planned performance audits ("Contraloría General de la República" of Costa Rica).

At the opposite end of the spectrum is the SAI of Venezuela, that reporting on five of the ten principle established by INTOSAI. Hardly better, complying with six principles, are another five SAIs (Chile, El Salvador, Paraguay, Peru and Uruguay). The remaining SAIs are in an intermediate position regarding the online provision of information about their activities.

Overall, the results for Latin American SAIs show a level of compliance with the criteria established by the ISSAIs very similar to those observed in the studies carried out in the Spanish regional SAIs (Alcaide-Muñoz et al., 2013; Garde-Sánchez et al., 2014). However, it is necessary to highlight the lower level observed in the dissemination of contracts (Principle 5) and the publication of conclusions drawn and recommendations (Principle 7). In this sense, the information provided to citizens cannot be understandable since they do not always offer the summarized and simplified information that presents the main findings of the audits. In addition, the non-publication of contracts implies a lack of transparency that should be avoided in this type of institution.

On the other hand, the analyzed entities have better compliance status of principle 9 (*provide formal mechanisms by which the public can express specific complaints and make suggestions regarding audits*) than those analyzed by Alcaide-Muñoz et al., (2013) and Garde-Sánchez et al., (2014). This situation supposes a better communication between the stakeholders and the SAIs.

With respect to the second part of this study, focused on the form of information disclosure, examining basic questions about the design, navigability and usability of each website, Table 5 and 6 present the data obtained and an overall summary for the 20 OLACEFS members.

The results show that these SAIs score well for the design and navigability of their websites, with an average total score of 2 out of 3. But only three institutions achieve the maximum rating and another two score 2.5 out of 3. In the same way, the usability parameters considered reflect similar results, with an average score of 2.03 out of 3. However, only one SAI (Mexico) reaches the maximum score and two others (Brasil and Uruguay) get a score of 2.75.

A detailed analysis of the data obtained for navigability and design shows that all of the websites state the corresponding title in the website heading. The content scores 0.75, but this result is due to the fact that all websites allow the user to directly print the information content, but only ten of them indicate that the content of the web it's of its own. The lowest-scoring parameter is that for navigability because only five SAIs include a map showing the content that is available.

The usability observe three aspects too. The availability of formats for data processing is very high, but "xls format" is only reachable in the case of Mexico. The accessibility scores 0.85 out of 1. The information can be downloaded from the websites for free in all the cases except in Chile, while five of twenty cases, the web does not include information in audio or visual format. The main weaknesses observed in the usability of these websites concern the item about search and interactivity. Only five SAIs provide the personal contacts of responsible persons for the information of the websites. A basic search tool was included in thirteen of the websites, but advanced search tools were present in ten cases.

By countries, the average score obtained was 4.03 out of 6, but there was considerable variance in the design and usability of their websites. Thus, the websites of "Auditoría Superior de la Federación" of Mexico had the best rating in this section (5.5 out of 6), followed by the websites of the Costa Rica (5.25 out of 6) and the SAIs of Dominican Republic (5 out of 6). The poorest performers in this respect were the websites of the SAI of El Salvador (3 out of 6) and those of the SAIs of Chile, Panama, Peru and Venezuela (3.25 out of 6 in each case).

The websites of the analyzed SAIs show better results than those obtained by Alcaide-Muñoz et al. (2013) and Garde-Sánchez et al. (2014) in the Spanish regional institutions both the score in design and navigability, also in usability. Although the interaction with the stakeholders is limited, the main difference is that the websites of the Latin American SAIs provide information that can be manipulated (in almost all the Webs the information can be obtained in Xml or Xbrl format). There is also multimedia information that helps to understand the reports and published documentation. This information, together with the channels to present complaints and suggestions (principle 9 mentioned above), allows us to affirm that the institutions that make up the OLACEFS have a considerable presence on the Internet, contrary to what was observed at the time by González-Díaz et al. (2013). Among the reforms of recent years, Latin American countries have enacted transparency laws. The article by Searson & Johnson (2010) found no relationship between transparency laws and the level of information disseminated on the websites of Latin American governments, although the authors themselves pointed out that *Transparency and freedom of information laws in most Latin American countries are remove new so it may take time to see the results exhibited on Latin American government Web sites* (Searson & Johnson, 2010, p.124). This could be the reason for the level achieved in the navigability and the usability of the websites of the SAIs in this study. Another possible justification is the pressure from international organizations. These entities receive resources to developing countries from international organizations, requesting in exchange, among other issues, the improvement in the transparency of governments (see, for example, International Monetary Fund, 2001).

Therefore, the supervisory entities that constitute OLACEFS should continue to further strengthen their online communication, so that the efforts being made to improve the transparency and accountability of public sector administrations in the area may be accompanied by a corresponding improvement in the transparency of the entities responsible for the control and supervision of governmental economic activity. However, in view of the specific cultural characteristics of the countries analysed, and their influence on economic management and information management systems (Caba & López, 2007, 2009; Araya et al., 2011; Caba et al., 2009), the authors consider it very satisfactory that many SAIs, in this initial analysis, obtained high scores for transparency and for the level of development of their websites. This outcome means that working groups can be created within this geographical area to facilitate website development and to foster the adoption of the transparency and accountability principles recommended by INTOSAI.

CONCLUSION

In recent years, the context in which governments and other public organisations operate has required them to provide greater transparency and accountability. However, in addition to public bodies' own efforts to respond more effectively to stakeholders' information needs, it is necessary to reinforce the activity of control and supervisory organisations. In this respect, the SAIs must contribute to increasing the credibility of the information provided by public administrations. Moreover, these institutions must respond to the challenge of improving their own policies regarding transparency and communication with citizens and with other public administrations. Hence, the SAIs themselves, through INTOSAI (2010, p. 2), consider communication to be a strategic element within audit practice.

Declarations have been made and improvement plans designed to increase the accountability and transparency of the SAIs. The goal of achieving effective internal and external communication has been addressed in two basic pronouncements: ISSAI 20, on principles of transparency and accountability, and ISSAI 21, which catalogues and presents good practices in the field of transparency. The application of these principles and practices has been studied mainly with respect to developed countries, particularly in Europe (Garde-Sánchez et al., 2014; González-Diaz et al., 2013), and much less so for other realities and sociopolitical contexts.

This study presents an initial analysis of the level of transparency and accountability of the SAIs that form part of OLACEFS, obtained from an evaluation of their respective websites, to determine the extent to which these organisations respond to the principles and criteria established by ISSAI 20 and 21, as well as to assess the design, navigability and usability of their websites.

The observation of Webs notes the interaction between the SAIs and their stakeholders must be improved. However, the websites examined are acceptable in terms of design and navigability, complying with many of the parameters considered. The level for usability is similar. In both cases it is higher than in previous studies, highlighting the efforts made by these SAIs in their IT infrastructures.

Regarding compliance with the principles and recommendations set out in ISSAI 20 and 21, the researchers find that there is heterogeneity among the SAIs considered, but the level of institutional information disclosure is, in general, quite high. Nevertheless some important issues are published in a limited number of cases, as the cases of the contracts they conclude, the divulgation of the conclusions and recommendations of the audits or even the audits planning.

Finally, the limitations of this study must be acknowledged. Firstly, the parameters studied regarding the implementation of the ISSAI principles are very generic, and future research should analyse the implementation of these principles in greater detail. It would also be interesting to study influential factors online transparency of audit institutions. In addition, it would be useful to compare the results obtained in this study with those from other geographic areas, such as Middle East or Southeast Asia, to enhance our understanding of the communication policies of SAIs in developing countries elsewhere and to identify their similarities and differences.

REFERENCES

Araya Leandro, C. E., Caba Pérez, C., & López Hernández, A. M. (2011). Innovation in governmental financial information systems in the central American region: Evidence from Costa Rica. *Innovar (Universidad Nacional de Colombia)*, *21*(41), 111–124.

Alcaide-Muñoz, L., Garde-Sánchez, R., & Rodríguez Bolívar, M. P. (2013). La transparencia de las entidades de fiscalización autonómicas en España. Un estudio empírico. *Revista de Control Externo*, *42*, 117–143.

Alcaide-Muñoz, L., Rodríguez-Bolívar, M. P., & López-Hernández, A. M. (2017). Transparency in governments: A meta-analytic review of incentives for digital versus hard-copy public financial disclosures. *American Review of Public Administration*, *47*(5), 550–573. doi:10.1177/0275074016629008

Baur, A. W. (2017). Harnessing the social web to enhance insights into people's opinions in business, government and public administration. *Information Systems Frontiers, 19*(2), 231–251. doi:10.100710796-016-9681-7

Bertot, J. C., Jaeger, P. T., & Grimes, J. M. (2010). Using ICTs to create a culture of transparency: E-government and social media as openness and anti-corruption tools for societies. *Government Information Quarterly, 27*(3), 264–271. doi:10.1016/j.giq.2010.03.001

Brunsson, N., & Sahlin-Andersson, K. (2000). Constructing organizations: The example of public sector reform. *Organization Studies, 21*(4), 721–746. doi:10.1177/0170840600214003

Caba Pérez, C., & López Hernández, A. M. (2007). Latin-American public administration reporting: Recent and future development. *Public Administration and Development, 27*(2), 139–157. doi:10.1002/pad.441

Caba Pérez, C., & López Hernández, A. M. (2009). Governmental financial transparency in MERCOSUR member countries. *International Review of Administrative Sciences, 75*(1), 169–181. doi:10.1177/0020852308099511

Caba Pérez, C., López Hernández, A. M., & Ortiz Rodríguez, D. (2009). Governmental financial information reforms and changes in the political systems: The Argentina, Chile and Paraguay experience. *Public Administration and Development, 29*(5), 429–440. doi:10.1002/pad.551

Caba, C., López, A. M., & Rodríguez, M. P. (2005). Citizens' access to on-line governmental financial information: Practices in the European Union countries. *Government Information Quarterly, 22*(2), 258–276. doi:10.1016/j.giq.2005.02.002

Caba Pérez, C., Rodríguez Bolívar, M. P., & López Hernández, A. M. (2008). E-Government process and incentives for online public financial information. *Online Information Review, 32*(3), 379–400. doi:10.1108/14684520810889682

Cicatiello, L., De Simone, E., & Gaeta, G. L. (2017). Political determinants of fiscal transparency: A panel data empirical investigation. *Economics of Governance, 18*(4), 315–336. doi:10.100710101-017-0192-x

de Renzio, P., & Krafchik, W. (2007). *Lessons from the field: The impact of civil society budget analysis and advocacy in six countries*. Washington, DC: International Budget Project.

Drake, P. W. (1989). *The money doctor in the Andes: US advisers, investors, and economic reform during the Kemmerer missions, 1923-1933*. Durham, NC: Duke University Press.

Estevez, E., Fillottrani, P., Janowski, T., & Ojo, A. (2012). Government information sharing. In Y.-C. Chen & P.-Y. Chu (Eds.), *Electronic governance and cross-boundary collaboration* (pp. 23–55). Hershey, PA: IGI Global. doi:10.4018/978-1-60960-753-1.ch002

Gallego, I., Rodríguez, L., & García, I. M. (2011). Information disclosed online by Spanish universities: Content and explanatory factors. *Online Information Review, 35*(3), 360–385. doi:10.1108/14684521111151423

Garde-Sánchez, R., Rodríguez-Bolívar, M. P., & Alcaide-Muñoz, L. (2014). Are Spanish SAIs accomplishing INTOSAI's best practices code of transparency and accountability? *Transylvanian Review of Administrative Sciences, 43*, 122–145.

González, B., García, R., & López, A. (2013). Communication as a transparency and accountability strategy in supreme audit institutions. *Administration & Society*, *45*(5), 583–609. doi:10.1177/0095399712438376

González, B., López, A., & García, R. (2008). Supreme Audit Institutions and their communication strategies. *International Review of Administrative Sciences*, *74*(3), 435–461. doi:10.1177/0020852308095312

Goodpaster, K. E. (1991). Business ethics and stakeholder analysis. *Business Ethics Quarterly*, *1*(1), 53–73. doi:10.2307/3857592

Ho, P., Tower, G., & Barako, D. (2008). Improving governance leads to improved corporate communication. *Corporate Ownership & Control*, *5*, 26–33.

International Monetary Fund. (2001). *Government Finance Statistics Manual* (2nd ed.). Washington, DC: IMF.

International Organization of Supreme Audit Institutions. (1977). *The Lima declaration*. Retrieved from http://www.issai.org/media(622,1033)/ISSAI_1_E.pdf

International Organization of Supreme Audit Institutions. (2006). *INTOSAI communication policy: A framework "Mutual exchange of information benefits all."* Retrieved from http://www.intosai.org/uploads/compolicyfin031106.pdf

International Organization of Supreme Audit Institutions. (2007). *ISSAI 1260: Communication with those charged with governance*. Retrieved from http://www.issai.org/media(635,1033)/ISSAI_1260_E.pdf

International Organization of Supreme Audit Institutions. (2009a). *ISSAI 20: Principles of transparency and accountability*. Author.

International Organization of Supreme Audit Institutions. (2009b). *ISSAI 21: Principles of transparency and accountability – Principles and good practices*. Author.

International Organization of Supreme Audit Institutions. (2010a). *INTOSAI communication guideline*. Retrieved from http://www.intosai.org/uploads/intkommrichtliniee.pdf

International Organization of Supreme Audit Institutions. (2010b). *INTOSAI GOV 9150: Co-operation and co-ordination between Internal Auditors and SAIs in the public sector*. Retrieved from http://www.issai.org/media(802,1033)/INTOSAI_GOV_9150_E_Exp-draft.pdf

International Organization of Supreme Audit Institutions. (2010c). *Strategic plan (2011-2016)*. Retrieved from http://www.intosai.org/blueline/upload/intosaispenglishv9web.pdf

International Organization of Supreme Audit Institutions. (2017). *Global SAI Stocktaking report 2017*. Retrieved from http://www.idi.no/en/all-news/idi-news/item/128-global-sai-stocktaking-report-2017

Jordana, J., & Levi-Faur, D. (2005). The diffusion of regulatory capitalism in Latin America: Sectoral and national channels in the making of a new order. *The Annals of the American Academy of Political and Social Science*, *528*(1), 102–104. doi:10.1177/0002716204272587

Krause, R. M., Feiock, R. C., & Hawkins, C. V. (2016). The administrative organization of sustainability within local government. *Journal of Public Administration: Research and Theory*, *26*, 113–127.

Lim, J. H., & Lee, E. (2012). Information technologies, community characteristics and environmental outcomes: Evidence from South Korea. *Journal of Environmental Planning and Management, 55*(3), 271–296. doi:10.1080/09640568.2011.597588

Marland, A., Lewis, J. P., & Flanagan, T. (2017). Governance in the age of digital media and branding. *Governance: An International Journal of Policy, Administration and Institutions, 30*(1), 125–141. doi:10.1111/gove.12194

Mol, A. P. (2015). China's transition to sustainability. Which direction to take? In Routledge international handbook of sustainable development (pp.351-363). Abingdon, UK: Routledge.

Neu, D., Warsame, H., & Pedwell, K. (1998). Managing public impressions: Environmental disclosures in annual reports. *Accounting, Organizations and Society, 23*(3), 265–282. doi:10.1016/S0361-3682(97)00008-1

Organization of Latin American and Caribbean Supreme Audit Institutions. (2010). *Declaración de Asunción. Principios sobre Rendición de cuentas*. Retrieved from http://www.olacefs.com/declaracion-de-asuncion-principios-sobre-rendicion-de-cuentas

Pettersen, I. J., & Solstad, E. (2007). The role of accounting information in a reforming area: A study of higher education institutions. *Financial Accountability & Management, 23*(2), 133–154. doi:10.1111/j.1468-0408.2007.00423.x

Puron-Cid, G., & Rodríguez-Bolívar, M. P. (2018). The effects of contextual factors into different features of financial transparency at the municipal level. *Government Information Quarterly, 35*(1), 135–150. doi:10.1016/j.giq.2017.10.005

Rios, A. M., Benito, B., & Bastida, F. (2013). Determinants of central government budget disclosure: An international comparative analysis. *Journal of Comparative Policy Analysis, 15*(3), 235–254. doi:10.1080/13876988.2013.798449

Ríos, A. M., Bastida, F., & Benito, B. (2017). Budget transparency and legislative budgetary oversight: An international approach. *American Review of Public Administration, 46*(5), 546–568. doi:10.1177/0275074014565020

Rodríguez Bolívar, M. P., Alcaide Muñoz, L., & López Hernández, A. M. (2013). Determinants of financial transparency in government organizations: A meta-analytic study. *International Public Management Journal, 16*(4), 557–602. doi:10.1080/10967494.2013.849169

Serrano Cinca, C., Rueda Tomas, M., & Portillo Tarragona, P. (2009). Factors influencing e-disclosure in local public administrations. *Environment and Planning. C, Government & Policy, 27*(2), 355–378. doi:10.1068/c07116r

Searson, E. M., & Johnson, M. A. (2010). Transparency laws and interactive public relations: An analysis of Latin American government web sites. *Public Relations Review, 36*(2), 120–126. doi:10.1016/j.pubrev.2010.03.003

Tolbert, C. J., Mossberger, K., & McNeal, R. (2008). Institutions, policy and egovernment in the American states. *Public Administration Review, 68*(3), 549–563. doi:10.1111/j.1540-6210.2008.00890.x

Wæraas, A. (2010). Communicating identity. the use of core value statements in regulative institutions. *Administration & Society*, *42*(5), 526–549. doi:10.1177/0095399710377435

Zuiderwijk, A., Janssen, M., Zhang, J., Puron-Cid, G., & GilGarcia, J. R. (2015). Towards decision support for disclosing data: Closed or open data? *Information Polity, 20*(2-3), 103–117.

KEY TERMS AND DEFINITIONS

Communication Strategy: Guidelines for action about what, how, and where to communicate the activities and results carried out by the institutions.

INTOSAI: International organization of public sector audit institutions. It issues pronouncements and guides of good practices for the realization of public audits.

ISSAIs: Professional standards and best practice guidelines for public sector auditors, officially authorized and endorsed by the International Organization of Supreme Audit Institutions (INTOSAI).

OLACEFS: Organization of public audit institutions in Latin America and the Caribbean. It is a forum to exchange ideas and experiences related to government control. It is one of the regional groups that make up INTOSAI.

Supreme Audit Institutions (SAIs): Independent public institutions; they are accountable to the stakeholders (mainly legislative bodies and citizens) controlling the use of public money by public entities.

APPENDIX

Table 1. OLACEFS members

Members	Foundation	Structure	Website
Auditoría General de la Nación de Argentina	1992	Committee (7 members)	www.agn.gov.ar
Auditoría General de Belice	1887	Auditor General	www.audit.gov.bz
Contraloría General del Estado Plurinacional de Bolivia	1929	Auditor General	www.contraloria.gob.bo
Tribunal de Cuentas de la Unión de Brasil	1891	Committee (9 members)	www.tcu.gov.br
Contraloría General de la República de Chile	1927	Auditor General	www.contraloria.cl
Contraloría General de la República de Colombia	1923	Auditor General and Vice-auditor	www.contraloria.gov.co
Contraloría General de la República de Costa Rica	1950	Auditor General	www.cgr.go.cr
Contraloría General del Estado de la República del Ecuador	1927	Auditor General and Vice-auditors(2)	www.contraloria.gob.ec
Corte de Cuentas de la República de El Salvador	1939	Committee (5 members)	www.cortedecuentas.gob.sv
Contraloría General de Cuentas de la República de Guatemala	1985	Auditor General and Vice-auditors(3)	www.contraloria.gob.gt
Tribunal Superior de Cuentas de la República de Honduras	2002	Committee (7 members)	www.tsc.gob.hn
Auditoría Superior de la Federación de México	2000	Auditor General	www.asf.gob.mx
Contraloría General de la República de Nicaragua	1979	Committee (5 members)	www.cgr.gob.ni
Contraloría General de la República de Panamá	1941	Auditor General and Vice-auditor	www.contraloria.gob.pa
Contraloría General de la República de Paraguay	1994	Auditor General and Vice-auditor	www.contraloria.gov.py
Contraloría General de la República de Perú	1929	Auditor General	www.contraloria.gob.pe
Oficina del Contralor del Estado Libre Asociado de Puerto Rico	1952	Auditor General and Vice-auditor	www.ocpr.gov.pr
Cámara de Cuentas de la República Dominicana	1942	Committee (5 members)	www.camaradecuentas.gob.do
Tribunal de Cuentas de la República del Uruguay	1934	Committee (7 members)	www.tcr.gub.uy
Contraloría General de la República Bolivariana de Venezuela	1938	Auditor General and Vice-auditor	www.cgr.gob.ve

Table 2. Compliance with the principles and good practices of ISSAI 21 on the SAIs' websites

Content Provided on the SAIs Websites	ISSAI 21	Score
1. Most websites have a heading entitled "Legislation" or "Legal mandate", which details the legal framework under which the SAI operates.	Principle 1	0/1
2. The majority of SAIs publish details of their mandate, responsibilities, mission and strategy.	Principle 2	0/1
3. Most websites have a section presenting the organisation's institutional activities.	Principle 3	0/1
4. The SAIs publish a list of planned audits on their website.	Principle 3	0/1
5. The SAIs publish the values, ethical code or standards of professional conduct to which they adhere.	Principle 4	0/1
6. The SAIs publish the contracts they conclude.	Principle 5	0/1
7. The SAIs publish an annual report including performance indicators and results.	Principle 6	0/1
8. The SAIs publish the conclusions drawn and recommendations arising from their audits.	Principle 7	0/1
9. Most of the SAIs meet the minimum requirement of publishing their complete audit reports on the website.	Principle 8	0/1
10. The SAIs provide formal mechanisms by which the public can express specific complaints and make suggestions regarding audits.	Principle 9	0/1

Table 3. Model evaluating the design, navigability and usability of websites

Concept	Item	Score
Design and Navigability of Websites		$DI = \sum_{i=1}^{m} g_i$
a) Headings	The SAI web pages each have a heading.	0/1 according to the absence / presence of this item
b) Characteristics of website content	b.1. The website allows the visitor to print the contents.	0/0.5 according to the absence / presence of each item
	b.2. The website indicates that its content is copyright.	
c) Characteristics of website navigability	A web map showing the contents is available	0/1 according to the absence / presence of this item
Usability		$UI = \sum_{i=1}^{m} gi$
d) Electronic formats used to process audit reports	.html	0/0.25 according to the absence / presence of each item
	.pdf or .doc	
	Xml and Xbrl	
	.xls	
e) Search and interactivity	e.1. A basic search tool is included.	0/0.25 according to the absence / presence of each item
	e.2. An advanced search tool is included.	
	e.3. A different e-mail address to the webmaster's is provided to request information or explanations.	
	e.4. Personal contacts with responsible persons of the SAI for the information provided are supplied on the website.	
f) Characteristics of accessibility	f.1. The website includes information in audio and/or visual formats.	0/0.5 according to the absence / presence of each item
	f.2. All information provided on the website is freeware and it can be downloaded.	

Table 4. Information disclosed on the SAIs' websites

Principles of Information Disclosure Laid Down by INTOSAI	Argentina	Belice	Bolivia	Brasil	Chile	Colombia	Costa Rica	Ecuador	El Salvador	Guatemala	Honduras	Mexico	Nicaragua	Panamá	Paraguay	Perú	Puerto Rico	Rep. Dominicana	Uruguay	Venezuela	Total	Average (%)
Most websites have a heading entitled "Legislation" or "Legal mandate", which details the legal framework under which the SAI operates - *Principle 1*	1	1	1	1	1	1	1	1	1	1	1	1	1	1	1	1	1	1	1	1	20	100%
The SAIs publish details of their mandate, responsibilities, mission and strategy - *Principle 2*	1	1	1	1	0	1	1	1	1	0	1	1	1	1	1	0	0	1	1	1	16	80%
Most websites have a section presenting the organization's institutional activities - *Principle 3*	1	0	1	1	0	1	1	1	1	1	1	1	1	1	0	1	1	1	1	0	16	80%
The SAIs publish a list of planned audits on their website- *Principle 3*	1	1	1	1	1	1	0	1	0	1	1	1	1	0	1	0	1	1	0	0	14	70%
The SAIs publish the values, ethical code or standards of professional conduct to which they adhere- *Principle 4*	1	1	1	1	0	1	1	1	0	0	1	1	1	1	1	1	1	1	1	1	17	85%
The SAIs publish on their website the contracts they conclude - *Principle 5*	0	0	1	0	0	0	1	1	0	1	0	0	1	0	0	0	1	1	0	0	7	35%
The SAIs publish an annual report including performance indicators and results- *Principle 6*	1	1	1	1	1	1	1	1	1	1	1	1	1	1	0	1	1	1	1	0	18	90%
The SAIs publish the conclusions drawn and recommendations arising from their audits- *Principle 7*	0	0	1	1	1	1	1	0	0	1	0	1	1	0	0	0	0	1	0	0	9	45%
The audit reports are published on the websites - *Principle 8*	1	1	1	1	1	1	1	1	1	1	1	1	1	1	1	1	1	1	1	1	20	100%
The SAIs provide formal mechanisms by which the public can express specific complaints and make suggestions regarding audits - *Principle 9*	1	1	1	1	1	1	1	0	1	1	1	1	1	1	1	1	1	1	0	1	18	90%
Total	**8**	**7**	**10**	**9**	**6**	**9**	**9**	**8**	**6**	**8**	**8**	**9**	**10**	**7**	**6**	**6**	**8**	**10**	**6**	**5**	**155**	**77,5%**

Table 5. Context of information disclosure – design and navigability

	Argentina	Belice	Bolivia	Brasil	Chile	Colombia	Costa Rica	Ecuador	El Salvador	Guatemala	Honduras	Mexico	Nicaragua	Panamá	Paraguay	Perú	Puerto Rico	Rep. Dominicana	Uruguay	Venezuela	Total	Average	Average (%)
Design And Navigability Of Websites	**1,5**	**3**	**2**	**2**	**1,5**	**2**	**3**	**2,5**	**2**	**1,5**	**2**	**2,5**	**2**	**1,5**	**1,5**	**1,5**	**2**	**3**	**1,5**	**1,5**	**40**	**2,00**	**66,67%**
a) Headings	1	1	1	1	1	1	1	1	1	1	1	1	1	1	1	1	1	1	1	1	20	1,00	100,00%
b) Characteristics of website content	0,5	1	1	1	0,5	1	1	0,5	1	0,5	1	0,5	1	0,5	0,5	0,5	1	1	0,5	0,5	15	0,75	75,00%
b.1. The website allows the visitor to print the contents with the option 'print page'.	*0,5*	*0,5*	*0,5*	*0,5*	*0,5*	*0,5*	*0,5*	*0,5*	*0,5*	*0,5*	*0,5*	*0,5*	*0,5*	*0,5*	*0,5*	*0,5*	*0,5*	*0,5*	*0,5*	*0,5*	*10*	*0,50*	*50,00%*
b.2. The website has the SAI copyright to indicate that the content of it is of its own.	*0,5*	*0*	*0,5*	*0*	*0,5*	*0*	*0,5*	*0*	*0*	*0*	*0,5*	*0,5*	*0*	*0*	*0,5*	*0*	*0,5*	*0*	*0,5*	*0*	*5*	*0,25*	*25,00%*
c) Characteristics of website navigability	0	1	0	0	0	0	1	1	0	0	0	1	0	0	0	0	0	1	0	0	5	0,25	25,00%

Table 6. Context of information disclosure - usability

	Argentina	Belice	Bolivia	Brasil	Chile	Colombia	Costa Rica	Ecuador	El Salvador	Guatemala	Honduras	Mexico	Nicaragua	Panamá	Paraguay	Perú	Puerto Rico	R. Dominicana	Uruguay	Venezuela	Total	Average	Average (%)
Usability	**2,25**	**1,5**	**1,5**	**2,75**	**1,75**	**2,5**	**2,25**	**2,25**	**1**	**2**	**1,75**	**3**	**2**	**1,75**	**2**	**1,75**	**2**	**2**	**2,75**	**1,75**	**40,5**	**2,03**	**67,50%**
d) Electronic formats used to process audit reports	0,5	0,5	0,5	0,75	0,75	0,75	0,75	0,75	0,5	0,75	0,75	1	0,75	0,75	0,75	0,75	0,75	0,75	0,75	0,75	14,25	0,71	71,25%
- .html format	0,25	0,25	0,25	0,25	0,25	0,25	0,25	0,25	0,25	0,25	0,25	0,25	0,25	0,25	0,25	0,25	0,25	0,25	0,25	0,25	5	0,25	25,00%
- .pdf or .doc format	0,25	0,25	0,25	0,25	0,25	0,25	0,25	0,25	0,25	0,25	0,25	0,25	0,25	0,25	0,25	0,25	0,25	0,25	0,25	0,25	5	0,25	25,00%
- Xml and Xbrl format	0	0	0	0,25	0,25	0,25	0,25	0,25	0	0,25	0,25	0,25	0,25	0,25	0,25	0,25	0,25	0,25	0,25	0,25	4	0,20	20,00%
- .xls format	0	0	0	0	0	0	0	0	0	0	0	0,25	0	0	0	0	0	0	0	0	0,25	0,01	1,25%
e) Search and interactivity	0,75	0,5	0,5	1	0,5	0,75	0,5	0,5	0	0,25	0,5	1	0,75	0	0,25	0	0,25	0,25	1	0	9,25	0,46	46,25%
e.1. A basic search tool is included in the SAI website.	0,25	0	0,25	0,25	0,25	0,25	0,25	0,25	0	0	0	0,25	0,25	0	0,25	0	0,25	0,25	0,25	0	3,25	0,16	16,25%
e.2. An advanced search tool is included in the SAI website.	0,25	0	0,25	0,25	0,25	0,25	0,25	0,25	0	0	0	0,25	0,25	0	0	0	0	0	0,25	0	2,5	0,13	12,50%
e.3. A different e-mail address to the webmaster's is provided to request information or explanations.	0,25	0,25	0	0,25	0	0,25	0	0	0	0,25	0,25	0,25	0,25	0	0	0	0	0	0,25	0	2,25	0,11	11,25%
e.4. Personal contacts with responsible persons of the SAI for the information provided are supplied on the website.	0	0,25	0	0,25	0	0	0	0	0	0	0,25	0,25	0	0	0	0	0	0	0,25	0	1,25	0,06	6,25%
f) Characteristics of accessibility	1	0,5	0,5	1	0,5	1	1	1	0,5	1	0,5	1	0,5	1	1	1	1	1	1	1	17	0,85	85,00%
f.1. The website includes information in audio and/or visual formats.	0,5	0	0	0,5	0,5	0,5	0,5	0,5	0	0,5	0	0,5	0	0,5	0,5	0,5	0,5	0,5	0,5	0,5	7,5	0,38	37,50%

continued on following page

Table 6. Continued

	Argentina	Belice	Bolivia	Brasil	Chile	Colombia	Costa Rica	Ecuador	El Salvador	Guatemala	Honduras	Mexico	Nicaragua	Panamá	Paraguay	Perú	Puerto Rico	R. Dominicana	Uruguay	Venezuela	Total	Average	Average (%)
f.2. All information provided on the website is freeware and it can be downloaded.	*0,5*	*0,5*	*0,5*	*0,5*	*0*	*0,5*	*0,5*	*0,5*	*0,5*	*0,5*	*0,5*	*0,5*	*0,5*	*0,5*	*0,5*	*0,5*	*0,5*	*0,5*	*0,5*	*0,5*	*9,5*	*0,48*	*47,50%*
TOTAL – Design and Usability	**3,75**	**4,5**	**3,5**	**4,75**	**3,25**	**4,5**	**5,25**	**4,75**	**3**	**3,5**	**3,75**	**5,5**	**4**	**3,25**	**3,5**	**3,25**	**4**	**5**	**4,25**	**3,25**	**80,5**	**4,03**	**67,08%**

Section 3
Fraud and Forensic Audit

Chapter 12
To Monitor and Detect Suspicious Transactions in a Financial Transaction System Through Database Forensic Audit and Rule-Based Outlier Detection Model

Harmeet Kaur Khanuja
Marathwada Mitra Mandal's College of Engineering, India

Dattatraya Adane
Shri Ramdeobaba College of Engineering and Management, India

ABSTRACT

The objective of this chapter is to monitor database transactions and provide information accountability to databases. It provides a methodology to retrieve and standardize different audit logs in a uniform XML format which are extracted from different databases. The financial transactions obtained through audit logs are then analyzed with database forensic audit. The transactions are examined, detected, and classified as per regulations and well-defined RBI antimony laundering rules to obtain outliers and suspicious transactions within audit logs. Bayesian network is used in this research to represent rule-based outlier detection model which identifies the risk level of the suspicious transactions.

INTRODUCTION

As per, FICCI- Federation of Indian Chambers of Commerce and Industry – Pinkerton India Risk Survey 2017, 'Information & Cyber Insecurity' has become more distinct due to the change that the nation which is undergoing towards digitization of various assets. It is said in the FICCI release, that the recent demonetization saw a spike in the number of people resorting to online platforms for financial transac-

DOI: 10.4018/978-1-5225-7356-2.ch012

tions. This is posturing greater risks for users, including businesses, e-commerce etc. Also there is tremendous increase in subscribers to the Unique Identification Number (UIN) where personal information is stored as data which are linked to the banking details. The businesses are legally required to retain certain types of information and data in their databases for various periods of time as per requirements in every state and country; hence it becomes critical to stop deleting any form of electronic records that might be related to the case. This is giving opportunities to hackers to commit a breach. This may also lead to increase in existing risks in the cyber domain, such as money laundering and identity theft.

In developing countries, the security is becoming complicated with rapid expansion of access to the Internet, an unprecedented understanding of technology, increasing economic competition, and the push to achieve greater efficiencies. The technological advancement and the globalization of online banking provisions for finance and the payment systems have widened the scope of concealing illegal money and easy mobility of funds across the borders. These are known as suspicious activities or illegal transactions incorporating money laundering. In financial transactions, people hide their actions through a series of steps that make it look like money coming from illegal or unethical sources which was earned legitimately. Financial institutions are required to keep an eye on database transactions to detect the abnormality or any suspicious activity carried out if any. This will prevent such cases and submit the detailed reports to the regulatory bodies.

Indeed, in today's business world, almost all applications use databases to manage data. Here the focus is on databases of banking transactions. Fraudulent banking activities are becoming more and more sophisticated which is threatening the security and trust of online banking business resulting as a major issue for handling financial crimes. It is now a global problem which can undermine the integrity and stability of financial markets and financial institutions. Moreover it is becoming challenging due to the Money Laundering practices carried over.

In view of this, the government act like Sarbanes-Oxley Audit Requirements (SOX) ("Sarbanes Oxley Audit Requirements", 2018) has an immense impact on database auditing requirements. Consequently, the monitoring systems and log collection must provide an audit trail of all the activities and access to sensitive business information. As per Reserve Bank of India (RBI) ("Master Direction - Know Your Customer (KYC) Direction", (2016)), the Banks and Financial institutions should exercise ongoing due diligence concerning every customer and carefully examine the transactions to ensure that they are consistent with the customer's profile and source of funds as per extant instructions. The Regulations of Reserve Bank of India for Anti-money Laundering (AML) defines the standard rules for suspecting the illegal transactions. The AML systems produce large volumes of work items, but very few results in quality investigations or actionable results. Effective and efficient detection of Anti Money Laundering is regarded as a major challenge to all the banks and is an increasing cause for concern. One way to ensure this is to keep end-to-end accountability of databases through continuous assurance technology and transaction monitoring with Digital forensics. This has motivated us to develop a methodology which monitors the database transactions and retain evidences to prove the transactions to be legitimate or suspicious. The suspicious transactions can then be used for investigations to reconstruct the illegal activity carried out in an organization. This can be achieved by incorporating information accountability in Database Management System.

This chapter presents a comprehensive discussion of a proposed methodology to detect suspicious transactions through forensic audit in a financial scenario which considers standard RBI rules implemented for countering frauds such as money laundering. The information retrieved through database audit logs is used to analyze hidden values. The suspected transactions are verified using Dempster-Shafer's theory of evidence, a reasoning technique that provides a way to encode uncertainty more naturally by determining risk level of the suspected transactions. The proposed methodology will facilitate digital investigators or auditors with decisive information for further investigations.

BACKGROUND OF THE STUDY

As per the survey, various crimes have taken place during the last decades. The Basel Institute on Governance shows the Basel AML Index (Base AML Index Report (2017)) which provides annual ranking assessment of country risk regarding money laundering/terrorism financing etc. It focuses on anti-money laundering and counters terrorist financing (AML/CTF) frameworks. The Annual Basel AML Index ranks 140 countries in terms of risk of money laundering and 'terrorism' financing. It released its annual Anti Money Laundering index in 2017. As per Basel AML Index report the risk statistics for some countries are shown in Figure 1a and Figure 1b. Each indicator is descaled into a 0 (low risk) to 10 (high risk) scale.

As per Basel AML Index, the factors which are leading to high risk ranking are predicted which are shown in Figure 2.

Thus the increasing intensity of risks and the ongoing changes in cybercrime requires database monitoring, auditing and digital investigations by digital forensic practitioners which is becoming mandate by different regulation bodies.

Database Auditing Requirement for Regulation Bodies

Figure 3 shows the various requirement and technology/techniques as said (Nick, 2016), which are adapted to the regulatory compliance.

Government regulations and increased awareness of security have increased the auditing requirements. The government regulations have impacted information technology systems and the auditing requirements of organizations. Some of these regulations have specifically influenced the auditing of the databases. The three government acts like, Payment Card Industry compliance PCI DSS (PCI Payment Card Industry Data Security Standard.), Health Insurance Portability and Accountability Act (HIPAA) and Sarbanes-Oxley have a significant impact on database auditing requirements. These Regulations require that access to sensitive data should be adequately monitored and managed. Ultimately, regardless

Figure 1a. Overall score based on a new FATF evaluation, which includes an effectiveness assessment

South Asia

Country	Overall Score
Afghanistan	**8.38**
Nepal	**7.57**
Sri Lanka *	**7.15**
Pakistan	**6.64**
Bangladesh *	**5.79**
India	**5.58**

Figure 1b. Overall score based on a new FATF evaluation, which includes an effectiveness assessment

Top 15 higher risk in Europe & Central Asia

Country	Overall Score
Tajikistan	8.28
Turkey	6.65
Ukraine	6.52
Kazakhstan	6.42
Kyrgyzstan	6.33
Russia	6.22
Uzbekistan	6.09
Bosnia-Herzegovina	5.91
Serbia *	5.76
Albania	5.75
Moldova	5.43
Hungary *	5.41
Italy *	5.41
Luxembourg	5.40
Georgia	5.37

Figure 2. Factors that can lead to high risk ranking

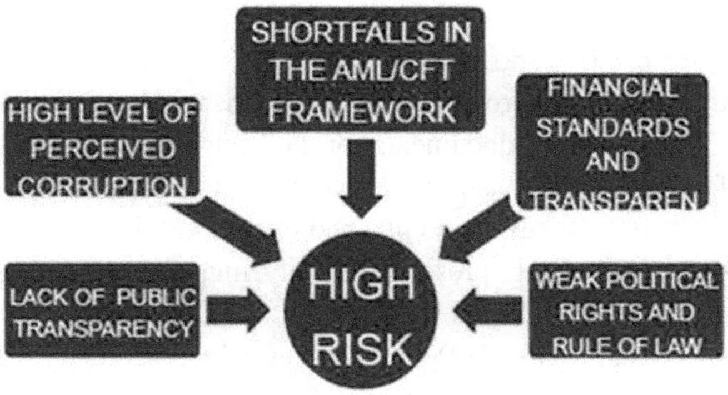

of whether an outside organization has mandated database monitoring if the stored data is of significant business value, the database should probably have appropriate monitoring in place to identify malicious attacks and inappropriate use of data. Activity monitoring should align with the business value of the information stored in the database and with the policies and requirements of the organization.

To get surety of compliance with government and industry regulations is a strenuous task. Database auditing on a regular basis if adapted can meet the regulatory requirements safely and proactively.

Figure 3. Regulation bodies

Need	SOX		HIPAA		PCI	
	Requirement	Technology / Technique	Requirement	Technology / Technique	Requirement	Technology / Technique
Confidentiality	Confidential Information cannot be exposed to unauthorized entities.	Use of encryption techniques and algorithms to ensure data is only divulged to authorized individuals.	All ePHI must be kept confidential to prevent unauthorized access.	Use of strong encryption when storing and transmitting confidential data in database.	Protect consumer credit Card information.	Encryption of data only authorized system or agents have access to sensitive account information.
Integrity	Software needs to support evidence that data has not been modified.	Cryptographic hashes and robust integrity checks.	Records should not modifiable by unauthorized people or entities.	Use integrity checking mechanism that apply principles of least privilege and minimize risk of privilege escalation.	---------	---------
Availability	Availability of financial data to authorized individuals.	General code reliability ,resistance of denial of service attacks, reliable data storage, recovery in case of system failure.	Record owners are guaranteed the right to access their own records.	Designed to properly handle errors and withstand denial of service attack. Maintain event logs to be able to reconstruct.	---------	---------
Access Controls	Support role- based access and revocation of accounts.	Integrating into larger identity management framework like LDAP. Review Access rights.	---------	---------	---------	---------
Auditing and Logging	Auditing and logging of events in system that process sensitive data Logs must not reveal information that system is	Logging of system events such as shutdown, restart or unusual events. Avoidance of logging of sensitive data.	Any action that might need to be traced must be documented.	Log information to be able to construct a clear audit trail of how a user or entity attempts to access and utilize resources. Logs should be backed up.	Comply with periodic audits to demonstrate standards are adequately being met.	Logging all pertinent account transactions and accesses.

DIGITAL FORENSICS

As per Digital Forensics Research Workshop (DFRWS) (Brian C., 2002), Digital forensics is defined as the use of scientifically derived and proven methods towards the preservation, collection, validation, identification, analysis, interpretation, documentation and presentation of digital evidence obtained from digital sources. It facilitates to reconstruct the events found to be criminal or helping to anticipate unauthorized actions shown to be disruptive to planned operations. The major phases of the processes in Figure 4 shows tasks like identifying, preserving, analyzing, and presenting which are in a legally acceptable manner.

Digital forensics as said (Raghavan, 2013) conducts investigations for the cases like an external intrusion, internal or external fraud, or if any compromise has happened with specific security policy. It investigates the crime scene and requires disciplines that include law enforcement and skills for presenting evidence. The process has to establish and maintain a chain of custody as explained in next section that has to be acceptable in a court of law.

Figure 4. Digital forensics process

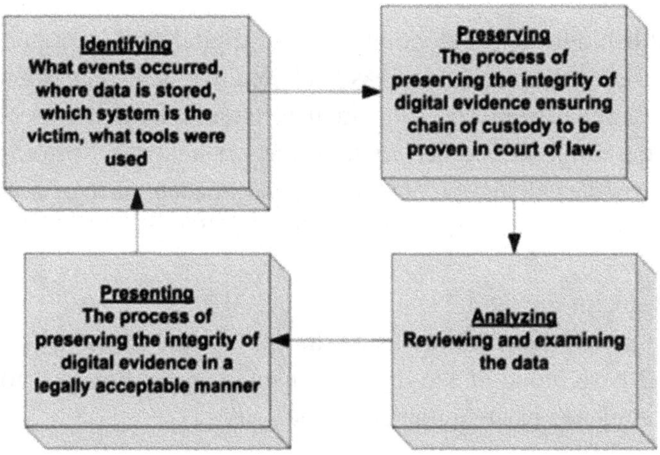

Establish and Maintain a Chain of Custody

While performing digital forensics for a civil lawsuit, a criminal investigation, or an administrative inquiry, the authenticity and integrity of the evidence examined are very critical. The first step in the process of Digital Forensics is to establish a chain of custody policy for an incident from victim's databases which often contain useful information during forensic investigations.

The goal of the policy ensures that each piece of evidence collected is accountable to an individual. To define a complete chain of custody, one must consider the following:

- Designate an evidence custodian and backup evidence custodian.
- Build a limited-access evidence storage facility.
- Log access and activity in the evidence storage facility.
- Establish a Standard Operating Procedure (SOP) for collecting, marking, transporting, and storing evidence.
- Forms created must include information for a chain of custody, evidence marks, evidence logs, etc.
- Each piece of evidence should be marked with a unique evidence number; the location, date, and time at which it is collected;
- Evidence logs track the evidence that enters and leaves the evidence storage facility and should contain (at a minimum) a description of the evidence item (to include identifying numbers).
- Audit the evidence storage facility and evidence logs and have someone other than the evidence custodian account for all evidence on a regular basis.

Establish Integrity

It is not enough to establish only the authenticity of your digital evidence; one also needs to verify its integrity. Because digital evidence consists of easily altered magnetic, electronic, or optical signals that cannot be seen or heard until hardware and software have interpreted them, special care must be taken to prove that your evidence is not modified during its collection, analysis, or storage. The primary method for determining integrity is the calculation of a hash value for each piece of evidence before and after it has been analyzed. The general procedure for establishing the integrity of digital evidence is as follows:

- Calculate a hash value of the digital evidence.
- Conduct a digital forensic examination using the appropriate methods.
- Calculate a second hash value of the digital evidence and compare it to the first value. If they match, the digital evidence has maintained its integrity.

Research by Access Data and NIST (E. Barker et al., 2015) take the position that MD5 and SHA-1 algorithms are secure for use in establishing digital evidence integrity and conducting forensic analysis.

DATABASE FORENSIC TOOL FOR AUDITING

Database forensics is a stream of Digital Forensics which has become an important field of study. As mention in the paper (M.S. Olivier, 2009) metadata contains useful information for investigation. Thus Digital forensics technique identifies preserves and analyzes digital information which can be used as evidences in civil and criminal legal proceedings. Also while investigation traditional forensic investigation focuses on volatile and non volatile operating system and selected application data. Applications such as Internet Explorer are typically targeted by traditional digital forensic investigations. These investigations often neglect the database.

Figure 5. Scope of traditional and database forensic investigations

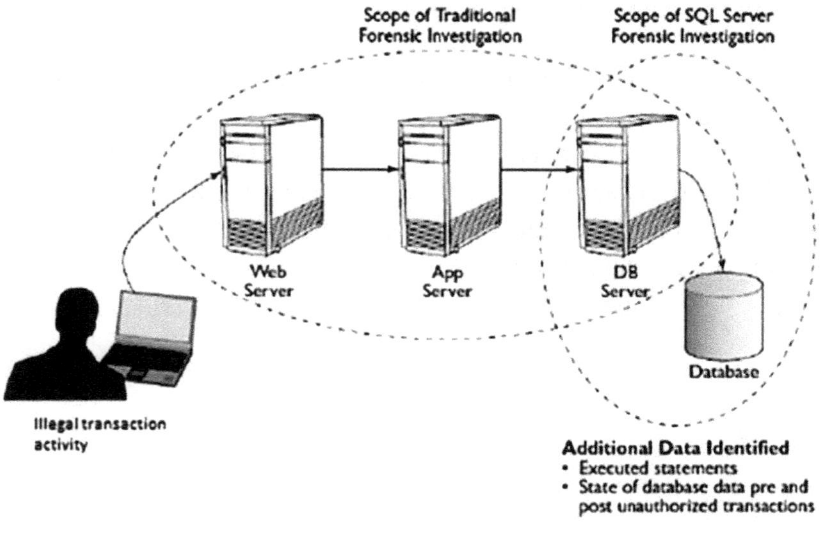

However, when the database is ignored, it is obviously difficult and in some cases impossible for investigators to determine database transactions that are suspicious during illegal activity. Database forensics picks up where traditional investigations end by focusing on the database and further qualifying and investigating digital intrusions to prove or disprove the occurrence of an unauthorized database transactions. Figure 5 shows the scope of traditional and database forensic investigations.

As said (Olivier, 2009) Database forensics is a subset of application-based digital forensics, which identifies preserves and analyses digital information within databases to produce evidence in a court of law. It involves the application of digital forensics techniques in gathering evidence admissible in a court of law from the database. It explores the use of different audit log files as key artifacts as the evidence in different databases for investigation which holds clues that will help to piece together the incident events for use as evidence in criminal legal proceedings. This field is now becoming an essential part of many investigations due to the increased volume of information which is helpful in solving different crimes and a large number of risks associated with the data stored on many databases.

As said in SQL Server database forensics (Fowler, 2009) with the database forensics procedure, we can retrace SQL operations performed, reconstruct the deleted information, also compromised data can be achieved with database artifacts as explained in next section. As said (Litchfield, 2007), SQL operations leave plenty of forensic data around database infrastructure in the Oracle server for forensic analysis. There is a LogMiner tool which allows an Oracle DBA and Forensic analyst to reconstruct the actions taken on an Oracle database even if the auditing features have been turned off.

Digital investigators can monitor the database audit logs and can perform various procedures to detect outliers within a database. The procedures of outlier detection can be done with data mining process. This is more explained in next section.

Outlier Detection in Database Audit Logs

An outlier as said (Kuna et al., 2014) is defined as an observation that is significantly different from the other data in its set. It is described (Kanhere et al., 2014) detecting these outliers in audit logs is extremely useful, as their existence can provide the auditor with crucial information but finding anomalies through manual queries or analyses of the audit logs' stored data requires highly trained staff and is a time-consuming process. Data mining techniques as said (Han et al., 2012) can be used to identify these entries and analyze the information. Real databases contain anomalies related to different causes, including errors in data collection, errors in the information systems, probable malicious actions, and illegal transactions and so on. As described (Rafal et al., 2012) data mining algorithms like clustering, mining frequent sets and data visualization techniques can be used for finding suspected transactions. The audit trails signifying the detection of anomalous values must be eventually analyzed by the auditor because the underlying cause of these outliers may imply a risk to the security or quality of the data.

As described in (Adedayo et al., 2015), the authors explained the ideal log setting for database forensics reconstruction. To process on audit trails it is important to identify database artifacts to retrieve the relevant information for investigations. It is more explained in next section.

The most popular databases mainly Oracle RDBMS, IBM DB2 and Microsoft SQL server are used for financial management systems where millions of transactions are carried out every day which results in massive amount of data in the databases. Oracle Forensics (D. Litchfield, 2007) and MS SQL Server Forensics (K. Fowler, 2009) tools have the scope of investigating the respective stand alone database with its own schema and audit log structure. As mentioned in the paper (Khanuja. H et al, 2014) the databases provide transaction logs where each transaction can be retraced but as per its own database structure. Sometimes it also results in difficult situations where the database becomes inaccessible due to technical failure or human errors.

It is a major problem with databases, that accidently while performing investigations on Oracle or SQL server, with sudden a power failure or breakdown there are chances where a log file can get corrupted or may also affect the transaction logs. So, there was indeed a requirement to build an investigation methodology which processes databases without the constraints of database structure and design. Hence we have designed and developed a process with database forensics which monitors, collects the traces of transactions irrespective of any database. With every transaction commit, the logs are extracted, transformed and loaded in database forensic XML file. This will save the risk of getting the evidences lost or corrupted from log files due to any breakdown. To begin with Database forensic investigations were experimented on Oracle 11g and MSSQL Server 2008.

Database Artifact Collection

The existing capabilities available for auditing in databases like MS SQL Server (Create a Server Audit and Database Audit Specification, 2018) and Oracle (Auditing Database Activity, 2018) are shown in Figure 6.

The database artifacts like audit logs, trace files, database objects, a data cache, data dictionary table, etc. contain valuable information. The most relevant database key artifacts are shown in Figure 7.

The digital investigations using relevant and appropriate artifacts can reduce the duration and financial cost of the respective investigation. It can increase the amount of relevant volatile data which can

Figure 6. Existing capabilities in databases

Function/Database	Oracle	MS SQL Server
What to log	Successful / not successful operations	All objects, tables, views, procedures and triggers
When to log	When Event-condition is satisfied	Database startup / shutdown
Where to log	Database or operating system or XML	Operating system
Fine-grained auditing	Yes	Yes
Result storage	Table	File or Table
Audit trail database name	SYS.AUD$ table	NA (User defined name for trace table)
Column based search possible	Yes	Yes
Mechanism	Selected user database action using audit features	Composing rules by GUI tools

Figure 7. Database key artifacts

Database	Key artifacts	Information collected
Oracle	DBA_Audit_Trail (SYS.AUD$)	Object Name, Action Name, Time Stamp, SQL_Text Session ID
MS SQL Server	SQL Server Profiler, Default Trace File	Text Data, Login Name, SPID (Server Process ID), End Time

be preserved after an incident. It also ensures that database investigation remains manageable. The SQL transactions are extracted from these database key artifacts (database audit logs etc.) and are transformed and loaded in Database Forensic XML. The section below explains the generation of Database Forensic XML through database audit logs.

Generation of Database Forensic XML Through Audit Logs

Three different processes like Extract, Transform and Load (ETL process) is done to get XML files through audit logs. The XML obtained gives the transaction records along with metadata of the transactions. This metadata gives the evidence to be kept and produced in court of law. Figure 8 shows the three subsequent processes of ETL.

The following steps explain the ETL process which can be implemented with Java programming language.

1. Establish the database connection.
2. EXTRACT the SQL transactions through database key artifacts (DBA_Audit_Trail, logs etc.) from different database systems. For this, create and execute SQL query on log table retrieving attributes username, time and text data (SQL Text).
3. Retrieve results from the resultset.
4. Create new audit XML file.
5. Iterate through the result set and read each record.
6. TRANSFORM the data from heterogeneous sources into one uniform format like uniform DATE structure, equivalence of different attributes name with the same context. For this, convert date and other numeric parameters into a uniform format.
7. LOAD/WRITE the resultant records along its metadata in audit XML file.

Figure 8. ETL process

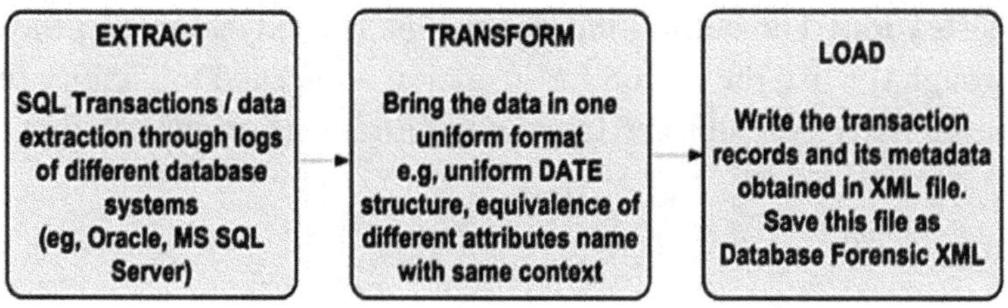

Figure 9. Generation of database forensic XML

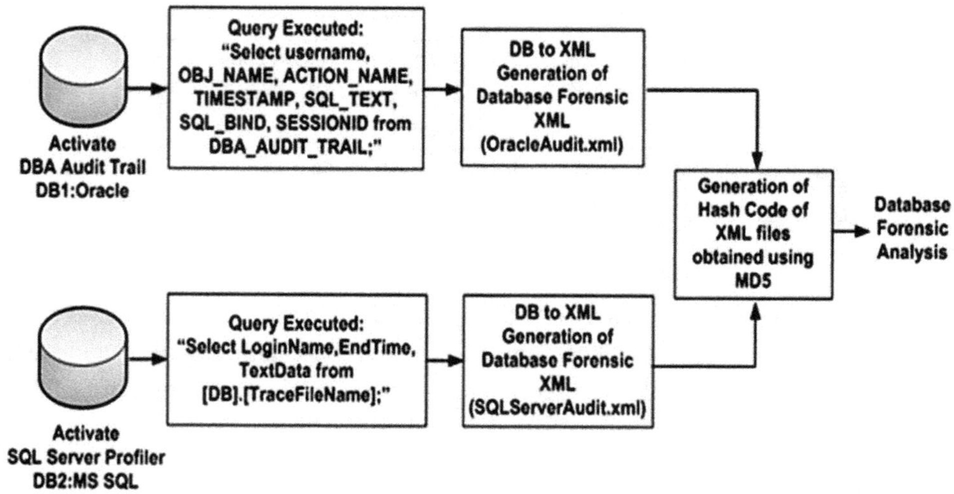

The generation of Database Forensic XML is shown in Figure 9.

The XML files obtained contain SQL transactions (DDL/DML statements) and detail information like date, time and user of the transaction records. The researchers call these XML files as Database Forensic XML.

During experimentation the researchers get OracleAudit.xml and SQLServerAudit.xml files which are shown in Figure 10. The Database Forensic XML file generated from different database systems should have at least three headers in common i.e., < username >, < timestamp > and < SQL Text >. The XML files obtained are stored on a separate storage for further forensic analysis by third party analyzer. To prevent the data from getting tampered, the researcher generates hash code of the XML segments using the MD5 algorithm. The Database Forensic XML files obtained are parsed using SAX parser (the Simple API for XML) in sequential order.

PROPOSED METHODOLOGY

1. **Rule-Based Outlier Detection:** For identifying outlier transactions the rules mentioned in Figure 11 are applied. Each and every transaction in the set of database forensic XML is checked against each of the rules one by one. If the transaction is found suspicious according to a rule, then the respective transaction is added to the outlier transactions list along with details of rule which marked it as suspicious. Once all transactions are checked, the researchers get the outlier transactions list which also contains the reason for suspicion.
2. **Bayesian Classification:** The outlier transactions list is used as input to Bayesian classification. While going through the list, the reason for suspicion is checked to identify that under which categories (Account Activity, Amount, and Location) the transaction is suspicious. This analysis is then

Figure 10. Database forensic XML

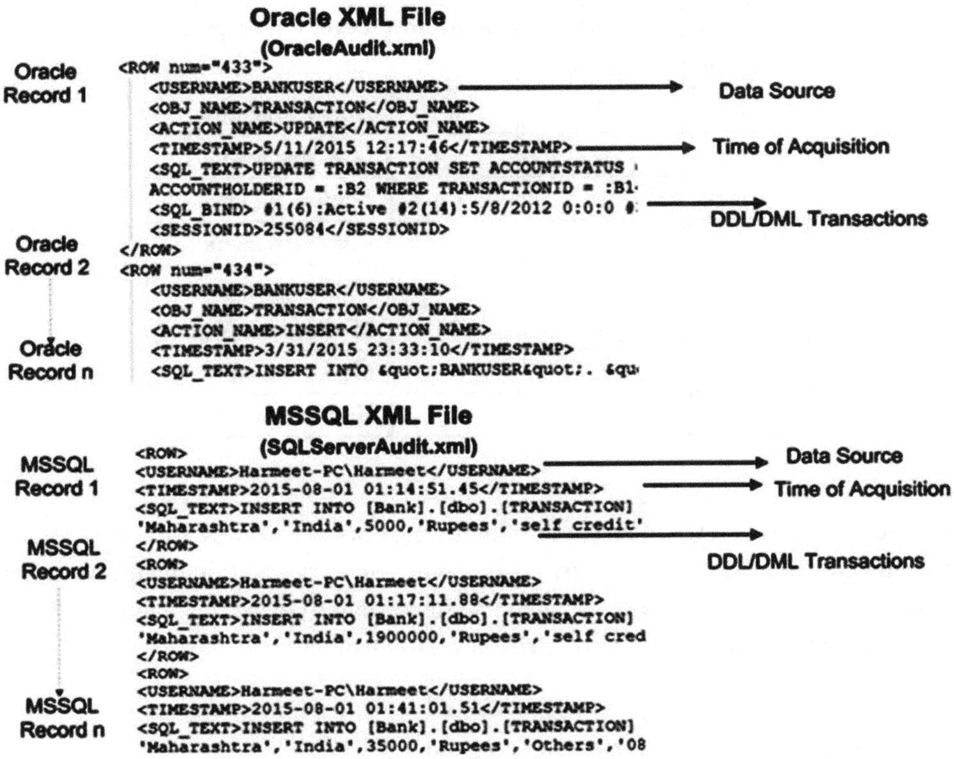

Figure 11. Rules for outlier detection

Rules	Suspicious Category	Description
Rule 1	Account Activity	Sudden transactions in dormant account i.e. previously inactive account.
Rule 2	Account Activity	Deposit or withdrawal transactions on same day in different accounts of the same person.
Rule 3	Transaction Amount	A customer makes large value deposit or withdrawal transactions in an account.
Rule 4	Transaction Amount	The deposit or withdrawal transactions of aggregate value greater than reporting threshold i.e. the amount of each deposit or withdrawal is not substantial, but the total of which is substantial.
Rule 5	Transaction Amount	A customer makes deposit or withdrawal transactions of value just under the reporting threshold.
Rule 6	Transaction Amount	The transactions in which cash is withdrawn immediately after it is deposited.
Rule 7	Transaction Amount	Frequency of withdrawal transactions is greater than threshold.
Rule 8	Location	The cash deposited to an account from high risk country.
Rule 9	Location	Cash deposited to same account from different locations on same day.

Figure 12. Rules for Bayesian classification

Account Activity	Transaction Amount	Location	Level Of Suspicion
0	0	0	Non-suspicious
0	0	1	Low-suspicious
0	1	0	Low-suspicious
1	0	0	Low-suspicious
0	1	1	Medium-suspicious
1	0	1	Medium-suspicious
1	1	0	Medium-suspicious
1	1	1	High-suspicious

used to describe the risk level of suspicion. Figure 12 shows the Rules for Bayesian classification, where 1 indicates the transaction is suspicious in the category and 0 indicates the transaction was not found suspicious in the respective category. According to these 0, 1 values in three categories the last column in the table indicates the risk level of suspicion.

RULE-BASED BAYESIAN CLASSIFICATION

Rule-based method is applied in sequential order on Database Forensic XML files. The XML files are frequently collected for particular duration and are parsed using SAX parser. The parser parses the data under three categories that is, Account, Amount or Location. The list of transaction records obtained after applying the Rule-based classification method gives the initial belief of the transactions to be suspicious. It says any activity violating the rules will be marked as suspicious. The Algorithm for each Rule is defined and shown in subsequent sections. The transactions are categorized as per rules defined.

Each transaction is verified against RBI rules. If the transaction is found suspicious, it is added to the outlier transactions list and marked as suspicious. The reason for suspicion is checked to identify that under which categories (Account, Amount or Location) or particularly which rule the transaction is suspicious. The Rule Based Bayesian Classification is implemented as explained in next section.

Proposed Algorithms for Rule-Based Outlier Detection

The notations used in algorithms are shown in Table 1.

Table 1. Notations used in algorithms

Notation	Meaning
TrnsAudRecList	list of audit records for customers' transactions in a bank.
outTrnsList	list of outlier transactions.

Figure 13.

Algorithm 1: for Rule 1, Activity in dormant account

```
For each Trns from TrnsAudRecList,
    get accountId for for Trns if(status
    of accountId is Dormant)
        mark Trns as outlier transaction
        set reason for outlier as activity in dormant account
        and add it to the outTrnsList
    End
if End
For
```

Algorithm 1: Category: Account Activity

This code is used to detect sudden transactions occurred in dormant account i.e previously inactive account.

Algorithm 2: Category: Account Activity

This code is used to detect transactions like deposit or withdrawal of amount done on same day in different accounts of the same person.

Algorithm 3: Category: Amount Activity

This code is used to detect transactions of a customer who makes large value deposit or withdrawal of amount in an account.

Figure 14.

Algorithm 2: for Rule 2, Transactions in different accounts of same person on same day

```
For each Transi from TrnsAudRecList,
    get transactionDatei, accountHolderNamei and accountIdi for Trnsi
    For each Trnsj from TrnsAudRecList,
        if (transactionDatej =transactionDatei)
            get accountHolderNamej and accountIdj for Trnsj
            if((accountHolderNamej = accountHolderNamei)and(accountIdj !=
                accountIdi)) mark transaction for accountIdi as outliertransaction
                set reason for outlier as Transactions in accounts of same person on same day
                and add it to the outTrnsList
            End if
        End if
    End For
End For
```

Figure 15.

Algorithm 3: for Rule 3, Large value transactions in an account

```
For each Trns fromTrnsAudRecList,
    get amount and accountRiskCategoryThreshold for Trns
    if(amount is greater than accountRiskCategoryThreshold)
        mark Trns as outlier transaction
        set reason for outlier as Large value transactions in an account
        and add it to the outTrnsList
    End if
End For
```

Algorithm 4: Category: Amount Activity

This code is used to detect the deposit or withdrawal of transactions with aggregate value greater than reporting threshold i.e. the amount of each deposit or withdrawal is not substantial, but the total of which is substantial.

Algorithm 5: Category: Amount Activity

This code is used to detect if a customer makes deposit or withdrawal transactions of value just under the reporting threshold.

Figure 16.

Algorithm 4: for Rule 4, Transactions of aggregate value greater than threshold

```
For each Transi from TrnsAudRecList,
    set aggregateAmount=0;
    get amounti, accountIdi, transactionTypei and accountRiskCategoryThresholdi for Trnsi
    For each Trnsj from TrnsAudRecList,
        if((accountIdj = accountIdi)and(transactionTypej =transactionTypei))
            set aggregateAmount=aggregateAmount +amountj
        End if
    End For
    if((aggregateAmount is greater than accountRiskCategoryThresholdi)
        mark transaction for accountIdi as outliertransaction
        set reason for outlier as aggregate value of transactions greater than threshold
        and add it to the outTrnsList
    End if
End For
```

Algorithm 6: Category: Amount Activity

This code is used to detect transactions where cash is withdrawn immediately after it is deposited.

Algorithm 7: Category: Amount Activity

This code is used to detect the transactions whose frequency of withdrawal is greater than threshold.

Algorithm 8: Category: Location Activity

This code is used to detect the transactions if the cash is deposited to an account from high risk country

Algorithm 9: Category: Location Activity

This is code is used to detect the transactions if cash is deposited to same account at different locations on same day

Figure 17.

Algorithm 5: for Rule 5, Transactions of value just under the reporting threshold

```
For each Trns fromTrnsAudRecList,
    get amount and accountRiskCategoryThreshold(arct) for Trns
    if((amount < arct)and(amount ≥(arct-10%)))
        mark Trns as outlier transaction
        set reason for outlier as transaction of value just under the reporting threshold
        and add it to theoutTrnsList
    End if
End For
```

Figure 18.

Algorithm 6: for Rule 6, Deposit transaction followed by immediate Withdrawal transaction

```
For each Transi from
    TrnsAudRecList,
    get accountIdi, transactionTypei, transactionDatei and transactionTimei for Trnsi
    For each Trnsj from TrnsAudRecList,
        if((accountIdj = accountIdi)and(transactionDatej = transactionDatei)and
        (transactionTimej > transactionTimei)and(transactionTypei is a Deposit
        transaction)and (trans actionTypej is a Withdrawl transaction))
            mark Trnsj as outlier transaction
            set reason for outlier as aggregate value of transactions greater than
            threshold and add it to theoutTrnsList
        End if
    End For
```

Figure 19.

Algorithm 7: for Rule 7, Frequency of withdrawal transactions is greater than threshold

```
For each Transi from TrnsAudRecList,
    get accountIdi, transactionTypei for Trnsi
    if(transactionTypei is withdrawal transaction)
        if(withdrawalHashtable doesnot contain
        accountIdi)
            add accountIdi to withdrawalHashtable and set withdrawalFrequency=1
        else
            set withdrawalFrequency=withdrawalFrequency +1 in hashtable for accountIdi
            if((withdrawalFrequency is greater than
                MaxWithdrawalFrequency) mark transaction for accountIdi
                as outliertransaction
                set reason for outlier as Withdrawal transaction frequency greater than threshold
                and add it to theoutTrnsList
            End if
        End if
    End if
End For
```

Figure 20.

Algorithm 8: for Rule 8, Deposit to an account from High riskcountry

```
For each Trns fromTrnsAudRecList,
    get transactionType and country for Trns
        if((country ∈ highRiskCountries)and(transactionType is
        withdrawal transaction)) mark Trns as outlier transaction

        set reason for outlier as Deposit to an account from High risk
        country and add it to theoutTrnsList
    End if
End For
```

Algorithm 10: Rule Based Bayesian Classification

This code is used to set the level of suspicion based upon the category (Amount, Account and Location) as shown in Figure 22.

Algorithmic Steps of Proposed System for Suspicious Transaction Detection

- Extract traces of transactions from audit logs of MS SQL and Oracle server.
- Perform ETL process on the records retrieved to generate Database Forensic XML.
- XML files obtained are verified using MD5 Hashing Algorithm.
- Parse Database Forensic XML using SAX Parser to get list of audit records.
- Rule Based Bayesian classification Algorithm is applied on list of audit records.

Figure 21.

```
Algorithm 9: for Rule 9, Cash deposited to same account at different locations on same day

For each Transi from TrnsAudRecList,
    get accountIdi, transactionTypei, transactionDatei, transactionCountryi for Trnsi
    if (transactionTypei is a Deposit
        transaction)) For each Trnsj
        from TrnsAudRecList,
            if((accountIdj is equal to accountIdi)and
            (transactionDatej is equal to transactionDatei)and
            (transactionCountryj is not same as
            transactionCountryi)and (transactionTypej is a
            Deposit transaction))

                mark Trnsj as outlier transaction
                set reason for outlier as Cash deposited to same account at different locations on
                same day and add it to the outTrnsList

            End if
    End if
```

- Generate outlier transaction report as per Rules.
- We get the list of transactions labeled as normal or suspicious. This gives the initial belief of the transactions to be suspicious.

The suspicious transactions received at various risk levels are represented using Bayesian network model ("Bayesian networks - an introduction", 2018), as explained in next section.

BAYESIAN NETWORK MODEL REPRESENTATION FOR SUSPICIOUS TRANSACTIONS

The Bayesian network model for rule-based outlier detection in Figure 8 explains how the level of suspicion is predicted for any transaction. The Transaction risk category value indicates the level of suspicion. It can be non-suspicious, low, medium or high. The transaction risk category depends on three values; the Account activity, Amount and Location.

- The Account activity can either be suspicious or non-suspicious. The Account activity value depends on the values of the transaction in dormant account and the value of transactions in different accounts of the same person.
- The Amount is indicated as either less than or greater than defined threshold value. The Amount value is the result of transaction amount compared with thresholds defined according to the account category.
- The location can be either suspicious or non-suspicious. The location depends on the frequency of the deposit transactions to same account at different locations on same day and whether the deposit transaction was carried out from the high risk country.

Figure 22.

Algorithm 10: Rule Based Bayesian Classification

```
Set accountActivityCount = 0, amountCount = 0, locationCount = 0 For each Trns from
outTrnsList get reasonForOutlier

switch(reasonForOutlier)
case 1:Activity in dormant account
   accountActivityCount = accountActivityCount + 1
case 2:Transactions in accounts of same person on same day
   accountActivityCount = accountActivityCount + 1
case 3:Large value transactions in an account
   amountCount = amountCount + 1
case 4:Aggregate value of transactions greater than threshold
   amountCount = amountCount + 1
case 5:Transaction of value just under the reporting threshold
   amountCount = amountCount + 1
case 6:Aggregate value of transactions greater than threshold
   amountCount = amountCount + 1
case 7:Frequency of withdrawal transactions is greater than threshold
   amountCount = amountCount + 1
case 8:Deposit to an account from High risk country
   locationCount = locationCount + 1
case 9:Cash deposited to same account at different locations on same day
   locationCount = locationCount + 1
End switch

if((accountActivityCount ≥ 1) and (amountCount ≥ 1) and (locationCount ≥ 1))
     set level of suspicion as High
else if[((accountActivityCount ≥ 1) and (amountCount ≥ 1) and (locationCount = 0))or
((accountActivityCount ≥ 1) and (amountCount = 0) and (locationCount ≥ 1))or
((accountActivityCount = 0) and (amountCount ≥ 1) and (locationCount ≥ 1))]
   set level of suspicion as Medium
else if[((accountActivityCount ≥ 1) and (amountCount = 0) and (locationCount = 0))or
((accountActivityCount = 0) and (amountCount = 0) and (locationCount ≥ 1))or
((accountActivityCount = 0) and (amountCount ≥ 1) and (locationCount = 0))]
   set level of suspicion as Low
else if((accountActivityCount = 0) and (amountCount = 0) and (locationCount = 0))
   set level of suspicion as NS(Non-suspicious)
```

Figure 24 shows that when the account activity is non-suspicious, amount is less than threshold value and the location is non-suspicious then the transaction risk category is non-suspicious.

Figure 25 shows that when the account activity is suspicious, amount is less than threshold value and the location is non-suspicious then the transaction risk category is less-suspicious.

Figure 26 shows that when the account activity is suspicious, amount is greater than threshold value and the location is non-suspicious then the transaction risk category is medium-suspicious.

Figure 12 shows that when the account activity is suspicious, amount is greater than threshold and the location is suspicious then the transaction risk category is High-suspicious.

Figure 23. Level of suspicion transactions

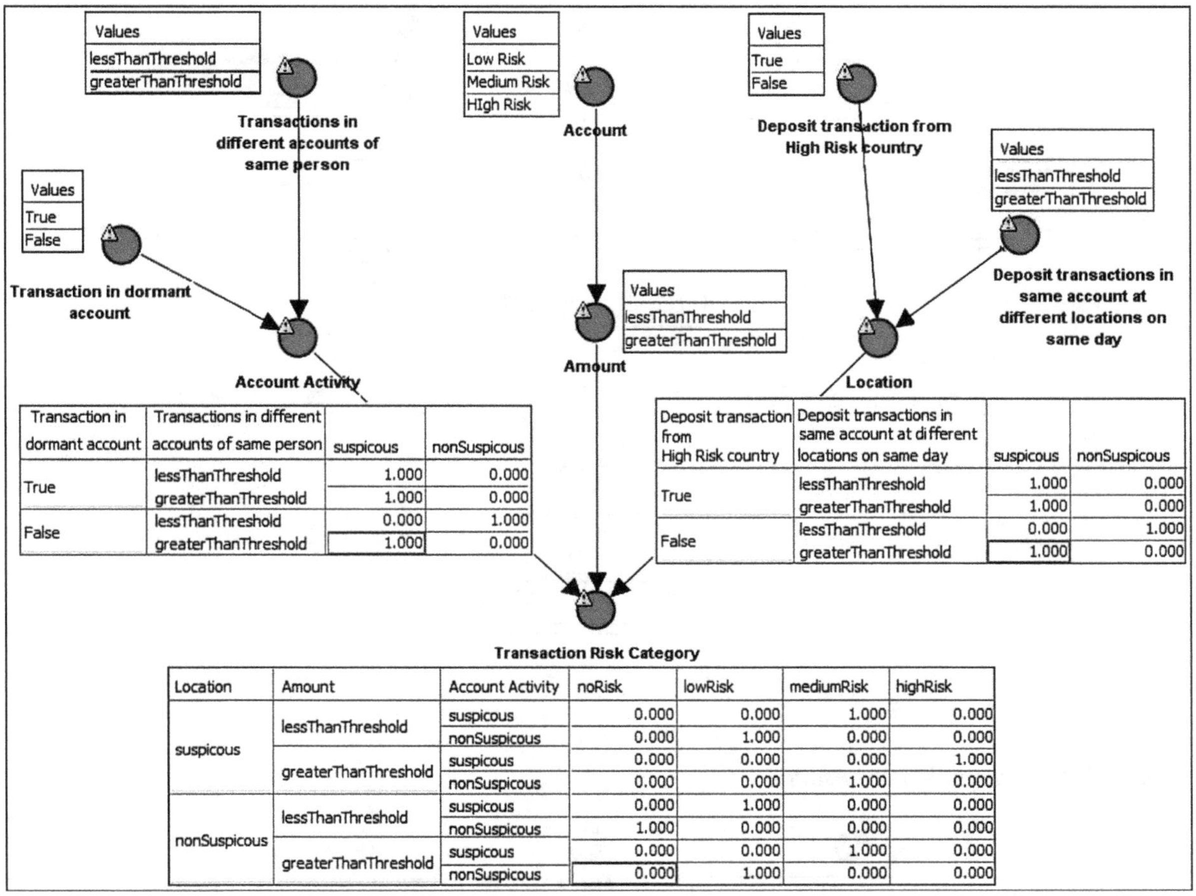

DEMPSTER - SHAFER THEORY

Dempster - Shafer theory is based on the work of Arthur Dempster during the 1960's and in particular by Glenn Shafer's treatise A Mathematical Theory of Evidence (Shafer 1976) or the theory of belief functions for representing and reasoning with uncertain and imprecise information. This particular theory is especially relevant for auditing and assurance as it focuses on evidence and evidential reasoning. This theory of evidence provides a framework to deal with a system with uncertain information. Moreover it is a generalization of the Bayesian theory of subjective probability such that it does not require probabilities for each evidence of interest, but bases belief in the truth of an event on the probabilities of other propositions or events related to it. Evidence theory provides an alternative to the traditional manner in which probability theory is used to represent uncertainty by means of the specification of two degrees of likelihood, belief and plausibility, for each event under consideration.

There are three basic functions that are important to understand and apply in Dempster Shafer theory (Shafer 2002): the basic belief mass function or basic probability assignment (bpa) function which specifies the belief mass distribution (e.g. m-values in our system) over all possible sub-sets of a frame of discernment(θ), the Belief function (Bel(s)), and the Plausibility function (Pl(s)). A frame of discernment

Figure 24. Non- suspicious transaction

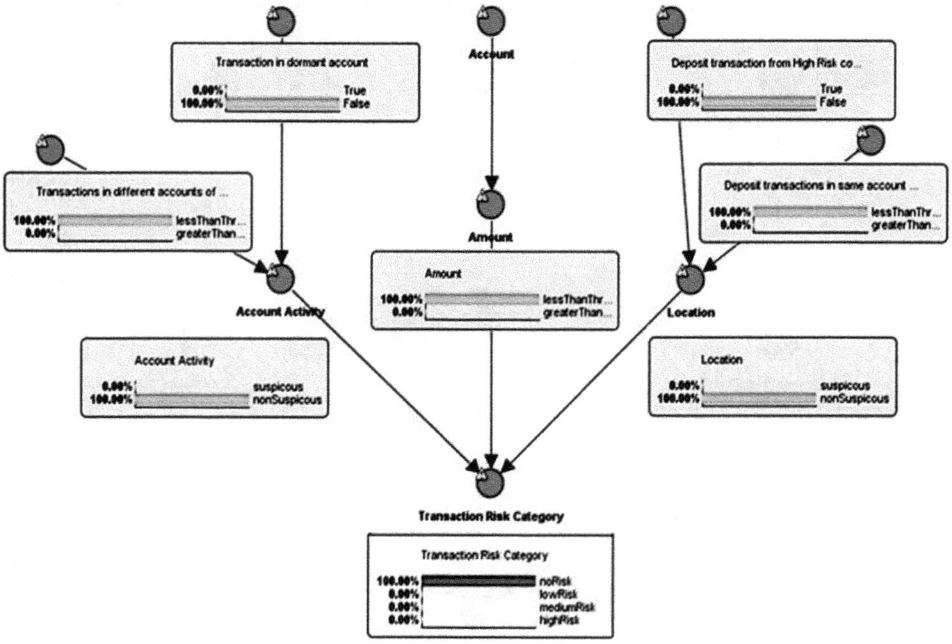

Figure 25. Less suspicious transaction

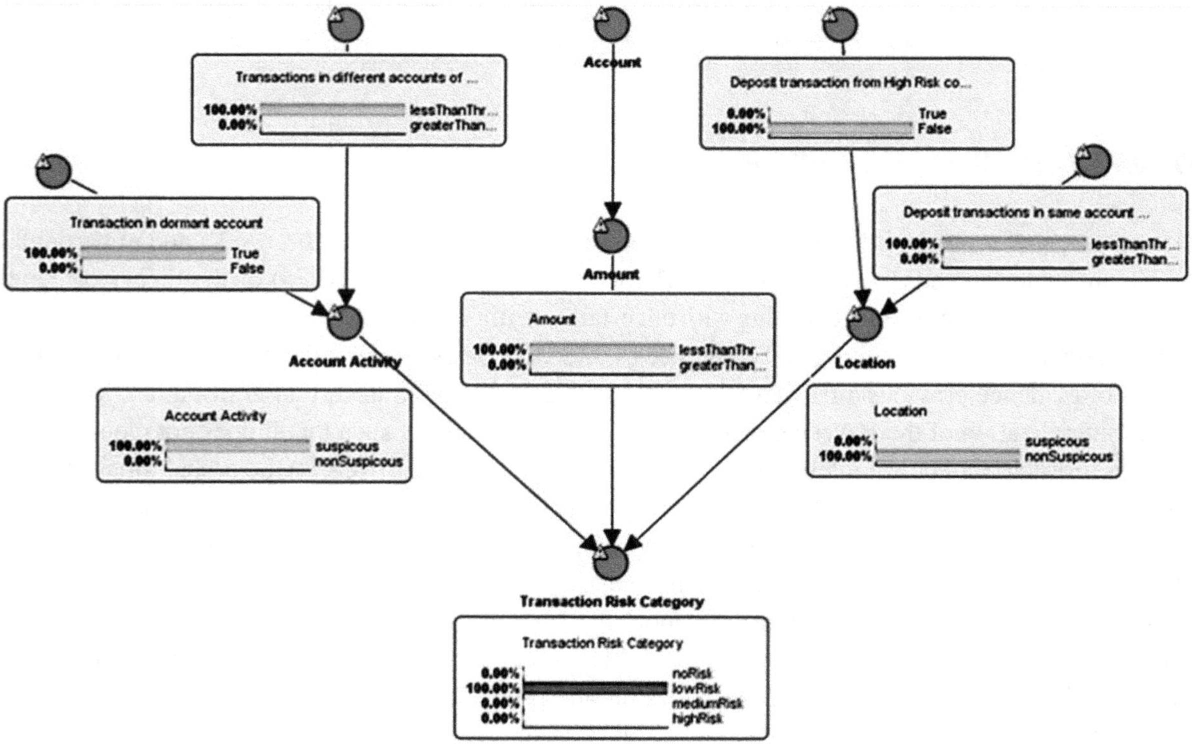

Figure 26. Medium suspicious transaction

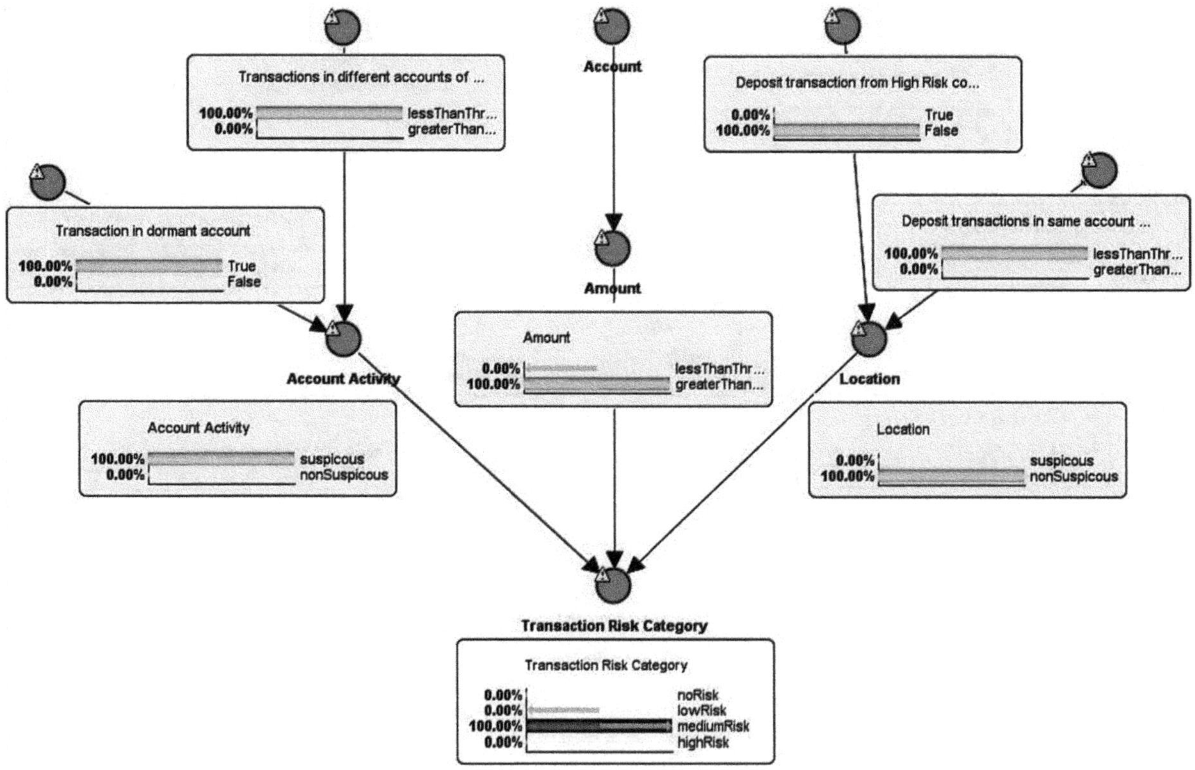

(also called a Universe of Discourse) in Dempster-Shafer is a set of mutually exclusive and exhaustive possibilities/evidence. The Dempster Shafer theory of evidence assigns a belief mass m to every element in the power set to the interval between 0 and 1, where the bpa of the null set is 0 and the summation of the bpa of all the subsets of the power set is 1. The relationship of belief function, plausibility function and ignorance (uncertainty) is shown in Figure 13.

Theory of Evidence: Rule of Combination

Dempster-Shafer is the theory of Evidence (Sentz K. et al, 2002) which is the practical way to combine information received from various sources. The general procedure in DST is to collect the evidence, combine the evidence and interpret the evidence. Individual evidences can be combined to form stronger evidences as said in paper (S. Panigrahi. et al., 2009). Say, two evidences, represented in terms of the bpa, m1 and m2 such that,

$$\sum_{P} m_1(P) = 1 \, and \sum_{Q} m_2(Q) = 1 \tag{1}$$

Figure 27. High suspicious transaction

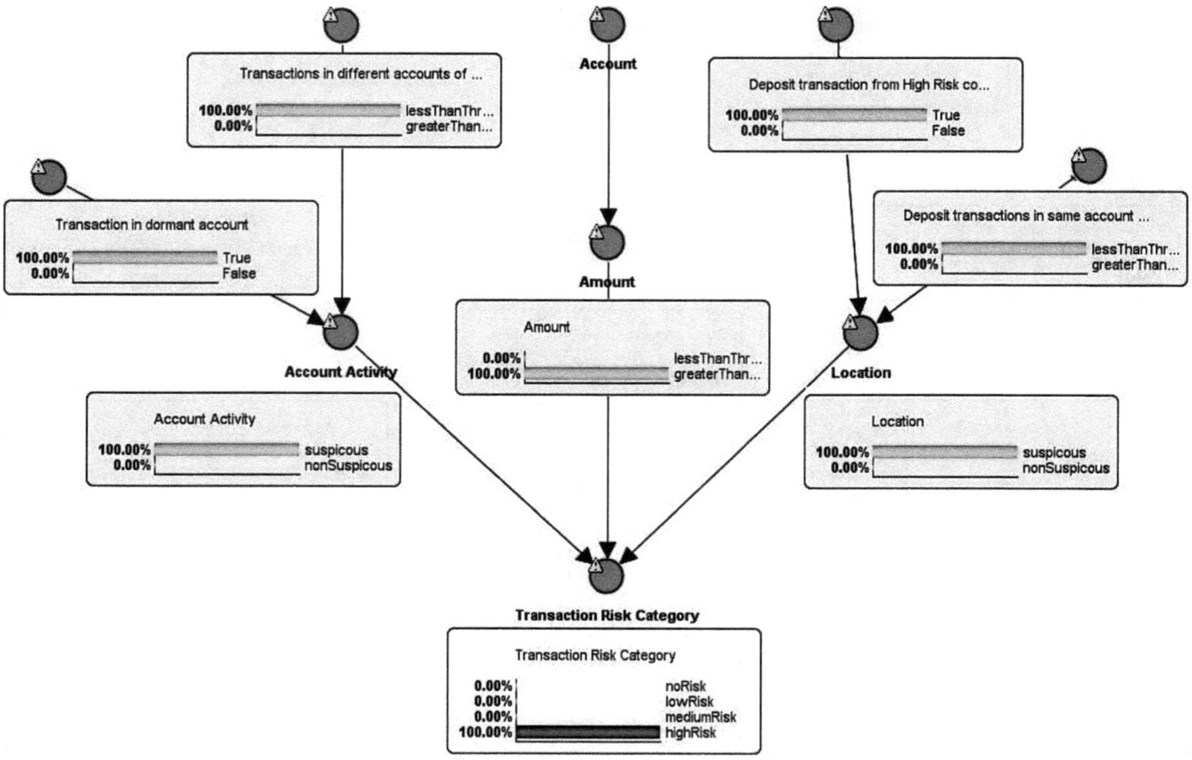

Figure 28. Relationship of belief function, plausibility function and ignorance (uncertainty)

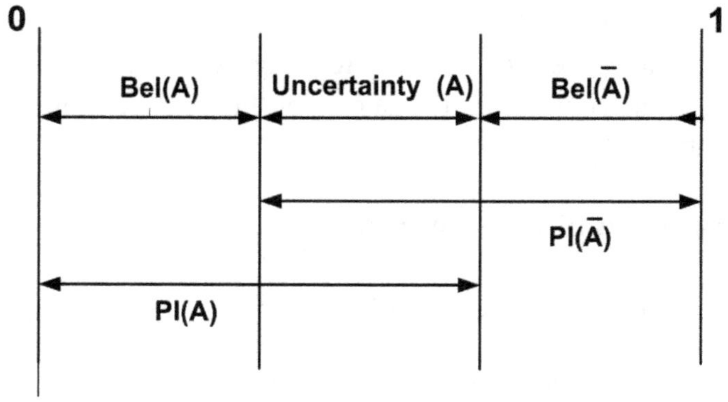

We have,

$$1 = \sum_{P} m_1(P) . \sum_{Q} m_2(Q) = \sum_{P,Q} m_1(P) . m_2(Q) \tag{2}$$

Thus,

$$= \sum_{P\cap Q=\varnothing} m_1(P).m_2(Q) + \sum_{A\neq\varnothing}\left[\sum_{P\cap Q=A} m_1(P).m_2(Q)\right] \quad (3)$$

The bpa, represented by 'm', is often thought of as Bayesian probability. In DST, the bpa is defined as a generalized Bayesian probability. Thus we can define the combination of basic probability assignments as

$$m_{12}(A) = \frac{\left[\sum_{P\cap Q=A} m_1(P).m_2(Q)\right]}{\left(1-\sum_{P\cap Q=\varnothing} m_1(P).m_2(Q)\right)} \quad (5)$$

for all A ≠∅, and m12 (∅) = 0. This satisfies ΣA = 1

The Belief function can be expressed in terms of the basic probability assignment, bpa:

$$m_{12}(A) = Bel(A) = \sum_{B\in A} m(B) \quad (6)$$

Given the belief function, Bel(A) and as shown in Figure 13 we have Plausibility function given as

$$Pl(A) = 1 - Bel(\bar{A}) \quad (7)$$

So a novel approach is used to analyze and assure the suspected transactions using Dempster Shafer theory. Here, initial belief is set on the basis of two parameters that are transaction amount (lower to higher value) and frequency of transactions (withdraw or deposit). These two parameters give the support of evidence for evaluating suspiciousness of the transaction. Secondly, a class is defined on Risk categories (Low, medium and high risk category) which classify the customers in a bank depending upon the Customer profile. It may contain information relating to Customer's identity, social/financial status, nature of business activity, information about his client's business and their location etc. This gives us additional support of evidence for evaluating the customer's transaction.

Evaluating Risk Level of Suspicious Transactions Using Theory of Evidence

The digital evidences like number of times the occurrences of suspected account (transactions) and high value transaction amount retrieved from the database audit logs is combined using theory of evidence. Algorithm of proposed system for finding risk of suspicious transactions using Dempster Shafer theory of evidence is as shown in Figure 29.

DST Analysis evaluates the suspicion of transaction which is combined output received from m1(s) which indicates number of times Account transaction occurs and m2(s) indicates transaction with high value amount.

Figure 29.

```
Algorithm 11: DST Analysis

Input evidence 1: No. Of Transactions (noOfTransactions),
Input evidence 2: High Value TransationAmt (highValueTransAmt) of each Account
Result: To get suspicion level of transactions
  while [each case (for the transactions of suspected Account)] do
      get the initial belief values of the transaction
        combine the evidences(noOfTransactions) m1(s), (highValueTransAmt) m2(s) and risk
        category m1(s), m2(s)
    calculate Belief (Bel(s)) and Plausability (Pl( s))
  if (Bel(s))> (Pl( s)) then
    degree of plausibility for transactions to be genuine is less
    suspected transactions = more suspicious
  else
    degree of plausibility for transactions to be genuine is more
    suspected transactions = less suspicious
  end if
end while
```

DATA ANALYSIS, FINDINGS, AND DISCUSSIONS

The experiments were carried out on Banking log files. Initially the researchers extracted the transaction records from the logs of Oracle and MS SQLServer. The transactions obtained from two different databases through audit logs were in different formats. These transaction records were then transformed and loaded in different but uniform XML segments as explained in subsections below.

ETL Process of Oracle Database

The traces of transactions in the Oracle database were recorded in data dictionary table DBA_AUDIT_TRAIL (SYS.AUD$) as shown in Figure 30. Specifically the attributes like username, TIMESTAMP and SQL_TEXT from 'BANKUSER' database was retrieved with the query as shown below:

The output extracted from the audit table is transformed and loaded into XML format as OracleAudit.xml. It contains three major heads < username >, < timestamp > and < sql_text >. The first XML segment is shown in Figure 32.

Figure 30.

```
select USERNAME, TIMESTAMP, SQL_TEXT from DBA_AUDIT_TRAIL where
username='BANKUSER' and OBJ_NAME='TRANSACTION' and (ACTION_NAME='SELECT'or
ACTION_NAME='UPDATE'or ACTION_NAME='INSERT' or ACTION_NAME='DROP') and
TIMESTAMP > = to_date ( '31-03-2015' , 'DD-MM-YYYY' ) and TIMESTAMP<to_date('30-07-
2015','DD-MM-YYYY')order by ACTION_NAME desc
```

Figure 31. Transaction records in DBA_AUDIT_TRAIL

	USERNAME	TIMESTAMP	SQL_TEXT
426	BANKUSER	01-04-15	UPDATE TRANSACTION SET ACCOUNTSTATUS = :B5 , DATEOFOPENING = :B4 , ACCOUNTBALANCE = :B3 , ACCOUNTHOLDERID = :B2 WHERE TR...
427	BANKUSER	01-04-15	UPDATE TRANSACTION SET ACCOUNTSTATUS = :B5 , DATEOFOPENING = :B4 , ACCOUNTBALANCE = :B3 , ACCOUNTHOLDERID = :B2 WHERE TR...
428	BANKUSER	01-04-15	UPDATE TRANSACTION SET ACCOUNTSTATUS = :B5 , DATEOFOPENING = :B4 , ACCOUNTBALANCE = :B3 , ACCOUNTHOLDERID = :B2 WHERE TR...
429	BANKUSER	01-04-15	UPDATE TRANSACTION SET ACCOUNTSTATUS = :B5 , DATEOFOPENING = :B4 , ACCOUNTBALANCE = :B3 , ACCOUNTHOLDERID = :B2 WHERE TR...
430	BANKUSER	01-04-15	UPDATE TRANSACTION SET ACCOUNTSTATUS = :B5 , DATEOFOPENING = :B4 , ACCOUNTBALANCE = :B3 , ACCOUNTHOLDERID = :B2 WHERE TR...
431	BANKUSER	01-04-15	UPDATE TRANSACTION SET ACCOUNTSTATUS = :B5 , DATEOFOPENING = :B4 , ACCOUNTBALANCE = :B3 , ACCOUNTHOLDERID = :B2 WHERE TR...
432	BANKUSER	31-03-15	UPDATE TRANSACTION SET ACCOUNTSTATUS = :B5 , DATEOFOPENING = :B4 , ACCOUNTBALANCE = :B3 , ACCOUNTHOLDERID = :B2 WHERE TR...
433	BANKUSER	31-03-15	UPDATE TRANSACTION SET ACCOUNTSTATUS = :B5 , DATEOFOPENING = :B4 , ACCOUNTBALANCE = :B3 , ACCOUNTHOLDERID = :B2 WHERE TR...
434	BANKUSER	12-05-15	INSERT INTO "BANKUSER". "TRANSACTION" (TRANSACTIONID, ACCOUNTID, TRANSACTIONDATE, TRANSACTIONTIME, TRANSACTIONMODE, TRAN...
435	BANKUSER	31-03-15	INSERT INTO "BANKUSER". "TRANSACTION" (TRANSACTIONID, ACCOUNTID, TRANSACTIONDATE, TRANSACTIONTIME, TRANSACTIONMODE, TRAN...
436	BANKUSER	11-05-15	INSERT INTO "BANKUSER". "TRANSACTION" (TRANSACTIONID, ACCOUNTID, TRANSACTIONDATE, TRANSACTIONTIME, TRANSACTIONMODE, TRAN...
437	BANKUSER	11-05-15	INSERT INTO "BANKUSER". "TRANSACTION" (TRANSACTIONID, ACCOUNTID, TRANSACTIONDATE, TRANSACTIONTIME, TRANSACTIONMODE, TRAN...
438	BANKUSER	11-05-15	INSERT INTO "BANKUSER". "TRANSACTION" (TRANSACTIONID, ACCOUNTID, TRANSACTIONDATE, TRANSACTIONTIME, TRANSACTIONMODE, TRAN...
439	BANKUSER	10-05-15	INSERT INTO "BANKUSER". "TRANSACTION" (TRANSACTIONID, ACCOUNTID, TRANSACTIONDATE, TRANSACTIONTIME, TRANSACTIONMODE, TRAN...
440	BANKUSER	10-05-15	INSERT INTO "BANKUSER". "TRANSACTION" (TRANSACTIONID, ACCOUNTID, TRANSACTIONDATE, TRANSACTIONTIME, TRANSACTIONMODE, TRAN...

ETL Process of MSSQL Server

The traces of transactions of Microsoft SQL Server 2008 were retrieved from SQL Server Profiler. The output from the SQL Server Profiler with attributes like LoginName, EndTime, TextData from 'Bank' database were extracted and transformed in user defined table called 'KeyArtifact' within the 'Bank' database as shown in Figure 34. The contents of the table were extracted with the query shown in Figure 33.

The output of the file obtained is transformed and loaded into XML format as SQLServerAudit.xml with three major heads < username >, < timestamp > and < sql_text >. The second XML segment is shown in Figure 35.

Figure 32. Oracle: database Forensic XML (OracleAudit.xml)

```
<ROW num="433">
    <USERNAME>BANKUSER</USERNAME>
    <OBJ_NAME>TRANSACTION</OBJ_NAME>
    <ACTION_NAME>UPDATE</ACTION_NAME>
    <TIMESTAMP>5/11/2015 12:17:46</TIMESTAMP>
    <SQL_TEXT>UPDATE TRANSACTION SET ACCOUNTSTATUS = :B5, DATEOFOPENING = :B4, ACCOUNTBALANCE = :B3,
    ACCOUNTHOLDERID = :B2 WHERE TRANSACTIONID = :B1</SQL_TEXT>
    <SQL_BIND> #1(6):Active #2(14):5/8/2012 0:0:0 #3(8):-1764300 #4(3):141 #5(3):577</SQL_BIND>
    <SESSIONID>255084</SESSIONID>
</ROW>
<ROW num="434">
    <USERNAME>BANKUSER</USERNAME>
    <OBJ_NAME>TRANSACTION</OBJ_NAME>
    <ACTION_NAME>INSERT</ACTION_NAME>
    <TIMESTAMP>3/31/2015 23:33:10</TIMESTAMP>
    <SQL_TEXT>INSERT INTO &quot;BANKUSER&quot;. &quot;TRANSACTION&quot; (TRANSACTIONID, ACCOUNTID,
    TRANSACTIONDATE, TRANSACTIONTIME, TRANSACTIONMODE, TRANSACTIONTYPE, TRANSACTIONCITY,
    TRANSACTIONSTATE, TRANSACTIONCOUNTRY, AMOUNT, CURRENCYCODE, PURPOSEOFTRANSACTION)
    VALUES (:B1, :B2, TO_DATE(:B3, 'YYYY-MM-DD HH24:MI:SS'),
    TO_TIMESTAMP(:B4, 'YYYY-MM-DD HH24:MI:SS.FF'), :B5, :B6, :B7, :B8, :B9, :B10, :B11, :B12)
    RETURNING ROWID INTO :O0 </SQL_TEXT>
    <SQL_BIND> #1(3):521 #2(2):40 #3(19):2015-03-31 00:00:00 #4(29):2015-03-31 19:26:28.030000000
    #5(4):Cash #6(6):Credit #7(6):Nagpur #8(11):Maharashtra #9(5):India #10(4):5000 #11(6):Rupees
    #12(11):self credit #13(0): </SQL_BIND>
    <SESSIONID>87788</SESSIONID>
</ROW>
```

Figure 33.

```
Select LoginName, EndTime, TextData from [Bank].[dbo].[KeyArtifact] where EndTime >=
(convert(datetime,'15-04-08 10:00:50 AM',5));
```

Figure 34. Outcome of SQL Profiler with active traces

	LoginName	EndTime	TextData
27	Harmeet-PC\...	2015-08-01 01:41:16.093	INSERT INTO [Bank].[dbo].[TRANSACTION] VALUES(525,43,'01-APR-15','Cash','Credit','Nagpur','Maharashtra','India',25000,'Rupees
28	Harmeet-PC\...	2015-08-01 01:41:22.727	INSERT INTO [Bank].[dbo].[TRANSACTION] VALUES(526,43,'01-APR-15','Cash','Debit','Pune','Maharashtra','India',10000,'Rupees','C
29	Harmeet-PC\...	2015-08-01 01:41:29.527	INSERT INTO [Bank].[dbo].[TRANSACTION] VALUES(527,43,'01-APR-15','Cash','Debit','Pune','Maharashtra','India',20000,'Rupees','C
30	Harmeet-PC\...	2015-08-01 01:41:35.343	INSERT INTO [Bank].[dbo].[TRANSACTION] VALUES(528,44,'01-APR-15','Cash','Credit','Nagpur','Maharashtra','India',35000,'Rupees
31	Harmeet-PC\...	2015-08-01 01:41:43.760	Select * from dbo."TRANSACTION";
32	Harmeet-PC\...	2015-08-01 01:42:00.013	set transaction isolation level read committed set implicit_transactions off
33	Harmeet-PC\...	2015-08-01 01:42:00.030	select LoginName,EndTime, TextData from [Bank].[dbo].[KeyArtifact] where EndTime >= (convert(datetime,'15-04-08 10:00:50 AM',5))a
34	Harmeet-PC\...	2015-08-01 01:43:23.073	SELECT dtb.name AS [Name], dtb.database_id AS [ID], CAST(case when dtb.name in ('master','model','msdb','tempdb') then 1 else dtb
35	Harmeet-PC\...	2015-08-01 01:44:58.440	SELECT dtb.name AS [Name], dtb.database_id AS [ID], CAST(case when dtb.name in ('master','model','msdb','tempdb') then 1 else dtb
36	Harmeet-PC\...	2015-08-01 01:46:15.583	SELECT dtb.name AS [Name], dtb.database_id AS [ID], CAST(case when dtb.name in ('master','model','msdb','tempdb') then 1 else dtb
37	Harmeet-PC\...	2015-08-01 01:47:43.783	SELECT dtb.name AS [Name], dtb.database_id AS [ID], CAST(case when dtb.name in ('master','model','msdb','tempdb') then 1 else dtb
38	Harmeet-PC\...	2015-08-01 01:48:56.420	SELECT dtb.name AS [Name], dtb.database_id AS [ID], CAST(case when dtb.name in ('master','model','msdb','tempdb') then 1 else dtb

Figure 35. SQLServer: database forensic XML (SQLServerAudit.xml)

```
<ROW>
<USERNAME>Harmeet-PC\Harmeet</USERNAME>
<TIMESTAMP>2015-08-01 01:14:51.45</TIMESTAMP>
<SQL_TEXT>INSERT INTO [Bank].[dbo].[TRANSACTION] VALUES(521,40,'31-3-15','Cash','Credit','Nagpur',
'Maharashtra','India',5000,'Rupees','self credit','01-12-14','Active',140);</SQL_TEXT>
</ROW>
<ROW>
<USERNAME>Harmeet-PC\Harmeet</USERNAME>
<TIMESTAMP>2015-08-01 01:17:11.88</TIMESTAMP>
<SQL_TEXT>INSERT INTO [Bank].[dbo].[TRANSACTION] VALUES(522,41,'31-3-15','Cash','Credit','Nagpur',
'Maharashtra','India',1900000,'Rupees','self credit','08-12-14','Dormant',140);</SQL_TEXT>
</ROW>
<ROW>
<USERNAME>Harmeet-PC\Harmeet</USERNAME>
<TIMESTAMP>2015-08-01 01:41:01.51</TIMESTAMP>
<SQL_TEXT>INSERT INTO [Bank].[dbo].[TRANSACTION] VALUES(523,43,'01-4-15','Cash','Credit','Nagpur',
'Maharashtra','India',35000,'Rupees','Others','08-12-12','Active',141);</SQL_TEXT>
</ROW>
```

As the outcome of ETL process we obtained two XML storage files, OracleAudit.xml and SQLServerAudit.xml. We processed these XML files separately and were parsed using SAX parser (the Simple API for XML).

EXPERIMENTATION

The experiment was carried on a financial banking dataset received from Financial Investigation Centre. The dataset received contained 600 accounts having more than 10,000 transaction records. These transaction records contained the data fields like ID, AccountID, Date, Time, ModeOfTransaction, TypeOfTransaction, City, State, Country, Amount, CodeOfCurrency. In experimentation proposed algorithms were applied. The transaction records were extracted from the log files of Oracle Database11g Release2 (11.2) and MSSQLServer 2008. The records extracted from two different databases were in different formats as shown in Figure 13 and 15. These transaction records were transformed into two different XML segments in uniform format as shown in Figure 14 and 16 as per ETL process.

The results obtained were two Database Forensic XML files named as OracleAudit.xml and SQLServerAudit.xml. Both XML segments have three common major heads, that is, < username >, < timestamp > and < sql_text >. These files were processed and parsed in sequential order. Initially, Rule Based Bayesian Classification algorithms were applied on both the XML segments. Suspected records were received with the following headers like Transaction ID, Account ID, IsSuspicious, RiskLevel, Category and Reason for Suspiciousness.

This gave the list of outlier transactions along with the reason of suspicious and marked with Rule number (eg, Rule 1, Rule 2......). The transaction records were received as per TransactionID indicating reason for suspiciousness for each record. The results obtained after first stage reduced the false alarms.

The suspected transactions are then assigned the probabilities on 0-1 scale based on the risk level as per evidences. This is shown in Figure 36. The evidences retrieved were portrait to find mainly the number of times account occurrences and the high value amount transaction in an account.

With Dempster Shafer theory the Degree of Belief and Plausibility values of the transactions are measured with the following equation (as explained in section 5).

$$m(s) = m_{12}(A) = \frac{\left[\sum_{P \cap Q = A} m_1(P).m_2(Q)\right]}{\left(1 - \sum_{P \cap Q = \varnothing} m_1(P).m_2(Q)\right)} \tag{5}$$

m(s) values: Risk Level For Account occurrences and Amount transactions
m(~s)values: Risk category (Low, medium and high risk category is assigned)
The evidence is considered Pure positive for suspicious transaction if:

(m(s) > 0, and m(~ s) = 0) and

Figure 36. Initial belief values on the evidence retrieved

No. of Account . Occ.	$m_1(s)$	$m_1(\sim s)$	$m_1(s,\sim s)$	High Value Transaction(Range) Amount(in lacs)	$m_2(s)$	$m_2(\sim s)$	$m_2(s,\sim s)$
1	0.2	0.6	0.2	Between 1 and 2	0.2	0.7	0.1
2	0.4	0.5	0.1	Between 2 and 3	0.3	0.6	0.1
3	0.4	0.5	0.1	Between 3 and 4	0.4	0.5	0.1
4	0.5	0.4	0.1	Between 4 and 5	0.4	0.5	0.1
5	0.5	0.4	0.1	Between 5 and 6	0.4	0.5	0.1
6	0.5	0.4	0.1	Between 6 and 7	0.7	0.2	0.1
7	0.5	0.4	0.1	Between 7 and 8	0.8	0.0	0.2
8	0.8	0.1	0.1	Between 8 and 9	0.9	0.1	0.0
9	0.8	0.1	0.1	Between 9 and 10	0.9	0.0	0.1
10	0.8	0.1	0.1	Between 10 and 11	0.9	0.0	0.1
11	0.8	0.1	0.1	Between 11 and 12	0.9	0.0	0.1
12	0.9	0.0	0.1	More than 12	0.9	0.0	0.1

The evidence is considered Pure negative for suspicious transaction if:

(m(s) = 0, and m(~s) > 0)

The initial belief values from Table 36 are used for getting the combined result from the two parameters. It is the probability of occurrences' of Account and Amount transaction.

Combining the two evidences P and Q we get value of $m\left(s\right)$ from eqn. (5) which is equivalent to Belief value Bel(s) as shown in eqn. (6) in above section. The transaction is considered suspicious if:

$m_{12}\left(A\right) > 0$ and thus Bel(s) > Pl(s)

This indicates the belief for transaction to be suspicious is more. So the suspected transactions are more suspicious.The transaction is not considered suspicious if:

$m_{12}\left(A\right) < 0$ and Bel(s) < Pl(s)

This indicates the belief for transaction to be suspicious is less. So the suspected transactions are less suspicious.

Figure 37 shows graphical analysis of risk level of suspected accounts as per number of account occurrences and high value transaction amount.

By using rule based and outlier detection technique in audit logs, the researchers have modeled a system for financial systems in order to monitor and detect suspicious transactions regularly and easily. Audit log is one of the important resources for suspicious transaction detection and this system provides efficient methods for analyzing audit logs. This system also reduces the need for skilled staff, as it doesn't demand to have a staff having thorough knowledge about the rules and also reduces the time required for detection and reporting by efficiently managing the whole process automatically.

Figure 37. Classification of transactions as per rules

Transaction ID	Account ID	IsSuspicious	Risk Level	Reason of Suspicion		
546	40	TRUE	1	Rule 3		
547	40	TRUE	1	Rule 3		
552	40	TRUE	1	Rule 3		
553	40	TRUE	1	Rule 3		
558	40	TRUE	1	Rule 3		
560	40	TRUE	1	Rule 3		
522	41	TRUE	3	Rule 1	Rule 2	Rule 4
575	42	FALSE	0			
523	43	TRUE	6	Rule 3	Rule 5	
524	43	TRUE	6	Rule 3	Rule 5	
525	43	TRUE	6	Rule 3	Rule 5	
526	43	TRUE	6	Rule 3	Rule 5	
527	43	TRUE	6	Rule 3	Rule 5	
567	43	TRUE	7	Rule 1	Rule 4	Rule 5
572	43	TRUE	6	Rule 4	Rule 5	
573	43	TRUE	6	Rule 4	Rule 5	
574	43	TRUE	7	Rule 1	Rule 4	Rule 5
576	43	TRUE	7	Rule 1	Rule 4	Rule 5
577	43	TRUE	6	Rule 4	Rule 5	
578	43	TRUE	6	Rule 4	Rule 5	

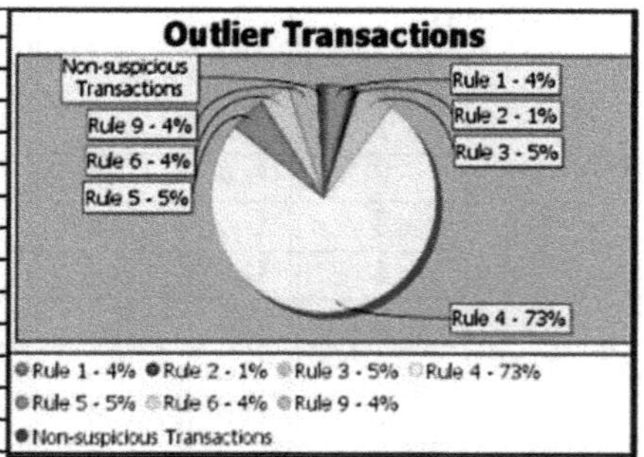

CONCLUSION AND FUTURE WORK

Commercial databases need to be monitored to comply with auditing requirements of government regulations for financial institutions. The majority of systems are still using traditional techniques to detect suspicious transactions. This chapter highlights a new dimension for accounting the databases with Digital forensics to detect suspicious and illegal transactions by incorporating database forensic practices and Dempster Shafer theory of evidence. This approach has been successfully verified using banking database implemented using Oracle and MS SQL Server. Moreover this architecture approach is designed for heterogeneous type of database.

However, in this research, the researchers have considered limited number of rules for outlier detection; the system can be extended to incorporate additional rules and more extracted evidence through database audit logs for outlier detection. In future, the rules will be trained with machine learning algorithms. This will automate the process for learning any new rule to be incorporated in the system and is implied by the regulation bodies. The research work can be extended with Blockchain technology which will keep time stamp of each record. The database will be decentralized which will make the transaction more secure with minimum probability of occurrences of suspicious transactions.

REFERENCES

Adedayo, O. M., & Olivier, M. S. (2015). Ideal log setting for database forensics reconstruction. *Digital Investigation: The International Journal of Digital Forensics & Incident Response.*, *12*(C), 27–40. doi:10.1016/j.diin.2014.12.002

Auditing Database Activity. (2018). Retrieved May 29, 2018, from https://docs.oracle.com/cd/E11882_01/server.112/e10575/tdpsg_auditing.htm

Barker, E. & Roginsky, A. (2015). *Transitions: Recommendation for Transitioning the Use of Cryptographic Algorithms and Key Lengths.* NIST Special Publication 800-131A.

Base AML Index Report. (2017). Retrieved from https://index.baselgovernance.org/sites/index/documents/Basel_AML_Index_Report_2017.pdf

Bayesian networks - an introduction. (2018). Retrieved May 29, 2018, from https://www.bayesserver.com/docs/introduction/bayesian-networks

Brian, C. (2002). *Defining Digital Forensic Examination and Analysis Tools.* Presented at The Digital Forensic Research Conference DFRWS 2002 USA, Syracuse, NY. Retrieved May 29, 2018, from https://www.dfrws.org/

Ed, M., & Craig, G. (2017). *Create a Server Audit and Database Audit Specification.* Retrieved May 29, 2018, from https://docs.microsoft.com/en-us/sql/relational- databases/security/auditing/create-a-server-audit-and-database-audit-specification?view=sql-server-2017

Fowler, K. (2009). SQL Server Forensic Analysis. Pearson Education.

Han, J., Kamber, M., & Pei, J. (2012). Data Mining: Concepts and Techniques (3rd ed.). Elsevier.

'Information & Cyber Insecurity' are the biggest risk in business operations: FICCI – Pinkerton India Risk Survey 2017. (n.d.). Retrieved from www.ficci.in/pressrelease/2806/india-risk-survey-ficci-press-release.pdf

Kanhere, P., & Khanuja, H. (2014). A Survey on Outlier Detection in Financial Transactions. *International Journal of Computers and Applications*, *108*(17).

Khanuja, H., & Adane, D. (2014, September). *Forensic Analysis for Monitoring Database Transactions*. Paper presented at Second International Symposium on Security in Computing and Communications (SSCC'14).

Kuna, H. D., Matinez, R. G., & Villatoro, F. R. (2014). Outlier detection in audit logs for application systems. *Information Systems*, *44*, 22–33. doi:10.1016/j.is.2014.03.001

Litchfield, D. (2007). *Oracle forensics part 1: dissecting the redo logs*. NISR Pub. Retrieved from https://oracle-base.com/articles/8i/logminer

Nick, E. (2016). *PCI, HIPAA, and SOX – Government Regulatory Compliance, Robin R., Easy Prey: How to Protect Your Business From Data Breach, Cybercrime & Employee Fraud*. Orlando, FL: Technology Press.

Olivier, M. S. (2009). On metadata context in Database Forensics. *Digital Investigation, Elsevier*, *5*(3), 115–123. doi:10.1016/j.diin.2008.10.001

Panigrahi, S., Sural, S., & Majumdar, A. K. (2009). *Detection of Intrusive Activity in Databases by Combining Multiple Evidences and Belief Update*. Paper presented at 2009 IEEE Symposium on Computational Intelligence in Cyber Security. 10.1109/CICYBS.2009.4925094

Rafal, D., Jan, S., & Wojciech, F. (2012). System supporting money laundering detection. *Digital Investigation, Elsevier*, *9*(1), 8–21. doi:10.1016/j.diin.2012.04.003

Raghavan, S. (2013). Digital forensic research: Current state of the art. *CSI Transactions on ICT*, *1*(1), 91–114. doi:10.100740012-012-0008-7

RBI. (2016). *Master Direction - Know Your Customer (KYC) Direction*. Retrieved on May 29, 2018 from https://rbi.org.in/scripts/NotificationUser.aspx?Mode=0&Id=10292

Sentz, K., & Ferson, S. (2002). *Combination of Evidence in Dempster–Shafer Theory*. Sandia National Laboratories. doi:10.2172/800792

SOX. (n.d.). *Sarbanes Oxley Audit Requirements*. Retrieved on May 29, 2018, from http://www.sarbanes-oxley-101.com/sarbanes-oxley-audits.htm

KEY TERMS AND DEFINITIONS

Audit Logs: An audit log is a document that records an event in digital format. It records when and what resources were accessed. It particularly includes user login information, source addresses and a timestamp. It keeps the record of the sequence of activities that has taken place at any time with specific operations or event. Audit log is also known as an audit trail. Audit trails keep the accountability of the task or actions taken place in systems.

Bayesian Network: Bayesian network is one of the graphical methodologies to build and represent models for problem solving with given data or expert opinion. This is a type of probabilistic graphical model which can be used for a wide range of tasks including prediction, anomaly detection, diagnostics, reasoning, decision making under uncertainty etc.

Chain of Custody: Chain of custody is a series of events viewed in sequence. It is a process to keep accountability of chain of actions and evidences revealed during a crime investigation. It keeps the chronological documentation or paper trail that records the sequence of physical or digital evidence. Evidence needs to follow a chain of custody which is the standard processes for collecting, documenting, and protecting evidence.

Database Forensics: Database forensics is a digital investigation process which deals with database contents and their related metadata to reveal malicious or suspicious activities carried onto or through database systems. It is a branch of digital forensics. It is a process which performs identification, artifact collection, analysis, documentation, and presentation of the suspected activities.

Digital Evidence: Digital evidence is any digital information which is received from computers, audio files, video recordings, digital images etc. The evidence obtained is essential in computer and cyber crimes. The digital evidences such as word processing documents, spreadsheets, internet browser histories, databases, the contents of computer memory and computer backup can be produced in Court of law. The authentic digital evidences are accepted for the cybercrime case.

ETL Process: ETL is a concept in data warehousing that deals with combining the data from various sources into data warehouse, data marts or relational database in order to analyze the data for patterns and insights. ETL takes the heterogeneous data and transforms it into a homogeneous data. ETL helps in programmatically analyzing heterogeneous data and derive business intelligence from it.

Outliers: An outlier is said to be an observation that is distant from other observations. Outlier detection is very important concept in data mining for data analysis. The application of outlier detection mainly focuses on the idea of detecting the suspicious or outlier financial transactions.

SAX Parser: SAX is a simple application program interface (API) for extensible markup language (XML). It is an event-based parser for parsing XML documents.

Suspicious Transactions: A suspicious transaction is one which on the grounds of digital evidences is suspected to involve activities like money laundering offences or a terrorist activity financing offence. The digital evidences are used to trace and proof unusual activity occurrence in accounts with respect to nature and value of transactions.

XML: XML is an extensible markup language (XML) file format which is used to create common information format. It defines a set of rules for encoding documents in a format. It is both a human-readable and machine-readable format.

Chapter 13
Forensic Auditing Tools in Detecting Financial Statements' Irregularities:
Benford's Law and Beneish Model in the Case of Toshiba

Radiah Othman
https://orcid.org/0000-0002-9772-0439
Massey University, New Zealand

Rashid Ameer
IPU New Zealand Tertiary Institute, New Zealand

Fawzi Laswad
Massey University, New Zealand

ABSTRACT

This chapter illustrates a three-stage analytical procedure to examine and detect the likelihood of financial statements manipulation and identify the accounts that were manipulated by Toshiba. It applies the Beneish model and Benford's law to Toshiba's balance sheet and income statement from 2002 to 2016. The results show significant deviation from Benford's law in the pre-fraud period in equity, long-term receivables and property, plant and equipment, long-term liabilities, and in the post-fraud period in the long-term liabilities, equity, long-term receivables, and total current assets. The results provide evidence of the usefulness of Beneish and Benford law as forensic auditing tools for detecting financial statements' irregularities and fraud that would be useful for the audit planning and sampling procedures.

DOI: 10.4018/978-1-5225-7356-2.ch013

INTRODUCTION: FRADULENT FINANCIAL REPORTING AND THE AUDITOR

Accounting and fraudulent financial reporting primarily consist of manipulating financial elements by overstating sales, profits and assets or by understating liabilities, expenses or losses (Spathis, 2002). Detecting accounting fraud using traditional internal audit procedures is difficult and complex (Fanning, Cogger, & Srivasta, 1995), and also expensive and time consuming (Buddhakulsomsiri & Parthanadee, 2008). Detection of fraud in financial statements requires more advanced procedures than just using the standard auditing procedures (Asllani & Naco, 2014).

While auditors are qualified to perform the auditing function, they may not necessarily have the experience, knowledge and skills to detect fraud. For example, frauds in Enron, AIG & Olympus were uncovered through whistleblowing and investigations by the regulators for suspicious transactions and accounting irregularities. In the Enron case in 2001, the revenues, income and assets had been significantly overstated. The Enron's auditor, Arthur Andersen was later dissolved and lost its reputation as provider of independent audits of financial statements (Albrecht, Albrecht, Albrecht and Zimbelman, 2016). Enron's use of special purpose entities for off-balance sheet financing was a common practice to maintain high credit rating and raise capital (Wilson and Key, 2012). In the WorldCom case, the company's total assets were inflated by approximately $11 billion and in India, Satyam manipulated both the balance sheets and income statements without the auditors (PWC) ever discovering the fraud for nearly 9 years. (Brown, Daugherty & Persellin, 2014; Bhasin, 2013). Most recently, Tesco was found overstating its profits by £263 million through revenue recognition irregularities (Williams, 2017). In these fraud cases, elements of financial statements were used and abused by keeping the debts off the balance sheets, underreporting line costs by capitalising expenses, inflating revenues with fake accounting entries, writing off large unapproved loans, converting unrealised investment losses into fee expenses and reporting losses as write-offs of goodwill.

The auditor has a responsibility to plan and perform the audit to obtain reasonable assurance about whether the financial statements are free from material misstatement, whether caused by error or fraud (International Standard on Auditing 240). One of the critical elements of auditors' work is assessing the materiality of errors. The auditor must take both the size of the error, i.e., its quantity and its qualitative characteristics into account when making the materiality decision. The forensic auditing tools provide a deeper level of insight towards materiality judgement; therefore addressing the need to enhance this skill is important to the auditing field.

BACKGROUND OF TOSHIBA FRAUD CASE

Toshiba with more than 140 years of history, is a world leader and innovator in pioneering high technology, a diversified manufacturer and marketer of advanced electronic and electrical products and systems spanning energy systems, infrastructure systems and storage devices. Toshiba was founded in 1875, and today operates a global network of more than 450 companies, with approx. 141,300 employees worldwide and annual sales of 3.9 trillion yen (US$37.2billion) ("Toshiba at a glance", 2018).

In 2017, Toshiba announced it was being sued by a group of foreign investors for JPY 43.9 billion ($400m) the latest in a series of continued reverberations from the 2015 accounting scandal that rocked the company (Connolly, 2017). In 2015, Toshiba which had been perceived as "a totem of strong and virtuous Japanese corporate governance" admitted that it had committed a multi-year $1.22 billion accounting fraud (Morang, 2017). On May 8, 2015 Toshiba established an Independent Investigation Committee (IIC) comprising independent and impartial experts who do not have any interest in Toshiba. IIC (2015) reported that top management, namely the President, the Executive Officer in charge of business groups, and CFO were aware of the intentional overstating of apparent current term profits and the postponement of recording expenses and losses, or the continuation therefore, but did not give instructions to stop or correct them thereof, in order to achieve the budget target (IIC, 2015, p. 307).

The accounting manipulation included the delay in the recording of material cost in projects that used the percentage-of-completion method and improper recording of operating expenses, channel stuffing, and the inappropriate valuation of inventory. Toshiba did not have a risk management structure or the like that could anticipate or prevent such inappropriate accounting treatment from being carried out, so it continued in an institutional way that involved top management. IIC (2015, p. 28) reported that there is a reasonable degree of possibility that those people intended to delay recording a provision for contract losses under heavy pressure to achieve their sales target. It was also reported that the root cause of the inappropriate carry-over amounts stems from excessive demands to meet challenges from certain top management at Corporate level (IIC, 2015, p.45). On p.37 of the report, IIC highlighted that the Overseas Sales & Marketing Department intended to prioritize improved profitability over appropriateness of accounting for the sake of achieving the budget due to excessive pressure from the Corporate (IIC, 2015). All these indicate that the pressure to conform to top management's instruction was so pervasive. IIC summarised that a corporate culture existed at Toshiba whereby employees could not act contrary to the intent of their superiors (IIC, 2015, p.68)

FORENSIC AUDITING TOOLS

This chapter illustrates the usefulness of two forensic auditing tools: Beneish Model and Digital analysis of Benford's Law. Previous studies provide support for using financial ratios, which are incorporated into the Beneish Model as an effective tool to detect fraud (Barksy, Catanach and Rhoades-Catanach, 2003). While Benford's Law improves sampling so auditors can concentrate on fraudulent or otherwise suspicious areas for detecting fraud, the Beneish Model has been used as a valuable tool for flagging up companies that are likely to have manipulated their financial statements. For instance, Barksy et al. (2003) argue that if these models are applied individually, the resulting accounting statements possibly reveal some warning signs for the auditors to take appropriate actions at the early stages. In their view, investors, internal and external auditors, and regulators can take advantage of the application of these tools as standard tools.

Beneish Model

The Beneish Model is a mathematical model developed by Professor Messod Daniel Beneish. Beneish (1999) profiled companies that manipulated earnings. The companies had either been charged with manipulation by the US SEC or admitted to manipulation in the public press. The model attained prominence for flagging Enron Corporation well in advance of its eventual demise. The MScore is composed of eight ratios that capture either financial statement distortions that can result from earnings manipulation or indicate a predisposition to engage in earnings manipulation (Beneish and Nichols, 2005). Thus, companies with higher Beneish scores are more likely to be manipulators (Warshavsky,

2012). It uses eight financial ratios to identify the occurrence of financial fraud or tendency to engage in earning manipulation.

$$M = -4.84 + 0.92(DSRI) + 0.528(GMI) + 0.404(AQI) + 0.892(SGI)$$
$$+0.115(DEPI) - 0.172(SGAI) + 4.679(Accruals) - 0.327(LEVI)$$

These eight ratios (variables) are weighted together in the formula shown above: where *DSRI* is the days' sales in the receivable index; *GMI* is the gross margin index. *AQI* is the asset quality index; *SGI* is the sales growth index; *DEPI* is the depreciation index; *SGAI* is the sales and general and administrative expenses index; *LVGI* is the leverage index, and Accruals is the total accruals to total assets. According to Beneish, if M > -1.78 then a firm is likely to be a manipulator.

The theoretical underpinning of the model and emergent M score is that the magnitude of these eight ratios signals deteriorating fundamentals and aggressive accounting. For example, manipulators are hypothesised to have decreasing *GMI* and increasing *SGAI.* Also, their *LEVI* is increasing and a greater proportion of their total assets reflect noncurrent and non- Property, Plant, and Equipment (PPE) investments. The manipulators have high *DSRI* and *DEPI* year to year indicates that manipulators tend to slow down their depreciation expense as a percentage of their gross PP&E. Lastly, the *Accruals* indicates that cash profits do not support the reported profits. Mantone (2013, p. 120) notes that Beneish model is an excellent tool for the financial forensic examiner. It allows scrutiny in detail of the financial statements by measuring changes that occur from period to period, whether it is monthly, quarterly or yearly, and therefore it can detect financial fraud (e.g., Mantone, 2013; Tarjo, 2015). Beneish model has been used in fraud cases such as Enron (Ofori, 2016; Mahama, 2015) and WorldCom (Impink, 2010). Cynthia (2005) claims that Beneish model did not have the ability to consistently discover problems in fraudulent financial reporting. However, Catanach & Rhoades-Catanach (2003) find a high probability of earnings manipulation in Enron"s financial statements for several years preceding its bankruptcy using Beneish model.

Benford Law

Benford's Law (hereafter BL) is named after Frank Benford, a physicist who published the seminal paper on the topic of the expected frequencies of the digits in a list of numbers (Benford, 1938). Benford (1938) hypothesised that more real-world numbers started with 1s and 2s than with 8s or 9s. Zero, by definition, is inadmissible as a first digit.He collected more than 20,000 observations from diverse data sets, including areas of rivers, atomic weights of elements and numbers appearing in the magazine articles, and his results showed that 1 was the first digit 30.6% of the time and 2 was the first digit 18.5% of the time. He found that for nearly one half of his numbers 49.1% had either 1 or 2 as the first digit. Using integral calculus, Benford then derived expected proportions for the digits and digit combinations in the tabulated data. These frequencies or proportions have since been known as BL. Under BL, the formula for the first and second digit frequencies is as follows:

$$p(D_1 = d_1) = \log(1 + 1/d_1); \qquad d_1 \in \{1, 2, \ldots 9\}$$

$$p(D_2 = d_2) = \sum_{d_1 -1}^{9} \log(1 + 1 / d_1 d_2); \qquad d_1 d_2 \in \{10, 11, 12, \ldots 99\}$$

d_1 represents the first digit and d_2 the second digit of a number: Where p indicates the probability of observing the digit in the parenthesis and log refers to the log to the base 10. The BL proportions for the digits in the first four positions of numbers are shown in Table 1. Therefore, if the actual distribution of the digits from a data set of accounting transactions does not follow these distributions, then there is a reason to believe that the data are probably manipulated by human intervention, thus auditors should ask further corroborating evidence is required for detailed examination.

Carslaw (1989) demonstrated the use of BL for the first time on corporate net incomes in the accounting literature. He used the expected second digit (d_2) of BL on New Zealand companies and showed that there were indeed more second digits 0, (d_2=0) and fewer second digits, 9 (d_2=9) than expected in the net income numbers, which supported his "rounding up" hypothesis – when corporate income is just below psychological boundaries, managers would round up these numbers. Previous research studies have mainly focused on proving (or disproving) BL's applicability to a variety of sets of data such as reported earnings (Shette & Kuntluru, 2014; Carslaw, 1988; Thomas, 1989); custom fraud (Barabesi, Cerasa, Cerioli, & Perrotta, 2018); accounts payable data, estimations in the general ledger, inventories, payments, and refunds (Nigrini, 1999); vendor kickbacks, fictitious vendors and divisional performance (Durtschi, Hillison, & Pacini, 2004); balance sheet and income statements (Grammatikos & Papanikolaou, 2016); taxpayer compliance (Nigrini, 1996); tax data (Javorcik & Pakel, 2018; Busta & Sundheim,1992); census statistics (Fu, Villas-Boas & Judge, 2018; Hill, 1995). Its simplicity and usefulness have encouraged researchers to test it in detecting data anomalies, irregularities and manipulation of accounting and corporate governance data (e.g. Mukherjee, 2016; Nigrini & Mittermaier, 1997).

BL can be used as an additional forensic tool. The traditional auditing analytical procedures analyse the magnitude, trends, and relationships of accounting data where large errors are typically detected, but not small errors (Durtschi et al., 2004). Busta and Weinberg (1998, p. 363) suggest the use of BL

Table 1. Benford's law expected digital frequencies

Digit	First Digit d_1	Second Digit d_2	Third Digit d_3	Fourth Digit d_4
0	-	0.11968	0.10178	0.10018
1	0.30103	0.11389	0.10138	0.10014
2	0.17609	0.10882	0.10097	0.10010
3	0.12494	0.10433	0.10057	0.10006
4	0.09691	0.10031	0.10018	0.10002
5	0.07918	0.09668	0.09979	0.09998
6	0.06695	0.09337	0.09940	0.09994
7	0.05799	0.09035	0.09902	0.09990
8	0.05115	0.08757	0.09864	0.09986
9	0.04576	0.08500	0.09827	0.09982

Source: Nigrini (1996, p. 96)

as part of the analytical procedures because it overcomes this limitation as the test is unaffected by the magnitude of error(s) and it is independent of the numbers relationship to other data. It is also less sensitive to the pattern of contamination as it analyses a data stream without regard to the time of the data, the location of the manipulation, or to the comparison of the data to any cumulative totals. BL provides a data analysis method that can help alert auditors to possible errors, potential fraud, manipulative biases, costly processing inefficiencies or other irregularities (Nigrini, 1999, p. 80). Indeed, International Standard of Auditing (ISA) 240 states that auditors should perform procedures to identify the risk of material misstatement due to fraud, which includes considering any unusual or unexpected relationships that have been identified in performing analytical procedures in audit planning.

Durtschi et al. (2004) claim that if correctly used, BL is a useful tool for identifying suspect accounts for further analysis. In the context of financial fraud detection, the more the observed set of accounting data deviates from the pattern predicted by BL so the higher the chance is that the data have been manipulated (Kumar & Bhattacharya, 2007, p. 82). The main reason is that human choices are not random. Therefore invented numbers are unlikely to follow BL (Nigrini, 1999). Previous studies that specifically used BL for detecting fraudulent accounting data are as follows: Amiram, Bozanic & Rouen (2015), Da Silva (2013), Durtschi et al. (2004), Zgela & Dobsã (2011), and Nigrini (2005). Previous studies analysed specific digit conformity to BL, e.g., Aerts, Van Camppenhout, and Van Caneghem, (2008); Verbruggen and Christiaens (2012); Jegers (2013); Omer and Yetman (2003); Krishnan, Yetman, and Yetman, (2006), and overall figures reported in the balance sheet and income statements (Luypaert, Van Caneghem and Van Uytbergen, 2016). The latter argued that it is doubtful that all financial statements users focus on the same figure. This chapter analyse both levels of analysis.

As demonstrated by Amiram et al. (2015), financial statements without error are distributed according to BL. However, those firms that misstate their financial results by manipulating accounts may report numbers with first digits to conform to BL. They show that there would be different levels of divergence from the BL in the financial statement data, two years before the errors were discovered by the regulatory (SEC) and in the years after the financial statements were restated. In Japanese context, Skousen, Guan, and Wetzel (2004) report that managers of Japanese firms tend to round up earning numbers to achieve key reference points. They also suggest that the pressure for meeting management forecasts of earnings may provide additional incentives for Japanese firms to round up earnings numbers.

In this chapter, the focus was on the first digit (d_1) distribution of Toshiba's financial statements data seven years prior to 2009 and seven years after. Toshiba's fraudulent financial reporting came to public attention in 2009. Further, the IIC also included the financial year starting 2009 as the period subject to investigation (IIC, 2015, p.15). The IIC investigation revealed that for the financial year 2009 alone, JPY 400 billion pre-tax income had been inflated by Toshiba. This accounted to 26% of the total pre-tax income to be adjusted. The Financial Times also reported that Toshiba was unable to report results for the financial year that ended in March 2015 and that it would need to trim its operating profit for fiscal years of 2009 to 2013 (Inagaki, 2015). Based on these information, the analysis was performed with the assumption that the fraud year is 2009. In total, 878 observations pre-crisis period, 437 observations during the crisis (fraud) period, and 441 observations post-fraud period were analysed. These numbers of observation meet the minimum threshold of 300 observations (Nigrini, 2011, p. 99). Following earlier studies, this chapter used the MAD (eMAD) test, which provides a forensic insight into whether or not Toshiba's financial data set conforms to BL, and the z-statistics specifically identifies the line items in the financial statement, for which certain first digits were observed showing significant deviations from BL. These tests are explained below in detail.

Z-Test

The general rule is that if the first digit test is a weak fit to BL, it is a signal that the data set might contain duplications and abnormalities. In other words, the first digit test shows signs of having the highest risks of errors or fraud (Nigrini, 2011, p. 100). In order to perform a significance test for the observed deviations of the actual proportion of (d_1) where $d_1 \varepsilon\{1, 2..., 9\}$ from the expected BL proportions, this chapter used a normally distributed z-statistic (Fleiss, 1981):

$$z = \frac{\left|p - p_0\right| - \frac{1}{2n}}{\sqrt{\frac{p_0(1 - p_0)}{n}}}$$

where p and p_0 are observed and expected BL proportions, respectively. N represents the sample size. The second term in the numerator is a correction term and is applied only when it is smaller than $|p - p_0|$ (Thomas, 1989). The z-statistics were calculated for the assets, liabilities, sales and expenses accounts that had 20 or more observations over the period of 15 years. Following Thomas (1989) and Skousen et al. (2004), the percentage observed deviations from expected BL proportions are used for analysis and discussion.

MAD (eMAD)

The chapter also used the Mean Absolute Deviation (MAD) test to assess digits' conformity to BL (Nigrini, 2011). The formula is, $\frac{\sum_{i=1}^{K}\left|AP - EP\right|}{K}$, where K represents the number of digits, $d_1 \varepsilon\{1, 2,..., 9\}$, AP denotes the actual proportion of the number of times a particular digit occurs within the data, and EP is the expected proportion according to BL. The values of the MADs for pre- and post-fraud were then compared. Nigrini (2011) proposed the level of acceptability as indicated in Table 2.

Recently, Barney and Schulzke (2016) proposed a new calculation, Excess MAD (eMAD), to further mitigate the effect of N on MAD, especially when N≥500. $eMAD \approx 1 / \sqrt{158.8N}$. The combination of MAD (eMAD) and z-statistics test is referred to as "smell test" (Nigrini, 2011, p. 11). The smell test provides indication of whether the financial statement data conform to BL or otherwise. If the data do not conform, this could imply that Toshiba was possibly manipulating its data and it could then be con-

Table 2. Level of acceptability

MAD-values	Conclusion
0.0000 to 0.0012	Close conformity
0.0012 to 0.0018	Acceptable conformity
0.0018 to 0.0022	Marginally acceptable conformity
Above 0.0022	Nonconformity

cluded where the manipulation was occurring based on the z-statistics. In short, the MAD (eMAD) test provides a forensic insight whether the data set overall conforms to BL and the z-statistics specifically identify the accounts in the financial statement with certain first digits show significant deviation from BL. The account(s) indicated by z-statistics as significant are then compared to the Independent Investigation Report (IIC, 2015). Not all the accounts were investigated due to limited scope of the Independent Investigation Committee; these are not included in the analysis.

DATA TESTED

Toshiba's annual financial statements data were downloaded in local currency (Japanese Yen) from the Thomson Reuters database. There are 499 and 501 financial statements data available for analysis for pre-fraud and post-fraud periods respectively. Next, in order to determine whether BL Law can be used, two restrictions suggested by Wallace (2002) were applied: (i) the mean of the number of observed digits is larger than the median, and (ii) the skewness value is positive. All data fulfil these two restrictions. Then each category under each Balance Sheet, Income Statements and Cash Flow Statement were checked to include only categories that have 20 line items or more (see Table 3). The final dataset were items as reported in the Income Statement and Balance Sheet. Cash Flow Statement items were excluded because their items were less than 20 per category. As a result, all Cash Flow Statement items were excluded.

Table 4 provides a description of line items extracted from Toshiba's balance sheet and income statements included in the analysis.

THREE STAGE PROCEDURES OF USING FORENSIC AUDITING TOOLS

The three-stage procedures are:

Stage 1: Beneish M-Score calculation to examine whether Toshiba has manipulated its financial statements data (pre-fraud and post-fraud);

Stage 2: Application of Benford's Law to identify the accounts that have been manipulated in Toshiba (pre-fraud and post-fraud); and

Table 3. Period of study and data

	Pre-fraud 2002 to 2008	**Post-fraud 2010 to 2016**	**Total**
Financial statements data	499	501	1,000
Mean is larger than the median, and skewness value is positive	0	0	0
	499	501	1,000
Categories with 20 or more line items	62	60	122
Final dataset	437	441	878

Table 4. The sample data

Line items – Balance sheet	Line items – Income statement
Assets	Net sales
Cash & Cash Equivalents	Interest and dividends
Trade Notes	Cost of sales
Trade Accounts receivable	Selling, general and administrative
Inventories	Interest expense
Deferred tax assets	Other expenses
Prepaid expenses and other current assets	Income from continuing Operations, before Income Taxes and Non-controlling Interests
LT receivables	Income taxes
Investments in and advances to affiliates	Deferred
Marketable securities and other investments	Net income
Land	Net loss
Buildings (Gross because the accumulated depreciation are for all PPE not shown individually)	
Machinery and equipment (Gross)	
Construction in progress (Gross)	
Other assets	
Liabilities and Shareholder equity	
Short-term borrowings	
Current portion of long-term debt	
Notes and accounts payable, trade	
Accounts payable, other, and accrued expenses	
Accrued income and other taxes	
Advance payments received	
Other current liabilities	
Long-term debt	
Accrued pension and severance costs	
Other liabilities	
Common Stock	
Additional Paid up Capital	
Retained Earnings	
Accumulated other comprehensive loss	
Treasury stock, at cost	

Stage 3: Match the financial statements line items as identified by Benford's Law to those line items, which were highlighted by the Independent Investigation Report (IIC, 2015). The IIC did not investigate matters that have been treated as uncorrected misstatements in accounting audits or quarterly reviews because they have already been recognised by the audit firm, Ernst & Young Shinnihon as having risks in the estimation of total costs of contract work for business management purpose.

The analysis of accounting figures was conducted mainly on Toshiba itself and subsidiaries that routinely record sales of JPY 10 billion or more by using the percentage of completion method or subsidiaries that have a project incurring a loss of roughly JPY 500 million or more.

Stage 1: Beneish Model

Beneish (1999) defines an earnings manipulator as a company that is growing extremely quickly, experiencing deteriorating fundamentals such as eroding profit margins, and adopting aggressive accounting practices. Based on the 8-variables model, M-score > -1.78 indicates a strong likelihood of manipulation. The analysis of Toshiba's M-scores pre-fraud (Table 5), fraud (Table 6), and post-fraud (Table 7) years seem to provide strong support of these assertions.

Stage 2: Digital Analysis of Benford's Law

The following tables indicate the percentage unit deviations (PUD), z-statistics, MAD and eMAD values in Toshiba's Income Statement and Balance Sheet. If manipulation has occurred in the financial statements pre-and post-fraud years, it will be observed that a line item will have a high percentage of the first digits being greater than five than expected as per BL, and also a low percentage of the first digits less than five than expected as per BL. The PUD will be in the upward direction for positive deviations and downward for negative deviation from BL.

The digital analysis results were organised as follows: (i) line items in the income statements that showed the most significant deviations from BL in the pre-and post-fraud period and the summary of income statements results in the tabular form; (ii) line items in the balance sheet pre-and post-fraud that showed most significant deviations from BL, and the summary of balance sheet results in the tabular form; and (iii) overall summary of income statement and balance sheet. MAD (eMAD) test provides substantial evidence that Toshiba's financial statements do not conform to BL in the pre-and post-fraud years.

Table 5. Toshiba's M-scores – pre fraud

Characteristics	2002	2003	2004	2005	2006	2007	2008
DSRI	0.99	0.93	0.85	1.01	1.02	0.97	1.00
GMI	1.11	0.92	0.99	1.02	0.99	1.05	1.02
AQI	1.02	1.03	0.98	1.01	1.05	0.99	1.06
DEPI	1.06	1.12	1.07	0.96	0.99	0.89	0.99
SGAI	1.14	0.92	1.00	0.96	0.98	0.89	0.99
LVGI	1.02	0.96	0.97	0.99	0.99	0.99	0.99
Accruals	-0.07	-0.05	-0.06	-0.06	-0.08	-0.07	-0.02
M-score	*-2.88*	*-2.72*	*-2.92*	*-2.66*	*-2.72*	*-2.71*	*-2.46*

Table 6. Toshiba's M-scores– fraud year

Characteristics	DSRI	GMI	AQI	DEPI	SGAI	LVGI	Accruals	*M-score*
	1.01	1.34	1.01	1.26	0.82	1.13	-0.06	-2.72

Table 7. Toshiba's M-scores – post fraud

Characteristics	2010	2011	2012	2013	2014	2015	2016
DSRI	1.10	0.96	1.19	1.08	0.95	0.98	0.90
GMI	0.81	0.96	0.99	0.97	0.99	1.08	1.53
AQI	0.98	1.06	1.00	0.99	0.97	1.06	1.00
DEPI	1.11	1.08	1.02	0.96	0.97	1.07	1.07
SGAI	1.16	0.71	1.04	1.03	1.01	1.25	1.07
LVGI	0.90	0.96	1.00	0.99	1.02	0.98	1.15
Accruals	-0.08	-0.03	-0.04	-0.01	-0.03	-0.05	-0.15
M-score	-2.88	-2.962	-2.54	-2.53	-2.59	-2.75	-3.12

Table 8. Percentage unit deviations of first digits in Toshiba's income statement

Items	N	Pre-fraud (2002–2008) Digit (z-statistics)									MAD /eMad
		1	2	3	4	5	6	7	8	9	
Sales and Other income:	21	-0.002 *0.153*	-0.003 *0.113*	-0.12 *1.402*	-0.05 *0.395*	+0.21 *3.101****	+0.03 *0.082*	+0.04 *0.263*	0.00 *0.073*	-0.05 *0.481*	0.06/ 0.043
Cost and expenses	28	+0.02 *0.209*	+0.04 *0.283*	-0.05 *0.571*	+0.08 *1.141*	+0.06 *0.898*	-0.07 *1.039*	-0.06 *0.909*	-0.05 *0.800*	+0.03 *0.198*	0.05/ 0.036
Items	**N**	**Post-fraud (2010-2016) Digit (z-statistics)**									**MAD /eMad**
		1	**2**	**3**	**4**	**5**	**6**	**7**	**8**	**9**	
Sales and Other income:	21	-0.02 *0.153*	-0.13 *1.259*	-0.12 *1.402*	-0.10 *1.132*	+0.02 *0.273*	+0.36 *6.194****	+0.04 *0.263*	0.00 *0.073*	-0.05 *0.481*	0.092/ 0.075
Cost and expenses	28	+0.20 *2.089***	-0.10 *1.206*	+0.05 *0.573*	+0.12 *1.780*	-0.04 *0.502*	-0.07 *1.039*	-0.06 *0.909*	-0.05 *0.800*	-0.05 *0.707*	0.082/ 0.067

Benford Law: Income Statement

Table 8 shows that the most significant deviations in the upward direction was in the Sales & Other Income in the pre-fraud (+21%) as well as in the post-fraud period (+36%). During the pre-fraud years, Sales & Other Income had digit 5 appear more frequently than expected, which seems to indicate that Toshiba tended to report revenue in bigger amounts. In the post-fraud years, the first digits 5 and 6 appear frequently. The annual report of Toshiba for the FY2010 shows a steady increase in revenues at least three years before its sudden drop in 2009 to nearly 13%.

The lesser occurrence of the first digit 4 and 9 than expected in both periods indicates that Toshiba made revenue numbers appear larger. This is because in 2010, sales still dropped, but not as much as in 2009, to just about 4%. The annual report of Toshiba for the FY2010 shows a steady increase in revenues and at least digits 1 and 5 were frequent, but the deviations were not statistically significant. These manipulations of expenses in the upward direction during the pre-fraud may have been motivated to ensure that they were fairly consistent with the increased in revenue accounts. According to Amiram et al. (2015), because of the sales manipulation, a firm likely needs to adjust the cost of goods sold and tax expense accordingly. Table 9 provides the summary of overall income statement results.

Benford Law: Balance Sheet Items (Assets)

The most significant deviations in the upward direction were during the pre-fraud period in the Long-term receivables and Investments (+25%) and PPE (+25%) (see Table 10). In contrast, the Total current assets had a significant deviation in the downward direction. In the pre-fraud period, Total current assets had a first digit 4 and 5 less frequently than expected, while the first digit 1 appeared more frequently than expected in the post-fraud period. Long-term receivables and Investments and Property, Plant and Equipment (PPE) had a first digit 2 and 8 more frequently than expected in the pre-fraud year as well as in the post-fraud period.

Benford Law: Balance Sheet Items (Total Equity)

The most significant deviations in the upward direction is in the Total Equity (+37%) during the pre-fraud and (+27%) during the post-fraud years. Also, during the pre-fraud years, the Total Equity had the digit 2 more frequently than expected. In the post-fraud years, Total Equity had the digit 4 more frequently than expected. This may be undertaken to make sure of consistent high ROE to give assurance to the capital providers that despite lower actual sales growth, Toshiba was still able to generate profit without needing as much capital.

Benford Law: Balance Sheet Items (Liabilities)

The results show that the most significant deviations in the downward direction in the long-term liabilities (-25%) during the pre-fraud years, but the deviations changed in the opposite direction in the post-fraud years (+28%). In the pre-fraud years, the results are not significant for current liabilities but in the post-fraud year, digit 3 is used more frequently than expected and significant at 1%. Table 11 provides the summary of the overall balance sheet results.

Table 9. Summary of results: Benford's law of income statement items

Income Statement Items	Pre-Fraud			Post-Fraud		
	Hypotheses	**Significant Account**	**Direction of Manipulation**	**Hypotheses**	**Significant Account**	**Direction of Manipulation**
Revenue	Increasing			Decreasing		
		Sales & Other Incomes	Increasing		Sales & Other Incomes	Increasing
Expenses	Decreasing			Decreasing		
		Operating Expenses			Operating Expenses	Increasing
		Non-operating expenses	Increasing		Non-operating Expenses	Increasing

Table 10. Percentage unit deviations of first digits in Toshiba's balance sheet

Items	N	Pre-fraud (2002–2008) Digit (z-statistics)									MAD/ eMAD
		1	2	3	4	5	6	7	8	9	
Total Current Assets	48	+0.03 0.33	+0.09 1.53	+0.04 0.66	-0.10 2.03**	-0.08 1.76**	+0.04 0.74	-0.06 1.41	+0.01 0.03	+0.02 0.21	0.05/ 0.04
Long-term Receivables and Investment	21	+0.18 1.51	+0.25 2.75***	-0.08 1.40	-0.10 0.74	-0.08 1.13	-0.07 0.94	-0.01 0.79	-0.05 0.57	-0.05 0.48	0.10/ 0.78
Property, Plant and Equipment	35	+0.13 1.46	+0.25 3.70***	-0.10 1.47	-0.10 1.65*	-0.05 0.80	-0.01 0.23	-0.06 1.11	-0.05 0.99	-0.02 0.08	0.08/ 0.07
Current Liabilities	49	-0.04 0.39	+0.04 0.14	+0.06 1.03	+0.03 0.36	-0.04 0.73	-0.03 0.45	0.00 0.10	+0.03 0.64	-0.03 0.51	0.03/ 0.02
Long-term Liabilities:	21	-0.25 3.29***	-0.18 2.72***	-0.12 2.15**	-0.02 0.20	-0.03 0.39	+0.06 1.15	+0.07 1.48	0.00 0.03	0.00 0.13	0.11/ 0.07
Total Equity	35	-0.13 1.49	+0.37 5.48***	-0.10 1.47	+0.02 0.06	-0.02 0.17	-0.04 0.57	-0.03 0.38	-0.02 0.22	-0.05 0.89	0.08/ 0.07

Items	N	Post-fraud (2010–2016) Digit (z-statistics)									MAD/ eMAD
		1	2	3	4	5	6	7	8	9	
Total Current Assets	49	+0.17 2.41**	-0.07 1.17	+0.04 0.60	+0.03 0.36	-0.06 1.23	-0.05 1.02	-0.02 0.21	-0.01 0.00	-0.03 0.51	0.05/ 0.04
Long-term Receivables and Investment	21	-0.25 2.29**	+0.16 1.61	+0.21 2.56***	+0.14 1.82*	-0.08 0.94	-0.07 0.79	-0.06 0.67	-0.05 0.57	0.00 0.04	0.11/ 0.10
Property, Plant and Equipment	35	-0.16 1.86*	+0.22 3.26***	-0.12 1.98**	-0.10 1.65*	-0.08 1.42	-0.07 1.25	0.00 0.02	-0.02 0.22	+0.33 8.82***	0.12/ 0.11
Current Liabilities	49	-0.06 0.70	0.03 0.33	0.06 3.19***	-0.02 0.12	0.02 0.33	-0.05 1.02	-0.02 0.21	-0.03 0.65	-0.05 1.19	0.047/ 0.04
Long-term Liabilities:	21	+0.08 0.56	-0.08 0.69	-0.12 1.40	-0.10 1.13	-0.03 0.13	-0.02 0.35	+0.28 4.98***	-0.05 0.57	+0.05 0.56	0.09/ 0.07
Total Equity	35	-0.07 0.70	-0.09 1.18	-0.01 0.19	+0.27 5.20***	+0.06 1.08	-0.01 0.23	-0.06 1.11	-0.05 0.90	-0.05 0.89	0.08/ 0.06

Stage 3: Matching Benford's Law Results and Independent Investigation Committee Findings

The results from the two-stage analysis are then compared with the IIC report to corroborate the findings. Specifically, the IIC analysed the changes in the total estimated income from contract work/total estimates cost of contract work for signs of overstatement or understatement. Toshiba's percentage of the completion method system had a framework in which the number of sales to be recorded and the amount of sales costs to be recorded are automatically calculated based on the percentage of completion method. For loss-making projects, according to the J-SOX rules, it was required to identify the loss-making projects, record provision for contract losses for each quarter, and reverse provision for contract loss for the previous quarter. However, these rules were not followed. Instead, a de facto rule was used where provision for contract losses could not be recorded without the approval of the Vice President and

Table 11. Summary of results – Benford's law of balance sheet items

Balance Sheet Items	Pre-Fraud			Post-Fraud		
	Hypotheses	Significant Account	Direction of Manipulation	Hypotheses	Significant Account	Direction of Manipulation
Asset	Increasing			Decreasing		
		Total Current Assets	Decreasing		Total Current Assets	Increasing
		Long-term receivables & Investment	Increasing		Long-term receivables & Investment	Excluded due to two or more significant results in opposite directions)
		Property, Plant, and Equipment	Excluded		Property, Plant, and Equipment	Increasing
					Other Assets	Increasing
Equities	Increasing		Increasing	Increasing		Increasing
Liabilities	Decreasing			Increasing		
		Long-term Liabilities	Decreasing		Current Liabilities	Increasing
					Long-term Liabilities	Increasing

the Company President except for recording of small provisions. With correction, the total estimated costs of contract work for the 4th quarter of FY 2011 would be JPY 9 billion and the amount of impact on profit and loss would be negative JPY 1.9 billion. Thus, overstated sales and understated provision for contract losses influenced gross profit (IIC, 2015).

The results of the first digit analysis supports that during the pre-fraud years, Sales & Other Income had digit 5 appear more frequently than expected, which proves that Toshiba reported revenue in bigger amounts because these numbers were not adjusted for the loss provisions. Also, the calculations, which use the *DSRI, GMI*, and *SGAI* in the Beneish Model, show Toshiba had been using aggressive accounting measures, and in particular, a mechanism known as Carry-over to overstate current year profits by adjusting profits and losses since 2008. The prime motivation was to meet profit targets. These were referred to in Toshiba as "Challenge" since it was customary for each business to aggregate their profit outlook by region in each quarter period for adjusting the gap with target sales.

Toshiba intentionally applied a temporary increase in the product prices to Overseas Affiliated Companies at the end of the quarter. As a result, inventories at these companies were overstated, and the sales and profit were overstated by the difference between the original product prices and the increased prices. Indeed, the first digit test on the inventory line item shows a significant deviation in the upward direction in the pre-fraud years. Furthermore, Toshiba understated operating expenses by requesting that vendors delay expenses that had already been provided.

According to IIC, there was little chance of this fraudulent act being detected in an accounting audit. Toshiba requested panel makers and ODM/OEM manufacturers to reduce their selling price to reflect the purchase price, even in cases where there was a low possibility of achieving cost reduction. The investigation report indicated that the overstatement of profits through the use of inappropriate carryovers is an "overstatement" of current profits more than real attainability, which reflects lack of awareness of appropriate accounting treatment. In fact, the accounting department itself played a proactive role by proposing inappropriate carryovers items, assessing the possibility of inappropriate carryovers, and communicating this to the accounting managers at overseas affiliated companies or preparing explanations for the auditors.

FUTURE RESEARCH DIRECTIONS

Future studies might want to focus on the role of national culture on the organisational culture which might had induced the perpetration of the fraud in Toshiba and other cases alike. It is also proposed that the future studies should examine the corporate governance failing in the years leading to fraud in 2009. It would provide researchers and policy makers with insight into developing new agendas for analysing such failures and how to create new frameworks to avoid such events in the future.

CONCLUSION

This chapter illustrates the usefulness of Beneish Model and Benford Law to examine and detect fraudulent financial statements of Toshiba Corporation in the pre-and post-fraud years. This indicates that the fraud could have been potentially committed much earlier than 2009 and prolonged further than 2015, the year when Toshiba was discovered as committing fraud.

The results show that when these models are applied individually to the financial statements in the pre-and post-fraud years, they both able to detect the deviation and direction of manipulation (upward or inward). Specifically, they were able to detect inflated revenues, profits and inventories and the reduction of operating expenses. If both tools were applied earlier, the auditors could potentially be alerted of the warning signs so that appropriate actions could be taken for further scrutiny but they failed in this regard.

Previous studies have suggested that the pressure to conform to top management's instruction was so pervasive among Japanese managers. The Independent Investigation Committee has also reported this particular issue as the main cause of the inappropriate accounting treatments in Toshiba's financial statements.

The authors are mindful of the limitation of forensic tools proposed in this chapter because these do not provide evidence of how the manipulation occurred. Although the chapter is able to trace back the results from the Beneish and BL model to the IIC report, its terms of reference were limited. The scope of the IIC investigation only includes: Accounting in relation to projects in which the percentage-of-completion method; Accounting in relation to recording of operating expenses in the Visual Products Business; Accounting in relation to the valuation of inventory in the Semiconductor Business; and Accounting in relation to parts transactions in the PC Business.

ACKNOWLEDGMENT

This research was supported by the Accounting and Finance Association of Australia and New Zealand (AFAANZ) [AFAANZ Research Grant scheme, approval letter dated 4th July 2017].

REFERENCES

Aerts, W., Van Camppenhout, G., & Van Caneghem, T. (2008). Clustering in dividends: Do managers rely on cognitive reference points? *Journal of Economic Psychology*, *29*(3), 276–284. doi:10.1016/j.joep.2007.10.003

Albrecht, W. S., Albrecht, C. O., Albrecht, C. C., & Zimbelman, M. F. (2016). *Fraud Examination*. Boston, MA: Cengage Learning.

Amiram, D., Bozanic, Z., & Rouen, E. (2015). Financial Statement Errors: Evidence from the Distributional Properties of Financial Statement Numbers. *Review of Accounting Studies*. Retrieved from http://link.springer.com/article/10.1007/s11142-015-9333-z

Asllani, A., & Naco, M. (2014). Using Benford's law for fraud detection in accounting practices. *Journal of Social Science Studies*, *1*(2), 129–143. doi:10.5296/jsss.v2i1.6395

Barabesi, L., Cerasa, A., Cerioli, A., & Perrotta, D. (2018). Goodness-of-Fit Testing for the Newcomb-Benford Law With Application to the Detection of Customs Fraud. *Journal of Business & Economic Statistics*, *36*(2), 346–358. doi:10.1080/07350015.2016.1172014

Barney, B. J., & Schulzke, K. S. (2016). Moderating "Cry Wolf" Events with Excess MAD in Benford's Law Research and Practice. *Journal of Forensic Accounting Research*, *1*(1), A66–A90. doi:10.2308/jfar-51622

Barsky, N. P., Catanach, A. H., & Rhoades-Catanach, S. C. (2003). Analyst tools for detecting financial reporting fraud. *Commercial Lending Review*, *18*(5), 31–36.

Beneish, M. (1999). Incentive and penalties related to earnings overstatements that violate GAAP. *The Accounting Review*, *74*(4), 425–457. doi:10.2308/accr.1999.74.4.425

Beneish, M. D. & Nichols, D. C. (2007). *The Predictable Cost of Earnings Manipulation*. SSRN-id1006840

Benford, F. (1938). The law of anomalous numbers. *Proceedings of the American Philosophical Society*, *78*(4), 551–572.

Bhasin, M. (2013). Corporate Accounting Scandal at Satyam: A Case Study of India's Enron. *European Journal of Business and Social Sciences*, *1*(12), 25–47.

Brown, V.L., Daugherty, B.E. & Persellin, J.S. (2014). Satyam Fraud: A Case Study of India's Enron. *Issues in Accounting Education*, *29*(3), 419-442. doi:10.2308/iace-50735

Buddhakulsomsiri, J., & Parthanadee, P. (2008). Stratified ransom sampling for estimating billing accuracy in health care systems. *Health Care Management Science*, *11*(1), 41–54. doi:10.100710729-007-9023-x

Busta, B., & Sundheim, R. (1992). *Tax return numbers tend to obey Benford's law* (Working Paper No. W93-106-94). Center for Business Research, St. Cloud State University.

Busta, B., & Weinberg, R. (1998). Using Benford's law and neural networks as a review procedure. *Managerial Auditing Journal*, *13*(6), 356–366. doi:10.1108/02686909810222375

Carslaw, C. (1988). Anomalies in income numbers: Evidence of goal-oriented behavior. *The Accounting Review*, *63*(2), 321–327.

Catanach, A. H., & Rhoades-Catanach, S. (2003). Enron : A Financial Reporting Failure. *Villanova Law Review*, *48*(4), 1057–1076.

Connoly, R. (2017). *Toshiba faces fresh $400m lawsuit over historic accounting scandal*. Retrieved from https://www.theneweconomy.com/business/toshiba-faces-fresh-400m-lawsuit-over-historic-accounting-scandal

Cynthia, H. (2005). Analysis ratios for detecting Financial Statement fraud. *ACFE Fraud Magazine*. Retrieved from http://www.fraud-magazine.com/article.aspx?id=4294967726

Da Silva, A. S. C. D. (2013). *The Application of Benford's Law in detecting accounting fraud in the financial sector* (Unpublished Masters Dissertation). Lisboa School of Economics and Management Lisbon, Portugal.

Das, S., & Zhang, H. (2003). Rounding-up in reported EPS, behavioral thresholds, and earnings management. *Journal of Accounting and Economics*, *35*(1), 31–50. doi:10.1016/S0165-4101(02)00096-4

Durtschi, C., Hillison, W., & Pacini, C. (2004). The effective use of Benford's Law to assist in detecting fraud in accounting data. *Journal of Forensic Accounting*, *5*, 17–34.

Fanning, K., Cogger, K. O., & Srivasta, R. (1995). Detection of management fraud: A neural network approach. *Intelligent Systems in Accounting, Finance & Management*, *4*(2), 113–126. doi:10.1002/j.1099-1174.1995.tb00084.x

Fleiss, J. L. (1981). *Statistical methods for rates and proportions* (2nd ed.). New York: John Wiley & Sons, Inc.

Fu, Q., Villas-Boas, S. B., & Judge, G. (2018). Does china income FSDs follow Benford? A comparison between Chinese income first significant digit distribution with Benford distribution. *China Economic Journal*, 1–9. doi:10.1080/17538963.2018.1477418

Grammatikos, T., & Papanikolaou, N. I. (2016, November). Applying Benford's law to accounting data manipulation in the banking industry. *LSF Research Working Paper Series, 16–11*, 1–36.

Guan, L., Lin, F., & Fang, W. (2008). Goal-oriented earnings management: Evidence from Taiwanese firms. *Emerging Markets Finance & Trade*, *44*(4), 19–32. doi:10.2753/REE1540-496X440402

Hill, T. (1988). Random-number guessing and the first digit phenomenon. *Psychological Reports*, *62*(3), 967–971. doi:10.2466/pr0.1988.62.3.967

Impink, J. (2010). *Earnings manipulation and bankruptcy: WorldCom*. Third version, Bachelor paper, Betzabeth Ignacius 5754992.

Inagaki, K. (2015). Accounting scandal set to shake up Toshiba. *Financial Times*. Retrieved from https://www.ft.com/content/b209abac-2bc0-11e5-acfb-cbd2e1c81cca

Independent Investigation Committee Report (IIC). (2015). *Investigation Report –Summary version, Independent Investigation Committee for Toshiba Corporation, 20 July 2015.* International Standard on Auditing 240, The Auditor's Responsibilities Relating to Fraud in an Audit of Financial Statements. Retrieve from http://www.ifac.org/system/files/downloads/a012-2010-iaasb-handbook-isa-240.pdf

Javorcik, B., & Pakel, B. D. (2018). *Forensics, Elasticities and Benford's Law: Detecting Tax Fraud in International Trade.* CEPR Discussion Papers 12798. Retrieved from https://ideas.repec.org/p/cpr/ceprdp/12798.html

Jegers, M. (2013). Do nonprofit organizations manage earnings? An empirical study. *Voluntas, 24*(4), 953–968. doi:10.100711266-012-9291-z

Krishnan, R., Yetman, M., & Yetman, R. (2006). Expense misreporting in a nonprofit organization. *The Accounting Review, 81*(2), 399–420. doi:10.2308/accr.2006.81.2.399

Kumar, K., & Bhattacharya, S. (2007, June). Detecting the dubious digits: Benford's law in forensic accounting. *Significance, 4*(2), 81–83. doi:10.1111/j.1740-9713.2007.00234.x

Luypaert, M., Van Caneghem, T., & Van Uytbergen, S. (2016). Financial statement siling lags: An empirical analysis among small firms. *International Small Business Journal, 34*(4), 506–531. doi:10.1177/0266242615569324

Mahama, M. (2015). Detecting Corporate fraud and financial distress using the Altman and Beneish models the case of Enron Corporation, *International Journal of Economics. Commerce and Management, III*(1), 1–18.

Mantone, P. S. (2013). *Using Analytics to Detect Possible Fraud: Tools and Techniques.* John Wiley & Sons Inc. doi:10.1002/9781118715789

Morang, S. C. (2017). In Toshiba's scandal, blame samurai code. *Fraud Magazine.* Retrieved from http://www.fraud-magazine.com/article.aspx?id=4294997970

Mosimann, J. E., Dahlberg, J. E., Davidian, N. M., & Krueger, J. W. (2002). Terminal digits and the examination of questioned data. *Accountability in Research, 9*(2), 75–92. doi:10.1080/08989620212969

Mosimann, J. E., Wiseman, C. V., & Edelman, R. E. (1995). Data fabrication: Can people generate random digits? *Accountability in Research, 4*(1), 31–55. doi:10.1080/08989629508573866

Mukherjee, S. (2016). Can Benford'd Law explain CEO pay? *Corporate Governance, 26*(2), 143–156. doi:10.1111/corg.12195

Nigrini, J. M. (2011). *Forensic analytics.* John Wiley & Sons. doi:10.1002/9781118386798

Nigrini, M. (1996). A taxpayer compliance analysis of Benford's law. *The Journal of the American Taxation Association, 18*(1), 72–91.

Nigrini, M. (1999a). Adding value with digital analysis. *The Internal Auditor, 56*, 21–23.

Nigrini, M. (1999b, May). I've got your number. *Journal of Accountancy, 187*(5), 79–83.

Nigrini, M., & Mittermaier, L., L. (1997). The use of Benford's Law as an aid in analytical procedures. *Auditing*, *16*(2), 52–67.

Nigrini, M. J. (2005). An assessment of the change in the incidence of earnings management around the Enron-Andersen episode. *Review of Accounting and Finance*, *4*(1), 92–110. doi:10.1108/eb043420

Ofori, E. (2016). Detecting Corporate Financial Fraud Using Modified Altman Z-Score and Beneish M-Score. The Case of Enron Corporation. *Research Journal of Finance and Accounting*, *7*(4), 59–65.

Omer, T. C., & Yetman, R. J. (2003). Near zero taxable income reporting by nonprofit organizations. *The Journal of the American Taxation Association*, *25*(2), 19–34. doi:10.2308/jata.2003.25.2.19

Shette, R., & Kuntluru, S. (2014). Rounding-up in reported income numbers: Evidence from Indian companies. *Review of Accounting and Finance*, *13*(2), 156–170. doi:10.1108/RAF-04-2013-0042

Skousen, C., Guan, L., & Wetzel, T. (2004). Anomalies and unusual patterns in reported earnings: Japanese managers round earnings. *Journal of International Financial Management & Accounting*, *15*(3), 212–234. doi:10.1111/j.1467-646X.2004.00108.x

Spathis, T. C. (2002). Detecting false financial statements using published data: Some evidence from Greece. *Managerial Auditing Journal*, *17*(4), 179–191. doi:10.1108/02686900210424321

Tarjo, N. H. (2015). Application of Beneish M-Score Models and Data Mining to Detect Financial Fraud. *2nd Global Conference on Business and Social Science-2015, GCBSS-2015*. 10.1016/j.sbspro.2015.11.122

Thomas, J. (1989). Unusual patterns in reported earnings. *The Accounting Review*, *64*(4), 773–787.

Toshiba at a Glance. (2018). Retrieved from https://www.toshiba.co.jp/about/ir/en/overview/index.htm

Verbruggen, S., & Christiaens, J. (2012). Do non-profit organizations manage earnings toward zero profit and does governmental financing play a role? *Canadian Journal of Administrative Sciences*, *29*(3), 205–217. doi:10.1002/cjas.1219

Wallace, W. (2002). Assessing the quality of data used for benchmarking and decision-making. *Journal of Government Financial Management*, *51*(3), 16–22.

Warshavsky, M. (2012). Analyzing Earnings Quality as a Financial Forensic Tool. *Financial Valuation and Litigation Expert Journal*, *39*, 16–20.

Williams, P. (2017). Accounting scandals are back in the big time. *ACCA Global*. Available at https://www.accaglobal.com/an/en/member/member/accounting-business/2017/03/in-focus/accounting-scandals.html

Wilson, A. C., & Key, K. G. (2012). Enron: A Case of Deception and Unethical Behavior. *Feature Edition*, *1*, 88–97.

Zgela, M., & Dobsä, J. (2011). Analysis of Top 500 Central and East European Companies Net Income Using Benford's Law. *Journal of Information and Organizational Sciences*, *35*(2), 214–228.

ADDITIONAL READING

Beneish, M. D., Lee, C. M. C., & Nichols, D. C. (2013). Earnings Manipulation and Expected Returns. *Journal of Financial Analysts*, *69*(2), 57–82. doi:10.2469/faj.v69.n2.1

Mantone, P. (2013). *Using Analytics to Detect Possible Fraud: Tools and Techniques*. Hoboken, New Jersey: John Wiley & Sons, Inc. doi:10.1002/9781118715789

Mehta, A., & Bhavani, G. (2017). Application of forensic tools to detect fraud: The case of Toshiba. *Journal of Forensic and Investigative Accounting*, *9*(1), 692–710.

Omar, N., Koya, R. K., Sanusi, Z. M., & Shafie, N. A. (2014). Financial Statement Fraud: A Case Examination Using Beneish Model and Ratio Analysis. *International Journal of Trade. Economics and Finance*, *5*(2), 184–186.

Paolone, F., & Pozzoli, M. (2017) Assessing the Effect of Financial Crisis of Earnings Manipulation. Empirical Evidence from the Top 1,000 World Listed Companies. In: Hošková-Mayerová Š., Maturo F., Kacprzyk J. (eds) Mathematical-Statistical Models and Qualitative Theories for Economic and Social Sciences. Studies in Systems, Decision and Control, 104, 249-263. Springer, Cham.

Peek, E., Meuwissen, R., Moers, F., & Vanstraelen, A. (2013). Comparing Abnormal Accruals Estimates across Samples: An International Test. *European Accounting Review*, *22*(3), 533–572. doi:10.1080/09638180.2012.746518

Stepanyan, A. (2014). Altman's Z-Score in the Airline Business. Case Study of Major U.S. Carriers. Are they Potential Bankruptcy Candidates? *International Journal of Advances in Management and Economics*, *3*, 116–124.

Stolowy, H., & Breton, G. (2004). Accounts Manipulation: A literature review and proposed conceptual framework. *Review of Accounting and Finance*, *3*(1), 5–66. doi:10.1108/eb043395

KEY TERMS AND DEFINITIONS

Audit: An independent examination of books and records by a qualified party based on specific criteria set in the engagement letter.

Detection: The process of discovery of items or facts being investigated.

Deviation: The departure of certain set of measurement from an established or accepted benchmark or standard.

Evidence: Anything that proves or disproves a proposition.

Forensic: The application of scientific and objective assessment on matters of inquiry.

Fraudulent: A deceitful subject matter that being produced with the intent to deceive or manipulate.

Manipulation: The state of manipulating to mislead the perception of others.

Chapter 14
Internal Control System in Cooperative Society

Norfaizah Manjah
Akademi Suruhanjaya Koperasi Malaysia (MCSC), Malaysia

Radiah Othman
https://orcid.org/0000-0002-9772-0439
Massey University, New Zealand

Haslinda Yusoff
Universiti Teknologi MARA, Malaysia

ABSTRACT

The increasing number of recent fraud cases involving the board of directors and top management in cooperative societies has raised concerns about the effectiveness of internal control systems (ICS) in these organizations. This chapter aims to examine the relationship between the effectiveness of the ICS and the likelihood of fraud occurrence by focusing on the control environment, risk assessment, and monitoring activities of cooperative societies in Malaysia. The results showed that the effectiveness of the control environment, risk assessment, and monitoring had no significant relationship with the likelihood of fraud occurrence in these organizations. However, this does not necessarily mean that the fraud risk is not an emerging issue. The study proposes that the internal auditors and audit committee oversee a pro-active fraud prevention check-up, as suggested by the Association of Certified Fraud Examiners (ACFE), which is to be implemented in co-operative societies to assess how vulnerable the organizations are to fraud.

INTRODUCTION

Fraud negatively impacts organisations in many ways including financial, reputation, psychological and social implications (IPPF, 2009). Fraud can be committed by an employee at any level within an organisation, as well as by those outside the organisation (IPPF 2009, p.2) indicating the importance of a good internal control system. The Committee of Sponsoring Organizations of the Treadway Commission (COSO)'s Internal Control – Integrated Framework (2013) describes an internal control as a process

DOI: 10.4018/978-1-5225-7356-2.ch014

consisting of ongoing tasks and activities that are effected by people at every level of an organisation. As such no industry or size of company is immune from fraud (Kapardis & Zopiatis, 2010) including the co-operative societies.

Fraud in cooperative societies is not new within developing countries context. In India for example, Adarsh Credit Co-operative ran Ponzi schemes promising a double in the deposits in six years and shifted most of the money deposited by the victims to shell companies being run by the realtives and friends of Mukesh Modi, the Chairman and the main promoter of Adarsh Credit ("Adarsh Credit Co-op", 2018). In another case, Sharmahan Multipurpose Cooperative Society had cheated customers in relation to their deposits and chit fund memberships. In Nigeria, the Niger State Government received reports of fraudulent activities going on in some of the Nigeria Union of Teachers (NUT). In Pakistan, Karimabad Ismailia Multipurpose Cooperative Society was involved in misappropriation of society funds, security deposits and transfer fees ("NAB arrests five", 2018). Close to home, two ex-employees duped the Singapore's oldest co-operative, Singapore Statutory Boards Employees; Co-operative Thrift and Loan Society, of S$5.1 million of members' savings by using names of phantom members to apply for a termination of their membership, withdrawal or loan ("Two charged", 2018). However, research on co-operative societies is limited. Previous scholarly academic research has focused on the perceived benefits and costs of implementing the framework (e.g. Beneish, Billings, & Hodder, 2008; DeFond & Francis, 2005), discussion and evaluation of the framework (e.g. Lawson, Muriel, & Sanders, 2017; Proviti, 2013), studies on the impact of the framework (Cohen, Krishnamoorthy, & Wright, 2010; Klamm & Watson, 2009), and on firm's existing controls (e.g. Janvrin, Payne, Byrnes, Schneider, & Curtis, 2012). Empirical research that provides similar evidence in NPO, especially the co-operative societies, is lacking. The pressing need is evidenced by the increasing fraud-related cases involving weaknesses in ICS in Malaysian cooperatives (see Table 1).

The British colonial administration introduced the concept of co-operative to Malaya (now Malaysia) for peasants, farmers and fisherman in 1922 (Fredericks, 1986) as part of its initiatives for poverty eradication in the rural areas. The co-operatives looked after the welfare of the members' children, education, housing ownership, employment and entrepreneurship opportunities. The mission was extended further to include better governance and management through the government's National Co-operative Policy, first launched in 2002. The Co-operative Societies (Amendment) Act, 2007 (hereafter the Act) defines a co-operative society as an autonomous association of persons united voluntarily to meet their common economic, social, and cultural needs and aspirations through a jointly owned and democratically con-

Table 1. Selected cases involving internal control 2010–2013

Cases/Year	2013	2012	2011	2010
Abuse of Authorisation System	9	9	10	7
Assets misappropriation		3	3	3
Inappropriate use of documents and records False (billing) claim Unjustified expenses	1 1	2		1
Misuse of funds	1	1		
Total	12	15	13	11

Source: (Investigation and Enforcement Unit of Malaysia Co-operative Society Commission, 2014)

trolled enterprise. In 2008, the Malaysian Co-operative Society Commission (MCSC) was established and good governance has since become a priority. Specifically, Section 45 requires that the board of a co-operative society exercise prudence and diligence of ordinary course of business, which includes the establishment of internal control systems (ICS) in order to protect the societies' members' interest. Failing which, they would be liable for any losses. However, in reality it is a different picture. For example, no action was taken against the directors of Koperasi Bir, which was involved in a multimillion ringgit (Malaysian currency) money laundering scheme (Shun, 2011). According to the Association of Certified Fraud Examiners' 2018 Report to the Nations on Occupational Fraud and Abuse, 83% of all frauds perpetrated against companies are asset misappropriation including billing claims, which is also reflected in Table 1 above. According to IPPF (2009), asset misappropriation involves stealing cash or assets and in many cases, the perpetrator tries to conceal the theft.

It is critical for the top management to seriously consider the possibility and consequences of fraud. However, the respected and trusted corporate executives being so morally corrupt that they were too busy stealing to think of the consequences for the employees, shareholders, customers, or themselves (Biegelman and Bartow, 2015). They tend to be in positions of trust, members of community organisations who are motivated by a personal need (IPPF, 2009). Despite financial and non-financial support by the Federal Government, the cooperatives' performance had not been satisfactory (Othman, Mansor, & Kari, 2014) in achieving its objectives of upholding members' interest. While the lack of managerial capacity was highlighted as the source of failure, including fraud, in these entities (Ismail & Mohd Sarif, 2010), Rittenberg, Martens, and Landes (2007) claim that the main reason is that the entities do not identify and control risks, therefore strong commitment to internal control is a matter of priority, not a matter of resources. As emphasised by Biegelman and Bartow (2012), although an outside audit can identify control gaps, only an honest inside assessment can truly gauge a company's risk of fraud.

The main objective of this chapter is to illustrate how a research was conducted to examine the insight of internal control elements in a co-operative society focussing on the control environment, risk assessment and monitoring activities of the COSO framework. Secondly, the chapter highlights the role of the internal auditing and Enterprise Risk Management in relation to fraud prevention. Thirdly, the chapter also implies the importance of the governing and the regulatory bodies to pro-actively monitor and make sure that the co-operatives management and staff are aware of the consequences of fraud through ongoing training and development and periodic assessment of fraud risk assessment.

INTERNAL AUDITING, RISK MANAGEMENT AND FRAUD PREVENTION

The recent 2018 ACFE fraud report (ACFE, 2018) reveals that organizations lose 5% of their revenues to fraud small businesses typically have fewer anti-fraud controls than larger organization, leaving them more vulnerable. The report also mention that and internal control weaknesses had led to nearly half of the fraud. Many firms across the globe have used the 1992 COSO framework to assess the design and effectiveness of the internal control systems (Murphy, 2015). An updated framework in 2013 retains many of the core elements of the 1992 Framework, including the five components of the internal control, and explicitly identifies 17 principles underlying each of these components (Lawson et al., 2017). The internal control components include control environment, risk assessment, control activities, information and communication, and monitoring activities. The recent 2013 Framework reemphasises the importance of applying internal controls to operational and compliance objectives and expands the reporting objectives to incorporate internal and non-financial reporting objectives (COSO, 2013). In addition, The Institute of Internal Auditors (IIA) has also published guidelines such as GTAG® 13 in addition to the IIA's Practice Guide, Internal Auditing and Fraud to provide guidance to chief audit executives and internal auditors on how to use technology to help prevent, detect, and respond to fraud (GTAG13, 2009). All these guidelines serve the seriousness of the regulatory and professional bodies to deal with fraud risk and conduct proper and adequate fraud risk assessments. As such, it is important for internal auditors to obtain a thorough understanding of the control framework(s) adopted either formally or informally by the organisation and to become familiar with globally recognized, comprehensive control frameworks such COSO frameworks (IG2130, 2017). IG2100 (2017) emphasizes that the internal auditors need to understand the business to perform a meaningful evaluations and may use established governance, risk management, and control frameworks as a guide in their evaluation.

As a profession, internal auditors have a critical role in curbing fraud occurrences. IPPF (2009) suggests that an effective internal audit activity can be extremely helpful in addressing fraud. They usually have a continual presence in the organisation that provides them with a better understanding of the organisation and its controls systems. They have to consider the possibility of significant errors, fraud, and noncompliance (IG1220, 2016, p.2) by using an established risk management or control framework such as COSO framework or ISO 310000 to assist in their work (IG2120, 2017). With the advances in technology (IT), they might be asked to participate in an IT fraud risk assessment which would systematically identifying where and how fraud may occur and who may be in a position to commit fraud (GTAG13, 2009). As such, as internal auditing assesses the organisation's efforts to complete a comprehensive fraud risk assessment, it is important that potential fraud schemes related to IT be identified and included in the enterprise wide risk assessment (IG2120, 2017; GTAG13, 2009, p.5). In addition, internal auditors may provide independent, objective assessments of the design and effectiveness of governance processes within the organisation which may be evidenced by statements of acknowledgement, signed by staff and business partners, to demonstrate the organisation's efforts to promote awareness of its ethics and values (IG2110, p. 5-6).

BACKGROUND OF PREVIOUS STUDIES

The importance of the internal controls has been emphasised by practitioners, academics and regulators (COSO, 2013; Tysiac, 2012; Landsittel, 2010). Often, an association is made of its implications for financial reporting reliability, efficiency, and being effective of an organisation's operation and compliance with laws and regulations (e.g. Hermanson, Smith, & Stephens, 2012). A strong internal control can deter and detect fraud occurrence. However, Kapardis and Zopiatis (2010) caution that no industry or size of company is immune from fraud. Fraud represents an "attempt to deceive another party to gain a benefit" (ACFE Report to the Nations on Occupational Fraud and Abuse, 2018). According to Albrecht and Zimbelman (2012), fraud occurs when the deception could instil some confidence in the victim to believe such an act is true when it is not. Kranacher, Riley, and Wells (2010) also state that this intention would cost the victim to suffer an economic loss, and the perpetrator to realise a gain or benefit. Kranacher et al. (2010) classified fraud into three major categories 1) asset misappropriations, 2) corruption, and 3) financial statements and other fraudulent statements. Various types of fraud are closely related to those that are committed against organisations and those that are committed on behalf of organisations. This includes employee embezzlement, vendor fraud, customer fraud, management fraud (financial statement fraud), investment scams and other consumer frauds (Albrecht, Albrecht, Albrecht & Zimbelman, 2016).

COSO framework has also been linked to the likelihood of fraud incidence and anti-fraud programmes. Previous studies suggest that poor internal control procedures were seen as factors that enabled fraud to occur (Hermanson et al., 2012; MacArthur, Waldrup, & Fane, 2004; (Peterson & Gibson, 2003; Buckhoff, 2002). In terms of fraud prevention (anti-fraud) programmes, Hoffman & Birnbrich, 2012; Hooks, Kaplan, Schultz, and Poneno, 1994) concur that good communication – an element of COSO's internal control to deter fraud – is compelling, as fraud usually involves concealment while communication fosters openness. Proactive actions towards fraud prevention are necessary since prevention is better than cure (Kapardis & Zopiatis, 2010). Rae and Subramaniam (2008) propose that risk management strategies relating to employee fraud will need to pay greater attention to organisational factors that affect both perceptions of justice at the workplace and internal control procedures' quality, including fostering a more ethical and equitable work environment, increasing internal auditing activities, and staff training in risk management.

Previous studies on Malaysian co-operatives have yet to explore internal control and likelihood of fraud. Most of these studies highlighted the challenges faced by co-operatives such as knowledge gap (Ismail & Mohd-Sarif, 2010) and lack of human resources (Kaur, Devi, Omar, Abd, & Samad, 2005). The co-operative employees were involved with these reported fraudulent activities. Guideline 4 under the Co-operatives Societies Regulation clearly spelt out the importance of Internal Audit Committee functions involving internal control systems and risk management. They have the authority to check all accounting records to ensure they comply with the relevant laws and decisions made in the Annual General Meeting. This is where the ICS plays its crucial role, which is to provide assurance in regard to fraud prevention mechanisms effectiveness. Nonetheless, the incidence of fraud is likely to be complex and a function of a combination of factors. The studies that examine the interactive effects of various situational factors on co-operatives' employee fraud are under-researched (Rae & Subramaniam, 2008). Following Rae and Subramaniam (2008), the chapter focuses on three organisational factors based on COSO ICS framework – control environment, risk assessment and monitoring activities – as they are seen to be distinct elements of a larger system of management controls.

In terms of the control environment, previous studies suggest that professional proficiency and objectivity significantly influence the control environment aspect of the internal control system (Gamage, Lock & Fernando, 2014; Fadzil et al., 2005). In a more ethical corporate environment, employees will be more willing and committed to adhere to the set rules and regulations within an organisation (Vardaman, Gondo & Allen, 2014; Rae & Subramaniam, 2008). Hermanson, Smith & Stephens (2012) and Kizirian and Leese (2004) found that the client's "management tone", particularly in terms of their attitudes towards security consciousness, has a significant effect on the strength of the client's security controls.

As emphasised by Dorminey, Fleming, Kranacher & Riley, Jr. (2012) and Hwang, Shin, & Han (2004), understanding the control environment is essential because it represents the control atmosphere for the entity and the foundation for other components. Within an information technology (IT) environment, GTAG13 (2009) suggests that the chief audit executives to discuss the overall assessment of the organisation's fraud control environment in IT. Long ago, Duncan, Flesher, and Stocks (1999) reported that fraudulent cases reveal that the top management contains little or no training in business management or accounting. Even recently, it is not surprising to note that the most common reported ICS weaknesses are deviations from policy and management override of control, which "create an atmosphere conducive to abuse and fraud" (Hermanson et al., 2012, p. 44). Merchant & White (2017) emphasizes the importance of ethics training to the top management as part of a good internal control environment

Controls are designed to mitigate risks at the entity, activity and transaction levels (IG 2130, 2017, p.2). COSO (2013, p. 7) stipulates that the effectiveness of control environment should have these components below in order for co-operative societies to detect fraud: the organisation demonstrates a commitment to integrity and ethical values; the board of directors demonstrates independence from management and exercises oversight of the development and performance of internal control; management establishes, with board oversight, structures, reporting lines, and appropriate authorities and responsibilities in the pursuit of the objectives; the organisation demonstrates a commitment to attract, develop, and retain competent individuals in alignment with objectives; and the organisation holds individuals accountable for their internal control responsibilities in the pursuit of the objectives. An organisation's exposure to fraud is a function of the fraud risks inherent in the business, the extent to which effective internal controls are present wither to prevent or detect fraud and the honesty and integrity of those involved in the process (IPPF, 2009, p.16). Thus, the more effective the control environment is, the higher the chance that fraud could be detected in the organisation (Spatacean, 2012). Therefore, the following hypothesis is proposed:

H1: *The effectiveness of control environment has a significant relationship with the absence of the likelihood of fraud occurrence.*

Risk is a condition in which there is a possibility of an adverse deviation from a desired outcome that is expected or hoped for (Bousquet & Dubiel-Teleszynski, 2017). The scope of fraud risk assessment may vary widely depending on the organisation's size, complexity or industry (IPPF, 2009). A fraud risk assessment concentrated on fraud schemes and scenarios to determine the presence of internal controls and whether or not the controls can be circumvented (IPPF, 2009). Premuroso and Houmes (2012) suggest that in order to assess the effectiveness of the risk assessment, the organisations should consider any susceptibility of fraud, potential for misstatements, and the risk of control failure. COSO (2013, p. 7) defines risk assessment as:

The possibility that an event will occur and adversely affect the achievement of objectives. Risk assessment involves a dynamic and iterative process for identifying and assessing risks to the achievement of objectives. Risks to the achievement of these objectives from across the entity are considered relative to established risk tolerances. Thus, risk assessment forms the basis for determining how risks will be managed.

The components of risk assessment should have the following: the organisation specifies objectives with sufficient clarity to enable the identification and assessment of risks relating to objectives; the organisation identifies risks to the achievement of its objectives across the entity and analyses the risks as a basis for determining how the risks should be managed; the organisation considers the potential for fraud in assessing risks to the achievement of objectives; and the organisation identifies and assesses changes that could significantly impact the system of internal control (COSO, 2013, p. 7).

Biegelman and Bartow (2015) suggest that the management must conduct periodic assessments of the risk of fraud at all levels and document the results based on past events and current circumstances. In an IT environment, GTAG13 (2009) suggest that fraud risk assessment is a component of an entity's larger enterprise risk management in which the management is responsible for. Thus, an effective risk assessment should be adequately designed to prevent or detect material misstatement, whether caused by errors or fraud (Spira & Page, 2003; Jones, 2008). In the Olympus fraud case, Fukukawa, Mock, and Srivastava (2014) comment that the fraud could have been discovered earlier if their auditor had practised professional scepticism in regard to risk assessment. This is also supported by Knapp and Knapp (2001), who suggest a relationship between identifying and evaluating risk factors with the heightened risk of fraud occurrence. As such, employees who are actively trained in risk management are likely to more accurately identify threats to the organisation as a result of weak or non-existent internal controls (N'Guilla Sow, Basiruddin, Mohamad & Abdul Rasid, 2018; Kramer, 2003). Therefore, the more that potential risks get taken care of, the higher the chance that fraud could be detected. Thus, the following hypothesis is proposed:

H2: *The effectiveness of risk assessment has a significant relationship with the absence of the likelihood of fraud occurrence.*

Hedley and Ben-Chorin (2011) suggest that monitoring activities could provide the management with crucial information in preventing, detecting and responding to fraud in the organisation. However, monitoring activities are only effective if the regular review and management commitment could be put in place. COSO (2013, p. 7) defines monitoring activities as:

Ongoing evaluations, separate evaluations, or some combination of the two are used to ascertain whether each of the five components of internal control, including controls to effect the principles within each components, is present and functioning. Ongoing evaluations, built into business processes at different levels of the entity, provide timely information. Separate evaluation, conducted periodically, will vary in scope and frequency depending on assessment of risks, effectiveness of ongoing evaluations, and other management considerations. Findings are evaluated against criteria established by regulators, recognized standard-setting bodies or management and the board of directors, and deficiencies are communicated to management and the board of director as appropriate.

The main objective of monitoring is to maintain effective internal control; therefore the management should monitor the quality and performance of the ICS that is always relevant and able to address the new risk. The internal control deficiencies must be communicated in a timely manner to those parties responsible for taking corrective action, including senior management and the board of directors, as appropriate (COSO, 2013). In an IT environment, IG2110 (2017) proposes continuous monitoring methods such as assigning internal auditors to observe meetings of governance-related bodies and advise them on an ongoing basis (p.4-5). This also includes continuous monitoring of critical data and related trends to identify unusual situations or variances; and routine and/ad hoc matching of public data and/or proprietary data (IPPF, 2009, p.22). Jones (2008) also indicated that checks and balance are crucial to guarding against loss and theft as an ongoing effort to prevent and detect dishonest activities (Adedokun & Oyewole, 2013; Wang & Kleiner, 2005). Therefore, a failure of monitoring may provide an opportunity for the top management to override the ICS (Mitra, Jaggi, & Hossain, 2013). In that regard, the more effective the monitoring activities are in an organisation, the earlier the fraud could be detected. Therefore, the following hypothesis is proposed:

H3: *The effectiveness of monitoring activities has a significant relationship with the absence of the likelihood of fraud occurrence.*

THEORETICAL FRAMEWORK

The Fraud Triangle theory was developed by Donald R. Cressey in 1953 to generalise the characteristics of white-collar offences. Albrecht et al. (2016) suggest that the reasons a person commits fraud are a perceived pressure, a perceived opportunity, and the ability to rationalise the fraud as acceptable. Cressey hypothesised that the fraud triangle elements must be presented together for fraud to be committed. Of importance is the perceived opportunity that primarily deals with the internal control effectiveness (Dorminey, Fleming, Kranacher, & Riley, 2012). Previous studies have reported that there is a relationship between the internal control and fraud triangle in that the fraudster prefers weak control in order to commit fraud, which provides an opportunity for a manager to override controls and the ability to conceal fraud (Huang, Lin, Chiu & Yen, 2017; Caplan, 1999). In this regard, Dorminey et al. (2012) introduce a meta-model of white-collar crime to show that the likelihood of fraud occurrence has a direct relationship with the control and procedures in the organisations. Specifically, the opportunity to use the control environment could encourage the fraudster to act in order to conceal and, to an extent, converse the act of fraud into something untraceable. Following Aghghaleh, Iskandar, and Mohamad (2014, p. 2), the COSO guidelines used in this chapter were developed from the fraud triangle theory and modified into the framework. Thus, the chapter attempts to test how the applicability of the fraud triangle elements of opportunity is best presented by the internal control framework and whether it can be used to examine the effectiveness of the internal control environment in detecting the likelihood of fraud occurrence in co-operatives. It is imperative that the co-operatives consider any susceptibility of fraud, potential for misstatements, and the risk of control failure (Premuroso & Houmes, 2012).

The primary objectives of an organisation's ICS are to provide administrative management with reasonable assurance that the financial information is accurate and reliable, the organisation complies with policies, plans and procedures, laws, regulations and contracts, assets are safeguarded against loss and theft, resources are used economically and efficiently and established objectives and goals for operations or programs can be met (Fadzil et al., 2005). Kummer, Singh and Best. (2015) highlights the importance of fraud control policies in smaller form of organisations. Nonetheless, adequate control is considered to be present if the administrative management has planned and organised controls in a manner that provides reasonable assurance that the organisation's objectives and goals will be achieved efficiently and economically (Akintoye & Adegbite, 2017; Fadzil et al., 2005). However, the quality of the ICS depends on how effective it is, thus an implementation merely suggests existence, not effectiveness. An effective control is present when the administrative management directs the system in such a way as to provide reasonable assurance that the organisation's objectives and goals will be achieved. In addition, fraud could also be prevented. In a recent study, Donelson, Ege and McInnis (2017) found a strong association between material weaknesses and future fraud revelation. Therefore, it is critical that the co-operative's board of directors continuously assesses the ICS adequacy and integrity.

RESEARCH METHOD

There are 809 registered co-operatives in Kuala Lumpur Federal State as per December 2013. For this chapter, 260 co-operative societies have been chosen to carefully represent the population of the cooperatives as suggested by Sekaran (2003) (refer to Table 2). This means for each function category, a simple random sampling was applied to maintain the similar percentage from the whole population (Sekaran & Bougie, 2011). A survey using questionnaires was used, which targeted internal auditors, boards of directors, managers, and those who have relevant experience with ICS implementation in their co-operatives (The questionnaire is attached in the Appendix).

The questionnaire is based on Hermanson et al. (2012)'s study and permission. Hermanson et al. (2012) reported that the control environment and risk assessment components are, on average, not as strong as those in monitoring component. They suggested for more work to be done to understand whether their findings hold in other setting thus, the inclusion of their questions into the questionnaire. Hermanson et al. also suggested for the survey to be conducted in industry specific organizations (2012, p.19). The questionnaire was divided into two sections: Section A and Section B. Section A asks the respondent about general information, which includes their co-operative function, their position, and amount of experience in the co-operative industry. Section B consists of the respondent's assessment towards the internal control, which is divided into three parts: 1) control environment, 2) risk assessment and 3) monitoring.

The details of the co-operatives were obtained from the Malaysia co-operative society commission (MCSC) federal state branch's registrar and then the questionnaires were mailed to randomly selected co-operatives in Kuala Lumpur. A stamped self-addressed envelope was attached with the questionnaire. Follow-up calls were also made after the deadline. Each of the questionnaires was pre-numbered with an associated calculated Altman z-score. Z score = 6.56 T1 + 3.26 T2 + 6.72 T3 + 1.05 T4 the score was used to measure the co-operative societies' financial distress indicator. A score of 1.10 and less suggests a high probability of bankruptcy, while scores that are above 2.60 suggest a low probability of bankruptcy. The variables and their measurements are shown in Table 3.

Table 2. Sample selection of respondent

Function	Number	Percentage (%)
Services	109	41.9
Consumer	63	24.2
Agriculture	24	9.2
Credit	44	16.9
Housing	10	3.8
Transportation	6	2.3
Industrial	3	1.1
Construction	1	0.6
Total	260	100

Table 3. Summary of variable measurement

Dependent Variables	Measurement	References
The likelihood of the fraud occurrence Red flags – by financial stress	Altman Z-Score A score of "1" is given if the organisation has financial distress and "0" if the organisation is in a safe position	Adedokun and Oyewole (2013) Shanmugam (2013)
Independent Variables	**Measurement**	
Effectiveness of Control Environment Effectiveness of Risk Assessment Effectiveness of Monitoring Activities	Five Likert scale Average value of each component	Jensen (1993) Knapp and Knapp (2001) Spira and Page (2003) Asare and Wright (2004) Wang and Kleiner (2005) Jones (2008) Spatacean (2012) Hermanson et al. (2012) Adedokun and Oyewole (2013) Mitra et al. (2013) Fukukawa et al. (2014)

FINDINGS

Demographic Profile

The profiles of respondents are shown in Table 4. The highest percentage of co-operative business function is consumers, which included education (31.5%), followed by credit (28.8%), services (26%), agriculture (6.8%), housing (4.1%), and transportation and construction with 1.4% each.

As shown in Table 5, the respondents are targeted as those who had the experience with the ICS implementation in the co-operatives. The majority of the respondents are board of directors/top management (43.8%), followed by manager (28.8%), internal auditor (20.5%), and other positions with 6.8%.

Most of the respondents had 1–4 years of experience in their position (38.4%) while the most experienced respondents are only 11%. This suggests that the majority of the respondents were still new in the co-operative business.

Table 4. Type of co-operatives

Type	Frequency	Percent
Services	19	26
Consumer	23	31.5
Agriculture	5	6.8
Credit	21	28.8
Housing	3	4.1
Transportation	1	1.4
Construction	1	1.4
Total	73	100

Table 5. Respondent position

Position	Percentage (%)
Board of Directors/Top Management	43.8
Manager	28.8
Internal Audit	20.5
Others	6.9
Total	100

Descriptive Analysis

Table 6 shows that the mean score is 0.33 (above 0), which indicates that that most of the co-operatives were not financially distressed. In this chapter, it is assumed that there is a high chance that fraud would occur in a financially distressed co-operative (a score of 1).

Table 7 indicates that for control environment, the highest mean comes from "information [that] is provided and presented in Annual General Meeting (AGM)" and the lowest is 3.56 from "meeting and discussion with internal audit staff". This finding showed that the respondents acknowledged that their co-operatives complied with the legislation to present the necessary information in the AGM. However, there seemed to be a minimal level of interaction between the board of directors and internal audit staff. Nine out of 15 items had a mean score of 4.00 or more, which indicates that the respondents agreed that the co-operatives had a controlled environment.

The Likert scale was used for this measurement, whereby 1 = strongly disagreed, 2 = disagreed, 3 = not sure, 4 = agreed and 5 = strongly agreed.

Meanwhile, in the risk assessment category, six out of seven questions scored less than 4.00, indicating that the respondents were not aware of risk assessment exercise in their organisation. Though it seemed that the cooperatives had fraud policies and procedures in place, budget allocations for fraud programmes could be an issue.

For the monitoring activities variable, the result shows that the co-operatives had conducted some form of monitoring activities, including inspection and follow-up. Most of the respondents agreed that the co-operatives had a good accountability mechanism (mean = 4.37). Unfortunately, the mechanism to control deficiencies was still lacking (mean = 3.85).

Table 6. Co-operatives financial distress

	Min	Max	Mean	Variance
Indicator	0	1	.33	.224

Legend: Indicator represents the financial distress of respective co-operative based on the Altman z-score

Table 7. Descriptive statistics

	Min	Max	Mean	Variance
Control Environment				
High quality and accurate financial reporting	2	5	4.44	.333
Knowledge, experience and training for internal audit staff	2	5	3.95	.803
Information is provided and presented in Annual General Meeting (AGM)	3	5	4.51	.281
Board of directors is committed to the ethics and integrity	2	5	4.26	.473
Meeting and discussion with internal audit staff	2	5	3.85	.852
Knowledge, industry experience and time to carry out the duties as board of directors	1	5	3.96	.957
Board of directors understand their role	2	5	4.12	.665
The co-operative's commitment to ethics and integrity is communicated throughout the organisation	2	5	4.07	.620
Top management appropriately responds to violations of behaviour	2	5	4.21	.499
The co-operative members understand ethics and integrity	2	5	3.95	.580
Employee knowledge and skills	2	5	4.25	.522
Appropriate tone at the top	2	5	4.11	.571
Sufficient time to carry out their responsibilities effectively	1	5	3.86	1.037
Management override	2	5	4.00	.417
Deviations policies	2	5	4.07	.509
Risk Assessment				
Fraud policies and procedures	3	5	4.16	.250
Risks consideration	2	5	3.99	.514
Analysing identified risks	2	5	3.85	.574
Changing management	2	5	3.66	.589
Fraud risk factors	2	5	3.71	.541
Adequate resources	2	5	3.56	.639
Assessment of fraud risks	2	5	3.64	.399
Monitoring Activities				
Deficiencies report management	2	5	4.04	.401
Internal auditors access	2	5	3.97	.638
Report on internal control deficiencies	2	5	4.03	.444
Mechanism to control deficiencies	2	5	3.85	.658
Follow-up on external auditor recommendation	2	5	4.23	.459
Follow-up on internal control deficiencies	2	5	4.15	.602
The internal audit function's scope, responsibilities, and audit plans are appropriate	2	5	4.08	.493
Competent and experienced internal audit staff	2	5	4.07	.731
Periodic inspection	2	5	4.18	.676
Accountability	2	5	4.37	.320

Normality Test

Skewness and kurtosis were used to test the normality distribution of the data based on how far they are from zero (Field, 2011). Park (2008) indicates that the ranges of acceptable skewness and kurtosis were equal or approximately to zero or in the value of +1.0 and -1.0.

Table 8 shows that most of the skewness and kurtosis of the three studied variables fell within the acceptable range of +1.0 to -1.0, ranging from .787 to -.738. Therefore, the data was normally distributed.

Factor Analysis

From Table 9, the result shows that the determinant of the variables correlation matrix is bigger than 0.00001, which indicates that the multi-collinearity is not the problem. The Kaiser-Meyer-Olkin (KMO) also has a value more than 0.5 as a bare minimum, which indicates that the sampling was adequate for running the test.

Furthermore, the results of Bartlett's Test of Sphericity have satisfied the requirement of significant at 5 per cent, which indicated the validity of the scales used in the analysis.

Reliability Test

As shown in Table 10, the Cronbach's Alpha for the Control Environment variables is .918, which indicates that the internal consistency for all 15 scaled items is excellent with risk assessment category scored at .879 and monitoring activities .879.

Table 8. Normality test (skewness and kurtosis)

Variables	Mean	Skewness	Kurtosis
Control Environment	4.1059	-.738	.56
Risk Assessment	3.7965	-.378	.407
Monitoring	4.0973	-.453	.787

Table 9. Factor analysis

		Control Environment	Risk Assessment	Monitoring Activities
Determinant		.000	.022	.007
Kaiser-Meyer-Olkin Measure of Sampling Adequacy		.841	.841	.821
Bartlett's Test of Sphericity	Approx. Chi-Square	597.092	262.897	338.986
	Df	105	21	45
	Sig	.000	.000	.000

Table 10. Reliability test

		Cronbach's Alpha	
Control Environment		.918	
Risk Assessment		.879	
Monitoring Activities		.879	

Correlation Analysis

In order to test the relationship of two variables, the correlations test was used in this chapter. Pallant (2005) suggests correlation coefficient of r =0.50 to 1.0 as strong correlation, r = 0.30 to 0.49 as medium correlation, and 0.10 to 0.29 as weak correlation. As indicated in Table 11, all three variables have positive but weak correlations of financial distress to control environment (r = .121), risk assessment (r = .173) and monitoring activities (r = .010). The result also shows that the relationship between financial stress and all three variables was not significant at 0.05 level.

Nonetheless, the direction of the relationship was positive and strongly correlated, whereas the control environment has a strong level positive relationship with risk assessment (r =.725) and monitoring activities. Risk assessment also has a positive and strong correlation with monitoring activities (r = .728). The result also shows that the relationship control environment and other indicators were significant at 0.05 level.

In summary, the result indicates that the financial distress, control environment, risk assessment and monitoring activities had a positive but weak relationship. This indicates that effective ICS could not be linked to the likelihood of fraud occurrence, which may also suggest that fraud could also occur in the organisations with effective ICS due to inherent limitation of the ICS collusion of two or more parties. This contradicts with Adedokun and Oyewole (2013), who show that the monitoring activities have a positive and strong relationship. It can also be inferred that the control environment had a positive and strong relationship with the risk assessment and monitoring activities, as expected.

Regression Analysis

Table 12 shows a summary of multiple regression results. It shows that 2.8 per cent of the variables studied contributed to the changes in the likelihood of fraud occurrence in the co-operatives with an F value of 1.69 ($p < 0.05$), which is considered to be good (Field, 2011). Hence, based on the result,

Table 11. Correlation analysis

	Indicator	Control Environment	Risk Assessment	Monitoring Activities
Indicator	1	.121	.173	.010
Control Environment		1	.725**	.779**
Risk Assessment			1	.728**
Monitoring Activities				1

**. Correlation is significant at the 0.05 level (2-tailed)

hypothesis 1 was rejected. The effectiveness of control environment had no significant relationship with the absence of the likelihood of fraud occurrence, shown by a p-value of 0.396 ($\beta = .335$; $P < .05$). This result contrasted with the findings of Hermanson et al. (2012), which suggests that frequent deviations from policy may create the likelihood of abuse and fraud. This may also be derived from the co-operative law enforcement, which supervises each co-operative compliance level. Hence, this finding suggested that the effectiveness of control environment did not determine the financial distress of the co-operative, and thus was not significantly related to the occurrence of fraud in that co-operative. As such, hypothesis 2 is rejected.

Table 12 also shows that the effectiveness of risk assessment had no significant relationship with the absence of the likelihood of fraud occurrence. This is shown by the p-value of 0.109 at significance level of 5 per cent ($\beta = .260$, $P < .05$). This finding supports the argument of Asare and Wright (2004) that risk assessment is not associated with fraud. However, the insignificant result contradicts Jones (2008), who emphasised that risk assessment should exist to deter any falsification. The result also contrasts with Fukukawa et al. (2014), Hermanson et al. (2012), and Knapp and Knapp (2001). The hypothesis for this variable was also rejected.

The results in Table 12 also show that the effectiveness of monitoring activities had no significant relationship with the absence of the likelihood of fraud occurrence ($\beta = -.314$, $P < .05$). Unlike Mitra et al. (2013), and Adedokun and Oyewole (2013), the results may suggest that even though the co-operatives had monitoring activities in their ICS, it was not adequate enough to escape the likelihood of fraud. Overall, all the hypotheses were rejected, which leaves the conclusion that there was no significant relationship between the effectiveness of the internal control system and the likelihood of fraud occurrence.

FUTURE RESEARCH DIRECTIONS

Future research should include other variables such as control activities, information and communication, and motivation to commit fraud. It should also extend the sampled co-operatives to include other states in Malaysia and consider a longitudinal analysis as well. With that, it might be possible to see if the likelihood of fraud occurrence could possibly build up over time. It is also suggested that future

Table 12. Multiple regression analysis

Dependent Variable	Likelihood of Fraud Occurrence		
R^2		.068	
Adjusted R^2		.028	
F statistic		1.6900	
Sig.		.177	
	Beta		**Sig.**
Constant			
Control Environment	.151		.396
Risk Assessment	.260		.109
Monitoring Activities	-.314		.096

research could be conducted in a particular business function such as consumer or credit, in order to look into the relationship between the internal control and business function nature.

CONCLUSION

The chapter illustrates a research which examined the relationship between the effectiveness of the ICS and the likelihood of fraud occurrence in co-operative societies in Malaysia framed by the fraud triangle theory and COSO framework. The chapter focused on three components as suggested by COSO – control environment, risk assessment and monitoring activities – in order to survey cooperative societies in Malaysia. The other two components were not observable and consistent throughout the organisations studied. The results showed that that the effectiveness of the control environment, risk assessment and monitoring had no significant relationship with the likelihood of fraud occurrence in the co-operative organisations. This indicated that internal control was not a major concern in the co-operatives surveyed in relation to fraud. Nonetheless, MCSC, the governing body, should ensure that the co-operatives were aware of the consequences of fraud and to arrange for ongoing training to the staff at all levels. The results seemed to suggest that even though the co-operatives had implemented an effective ICS, it might not be sufficient to assist them in detecting the likelihood of fraud occurrence. As widely reported, human nature and greed guarantee that society and corporations would always face the issue of fraud, so lessening or removing the opportunity is one way to fight fraud (Biegelman & Bartow, 2015). Ideally, a compliance programme should be both industry-specific and unique to the co-operative, tailored to fit its requirements, and the compliance and ethics programme should be comprehensive to cover not only the risk of fraud but also corruption and other critical programme aspects.

The authors propose that MCSC should also oversee a pro-active Fraud Prevention Check-up as suggested by the Association of Certified Fraud Examiner (ACFE, 2012) to critically assess how vulnerable the organisations are to fraud. The check-up consists of a series of questions on fraud risk oversight, fraud risk ownership, fraud risk assessment, fraud risk tolerance and risk management policy. Biegelman and Bartow (2015) suggest that in designing an anti-corruption compliance programme for an organisation, compliance programme individuality should be a key consideration.

The chapter is not without its limitations. Firstly, the sample only covered the Federal State of Kuala Lumpur area. This is mainly due to time constraint and data collection cost, which could suggest potential bias in the chapter. Furthermore, this chapter only uses the z-score as an indicator for financial distress of the co-operatives. Perhaps by using another model, the likelihood of fraud occurrence could be captured more precisely. Lastly, the results of this chapter are not be extrapolated or generalised to the global internal audit profession but are rather limited to the context of the research population, the Malaysian cooperative societies and the domestic internal audit profession. One of the contributions of the chapter is highlighting the role of the internal auditing and Enterprise Risk Management in relation to fraud prevention. The chapter also implies the importance of the governing and the regulatory bodies to pro-actively monitor and make sure that the co-operatives management and staff are aware of the consequences of fraud through ongoing training and development and periodic assessment of fraud risk assessment.

REFERENCES

Adarsh Credit Co-op must pass through the acid-test. (2018, May). Retrieved from http://www.indian-cooperative.com/banks/adarsh-credit-co-op-must-pass-through-the-acid-test/

Adedokun, I. A., & Oyewole, T. (2013). Evaluation of the effect of monitoring and control activities on fraud detection in selected Nigerian commercial banks. *Research Journal of Finance and Accounting*, *4*(6), 57–63.

Aghghaleh, S. F., Iskandar, T. M., & Mohamed, Z. M. (2014). Fraud risks factor of fraud triangle and the likelihood of fraud occurrence: Evidence from Malaysia. *Information Management and Business Review*, *6*(1), 1–7.

Akintoye, S., & Adegbite, E. (2017, July). The impact of control fraud on the banking system: evidence from a developing country. *Global Research Institute for Business Academics*. Retrieved from https://www.dora.dmu.ac.uk/handle/2086/14713

Albrecht, C. C., & Zimbelman, M. F. (2012). *Forensic accounting*. South-Western Cengage Learning.

Albrecht, W. S., Albrecht, C. O., Albrecht, C. C., & Zimbelman, M. F. (2016). Fraud examination (5th ed.). Mason, OH: South Western Cengage Learning.

Asare, S. K., & Wright, A. M. (2004). The effectiveness of alternative risk assessment and program planning tools in a fraud setting. *Contemporary Accounting Research*, *21*(2), 325–352. doi:10.1506/L20L-7FUM-FPCB-7BE2

Association of Certified Fraud Examiners. (2010). *2010 Report to the Nations on Occupational Fraud and Abuse*. Austin, TX: ACFE.

Association of Certified Fraud Examiners (ACFE). (2018). Report to the nations on occupational fraud and abuse 2018 global fraud study. Austin, TX: ACFE.

Beneish, M. D., Billings, M. B., & Hodder, L. D. (2008). Internal control weaknesses and information uncertainty. *The Accounting Review*, *83*(3), 665–703. doi:10.2308/accr.2008.83.3.665

Biegelman, M. T., & Bartow, J. T. (2015). *Executive roadmap to fraud prevention and internal control: Creating a culture of compliance* (2nd ed.). John Wiley and Sons.

Bousquet, A., & Dubiel-Teleszynski, T. (2017). Operational Risk Module of the Top-Down Stress Test Framework. *Satellite Models*, 95-103.

Buckhoff, T. A. (2002). Preventing employee fraud by minimizing opportunity. *The CPA Journal*, *72*(5), 64–66.

Caplan, D. (1999). Internal controls and the detection of management fraud. *Journal of Accounting Research*, *37*(1), 101–117. doi:10.2307/2491398

Co-operative Act. 1993 (Amendment). (2012). Laws of Malaysia. In The M. Commissioner of Law Revision (Ed.), Act 502. Kuala Lumpur: Percetakan Nasional Malaysia Berhad.

Cohen, J., Krishnamoorthy, R., & Wright, A. (2010). Corporate governance in the post-Sarbanes-Oxley era: Auditors' experiences. *Contemporary Accounting Research*, *27*(3), 751–786. doi:10.1111/j.1911-3846.2010.01026.x

Committee of Sponsoring Organizations (COSO). (2013, April). *Internal control-integrated framework COSO*. Retrieved from http://www.coso.org

Committee of Sponsoring Organizations of the Treadway Commission (COSO). (2013). *Internal Control – Integrated Framework*. New York: COSO.

Cressey, D. R. (1953). *Other people's money: The social psychology of embezzlement*. New York: The Free Press.

DeFond, M. L., & Francis, J. R. (2005). Audit research after Sarbanes-Oxley. *Auditing*, *24*(Suppl.), 5–30.

Din, J. (2006). *Applying data envelopment analysis to evaluate the efficiency of fishermen associations in Malaysia* (PhD thesis). University Putra Malaysia, Selangor, Malaysia.

Donelson, D. C., Ege, M. S., & McInnis, J. M. (2017). Internal control weaknesses and financial reporting fraud. *Auditing*, *36*(3), 45–69. doi:10.2308/ajpt-51608

Dorminey, J., Fleming, A. S., Kranacher, M. J., Richard, A., & Riley, J. (2012). The evolution of fraud theory. *Issues in Accounting Education*, *27*(2), 555–579. doi:10.2308/iace-50131

Duncan, J. B., Flesher, D. L., & Stocks, M. H. (1999). Internal control systems in US churches: An examination of the effects of church size and domination on systems of internal control. *Accounting, Auditing & Accountability Journal*, *12*(2), 142–163. doi:10.1108/09513579910270084

Fadzil, F. H., Haron, H., & Jantan, M. (2005). Internal auditing practices and internal control system. *Managerial Auditing Journal*, *20*(8), 844–866. doi:10.1108/02686900510619683

Field, A. (2011). *Discovering statistics using SPSS*. London: SAGE Publications Ltd.

Fredericks, L. J. (1986). *The co-operative movement in West Malaysia: Policy, structure and institutional growth*. Kuala Lumpur: University of Malaya.

Fukukawa, H., Mock, T. J., & Srivastava, R. P. (2014). Assessing the risk fraud at Olympus and identifying an effective audit plan. *The Japanese Accounting Review*, *4*(2014), 1–25. doi:10.11640/tjar.4.2014.01

Gamage, C. T., Lock, K. L., & Fernando, A. A. J. (2014). A proposed research framework: Effectiveness of internal control system in state commercial banks in Sri Lanka. *International Journal of Scientific Research and Innovative Technology*, *1*(5), 25–44.

GTAG13. (2009). *Global Technology Audit Guide (GTAG®) 13 Fraud Prevention and Detection in an Automated World*. Altamonte Springs, FL: The Institute of Internal Auditors.

Hedley, T. P., & Ben-Chorin, O. (2011). *Auditing and monitoring activities help uncover fraud and assess control effectiveness*. Retrieved from https://www.kpmg.com/US/en/IssuesAndInsights/ArticlesPublications/Documents/auditing-and-monitoring.pdf

Hermanson, D. R., Smith, J. L., & Stephens, N. M. (2012). How effective are organizations' internal controls? Insights into specific internal control elements. *Current Issues in Auditing*, *6*(1), 31–50. doi:10.2308/ciia-50146

Hoffman, A. O. I., & Birnbrich, C. (2012). The impact of fraud prevention on bank-customer relationships: An empirical investigation in retail banking. *International Journal of Bank Marketing*, *30*(5), 390–407. doi:10.1108/02652321211247435

Hooks, K. L., Kaplan, S. E., Schultz, J. Jr, & Poneno, L. A. (1994). Enhancing communication to assist in fraud prevention and detection. *Auditing*, *13*(2), 86–117.

Huang, S. Y., Lin, C. C., Chiu, A. A., & Yen, D. C. (2017). Fraud detection using fraud triangle risk factors. *Information Systems Frontiers*, *19*(6), 1343–1356. doi:10.100710796-016-9647-9

Hwang, S. S., Shin, T., & Han, I. (2004). CRAS-CBR: Internal control assessment system using case-based reasoning. *Expert Systems: International Journal of Knowledge Engineering and Neural Networks*, *21*(1), 23–32. doi:10.1111/j.1468-0394.2004.00260.x

IG1220. (2016). *Implementation Guide 1220 Due Professional Care*. The Institute of Internal Auditors. Retrieved from https://na.theiia.org/standards-guidance/Public%20Documents/IPPF%202013%20 English.pdf

IG2100. (2017). *Implementation Guide 2100 Nature of Work*. The Institute of Internal Auditors. Retrieved from https://na.theiia.org/standards-guidance/Public%20Documents/IPPF%202013%20English.pdf

IG2110. (2017). *Implementation Guide 2130 Control*. The Institute of Internal Auditors. Retrieved from https://na.theiia.org/standards-guidance/Public%20Documents/IPPF%202013%20English.pdf

IG2120. (2017). *Implementation Guide 2120 Risk Management*. The Institute of Internal Auditors. Retrieved from https://na.theiia.org/standards-guidance/Public%20Documents/IPPF%202013%20English.pdf

IG2130. (2017). *Implementation Guide 2120 Risk Management*. The Institute of Internal Auditors. Retrieved from https://na.theiia.org/standards-guidance/Public%20Documents/IPPF%202013%20English.pdf

Investigation and Enforcement Unit of Malaysia Co-operative Society Commission. (2014). *Cases involving internal controls*. Unpublished raw data.

IPPF. (2009). *IPPF-Practice Guide Internal Auditing and Fraud*. The Institute of Internal Auditors. Retrieved from https://na.theiia.org/standards-guidance/Pages/Standards-and-Guidance-IPPF.aspx

Ismail, Y., & Mohd-Sarif, S. (2010). Convergence of global and traditional managers' characteristics: A case of senior management of cooperatives in Malaysia. *Journal of International Business and Entrepreneurship Development*, *5*(1), 28–47. doi:10.1504/JIBED.2010.035198

Janvrin, D. J., Payne, E. A., Byrnes, P., Schneider, G. P., & Curtis, M. B. (2012). The updated COSO internal control-integrated framework: Recommendations and opportunities for future research. *Journal of Information Systems*, *26*(2), 189–213. doi:10.2308/isys-50255

Jensen, M. C. (1993). The modern industrial revolution, exit and the failure of internal control system. *The Journal of Finance*, *48*(3), 831–880. doi:10.1111/j.1540-6261.1993.tb04022.x

Jones, M. J. (2008). Internal control, accountability and corporate governance: Medieval and modern Britain compared. *Accounting, Auditing & Accountability Journal*, *21*(7), 1052–1075. doi:10.1108/09513570810907474

Kapardis, M. K., & Zopiatis, A. (2010). Investigating incidents of fraud in small economies: The case for Cyprus. *Journal of Financial Crime*, *17*(2), 195–209. doi:10.1108/13590791011033890

Kaur, I., Devi, S., Omar, R., Abd, R., & Samad, R. (2005). *Kajian Kedudukan Tenaga Kerja dan Kepuasan Kerja dalam Kalangan Kakitangan Gerakan Koperasi di Malaysia (Research monograph)*. Cooperative College of Malaysia.

Kizirian, T., & Leese, W. R. (2004). Security controls and management tone. *Internal Auditing*, *19*(2), 42–46.

Klamm, B. K., & Watson, M. W. (2009). SOX 404 reported internal control weaknesses: A test of COSO framework components and information technology. *Journal of Information Systems*, *23*(2), 1–23. doi:10.2308/jis.2009.23.2.1

Knapp, C. A., & Knapp, M. C. (2001). The effects of experience and explicit fraud risk assessment in detecting fraud with analytical procedures. *Accounting, Organizations and Society*, *26*(1), 25–37. doi:10.1016/S0361-3682(00)00005-2

Kramer, W. M. (2003). The rules of fraud. *Risk Management*, *50*(11), 54.

Kranacher, M. J., Riley, R. A. Jr, & Wells, J. T. (2011). *Forensic accounting and fraud examination*. New York: John Wiley & Sons, Inc.

Kummer, T., Singh, K., & Best, P. (2015). The effectiveness of fraud detection instruments in not-for-profit organizations. *Managerial Auditing Journal*, *30*(4/5), 435–455. doi:10.1108/MAJ-08-2014-1083

Landsittel, D. L., & Rittenberg, L. E. (2010). COSO: Working with the academic community. *Accounting Horizons*, *24*(3), 455–469. doi:10.2308/acch.2010.24.3.455

Lawson, B. P., Muriel, L., & Sanders, P. R. (2017). A survey on firms' implementation of COSO's 2013 Internal control-integrated framework. *Research in Accounting Regulation*, *29*(1), 30–43. doi:10.1016/j.racreg.2017.04.004

MacArthur, J. B., Waldrup, B. E., & Fane, G. R. (2004). Caution: Fraud overhead. *Strategic Finance*, *86*(4), 28–33.

Malaysia Co-operative Society Commission Act 2007. (2012). Laws of Malaysia. In The M. Commissioner of Law Revision (Ed.), Act 665. Kuala Lumpur: Percetakan Nasional Malaysia Berhad.

Merchant, K. A., & White, L. F. (2017). Linking the Ethics and Management Control Literatures. In *Advances in Management Accounting* (pp. 1–29). Emerald Publishing Limited. doi:10.1108/S1474-787120170000028001

Mitra, S., Jaggi, B., & Hossain, M. (2013). Internal control weaknesses and accounting conservatism: Evidence from the post-Sarbanes-Oxley period. *Journal of Accounting, Auditing & Finance*, *28*(2), 152–191. doi:10.1177/0148558X13479057

Murphy, M. (2015). Companies drag feet on updating fraud safeguards. *Wall Street Journal*. Retrieved from https://www.wsj.com/articles/companies-drag-feet-on-updating-fraud-safeguards-1425346394

Mwakajumilo, S. L. I. (2011). *The role of informal microfinance institutions in saving mobilization, investment and poverty reduction. A case of savings and credit cooperative societies (SACCOs) in Tanzania from 1961–2008* (PhD thesis). St. Clements University, Turks and Caico. Retrieved from: http://www.academia.edu/3418480/THE_ROLE_OF_INFORMAL_MICROFINANCE_INSTITUTIONS_IN_SAVING_MOBILIZATION_INVESTMENT_AND_POVERTY_REDUCTION._A_CASE_OF_SAVINGS_

N'Guilla Sow, A., Basiruddin, R., Mohammad, J., & Abdul Rasid, S. Z. (2018). Fraud prevention in Malaysian small and medium enterprises (SMEs). *Journal of Financial Crime*, *25*(2), 499–517.

NAB arrests five. (2018). *NAB arrests five in cooperative society fraud case*. Retrieved from https://www.dawn.com/news/1420332

Niger warns cooperative societies against fraud. (2017). Retrieved from http://www.thetidenewsonline.com/2017/04/24/niger-warns-cooperative-societies-against-fraud/

Othman, A., Mansor, N., & Kari, F. (2014). Assessing the performance of co-operatives in Malaysia: An analysis of co-operative groups using a data envelopment analysis approach. *Asia Pacific Business Review*, *20*(3), 484–505. doi:10.1080/13602381.2014.933065

Pallant, J. (2005). *SPSS survival manual*. Allen & Unwin.

Park, H. M. (2008). *Univariate analysis and normality test using SAS, Stata, and SPSS* (Technical Working Paper). The University Information Technology Services (UITS) Center for Statistical and Mathematical Computing, Indiana University.

Petersn, B. K., & Gibson, T. H. (2003). Student health services: A case of employee fraud. *Journal of Accounting Education*, *21*(1), 61–73. doi:10.1016/S0748-5751(02)00016-7

Premuroso, R. F., & Houmes, R. (2012). Financial statement risk assessment following the COSO framework: An instructional case study. *International Journal of Accounting and Information Management*, *20*(1), 26–37. doi:10.1108/18347641211201063

Protiviti. (2013). *The updated COSO internal control framework. Frequently asked questions* (3rd ed.). Retrieved from https://www.protiviti.com/sites/default/files/united_states/insights/updated-coso-internal-control-framework-faqs-third-edition-protiviti.pdf

Rae, K., & Subramaniam, N. (2008). Quality of internal control procedures: Antecedents and moderating on organizational justice and employee fraud. *Managerial Auditing Journal*, *23*(2), 104–124. doi:10.1108/02686900810839820

Rittenberg, L. E., Martens, F., & Landes, C. E. (2007, March). Internal control guidance – not just a small matter. *Journal of Accountancy*, 46–50.

Schwarcz, S. L. (2009). The "principles" paradox. *European Business Organization Law Review, 10*(02), 175–184. doi:10.1017/S156675290900175X

Sekaran, U. (2003). *Research Methods for Business*. New York: John Wiley & Sons, Inc.

Sekaran, U., & Bougie, R. (2011). *Research methods for business: A skill-building approach*. New York: John Wiley and Sons, Inc.

Shanmugam, J.K., Haat, M.H.C., & Ali, A. (n.d.). An exploratory study of internal control and fraud prevention measures in SMEs. *International Journal of Business Research and Management, 3*(2), 90–99.

Shun, T. (2011, May 1). *The great Malaysian cooperative scam.* Retrieved from http://www.freemalaysiatoday.com/category/opinion/2011/11/24/the-great-malaysian-cooperative-scam/

Spatacean, I. O. (2012). Addressing fraud risk by testing the effectiveness of internal control over financial reporting – case of Romanian financial investment companies. *Procedia Economics and Finance, 3*, 230–235. doi:10.1016/S2212-5671(12)00145-1

Spira, L. F., & Page, M. (2003). Risk management: The reinvention of internal control and the changing role of internal audit. *Accounting, Auditing & Accountability Journal, 16*(4), 640–661. doi:10.1108/09513570310492335

Two charged. (2018). *Two charged with stealing S$5m from Stat Boards co-op*. Retrieved from https://www.todayonline.com/singapore/two-former-co-op-employees-charged-s5m-fraud

Tysiac, K. (2012). Internal control, revisited. *Journal of Accountancy, 213*(3), 24–29.

Vardaman, J. M., Gondo, M. B., & Allen, D. G. (2014). Ethical climate and pro-social rule breaking in the workplace. *Human Resource Management Review, 24*(1), 108–118. doi:10.1016/j.hrmr.2012.05.001

Wang, Y., & Kleiner, B. H. (2005). Defining employee dishonesty. *Management Research News, 28*(2/3), 11–22. doi:10.1108/01409170510785057

ADDITIONAL READING

Biegelman, M. T., & Bartow, J. T. (2012). Executive Roadmap to Fraud Prevention and Internal Control: Creating a Culture of Compliance, (2nd. Ed.), Hoboken, New Jersey: John Wiley & Sons, Inc. doi:10.1002/9781119202356

Bruwer, J. P., Petersen, A., & Le Roux, S. (2018). Occupational fraud risk, internal control initiatives and the sustainability of Small, Medium and Micro Enterprises in a developing country: A Literature Review. *Acta Universitatis Danubius. Œconomica, 14*(4), 567-580.

Cascarino, R. E. (2013). Corporate Fraud and Internal Control- A Framework for Prevention, (2nd. Ed.), Hoboken, New Jersey: John Wiley & Sons, Inc.

Germann, S., & Manasseh, S. (2017). Internal Controls in Small and Medium Size Enterprises: A Study of Matamata. *AMR*, 51-62.

Lawson, B. P., Muriel, L., & Sanders, P. R. (2017). A survey on firms' implementation of COSO's 2013 Internal Control–Integrated Framework. *Research in Accounting Regulation*, *29*(1), 30–43. doi:10.1016/j.racreg.2017.04.004

Merchant, K. A., & White, L. F. (2017). Linking the Ethics and Management Control Literatures. In Advances in Management Accounting (pp. 1-29). Emerald Publishing Limited. doi:10.1108/S1474-787120170000028001

Suh, J. B., Shim, H. S., & Button, M. (2018). Exploring the impact of organizational investment on occupational fraud: Mediating effects of ethical culture and monitoring control. *International Journal of Law, Crime and Justice*, *53*, 46–55. doi:10.1016/j.ijlcj.2018.02.003

Tomas, D., Todorovic, I., & Todorovic, Z. (2017). The Coso Framework and the Organization of Internal Audit for Fighting Against Fraud. *Casopis Za Ekonomiju I Trzisne Komunikacije*, *7*(2), 235-251.

KEY TERMS AND DEFINITIONS

Control Environment: The environment within an entity that sets the tone and control consciousness of the people working in it.

Fraud: A deception or manipulation in which an individual/entity to get advantage over another by false representation.

Internal Auditor: An individual or a unit employed by an entity to audit the efficiency and effectiveness of operation including risk assessment and monitoring activities.

Internal Control: Control activities and procedures established by the management and those charged with the governance to prevent error or fraud from occurring.

Management Fraud: Fraud perpetrated by the top management of an entity.

Risk Assessment: Activities typically performed by an internal audit unit or auditors in identifying, analyzing, and managing risk including fraud risk.

Society: A small entity typically established for not profit motives or mutual benefits of its members.

Whistle-Blowing: An act in which the employees or others giving a typically an anonymous tip of a suspicions of fraud.

Table 13.

	Board of Directors/ Top Management
	Manager
	Internal Audit
	Others

APPENDIX: QUESTIONNAIRE

Section A: Co-Operative Societies and Respondence Profile

Please respond to the following questions by selecting (/) from the dropdown list or completing the space provided.

1. Position (Table 13).
2. Experiences is co-operative movement (Table 14).
3. Experiences in current co-operative societies (Table 15).
4. Function/Industry:
5. Main contributor to the revenue/sales:

Section B: Assessment Towards Internal Control System

To what extent do you agree or disagree with each of the statements shown in Table 16-18? For each of the following statements, please select from the dropdown list the number that best represents your level of agreement using the scale.

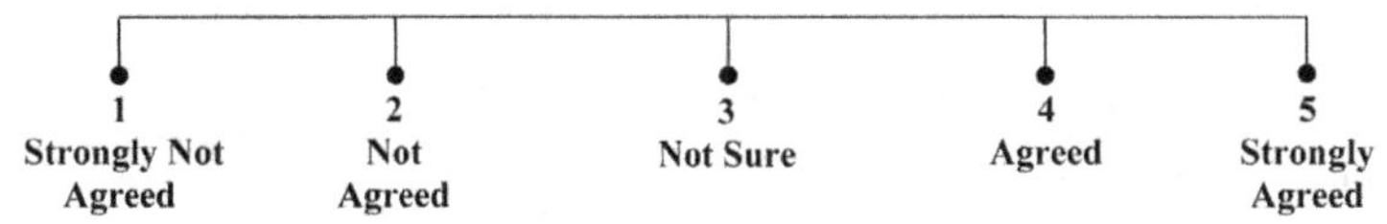

Thank you for your participation.

Table 14.

	20+ years
	15 – 19 years
	10 – 14 years
	5 – 9 years
	1 – 4 years

Table 15.

	20+ years
	15 – 19 years
	10 – 14 years
	5 – 9 years
	1 – 4 years

Table 16. Part 1: Control environment

1	Top management is committed to the high quality, accurate financial reporting to fulfill the co-operative societies legislative requirement.	**1 2 3 4 5**
2	Internal audit in charge have the required knowledge, experience, and training to perform their duties.	**1 2 3 4 5**
3	Necessary information is provided and presented in Annual General Meeting (AGM).	**1 2 3 4 5**
4	Board of directors is committed to ethics and integrity in business.	**1 2 3 4 5**
5	The audit committee meets privately with the internal audit to discuss issues relating to internal control, the financial reporting process, and co-operatives performances.	**1 2 3 4 5**
6	Board of directors have sufficient knowledge, industry experience, and time to carry out their duties.	**1 2 3 4 5**
7	Board of directors understand their role.	**1 2 3 4 5**
8	The co-operatives's commitment to ethics and integrity is communicated throughout the organization.	**1 2 3 4 5**
9	Top management appropriately responds to violations of behavior.	**1 2 3 4 5**
10	The co-operative members understand the expectations of top management regarding ethics and integrity.	**1 2 3 4 5**
11	Existing employee have adequate knowledge and skills to perform their jobs.	**1 2 3 4 5**
12	Board of directors take adequate steps to ensure an appropriate tone at the top.	**1 2 3 4 5**
13	The management have sufficient time to carry out their responsibilities effectively.	**1 2 3 4 5**
14	Management override of controls is appropriately documented and explained.	**1 2 3 4 5**
15	All deviations from established policies are investigated and documented.	**1 2 3 4 5**

Table 17. Part 2: Risk assessment

1	Responsibility and accountability for fraud policies and procedures reside with management.	**1 2 3 4 5**
2	Management adequately consider risks relating to information system.	**1 2 3 4 5**
3	Appropriate levels of management are involved with analyzing identified risks.	**1 2 3 4 5**
4	Mechanism exist in the entity to identify and react to changes that can have a more dramatic and pervasive effect on the entity, and may demand the attention of top management.	**1 2 3 4 5**
5	The co-operative's assessment considers fraud risk factors that influence the likelihood of someone committing a fraud, and the impact of a fraud on financial reporting.	**1 2 3 4 5**
6	Adequate resources exist to achieve activity-level objectives.	**1 2 3 4 5**
7	The co-operative's assessment of fraud risks considers incentives and pressures, attitudes and rationalizations, as well as opportunity to commit fraud.	**1 2 3 4 5**

Table 18. Part 3: Monitoring

1	Deficiencies in internal control are reported to the person directly responsible for the activity and to a person at least one level higher.	**1 2 3 4 5**
2	The internal auditors have access to the board of directors or audit committee.	**1 2 3 4 5**
3	Specified types of internal control deficiencies are reported to the top management and to the board.	**1 2 3 4 5**
4	There exists a mechanism for capturing and reporting identified internal control deficiencies.	**1 2 3 4 5**
5	External auditor recommendations that have been selected for implementation are followed up to verify implementation.	**1 2 3 4 5**
6	Follow-up on internal control deficiencies occurs to ensure that corrective action is taken.	**1 2 3 4 5**
7	The internal audit function's scope, responsibilities, and audit plans are appropriate to the co-operative's needs.	**1 2 3 4 5**
8	The co-operatice's has appropriate levels of competent and experienced internal audit staff.	**1 2 3 4 5**
9	Periodic comparisons of amounts recorded by the accounting system with the physical assets are performed.	**1 2 3 4 5**
10	Operating personnel are required to sign off on the accuracy of their unit financial statements, and are held responsible if errors are discovered.	**1 2 3 4 5**

Chapter 15
Internal Audit Structure and Fraud Risk Assessment From a Regulatory Perspective:
An Insight Into the Turkish Financial Services Sector

Lale Aslan
Istanbul Yeni Yuzyil University, Turkey

ABSTRACT

This chapter aims to depict the role of internal audit in Turkish capital markets by comparing the internal audit structure and its role in detecting fraud in financial institutions and developing a framework for assessing fraud risk in intermediary institutions. The newly constructed regulations concerning banks, intermediary institutions, and portfolio management companies are compared to a global benchmark by using a conceptual and descriptive approach. According to the results of this comparison, it is clear that Turkish legislation needs to be improved in critical areas. "Integrity" should be incorporated as a founding concept of the internal audit function. Certification of internal auditors needs to be encouraged, and internal audit standards need to be adapted. As a result, a fraud risk assessment template influenced by the new regulatory framework is developed for intermediary institutions.

INTRODUCTION

As generally acknowledged, the finance sector is the powerhouse of the economy on a global scale, and capital markets act like the spinal cord of the global economy. The reason behind the importance of financial sector is partly due to globalization effect, which has also caused financial markets all over the world to become integrated, and as a result, the majority of stock markets felt the effects of the 2008 crisis. It is possible to say that financial institutions took the hardest blow in the conjuncture after 2008. Thus, the main changes in the regulation were made in the areas that concern financial institutions and capital markets to address the public pressure in the aftermath of the crisis. The internal audit took the

DOI: 10.4018/978-1-5225-7356-2.ch015

lion's share during this phase; meaning that the majority of the changes made were in touch with the concepts of fraud, corporate governance, transparency, and internal auditing.

With the influence of the events described above, fraud started to become more and more signified especially in financial markets. Fraud in capital markets results not only in financial loss for shareholders but has a more significant cost to the overall economy. Since it is not possible to single out a specific country from the world economy, an essential corporate loss can easily be signified in global financial markets.

Fraud risk is notably increased in economic downturns due to mounting financial pressure toward individuals. Most frequently committed fraud type is asset misappropriation, followed by corruption, although these fraud types are not very costly when compared to fraudulent reporting. The increasing fraud trend is living proof of deficiency in focusing on fraud risk. Mostly top management levels lack understanding of fraud risk and generally over trusting in employees cause a lapse in objective assessment concerning this issue. There have been many fraud cases affecting corporations and overall economy on a global scale. However, companies do not feel urged to take precautions if not pressured by government-imposed regulations. That is why increased regulation is a vital top-down approach to increasing awareness of fraud risk both for management and internal audit.

In Turkey, the contribution of the finance sector to the overall state of the economy is paramount. Thus regulation of this area is vital to have a fully functioning capital market. With the effects of recent developments in the global economy and public pressure; regulators have imposed and introduced new rules concerning finance sector actors, and internal audit plays a significant part in the new regulations. In addition to developments explained above a new venture of the government, called Istanbul International Finance Center Project, echoes the significance of this sector as a part of a new brand to be introduced to world finance arena. Consequently, the magnitude of the role of the financial sector for Turkish economy cannot be denied and because of that phenomenon, internal audit in financial institutions should have a much active role than the one it is considered to have today.

The primary objective of this chapter is to compare existing financial sector regulations and recent updates in these regulations to show the increasing importance of internal audit and fraud prevention and to develop a fraud risk assessment template for intermediary institutions as complementary to current legislation.

BACKGROUND

Internal audit acts like insurance against the pitfalls in corporations. Thus trustworthy internal audit departments are perceived as the go-to department for fraud related precautions and workflow. The structure and foundations of an internal audit department are crucial to success in the prevention of fraud. Thus, in this section, the internal audit structures in Turkish finance sector will be presented.

Internal Audit Structure and Foundations

Organizational governance demands management of all risks that the organization faces, securing efforts put in for reaching its ultimate goal of maximizing shareholder value. The importance of assurance services in this endeavor is signified in the Institute of Internal Auditors' (IIA) definition of governance: "The monitoring of organizational risks and the assurance that controls adequately mitigate those risks both contribute directly to the achievement of organizational goals and the preservation of organizational value" (Hermanson & Rittenberg, 2003, p. 27).

There are four dimensions to assurance related departments established in organizations. These are Internal Audit, Internal Control, Risk Management and Compliance Departments. The joint mission of these departments is to manage the risks the organization faces. Whether internal or external, fraud is a significant risk that needs to be addressed, even though it is not under the full responsibility of solely one department. In addition to this, Internal Audit has a different position when compared to the other assurance departments in the organization. Its mission is to be independent in its activities, whether these activities be performing daily operations unrelated to auditing activities or having an independent stance in the department structure, which positions this department in a suitable position for fraud prevention-related activities. The importance of an independent internal audit department is also signified in BIS's Corporate Governance Principles for Banks (2015).

The structure of internal audit departments dramatically influences the likelihood of its success in fraud prevention and detection. Coram, Ferguson, and Moroney (2008) have shown that there is "a significant positive relationship between an organization having an internal audit function and the number and value of self-reported frauds" (p. 544). Thus, internal audit is critical for the finance sector, where fraud cases cause extensive damage both to the sector and economy.

COMPARISON OF TURKISH INTERNAL AUDIT LEGISLATION IN FINANCIAL SERVICES SECTOR WITH A GLOBAL BENCHMARK

Bank for International Settlements' (BIS) Basel Committee on Banking Supervision has formed a set of principles concerning the internal audit functions in banks in 2012. Since this set of principles is a reference point in evaluating the soundness of internal audit function in banks, the adequacy of Turkish regulations is compared to these principles. BIS has dictated compelling principles that guide banks to improve and enhance their internal audit functions. By doing so various risks such as noncompliance and reputation risks can be diminished. In turn, governance will be improved, and better management practices will be adopted with the aid of a well-functioning internal audit department.

Generally, in the finance sector, it is possible to see complex organization ownership structures. A conglomerate may own a bank, and the bank may own an intermediary institution. The intermediary institution in question may own a portfolio management company. While this ownership type is undoubtedly legal, the internal audit functions of the Intermediary Institutions and Portfolio Management Companies, have to be compliant with the BIS principles, because these institutions have become integrated with the bank. Therefore, this chapter also includes a comparison of Turkish legislation concerning Intermediary Institutions and Portfolio Management Companies with BIS principles. This comparison aims to point out areas that need improvement to secure a well-functioning internal audit in these institutions. Table 1 shows a summary of this comparison.

In some European countries and the U.S., the authority responsible for regulating and auditing the banking industry is also responsible for regulating and auditing capital markets and related institutions. In Turkey, there are two different authorities responsible for regulating the finance sector. The Banking Regulation and Supervision Agency (BRSA) is responsible for regulating and auditing banks according to Banking Law No 5411 (2005), Capital Markets Board (CMB) is responsible for regulating and auditing Istanbul Stock Exchange, Intermediary Institutions, Portfolio Management Companies, Funds, Real

Estate Appraisal Companies, Investment Trusts and Independent Auditing Firms according to Regulation on Organization, Tasks and Working Principles of Capital Markets Board (1982) Article 9. Thus, regulations concerning banks and other capital market institutions differ according to the regulatory authority. Even though there are similar points, some contradictions exist.

The BIS principles consist of six categories, and these are Auditor Qualities, Documentation, Responsibility and Reporting, Scope, Structure, and Supervision. The category called 'Auditor Qualities' defines the main points about auditors' characteristics with two principles; Principle no. 3 and 4. Principle 3 requires auditors to be competent to perform audits in all banking functions, and Chief Audit Executive (CAE) is responsible for hiring professionally competent people, and their continuous training. Rose (2015) defines competency as "the knowledge, skills, abilities and other characteristics needed for effective performance in a given role" in IIA's common body of knowledge (p. 5). IIA's Competency Framework has four main tiers, and the first tier is professional ethics; signifying the importance IIA gives to the concept. IIA's code of ethics (2010) has four core principles: integrity, objectivity, confidentiality, and competency. Integrity is the most critical principle because auditors are expected to behave honestly and responsibly while showing diligence in their work.

Furthermore, auditors should maintain an objective mindset and form judgments without any influences. Auditors frequently come across sensitive information, and they need to keep such information private unless there is a legal request to make it available to third parties. The final principle concerns auditors' knowledge, skills and expertise level.

In Turkey, Article 22 of Regulation on Internal Systems and Internal Capital Adequacy Evaluation Process of Banks (ISR, 2014) also gives the responsibility to the CAE in assessing the competency level of auditors. However, CAE is also responsible for preparing training programs and developing the skills of auditors. Article 23 states that auditors assigned to audit Information Systems, need to provide training certificates that prove their skills and knowledge. In order to become a CAE, an individual is required to have seven years of banking experience according to ISR's Article 22. However, having just seven years of experience in banking does not guarantee the extensive knowledge and skills auditing function demands. Certification should also be mandatory. It is possible to say that auditor competency is considered quite valuable, but not adequately addressed in Turkish legislation concerning banks.

In Intermediary Institutions, CAE is not given the responsibility to assess the competency of auditors. However, competency requirements are listed in Capital Markets Regulation. According to Communiqué on Principles Regarding the Internal Auditing Systems of Brokerage Houses, Serial V, No. 68 (2003) Article 16, auditors are required to be graduated from a 4-year bachelor's program and have at least 3 years of work experience in capital markets, accounting, banking, information systems audit, independent audit, or practice of law. If the auditor is responsible for information systems audit, then she/he should be able to prove her/his expertise with training certificates. In addition to this, auditors need to obtain a CMB Level 3 License, which proves extensive theoretical knowledge on capital markets, related legislation and financial instruments with regard to Communiqué on Principles Regarding Licensing and Record Keeping for Those Engaged in Capital Markets, VII-128.7, Appendix 1 (2014). Auditors employed in Portfolio Management Companies also have to obtain the CMB Level 3 License according to the Communiqué stated above. However, Communiqué on Portfolio Management Companies and Activities of Such Companies, III-55.1 (2013a) fails to report any other legal requirements for auditors. Since auditor competency is paramount, auditors have to have certification concerning auditing practices. Thus there is room for improvement for this area in Turkish regulation.

There are some global certification systems concerning internal auditors; these are IIA's Certified Internal Auditor (CIA), AICPA's Accounting and Auditing Certification Programs and ACCA's Certificate in Audit. The certificate most compatible with the internal audit is CIA. Thus the contents of CIA will be presented here. The CIA exam consists of three parts; (i) Essentials of internal auditing, ii) Practice of internal auditing, and iii) Business knowledge for internal auditing (IIA, 2018a). Essentials of internal auditing include the founding context of internal audit such as independence, objectivity, risk management and fraud. The practice of internal auditing involves steps like audit planning, audit application stages and audit findings reporting and monitoring. The final part of the CIA exam includes business-related topics, such as business ethics, communication, organizational structure, Information Technology (IT) and finance. For internal auditors who are employed in the financial services sector, another IIA certificate can be considered, as well. This certificate is called Certified Financial Services Auditor (CFSA) which tests proficiency on the audit process, auditing financial statements, financial services products, financial services processes and regulatory environment (IIA, 2018b).

On the other hand, Turkish regulation requires financial services auditors to obtain CMB Level 3 License. The topics tested for CMB Level 3 License are capital markets regulations, capital market instruments, investment institutions, financial markets, settlement, custody and clearing operations, financial management and financial analysis, commercial law, accounting and financial reporting, general economics, financial mathematics and taxation in corporations and capital markets (Capital Market Licensing Registry and Training Institution, 2018). As can be seen above, capital markets are extensively covered in the CMB Level 3 License. However, there aren't any topics tested concerning auditing practices. IIA's standards (2017) clearly articulate that an auditor needs to have extensive knowledge in the area of audit, as well as auditing techniques. Thus, auditors in Turkish financial services need to obtain a certification concerning auditing practices, like CIA.

Principle 4 defines the most significant ethical standard for auditors, which is integrity. Although integrity is the headline for this principle, the ethical standard covers other aspects such as respecting information confidentiality, avoiding conflicts of interest, respecting a cool – off period and respecting the banks' code of ethics. In ISR (2014), integrity is not mentioned. However other ethical concepts are covered, such as due diligence, independence, objectivity, and avoiding conflicts of interest. However, integrity is the essential ingredient in the making of an auditor, so ignoring this concept will weaken the Internal Audit function.

Even though "integrity" is not mentioned in writing, a similar word, "honesty" is mentioned instead in Communiqué on Principles of Establishment and Activities of Investment Firms, III-39.1 (2013b), Article 22 states that the intermediary institution and personnel have to act honestly and objectively throughout their work. An exact copy of this sentence is found in Article 22 of Communiqué III-55.1 (2013a). The only difference is Communiqué III-55.1 spells "auditors" as well, making the article more meaningful from an auditor's perspective. The concept of integrity and a code of conduct are entirely necessary to establish a responsible audit department.

The second category of principles is called 'Documentation,' and it consists of the preparation of a mandatory internal audit charter. The internal audit charter is the document that gives the internal audit function much-needed authority. It also covers responsibilities and describes essential activities. In ISR (2014), the internal audit charter is not explicitly stated as a separate article, it is just mentioned in a general article about the competencies of auditors which should be included in the charter along with risk-based auditing, internal audit plan, auditing terms, audit programs, sampling methods, reporting and monitoring as well as consulting activities, providing well-constructed guidance for internal auditors in preparing the internal audit charter.

Communiqué Serial V No 68 (2003) Article 10 recites the internal audit charter as a mandatory document for Intermediary Institutions, which has to be approved by the Board of Directors (BOD). On the other hand, Communiqué III-55.1 Article 11 only paints a vague picture on the subject, by stating all mandatory documents concerning internal control system have to be written and approved by BOD, however, an internal audit charter is not explicitly mentioned, thus leaving a gray area in this particular spot.

The third category of principles is called 'Responsibility and Reporting,' and it covers five principles on the responsibilities of each actor and their reporting lines. Principle 8 states the responsibility of the BOD for setting up and securing a well-functioning internal audit department. Banking Law No. 5411 (2005) Article 23 clearly states that it is the responsibility of BOD to establish internal systems including risk management, internal control, and internal audit. ISR (2014) Article 5 states that "BOD is responsible for securing the accuracy, reliability, and maintenance of information provided by internal systems." As a result, Turkish regulation covers this BIS principle wholly. Principle 8 states that each bank in a banking group should have an internal audit function. However, the opposite is exact for Turkish regulation concerning Intermediary Institutions and Portfolio Management Companies. Article 12 of Communiqué Serial V, No. 68 (2003) states that while it is mandatory for Intermediary Institutions to establish an internal audit department; if the Intermediary Institution belongs to a group, the internal audit function may be outsourced to the group internal audit, or the owner bank's internal audit department. The same goes for Portfolio Management Companies as well; they can use the owner company's internal audit team. This clause somewhat weakens the control strength obtained by an in-house auditor, because the auditors from another company would not be able to audit the company as frequently as an in-house auditor could. Thus, this creates a high-risk area concerning compliance and fraud (James, 2003).

Principle 10 gives the audit committee full responsibility for supervising internal audit activities. Responsibilities of the audit committee are defined in Article 24 of Banking Law 5411 (2005). Article 24 deems it compulsory for banks to establish an audit committee, which is responsible for supervision of internal systems. Internal system departments are required to provide periodical reports on their activities to the audit committee. In return, the audit committee is required to report BOD at least biannually the results of internal systems activities, and any possible remedies for improvement of legal discrepancies. Once again Turkish legislation covers this principle entirely.

It is not compulsory for an Intermediary Institution to have an audit committee. However, BODs are responsible for overseeing the work of internal audit. If the BOD wishes to delegate this task, they are allowed to select an internal control responsible who can take over this duty, valid for both Intermediary Institutions and Portfolio Management Companies according to Article 13 III-55.1 (2013a) and Article 8 Serial V No. 68 (2003).

Principle 11 states that CAE is responsible for the application of internal audit standards and code of ethics in auditing activities by auditors. CAE should be a person of integrity in order to present a reliable façade for other departments. ISR (2014) Article 22 gives authority to the CAE to decide on the policies and application methods. Audit committee validates, and BOD approves the policies and methods used. However, IIA standards are not imposed, and since there aren't any local standards on internal audit, standards are overlooked in the regulation. In addition to this, there isn't a specific code of conduct that auditors are required to adhere or any clauses related to the integrity of CAE. CAE's character is a crucial element in constructing a sound and well-functioning internal audit department. Therefore, such deficiencies have to be improved in the legislation. Both Portfolio Management Companies and Intermediary Institutions do not have to apply international auditing standards, and CAEs are not directed to follow any auditing standards at any rate.

Principle 12 mandates accountability towards BOD or audit committee. Article 4 of Regulation on Internal Systems and Internal Capital Adequacy Evaluation Process of Banks, clearly defines the reporting line of internal audit as BOD and if BOD sees appropriate it can delegate its responsibilities concerning internal systems to a BOD member. This article clearly shows that internal audit is directly reporting and accountable to BOD. Both Portfolio Management Companies' and Intermediary Institutions' internal auditors are required to report to and duly responsible to BOD, which is stated in Communiqué III-55.1 (2013a) Article 13 and Communiqué Serial V No 68 (2003) Article 7 and 12.

Principle 15 mandates BOD as responsible for outsourced internal audit activities. However, Regulation on Outsourced Activities of Banks (2011) Article 4 forbids any outsourcing activities concerning internal systems of Banks. These internal activities are considered crucial for activities of Banks; therefore outsourcing is banned to diminish related risks. The same principle is valid for Intermediary Institutions according to Communiqué III-39.1 (2013b) Article 49. The company is responsible for outsourced activities in Intermediary Institutions with Communiqué III-39.1 Article 50/2, and similarly, for Portfolio Management Companies, Communiqué III-55.1 (2013a) Article 19 states that the 'Company' is responsible for outsourced activities.

The fourth category is called 'Scope,' and it concerns principles that are related to drawing a framework for internal audit activities. Principle 2 in this category bans auditors from engaging in any daily operations that they are considered to be auditing. If otherwise, it would endanger the auditors' independence, and it would not be possible to trust audit results or the lack of findings consequently. In Turkish legislation, precisely on Article 23 of ISR (2014), it is imposed that auditors have to be independent and objective in their work. Even though ISR tries to secure independence; it fails to secure objectivity by defining clear-cut rules. The vagueness concerning objectivity should be improved in order to maintain a sound internal audit department. This rule is mentioned under the competencies of auditors in ISR; however in no part of the Regulation, this rule is elaborated; thus, leaving a gray area concerning the involvement of auditors in daily operations. The independence of auditors is secured by freeing them from reporting to parties other than CAE, BOD or the Audit Representative of the BOD (an independent BOD member, who is delegated major responsibilities of BOD concerning auditing in the Bank). Unfortunately for Intermediary Institutions and Portfolio Management Companies, the opposite is imposed in Turkish regulation. In Communiqués Serial V No 68 (2003) Article 21 and III-55.1 (2013a) Article 13 CMB gives the responsibility to perform internal controls under one department called 'Internal Control,' instead of making it a responsibility of all personnel in the organization.

Furthermore, CMB allows the internal auditor to perform internal controls, as well. This statement undermines the independence of the internal audit function since it is required to audit its work concerning internal controls. CMB regulations need to be updated with regard to the independence principle.

Principle 6 can be summarized as a principle that includes all activities of the bank including outsourced activities, in the perimeter of internal audit. The reason behind this principle is to ensure that no process falls under the radar. Thus it becomes possible to eliminate specific risks borne by day-to-day operations, notwithstanding outsourced activities. Article 21 of ISR (2014) defines the scope of internal audit activities as all activities of the bank without any internal restrictions, including local and foreign subsidiaries and head office. Although all internal activities of banks are included in the internal audit scope, outsourced activities are not mentioned in ISR. However, Regulation on Outsourced Activities of Banks (2011), Article 5 states that the effects of the outsourced activity on Banks' internal audit has to be considered and Article 9 regulates how outsourcing companies should be audited by the internal audit department of the bank. Turkish regulation requires all activities of Intermediary Institutions and Portfolio Management Companies to be subject to internal audit with Communiqué Serial V No 68 (2003) Article 12 and Communiqué III-55.1 (2013a) Article 13 consecutively.

The next principle or Principle 7 under the category 'Scope' is about covering all audit mission-related regulations in the audit plan. This principle ensures compliance with the rules imposed by regulatory authorities, thus assuring a sound foundation for operations of the bank, meanwhile reducing reputation risk. Article 21 of ISR (2014) defines the scope of internal audit activities in detail, such as stating what issues to cover in audit missions. This article also states that "operations' compliance with the Law and other related legislation, internal strategy, policy and procedures of the bank should be audited." Thus, this specific clause of Article 21 wholly covers Principle 7, ensuring a sound base for banks' operations while decreasing reputation risk, as well as providing assurance for institutionalization process of the bank and applications of corporate governance principles. There aren't any clauses concerning audit plan or its contents in Regulation concerning Intermediary Institutions or Portfolio Management Companies.

Principle 13 is the last principle under the category 'Scope.' As a summary, it states that internal control, risk management and governance systems and processes should be assessed by the internal audit function. Similar to the previous principle, this requirement is met with Article 21 of ISR (2014), which states that internal control and risk management systems' adequacy and effectiveness should be assessed by internal audit. While there aren't any regulations that require Intermediary Institutions' internal audit function to assess internal control or risk management, Communiqué III-55.1 (2013a) Article 13 requires the internal audit department of Portfolio Management Companies to evaluate internal control and risk management systems, as well as governance systems. The main reason behind such a difference in regulations both written by CMB is that Communiqué Serial V No 68 dates back to 2003, whereas Communiqué III-55.1 was published in 2013. Some of the significant Turkish regulations have been gradually updated since 2012 within the context of Istanbul International Finance Center Project, and Communiqué Serial V No 68 is one of the few that is not updated.

The fifth category of principles is called 'Structure,' and it concerns the foundations of the internal audit function in banks. Principle 1 in this category involves the independence of the internal audit, which is ensured in Turkish Banking Law No. 5411 (2005) Article 32. The independence of internal audit is also secured with Article 18 of Communiqué Serial V No 68 (2003) and Article 22 of Communiqué III-55.1 (2013a) for capital markets. However, as mentioned above in Principle 2, there are some different clauses in these regulations that prevent the formation of an entirely independent internal audit paradigm.

The following principle in 'Structure' category is Principle 9. This principle states that each bank in a banking group/holding should have an internal audit function. Article 32 of Banking Law No. 5411 (2005) states that all undertakings subject to consolidation should be involved in the internal audit. However, it does not explicitly state that all banks under one banking group should have separate internal audit functions, on the contrary, internal audit function of the bank may be responsible for auditing activities concerning the activities of undertakings subject to consolidation. All companies should have an independent audit function, in order to provide the maximum possible assurance. Thus, Turkish legislation needs an update in this article. Communiqué Serial V No 68 (2003) Article 21 and Communiqué III-55.1 (2013a) Article 11 and 12 give the responsibility of internal controls to BOD.

Principle 14 requires all financial institutions to have an internal audit department. For intermediary institutions, if the owner of the institution is a financial group or a bank, it is not mandatory for the institution to have an internal audit department. The institution is allowed merely to outsource its internal audit function from the bank or the group, according to Communiqué Serial V No 68 (2003), Article 12. Communiqué III-39.1 (2013) Article 49 explicitly forbids the outsourcing of internal systems activities (other than above-stated situation). For Portfolio Management Companies Communiqué III-55.1 (2013) Article 9 allows the companies to outsource internal control and internal audit services from Intermediary Institutions or other expert establishments.

The final category is called 'Supervision,' and it contains principles concerning the role of Regulatory Authority in the supervision of the banks' internal audit functions. Principle 16 states that supervisors are required to communicate risk areas, risk mitigation measures, weaknesses and responses with the internal audit department. Regulation on Banking Regulation and Supervision Agency Auditing Methods and Principles (2006) Article 17 states that audit findings should be conveyed to bank management and their views are considered in finalizing the report. This article fully covers Principle 16's contents.

Principle 17 requires supervisors to assess the authority within the bank. This principle is stated in a closed expression in Article 14 of Regulation on Banking Regulation and Supervision Agency Auditing Methods and Principles (2006). Article 14 states that BRSA should be investigating the adequacy and effectiveness of Risk management, internal control, and internal audit systems. Since the effectiveness of any internal audit function depends significantly on the authority of the internal audit department, this principle is present as defacto, even if it is not openly dictated. However, it would be more prudent to include Principle 17 in writing as an addendum to Article 14.

The last three principles left in 'Supervision' category are Principles 18, 19 and 20. To sum up, Principle 18 states that supervisors should report all weaknesses, Principle 19 asks supervisors to consider the impact of internal audit assessments and Principle 20 gives the authority to ask for remedies covering up any weaknesses and deficiencies of banks. Principle 20's requirements are covered with Banking Law No 5411 (2005) Article 93. For CMB Principle 16, 17, 18 and 19 are not publicly stated. The authority of CMB asking for remedies is described in detail in Capital Market Law No. 6263 (2012) with Articles 91, 92, 93, 94, 95, 96, 97, 98, 99, 100 and 101.

FRAUD RISK ASSESSMENT IN INTERMEDIARY INSTITUTIONS

Fraud is almost as old as human history. There have always been some people who are greedy and do not content themselves with what they have. The first known fraud case belongs to a Greek merchant called Hegestratos, who took a loan and tried to get away without paying it back in 300 B.C. (Beattie, 2017, para. 1-2). Things have gotten quite complicated since then. With global banking and complex transactions of today, it is a complicated process to become aware of the fraud. Some examples of modern fraud are Wells Fargo, where a vast number of fake accounts were used for cross-selling and manipulating the market by increasing volume; Theranos where investors were manipulated with misstatement; Enron, where financial statements were manipulated to show revenue that was fictitious; and WorldCom, where declining earnings were covered with false expenditures (Michaels, 2018). It is possible to elongate the list with many more incidents. However, the constructive paradigm would require focusing on the solution, which cannot be achieved without sound internal audit departments. Even though there are many aspects that need to work in harmony to prevent fraud, the one aspect that is closest to the solution is internal audit functions of corporations. A sound internal audit department is the key to good corporate governance, without it the fight against fraud would lose its meaning.

Table 1. Comparison of BIS principles and Turkish regulations on internal audit in financial services sector

Category	BIS Principle Summary	Turkish Regulation on Banks	Turkish Regulation on Intermediary Institutions	Turkish Regulation on Portfolio Management Companies
Auditor Qualities	3. Auditors must be professionally competent.	Partially covered	Partially covered	Partially covered
	4. Auditors must act with integrity.	Partially covered	Partially covered	Partially covered
Documentation	5. Mandatory internal audit charter.	Partially covered	Fully compliant	Partially covered
Responsibility & Reporting	8. BOD is responsible for establishing & maintaining an IA function.	Fully compliant	Fully compliant	Fully compliant
	10. Audit Committee is responsible for overseeing IA function.	Fully compliant	Non-compliant	Non-compliant
	11. Chief Audit Executive is responsible for applying IA standards & code of ethics.	Non-compliant	Non-compliant	Non-compliant
	12. IA should be accountable to BOD or AC.	Fully compliant	Fully compliant	Fully compliant
	15. BOD is responsible for outsourced IA activities.	Non-compliant	Non-compliant	Non-compliant
Scope	2. IA must not engage in audited activities.	Non-compliant	Non-compliant	Non-compliant
	6. IA should cover all activities of the bank (including outsourced activities)	Fully compliant	Fully compliant	Fully compliant
	7. IA should cover all related regulations in the audit plan.	Fully compliant	Non-compliant	Fully compliant
	13. IA should assess internal control, risk management, and governance systems & processes.	Fully compliant	Fully compliant	Fully compliant
Structure	1. IA must be independent.	Fully compliant	Fully compliant	Fully compliant
	9. Each bank in a banking group/ holding should have IA function.	Fully compliant	Fully compliant	Fully compliant
	14. All banks are required to have their own IA department.	Partially covered	Fully compliant	Partially covered
Supervision	16. Supervisors should communicate risk areas, risk mitigation measures, weaknesses & responses with IA Department.	Fully compliant	Non-compliant	Non-compliant
	17. Supervisors should assess IA authority within the bank.	Non-compliant	Non-compliant	Non-compliant
	18. Supervisors should report all weaknesses.	Non-compliant	Non-compliant	Non-compliant
	19. Supervisors should consider the impact of IA assessments.	Non-compliant	Non-compliant	Non-compliant
	20. Supervisors should be able to ask for remedies.	Fully compliant	Fully compliant	Fully compliant
AC: Audit Committee, IA: Internal Audit				

"Research on such disasters, particularly financial fraud, consistently documents an association between weak governance (e.g., Less independent boards, lower quality audit committees, or the absence of an internal audit function) and the incidence of problems" (Hermanson & Rittenberg, 2003, p.38). The primary objective of this chapter is to look at the structure of internal audit functions that exist in today's reality and try to reach an ideal structure form, which can be beneficial to financial institutions. From this point on the chapter identifies critical risk points that can be subject to fraud and offers a new format to be used in risk management in intermediary institutions.

Recent Developments in Regulations Concerning Fraud

Generally, in literature when fraud is mentioned it may fall into one of such categories; fraudulent financial reporting, misappropriation of assets, revenue or assets gained by fraudulent acts or illegal acts, expenses or liabilities avoided by fraudulent or illegal acts, expenses or liabilities incurred for fraudulent or illegal acts or securities fraud which is mostly referred to as 'other misconduct' due to limited areas of research by audit community concerning this context (KPMG, 2006). This definition includes conflicts of interest, insider trading, manipulation and market abuse.

In an international perspective, fraud has been a top priority topic in the latest regulations all over the world. Due to the increased cost of fraud, regulatory authorities have felt the pressure to apply stricter rules to ensure prevention of fraud. Perhaps the most important legislation is the Sarbanes Oxley Act of 2002, which was specially enacted to secure financial reporting requirements associated with corporate governance principles, by inflicting several clauses on the work of internal and external auditors. "The Act mandated some reforms to enhance corporate responsibility, enhance financial disclosures and combat corporate and accounting fraud, and created the 'Public Company Accounting Oversight Board,' also known as the PCAOB, to oversee the activities of the auditing profession (Securities Exchange Commission, 2013)." This act is considered as a fundamental reform concerning business practices.

Dodd-Frank Wall Street Reform and Consumer Protection Act of 2010 (Securities Exchange Commission, 2013) is also shaped by the effects of the recent crisis aimed to regulate financial products. However, in economic literature, there is a general criticism towards how shadow banking is handled in the regulation above. "Although Dodd-Frank takes some useful steps in the regulation of shadow banking, there are still large gaps where it is almost silent. Three important gaps involve the regulation of MMMFs [Money Market Mutual Funds], securitization, and repos. Fortunately, the law also created a council of regulators, the Financial Stability Oversight Council, with significant power to identify and manage systemic risks, including the power to recommend significant changes in regulation, if deemed necessary for financial stability" (Gorton & Metrick, 2012, p. 262).

Hanson, Kashyap, and Stein (2011) state that the Dodd-Frank act falls short of expectations concerning regulations on shadow banking practices. The reason shadow banking is emphasized so much is that usually in an economic crisis run on banks is the finalization point, where all investors try to withdraw their investments from the financial system, due to diminished trust in the economy caused by ambiguity.

One of the essential regulations passed after 2005 is called the Foreign Account Tax Compliance Act (FATCA). "FATCA is an important development in U.S. efforts to improve tax compliance involving foreign financial assets and offshore accounts. Under FATCA, U.S. taxpayers with specified foreign financial assets that exceed certain thresholds must report those assets to the IRS (Internal Revenue Service)" (U.S. Embassy in Nicaragua, 2018). When it becomes active, FATCA will bring essential requirements concerning financial institutions on prevention of tax evasion of U.S. citizens.

There have been several updates in foreign regulations, as described above. However, fraud seems to be ignored in Turkish regulations even though it is such a critical matter. Thus, a complementary fraud risk assessment will be developed to emphasize this point. However, the foundations of fraud risk need to be explained beforehand.

Fraud Risk

Fraud is best explained by Cressey's fraud triangle where there are three main components that have to be present at the same time.

Trusted persons become trust violators when they conceive of themselves as having a financial problem which is non-shareable, are aware this problem can be secretly resolved by violation of the position of financial trust, and are able to apply to their own conduct in that situation verbalizations which enable them to adjust their conceptions of themselves as trusted persons with their conceptions of themselves as users of the entrusted funds or property. (Cressey, 1973, p.30).

First of all, there should be an incentive in the person who commits fraud. This incentive can be best explained by a motive such as financial or personal problems and pressure. The second component is necessary at this point. The fraudster in question has to justify the act of fraud to oneself, by stating excuses similar to having earned the right to the action they are planning to commit. Finally, there has to be an opportunity to realize the planned act of fraud. Generally, this opportunity presents itself as a deficiency in the control environment. For instance, in case of theft concerning petty cash, lack of daily cash counts including supervision by the financial controller would create a significant deficiency in the control environment.

When identification of fraud is investigated, it is possible to see that generally fraud is discovered by notification of other employees, rather than internal audit (Bozkurt, 2009), which in turn signifies a lack of proper fraud risk assessment in companies. However, IIA (Araj, 2015) clearly states that fraud prevention and detection is one of the primary responsibilities of the internal audit function. Fraud risk assessment consists of identifying sources both internal and external and deciding on the percentage of likelihood of occurrence and financial and reputational impact on the firm as well as risk rating. According to these results, the internal auditor decides on the methodology to manage related fraud risks, which should include fraud scenarios and responsive actions.

R isk is one of the most popular concepts in financial markets today, and it is possible to see a significant effort to reduce risk to create a safe environment for the investors. Even though risk does not have a universal meaning that academicians have agreed on, in financial markets, it is considered as a part of bigger picture and defined as "the probability of reduced economic benefit as the result of a monetary loss or an expense or loss about an operation or activity" according to BRSA (ISR, 2014, Article 3).

There are numerous risk factors that financial markets are facing. However the core of this study is internal audit, thus "risk" concept will be reviewed from an auditor's point of view in the intermediation process.

According to BRSA regulations, Banks established under Turkish legislation are required to perform a risk evaluation concerning all banking activities. Risks included in this assessment are major risk categories that may affect its financial situation and the way a bank runs its operations as well. These risks are depicted as credit risk, liquidity risk, operational risk and market risk. Evaluation of these risks should be performed by using the Risk Evaluation Matrix as defined by the Regulation on the Internal Systems of Banks of BRSA. A copy of this risk matrix is present in Appendix 2.

Even though fraud risk makes up an essential part of the financial system, it is ignored in risk calculation process presented by BRSA, which is roughly based on the Basel II framework. There is a small part included for other risks, which may be used to include reputational risks and fraud risk, which in reality have a significant impact on the credit risk and liquidity risk in turn. A bank that is subject to a high fraud risk level would have a low reputation in the industry and have difficulties in maintaining a liquid portfolio. Accordingly, the Turkish Banking Sector has witnessed several similarities in the past and even a banking sector crisis related to liquidity in 2001 (Conkar, Keskin & Kayahan, 2009; Atici & Gursoy, 2011). However increased regulatory requirements have great importance as preventive countermeasures (Ganioglu, 2007). Perhaps the most significant countermeasure in managing liquidity risk is the BIS's Liquidity Coverage Ratio in Basel III Accord (2013). The importance of decreasing and managing fraud risk is emphasized when the sensitivities of this sector are considered.

Although the regulation above does stress measures to be taken to eliminate fraud risk in "functional division of tasks," it is otherwise nonexistent in the related communiqué. Banks are required to employ professional internal auditors responsible for internal control systems, who prepare a risk assessment of all banking activities, and most dangerous areas are given priority for the upcoming audit plan. Thus, lack of assessment of internal and external fraud risks may result in a poor judgment of the total risk a bank is facing and a non-realistic audit plan will not answer the needs of an organization. Since it is the primary task of an internal auditor to make sure all assets of the organization are safeguarded, fraud risk may not be exempt from any risk assessment project. All risk types require a signified amount of capital to be set aside for securing the capital adequacy ratio. Accordingly, requesting a particular amount of capital for fraud risk will increase the cost of capital for banks, however, when this is compared to the losses that finance sector faces, it is only prudent to have a countermeasure for the worst-case scenario.

In addition to this, it is possible to say that fraud risk assessment is left to the Risk Control Self-Assessment (RCSA) of operational risk in banks, due to Basel II requirements. Basel II lists fraud risk as part of operational risk concerning employees (KPMG, 2006). There are many templates for fraud risk assessment that provides a roadmap for assessing the fraud risk an entity faces. An exemplary fraud risk assessment template by IIA is also presented in Appendix 3. In this report; only financial statements fraud is considered, while external fraud is ignored. However, the measurement side is more effective than the BRSA format. Likelihood of fraud risk is crucial because it would not be a sound choice if the company focused on risks with low probabilities instead of focusing on risks with high probabilities. Moreover, the significance of the risk is an important issue that allows for calculating the damage of the risk in question in a worst-case scenario.

For firms, and especially banks, credit risk is seen as the most critical risk source. The origin of credit risk reveals a vital concept: asymmetric information. Asymmetric information prevents banks from being entirely informed about firms' financial situations; thus, banks end up giving credits to firms with low credit ratings and insufficiently credible performance [see for example Berger & Espinosa-Vega (2005), Carey & Hyrcay (2001)]. The current liquidity excess results in a different view of risk by investors. Frankel and Schmukler (1997) state that "less sophisticated investors with little capital have begun to find international diversification easier to achieve." Consequently, asymmetric information sourced credit risk, which causes banking crises, is always a current issue in financial markets.

As stated in the Basel II Amendment (Bank for International Settlements, 2016), another factor that has an impact on credit risk is an imbalance in a firms' capital structure. It is observed that a successful firm operation is closely related to firm income. When operating cash flows are inadequate, financing with over debt will increase a firm's credit risk. It is stated that this situation is greatly affected by macroeconomic factors because such factors determine the cost of financing methods on a firm's capital structure. That is why evaluating credit risk, capital structure and macroeconomic factors together would be a correct way of applying a risk management system. In 2003 Koopman and Lucas found that default and credit risk cycles are in correlation with macroeconomic factors. This paper shows that a change in GDP creates two cycles in credit spreads and firm bankruptcies.

Moreover, Hackbarth, Miao, and Morellec completed a study in 2005 which indicates the impact of macroeconomic conditions on the capital structure and credit risk. In this model, there is a "regime shift" between low and high economic conditions. The result is that firms decide to default and adjust their capital structure on business cycles. There are some papers in the literature covering several macroeconomic aspects and their link to debt. According to Dreher, Herz and Karb's research in 2005, "there is a negative lagged influence of currency crises on debt crises, the occurrence of a currency crisis significantly increases the risk of a contemporaneous debt crisis and vice versa" (p. 1). In addition to this, credit risk is affected by other factors such as liquidity risk [see Zheng on liquidity risk (2006) or Duffie & Singleton (2003)] on the impact of macroeconomic factors on the probability of default). Also, Arestis and Demetriades (2002) state that the effect of lending interest rates, reserve and liquidity requirement policies are different in every country. Such a research shows the significant effect of macroeconomic factors on credit risk and these factors are unique for each country [see for example Isgut (2001) & Jakubik (2006)] although, in some papers there is a global approach to modeling the effect of macroeconomy on credit risk [Pesaran & Shuermann (2006)].

Since there aren't any templates imposed by any regulatory authorities, it is possible to say that fraud risk is not adequately addressed by intermediary institutions at any rate. For investment firms, it becomes an entirely different story than banks because internal fraud includes market abusing acts such as manipulation and insider trading due to the operations performed by these institutions. Any financial statements fraud may involve insider trading if the company is a publicly held corporation. However, this becomes the primary issue for the intermediation process. Thus, internal audit should include proper and adequate fraud risk.

Internal fraud concern areas may be unauthorized access to classified information such as client account information or theft of classified information, i.e., client contact information may also be subject to external fraud as well. Unauthorized personnel could use client information for gaining access to client's funds and external parties, or rival companies may merely use client information to approach them for business purposes, which could result in loss of business and profit. This fraud scheme may be performed by both external parties and employees. Concerning operations, commission rates may be intercepted due to third parties. As a result, constant monitoring of transactions in financial statements is vital.

Moreover, these transfers from or to client accounts should continuously be monitored to keep unauthorized transactions in check. Furthermore, client confirmations should be carefully monitored to ensure that correct information on client's assets is stated in the account statements. Concerning external fraud, client collaterals are a sensitive issue, since embezzlement of funds placed as collateral or margin to the client when the client is still obliged to the company is a risk-bearing point.

In addition to this, financial statements fraud should not be neglected in financial institutions as well. In some cases, accounting departments may be shadowed by the high risks of stocks and derivatives trading. Thus it is recommended that a separate assessment for accounting departments should be put in place, especially the manipulation of suspense accounts should frequently be questioned. Due to significant sums involved, segregation of duties concerning cash management and settlement is of paramount importance.

Conflicts of interest issues are another major risk area, where research and corporate finance activities are involved, especially concerning Initial Public Offering processes. Thus, imposing Chinese walls between research and corporate finance departments and research and trading platforms is quite essential. The use of Chinese walls is proposed to ensure restricting any information on draft research reports to be accessed by these departments, which can be used as a source for inside information.

Finally, security of technological infrastructure and related platforms are paramount, because all transactions performed in capital markets are classified in nature. Information on client identity, client accounts, performed transactions and current market positions are considered as top secret and revealing of these facts to external parties would cause breaching of inside information, which would be used to manipulate the capital markets for personal gain by external parties.

Since breaching of these platforms by third parties would have devastating consequences not only for the investment firm in question but the whole capital market volumes and prices, auditing IT departments according to Control Objectives for Information and Related Technologies (COBIT) requirements is recommended to ensure due diligence concerning security, which is only mandatory for banks and investment firms owned by banks. Thus, a clear path for fraud concerning investment firms that are not institutional by nature is left under the spotlight.

Risk Assessment Template

Since there aren't any templates imposed by regulatory authorities for risk assessment in investment firms, a template report is constructed according to the information stated above on the fraud risk bearing areas, and presented in Appendix 1. This template is supported by the analysis results presented by Aslan (2017). CMB fines concerning investment fraud define some specific qualities in investment firms that bring about areas inflicted with fraud risk. Thus, internal audit departments should consider the following areas while assessing fraud risk.

The first part of this risk assessment template considers five different risk categories associated with investment fraud and sanctions imposed by CMB. These are Customer Relations and Compliance, Compliance with Transactions and Developments in the Sector, Financial Risk, and Security, Conflicts of Interest, Compliance with Regulations and Internal Policies. Since client identification is found to be of paramount importance in financial markets and a frequent cause for CMB sanctions, it is included in the risk assessment process. Also, client relations may be subject to lawsuits which are again linked to CMB sanctions with the results presented above. On the financial side, it is essential to consider the effects of financial inconvenience on the clients as well. Thus, Customer Relations and Compliance title cover the following risk issues:

- Failure of compliance with 'Know Your Client' (KYC) rules
- Failure of safekeeping of client documentation
- Failure to update the documentation with limited validation

- Failure to respect internal account opening and KYC rules
- Failure to respect anti-money laundering regulations
- Failure to respect combating of financing of terrorism including embargoes and related regulations
- Failure to respect restrictions of regulators concerning banned clients
- Failure to respect international regulations concerning the client
- Failure to assess client risk and insufficient due diligence correctly
- Failure to meet client's expectations and improper (aggressive) marketing
- Failure to meet margin calls and Fee Schedule
- Failure to respect client complaint procedure
- Failure to provide equal treatment of clients (time and order basis)

CMB generally refers to necessary documentation as audit proof against any investment fraud thus this is included in the risk assessment template. Also, cross-border and complex transactions are more frequently involved in money laundering and market abuse. Such fraudulent activities can only be prevented by strengthening the control environment in the Intermediary Institutions. Compliance with Transactions and Developments in the Sector part tries to assess the following risk issues.

- Lack of proper formalization of client relations, order transmission process, and other mandatory documentation
- Failure to respect conveying information to clients concerning new products or changes in regulations
- Failure to audit complex and transborder (overseas) transactions
- Failure to implement ethical rules and code of conduct
- Financial situation, especially capital adequacy ratio and accruals for different risk types come off as a critical issue concerning the assessment of fraud risk.
- Failure to respect client data security principles (compliance with COBIT measures)
- Lack of financial security policy
- Lack of surveillance of financial reporting and budgeting process
- Lack of surveillance of capital adequacy ratio and risk accruals
- Lack of IT audit concerning information security
- Lack of Business Continuity and Disaster Recovery Principles

Conflicts of Interest is probably the Achilles' heel of Intermediary Institutions because rules concerning this field are not included in the regulations, but only referred to in ethical principles of the sector, which has consultative status. Nevertheless, conflicts of interest are the major issues in financial markets that can cause investment fraud. Especially concerning authorization certificates variable, implementation of Chinese Walls and secure online access to confidential information is depicted as crucial. The following are essential risk issues to be considered in this context.

- Lack of ethical rules, code of conduct and conflicts of interest policy
- Lack of controls over analyst recommendations
- Lack of inducements policy and procedure
- Lack of policy and supervisions concerning use and access to inside information
- Lack of Chinese Walls principle

- Lack of policy and supervisions over personnel transactions

The final point to be considered in risk assessment by internal audit should comply with regulations and internal policies. Since Corporate Governance principles of CMB include articles on announcing remuneration information of top management and key personnel, an HR policy is vital. Also, surveillance over public announcements and authorization certificates are other important outcomes, and they are included in this part of the risk assessment template.

- Lack of proper HR policies including remuneration and performance pay principle
- Lack of principles concerning prevention of market abuse
- Failure to respect CMB regulations concerning credit transactions
- Failure to respect CMB regulations concerning mandatory documentation keeping
- Failure to respect CMB regulations concerning accounting principles
- Failure to provide regulatory authorities with timely and accurate information
- Lack of surveillance of published announcements
- Failure to gain related licenses (for personnel)
- Lack of follow up on lawsuits
- Failure to gain related licenses (for performing related activities)
- Engaging in both sales, trading, research and corporate finance activities
- Failure to meet training regulations
- Failure in applying the Segregation of Duties principle

The other parts of the template only offer assessment aspects such as the impact of the risk, whether it has a reputational impact or only financial impact, whether the risk has a recurring nature or exceptional nature and internal control environment is to be assessed within this context as well, by questioning previously given sanctions by CMB, current internal controls concerning risk bearing points and last audit rating on the subject.

SOLUTIONS AND RECOMMENDATIONS

The sections above presented an outlook for the internal audit structure in Turkish financial services sector and how fraud, if not ignored altogether, lacked sophistication even in the advanced regulations for banks. Therefore, the significant gap borne by the lack of fraud related articles in the regulation is addressed with a risk assessment template constructed specially for fraud related issues. Intermediary institutions are recommended to use or adapt this framework as necessary in constructing a fraud risk assessment methodology and perform fraud risk assessment at least once a year.

This fraud risk assessment template is tailored according to industry-specific needs and when performed on an annual basis is expected to help financial institutions to manage fraud risk. Internal auditors are recommended to develop company-specific risk assessment templates or integrate this framework into their annual audit plans. Even though applying only fraud risk assessment does not eliminate fraud risk, it would be a good starting point for institutions that do not address fraud risk at all.

FUTURE RESEARCH DIRECTIONS

Currently, management of fraud risk is entirely signified in financial markets and finance literature. To assure the soundness of capital markets fraud risk has to be controlled and managed correctly and this cannot be achieved without performing fraud risk assessment. Even though existing regulations lack templates or definitions concerning fraud, organizations have to step forward, and C-suite executives should put their power behind internal auditors and support them in this endeavor. For future studies, detailed Enterprise Risk Management templates can be developed, and fraud risk assessment can be included as a part of this system.

CONCLUSION

Financial institutions make up the foundations of the modern-day economy, and the basis of this is built on trust on both sides of the equation, which are agencies and consumers. Any disruption on the financial institution's side will damage the reputation of these establishments. Thus, having an internal audit as an independent function is like insurance in financial markets especially against fraudulent activities.

On the other hand, internal audit needs support from top management and regulators, since internal audit only develops with a top-down approach in Turkish financial institutions. If internal audit lacks the necessary tools and conditions, it is not fair to expect desirable results. Thus regulators need to work with diligence in case of internal audit. Especially for brokerage houses, the regulation that enables one person to be employed for both internal control and internal audit departments should be revised with the influence of segregation of duties principle.

Another point is that internal audit system in portfolio management companies should be strengthened by imposing a mandatory risk-based audit plan and specific Information Technology audit, or controls since Information Technology is a risky area where increased security measures are necessary.

As a result, it is an undeniable fact that banks in Turkey have a superior internal audit system when compared to brokerage houses and portfolio management companies. However, the new regulation has imposed some new rules which try to bring all financial institutions to a central standard.

Unfortunately, this cannot be wholly achieved unless the definition of an internal audit is not changed in regulation concerning brokerage houses. Even though the new rules promise a better future for internal audit in financial institutions, some improvement is deemed necessary.

ACKNOWLEDGMENT

This research received no specific grant from any funding agency in the public, commercial, or not-for-profit sectors.

REFERENCES

Araj, F. G. (2015). Responding to fraud risk: Exploring where internal auditing stands. *IIA Common Body of Knowledge*. Retrieved August 3, 2018 from https://www.iia.nl/SiteFiles/Publicaties/IIARF%20CBOK%20Responding%20to%20Fraud%20Risk%20October%202015.pdf

Arestis, P., Demetriades, P., Fattouh, B., & Mouratidis, K. (2002). The impact of financial liberalisation policies on financial development: Evidence from developing economies. *International Journal of Finance & Economics*, *7*(2), 109–121. doi:10.1002/ijfe.181

Aslan, L. (2017). The Determinants of Employee Fraud in Turkish Intermediary Institutions. *1st International Symposium on Economics, Finance and Econometrics. Proceedings*, *1*, 170–188.

Atici, G., & Gursoy, G. (2011). Financial crises and capital buffer: Evidence from the Turkish banking sector, business perspectives. *Banks and Bank Systems International Research Journal*, *6*(1), 72–86.

Bank for International Settlements. (2006). *International convergence of capital measurement and capital standards*. Retrieved August 3, 2018 from https://www.bis.org/publ/bcbs128.htm

Bank for International Settlements. (2012). *The internal audit function in banks*. Retrieved August 3, 2018 from https://www.bis.org/publ/bcbs223.pdf

Bank for International Settlements. (2013). *Basel III: The liquidity coverage ratio and liquidity risk monitoring tools*. Retrieved August 3, 2018 from https://www.bis.org/publ/bcbs238.pdf

Bank for International Settlements. (2015). *Corporate governance principles for banks*. Retrieved August 3, 2018 from https://www.bis.org/bcbs/publ/d328.pdf

Banking Regulation and Supervision Agency. (2005). *Banking law no. 5411*. Retrieved August 3, 2018 from https://www.tbb.org.tr/en/banking-legislation/banking-law/14

Banking Regulation and Supervision Agency. (2006). *Regulation on Banking Regulation and Supervision Agency auditing methods and principles*. Retrieved August 3, 2018 from http://www.mevzuat.gov.tr/Metin.Aspx?MevzuatKod=7.5.10522&MevzuatIliski=0&sourceXmlSearch=denetleme%20kurumu%20taraf%C4%B1ndan

Banking Regulation and Supervision Agency. (2011). *Regulation on outsourced activities of banks*. Retrieved August 3, 2018 from http://www.mevzuat.gov.tr/Metin.Aspx?MevzuatKod=7.5.15481&MevzuatIliski=0&sourceXmlSearch=destek%20hizmeti

Banking Regulation and Supervision Agency. (2014). *Regulation on internal systems and internal capital adequacy evaluation process of banks*. Retrieved August 3, 2018 from http://www.mevzuat.gov.tr/Metin.Aspx?MevzuatKod=7.5.19864&MevzuatIliski=0&sourceXmlSearch=i%C3%A7%20sistemleri

Beattie, A. (2017). *The pioneers of financial fraud*. Retrieved August 3, 2018 from https://www.investopedia.com/articles/financial-theory/09/history-of-fraud.asp

Berger, A. N., & Espinosa-Vega, M. A. (2005). *Debt maturity, risk and asymmetric information*. Retrieved June 4, 2007 from http://www.imf.org/external/pubs/ft/wp/2005/wp05201.pdf

Bozkurt, N. (2009). *Isletmelerin kara deligi hile*. Istanbul: Alfa.

Capital Market Licensing Registry and Training Institution. (2018). *Exam subjects and subtitles*. Retrieved August 3, 2018 from https://www.spl.com.tr/spl/eep/kurumportal/Content/sinav-konulari-ve-alt-konu-basliklari/53/

Capital Markets Board of Turkey. (1982). *Regulation on organization, tasks and working principles of Capital Markets Board*. Retrieved August 3, 2018 from http://www.mevzuat.gov.tr/MevzuatMetin/3.5.84644.pdf

Capital Markets Board of Turkey. (2003). *Communiqué on principles regarding the internal auditing systems of brokerage houses serial V no 68*. Retrieved August 3, 2018 from http://www.cmb.gov.tr/SiteApps/Teblig/File/252

Capital Markets Board of Turkey. (2012). *Capital market law no. 6263*. Retrieved August 3, 2018 from http://www.cmb.gov.tr/Sayfa/Dosya/87

Capital Markets Board of Turkey. (2013a). *Communiqué on portfolio management companies and activities of such companies serial III-55.1*. Retrieved August 3, 2018 from http://www.cmb.gov.tr/SiteApps/Teblig/File/472

Capital Markets Board of Turkey. (2013b). *Communiqué on principles of establishment and activities of investment firms serial III-39.1*. Retrieved August 3, 2018 from http://www.cmb.gov.tr/SiteApps/Teblig/File/510

Capital Markets Board of Turkey. (2014). *Communiqué on principles regarding licensing and record keeping for those engaged in capital market activities serial VII-128.7*. Retrieved August 3, 2018 from http://www.cmb.gov.tr/SiteApps/Teblig/File/511

Carey, M., & Hrycay, M. (2001). Parameterizing credit risk models with rating data. *Journal of Banking & Finance*, *25*(1), 197–270. doi:10.1016/S0378-4266(00)00124-2

Conkar, K., Keskin, A., & Kayahan, C. (2009). Banking crises and financial system in Turkey. *Journal of Modern Accounting and Auditing*, *5*(7), 21–34.

Coram, P., Ferguson, C., & Moroney, R. (2008). Internal audit, alternative internal audit structures and the level of misappropriation of assets fraud. *Accounting and Finance*, *48*, 543–559.

Cressey, D. R. (1973). *Other people's money*. Montclair: Patterson Smith.

Dreher, A., Herz, B., & Kard, V. (2005). *Is there a causal link between currency debt crises?* Retrieved June 4, 2007 from http://papers.ssrn.com/sol3/papers.cfm?abstract_id=528063

Duffie, D., & Singleton, K. J. (2003). *Credit risk pricing, measurement and management*. Princeton.

Frankel, J. A., & Schmukler, S. L. (1997). *Country funds and asymmetric information*. Retrieved June 4, 2007 from http://repositories.cdlib.org/iber/cider/C97-087

Ganioglu, A. (2007). Prudential regulation and supervision of the banking sector and banking crises: A cross-country empirical investigation. *BDDK Bankacilik ve Finansal Piyasalar Dergisi*, *1*, 11–29.

Gorton, G., & Metrick, A. (2012). The shadow banking system (with comments and discussion). *Brookings Papers on Economic Activity*, *2*, 261–312. Retrieved from https://www.brookings.edu/bpea-articles/regulating-the-shadow-banking-system-with-comments-and-discussion/

Hackbarth, D., Miao, J., & Morellec, E. (2005). *Capital structure, credit risk and macroeconomic conditions*. Retrieved November 8, 2006 from http://www.defaultrisk.com/ps_other.htm

Hanson, S. G., Kashyap, A. K., & Stein, J. C. (2011). A macroprudential approach to financial regulation. *The Journal of Economic Perspectives*, *25*(1), 3–28. doi:10.1257/jep.25.1.3 PMID:21595323

Hermanson, D. R., & Rittenberg, L. E. (2003). Chapter 2: Internal audit and organizational governance. *Research Opportunities in Internal Auditing*. Retrieved August 3, 2018 from https://na.theiia.org/iiarf/Public%20Documents/Chapter%202%20Internal%20Audit%20and%20Organizational%20Governance.pdf

Institute of Internal Auditors. (2010). *Code of ethics*. Retrieved August 3, 2018 from https://na.theiia.org/standards-guidance/mandatory-guidance/Pages/Code-of-Ethics.aspx

Institute of Internal Auditors. (2017). *International standards for the professional practice of internal auditing (standards)*. Retrieved August 3, 2018 from https://na.theiia.org/standards-guidance/Public%20Documents/IPPF-Standards-2017.pdf

Institute of Internal Auditors. (2018a). *CIA exam: Why, how and what is changing January 2019*. Retrieved August 3, 2018 from https://global.theiia.org/certification/CIA-Certification/Pages/cia-exam-why-and-how-its-changing.aspx

Institute of Internal Auditors. (2018b). *Certified financial services auditor exam syllabus*. Retrieved August 3, 2018 from https://global.theiia.org/certification/cfsa-certification/Pages/Exam-Syllabus.aspx

Isgut, A. E. (2001). Developing countries borrowing in the international financial market with an uncertain credit ceiling. *International Journal of Finance & Economics*, *6*(2), 171–183. doi:10.1002/ijfe.153

Jakubik, P. (2006). *Does credit risk vary with economic cycles? The case of Finland*. Retrieved January 12, 2007 from http://ideas.repec.org/p/fau/wpaper/wp2006_11.html

James, K. L. (2003). The effects of internal audit structure on perceived financial statement fraud prevention. *Accounting Horizons*, *17*(4), 315–327. doi:10.2308/acch.2003.17.4.315

Koopman, S. J., & Lucas, A. (2005). Business and default cycles for credit risk. *Journal of Applied Econometrics*, *20*(2), 311–323. doi:10.1002/jae.833

KPMG. (2006). *Fraud risk management*. Retrieved October 30, 2012 from http://www.kpmg.com/CN/en/IssuesAndInsights/ArticlesPublications/documents/Fraud-Risk-Management-O-200610.pdf

Michaels, M. (2018). The most memorable and expensive financial fraud cases of all time. *Business Insider*. Retrieved August 3, 2018 from https://www.businessinsider.com/fraud-financial-scandals-notable-and-expensive-2018-4#wells-fargo-

Pesaran, H., & Shuermann, T. (2006). Macroeconomic dynamics and credit risk: Global perspective. *Journal of Money, Credit and Banking*, *38*(5), 1211–1261. doi:10.1353/mcb.2006.0074

Rose, J. (2015). Mapping your career: Competencies necessary for internal audit excellence. *IIA Common Body of Knowledge*. Retrieved August 3, 2018 from http://contentz.mkt5790.com/lp/2842/197389/IIARF%20CBOK%20Mapping%20Your%20Career%20Dec%202015_1.pdf

Sarbanes Oxley Act. (2002). Retrieved August 3, 2018 from http://www.soxlaw.com/

Securities Exchange Commission. (2013). *The laws that govern the securities industry*. Retrieved August 3, 2018 from https://www.sec.gov/answers/about-lawsshtml.html

US Embassy in Nicaragua. (2018). *Foreign account tax compliance act (FATCA) – April 15th is tax day*. Retrieved August 3, 2018 from https://ni.usembassy.gov/foreign-account-tax-compliance-act-fatca-april-15th-tax-day/

Zheng, H. (2006). Interaction of credit and liquidity risks: Modeling and valuation. *Journal of Banking & Finance*, *30*(2), 391–407. doi:10.1016/j.jbankfin.2005.04.026

ADDITIONAL READING

ACFE. (2018). Fraud risk assessment tool, Retrieved June 2, 2018 from http://www.acfe.com/frat.aspx?id=6797

Aslan, L. (2014). The influence of European and U.S. legislation on Turkish capital markets regulation. *Journal of Business Economics and Finance*, *3*(1), 60–70.

Aslan, L. (2017). The determinants of employee fraud in Turkish intermediary institutions. *1st International Symposium on Economics, Finance and Econometrics. Proceedings*, *1*, 170–188.

CIMA. (2008). Fraud risk management: A guide to good practice. Retrieved June 2, 2018 from http://www.cimaglobal.com/Documents/ImportedDocuments/cid_techguide_fraud_risk_management_feb09.pdf.pdf

COSO. (2016). Fraud risk management guide, Retrieved June 2, 2018 from https://www.coso.org/Documents/COSO-Fraud-Risk-Management-Guide-Executive-Summary.pdf

Marshall, R., & Magliozzi, R. (2009). The changing landscape for internal auditors in financial institutions. *Bank Accounting & Finance*, (February –March): 43–46.

Utica College & Protiviti Risk and Business Consulting. (2016). Taking the best route to managing fraud and corruption risks, Retrieved June 2, 2018 from https://www.protiviti.com/sites/default/files/united_states/insights/white-collar-crime-fraud-corruption-risks-survey-utica-college-protiviti.pdf

KEY TERMS AND DEFINITIONS

Chinese Walls: Physical separation of departments in intermediary institutions.

Financial Services Regulation: Legislation penned by regulators in capital markets.

Fraud Prevention: Precautions taken by management towards preventing employees or other related parties in taking place in fraudulent activities.

Fraud Risk: The possibility of the organization being subject to fraudulent activity.

Intermediary Institutions: According to Capital Market Law No. 6263 Brokerage Houses and Banks established in Turkey are called Intermediary Institutions.

Risk Assessment: Evaluation of components that have uncertainty in organizational activities.

Risk Management: Managing the uncertainty of components in such a way that either they are eliminated or reduced.

APPENDIX 1

Risk Assessment for Intermediary Institutions

See Table 2.

APPENDIX 2

Bank Risk Evaluation Matrix

See Tables 3 and 4.

APPENDIX 3

Sample Fraud Risk Assessment Matrix by IIA

See Table 5.

Table 2.

RISK CATEGORIES	RISK ISSUES	RECURRING RISK		EXCEPTIONAL RISK		CONTROL ENVIRONMENT						LAST INTERNAL AUDIT RATING	TOTAL RISK ASSESSMENT
		Financial Impact	Reputational Impact	Financial Impact	Reputational Impact	Internal Policy & Procedures	Level 1 Internal Controls	Level 2 Internal Controls	CMB Sanctions	Changes in Organization	Changes in Rules & Regulation		
CUSTOMER RELATIONS & COMPLIANCE	Failure of compliance with KYC rules												
	Failure of safekeeping of Client Documentation												
	Failure to update Documentation with limited validation												
	Failure to respect internal account opening & KYC rules												
	Failure to respect AML regulations												
	Failure to respect CFT incl. Embargoes and related regulations												
	Failure to respect restrictions of regulators concerning banned clients												
	Failure to respect international regulations concerning the client												
	Failure to assess client risk and insufficient due diligence correctly												
	Failure to meet client's expectations and improper(aggressive) marketing												
	Failure to meet margin calls and fee schedule												
	Failure to respect client complaint procedure												

continued on following page

Table 2. Continued

RISK CATEGORIES	RISK ISSUES	RECURRING RISK		EXCEPTIONAL RISK		CONTROL ENVIRONMENT						LAST INTERNAL AUDIT RATING	TOTAL RISK ASSESSMENT
	Failure to provide equal treatment of clients (time and order basis)												
COMPLIANCE OF TRANSACTIONS AND DEVELOPMENTS IN THE SECTOR	Lack of proper formalization of client relations, order transmission process, and other mandatory documentation												
	Failure to respect conveying information to clients concerning new products or changes in regulations												
	Failure to audit complex and transborder (overseas) transactions												
	Failure to implement ethical rules and code of conduct												
FINANCIAL RISK AND SECURITY	Failure to respect client data security principles (compliance with COBIT measures)												
	Lack of financial security policy												
	Lack of surveillance of financial reporting and budgeting process												
	Lack of surveillance of capital adequacy ratio and risk accruals												
	Lack of IT audit concerning information security												
	Lack of Business Continuity and Disaster Recovery Principles												
CONFLICTS OF INTEREST	Lack of ethical rules, code of conduct and conflicts of interest policy												

continued on following page

Table 2. Continued

RISK CATEGORIES	RISK ISSUES	RECURRING RISK		EXCEPTIONAL RISK		CONTROL ENVIRONMENT						LAST INTERNAL AUDIT RATING	TOTAL RISK ASSESSMENT
	Lack of controls over analyst recommendations Lack of inducements policy and procedure												
	Lack of policy and supervisions concerning use and access to inside information												
	Lack of Chinese Walls principle												
	Lack of policy and supervisions over personnel transactions												
COMPLIANCE WITH REGULATIONS AND INTERNAL POLICIES	Lack of proper HR policies including remuneration and performance pay principle												
	Lack of principles concerning prevention of market abuse												
	Failure to respect CMB regulations concerning credit transactions												
	Failure to respect CMB regulations concerning mandatory documentation keeping												
	Failure to respect CMB regulations concerning accounting principles												
	Failure to provide regulatory authorities with timely and accurate information												
	Lack of surveillance of Announcements published on KAP												
	Failure to gain related licenses (for personnel)												

continued on following page

Table 2. Continued

RISK CATEGORIES	RISK ISSUES	RECURRING RISK		EXCEPTIONAL RISK		CONTROL ENVIRONMENT						LAST INTERNAL AUDIT RATING	TOTAL RISK ASSESSMENT
	Lack of follow up of lawsuits												
	Failure to gain related licenses (for performing related activities)												
	Engaging in both sales, trading, research and corporate finance activities												
	Failure to meet training regulations												
	Failure in applying the Segregation of Duties principle												

Table 3.

Operational Activities in the Bank	Volume or Relative Weight	Risks Concerning Operational Activities							Risk Management Systems				Consolidated Average Risk Level
		Credit Risk	Market Risk	Liquidity Risk	Operational Risk	Regulatory Risk	Credibility Risk	Other Risks	Supervision by Senior Management	Policies, Procedures and Limits	Risk Management, Monitoring and MIS	Internal Controls	
Lending													
Individual Banking Operations													
Deposit Collecting and Investment Products													
Fund Management													
Financial Investments and Placements													
Administration and Custody of Client Funds													
Mergers and Takeovers													
Insurance Services													
Payments System													
Information Systems													
Human Resources													
Legal Transactions													
New Technologies													
Other Activities													
Final Risk Level													

Table 4.

Operational Activities in the Bank	**Volume or Relative Weight**	**Risks Concerning Operational Activities**							**Risk Management Systems**				**Consolidated Average Risk Level**
		Credit Risk	**Market Risk**	**Liquidity Risk**	**Operational Risk**	**Regulatory Risk**	**Credibility Risk**	**Other Risks**	**Supervision by Senior Management**	**Policies, Procedures and Limits**	**Risk Management, Monitoring and MIS**	**Internal Controls**	
Lending													
Individual Banking Operations													
Deposit Collecting and Investment Products													
Fund Management													
Financial Investments and Placements													
Administration and Custody of Client Funds													
Mergers and Takeovers													
Insurance Services													
Payments System													
Information Systems													
Human Resources													
Legal Transactions													
New Technologies													
Other Activities													
Final Risk Level													

Table 5.

Fraud Schemes & Scenarios	Likelihood	Significance	People and/or Department	Existing Anti-fraud Controls	Controls Effectiveness Assessment	Residual Risks	Fraud Risk Response
Financial reporting	Reasonably Possible	Material	Sales personnel	Controlled contract administration system	Tested by IA	N/A	Periodic testing by IA
Revenue recognition							
Backdating agreements							
Channel stuffing	Remote	Insignificant	N/A	N/A	N/A	N/A	N/A
Holding books open	Reasonably possible	Material	Accounting	Standard monthly close process	Tested by management	Risk of management override	Testing of late journal entries
Late shipments	Probable	Significant	Shipping department	Integrated shipping system, linked to invoicing and sales register	Tested by IA	Risk of override	Cut off testing by IA

Chapter 16
External vs. Internal Auditors in Prevention and Detection of Fraud:
The Perception of Portuguese Tax Auditors

Rui Robalo
School of Management and Technology of Santarém, Portugal

Sérgio Antunes da Silva
Portuguese Tax and Customs Authority, Portugal

ABSTRACT

This chapter aims to analyze, from the perspective of tax inspectors, what appreciation these tax auditors have to the collaboration between external and internal auditors for the prevention and detection of fraud in organizations. The investigation, based on the opinion of 142 Portuguese tax inspectors, reveals that tax inspectors attach a greater importance to the absence of barriers of communication between external and internal auditors, to the indications of the external to the internal auditors, on situations enhancing risk, and to the fact that, in dubious situations, the internal auditors must listen the opinion of the external auditors. In turn, tax inspectors value less the consideration of the external auditors in the work developed by the internal auditors, the frequency of meetings between the external and internal auditors, and the confidence of the external auditors in the technical work quality of the internal auditors. Despite the consistency of these results, the present study has allowed us to detect some differences between the tax inspectors surveyed.

INTRODUCTION

The responsibility of the auditors directed towards the detection of fraud has been increasing, notably through the improvement of the norms. For example, the International Standard on Auditing (ISA) 240 (2009) represents a significant advance in extending the functions of the work teams in the planning and execution phase of the audit, positioning itself as a primary agent in restoring the confidence of

DOI: 10.4018/978-1-5225-7356-2.ch016

investors, by increasing the quality of audits and strengthening the values of the profession, as well as in the fight against fraud. In the Portuguese context, Almeida (2017) produces evidence that the research and disclosure of fraud and illegal acts carried out by the major companies follow international trends.

However, studies have focused particularly on a type of external auditors: the typical financial auditors of audit companies. But we believe that there is also the need to meet another type of external auditors: the tax auditors. Thus, in view of the work of audit and fraud, we developed a study for analyzing the perception of tax inspectors (TIs), auditors of the Tax and Customs Authority (TCA), regarding the importance of collaboration between external and internal auditors in prevention and detection of fraud. Through a questionnaire, we asked the TIs to value a set of nine sentences related with the collaboration between external and internal auditors to find out which elements of collaboration that best contribute to the detection and prevention of fraud. This work seeks to obtain the opinion of the TIs, external auditors who often find diverse situations of fraud. Although TIs mission is focused on preventing and detecting irregularities and tax evasions, their performance resorts to detailed analysis of individuals and organizations. Given the lack of work that focuses on this type of external auditors, this study presents an innovative and, simultaneously, exploratory nature.

Due to the high importance of cooperation between the external and internal auditors the international Federation of Accountants (IFAC) has issued the International Standard on Auditing (ISA) 610 (2009), which has clarified the responsibilities of external auditors face to the work of the internal auditors. When examining the tasks and work carried out by the internal auditors, the external auditors must have enough knowledge to carry out additional audit procedures to be able to assess and minimize any risks inherent to the quality and accuracy of the work of the internal auditors.

External auditors should also assess the objectivity of the internal audit function, the technical competence of the human resources of the internal audit structure, their professional zeal, and should promote periodic meetings with the internal auditors. It should also be stressed that ISA 610 (2009) does not prevent external auditors from using the work of internal auditors. However, it prescribes that evaluations and analyses should be carried out to determine the quality of the internal audit and, consequently, of the information that it produces.

The next section meets the literature review on the several types of financial auditors, tax inspection and fraud, and the importance of collaboration between auditors in preventing and detecting fraud. In the third section, the methodology adopted in this study is presented. Subsequently, in the fourth section, the results are presented and discussed. In the fifth and closing section, the final remarks are presented, considering the limitations of the study and the suggestions for future research.

LITERATURE REVIEW

Financial Auditor vs. Tax Inspector

Talking about financial auditor implies talking about financial audit. This fundamentally focuses on the expression of an opinion on the financial statements of a given organization contributing to the increase in the credibility of financial information. A financial audit must appear to be effective and receive everyone's confidence and should be carried out by an independent auditor (Costa, 2017). The auditor is generally presented as a guarantor of the credibility of the financial information of the organizations. But to ensure this credibility, the auditor needs to take advantage of the necessary autonomy to ensure the maximum effectiveness of his/her work (Rezaee, 2004; Taborda, 2015) and, as Attie refers to (2011), his/her opinion needs to be supported on a solid basis so that his/her conclusions are not object of dispute. These solid bases allow the performance of the auditor's objective, which, according to Hopwood, Leiner, & Young (2012), is to determine whether the financial information is free of relevant inaccuracies, whether due to error or fraud. Thus, the ethics and deontology of auditors are key factors for a financial audit to be looked at with less distrust. It should be noted that according to the ISA 200 (2009), the auditors has a duty to respect what is ethically required of them, namely to ensure that they are independent. As referred by the CEOROC (2011), besides being independent of their customers, the auditors must act with integrity, competency, professional zeal and should display an unimpeachable professional behaviour.

Financial auditors may be internal or external (Costa, 2017). Internal financial auditors tend to conduct analyses, assessments, recommendations, suggestions and information regarding the activities examined, including the promotion of effective internal control. They should also identify and disseminate the strengths and weaknesses, determine the causes, assess the consequences, and find a solution so that the top-level managers can in advance minimize any serious and irregular situation. In turn, external financial auditors tend to have an increasingly key role in organizations, testing and asserting the credibility of the financial statements, governing themselves by specific auditing standards, which have as purpose the discovery of relevant distortions.

In addition to the typical financial auditors, which may be external or internal, there are other auditors who may be considered (external) financial auditors. This is what happens in the tax audits carried out by TIs, which aim at the observation of the tax facts, the verification of compliance with the tax obligations and, also, the prevention of tax violations.

In the past, the tax inspection arose as a dissonant element of the financial audit. However, despite the existence of specific characteristics, the Ministry of Finance (1996, § 2.5.2) intended to supply such a position, approaching the tax inspection to the financial audit, pointing out synergies at the level of the procedures, referring that "inspection methods must follow the procedures normally used in auditing". Canedo, Guedes, & Monteiro (2009) refer that, given the absence of proper norms inherent in the work of tax audit, the TIs must, with the necessary adjustments judged, follow part of its audit procedures based on audit standards generally accepted More recently, the Ministry of Finance (2015, pp. 55), states that the tax inspection must "develop internal quality control mechanisms at the level of the inspection procedures, covering the various phases of the audit (planning, implementation and reporting), notably through the generalization of the use of questionnaires for audit review to ensure compliance with the various formalisms relating to inspection procedures, compliance with the technical standards of audit and appropriate support, through the reference to doctrine and/or jurisprudence, of the most complex fixes and/or materially relevant". We can therefore say that the tax audit methodologies used by TIs have strong similarities to those followed by financial auditors.

As external financial auditors, the TIs presents some peculiarities. They are part of the functional and organic structure of TCA, created by Decree-Law No. 118/2011 of 15 December, through the merger (1) of the Directorate-General for Customs and Excise Duties, (2) Directorate-General for Taxes, and (3) General Directorate of Information and Support for Tax and Customs Services. Hence, the TCA shall administer taxes, customs duties and other tributes assigned to it, as well as to exercise control of the external frontier of the European Union and of the national customs territory for tax, economic and protection purposes, in accordance with the policies defined by the Government and the law of the European Union, as provided in article 14 (1) of Decree-Law No. 117/2011 of 15 December.

As a general role, the TIs are part of the TCA's tax inspection, which presents its functions defined in the Supplementary Regime of the Tax and Customs Inspection Procedures (SRTCIP), created by Decree-Law n. ° 413/98, of 31 December, which entered into force in January 1, 1999. The various aspects of operation of the tax inspection are identified in article 2 of the SRTCIP, highlighting the following: "Confirmation of the elements declared by taxable persons and other tax-bound individuals; The conduct of individual, sectoral or territorial studies on the behaviour of taxable persons and other tax-bound individuals and the evolution of the economic sectors in which their activity is inserted; The conduct of technical expertise or examinations of any kind; Cooperation in accordance with international conventions or Community regulations, in the context of the prevention and repression of evasion and fraud". The work of TIs is guided by the promotion of responsible attitudes, competence and professional scepticism, minimizing the practice of errors, as in the performance inherent in other financial auditors, governing the performance of TIs by principles of truth, proportionality, contradiction and cooperation (article 5 of the SRTCIP).

In terms of specific work, the TIs develop their work, breaking it up into three phases: (1) planning, (2) execution and (3) reporting (Canedo et al., 2009). The first phase involves an assessment of the risk of tax failure, a definition of strategy, with a plan of approach to audit and a work schedule. Already the second phase, implementation, corresponds to the work of applying the procedures and substantive tests of details of transactions and balances defined in the work programmes and final analytical review. The third stage, reporting, focuses on the general conclusions, verifying that the evidence obtained is competent and enough to adequately substantiate the irregularities detected and the subsequent preparation of the inspection report.

Despite the different objectives, there are many similarities between the financial auditor and the tax auditor/inspector. They both use similar methodologies, considering the principles of legality, prudence, among others, that guide their performances. About the type of diligence that can be done by TIs, article 63 of the general tax law, created by Decree-Law n. ° 398/98, of 17 December, identifies several, particularly the free access to facilities, books and accounting records. It points out a "privileged" act of TIs, which in addition to their performance result from the law, they are invested in the power of legal authority, which does not happen with traditional financial auditors.

Auditor and Fraud Prevention and Detection

Although fraud designations are diverse, they all point in the same direction. According to ISA 240 (2009, § 11a), fraud is defined as "an intentional act practiced by one or more individuals from management, in charge of governance, employees or third parties, involving the deliberate use of falsehoods to obtain an unfair or illegal advantage". This standard refers to various situations that are the source of fraud, such as: manipulation, falsification or alteration of records or documents, improper appropriation of assets, among others. We can thus conceive the concept of fraud as a deliberate act, aiming to obtain illicit benefits, thus distinguishing itself from the error, which can be practiced in an unintentional way.

Fraud is a complex subject. The auditors address the prevention and detection of fraud as a delicate subject, and there is a greater need to alert the auditors in times of crisis (OROC, 2013). But the prevention and detection of fraud does not only stand out as a responsibility of the external auditor, but also of the internal auditor and the environment in which it is inserted, namely the management of the organisation and the internal control system implemented. Marques and Marçal (2011, pp. 55) argue that "only an adequate internal control system allows reasonable safety in the prevention, limitation and detection of errors and irregularities". However, it is in the top management of each organization that lies most of the responsibility for the prevention and detection of fraud, since it is through their actions that the mechanisms of control are constructed.

In the organizations fraud in the financial reporting may involve the falsification of the financial statements and may present two separate guidelines. Fraud sometimes seeks to present a better financial situation than it does (for example, to influence its stock quotes or to evade potential investors). In other cases, fraud follows the goal of presenting a more degraded financial situation, seeking to pay less taxes.

As far as tax fraud is concerned, TIs are essentially against four types of fraud: (1) tax evasion, (2) credit frustration, (3) fraud and (4) abuse of trust. These 4 types of fraud are identified in the Tax Violations General Scheme (TVGS), approved by Law No. 15/2001, of 5 June. The first type of fraud, tax evasion, is identified in article 87 of the TVGS and is essentially substantiated in the rendering of false declarations, in the falsification or addiction of tax-relevant documents, resulting from these enrichment acts of several people. The second type, frustration of credits, is identified in article 88 of the TVGS and results from the knowledge of the existence of a tribute already settled, or in the process of liquidation, having the intention to frustrate wholly or partially the tax credit. In turn, the fraud, presented here as the third type, is identified in article 103 of the TVGS and is related to illegitimate conducts aimed at the non-settlement, delivery or payment of the tax provision or the improper obtaining of tax benefits. Finally, the fourth and last type of fraud more common, abuse of confidence, is identified in article 105 of the TVGS and results from the fact that someone does not deliver to the tax administration, wholly or partially, tax provision of value greater than €7500, and that s/he was legally obliged to deliver it. In the next section we will address the importance of collaboration between external and internal auditors to prevent and detect these types of fraud.

Collaboration Between External and Internal Auditors in the Prevention and Detection of Fraud

The tasks developed by TIs, external financial auditors, are substantiated in analysis based on accounting with resources to audit techniques, using various means at their disposal, the relevance of which leads to more efficient and effective work in preventing and detecting fraud situations. In turn, and as already mentioned in this chapter, the work of the internal financial auditor presents a high relevance and influence on the work of the external financial auditor, resulting in the success of the global work, in combining the tasks of each one. Let's see, then, a set of collaboration situations between external and internal auditors that may be relevant to the prevention and detection of fraud.

The Absence of Communication Barriers Between the Auditors

The existence of effective communication between the auditors is fundamental and has increasingly a decisive role in organizations. Renard (2002) states that the development of the work of auditors (external and internal) is complementary, since the external auditor is more determined to appreciate the reliability of the results presented by the internal auditor, and this, after the work presented by the latter, it benefits from arguments and recommendations dictated by the external Auditor. A study by Suwaidan & Qasim (2010) concluded that external auditors consider the objectivity, competence and performance in the work of internal auditors as very important factors that affect their decisions. Paino, Razali, & Jabar (2015) argue that the non-existence of communication barriers enhances the confidence of the external auditor in the work of the internal auditor. In short, the mutual exchange of information and respect for each other's work leads to a decrease in the barriers of communication between the two auditors, determining the level of success of their work.

The Information Provided by the External Auditor Improves the Quality of the Work of the Internal Auditor

The technical skills allied to behavioural skills are essential for an internal auditor to achieve success in his work, emphasizing in his/her skills, among others, the knowledge of the business, the use of information technologies, the Training of the work team and the interpersonal relationship. However, Gramling & Schneider (2018) found that internal auditors are less likely to assess a specific deficiency in the internal control of the process arising from some influences from the management of organizations. Thus, in the case of weaknesses in internal control by the external auditor and being referred to the internal auditor, the latter, consequently, after the necessary adjustments, will improve the quality of his/her work.

The External Auditor's Consideration in the Work Carried Out by the Internal Auditor

Both auditors (external and internal) work for a common goal, seeking to show a true and real image of the organization. By appreciating and retaking the work of the internal auditor, the external auditor not only give credibility to the work of the internal auditor but creates conditions to improve the credibility of the financial information presented. Chan & Vasarhelyi (2018) noted that using technology and automation in the continuous audit methodology increases the efficiency and effectiveness of the audit process. Thus, improving the quality of their work, the internal auditor, both for independence and for continuous auditing methods, will have a better consideration of the external auditor for the work s/he has done.

The Frequency of Meetings Between External and Internal Auditors in Relation to the Audit Work

The emergence of new business (e.g. online transactions, privacy policies, validation of the electronic signature, etc.) leads to the meetings between the auditors (external and internal) to have a higher frequency, because it allows a better and more rapid monitoring of the mutations that may exist in the economy and in society. The increase of meetings will increase mutual confidence, leading to a decrease in surplus spending as referred to by Haron, Chambers, Ramsi, & Ismail (2004). In this way, the frequency of meetings between auditors improves mutual confidence and increases their professional skills.

The Instructions of the External Auditor to the Internal Auditor on Risk-Enhancing Situations (Red Flags)

External auditors are more likely to use the internal audit for analysis of internal control assessment situations and risk situations, thus leading to an identification of potentially "dangerous" situations (Munro & Stewart, 2011). The risk situations in the organizations are real and the recent past has demonstrated it. The external auditor, as an element that is "out" of the organizations, has a different view of the one that is presented by the internal auditor, thus reinforcing the relevance of the quality of his/her indications, which lead to a decrease in situations that enhance red flags (elevated risk situations). On the other hand, as Chalmers, Hay, & Khlif (2018) refer, the quality of internal control can have a significant effect on the users' decision making of financial information, as the risk is diminished. Thus, the work of internal and external auditors should be as complementary, there are several points of approximation between the two, mitigating the risk, and contributing in an extremely valid and positive way in the final work to be presented (Morais & Martins, 2013).

The External Auditor's Confidence in the Technical Quality of the Internal Auditor's Work

The external Auditor, during his/her work, shall assess the technical qualities of the internal auditor, his/her training for the implementation of the tasks assigned to him/her and whether his/her work is subject to supervision, revision and documentation, thus subsisting more confidence in the quality of the work of the internal auditor. Scheider (2009) states that by relying on the work of the internal auditors, the external auditors avoid duplication of procedures, although the internal auditors are more aware of the functioning of the organizations. In fact, the professional competence, responsibility and objectivity of an auditor have a significant effect on the quality of the audit performed (Zahmatkesh & Rezazadeh, 2017). Thus, the technical quality of the work of an internal auditor tends to increase the confidence of the external auditor in the information provided by the former.

The Frequency of Meetings Between External Auditor and the Management in Relation to the Internal Control System

The verification of the procedures and the validation of the controls used in the organizations enable the external auditor to issue an opinion of advice to the managers of the organization, ensuring greater security in the decision-making. In a recent study, Cao & Lu (2018) verified that the quality of internal control is better in companies where its members of the administration have higher qualifications. Thus, the meetings between the external auditor and the managers of the organizations have a high relevance for the quality of the information presented, always on the assumption of the validity of the information transmitted to the external auditor by the internal auditor.

In Dubious Situations, the Internal Auditor Must Apply to the Opinion of the External Auditor

The technical skills of the internal auditors are essential for the proper performance of the functions they exercise in organizations, subsisting as a basis for the internal controls implemented. The frequent decision-making by the internal auditor, being simpler and other extremely complex, leads to the need to obtain many information to reduce its risk. It is therefore normal that in more complex decisions the internal auditor will use the opinion of the external auditor and may lead to adjustments to the defined control programmes (Margheim, 1986). More recently, Hung & Cheng (2018) refer that auditors should pay extremely high attention when organizations perform complex transactions with related parties and when they have situations of great product diversification. It is thus expected, in situations of high complexity, the appeal of the internal auditor to the opinion of the external auditor.

The External Auditor's Confidence in the Suitability of the Internal Auditor

Internal auditors are required to conduct themselves above suspicion, both in the field of ethics and integrity. Also, its independence in the realization of the actions is one of the fundamental aspects for the good performance of the tasks carried out by the internal auditor. Svanberg & Öhman (2016) claim that auditors in a strong ethical culture are more likely to maintain the auditor's objectivity than auditors in less favourable cultures, leading companies to promote a strong ethical culture to reduce adversity in the work of auditors. Thus, the external auditor's confidence in the integrity of the internal auditor is of high importance, given that it will lead to the former having a better empathy and acceptance of the work of the latter.

RESEARCH METHODOLOGY

As already presented in the "Introduction" section, this work aims to study the perception of TIs regarding the importance of collaboration between external and internal auditors in the prevention and detection of fraud. Thus, we proceed to collect the opinions of TIs through a questionnaire, anonymous, delivered randomly to these auditors, who belong to the different Directorates of the Portuguese Tax and Customs Authority. The elaboration of a questionnaire covers fundamentally the transposition of research objectives into their own issues, so the answers will provide the data required to describe the characteristics of the population in analysis. It was thus sought the most globalized vision possible about how TIs value the collaboration between external and internal auditors in the prevention and detection of fraud.

The questionnaire is made up of two parts. The first part meets the TIs profile and contains a set of 7 questions. These questions focus on (1) the Professional category, (2) the professional experience, (3) the geographical location of activity exercise, (4) the academic qualifications, (5) the academic area of qualifications, (6) the business area/ more sensitive to fraud and, finally, (7) if they have already detected fraud.

The second part of the questionnaire meets the perception of TIs relative to the importance of collaboration between external and internal auditors in the prevention and detection of fraud. Thus, the following question was put to the TIs: "Following the work of audit carried out in the organizations, and in view of their professional functions, how important are these sentences in the prevention and detection of fraud?". The nine sentences placed to TIs, resulting from the revision of literature (being not a replication of another questionnaire), were in Table 1.

For each of the nine sentences the TIs was requested to value them according to the following scale: *1. Nothing important; 2. Little important; 3. Important; 4. Very important; 5. Extremely important.* With the graduations to the 9 sentences we want to have a vision of what the external Auditor, in this case TIs, more value and less value in the collaboration between external and internal auditors regarding the detection and prevention of fraud in organizations. The choice of this graduation resulted from the adaptation of the following typical Likert scale format: 1. I do not agree entirely; 2. I do not agree partially; 3. Indifferent; 4. I agree partially; 5. Totally agree. A pre-test was also performed on the questionnaire, based on 10 TIs, with the objective of assessing whether the questionnaire was understandable by the respondents. It was found that the TIs understood what was requested, not being detected abnormal situations in the questionnaire that lacked changes and revisions.

Table 1. Sentences placed to TIs

S1	*The absence of communication barriers between the auditors*
S2	*The information provided by the external auditor improves the quality of the work of the internal auditor*
S3	*The external auditor's consideration in the work carried out by the internal auditor*
S4	*The frequency of meetings between the external auditor and the internal auditor in relation to the audit work*
S5	*The instructions of the external auditor to the internal auditor on risk-enhancing situations (red flags)*
S6	*The external auditor's confidence in the technical quality of the internal auditor's work*
S7	*The frequency of meetings between the external auditor and the management in relation to the internal control system*
S8	*In dubious situations, the internal auditor must use the opinion of the external auditor*
S9	*The external auditor's confidence in the suitability of the internal auditor*

About the use of a Likert scale, we stress the advantage of its simplicity and the ease of a respondent to issue a degree of agreement on any statement. Also, it is noteworthy its ease of construction and the clarity of answers. To the respondent are offered several possibilities of response and, being extremely visual, the respondent understands easily the logic of this scale, and can compare the items in analysis, changing them according to their will. The confirmation of psychometric consistency in the metrics used by the Likert scale contributes a lot for its adoption by researchers (Costa, 2011).

According to Ghiglione & Cotalon (2001, pp. 29) "it is very rare that we can study exhaustively a population, that is, to inquire all its members would be so long and costly, that it would become virtually impossible", so the constitution of a representative sample of the population presents itself as an essential condition so that what is inferred from the observations can also be widespread to the entire population. The TCA possessed in 2013 about 2,000 TIs that were affections to the tax inspection (Ministry of Finance, 2013), number that at the date of the questionnaire slight variation suffered. Those employees are working either in district directions of finance (headquartered in all the districts of the country) or in the central services of the TCA (located in Lisbon and Porto). Being certain that not all TIs are aggregated to the functions of tax inspection, since some are dispersed by other services of TCA, other than the tax inspection, were sent 200 questionnaires to TIs with effective tax inspection functions belonging to several district directions of finance, having received 146 questionnaires.

The questionnaires were applied, in paper support, between the days 02 and 23 June 2014. The delivery and collection of the questionnaires in the district direction of Santarém was carried out by one of the researchers, and in the other district directions of finance the delivery and collection of the questionnaires was carried out by several TIs. It was personally transmitted to all TIs what the scope and purpose of the questionnaire was.

In data analysis was given order, organization and interpretation to the elements collected, for drawing out useful and credible conclusions. Of the 146 questionnaires obtained, 4 were invalidated because they did not have answers to all the items. The replies collected by the 142 questionnaires were grouped quantitatively in view of the valuation that each respondent attributed to each of the nine sentences related to the prevention and detection of fraud, catalogued from S1 to S9, according to the Likert scale used. There were also groupings between degrees near this scale for the whole of the nine sentences. Subsequently, the valuations attributed by TIs to each of the nine sentences were grouped in view of the professional experience and academic training area, with the aim of identifying different perceptions of the importance of the collaboration between external and internal auditors in the prevention and detection of fraud in organizations.

ANALYSIS OF RESULTS

Analysis of the Profile of TIs Surveyed

Analysis of the profile of respondents emphasize five general considerations. The first one has to do with the professional experience of these auditors. About the years of the profession of TIs, we find that 58% of respondents have more than 8 years of professional experience and that, in turn, 28% have between 5 and 8 years of profession. We easily understand that about 86% of TIs surveyed have more than 5 years of professional experience.

The second general consideration of the analysis of the profile of TIs surveyed has to do with the academic qualifications. The overwhelming majority (88%) of TIs have a degree, and there are still 6% who have the master's degree. The fact that 94% of TIs surveyed has at least one degree arises from the requirement currently provided by the competitions for access to the tax inspector category.

The third general consideration related to the profile of TIs surveyed has to do with the specific area of its academic qualifications. We verify that the TIs surveyed have higher studies in the following five areas: management, law, accounting, economics and auditing. It should be noted that most TIs surveyed (77%) has an academic degree in the managerial area, while the remaining 23% have an academic degree in law. The existence of TIs in this area concerns the need of juristic tax inspectors in the TCA.

The fourth general consideration has to do with the perception of the TIs surveyed in relation to the area's most susceptible to fraud situations in the organizations. About 80% of TIs associated fraud more with the financial and accounting areas. These answers may not be oblivious to the fact that most of these professionals have a training in the areas of management, accounting and economics.

Finally, the fifth general consideration has to do with fraud situations already detected by TIs. Only 9% of respondents had not yet detected fraud situations. Since 86% of TIs have 5 or more years of experience, it is understandable that 91% of these TIs have already detected fraud situations (e.g. tax evasion, credit frustration, fraud and abuse of confidence).

Collaboration Between External and Internal Auditors

This section presents the analysis of TIs responses in relation to the nine sentences related to the collaboration between external and internal auditors in the prevention and detection of fraud. In the first phase, we proceed to a general analysis of the evidence obtained (see Table 2). In this analysis we have found three relevant aspects. The first of these concerns the fact that there have been few TIs that value the nine sentences as "1. Nothing important" or "2. Little important". These results are an indicator of the relevance of each of these nine sentences for the prevention and detection of fraud in organizations. Despite the ongoing audit work in these sentences are considered important in the prevention and detection of fraud by several authors in the literature in financial audit (e.g. Munro & Stewart, 2011; Morais & Martins, 2013; Svanberg & Öhman, 2016), we verify that they are also important in the tax audit (in the Portuguese context).

The second relevant aspect of the current analysis has to do with the appreciation most chosen by the Tis surveyed. We found that the most chosen appreciation for these was "4. Very important" in all sentences, except for the sentence S4 (*the frequency of meetings between the external auditor and the internal auditor in relation to the audit work*). This allows us to say that this will be one of the least relevant sentences for the whole of TIs surveyed. In turn, when analysing only the sentences valued as "4. Very important", we find that the sentences most valued by the TIs surveyed are the S1 (*the absence of communication barriers between the auditors*) and the S2 (*the information provided by the external auditor improves the quality of the work of the internal auditor*), following in third place several sentences (S3, S5 and S8).

However, we must not forget that in appreciation "5. Extremely important", the order of importance of sentences is different from the previous one. In this case, in the three sentences most valued by the TIs surveyed, we find, in addition to S1, the S5 (*the instructions of the external auditor to the internal auditor on risk-enhancing situations*) and the S9 (*the external auditor's confidence in the suitability of the internal auditor*). In face of this situation, it was decided to analyse the more (and less) sentences valued by TIs by joining the valued responses as "4. Very important" and "5. Extremely important" (see the last column in Table 2). This junction results that the most valued sentences are S1, S5 and S8. These results find adherence to the importance of the non-existence of communication between external and internal auditors (e.g. Suwaidan & Qasim, 2010); Paino et al., 2015), on the importance of the external auditor's instructions to the internal auditor, on risk-enhancing situations (e.g. Munro & Stewart, 2011; Morais & Martins, 2013; Chalmers et al., 2018), and in the importance that, in dubious situations, the internal auditor must use the opinion of the external auditor (e.g. Margheim, 1986; Hung & Cheng, 2018).

The third relevant aspect of the current analysis has to do with the sentences less valued by the Tis surveyed. To this end, a similar methodology to the one used in identifying the sentences most valued by these professionals was followed, analysing together the responses with "4. Very important" and "5. Extremely important". From this analysis it follows that the less valued sentences are the S3 (*the external auditor's consideration in the work carried out by the internal auditor*), the S6 (*the external auditor's confidence in the technical quality of the internal auditor's work*), and particularly the S4 (*the frequency of meetings between the external auditor and the internal auditor in relation to the audit work*).

Analysis According to the Years of Profession of TIs

Experience is a determining factor in the exercise of a profession and auditors of the tax inspection are no exception. In this sense, it was decided to deepen the analysis of the previous section, considering the number of years of profession exercised by TIs. To be able to compare the results of this analysis with those of the previous section, a similar methodology was followed by the identification of the sentences more and less valued by these professionals, having grouped the replies of the TIs of "4. Very important" and "5. Extremely important" (see Table 3).

Except for TIs integrated in the group "< 5 years", the less experienced group, the sentence most valued by the other groups was the S1 (*the absence of communication barriers between the auditors*), i.e. the same as the general analysis. In turn, the TIs integrated in the group "< 5 years", value more the sentence S5 (*the instructions of the external auditor to the internal auditor on risk-enhancing situations*), the second most valued in the general analysis. About the sentence less valued by TIs there is consistency, since all groups of TIs have chosen the sentence S4 (*the frequency of meetings between the external auditor and the internal auditor in relation to the audit work*).

Table 2. Analysis of the evidence obtained from TIs

	The sentences under analysis	Scale (a)					Accum. values (b)
		1	2	3	4	5	4+5
S1	The absence of communication barriers between the auditors	0	0	37	73	32	105
		0%	0%	26%	51%	23%	74%
S2	The information provided by the external auditor improves the quality of the work of the internal auditor	0	3	46	72	21	93
		0%	2%	32%	51%	15%	65%
S3	The external auditor's consideration in the work carried out by the internal auditor	0	5	58	69	10	79
		0%	4%	41%	49%	7%	56%
S4	The frequency of meetings between the external auditor and the internal auditor in relation to the audit work	0	15	70	48	9	57
		0%	11%	49%	34%	6%	40%
S5	The instructions of the external auditor to the internal auditor on risk-enhancing situations (red flags)	0	2	38	69	33	102
		0%	1%	27%	49%	23%	72%
S6	The external auditor's confidence in the technical quality of the internal auditor's work	1	7	55	57	22	79
		1%	5%	39%	40%	15%	56%
S7	The frequency of meetings between the external auditor and the management in relation to the internal control system	0	8	49	65	20	85
		0%	6%	35%	46%	14%	60%
S8	In dubious situations, the internal auditor must use the opinion of the external auditor	0	6	41	69	26	95
		0%	4%	29%	49%	18%	67%
S9	The external auditor's confidence in the suitability of the internal auditor	1	7	49	56	29	85
		1%	5%	35%	39%	20%	60%

(a) *Scale:scale: 1. Nothing important; 2. Little important; 3. Important; 4. Very important; 5. Extremely import*

(b) *These values result from the sum of the valuations "4. Very important" and "5. Extremely important"*

Analysis According to the Area of Academic Qualifications of TIs

As in the previous section, this section intends to deepen the general analysis on the replies of TIs, considering the area of its academic qualifications. The goal is to verify if the perceptions of TIs vary according to their academic background. To be able to compare the results of this analysis by areas of academic qualifications with previous analysis, a similar methodology was followed to identify the sentences more and less valued by TIs (see Table 4).

We noticed that, although there is dispersal in the responses arising from different areas of study, the sentences most valued by each of the groups of TIs find adherence to the general results, highlighting the sentence S1 (*the absence of communication barriers between the auditors*) and the sentence S5 (*the instructions of the external auditor to the internal auditor on risk-enhancing situations*). About the less-valued sentenced, all groups of TIs have chosen the sentence S4 (*the frequency of meetings between the external auditor and the internal auditor in relation to the audit work*).

Table 3. Analysis of TIs responses for years of profession

The sentences under analysis		< 5 years	5 a 8 years	8 a 15 years	> a 15 years
		Accumulated values (a)			
		4+5	4+5	4+5	4+5
S1	The absence of communication barriers between the auditors	12	27	22	44
S2	The information provided by the external auditor improves the quality of the work of the internal auditor	10	21	22	40
S3	The external auditor's consideration in the work carried out by the internal auditor	9	23	14	33
S4	The frequency of meetings between the external auditor and the internal auditor in relation to the audit work	4	16	12	25
S5	The instructions of the external auditor to the internal auditor on risk-enhancing situations (red flags)	17	26	16	43
S6	The external auditor's confidence in the technical quality of the internal auditor's work	10	19	18	32
S7	The frequency of meetings between the external auditor and the management in relation to the internal control system	4	26	19	36
S8	In dubious situations, the internal auditor must use the opinion of the external auditor	15	25	17	38
S9	The external auditor's confidence in the suitability of the internal auditor	12	20	19	34

(a) These values result from the sum of the valuations "4. Very important" and "5. Extremely important"

Table 4. Analysis of TIs responses by academic qualifications Area

The sentences under analysis		Accounting	Managt.	Law	Economy
		Accumulated values (a)			
		4+5	4+5	4+5	4+5
S1	The absence of communication barriers between the auditors	23	40	23	18
S2	The information provided by the external auditor improves the quality of the work of the internal auditor	21	37	20	14
S3	The external auditor's consideration in the work carried out by the internal auditor	17	32	19	10
S4	The frequency of meetings between the external auditor and the internal auditor in relation to the audit work	15	20	15	7
S5	The instructions of the external auditor to the internal auditor on risk-enhancing situations (red flags)	20	42	26	13
S6	The external auditor's confidence in the technical quality of the internal auditor's work	17	33	21	8
S7	The frequency of meetings between the external auditor and the management in relation to the internal control system	18	39	14	14
S8	In dubious situations, the internal auditor must use the opinion of the external auditor	20	36	23	16
S9	The external auditor's confidence in the suitability of the internal auditor	21	33	21	10

(a) These values result from the sum of the valuations "4. Very important" and "5. Extremely important"

CONCLUSION

We intend with this study to know what TIs in Portugal consider more and less relevant in terms of collaboration between external and internal auditors for the prevention and detection of fraud situations in organizations. Given the lack of work that focuses on this type of external auditors, this study presents an innovative and simultaneously exploratory strand.

This study provides tree contributions. The first is that TIs value differently the various forms of collaboration between external and internal auditors for the prevention and detection of fraud in organizations. They value more the absence of communication between the auditors, the instructions of the external auditor to the internal auditor on risk-enhancing situations (on risk-enhancing situations) and that, in dubious situations, the internal auditor must use the opinion of the external auditor.

The second contribution that this study gives us is related to the professional experience. As evidenced in previous studies for external auditors, the practice time of the profession is also important for TIs in the appreciation of the importance of the tasks of the audit work for the prevention and detection of fraud situations in organizations.

Finally, the third contribution provided by this study is related to academic education. Regarding what is most relevant to the prevention and detection of fraud in organizations, there are some differences between TIs with different academic backgrounds. However, there is agreement on the less relevant aspects of collaboration between external and internal auditors.

There is no study without limitations and this is no exception. The main limitation of this study is related to its exploratory nature and the difficulty of inference of the results of it to other contexts, beyond the Portuguese context. We therefore suggest that in future research there are other national contexts, notably European contexts.

Another suggestion of future research may be the replication of this study in the national context to another type of internal and/or external auditors (e.g. statutory auditors). The analysis of those two types of auditors will allow us to study common and different perceptions in the same economic context, in relation to the best forms of collaboration between externals and internal auditors for the prevention and detection of fraud in organizations.

REFERENCES

Almeida, B. (2017). Audit role in today's society: The Portuguese perspective. *TÉKHNE - Review of Applied Management Studies*, *15*(1), 42-57.

Attie, W. (2011). *Auditoria: Conceitos e aplicações*. São Paulo: Atlas.

Canedo, J., Guedes, O., & Monteiro, A. (2009). *Manual de auditoria tributária*. Lisboa: Direcção-Geral dos Impostos.

Cao, Y., & Lu, Y. (2018). (in press). The individual characteristics of board members and internal control weakness: Evidence from China. *Pacific-Basin Finance Journal*.

CEOROC. (2011). Diário da República Portuguesa N.° 198, 2ª Série.

Chalmers, K., Hay, D., & Khlif, H. (2018). (in press). Internal control in accounting research: A review. *Journal of Accounting Literature*. doi:10.1016/j.acclit.2018.03.002

Chan, D. Y., & Vasarhelyi, M. A. (2018). Innovation and Practice of Continuous Auditing. In D. Y. Chan, V. Chiu, & M. A. Vasarhelyi (Eds.), *Continuous Auditing* (pp. 271–283). Emerald Publishing Limited. doi:10.1108/978-1-78743-413-420181013

Costa, C. (2017). *Auditoria financeira: Teoria e* prática. Lisboa: Rei dos Livros.

Costa, F. (2011). *Mensuração e desenvolvimento de escalas: aplicações em administração*. Rio de Janeiro: Ciência Moderna.

Decree-Law No. 117/2011 of 15 December. Portuguese Republic Journal No. 239, 1st Serie.

Decree-Law No. 118/2011 of 15 December. Portuguese Republic Journal No. 239, 1st Serie.

Decree-Law No. 398/1998 of 17 December. Portuguese Republic Journal No. 290, 1st Serie.

Decree-Law No. 413/1998 of 31 December. Portuguese Republic Journal No. 301, 1st Serie.

Edge, W. R., & Farley, A. A. (1991). External auditor evaluation of the internal audit function. *Accounting and Finance*, *31*(1), 69–83. doi:10.1111/j.1467-629X.1991.tb00254.x

Ghiglione, R., & Matalon, B. (2001). *O inquérito: Teoria e prática*. Oeiras: Celta Editora.

Gramling, A., & Schneider, A. (2018). Effects of reporting relationship and type of internal control deficiency on internal auditors' internal control evaluations. *Managerial Auditing Journal*, *33*(3), 318–335. doi:10.1108/MAJ-07-2017-1606

Haron, H., Chambers, A., Ramsi, R., & Ismail, I. (2004). The reliance of external auditors on internal auditors. *Managerial Auditing Journal*, *19*(9), 1148–1159. doi:10.1108/02686900410562795

Hopwood, W., Leiner, J., & Young, G. (2012). *Forensic accounting and Fraud Examination*. New York: McGraw-Hill.

Hung, Y. S., & Cheng, Y. C. (2018). The impact of information complexity on audit failures from corporate fraud: Individual auditor level analysis. *Asia Pacific Management Review*, *23*(2), 72–85. doi:10.1016/j.apmrv.2017.09.002

ISA 200. (2009). *Objetivos gerais do auditor independente e condução de uma auditoria de acordo com as normas internacionais de auditoria*. International Federation of Accountants.

ISA 240. (2009). *As responsabilidades do auditor relativas a fraude numa auditoria de demonstrações financeiras*. International Federation of Accountants.

ISA 610. (2009). *Usar o Trabalho de Auditores Internos*. International Federation of Accountants.

Law No. 15/2001 of 5 June. Portuguese Republic Journal No. 130, 1st Serie.

Margheim, L. L. (1986). Further evidence on external auditors' reliance on internal auditors. *Journal of Accounting Research*, *24*(1), 194–205. doi:10.2307/2490813

Marques, F., & Marçal, N. (2011). *Manual de auditoria e controlo interno no sector público*. Lisboa: Edições Sílabo.

Ministry of Finance. (1996). *Relatório da Comissão para o desenvolvimento da reforma fiscal*. Available at: http://purl.sgmf.pt/COL-MF-0028/1/

Ministry of Finance. (2013). *Balanço Social da Autoridade Tributária e Aduaneira*. Direção de Serviços de Gestão de Recursos Humanos.

Ministry of Finance (2015). *Plano Estratégico de combate à fraude e evasão fiscais*. Gabinete do Secretario de Estado dos Assuntos Fiscais.

Morais, G., & Martins, I. (2013). *Auditoria Interna: Função e processo*. Lisboa: Áreas Editora.

Munro, L., & Stewart, J. (2011). External auditors' reliance on internal auditing: Further evidence. *Managerial Auditing Journal*, *26*(6), 464–48. doi:10.1108/02686901111142530

OROC. (2013). *Continuidade: Estudo de um caso*. Newsletter abril/junho.

Paino, H. I., Razali, F. M., & Jabar, F. A. (2015). The Influence of External Auditor's Working Style, Communication Barriers and Enterprise Risk Management toward Reliance on Internal Auditor's Work. *Procedia Economics and Finance*, *28*, 151–155. doi:10.1016/S2212-5671(15)01094-1

Renard, J. (2002). *Teoria si practica auditului intern. Editia a IV-a*. Bucuresti: Ministerul Finantelor Publice.

Rezaee, Z. (2004). Restoring public trust in the accounting profession by developing anti-fraud education, programs, and auditing. *Managerial Auditing Journal*, *19*(1), 134–148. doi:10.1108/02686900410509857

Scheider, A. (2009). The nature, impact and facilitation of external auditor reliance on internal auditing. *Academy of Accounting and Financial Studies Journal*, *13*(4), 40–53.

Suwaidan, M. S., & Qasim, A. (2010). External auditors' reliance on internal auditors and its impact on audit fees: An empirical investigation. *Managerial Auditing Journal*, *25*(6), 509–525. doi:10.1108/02686901011054845

Svanberg, J., & Öhman, P. (2016). Does Ethical Culture in Audit Firms Support Auditor Objectivity? *Accounting in Europe*, *13*(1), 65–79. doi:10.1080/17449480.2016.1164324

Taborda, D. (2015). *Auditoria: Revisão legal das contas e outras funções do revisor oficial de contas*. Lisboa: Sílabo.

Zahmatkesh, S. & Rezazadeh, J. (2017). The effect of auditor features on audit quality. *TÉKHNE - Review of Applied Management Studies*, *15*(2), 79-87.

KEY TERMS AND DEFINITIONS

External Auditor: From the financial auditor's perspective is a professional who carries out an audit in accordance with the specific laws or rules on the financial statements of a company, government entity or other legal person or organization, which is independent of the entity being audited, governed by ethical principles.

Finance Directorate: Is a decentralized structure, at a regional level, depending on the Tax and Customs Authority, which has the purpose to answer to the requests for clarification raised by taxpayers, to ensure the activities related to the tax inspection, to develop research procedures of tax irregularities, to coordinate and control the performance of financial services, and to ensure the activities related to tax justice.

Fraud: Is a deviant behavior on the part of individuals who are part of a society, characterized as a fraudulent or bad-faith act that is practiced with the intention of damaging a third entity, having the intention of obtaining gains and the non- assuming of obligations.

Internal Auditor: Is a professional responsible for observing the internal regulations of its employer, acting independently, maintaining a high standard of moral and functional behavior, reporting any suggestions on possible improvements on control systems or work, aiming to add value and to improve of existing practices.

Materiality: Is a concept that postulates that all information that is liable to influence the decision of users should always be assessed considering the cost-benefit ratio for their production, being material the procedure or value which, evidenced, omitted, or distorted, may alter the basis of the judgment which the information user makes about the value of organization and their tendencies, and that affects the quality of the information delivered.

Tax and Customs Authority: Is an organism of the Portuguese State, depending on the Ministry of Finance, which has the mission to administer taxes, customs duties and other taxes assigned to it, as well as to exercise control of the external border of the European Union and of the national customs territory, for tax purposes, economic and protection of society, enabling the State to redistribute its wealth for public purposes of a financial, economic, and social nature.

Tax Inspector: Is an official of the Tax and Customs Authority, which carries out the necessary steps to ascertain the tax situation of taxpayers, including the investigation of facts and tax situations, the fulfilment of duties and the prevention of violations of tax rules, which must follow the principles of material truth, proportionality, adversarial and cooperation.

Compilation of References

'Information & Cyber Insecurity' are the biggest risk in business operations: FICCI – Pinkerton India Risk Survey 2017. (n.d.). Retrieved from www.ficci.in/pressrelease/2806/india-risk-survey-ficci-press-release.pdf

Abbass, D. A., & Aleqab, M. M. (2013). Internal Auditors ' Characteristics and Audit Fees : Evidence from Egyptian Firms. *International Business Research*, *6*(4), 67–80. doi:10.5539/ibr.v6n4p67

Abbot, A., Parker, S., & Peters, G. (2012). Audit Fee Reductions from Internal Audit-Provided Assistance: The Incremental Impact of Internal Audit Characteristics. *Contemporary Accounting Research*, *29*(1), 94–118. doi:10.1111/j.1911-3846.2011.01072.x

Abbott, L. J., Parker, S., Peters, G. F., & Raghunandan, K. (2003). The Association between Audit Committee Characteristics and Audit Fees. *Auditing*, *22*(2), 17–32. doi:10.2308/aud.2003.22.2.17

Abdul-Rahman, O., Benjamin, A., & Olayinka, O. (2017). Effect of audit fees on audit quality: Evidence from cement manufacturing companies in Nigeria. *European Journal of Accounting. Auditing and Finance Research*, *5*(1), 6–17.

Adarsh Credit Co-op must pass through the acid-test. (2018, May). Retrieved from http://www.indiancooperative.com/banks/adarsh-credit-co-op-must-pass-through-the-acid-test/

Adedayo, O. M., & Olivier, M. S. (2015). Ideal log setting for database forensics reconstruction. *Digital Investigation: The International Journal of Digital Forensics & Incident Response.*, *12*(C), 27–40. doi:10.1016/j.diin.2014.12.002

Adedokun, I. A., & Oyewole, T. (2013). Evaluation of the effect of monitoring and control activities on fraud detection in selected Nigerian commercial banks. *Research Journal of Finance and Accounting*, *4*(6), 57–63.

Adeyemi, S., & Olowookere, J. (2011). Stakeholders' perception of audit performance gap in Nigeria. *International Journal of Accounting and Financial Reporting*, *1*(1), 152–172. doi:10.5296/ijafr.v1i1.808

Adznan, S., & Nelson, S. (2014). Financial instruments disclosure practices: Evidence from Malaysian listed firms. *Procedia: Social and Behavioral Sciences*, *164*, 62–67. doi:10.1016/j.sbspro.2014.11.051

Aerts, W., Van Camppenhout, G., & Van Caneghem, T. (2008). Clustering in dividends: Do managers rely on cognitive reference points? *Journal of Economic Psychology*, *29*(3), 276–284. doi:10.1016/j.joep.2007.10.003

Aggarwal, R., & Simkins, B. (2004). Evidence on voluntary disclosures of derivatives usage by large US companies. *Journal of Derivatives Accounting*, *1*(1), 61–81. doi:10.1142/S0219868104000063

Aghghaleh, S. F., Iskandar, T. M., & Mohamed, Z. M. (2014). Fraud risks factor of fraud triangle and the likelihood of fraud occurrence: Evidence from Malaysia. *Information Management and Business Review*, *6*(1), 1–7.

Akintoye, S., & Adegbite, E. (2017, July). The impact of control fraud on the banking system: evidence from a developing country. *Global Research Institute for Business Academics*. Retrieved from https://www.dora.dmu.ac.uk/handle/2086/14713

Al Rashdi, Z., Dick, M., & Storey, I. (2016). *A Conceptual Framework for Accountability in Cloud Computing Service Provision*. Pearson. Retrieved from http://arxiv.org/abs/1606.03540

Albrecht, W. S., Albrecht, C. O., Albrecht, C. C., & Zimbelman, M. F. (2016). Fraud examination (5th ed.). Mason, OH: South Western Cengage Learning.

Albrecht, C. C., & Zimbelman, M. F. (2012). *Forensic accounting*. South-Western Cengage Learning.

Albrecht, W. S., Albrecht, C. O., Albrecht, C. C., & Zimbelman, M. F. (2016). *Fraud Examination*. Boston, MA: Cengage Learning.

Alcaide-Muñoz, L., Garde-Sánchez, R., & Rodríguez Bolívar, M. P. (2013). La transparencia de las entidades de fiscalización autonómicas en España. Un estudio empírico. *Revista de Control Externo*, *42*, 117–143.

Alcaide-Muñoz, L., Rodríguez-Bolívar, M. P., & López-Hernández, A. M. (2017). Transparency in governments: A meta-analytic review of incentives for digital versus hard-copy public financial disclosures. *American Review of Public Administration*, *47*(5), 550–573. doi:10.1177/0275074016629008

Alçın, S. (2016). A new theme for production: Industry 4.0. *Journal of Life Economics*, *2*, 19–30.

Al-Harshani, M. O. (2008). The pricing of audit services: Evidence from Kuwait. *Managerial Auditing Journal*, *23*(7), 685–696. doi:10.1108/02686900810890643

Ali, A., Heang, L., Mohamad, R., & Ojo, M. (2008). Internship and audit expectation gap among undergraduate students in Universiti Utara Malaysia. *Journal of Financial Reporting & Accounting*, *6*(1), 55–74. doi:10.1108/19852510880000635

Ali, J., Ahmed, M., & Henry, K. (2004). Disclosure compliance with national accounting standards by listed companies in South Asia. *Accounting and Business Research*, *34*(3), 183–199. doi:10.1080/00014788.2004.9729963

Alles, M. G., & Gray, G. L. (2015). *The Pros and Cons of Using Big Data in Auditing: a Synthesis of the Literature and a Research Agenda*. Academic Press.

Alles, G. A. (2015). Drivers of the use and facilitators and obstacles of the evolution of big data by the audit profession. *Accounting Horizons*, *29*(2), 439–449. doi:10.2308/acch-51067

Alles, M. G., Kogan, A., & Vasarhelyi, M. A. (2004). Reply Restoring auditor credibility: Tertiary monitoring and logging of continuous assurance systems. *International Journal of Accounting Information Systems*, *5*(2), 211–212. doi:10.1016/j.accinf.2004.02.008

Alles, M. G., Kogan, A., & Vasarhelyi, M. A. (2008). Putting continuous auditing theory into practice: Lessons from two pilot implementations. *Journal of Information Systems*, *22*(2), 195–214. doi:10.2308/jis.2008.22.2.195

Alles, M. G., Riccio, E. L., Vasarhelyi, M. A., & Tostes, F. (2006). Continuous auditing: The USA experience and considerations for its implementation in brazil. *Journal of Information Systems and Technology Management*, *3*(2), 211–224. doi:10.4301/S1807-17752006000200007

Alles, M., Brennan, G., Kogan, A., & Vasarhelyi, M. A. (2006). Continuous monitoring of business process controls: A pilot implementation of a continuous auditing system at Siemens. *International Journal of Accounting Information Systems*, *7*(2), 137–161. doi:10.1016/j.accinf.2005.10.004

Almeida, B. (2017). Audit role in today's society: The Portuguese perspective. *TÉKHNE - Review of Applied Management Studies*, *15*(1), 42-57.

Almeida, B. (2005). *Auditoria e sociedade: diferenças de expetativas*. Lisboa: Publisher Team.

Almeida, B. (2012). The Portuguese expectation gap: Empirical evidence. *Business and Management Review*, *2*(10), 28–46.

Almeida, B., & Almeida, J. (2011). En torno a las teorías justificativas de la auditoría. *Partida Doble*, *228*, 55–66.

Almeida, B., & Colomina, C. (2009). Evidencia de las diferencias de expectativas en auditoria en mercados bursátiles de reducida dimensión: El caso portugués. *Revista Universo Contábil*, *5*(1), 100–114.

Almeida, J. R. (2000). *Contabilidade de custos para autarquias locais* [Cost accounting for local authorities]. Porto: Vida Económica – Editorial.

Al-Najjar, B. (2018). Corporate governance and audit features: SMEs evidence. *Journal of Small Business and Enterprise Development*, *25*(1), 163–179. doi:10.1108/JSBED-08-2017-0243

Al-Twaijry, A., Brierley, J., & Gwilliam, D. (2004). An examination of the relationship between internal and external audit in the Saudi Arabian corporate sector. *Managerial Auditing Journal*, *19*(7), 924–944.

Al-Twaijry, A. (2017). Internal Audit Quality Evaluation and Reliance Decision: External Auditors' Perception. *International Journal of Economics & Management Sciences*, *6*(5).

Alves, S. (2012). Ownership Structure and Earnings Management: Evidence from Portugal. *Australasian Accounting Business and Finance*, *6*(1), 57–74.

Amaral, D. F. (2007). *Curso de Direito Administrativo* [Course of Administrative Law] (3rd ed.). Coimbra: Almedina.

Amiram, D., Bozanic, Z., & Rouen, E. (2015). Financial Statement Errors: Evidence from the Distributional Properties of Financial Statement Numbers. *Review of Accounting Studies*. Retrieved from http://link.springer.com/article/10.1007/s11142-015-9333-z

Anderson, D., & Chambers, R. (2006). State of the internal audit profession study: Continuous auditing gains momentum. *Pricewaterhouse Coopers*, *30*, 5–12.

Anderson, T., & Zéghal, D. (1994). The Pricing of Audit Services: Further Evidence From the Canadian Market. *Accounting and Business Research*, *24*(95), 195–207. doi:10.1080/00014788.1994.9729479

ANSOL. (2018). *ANSOL - Associação Nacional para o Software Livre*. Retrieved June 16, 2018, from https://ansol.org/

Antonelli, C. (1999). *Localized technological change and the evolution of standards as economic institutions*. Oxford, UK: Oxford University Press. doi:10.1093/0198296045.003.0005

Aparicio, M., & Costa, C. J. (2012). Macroeconomics Leverage Trough Open Source. In *Proceedings of the Workshop on Open Source and Design of Communication* (pp. 19–24). Academic Press. 10.1145/2316936.2316941

Appelbaum, D., Kogan, A., & Vasarhelyi, M. A. (2017). Big Data and Analytics in the Modern Audit Engagement: Research Needs. *Auditing*, *36*(4), 1–27. doi:10.2308/ajpt-51684

Araj, F. G. (2015). Responding to fraud risk: Exploring where internal auditing stands. *IIA Common Body of Knowledge*. Retrieved August 3, 2018 from https://www.iia.nl/SiteFiles/Publicaties/IIARF%20CBOK%20Responding%20to%20Fraud%20Risk%20October%202015.pdf

Araya Leandro, C. E., Caba Pérez, C., & López Hernández, A. M. (2011). Innovation in governmental financial information systems in the central American region: Evidence from Costa Rica. *Innovar (Universidad Nacional de Colombia)*, *21*(41), 111–124.

Archer, J., Boehme, A., Cullinance, D., Puhlmann, N., Kurz, P., & Reavis, J. (2012, December). Security Guidance for Critical Areas of Mobile Computing. *Cloud Security Alliance*, 1–60. doi:10.1017/CBO9781107415324.004

Arens, A. A., Elder, R. J., & Beasley, M. S. (2012). *Auditing and Assurance Servies: An Integrated Approach* (14th ed.). Pearson Prentice Hall.

Arestis, P., Demetriades, P., Fattouh, B., & Mouratidis, K. (2002). The impact of financial liberalisation policies on financial development: Evidence from developing economies. *International Journal of Finance & Economics, 7*(2), 109–121. doi:10.1002/ijfe.181

Arıksoy, G. (2016). *Endüstri 4.0: Akıllı fabrikaların akıllı güvenliği*. Retrieved April 15, 2018, from https://hbrturkiye.com/blog/endustri-4-0-akilli-fabrikalarin-akilli-guvenligi

Aronmwan, E., Ashafoke, T., & Mgbame, C. (2013). Audit firm reputation and audit quality. *European Journal of Business and Management, 5*(7), 66–75.

Asare, S. K., & Wright, A. M. (2004). The effectiveness of alternative risk assessment and program planning tools in a fraud setting. *Contemporary Accounting Research, 21*(2), 325–352. doi:10.1506/L20L-7FUM-FPCB-7BE2

Ashton, K. (2009). That internet of things. *RFID Journal*. Retrieved April 15, 2018, from http://www.rfidjournal.com/articles/view?4986

Aslan, L. (2017). The Determinants of Employee Fraud in Turkish Intermediary Institutions. *1st International Symposium on Economics, Finance and Econometrics. Proceedings, 1*, 170–188.

Asllani, A., & Naco, M. (2014). Using Benford's law for fraud detection in accounting practices. *Journal of Social Science Studies, 1*(2), 129–143. doi:10.5296/jsss.v2i1.6395

Association of Certified Fraud Examiners (ACFE). (2018). Report to the nations on occupational fraud and abuse 2018 global fraud study. Austin, TX: ACFE.

Association of Certified Fraud Examiners. (2010). *2010 Report to the Nations on Occupational Fraud and Abuse*. Austin, TX: ACFE.

Association of Certified Fraud Examiners. (2018). *2018 Report to the Nations: Global study on occupational fraud and abuse*. Association of Certified Fraud Examiners.

Asthana, S., Kalelkar, R., & Raman, K. (2018). Unintended consequences of Big 4 auditor office-level industry specialization. *International Journal of Accounting, Auditing, and Performance Evaluation, 14*(2-3), 254–289. doi:10.1504/IJAAPE.2018.091066

Atici, G., & Gursoy, G. (2011). Financial crises and capital buffer: Evidence from the Turkish banking sector, business perspectives. *Banks and Bank Systems International Research Journal, 6*(1), 72–86.

Attie, W. (2011). *Auditoria: Conceitos e aplicações*. São Paulo: Atlas.

Auditing Database Activity. (2018). Retrieved May 29, 2018, from https://docs.oracle.com/cd/E11882_01/server.112/e10575/tdpsg_auditing.htm

Azevedo, S. R. C. (2014). Auditoria aos municípios estudo de caso – uma aplicação à Área Metropolitana do Porto [Audit to municipalities case study – an application to the Metropolitan Area of Porto]. Master's work project. Porto: Instituto Superior de Contabilidade e Administração do Porto do Politécnico do Porto.

Babatolu, A., Aigienohuwa, O., & Uniamikogbo, E. (2016). Auditor's independence and audit quality: A study of selected deposit money banks in Nigeria. *International Journal of Finance and Accounting, 5*(1), 13–21.

Baffa, A. (2017). The differential effect of auditor type on the value relevance of earnings and book values: Evidence from listed firms in Nigeria. *European Journal of Multidisciplinary Studies, 6*(1), 187–204. doi:10.26417/ejms.v6i1.p187-204

Bagheri, B., Yang, S., Kao, H., & Lee, J. (2015). Cyber-physical systems architecture for self-aware machines in industry 4.0 environment. *IFAC-PapersOnLine*, *48*(3), 1622–1627. doi:10.1016/j.ifacol.2015.06.318

Bailey, K., Bylinski, J., & Shields, M. (1983). Effects of audit report wording changes on the perceived message. *Journal of Accounting Research*, *21*(2), 355–370. doi:10.2307/2490779

Baker, N. (2009). Software trend spotting: Recent IIA survey results show many auditors use software to automate key tasks, though a surprising number have yet to adopt popular tools. *Internal Auditor*, *66*(4), 30–35.

Bamber, E., Bamber, L., & Schoderbeck, M. (1993). Audit structure and other determinants of audit report lag: An empirical analysis. *Auditing*, *12*(1), 1–23.

Bank for International Settlements. (2006). *International convergence of capital measurement and capital standards.* Retrieved August 3, 2018 from https://www.bis.org/publ/bcbs128.htm

Bank for International Settlements. (2012). *The internal audit function in banks.* Retrieved August 3, 2018 from https://www.bis.org/publ/bcbs223.pdf

Bank for International Settlements. (2013). *Basel III: The liquidity coverage ratio and liquidity risk monitoring tools.* Retrieved August 3, 2018 from https://www.bis.org/publ/bcbs238.pdf

Bank for International Settlements. (2015). *Corporate governance principles for banks.* Retrieved August 3, 2018 from https://www.bis.org/bcbs/publ/d328.pdf

Banking Regulation and Supervision Agency. (2005). *Banking law no. 5411.* Retrieved August 3, 2018 from https://www.tbb.org.tr/en/banking-legislation/banking-law/14

Banking Regulation and Supervision Agency. (2006). *Regulation on Banking Regulation and Supervision Agency auditing methods and principles.* Retrieved August 3, 2018 from http://www.mevzuat.gov.tr/Metin.Aspx?MevzuatKod=7.5.10522&MevzuatIliski=0&sourceXmlSearch=denetleme%20kurumu%20taraf%C4%B1ndan

Banking Regulation and Supervision Agency. (2011). *Regulation on outsourced activities of banks.* Retrieved August 3, 2018 from http://www.mevzuat.gov.tr/Metin.Aspx?MevzuatKod=7.5.15481&MevzuatIliski=0&sourceXmlSearch=destek%20hizmeti

Banking Regulation and Supervision Agency. (2014). *Regulation on internal systems and internal capital adequacy evaluation process of banks.* Retrieved August 3, 2018 from http://www.mevzuat.gov.tr/Metin.Aspx?MevzuatKod=7.5.19864&MevzuatIliski=0&sourceXmlSearch=i%C3%A7%20sistemleri

Barabesi, L., Cerasa, A., Cerioli, A., & Perrotta, D. (2018). Goodness-of-Fit Testing for the Newcomb-Benford Law With Application to the Detection of Customs Fraud. *Journal of Business & Economic Statistics*, *36*(2), 346–358. doi:10.1080/07350015.2016.1172014

Barako, D., Hancock, P., & Izan, H. (2006). Factors influencing voluntary corporate disclosure by Kenyan companies. *Corporate Governance*, *14*(2), 107–125. doi:10.1111/j.1467-8683.2006.00491.x

Barker, E. & Roginsky, A. (2015). *Transitions: Recommendation for Transitioning the Use of Cryptographic Algorithms and Key Lengths.* NIST Special Publication 800-131A.

Barney, B. J., & Schulzke, K. S. (2016). Moderating "Cry Wolf" Events with Excess MAD in Benford's Law Research and Practice. *Journal of Forensic Accounting Research*, *1*(1), A66–A90. doi:10.2308/jfar-51622

Baron, C., Johnson, D., Searfoss, D., & Smith, C. (1977). Uncovering corporate irregularities: Are we closing the expectation gap? *Journal of Accountancy*, *144*(4), 56–66.

Barsky, N. P., Catanach, A. H., & Rhoades-Catanach, S. C. (2003). Analyst tools for detecting financial reporting fraud. *Commercial Lending Review*, *18*(5), 31–36.

Base AML Index Report. (2017). Retrieved from https://index.baselgovernance.org/sites/index/documents/Basel_AML_Index_Report_2017.pdf

Basir, S. A., Davies, J., Douglas, J., & Douglas, A. (2017). The influence of academic culture on quality management system ISO 9001 maintenance within Malaysian universities. *Journal of Higher Education Policy and Management*, *39*(3), 320–340. doi:10.1080/1360080X.2017.1298199

Batista, M., Costa, C. J., & Aparicio, M. (2013). ERP OS Localization Framework. In *Proceedings of the Workshop on Open Source and Design of Communication* (pp. 1–8). New York: ACM. 10.1145/2503848.2503849

Baur, A. W. (2017). Harnessing the social web to enhance insights into people's opinions in business, government and public administration. *Information Systems Frontiers*, *19*(2), 231–251. doi:10.100710796-016-9681-7

Bayesian networks - an introduction. (2018). Retrieved May 29, 2018, from https://www.bayesserver.com/docs/introduction/bayesian-networks

Beasley, M. S. (1996). An Empirical Analysis of the Relation Between the Board of Director Composition and Financial Statement Fraud. *The Accounting Review*, *71*(4), 443–465.

Beattie, A. (2017). *The pioneers of financial fraud*. Retrieved August 3, 2018 from https://www.investopedia.com/articles/financial-theory/09/history-of-fraud.asp

Bendovschi, A. C., & Ionescu, B. Ş. (2015). The gap between cloud computing technology and the audit and information security supporting standards and regulations. *Audit Financiar*, *5*(125), 115–121.

Beneish, M. D. & Nichols, D. C. (2007). *The Predictable Cost of Earnings Manipulation*. SSRN-id1006840

Beneish, M. (1999). Incentive and penalties related to earnings overstatements that violate GAAP. *The Accounting Review*, *74*(4), 425–457. doi:10.2308/accr.1999.74.4.425

Beneish, M. D., Billings, M. B., & Hodder, L. D. (2008). Internal control weaknesses and information uncertainty. *The Accounting Review*, *83*(3), 665–703. doi:10.2308/accr.2008.83.3.665

Benford, F. (1938). The law of anomalous numbers. *Proceedings of the American Philosophical Society*, *78*(4), 551–572.

Berger, A. N., & Espinosa-Vega, M. A. (2005). *Debt maturity, risk and asymmetric information*. Retrieved June 4, 2007 from http://www.imf.org/external/pubs/ft/wp/2005/wp05201.pdf

Bertot, J. C., Jaeger, P. T., & Grimes, J. M. (2010). Using ICTs to create a culture of transparency: E-government and social media as openness and anti-corruption tools for societies. *Government Information Quarterly*, *27*(3), 264–271. doi:10.1016/j.giq.2010.03.001

Bharati, P., Lee, I., Chaudhury, A., Qureshi, S., Kamal, M., & Wolcott, P. (2009). Information technology interventions for growth and competitiveness in micro-enterprises. *International Journal of E-Business Research*, *5*(1), 117–140. doi:10.4018/jebr.2009010106

Bhasin, M. (2013). Corporate Accounting Scandal at Satyam: A Case Study of India's Enron. *European Journal of Business and Social Sciences*, *1*(12), 25–47.

Biegelman, M. T., & Bartow, J. T. (2015). *Executive roadmap to fraud prevention and internal control: Creating a culture of compliance* (2nd ed.). John Wiley and Sons.

Bircan, G. (2017). *Nesnelerin interneti nedir?* Retrieved April 15, 2018, from https://www.voltimum.com.tr/haberler/nesnelerin-interneti-ve-kullanim

Birt, J., Rankin, M., & Song, C. (2013). Derivatives use and financial instrument disclosure in the extractives industry. *Accounting and Finance*, *53*(1), 55–83. doi:10.1111/acfi.12001

Blanco, H., & Bustos, B. (2004). *Normalización y comercio sustentable en Sudamérica* [Standardization and sustainable trade in South America]. Santiago de Chile: RIDES.

Blind, K. (2004). *The economics of standards: Theory, evidence, policy.* Edward Elgar Publishing.

Bliss, M. A. (2011). Does CEO Duality Constrain Board Independence? Some Evidence From Audit Pricing. *Accounting and Finance*, *51*(2), 361–380. doi:10.1111/j.1467-629X.2010.00360.x

Boolaky, P. K., & Soobaroyen, T. (2017). Adoption of International Standards on Auditing (ISA): Do institutional factors matter? *International Journal of Auditing*, *1*(21), 59–81. doi:10.1111/ijau.12081

Bousquet, A., & Dubiel-Teleszynski, T. (2017). Operational Risk Module of the Top-Down Stress Test Framework. *Satellite Models*, 95-103.

Boynton, W. C., Johnson, R. N., & Kell, W. G. (2003). *Modern auditing* (7th ed.). New York: John Willey & Sons Inc.

Bozkurt, N. (2009). *Isletmelerin kara deligi hile*. Istanbul: Alfa.

Brandas, C., Megan, O., & Didraga, O. (2015). Global Perspectives on Accounting Information Systems: Mobile and Cloud Approach. *Procedia Economics and Finance*, *20*(15), 88–93. doi:10.1016/S2212-5671(15)00051-9

Braun, R. L., & Davis, H. E. (2003). Computer-assisted audit tools and techniques: Analysis and perspectives. *Managerial Auditing Journal*, *18*(9), 725–731. doi:10.1108/02686900310500488

Breesch, D., & Branson, J. (2009). The effects of auditor gender on audit quality. *The IUP Journal of Accounting Research & Audit Practices*, *8*(3-4), 78–107.

Bresnahan, T., & Greenstein, S. (2014). Mobile Computing: The Next Platform Rivalry. *The American Economic Review*, *104*(5), 475–480. doi:10.1257/aer.104.5.475

Brian, C. (2002). *Defining Digital Forensic Examination and Analysis Tools.* Presented at The Digital Forensic Research Conference DFRWS 2002 USA, Syracuse, NY. Retrieved May 29, 2018, from https://www.dfrws.org/

Brown, V.L., Daugherty, B.E. & Persellin, J.S. (2014). Satyam Fraud: A Case Study of India's Enron. *Issues in Accounting Education*, *29*(3), 419-442. doi:10.2308/iace-50735

Brown, C. E., Wong, J. A., & Baldwin, A. A. (2007). A Review and Analysis of the Existing Research Streams in Continuous Auditing. *Journal of Emerging Technologies in Accounting*, *4*(1), 1–28. doi:10.2308/jeta.2007.4.1.1

Brown-Liburd, H., Issa, H., & Lombardi, D. (2015). Behavioral implications of big data's impact on audit judgment and decision making and future research directions. *Accounting Horizons*, *29*(2), 451–468. doi:10.2308/acch-51023

Brunsson, N., & Jacobsson, B. (2000). The contemporary expansion of standardization. In N. Brunsson & B. Jacobsson (Eds.), *A world of standards* (pp. 1–17). Oxford, UK: Oxford University Press.

Brunsson, N., & Sahlin-Andersson, K. (2000). Constructing organizations: The example of public sector reform. *Organization Studies*, *21*(4), 721–746. doi:10.1177/0170840600214003

Buckhoff, T. A. (2002). Preventing employee fraud by minimizing opportunity. *The CPA Journal*, *72*(5), 64–66.

Buddhakulsomsiri, J., & Parthanadee, P. (2008). Stratified ransom sampling for estimating billing accuracy in health care systems. *Health Care Management Science, 11*(1), 41–54. doi:10.100710729-007-9023-x

Bulut, C. (2017). *Bulut bilişim (cloud computing) nedir?* Retrieved April 15, 2018, from http://www.endustri40.com/bulut-bilisim-cloud-computing-nedir

Bulut, E., & Akçacı, T. (2017). Industry 4.0 and within the scope of innovation indicators analysis of Turkey. *ASSAM International Refereed Journal, 7*, 50–72.

Busta, B., & Sundheim, R. (1992). *Tax return numbers tend to obey Benford's law* (Working Paper No. W93-106-94). Center for Business Research, St. Cloud State University.

Busta, B., & Weinberg, R. (1998). Using Benford's law and neural networks as a review procedure. *Managerial Auditing Journal, 13*(6), 356–366. doi:10.1108/02686909810222375

Byrnes, P. E., Ames, B., & Vasarhelyi, M. (2015). The current state of continuous auditing and continuous monitoring. *Audit Analytics and Continuous Audit: Looking Toward the Future*, 53–70.

Byrnes, P. E., Criste, T. R., Stewart, T. R., & Vasarhelyi, M. (2015). Reimagining auditing in a wired world. *Audit Analytics and Continuous Audit: Looking Toward the Future*, 87–103.

Caba Pérez, C., & López Hernández, A. M. (2007). Latin-American public administration reporting: Recent and future development. *Public Administration and Development, 27*(2), 139–157. doi:10.1002/pad.441

Caba Pérez, C., & López Hernández, A. M. (2009). Governmental financial transparency in MERCOSUR member countries. *International Review of Administrative Sciences, 75*(1), 169–181. doi:10.1177/0020852308099511

Caba Pérez, C., López Hernández, A. M., & Ortiz Rodríguez, D. (2009). Governmental financial information reforms and changes in the political systems: The Argentina, Chile and Paraguay experience. *Public Administration and Development, 29*(5), 429–440. doi:10.1002/pad.551

Caba Pérez, C., Rodríguez Bolívar, M. P., & López Hernández, A. M. (2008). E-Government process and incentives for online public financial information. *Online Information Review, 32*(3), 379–400. doi:10.1108/14684520810889682

Caba, C., López, A. M., & Rodríguez, M. P. (2005). Citizens' access to on-line governmental financial information: Practices in the European Union countries. *Government Information Quarterly, 22*(2), 258–276. doi:10.1016/j.giq.2005.02.002

Cahan, S., & Sun, J. (2015). The effect of audit experience on audit fees and audit quality. *Journal of Accounting, Auditing & Finance, 30*(1), 78–100. doi:10.1177/0148558X14544503

Calder, A. (2008). *Governo das sociedades: A Pratical Guide to the Legal Frameworks and International Codes of Practice*. London: Kogan Page Limited.

Cameron, A. (1993). Do chartered accountants live up to small business expectation? *Accountants Journal, 72*, 76–78.

Campa, D. (2013). Big 4 fee premium" and audit quality: Latest evidence from UK listed companies. *Managerial Auditing Journal, 28*(8), 680–707. doi:10.1108/MAJ-11-2012-0784

Canedo, J., Guedes, O., & Monteiro, A. (2009). *Manual de auditoria tributária*. Lisboa: Direcção-Geral dos Impostos.

Cao, Y., & Lu, Y. (2018). (in press). The individual characteristics of board members and internal control weakness: Evidence from China. *Pacific-Basin Finance Journal.*

Capital Market Licensing Registry and Training Institution. (2018). *Exam subjects and subtitles.* Retrieved August 3, 2018 from https://www.spl.com.tr/spl/eep/kurumportal/Content/sinav-konulari-ve-alt-konu-basliklari/53/

Capital Markets Board of Turkey. (1982). *Regulation on organization, tasks and working principles of Capital Markets Board*. Retrieved August 3, 2018 from http://www.mevzuat.gov.tr/MevzuatMetin/3.5.84644.pdf

Capital Markets Board of Turkey. (2003). *Communiqué on principles regarding the internal auditing systems of brokerage houses serial V no 68*. Retrieved August 3, 2018 from http://www.cmb.gov.tr/SiteApps/Teblig/File/252

Capital Markets Board of Turkey. (2012). *Capital market law no. 6263*. Retrieved August 3, 2018 from http://www.cmb.gov.tr/Sayfa/Dosya/87

Capital Markets Board of Turkey. (2013a). *Communiqué on portfolio management companies and activities of such companies serial III-55.1*. Retrieved August 3, 2018 from http://www.cmb.gov.tr/SiteApps/Teblig/File/472

Capital Markets Board of Turkey. (2013b). *Communiqué on principles of establishment and activities of investment firms serial III-39.1*. Retrieved August 3, 2018 from http://www.cmb.gov.tr/SiteApps/Teblig/File/510

Capital Markets Board of Turkey. (2014). *Communiqué on principles regarding licensing and record keeping for those engaged in capital market activities serial VII-128.7*. Retrieved August 3, 2018 from http://www.cmb.gov.tr/SiteApps/Teblig/File/511

Caplan, D. (1999). Internal controls and the detection of management fraud. *Journal of Accounting Research*, *37*(1), 101–117. doi:10.2307/2491398

Capriotti, R. J. (2014). Big Data Bringing Big Changes to Accounting. *Pennsylvania CPA Journal*, 1–3.

Carcello, J. V., Hermanson, D. R., Neal, T. L., & Riley, R. A. Jr. (2002). Board Characteristics and Audit Fees. *Contemporary Accounting Research*, *19*(3), 365–384. doi:10.1506/CHWK-GMQ0-MLKE-K03V

Carey, M., & Hrycay, M. (2001). Parameterizing credit risk models with rating data. *Journal of Banking & Finance*, *25*(1), 197–270. doi:10.1016/S0378-4266(00)00124-2

Carlin, S., & Curran, K. (2011). Cloud Computing Security. *International Journal of Ambient Computing and Intelligence*, *3*(1), 14–19. doi:10.4018/jaci.2011010102

Carslaw, C. (1988). Anomalies in income numbers: Evidence of goal-oriented behavior. *The Accounting Review*, *63*(2), 321–327.

Carvalho, R. (2013). Auditoria da Administração Pública – Factores de risco mais comuns na Administração Pública [Audit of Public Administration – Most common risk factors in Public Administration]. Visual Projection, Master's in Auditing, Edition 2013-2015. Porto: Instituto Superior de Contabilidade e Administração do Porto do Politécnico do Porto.

Castells, A. R., Sanz, F. L., & Chiner, N. L. (2013). Corporate Boards in Spain. In P. Davies, K. J. Hopt, R. Nowak, & G. Van Solinge (Eds.), *Corporate Boards in Law and Practice: A Comparative Analysis in Europe* (pp. 549–616). New York: Oxford University Press. doi:10.1093/acprof:oso/9780198705154.003.0008

Catanach, A. H., & Rhoades-Catanach, S. (2003). Enron : A Financial Reporting Failure. *Villanova Law Review*, *48*(4), 1057–1076.

Çelen, S. (2017). Industry 4.0 and simulation. *International Journal of 3D Printing Technologies and Digital Industry*, *1*, 9-26.

CEOROC. (2011). Diário da República Portuguesa N.º 198, 2ª Série.

Chalmers, K., & Godfrey, J. (2004). Reputation costs: The impetus for voluntary derivative financial instrument reporting. *Accounting, Organizations and Society*, *29*(2), 95–125. doi:10.1016/S0361-3682(02)00034-X

Chalmers, K., Hay, D., & Khlif, H. (2018). (in press). Internal control in accounting research: A review. *Journal of Accounting Literature*. doi:10.1016/j.acclit.2018.03.002

Chan, D. Y., & Vasarhelyi, M. A. (2011). Innovation and practice of continuous auditing. *International Journal of Accounting Information Systems*, *12*(2), 152–160. doi:10.1016/j.accinf.2011.01.001

Chan, D. Y., & Vasarhelyi, M. A. (2018). Innovation and Practice of Continuous Auditing. In D. Y. Chan, V. Chiu, & M. A. Vasarhelyi (Eds.), *Continuous Auditing* (pp. 271–283). Emerald Publishing Limited. doi:10.1108/978-1-78743-413-420181013

Chan, Y., & Walter, T. (1996). Qualified audit reports and costly contracting. *Asia Pacific Journal of Management*, *13*(1), 37–63. doi:10.1007/BF01739681

Chen, C., Su, X., Zhao, R., & Kong, C. U. H. (2000). An emerging market's reaction to initial modified audit opinions: Evidence for the Shanghai Stock Exchange. *Contemporary Accounting Research*, *17*(3), 429–455. doi:10.1506/GCJP-5599-QUWB-G86D

Cheng, C., & Flasher, R. (2018). Two short case studies in staff auditor and student ethical decision making. *Issues in Accounting Education*, *33*(1), 45–52. doi:10.2308/iace-51881

Chen, M. C., Wang, R. J., & Chen, A. P. (2007). An empirical study for the detection of corporate financial anomaly using outlier mining techniques. *2007 International Conference on Convergence Information Technology, ICCIT 2007*, 612–617. 10.1109/ICCIT.2007.237

Chiang, H., & Lin, S. (2012). Auditor's industry specialization and disclosure quality of IAS No. 39 -Related accounts. *Journal of Applied Finance & Banking*, *2*(2), 59–98.

Chiu, V., Liu, Q., & Vasarhelyi, M. A. (2014). The development and intellectual structure of continuous auditing research. *Journal of Accounting Literature*, *33*(1–2), 37–57. doi:10.1016/j.acclit.2014.08.001

Chi, W., Myers, L., Omer, T., & Xie, H. (2017). The effects of audit partner pre-client and client-specific experience on audit quality and on perceptions of audit quality. *Review of Accounting Studies*, *22*(1), 361–391. doi:10.100711142-016-9376-9

Chou, D. C. (2015). Cloud computing risk and audit issues. *Computer Standards & Interfaces*, *42*, 137–142. doi:10.1016/j.csi.2015.06.005

Cicatiello, L., De Simone, E., & Gaeta, G. L. (2017). Political determinants of fiscal transparency: A panel data empirical investigation. *Economics of Governance*, *18*(4), 315–336. doi:10.100710101-017-0192-x

Código das Sociedades Comerciais (CSC), Decreto-Lei n.o 262/1986 de 2 de Setembro da Assembleia da Républica. Diário da República: I série, No 201 (1986).

Cohen, J., Krishnamoorthy, R., & Wright, A. (2010). Corporate governance in the post-Sarbanes-Oxley era: Auditors' experiences. *Contemporary Accounting Research*, *27*(3), 751–786. doi:10.1111/j.1911-3846.2010.01026.x

Colbert, G., & Murray, D. (1998). The association between auditor quality and auditor size: An analysis of small CPA firms. *Journal of Accounting, Auditing & Finance*, *13*(2), 135–150. doi:10.1177/0148558X9801300203

Committee of Sponsoring Organizations (COSO). (2013, April). *Internal control-integrated framework COSO*. Retrieved from http://www.coso.org

Committee of Sponsoring Organizations of the Treadway Commission (COSO). (2013). *Internal Control – Integrated Framework*. New York: COSO.

Committee of Sponsoring Organizations of the Treadway Commission. (2017). *Enterprise risk management integrating with strategy and performance*. Available at https://www.coso.org/Documents/2017-COSO-ERM-Integrating-with-Strategy-and-Performance-Executive-Summary.pdf

Conger, J. A., Finegold, D., & Lawler, E. E. (1998). Appraising Boardroom performance. *Harvard Business Review*, *76*(1), 136–148. PMID:10176916

Conheady, B., McIlkenny, P., Opong, K. K., & Pignatel, I. (2015). Board effectiveness and firm performance of Canadian listed firms. *The British Accounting Review*, *47*(3), 290–303. doi:10.1016/j.bar.2014.02.002

Conkar, K., Keskin, A., & Kayahan, C. (2009). Banking crises and financial system in Turkey. *Journal of Modern Accounting and Auditing*, *5*(7), 21–34.

Connoly, R. (2017). *Toshiba faces fresh $400m lawsuit over historic accounting scandal*. Retrieved from https://www.theneweconomy.com/business/toshiba-faces-fresh-400m-lawsuit-over-historic-accounting-scandal

Co-operative Act. 1993 (Amendment). (2012). Laws of Malaysia. In The M. Commissioner of Law Revision (Ed.), Act 502. Kuala Lumpur: Percetakan Nasional Malaysia Berhad.

Coram, P., Ferguson, C., & Moroney, R. (2008). Internal audit, alternative internal audit structures and the level of misappropriation of assets fraud. *Accounting and Finance*, *48*, 543–559.

Corkern, S. M., Kimmel, S. B., & Morehead, B. (2015). Accountants Need To Be Prepared For The Big Question : Should I Move To The Cloud? *International Journal of Management & Information Systems*, *19*(1), 13–20.

Costa, C. (2017). *Auditoria financeira: Teoria e* prática. Lisboa: Rei dos Livros.

Costa, C. J., & Aparicio, M. (2006). Organizational Tools in the Web: ERP Open Source. In *Proceedings of the IADIS International Conference on WWW/Internet* (pp. 401–408). Academic Press.

Costa, C. (2007). In C. J. Costa (Ed.), *"ERP Open Source," in Information Technology, Organizations and Teams* (pp. 159–170)., press.itml.org

Costa, C. J. (2010). Testing Usability of ERP Open Source Systems. In *Proceedings of the Workshop on Open Source and Design of Communication* (pp. 25–30). New York: ACM. 10.1145/1936755.1936763

Costa, F. (2011). *Mensuração e desenvolvimento de escalas: aplicações em administração*. Rio de Janeiro: Ciência Moderna.

Costa, R., Serra, S., & Gomes, P. (2013). Fatores determinantes da opinião do auditor: estudo empírico das empresas portuguesas, *Proceedings of XIV Congresso Internacional de Contabilidade e Auditoria.*

CPE. (2016). *Auditing cloud computing security*. Retrieved April 15, 2018, from http://www.cpeinteractive.com/session/cloud/

Craswell, A., Francis, J., & Taylor, S. (1995). Auditor brand name reputations and industry specializations. *Journal of Accounting and Economics*, *20*(3), 297–322. doi:10.1016/0165-4101(95)00403-3

Cressey, D. R. (1953). *Other people's money: The social psychology of embezzlement*. New York: The Free Press.

Cressey, D. R. (1973). *Other people's money*. Montclair: Patterson Smith.

Cristobal, E. de las H., Ucieda, J. L., & Navallas, B. (2011). Law, Corporate Governance, and Accounting: European Perspectives. New York: Routledge.

Crook, S. K., & Hopkins, S. (2013). *SAP Enterprise Mobility: Bringing a Cohesive Approach to a Complex Market*. Academic Press.

Cruz, N. F., & Sousa, L. (2014). *Local integrity system assessment Portugal*. Lisboa: TIAC.

Cukier, K., & Mayer-Schoenberger, V. (2014). The Rise of Big Data. *Foreign Affairs*, *92*(3), 28–40.

Cynthia, H. (2005). Analysis ratios for detecting Financial Statement fraud. *ACFE Fraud Magazine*. Retrieved from http://www.fraud-magazine.com/article.aspx?id=4294967726

Da Costa, G. P. C. & Dutra, T. A. G. L. (2014). Financial audit the era of big data: New possibilities for evaluating and responding to risks in financial statements of the federal government. *Revista do TCU*, 54-61.

Da Silva, A. S. C. D. (2013). *The Application of Benford's Law in detecting accounting fraud in the financial sector* (Unpublished Masters Dissertation). Lisboa School of Economics and Management Lisbon, Portugal.

Dai, J., & Vasarhelyi, M. A. (2016). Imagineering audit 4.0. *Journal of Emerging Technologies in Accounting*, *13*(1), 1–15. doi:10.2308/jeta-10494

Darus, F., & Taylor, D. (2009). Influences of proprietary and political costs on voluntary disclosure relating to financial instruments before and after mandatory requirements. *Corporate Ownership and Control*, *6*(4), 391–406. doi:10.22495/cocv6i4c3p5

Das, S., & Zhang, H. (2003). Rounding-up in reported EPS, behavioral thresholds, and earnings management. *Journal of Accounting and Economics*, *35*(1), 31–50. doi:10.1016/S0165-4101(02)00096-4

David Coderre. (2015). *Global technology audit guide (GTAG) 3: Continuous auditing: coordinating continuous auditing and monitoring to provide continuous assurance* (2nd ed.). The Institute of Internal Auditors.

de Renzio, P., & Krafchik, W. (2007). *Lessons from the field: The impact of civil society budget analysis and advocacy in six countries*. Washington, DC: International Budget Project.

De Sousa, L. (2010). *A corrupção participada em Portugal 2004-2008. Resultados globais de uma pesquisa em curso*. Lisboa: PGR/DCIAP and CIES-ISCTE.

Debreceny, R. S., & Gray, G. L. (2011). Data Mining of Electronic Mail and Auditing: A Research Agenda. *Journal of Information Systems*, *25*(2), 195–226. doi:10.2308/isys-10167

Decree-Law No. 117/2011 of 15 December. Portuguese Republic Journal No. 239, 1st Serie.

Decree-Law No. 118/2011 of 15 December. Portuguese Republic Journal No. 239, 1st Serie.

Decree-Law No. 398/1998 of 17 December. Portuguese Republic Journal No. 290, 1st Serie.

Decree-Law No. 413/1998 of 31 December. Portuguese Republic Journal No. 301, 1st Serie.

DeFond, M. (1992). The association between changes in client firm agency costs and auditor switching. *Auditing*, *11*(1), 16–31.

DeFond, M. L., & Francis, J. R. (2005). Audit research after Sarbanes-Oxley. *Auditing*, *24*(Suppl.), 5–30.

Deloitte. (2010). *Continuous monitoring and continuous auditing: From idea to implementation*. Retrieved from https://www2.deloitte.com/content/dam/Deloitte/uy/Documents/audit/Monitoreo continuo y auditoria continua.pdf

Deming, W. (1989). *Calidad, productividad y competitividad. La salida de la crisis* [Quality, productivity and competitiveness. The way out of the crisis]. Madrid: Díaz de Santos.

Depoers, F. (2000). A cost-benefit study of voluntary disclosure: Some empirical evidence from French listed companies. *European Accounting Review*, *9*(2), 245–263. doi:10.1080/09638180050129891

Desai, V., Roberts, R. & Srivastava, R. (2010). An Analytical Model for External Auditor Evaluation of the Internal Audit Function Using Belief Functions. *Contemporary Accounting Research*, *27*(2), 346. doi:10.1111/j.1911-3846.2010.01023_4.x

Desender, K. A., Aguilera, R. V., Crespi, R., & García-Cestona, M. (2013). When Does Ownership Matter? Board Characteristics and Behavior. *Strategic Management Journal*, *34*(7), 823–842. doi:10.1002mj.2046

Deutsch, Y. (2005). The impact of board composition on firms' critical decisions: A meta-analytic review. *Journal of Management*, *31*(3), 424–444. doi:10.1177/0149206304272185

Devi, A., & Devi, S. (2014). Audit expectation gap between auditors and users of financial statements. *European Journal of Business and Management*, *6*(14), 75–82.

Dhaliwal, D. S. (1980). The effect of firm's capital structure on the choice of accounting methods. *The Accounting Review*, *LV*(1), 78–84.

Dias, A. (2006). *A Auditoria e a Tomada de Decisão*. Paper presented at the XI Congresso Internacional de Contabilidade e Auditoria, Coimbra.

Dias, A. (2009). Quality management systems for global business as a competitive advantage. Journal Many faces of Innovation – from literature synthesis to empirical studies, 78-103.

Dias, A. (2010). Quality management systems for globally competing. *Revista de Gestão e Sustentabilidade – Portuguese Review of Management and Sustainability*, *1*, 79-96.

Dias, A. (2013). *Diffusion and efficiency of ISO standards within the European Union: A qualitative and quantitative analysis in Portuguese organizations* (PhD Thesis). Proquest LLC UMI 3570823.

Dias, A. (2014). *Diffusion and efficiency of ISO 9000 standards in EU*. Lambert Academic Publishers.

Dias, A. (2017). A more effective audit after COSO ERM 2017 or after ISO 31000:2009? *Perspectiva Empresarial*, *4*(2), 73–82. doi:10.16967/rpe.v4n2a7

Dias, A., & Lima, L. (2010). Quality systems for global business as a competitive advantage. In T. Riihelä & M. Mattila (Eds.), *Many faces of Innovation – from literature synthesis to empirical studies* (pp. 78–103). Hyvinkaa, Finland: Laurea University of Applied Sciences.

Dimitriu, O., & Matei, M. (2014). A New Paradigm for Accounting through Cloud Computing. *Procedia Economics and Finance*, *15*(14), 840–846. doi:10.1016/S2212-5671(14)00541-3

Din, J. (2006). *Applying data envelopment analysis to evaluate the efficiency of fishermen associations in Malaysia* (PhD thesis). University Putra Malaysia, Selangor, Malaysia.

Dixon, R., Woodhead, A., & Soliman, M. (2006). An investigation of the expectation gap in Egypt. *Managerial Auditing Journal*, *21*(3), 293–302. doi:10.1108/02686900610653026

Doelitzscher, F. H. (2014). *Security audit compliance for cloud computing* (Doctoral Dissertation). Plymouth University, School of Computing, Communication & Electronics.

Donelson, D. C., Ege, M. S., & McInnis, J. M. (2017). Internal control weaknesses and financial reporting fraud. *Auditing*, *36*(3), 45–69. doi:10.2308/ajpt-51608

Dorminey, J., Fleming, A. S., Kranacher, M. J., Richard, A., & Riley, J. (2012). The evolution of fraud theory. *Issues in Accounting Education, 27*(2), 555–579. doi:10.2308/iace-50131

Drake, P. W. (1989). *The money doctor in the Andes: US advisers, investors, and economic reform during the Kemmerer missions, 1923-1933.* Durham, NC: Duke University Press.

Dreher, A., Herz, B., & Kard, V. (2005). *Is there a causal link between currency debt crises?* Retrieved June 4, 2007 from http://papers.ssrn.com/sol3/papers.cfm?abstract_id=528063

Drucker, P. (1986). *Managing for results.* New York: Harper & Row.

Duffie, D., & Singleton, K. J. (2003). *Credit risk pricing, measurement and management.* Princeton.

Du, H., & Roohani, S. (2007). Meeting Challenges and Expectations of Continuous Auditing in the Context of Independent Audits of Financial Statements. *International Journal of Auditing, 11*(2), 133–146. doi:10.1111/j.1099-1123.2007.00359.x

Duncan, B., & Whittington, M. (2016). Enhancing Cloud Security and Privacy: The Cloud Audit Problem. *Cloud Computing 2016: The Seventh International Conference on Cloud Computing, GRIDs, and Virtualization*, 119–124.

Duncan, B., & Whittington, M. (2016). Cloud cyber-security: Empowering the audit trail. *International Journal on Advances in Security, 9*(3&4), 169–183.

Duncan, J. B., Flesher, D. L., & Stocks, M. H. (1999). Internal control systems in US churches: An examination of the effects of church size and domination on systems of internal control. *Accounting, Auditing & Accountability Journal, 12*(2), 142–163. doi:10.1108/09513579910270084

Dunn, K., & Mayhew, B. (2004). Audit firm industry specialization and client disclosure quality. *Review of Accounting Studies, 9*(1), 35–58. doi:10.1023/B:RAST.0000013628.49401.69

Duréndez, A. (2003). The usefulness of the audit report in investment and financing decisions. *Managerial Auditing Journal, 18*(6/7), 549–559. doi:10.1108/02686900310482687

Durtschi, C., Hillison, W., & Pacini, C. (2004). The effective use of Benford's Law to assist in detecting fraud in accounting data. *Journal of Forensic Accounting, 5*, 17–34.

EBSO. (2015). *Sanayi 4.0.* Ege Bölgesi Sanayiler Odası Araştırma Müdürlüğü. Retrieved April 15, 2018, from http://www.ebso.org.tr/ebsomedia/documents/sanayi-40_88510761.pdf

Ed, M., & Craig, G. (2017). *Create a Server Audit and Database Audit Specification.* Retrieved May 29, 2018, from https://docs.microsoft.com/en-us/sql/relational- databases/security/auditing/create-a-server-audit-and-database-audit-specification?view=sql-server-2017

Edge, W. R., & Farley, A. A. (1991). External auditor evaluation of the internal audit function. *Accounting and Finance, 31*(1), 69–83. doi:10.1111/j.1467-629X.1991.tb00254.x

Eisenhardt, K. (1989). Agency theory: An assessment and review. *Academy of Management Review, 14*(1), 57–74. doi:10.5465/amr.1989.4279003

Elad, F. (2017). *The Impact of Audit Education on the Audit Expectation Gap Evidence from Civilekonom Students in Sweden* (Business Administration Master's Thesis). Karlstand University, Karlstad.

Elefterie, L., & Badea, G. (2016). The impact of information technology on the audit process. *Economics, Management and Financial Markets, 11*(1), 303–309. Retrieved from http://www.addletonacademicpublishers.com/economics-management-and-financial-markets

Enes, E. (2013). *A educação como contributo para a redução das diferenças de expectativas em auditoria: o caso Português* (Unpublished Master's Thesis). Instituto Politécnico de Tomar, Tomar.

Engel, E., Hayes, R. M., & Wang, X. (2010). Audit Committee Compensation and the Demand for Monitoring of the Financial Reporting Process. *Journal of Accounting and Economics, 49*(1-2), 136–154. doi:10.1016/j.jacceco.2009.08.001

Enofe, A., Mgbane, C., Aronmwan, E., & Ogbeide, I. (2013). Audit reasonableness expectation gap: Users' perception in Nigeria. *International Journal of Business and Social Research, 3*(3), 154–163.

Epstein, M., & Geiger, M. (1994). Investor views of audit assurance: Recent evidence of the expectation gap. *Journal of Accountancy, 177*(1), 60–66.

Ernst and Young. (2015). Big data and analytics in the audit process. *BoardMatters Quarterly, 9*, 6–9.

Erturan, E. İ., & Ergin, E. (2017). Internet of things in auditing: Inventory cycle. *The Journal of Accounting and Finance, 75*, 13–30.

ESOP. (2018). *ESOP - Associação de Empresas de Software Open Source Portuguesas.* Retrieved June 1, 2018, from http://www.esop.pt/

Estevez, E., Fillottrani, P., Janowski, T., & Ojo, A. (2012). Government information sharing. In Y.-C. Chen & P.-Y. Chu (Eds.), *Electronic governance and cross-boundary collaboration* (pp. 23–55). Hershey, PA: IGI Global. doi:10.4018/978-1-60960-753-1.ch002

European Confederation of Institutes of Internal Auditing. (2007). *The role of internal audit in corporate governance in Europe : current status, necessary improvements, future tasks.* Berlin: Erich Schmidt Verlag.

Evans, L. (2003). Auditing and audit firms in Germany before 1931. *The Accounting Historians Journal, 30*(2), 29–65. doi:10.2308/0148-4184.30.2.29

Fadzil, F. H., Haron, H., & Jantan, M. (2005). Internal auditing practices and internal control system. *Managerial Auditing Journal, 20*(8), 844–866. doi:10.1108/02686900510619683

Fadzly, M., & Ahmad, Z. (2004). Audit expectation gap: The case of Malaysia. *Managerial Auditing Journal, 19*(7), 897–915. doi:10.1108/02686900410549420

Fan, J., & Wong, T. (2005). Do external auditors perform a corporate governance role in emerging markets? Evidence from East Asia. *Journal of Accounting Research, 43*(1), 35–72. doi:10.1111/j.1475-679x.2004.00162.x

Fanning, K., Cogger, K. O., & Srivasta, R. (1995). Detection of management fraud: A neural network approach. *Intelligent Systems in Accounting, Finance & Management, 4*(2), 113–126. doi:10.1002/j.1099-1174.1995.tb00084.x

Farooq, M., Kazim, I., Usman, M., & Latif, I. (2018). Corporate Governance and Audit Fees: Evidence from a Developing Country. *Pakistan Journal of Commerce and Social Sciences, 12*(1), 94–110.

Félix, S. A. L. (2013). Uma análise sistémica da auditoria interna nos municípios em Portugal [A systemic analysis of internal auditing in municipalities in Portugal]. Master's work project. Coimbra: Instituto Superior de Contabilidade e Administração de Coimbra do Politécnico de Coimbra.

Felix, W. L. J. Jr, Gramling, A. A., & Maletta, M. J. (2001). The Contribution of Internal Audit as a Determinant of External Audit Fees and Factors Influencing This Contribution. *Journal of Accounting Research, 39*(3), 513–534. doi:10.1111/1475-679X.00026

Ferguson, A., Stokes, D., & Technology, U. (2002). Brand name audit pricing, industry specialization, and leadership premiums post-Big 8 and Big 6 Mergers. *Contemporary Accounting Research*, *19*(1), 77–110. doi:10.1506/VF1T-VRT0-5LB3-766M

Ferguson, C., Richardson, G., & Wines, G. (2000). Audit education and training: The effect of formal studies and work experience. *Accounting Horizons*, *14*(2), 137–167. doi:10.2308/acch.2000.14.2.137

Fernandes, N. (2011). *O software open source como suporte à infra-estrutura de TI na administração pública local portuguesa: Factores determinantes na sua adopção - Mestrado em Gestão de Sistemas de informação*. ISCTE-IUL.

Fernando, G., Elder, R., & Abdel-Meguid, A. (2010). Audit quality attributes, client size, and cost of equity capital. *Review of Accounting and Finance*, *9*(4), 363–381. doi:10.1108/14757701011094571

Fernando, N., Loke, S. W., & Rahayu, W. (2013). Mobile cloud computing: A survey. *Future Generation Computer Systems*, *29*(1), 84–106. doi:10.1016/j.future.2012.05.023

Fichman, R. G. (1992). *Information Technology Diffusion: A Review of Empirical Research*. MIT Sloan School of Management.

Fichman, R. G., & Kemerer, C. F. (1997). The Assimilation of Software Process Innovations: An Organizational Learning Perspective. *Management Science*, *43*(10), 1345–1363. doi:10.1287/mnsc.43.10.1345

Field, A. (2011). *Discovering statistics using SPSS*. London: SAGE Publications Ltd.

Fleischer, R., & Goettsche, M. (2012). Size effects and audit pricing: Evidence from Germany. *Journal of International Accounting, Auditing & Taxation*, *21*(2), 156–168. doi:10.1016/j.intaccaudtax.2012.07.005

Fleiss, J. L. (1981). *Statistical methods for rates and proportions* (2nd ed.). New York: John Wiley & Sons, Inc.

Flowerday, S., Blundell, A. W., & Von Solms, R. (2006). Continuous auditing technologies and models: A discussion. *Computers & Security*, *25*(5), 325–331. doi:10.1016/j.cose.2006.06.004

Flowerday, S., & Von Solms, R. (2005). Continuous auditing: Verifying information integrity and providing assurances for financial reports. *Computer Fraud & Security*, *2005*(7), 12–16. doi:10.1016/S1361-3723(05)70232-3

Fosso Wamba, S., Akter, S., Edwards, A., Chopin, G., & Gnanzou, D. (2015). How "big data" can make big impact: Findings from a systematic review and a longitudinal case study. *International Journal of Production Economics*, *165*, 234–246. doi:10.1016/j.ijpe.2014.12.031

Fowler, K. (2009). SQL Server Forensic Analysis. Pearson Education.

Francis, J., & Stokes, D. (1986). Audit prices, product differentiation and scale economies: Further evidence from the Australian market. *Journal of Accounting Research*, *24*(2), 383–393. doi:10.2307/2491141

Francis, J., & Wilson, E. (1988). Auditor changes: A joint test of theories relating to agency costs and auditor differentiation. *The Accounting Review*, *13*(4), 663–707.

Frankel, J. A., & Schmukler, S. L. (1997). *Country funds and asymmetric information*. Retrieved June 4, 2007 from http://repositories.cdlib.org/iber/cider/C97-087

Fredericks, L. J. (1986). *The co-operative movement in West Malaysia: Policy, structure and institutional growth*. Kuala Lumpur: University of Malaya.

FSF. (2017). *Free software is a matter of liberty, not price — Free Software Foundation — working together for free software*. Retrieved January 21, 2017, from http://www.fsf.org

Fuentes, C. De, & Pucheta-Martínez, M. C. (2009). Auditor independence, joint determination of audit and non-audit fees and the incidence of qualified audit reports. *Revista Latinoamericana de Administración, 43*(2), 63–92.

Fukukawa, H., & Kim, H. (2017). Effects of audit partners on clients' business risk disclosure. *Accounting and Business Research, 47*(7), 780–809. doi:10.1080/00014788.2017.1299619

Fukukawa, H., Mock, T. J., & Srivastava, R. P. (2014). Assessing the risk fraud at Olympus and identifying an effective audit plan. *The Japanese Accounting Review, 4*(2014), 1–25. doi:10.11640/tjar.4.2014.01

Fu, Q., Villas-Boas, S. B., & Judge, G. (2018). Does china income FSDs follow Benford? A comparison between Chinese income first significant digit distribution with Benford distribution. *China Economic Journal*, 1–9. doi:10.1080/17538963.2018.1477418

Gallego, I., Rodríguez, L., & García, I. M. (2011). Information disclosed online by Spanish universities: Content and explanatory factors. *Online Information Review, 35*(3), 360–385. doi:10.1108/14684521111151423

Gamage, C. T., Lock, K. L., & Fernando, A. A. J. (2014). A proposed research framework: Effectiveness of internal control system in state commercial banks in Sri Lanka. *International Journal of Scientific Research and Innovative Technology, 1*(5), 25–44.

Gandomi, A., & Haider, M. (2015). Beyond the hype: Big data concepts, methods, and analytics. *International Journal of Information Management, 35*(2), 137–144. doi:10.1016/j.ijinfomgt.2014.10.007

Ganioglu, A. (2007). Prudential regulation and supervision of the banking sector and banking crises: A cross-country empirical investigation. *BDDK Bankacilik ve Finansal Piyasalar Dergisi, 1*, 11–29.

Gantz, J., & Reinsel, D. (2012). The digital universe in 2020: Big data, bigger digital shadows, and biggest growth in the far east. *IDC IView: IDC Analyze the Future*, 1–16.

Garcia, M. N., dos Santos, S., Pereira, R. da S., & Rossi, G. B. (2010). Software livre em relação ao software proprietário: Aspectos favoráveis e desfavoráveis percebidos por especialistas. *Gestão & Regionalidade, 26*(78), 106–120.

García, M., Garrido, P., Vico, A., Moizer, P., & Humphrey, C. (1999). La calidad del servicio de auditoría: Los auditores vistos por sus clientes. *Revista Española de Financiación y Contabilidad, 28*(102), 1005–1041.

García, M., Humphrey, C., Moizer, P., & Turley, S. (1993). Auditing expectations and performance in Spain and Britain: A comparative analysis. *The International Journal of Accounting, 28*(4), 281–307.

Garde-Sánchez, R., Rodríguez-Bolívar, M. P., & Alcaide-Muñoz, L. (2014). Are Spanish SAIs accomplishing INTOSAI's best practices code of transparency and accountability? *Transylvanian Review of Administrative Sciences, 43*, 122–145.

Garg, N., & Bawa, S. (2017). RITS-MHT: Relative indexed and time stamped Merkle hash tree based data auditing protocol for cloud computing. *Journal of Network and Computer Applications, 84*, 1–13. doi:10.1016/j.jnca.2017.02.005

Gay, G., Schelluch, P., & Baines, A. (1998). Perceptions of messages conveyed by review and audit reports. *Accounting, Auditing & Accountability Journal, 11*(4), 472.494.

Gebrayel, E., Jarrar, H., Salloum, C., & Lefebvre, Q. (2018). Effective association between audit committees and the internal audit function and its impact on financial reporting quality: Empirical evidence from Omani listed firms. *International Journal of Auditing, 22*(1), 1–17.

Geeta, C. M., Raghavendra, S., Buyya, R., & Venugopal, K. R. (2018). Data Auditing and Security in Cloud Computing : Issues, Challenges and Future Directions. *International Journal of Computer, 28*(1), 8–57.

Gepp, A., Linnenluecke, M. K., O'Neill, T. J., & Smith, T. (2018). Big Data TECHNIQUES in Auditing RESEARCH AND PRACTICE: current trends and future opportunities. *Journal of Accounting Literature*, 1–42.

Gerrard, I., Houghton, K., & Woodliff, D. (1994). Audit Fees: The Effects of Auditee, Auditor and Industry Differences. *Managerial Auditing Journal*, *9*(7), 3–11. doi:10.1108/02686909410067534

Ghafory, I. (2017). *Siber-fiziksel sistemler nedir?* Retrieved April 15, 2018, from http://www.endustri40.com/siber-fiziksel-sistemler

Ghafran, C., & O' Sullivan, N. (2017). The impact of audit committee expertise on audit quality: Evidence from UK audit fees. *The British Accounting Review*, *49*(6), 578–593. doi:10.1016/j.bar.2017.09.008

Ghiglione, R., & Matalon, B. (2001). *O inquérito: Teoria e prática.* Oeiras: Celta Editora.

Giovannucci, D., & Ponte, S. (2005). Standards as a new form of social contract? Sustainability initiatives in the coffee industry. *Food Policy*, *30*(3), 284–301. doi:10.1016/j.foodpol.2005.05.007

Gist, W. E. (1992). Explaining Variability in External Audit Fees. *Accounting and Business Research*, *23*(89), 79–84. doi:10.1080/00014788.1992.9729863

Gloeck, J., & Jager, H. (1993). *The focus point of the audit expectation gap in the Republic of South Africa.* Working paper, School of Accountancy, University of Pretoria.

Glynn, E., Fitzgerald, B., & Exton, C. (2005). Commercial Adoption of Open Source Software : An Empirical Study. In *2005 International Symposium on Empirical Software Engineering, 2005* (pp. 225–234). Academic Press. 10.1109/ISESE.2005.1541831

Godinho, R. (2012). *O Open Source Software na Administração Pública Central Portuguesa.* ISCTE-IUL.

Godsell, D. (1991). Auditors' legal liability and the expectation gap. *Australian Accountant*, *61*(1), 22–28.

Golen, S. (2008). Communication Barriers Between Internal and External Auditors. *ABEA Journal*, *27*(Fall), 35–43.

Gómez, N. (2003). *El Informe de auditoría y su efecto sobre la decisión del cambio de Auditor. Premio de Investigación Contable José Mª Fernández Pirla.* XI Edición, Instituto de Contabilidad y Auditoría de Cuentas.

González, B., García, R., & López, A. (2013). Communication as a transparency and accountability strategy in supreme audit institutions. *Administration & Society*, *45*(5), 583–609. doi:10.1177/0095399712438376

González, B., López, A., & García, R. (2008). Supreme Audit Institutions and their communication strategies. *International Review of Administrative Sciences*, *74*(3), 435–461. doi:10.1177/0020852308095312

Gonzalez, G. C., Sharma, P. N., & Galletta, D. (2012). Factors influencing the planned adoption of continuous monitoring technology. *Journal of Information Systems*, *26*(2), 53–69. doi:10.2308/isys-50259

Goodpaster, K. E. (1991). Business ethics and stakeholder analysis. *Business Ethics Quarterly*, *1*(1), 53–73. doi:10.2307/3857592

Goodwin, J., & Seow, J. (2002). The Influence of Corporate Governance Mechanisms on the quality of financial reporting and Auditing: Perceptions of auditors and directors in Singapor. *Accounting and Finance*, *42*(3), 195–223. doi:10.1111/1467-629X.t01-1-00074

Goodwin-Stewart, J., & Kent, P. (2006). Relation between external audit fees, audit committee characteristics and internal audit. *Accounting and Finance*, *46*(3), 387–404. doi:10.1111/j.1467-629X.2006.00174.x

Gorton, G., & Metrick, A. (2012). The shadow banking system (with comments and discussion). *Brookings Papers on Economic Activity*, *2*, 261–312. Retrieved from https://www.brookings.edu/bpea-articles/regulating-the-shadow-banking-system-with-comments-and-discussion/

Gramling, A., Schatzberg, J., & Wallace, W. (1996). The role of undergraduate auditing coursework in reducing the expectation gap. *Issues in Accounting Education*, *11*(1), 131–161.

Gramling, A., & Schneider, A. (2018). Effects of reporting relationship and type of internal control deficiency on internal auditors' internal control evaluations. *Managerial Auditing Journal*, *33*(3), 318–335. doi:10.1108/MAJ-07-2017-1606

Grammatikos, T., & Papanikolaou, N. I. (2016, November). Applying Benford's law to accounting data manipulation in the banking industry. *LSF Research Working Paper Series, 16–11*, 1–36.

Griffin, P., Lont, D. H., & Sun, Y. (2008). Corporate Governance and Audit Fees: Evidence of Countervailing Relations. *Journal of Contemporary Accounting & Economics*, *4*(1), 18–49. doi:10.1016/S1815-5669(10)70028-X

Groomer, S. M., & Murthy, U. S. (1989). Continuous Auditing of Database Applications: An Embedded Audit Module Approach. *Journal of Information Systems*.

GTAG13. (2009). *Global Technology Audit Guide (GTAG®) 13 Fraud Prevention and Detection in an Automated World*. Altamonte Springs, FL: The Institute of Internal Auditors.

Guan, L., Lin, F., & Fang, W. (2008). Goal-oriented earnings management: Evidence from Taiwanese firms. *Emerging Markets Finance & Trade*, *44*(4), 19–32. doi:10.2753/REE1540-496X440402

Gul, F., Fung, S., & Jaggi, B. (2009). Earnings quality: Some evidence on the role of auditor tenure and auditors' industry expertise. *Journal of Accounting and Economics*, *47*(3), 265–287. doi:10.1016/j.jacceco.2009.03.001

Gupta, A., Briscoe, F., & Hambrick, D. C. (2017). Red, blue, and purple firms: Organizational political ideology and corporate social responsibility. *Strategic Management Journal*, *38*(5), 1018–1040. doi:10.1002mj.2550

Gupta, A., & Shakya, S. (2015). Information System Audit. *Cloud Computing Security and Challenges*, *4*(11), 48–56.

Hackbarth, D., Miao, J., & Morellec, E. (2005). *Capital structure, credit risk and macroeconomic conditions*. Retrieved November 8, 2006 from http://www.defaultrisk.com/ps_other.htm

Halper, F., Snively, J., & Vasarhelyi, M. (1992). The Continuous Process Audit System: Knowledge Acquisition and Representation. *Edpacs*, 1-13.

Han, J., Kamber, M., & Pei, J. (2012). Data Mining: Concepts and Techniques (3rd ed.). Elsevier.

Hans, C., Edward, L., Martin, W., & Cheng, Z. (2015). Incentives or standards: What determines accounting quality changes around IFRS adoption? *Journal of European Accounting Review*, *24*(01), 31–61. doi:10.1080/09638180.2015.1009144

Hansmann, H., & Kraakman, R. (2004). *Agency problems and legal strategies*. Center for Law, Economics and Public Policy, Research paper no. 301.

Hanson, S. G., Kashyap, A. K., & Stein, J. C. (2011). A macroprudential approach to financial regulation. *The Journal of Economic Perspectives*, *25*(1), 3–28. doi:10.1257/jep.25.1.3 PMID:21595323

Hardies, K., Breesch, D., & Branson, J. (2016). Do (fe)male auditors impair audit quality? Evidence from going-concern opinions. *European Accounting Review*, *25*(1), 7–34. doi:10.1080/09638180.2014.921445

Hardy, C. A. (2015). Business analytics and continuous assurance: Theoretical matters, practice issues, and future directions. In *48th Hawaii International Conference on System Sciences (HICSS)* (pp. 4732–4741). IEEE. 10.1109/HICSS.2015.563

Hardy, C. A., & Laslett, G. (2015). Continuous auditing and monitoring in practice: Lessons from Metcash's Business Assurance Group. *Journal of Information Systems, 29*(2), 183–194. doi:10.2308/isys-50969

Haron, H., Chambers, A., Ramsi, R., & Ismail, I. (2004). The reliance of external auditors on internal auditors. *Managerial Auditing Journal, 19*(9), 1148–1159. doi:10.1108/02686900410562795

Hassan, M., Percy, M., & Stewart, J. (2006). The transparency of derivative disclosures by Australian firms in the extractive industry. *Corporate. Ownership and Control, 4*(2), 257–270.

Hassan, M., Salleh, N., Yatim, P., & Rahman, M. (2012). Risk management committee and financial instrument disclosure. *Asian Journal of Accounting and Governance, 3*(1), 13–28. doi:10.17576/ajag-2012-3-6512

Hatefi, M., & Fasanghari, M. (2016). A DEA-Based Approach for Information Technology Risk Assessment through Risk Information Technology Framework. *The International Arab Journal of Information Technology, 13*(1), 51–58.

Hay, D., & Davis, D. (2004). The voluntary choice of an audit of any level of quality. *Auditing, 23*(September), 37–53. doi:10.2308/aud.2004.23.2.37

Hay, D., Knechel, W. R., & Ling, H. (2008). Evidence on the Impact of Internal Control and Corporate Governance on Audit Fees. *International Journal of Auditing, 12*(1), 9–24. doi:10.1111/j.1099-1123.2008.00367.x

Hedley, T. P., & Ben-Chorin, O. (2011). *Auditing and monitoring activities help uncover fraud and assess control effectiveness.* Retrieved from https://www.kpmg.com/US/en/IssuesAndInsights/ArticlesPublications/Documents/auditing-and-monitoring.pdf

Heliodoro, P. (2009). Expectation gap em auditoria. XIV *Encuentro AECA Innovación y responsabilidade: desafíos y soluciones*.

Henson, S., & Loader, R. (2001). Barriers to agricultural exports from developing countries: The role of sanitary and phytosanitary requirements. *World Development, 29*(1), 85–102. doi:10.1016/S0305-750X(00)00085-1

Heras, I. (Coord.). (2006). ISO 9000, ISO 14001 y otros estándares de gestión: Pasado, presente y futuro [ISO 9000, ISO 14001 and other management standards: Past, present and future]. Madrid: Editorial Civitas.

Heras, I., Dick, G., & Casadesús, M. (2002). ISO 9000 registration's impact on sales and profitability. A longitudinal analysis of performance before and after accreditation. *International Journal of Quality & Reliability Management, 19*(6), 774–791. doi:10.1108/02656710210429618

Hermanson, D. R., & Rittenberg, L. E. (2003). Chapter 2: Internal audit and organizational governance. *Research Opportunities in Internal Auditing.* Retrieved August 3, 2018 from https://na.theiia.org/iiarf/Public%20Documents/Chapter%202%20Internal%20Audit%20and%20Organizational%20Governance.pdf

Hermanson, D. R., Smith, J. L., & Stephens, N. M. (2012). How effective are organizations' internal controls? Insights into specific internal control elements. *Current Issues in Auditing, 6*(1), 31–50. doi:10.2308/ciia-50146

Hill, T. (1988). Random-number guessing and the first digit phenomenon. *Psychological Reports, 62*(3), 967–971. doi:10.2466/pr0.1988.62.3.967

Hines, C. S., Masli, A., Mauldin, E. G., & Peters, G. F. (2015). Board Risk Committees and Audit Pricing. *Auditing, 34*(4), 59–84. doi:10.2308/ajpt-51035

Hoffman, A. O. I., & Birnbrich, C. (2012). The impact of fraud prevention on bank-customer relationships: An empirical investigation in retail banking. *International Journal of Bank Marketing, 30*(5), 390–407. doi:10.1108/02652321211247435

Hogan, C., & Jeter, D. (1999). Industry specialization by auditors. *Auditing, 18*(1), 1–17. doi:10.2308/aud.1999.18.1.1

Hooks, K. L., Kaplan, S. E., Schultz, J. Jr, & Poneno, L. A. (1994). Enhancing communication to assist in fraud prevention and detection. *Auditing*, *13*(2), 86–117.

Ho, P., Tower, G., & Barako, D. (2008). Improving governance leads to improved corporate communication. *Corporate Ownership & Control*, *5*, 26–33.

Hopwood, W., Leiner, J., & Young, G. (2012). *Forensic accounting and Fraud Examination*. New York: McGraw-Hill.

Ho, S., & Hutchinson, M. (2010). Internal audit department characteristics/activities and audit fees: Some evidence from Hong Kong firms. *Journal of International Accounting, Auditing & Taxation*, *19*(2), 121–136. doi:10.1016/j.intaccaudtax.2010.07.004

Huang, S. Y., Lin, C. C., Chiu, A. A., & Yen, D. C. (2017). Fraud detection using fraud triangle risk factors. *Information Systems Frontiers*, *19*(6), 1343–1356. doi:10.100710796-016-9647-9

Humphrey, C. (1997). Debating audit expectations. *Current Issues in Auditing*, *3*, 3–30.

Humphrey, C., Moizer, P., & Turley, S. (1993). The audit expectation gap in Britain: An empirical investigation. *Accounting and Business Research*, *23*(1), 395–411. doi:10.1080/00014788.1993.9729907

Hung, Y. S., & Cheng, Y. C. (2018). The impact of information complexity on audit failures from corporate fraud: Individual auditor level analysis. *Asia Pacific Management Review*, *23*(2), 72–85. doi:10.1016/j.apmrv.2017.09.002

Hunton, J. E. (2003). Core Concepts of Information Systems Auditing. John Wiley & Sons.

Hunton, J. E., Mauldin, E. G., & Wheeler, P. R. (2008). Potential functional and dysfunctional effects of continuous monitoring. *The Accounting Review*, *83*(6), 1551–1569. doi:10.2308/accr.2008.83.6.1551

Hwang, S. S., Shin, T., & Han, I. (2004). CRAS-CBR: Internal control assessment system using case-based reasoning. *Expert Systems: International Journal of Knowledge Engineering and Neural Networks*, *21*(1), 23–32. doi:10.1111/j.1468-0394.2004.00260.x

Hyvönen, J. (2007). Strategy, performance, measurement techniques and information technology of the firm and their links to organizational performance. *Management Accounting Research*, *18*(3), 343–366. doi:10.1016/j.mar.2007.02.001

Idowu, A., & Oluwatoyin, A. (2014). Impact of auditing education on audit expectation gap in Nigeria. *International Journal of Academic Research in Accounting. Finance and Management Sciences*, *4*(3), 109–116.

IFAC. (2009). *International Standard on Auditing 200: Overall objectives of the independent auditor and the conduct of an audit in accordance with international standards on auditing*. New York: International Federation of Accountants.

IFAC. (2016). *International Standard on Auditing 570: Going Concern*. New York: International Federation of Accountants.

IFAC. (2016). ISA 330: The auditor's responses to assessed Risks. In *Handbook of International Quality Control, Auditing, Review, Other Assurance, and Related Services Pronouncements* (pp. 347–369). New York: International Federation of Accountants.

IG1220. (2016). *Implementation Guide 1220 Due Professional Care*. The Institute of Internal Auditors. Retrieved from https://na.theiia.org/standards-guidance/Public%20Documents/IPPF%202013%20English.pdf

IG2100. (2017). *Implementation Guide 2100 Nature of Work*. The Institute of Internal Auditors. Retrieved from https://na.theiia.org/standards-guidance/Public%20Documents/IPPF%202013%20English.pdf

IG2110. (2017). *Implementation Guide 2130 Control*. The Institute of Internal Auditors. Retrieved from https://na.theiia.org/standards-guidance/Public%20Documents/IPPF%202013%20English.pdf

IG2120. (2017). *Implementation Guide 2120 Risk Management*. The Institute of Internal Auditors. Retrieved from https://na.theiia.org/standards-guidance/Public%20Documents/IPPF%202013%20English.pdf

IG2130. (2017). *Implementation Guide 2120 Risk Management*. The Institute of Internal Auditors. Retrieved from https://na.theiia.org/standards-guidance/Public%20Documents/IPPF%202013%20English.pdf

Ihendinihu, J., & Robert, S. (2014). Role of audit education in minimizing audit expectation gap (AEG) in Nigeria. *International Journal of Business and Management*, *9*(2), 203–211. doi:10.5539/ijbm.v9n2p203

IIA. (2017a). *Understanding and auditing big data*, The Institute of Internal Auditors. Retrieved April 15, 2018, from https://www.iia.nl/SiteFiles/Publicaties/GTAG-Understanding-and-Auditing-Big-Data.pdf

IIA. (2017b). *Global perspectives and insights artificial intelligence - considerations for the profession of internal auditing*. The Institute of Internal Auditors. Retrieved April 15, 2018, from https://na.theiia.org/periodicals/Public%20Documents/GPI-Artificial-Intelligence.pdf

Impink, J. (2010). *Earnings manipulation and bankruptcy: WorldCom*. Third version, Bachelor paper, Betzabeth Ignacius 5754992.

Inácio, H. (2014). *Controlo Interno - Enquadramento teórico e aplicação prática*. Escolar Editora.

Inagaki, K. (2015). Accounting scandal set to shake up Toshiba. *Financial Times*. Retrieved from https://www.ft.com/content/b209abac-2bc0-11e5-acfb-cbd2e1c81cca

Independent Investigation Committee Report (IIC). (2015). *Investigation Report –Summary version, Independent Investigation Committee for Toshiba Corporation, 20 July 2015*. International Standard on Auditing 240, The Auditor's Responsibilities Relating to Fraud in an Audit of Financial Statements. Retrieve from http://www.ifac.org/system/files/downloads/a012-2010-iaasb-handbook-isa-240.pdf

Institute of Internal Auditors. (2010). *Code of ethics*. Retrieved August 3, 2018 from https://na.theiia.org/standards-guidance/mandatory-guidance/Pages/Code-of-Ethics.aspx

Institute of Internal Auditors. (2017). *International standards for the professional practice of internal auditing (standards)*. Retrieved August 3, 2018 from https://na.theiia.org/standards-guidance/Public%20Documents/IPPF-Standards-2017.pdf

Institute of Internal Auditors. (2018a). *CIA exam: Why, how and what is changing January 2019*. Retrieved August 3, 2018 from https://global.theiia.org/certification/CIA-Certification/Pages/cia-exam-why-and-how-its-changing.aspx

Institute of Internal Auditors. (2018b). *Certified financial services auditor exam syllabus*. Retrieved August 3, 2018 from https://global.theiia.org/certification/cfsa-certification/Pages/Exam-Syllabus.aspx

International Federation of Accountants. (2010). ISA 610: Using the Work of External Auditors. In Handbook of International Quality Control, Auditing, Review, Other Assurances, and Related Services Pronouncements. Author.

International Monetary Fund. (2001). *Government Finance Statistics Manual* (2nd ed.). Washington, DC: IMF.

International Organization of Supreme Audit Institutions. (1977). *The Lima declaration*. Retrieved from http://www.issai.org/media(622,1033)/ISSAI_1_E.pdf

International Organization of Supreme Audit Institutions. (2006). *INTOSAI communication policy: A framework "Mutual exchange of information benefits all."* Retrieved from http://www.intosai.org/uploads/compolicyfin031106.pdf

International Organization of Supreme Audit Institutions. (2007). *ISSAI 1260: Communication with those charged with governance*. Retrieved from http://www.issai.org/media(635,1033)/ISSAI_1260_E.pdf

International Organization of Supreme Audit Institutions. (2009a). *ISSAI 20: Principles of transparency and accountability*. Author.

International Organization of Supreme Audit Institutions. (2009b). *ISSAI 21: Principles of transparency and accountability – Principles and good practices*. Author.

International Organization of Supreme Audit Institutions. (2010a). *INTOSAI communication guideline*. Retrieved from http://www.intosai.org/uploads/intkommrichtliniee.pdf

International Organization of Supreme Audit Institutions. (2010b). *INTOSAI GOV 9150: Co-operation and co-ordination between Internal Auditors and SAIs in the public sector*. Retrieved from http://www.issai.org/media(802,1033)/INTOSAI_GOV_9150_E_Exp-draft.pdf

International Organization of Supreme Audit Institutions. (2010c). *Strategic plan (2011-2016)*. Retrieved from http://www.intosai.org/blueline/upload/intosaispenglishv9web.pdf

International Organization of Supreme Audit Institutions. (2017). *Global SAI Stocktaking report 2017*. Retrieved from http://www.idi.no/en/all-news/idi-news/item/128-global-sai-stocktaking-report-2017

Investigation and Enforcement Unit of Malaysia Co-operative Society Commission. (2014). *Cases involving internal controls*. Unpublished raw data.

IPPF. (2009). *IPPF-Practice Guide Internal Auditing and Fraud*. The Institute of Internal Auditors. Retrieved from https://na.theiia.org/standards-guidance/Pages/Standards-and-Guidance-IPPF.aspx

ISA 200. (2009). *Objetivos gerais do auditor independente e condução de uma auditoria de acordo com as normas internacionais de auditoria*. International Federation of Accountants.

ISA 240. (2009). *As responsabilidades do auditor relativas a fraude numa auditoria de demonstrações financeiras*. International Federation of Accountants.

ISA 610. (2009). *Usar o Trabalho de Auditores Internos*. International Federation of Accountants.

Isgut, A. E. (2001). Developing countries borrowing in the international financial market with an uncertain credit ceiling. *International Journal of Finance & Economics*, *6*(2), 171–183. doi:10.1002/ijfe.153

Ismail, Y., & Mohd-Sarif, S. (2010). Convergence of global and traditional managers' characteristics: A case of senior management of cooperatives in Malaysia. *Journal of International Business and Entrepreneurship Development*, *5*(1), 28–47. doi:10.1504/JIBED.2010.035198

Issa, H., Sun, T., & Vasarhelyi, M. A. (2016). Research ideas for artificial intelligence in auditing: The formalization of audit and workforce supplementation. *Journal of Emerging Technologies in Accounting*, *13*(2), 1–20. doi:10.2308/jeta-10511

Ittonen, K., Miettinen, J., & Sami, V. (2010). Does Female Representation on Audit Committees Affect Audit Fees? Quarterly Journal of Finance and Accounting. *Quarterly Journal of Finance and Accounting*, *49*(3-4), 113.

Ittonen, K., Vähämaa, E., & Vähämaa, S. (2013). Female auditors and accruals quality. *Accounting Horizons*, *27*(2), 205–228. doi:10.2308/acch-50400

Jackson, R. A. (2013). *Audit in a digital business world: Big data, cloud, mobile, and social media technologies are transforming the business environment as well as the risks*. Retrieved April 15, 2018, from https://www.highbeam.com/doc/1G1-340425202.html

Jacobson, D. D. (2009). Revisiting IT governance in the light of institutional theory. In *2009 42nd Hawaii International Conference on System Sciences* (pp. 1–9). IEEE.

Jakubik, P. (2006). *Does credit risk vary with economic cycles? The case of Finland.* Retrieved January 12, 2007 from http://ideas.repec.org/p/fau/wpaper/wp2006_11.html

James, O. A. (2013). The Impact of Information and Communication Technology on Internal Control's Prevention and Detection of Fraud. *Ph.D Thesis, 3*(13), 1738–1752.

James, K. L. (2003). The effects of internal audit structure on perceived financial statement fraud prevention. *Accounting Horizons, 17*(4), 315–327. doi:10.2308/acch.2003.17.4.315

Janvrin, D. J., Payne, E. A., Byrnes, P., Schneider, G. P., & Curtis, M. B. (2012). The updated COSO internal control-integrated framework: Recommendations and opportunities for future research. *Journal of Information Systems, 26*(2), 189–213. doi:10.2308/isys-50255

Janvrin, D., Bierstaker, J. L., & Lowe, D. J. (2009). An Investigation of Factors Influencing the Use of Computer-Related Audit Procedures. *Journal of Information Systems, 23*(1), 97–118. doi:10.2308/jis.2009.23.1.97

Javorcik, B., & Pakel, B. D. (2018). *Forensics, Elasticities and Benford's Law: Detecting Tax Fraud in International Trade.* CEPR Discussion Papers 12798. Retrieved from https://ideas.repec.org/p/cpr/ceprdp/12798.html

Jegers, M. (2013). Do nonprofit organizations manage earnings? An empirical study. *Voluntas, 24*(4), 953–968. doi:10.100711266-012-9291-z

Jensen, M. C. (1993). The modern industrial revolution, exit and the failure of internal control system. *The Journal of Finance, 48*(3), 831–880. doi:10.1111/j.1540-6261.1993.tb04022.x

Jensen, M. C., & Meckling, W. H. (1976). Theory of the firm : Managerial behavior, agency Costs and ownership structure. *Journal of Financial Economics, 3*(4), 305–360. doi:10.1016/0304-405X(76)90026-X

Jermias, J., & Gani, L. (2014). The impact of board capital and board characteristics on firm performance. *The British Accounting Review, 46*(2), 135–153. doi:10.1016/j.bar.2013.12.001

Jiang, L., André, P., & Richard, C. (2017). An international study of internal audit function quality. *Accounting and Business Research, 19*(9), 264–298. doi:10.1080/00014788.2017.1357461

Jiang, J., Wang, I., & Wang, K. (2018). *Big N auditors and audit quality: New evidence from quasi-experiments.* The Accounting Review. In-Press.

Jie, S., & Fang, Z. (2015). *Research on the technology of on-line audit warning in big data environment.* Paper presented at 5th International Conference on Information Engineering for Mechanics and Materials.

Jones, M. J. (2008). Internal control, accountability and corporate governance: Medieval and modern Britain compared. *Accounting, Auditing & Accountability Journal, 21*(7), 1052–1075. doi:10.1108/09513570810907474

Jordana, J., & Levi-Faur, D. (2005). The diffusion of regulatory capitalism in Latin America: Sectoral and national channels in the making of a new order. *The Annals of the American Academy of Political and Social Science, 528*(1), 102–104. doi:10.1177/0002716204272587

Kanchana, M., Praveen, C., Kumar, M. K., Hussain, S. N., & Kumar, E. P. (2013). Privacy -preserving audit of secure data storage services in cloud computing. *International Journal of Advanced Research in Computer Science and Software Engineering, 3*(5), 901–905.

Kanhere, P., & Khanuja, H. (2014). A Survey on Outlier Detection in Financial Transactions. *International Journal of Computers and Applications, 108*(17).

Kapardis, M. K., & Zopiatis, A. (2010). Investigating incidents of fraud in small economies: The case for Cyprus. *Journal of Financial Crime, 17*(2), 195–209. doi:10.1108/13590791011033890

Kaplan, R., & Norton, D. (1992). The balanced scorecard – Measures that drive performance. *Harvard Business Review, 70*(1), 71–79.

Karim, K., Robin, A., & Suh, S. (2015). Board Structure and Audit Committee Monitoring: Effects of Audit Committee Monitoring Incentives and Board Entrenchment on Audit Fees. *Journal of Accounting, Auditing & Finance, 31*(2), 249–276. doi:10.1177/0148558X15583412

Kaur, I., Devi, S., Omar, R., Abd, R., & Samad, R. (2005). *Kajian Kedudukan Tenaga Kerja dan Kepuasan Kerja dalam Kalangan Kakitangan Gerakan Koperasi di Malaysia (Research monograph).* Cooperative College of Malaysia.

Kavanagh, P. (2004). Open source software: implementation and management. Elsevier.

Kavya, A., & Lobo, P. (2017). An Analysis of Security Issues and Solutions in Cloud Computing. *International Journal of Emerging Research in Management &Technology, 6*(6), 279–285. doi:10.9790/0661-1902046772

Keasey, K., Watson, R., & Wynarczk, P. (1988). The small company audit qualifications: A preliminary investigation. *Accounting and Business Research, 18*(72), 323–333. doi:10.1080/00014788.1988.9729379

Khan, A. R., Hossain, D. M., & Siddiqui, J. (2011). Corporate ownership concentration and audit fees: The case of an emerging economy. *Advances in Accounting, 27*(1), 125–131. doi:10.1016/j.adiac.2011.04.007

Khanuja, H., & Adane, D. (2014, September). *Forensic Analysis for Monitoring Database Transactions.* Paper presented at Second International Symposium on Security in Computing and Communications (SSCC'14).

Kiesow, A., Zarvic, N., & Thomas, O. (2014). Continuous auditing in big data computing environments: Towards an integrated audit approach by using CAATTs. *GI-Jahrestagung,* 901-912.

Kiesow, A., Schomaker, T., & Thomas, O. (2016). *Transferring continuous auditing to the Digital Age – The Knowledge Base after three decades of research.* Research Papers.

Kiesow, A., Schomaker, T., & Thomas, O. (2016). Transferring Continuous Auditing to the Digital Age – The Knowledge Base after Three Decades of Research. *Twenty-Fourth European Conference on Information Systems (ECIS),* 1–18.

Kiesow, A., Zarvic, N., & Thomas, O. (2014). Continuous Auditing in Big Data Computing Environments: Towards an Integrated Audit Approach by Using CAATTs. *Management of Complex IT-Systems and Applications (MITA) - INFORMATIK, P-232,* 901–912.

Kikhia, H. Y. (2014). Board Characteristics, Audit Committee Characteristics, and Audit Fees: Evidence from Jordan. *International Business Research, 7*(12), 98–111. doi:10.5539/ibr.v7n12p98

Kimeli, E. K. (2016). Determinants of Audit Fees Pricing : Evidence from Nairobi Securities Exchange (NSE). *International Journal of Research in Business Studies and Management, 3*(1), 23–35.

Kim, H.-J., Mannino, M., & Nieschwietz, R. J. (2009). Information technology acceptance in the internal audit profession: Impact of technology features and complexity. *International Journal of Accounting Information Systems, 10*(4), 214–228. doi:10.1016/j.accinf.2009.09.001

Kinkela, K. (2012). Practical and ethical considerations on the use of cloud computing in accounting. *Journal of Finance and Accountancy,* 1–10.

Kinney, W., & Martin, R. (1994). Does Auditing Reduce Bias in Financial Reporting? A Review of Audit-Related Adjustment Studies. *Auditing*, *13*, 149–156.

Kizirian, T., & Leese, W. R. (2004). Security controls and management tone. *Internal Auditing*, *19*(2), 42–46.

Klamm, B. K., & Watson, M. W. (2009). SOX 404 reported internal control weaknesses: A test of COSO framework components and information technology. *Journal of Information Systems*, *23*(2), 1–23. doi:10.2308/jis.2009.23.2.1

Klein, A. (2002). Audit committee, board of director characteristics, and earnings management. *Journal of Accounting and Economics*, *33*(3), 375–400. doi:10.1016/S0165-4101(02)00059-9

Knapp, C. A., & Knapp, M. C. (2001). The effects of experience and explicit fraud risk assessment in detecting fraud with analytical procedures. *Accounting, Organizations and Society*, *26*(1), 25–37. doi:10.1016/S0361-3682(00)00005-2

Knechel, W. R., & Willekens, M. (2006). The Role of Risk Management and Governance in Determining Audit Demand. *Journal of Business Finance & Accounting*, *33*(9-10), 1344–1367. doi:10.1111/j.1468-5957.2006.01238.x

Koch, H. S. (1981). Online Computer Auditing through Continuous and Intermittent Simulation. *Management Information Systems Quarterly*, *5*(1), 29–41. doi:10.2307/249156

Kogan, A., Sudit, E. F., & Vasarhelyi, M. A. (1999). Continuous Online Auditing:A Program of Research. *Journal of Information Systems*, *13*(2), 87–103. doi:10.2308/jis.1999.13.2.87

Koopman, S. J., & Lucas, A. (2005). Business and default cycles for credit risk. *Journal of Applied Econometrics*, *20*(2), 311–323. doi:10.1002/jae.833

Koşan, L. (2014). Augmented reality applications in accounting education. *Cukurova University Faculty of Economics and Administrative Sciences*, *2*, 37–47.

Kose, Y., & Erdogan, S. (2015). The audit expectation gap in Turkey. *Journal of Accounting & Finance,* 193-214.

Koskivaara, E. (2006). Integrating analytical procedures into the continuous audit environment. *JISTEM-Journal of Information Systems and Technology Management*, *3*(3), 331–346. doi:10.4301/S1807-17752006000300005

Koskivaara, E., & Back, B. (2007). Artificial Neural Network Assistant (ANNA) for Continuous Auditing and Monitoring of Financial Data. *Journal of Emerging Technologies in Accounting*, *4*(1), 29–45. doi:10.2308/jeta.2007.4.1.29

KPMG. (2006). *Fraud risk management.* Retrieved October 30, 2012 from http://www.kpmg.com/CN/en/IssuesAndInsights/ArticlesPublications/documents/Fraud-Risk-Management-O-200610.pdf

KPMG. (2012). *Continuous auditing and continuous monitoring: The current status and the road ahead.* Retrieved from http://mcr.doingbusiness.ro/uploads/517518efdd1e7CA and CM WEB DE-Survey.pdf

KPMG. (2013). *A survey of fraud, bribery and corruption in Australia & New Zealand 2012.* Retrieved from https://www.kpmg.com/AU/en/IssuesAndInsights/ArticlesPublications/Fraud-Survey/Documents/fraud-bribery-corruption-survey-2012v2.pdf

Krahel, J. P., & Titera, W. R. (2015). Consequences of big data and formalization on accounting and auditing standards. *Accounting Horizons*, *29*(2), 409–422. doi:10.2308/acch-51065

Kramer, W. M. (2003). The rules of fraud. *Risk Management*, *50*(11), 54.

Kranacher, M. J., Riley, R. A. Jr, & Wells, J. T. (2011). *Forensic accounting and fraud examination.* New York: John Wiley & Sons, Inc.

Krause, R. M., Feiock, R. C., & Hawkins, C. V. (2016). The administrative organization of sustainability within local government. *Journal of Public Administration: Research and Theory*, *26*, 113–127.

Kress, R. E. (2016). Transforming the IT audit function: Taking the digital journey. *ISACA*. Retrieved from https://www.isaca.org/Journal/archives/2016/Volume-1/Pages/transforming-the-it-audit-function.aspx

Krishnan, G., & Visvanathan, G. (2009). Do Auditors Price Audit Committee's Expertise? The Case of Accounting versus Nonaccounting Financial Experts. *Auditing*, *28*(1), 241–261. doi:10.2308/aud.2009.28.1.241

Krishnan, J., & Krishnan, J. (1996). The role of economic trade-offs in the audit opinion decision: An empirical analysis. *Journal of Accounting, Auditing & Finance*, *4*(4), 565–586. doi:10.1177/0148558X9601100403

Krishnan, R., Yetman, M., & Yetman, R. (2006). Expense misreporting in a nonprofit organization. *The Accounting Review*, *81*(2), 399–420. doi:10.2308/accr.2006.81.2.399

Kuhn, J. R. Jr, & Sutton, S. G. (2010). Continuous Auditing in ERP System Environments: The Current State and Future Directions. *Journal of Information Systems*, *24*(1), 91–112. doi:10.2308/jis.2010.24.1.91

Kumar S, K. (2016). Secure Auditing and Deduplication of Data on Cloud. *International Journal of Engineering Sciences & Research Technology, 5*, 289–292.

Kumar, P. R., Raj, P. H., & Jelciana, P. (2018). Exploring Data Security Issues and Solutions in Cloud Computing. *Procedia Computer Science, 125*(2009), 691–697. doi:10.1016/j.procs.2017.12.089

Kumari, J., Dissabandara, D., & Ajward, A. (2018). The Audit Expectations Gap and the Role of Audit Education: Evidence from Sri Lanka. *Vidyodaya Journal of Management*, *3*(1), 1–26. doi:10.31357/vjm.v3i1.3386

Kumar, K., & Bhattacharya, S. (2007, June). Detecting the dubious digits: Benford's law in forensic accounting. *Significance*, *4*(2), 81–83. doi:10.1111/j.1740-9713.2007.00234.x

Kummer, T., Singh, K., & Best, P. (2015). The effectiveness of fraud detection instruments in not-for-profit organizations. *Managerial Auditing Journal*, *30*(4/5), 435–455. doi:10.1108/MAJ-08-2014-1083

Kuna, H. D., Matinez, R. G., & Villatoro, F. R. (2014). Outlier detection in audit logs for application systems. *Information Systems*, *44*, 22–33. doi:10.1016/j.is.2014.03.001

Kuntari, Y., Chariri, A., & Nurdhiana, N. (2017). The effect of auditor ethics, auditor experience, audit fees and auditor motivation on audit quality. *Sriwijaya International Journal of Dynamic Economics and Business*, *1*(2), 203–218. doi:10.29259ijdeb.v1i2.203-218

Landsittel, D. L., & Rittenberg, L. E. (2010). COSO: Working with the academic community. *Accounting Horizons*, *24*(3), 455–469. doi:10.2308/acch.2010.24.3.455

Lanza, P. (1998). La informática en el trabajo de auditoria. *Auditoria Publica*, *13*, 93–98.

Laslett, G., & Hardy, C. A. (2015). Implementing continuous auditing and continuous monitoring in metcash: Change, capabilities, and culture. *Audit Analytics and Continuous Audit: Looking Toward the Future*, 157–167.

Laslett, G., & Hardy, C. C. (2015). Case Study B. *Audit Analytics*, 157-168.

Laurent, A. M. S. (2004). *Understanding open source and free software licensing: guide to navigating licensing issues in existing & new software*. O'Reilly Media.

Law No. 15/2001 of 5 June. Portuguese Republic Journal No. 130, 1st Serie.

Law, C., & Ngai, E. (2005). IT business value research: A critical review and research agenda. *International Journal of Enterprise Information Systems, 1*(3), 35–55. doi:10.4018/jeis.2005070103

Lawson, B. P., Muriel, L., & Sanders, P. R. (2017). A survey on firms' implementation of COSO's 2013 Internal control-integrated framework. *Research in Accounting Regulation, 29*(1), 30–43. doi:10.1016/j.racreg.2017.04.004

Lee, H.-Y., & Park, H.-Y. (2016). Characteristics of the internal audit and external audit hours: Evidence from S. Korea. *Managerial Auditing Journal, 31*(6/7), 629–654. doi:10.1108/MAJ-05-2015-1193

Lee, T., Azham, M., & Kandasamy, S. (2008). Towards reducing the audit expectation gap: Possible mission? *Accounting Today, 21*(2), 18–22.

Lemos, K. (2011). *Contabilidade de instrumentos derivados. Estudo da informação divulgada pelas empresas portuguesas* (Unpublished doctoral dissertation). Facultad de Ciencias Económicas y Empresariales, Universidad de Santiago de Compostela.

Lemos, K., Rodrigues, L., & Rodríguez Ariza, L. (2009). Determinantes do nível de divulgação de informação sobre instrumentos derivados. Evidência empírica no mercado de capitais português. *Tékhne – Revista de Estudos Politécnicos, 7*(12), 145-175.

Libby, R., & Frederick, D. (1990). Experience and the ability to explain audit findings. *Journal of Accounting Research, 28*(2), 348–367. doi:10.2307/2491154

Liburd, H. B., & Vasarhelyi, M. A. (2015). Big data and audit evidence. *Journal of Emerging Technologies in Accounting, 12*(1), 1–16. doi:10.2308/jeta-10468

Liddy, J. P. (2014). The Future of Audit. *Forbes*, 1–3.

Liggio, C. (1974). The expectation gap: The accountant's Waterloo. *Journal of Contemporary Business, 3*(3), 27–44.

Lim, J. H., & Lee, E. (2012). Information technologies, community characteristics and environmental outcomes: Evidence from South Korea. *Journal of Environmental Planning and Management, 55*(3), 271–296. doi:10.1080/09640568.2011.597588

Lin, W. & Hwang I. (2010). Audit Quality, Corporate Governance, and Earnings Management: A Meta-Analysis. *International Journal of Auditing, 14*, 57-77. doi:10.1111/j.1099-1123.2009.00403.x

Lins, S., Teigeler, H., & Sunyaev, A. (2016). Towards A Bright Future: Enhancing Diffusion of Continuous Cloud Service Auditing by Third Parties. *Twenty-Fourth European Conference on Information Systems (ECIS)*, 1–17. Retrieved from https://www.researchgate.net/profile/Sebastian_Lins/publication/301287731_TOWARDS_A_BRIGHT_FUTURE_ENHANCING_DIFFUSION_OF_CONTINUOUS_CLOUD_SERVICE_AUDITING_BY_THIRD_PARTIES/links/570f93d308aec95f0614c528.pdf

Lins, S., Thiebes, S., Schneider, S., & Sunyaev, A. (2015). What is really going on at your cloud service provider? Creating trustworthy certifications by continuous auditing. In *2015 48th Hawaii International Conference on System Sciences* (pp. 5352–5361). IEEE. 10.1109/HICSS.2015.629

Lins, S., Schneider, S., & Sunyaev, A. (2016). *Trust is Good, Control is Better: Creating Secure Clouds by Continuous Auditing. IEEE Transactions on Cloud Computing.*

Litchfield, D. (2007). *Oracle forensics part 1: dissecting the redo logs.* NISR Pub. Retrieved from https://oracle-base.com/articles/8i/logminer

Liu, C., Chen, J., Member, S., Yang, L. T., & Zhang, X. (2014). *Authorized Public Auditing of Dynamic Big Data Storage on Cloud with Efficient Verifiable Fine-Grained Updates*. Academic Press.

Lombardi, D. R., Bloch, R., & Vasarhelyi, M. A. (2014). The Future of Audit. *Journal of Information Systems and Technology Management, 11*(1), 21–32. doi:10.4301/S1807-17752014000100002

Lopes, N. G., & Costa, C. J. (2008). ERP Localization: Exploratory Study in Translation: European and Brazilian Portuguese. In *Proceedings of the 26th Annual ACM International Conference on Design of Communication* (pp. 93–98). New York: ACM. 10.1145/1456536.1456555

Lopes, P., & Rodrigues, L. (2007). Accounting for financial instruments: An analysis of the determinants of disclosure in the Portuguese stock exchange. *The International Journal of Accounting, 42*(1), 25–56. doi:10.1016/j.intacc.2006.12.002

Lourenço, I. M. E. C., & Castelo Branco, M. E. M. A. D. (2015). Principais consequências da adoção das IFRS: Análise da literatura existente e sugestões para investigação futura [Main consequences of adopting IFRS: Analysis of existing literature and suggestions for future research]. *Revista Contabilidade & Finanças, 26*(68), 126–139.

Low, A., Foo, S., & Koh, H. (1988). The expectation gap between financial analysts and auditors – some empirical evidence. *Singapore Accountant, 4*, 10–13.

Luo, Y., Xu, M., Huang, K., Wang, D., & Fu, S. (2018). Efficient auditing for shared data in the cloud with secure user revocation and computations outsourcing. *Computers & Security, 73*, 492–506. doi:10.1016/j.cose.2017.12.004

Luypaert, M., Van Caneghem, T., & Van Uytbergen, S. (2016). Financial statement siling lags: An empirical analysis among small firms. *International Small Business Journal, 34*(4), 506–531. doi:10.1177/0266242615569324

MacArthur, J. B., Waldrup, B. E., & Fane, G. R. (2004). Caution: Fraud overhead. *Strategic Finance, 86*(4), 28–33.

Madsen, P. (2013). *Commercial loan officers and the audit expectation gap* (Master's thesis). Uppsala Universitet Department of Business Studies.

Magalhães, M., & Dias, A. (2017). Modelo integrado de gestão do risco para o sector público português. Estudo de caso – O município da Maia [Integrated risk management model for the Portuguese public sector. Case study – The municipality of Maia]. Master's work project. Porto: Instituto Superior de Contabilidade e Administração do Politécnico do Porto.

Mahama, M. (2015). Detecting Corporate fraud and financial distress using the Altman and Beneish models the case of Enron Corporation, *International Journal of Economics. Commerce and Management, III*(1), 1–18.

Mahzan, N., & Lymer, A. (2014). Examining the adoption of computer-assisted audit tools and techniques: Cases of generalized audit software use by internal auditors. *Managerial Auditing Journal, 29*(4), 327–349. doi:10.1108/MAJ-05-2013-0877

Malaysia Co-operative Society Commission Act 2007. (2012). Laws of Malaysia. In The M. Commissioner of Law Revision (Ed.), Act 665. Kuala Lumpur: Percetakan Nasional Malaysia Berhad.

Mantone, P. S. (2013). *Using Analytics to Detect Possible Fraud: Tools and Techniques*. John Wiley & Sons Inc. doi:10.1002/9781118715789

Mapurunga, P., Ponte, V., Coelho, A., & Meneses, A. (2011). Determinantes do nível de *disclosure* de instrumentos financeiros derivativos em firmas brasileiras. *Revista Contabilidade e Finanças. USP São Paulo, 22*(57), 263–278.

Margheim, L. L. (1986). Further evidence on external auditors' reliance on internal auditors. *Journal of Accounting Research, 24*(1), 194–205. doi:10.2307/2490813

Marks, N. (2009). *A Look into the future: The next evolution of internal audit*. Retrieved from https://www.iia.nl/SiteFiles/CRCA Final.pdf

Marland, A., Lewis, J. P., & Flanagan, T. (2017). Governance in the age of digital media and branding. *Governance: An International Journal of Policy, Administration and Institutions*, *30*(1), 125–141. doi:10.1111/gove.12194

Marôco, J. (2010). Análise Estatistica com o SPSS Statistics (6th ed.). Pêro Pinheiro. Report Number Análise e Gestão de Informação, Lda.

Marques, R. P., & Santos, C. (2017). Research on continuous auditing: A bibliometric analysis. In *2017 12th Iberian Conference on Information Systems and Technologies (CISTI)* (pp. 1–4). IEEE. 10.23919/CISTI.2017.7976048

Marques, F., & Marçal, N. (2011). *Manual de auditoria e controlo interno no sector público*. Lisboa: Edições Sílabo.

Masoud, N. (2017a). Audit expectation gap among undergraduate accounting at Jordanian Universities. *Journal of Private Equity*, *20*(2), 73–89. doi:10.3905/jpe.2017.20.2.073

Masoud, N. (2017b). An empirical study of audit expectation-performance gap: The case of Libya. *Research in International Business and Finance*, *41*, 1–15. doi:10.1016/j.ribaf.2017.04.012

Massonet, P., Naqvi, S., Ponsard, C., Latanicki, J., Rochwerger, B., & Villari, M. (2011, May). *A monitoring and audit logging architecture for data location compliance in federated cloud infrastructures*. Paper presented at 25th IEEE International Symposium on Parallel and Distributed Processing, IPDPS 2011, Anchorage, AK. 10.1109/IPDPS.2011.304

McAfee, A., & Brynjolfsson, E. (2012). Big data: The Management Revolution. *Harvard Business Review*, *90*(10), 61–67. PMID:23074865

McEnroe, J., & Martens, S. (2001). Auditors' and investors' perceptions of the expectation gap. *Accounting Horizons*, *15*(4), 345–358. doi:10.2308/acch.2001.15.4.345

Medinets, A. F., Gross, J. A., & Brennan, G. (2015). Developing Continuous Assurance at Siemens. *Audit Analytics and Continuous Audit: Looking Toward the Future*, 147–155.

Medinets, A.F., Gross, J.A., Brennan, G. (2015). Case Study A. *Audit Analytics*, 147-156.

Mehri, F., Khakzadi, M., & Shamsi, M. (2016). *A Survey of Third-party Audit for Data Storage Security in Cloud Computing*. Academic Press.

Menon, K., & Williams, J. (1994). The use of audit committees for monitoring. *Journal of Accounting and Public Policy*, *13*(2), 121–139. doi:10.1016/0278-4254(94)90016-7

Merchant, K. A., & White, L. F. (2017). Linking the Ethics and Management Control Literatures. In *Advances in Management Accounting* (pp. 1–29). Emerald Publishing Limited. doi:10.1108/S1474-787120170000028001

Meservy, R. D., Denna, E. L., & Hansen, J. V. (1992). Application of artificial intelligence to accounting, tax, and audit services: Research at Brigham Young University. *Expert Systems with Applications*, *4*(2), 213–218. doi:10.1016/0957-4174(92)90112-6

Meyer, A., & Goes, J. (1988). Organizational Assimilation of Innovations: A multilevel Contextual Analysis. *Academy of Management Journal*, *31*(4), 897–924.

Michaels, M. (2018). The most memorable and expensive financial fraud cases of all time. *Business Insider*. Retrieved August 3, 2018 from https://www.businessinsider.com/fraud-financial-scandals-notable-and-expensive-2018-4#wells-fargo-

Mihret, D. G., & Yismaw, A. W. (2007). Internal audit effectiveness: An Ethiopian public sector case study. *Managerial Auditing Journal, 22*(5), 470–484. doi:10.1108/02686900710750757

Ministry of Finance (2015). *Plano Estratégico de combate à fraude e evasão fiscais*. Gabinete do Secretario de Estado dos Assuntos Fiscais.

Ministry of Finance. (1996). *Relatório da Comissão para o desenvolvimento da reforma fiscal*. Available at: http://purl.sgmf.pt/COL-MF-0028/1/

Ministry of Finance. (2013). *Balanço Social da Autoridade Tributária e Aduaneira*. Direção de Serviços de Gestão de Recursos Humanos.

Mintzberg, H. (1987). The strategy concept II: Another look at why organizations need strategies. *California Management Review, 30*(1), 25–32. doi:10.2307/41165264

Mir Fernández, C., Moreno, D., & Olmeda, I. (2006). *Determinantes de la Revelación de Información sobre derivados financieros en el mercado Español*. Paper presented at the I Jornada de Investigación de la REFC, Madrid.

Mitra, S., Hossain, M., & Deis, D. R. (2007). The empirical relationship between ownership characteristics and audit fees. *Review of Quantitative Finance and Accounting, 28*(3), 257–285. doi:10.100711156-006-0014-7

Mitra, S., Jaggi, B., & Hossain, M. (2013). Internal control weaknesses and accounting conservatism: Evidence from the post-Sarbanes-Oxley period. *Journal of Accounting, Auditing & Finance, 28*(2), 152–191. doi:10.1177/0148558X13479057

Moctezuma, J. (2017). Why the Big 4 are leaders in the audit market? A literature review. *Archives of Business Research, 5*(12), 227–244.

Moffitt, K. C., & Vasarhelyi, M. A. (2013). AIS in an Age of Big Data. *Journal of Information Systems, 27*(2), 1–19. doi:10.2308/isys-10372

Mohamed, Z., Zain, M. M., Subramaniam, N., Fadzilah, W., & Yusoff, W. (2012). Internal Audit Attributes and External Audit ' s Reliance on Internal Audit. *Implications for Audit Fees, 285*, 268–285. doi:10.1111/j.1099-1123.2012.00450.x

Mol, A. P. (2015). China's transition to sustainability. Which direction to take? In Routledge international handbook of sustainable development (pp.351-363). Abingdon, UK: Routledge.

Monroe, G., & Woodliff, D. (1993). The effect of education on the audit expectation gap. *Accounting and Finance, 33*(1), 61–78. doi:10.1111/j.1467-629X.1993.tb00195.x

Monroe, G., & Woodliff, D. (1994). An empirical investigation of the audit expectation gap: Australian evidence. *Accounting and Finance, 34*(1), 47–74. doi:10.1111/j.1467-629X.1994.tb00262.x

Monteiro, S. C. (2012). *Percursos de excelência académica no ensino superior: Estudo em alunos de engenharia em Portugal* [Courses of academic excellence in higher education: Study in engineering students in Portugal] (PhD Thesis). Braga: Escola de Psicologia da Universidade do Minho.

Monterry, J., & Sánchez, A. (2007). Rotación y dependencia económica de los auditores: Sus efectos sobre la calidad del resultado en las compañías cotizadas españolas. *Investigacion Economica, XXXI*(1), 119–159.

Morais, A., & Fialho, A. (2008). Do harmonized accounting standards lead to harmonized accounting practices? An empirical study of IAS 39 measurement requirements in some European Union countries. *Australian Accounting Review, 46*(18), 225–235.

Morais, G., & Martins, I. (2013). *Auditoria Interna: Função e processo*. Lisboa: Áreas Editora.

Morang, S. C. (2017). In Toshiba's scandal, blame samurai code. *Fraud Magazine.* Retrieved from http://www.fraud-magazine.com/article.aspx?id=4294997970

Mosimann, J. E., Dahlberg, J. E., Davidian, N. M., & Krueger, J. W. (2002). Terminal digits and the examination of questioned data. *Accountability in Research, 9*(2), 75–92. doi:10.1080/08989620212969

Mosimann, J. E., Wiseman, C. V., & Edelman, R. E. (1995). Data fabrication: Can people generate random digits? *Accountability in Research, 4*(1), 31–55. doi:10.1080/08989629508573866

Moura, N. J. (2011). Procedimentos de auditoria a adoptar na revisão legal das contas dos municípios: enquadramento teórico e aplicação prática. *Revista Revisores & Auditores, Ordem dos Revisores Oficiais de Contas, 52*, 22-34.

Mukherjee, S. (2016). Can Benford'd Law explain CEO pay? *Corporate Governance, 26*(2), 143–156. doi:10.1111/corg.12195

Mukhlisin, M., & Antonio, M. S. (2018). Meta-analysis on direction of accounting standards for islamic financial institutions: Case studies in United Kingdom and Indonesia. *Al-Iqtishad: Jurnal Ilmu Ekonomi Syariah, 10*(1), 231–254. doi:10.15408/aiq.v10i1.5676

Munro, L., & Stewart, J. (2011). External auditors' reliance on internal auditing: Further evidence. *Managerial Auditing Journal, 26*(6), 461–481. doi:10.1108/02686901111142530

Murmura, F., Liberatore, L., Bravi, L., & Casolani, N. (2018). Evaluation of Italian companies' perception about ISO 14001 and Eco Management and Audit Scheme III: Motivations, benefits and barriers. *Journal of Cleaner Production, 174*, 691–700. doi:10.1016/j.jclepro.2017.10.337

Murphy, M. (2015). Companies drag feet on updating fraud safeguards. *Wall Street Journal.* Retrieved from https://www.wsj.com/articles/companies-drag-feet-on-updating-fraud-safeguards-1425346394

Mwakajumilo, S. L. I. (2011). *The role of informal microfinance institutions in saving mobilization, investment and poverty reduction. A case of savings and credit cooperative societies (SACCOs) in Tanzania from 1961–2008* (PhD thesis). St. Clements University, Turks and Caico. Retrieved from: http://www.academia.edu/3418480/THE_ROLE_OF_INFORMAL_MICROFINANCE_INSTITUTIONS_IN_SAVING_MOBILIZATION_INVESTMENT_AND_POVERTY_REDUCTION._A_CASE_OF_SAVINGS_

N'Guilla Sow, A., Basiruddin, R., Mohammad, J., & Abdul Rasid, S. Z. (2018). Fraud prevention in Malaysian small and medium enterprises (SMEs). *Journal of Financial Crime, 25*(2), 499–517.

NAB arrests five. (2018). *NAB arrests five in cooperative society fraud case.* Retrieved from https://www.dawn.com/news/1420332

Navarro, J., & Martínez, I. (2004). Manipulación contable y calidad del auditor: Un estudio empírico de la realidad española. *Revista Española de Financiación y Contabilidad, 33*(123), 1025–1061.

Neto, P. (2011). Demystifying Cloud Computing. In *Proceeding of Doctoral Symposium on Informatics Engineering* (*Vol. 24*, pp. 16–21). Academic Press. 10.1007/978-1-84996-241-4

Neu, D., Warsame, H., & Pedwell, K. (1998). Managing public impressions: Environmental disclosures in annual reports. *Accounting, Organizations and Society, 23*(3), 265–282. doi:10.1016/S0361-3682(97)00008-1

Nick, E. (2016). *PCI, HIPAA, and SOX – Government Regulatory Compliance, Robin R., Easy Prey: How to Protect Your Business From Data Breach, Cybercrime & Employee Fraud.* Orlando, FL: Technology Press.

Niger warns cooperative societies against fraud. (2017). Retrieved from http://www.thetidenewsonline.com/2017/04/24/niger-warns-cooperative-societies-against-fraud/

Nigrini, J. M. (2011). *Forensic analytics*. John Wiley & Sons. doi:10.1002/9781118386798

Nigrini, M. (1996). A taxpayer compliance analysis of Benford's law. *The Journal of the American Taxation Association, 18*(1), 72–91.

Nigrini, M. (1999a). Adding value with digital analysis. *The Internal Auditor, 56*, 21–23.

Nigrini, M. (1999b, May). I've got your number. *Journal of Accountancy, 187*(5), 79–83.

Nigrini, M. J. (2005). An assessment of the change in the incidence of earnings management around the Enron-Andersen episode. *Review of Accounting and Finance, 4*(1), 92–110. doi:10.1108/eb043420

Nigrini, M., & Mittermaier, L., L. (1997). The use of Benford's Law as an aid in analytical procedures. *Auditing, 16*(2), 52–67.

Nogueira, S. P. S., & Jorge, S. M. F. (2017). The perceived usefulness of financial information for decision making in Portuguese municipalities: The importance of internal control. *Journal of Applied Accounting Research, 18*(1), 116–136. doi:10.1108/JAAR-05-2014-0052

Novie, S. (2013). An empirical analysis of auditor independence and audit fees on audit quality. *International Journal of Management and Business, 3*(3), 82–87.

Nwanyanwu, L. (2017). Audit quality practices and financial reporting in Nigeria. *International Journal of Academic Research in Accounting. Finance and Management Sciences, 7*(2), 145–155.

O'Keefe, T. B., Simunic, D., & Stein, M. T. (1994). The Production of Audit Services: Evidence from a Major Public Accounting Firm. *Journal of Accounting Research, 32*(2), 241–261. doi:10.2307/2491284

O'Keefe, T., King, R., & Gaver, K. (1994). Audit fees, industry specialization, and compliance with GAAS reporting standards. *Auditing, 13*(2), 41–55.

O'Sullivan, N. (2000). The Impact of Board Composition and Ownership on Audit Quality: Evidence From Large Uk Companies. *The British Accounting Review, 32*(4), 397–414. doi:10.1006/bare.2000.0139

Oakland, J., & Tanner, S. (2007). A new framework for managing change: Total Quality Management & business excellence. *Journal of Quality & Reliability Management, 18*(1-2), 1-19.

Ofori, E. (2016). Detecting Corporate Financial Fraud Using Modified Altman Z-Score and Beneish M-Score. The Case of Enron Corporation. *Research Journal of Finance and Accounting, 7*(4), 59–65.

Ogundana, O., Ojeka, S., Ojua, M., & Nwaze, C. (2017). Quality of accounting information and internal audit characteristics in Nigeria. *Journal of Modern Accounting and Auditing, 13*(8), 333–344.

Okafor, C., & Otalor, J. (2013). Narrowing the expectation gap in auditing: The role of the auditing profession. *Research Journal of Finance and Accounting, 4*(2), 43–52.

Oktorina, M., & Wedari, L. K. (2015). An Empirical Investigation on Ownership Characteristics, Activities of the Audit Committee, and Audit Fees in Listed companies on Indonesia Stock Exchange. *Applied Finance and Accounting, 1*(1), 20–29. doi:10.11114/afa.v1i1.639

Oliveira, U. R., Marins, F. A. S., Rocha, H. M., & Salomon, V. A. P. (2017). The ISO 31000 standard in supply chain risk management. *Journal of Cleaner Production, 151*, 616–633. doi:10.1016/j.jclepro.2017.03.054

Olivier, M. S. (2009). On metadata context in Database Forensics. *Digital Investigation, Elsevier*, *5*(3), 115–123. doi:10.1016/j.diin.2008.10.001

Omer, T. C., & Yetman, R. J. (2003). Near zero taxable income reporting by nonprofit organizations. *The Journal of the American Taxation Association*, *25*(2), 19–34. doi:10.2308/jata.2003.25.2.19

Omoteso, K. (2012). The application of artificial intelligence in auditing: Looking back to the future. *Expert Systems with Applications*, *39*(9), 8490–8495. doi:10.1016/j.eswa.2012.01.098

Oral, O., & Çakır, M. (2017). The concept of internet of things (IoT) and creating a sample prototype. *The Journal of Graduate School of Natural and Applied Sciences of Mehmet Akif Ersoy University*, 172-177.

Organisation for Economic Co-operation and Development. (2004). *OECD Principles of Corporate Governance*. Paris: OECD.

Organization of Latin American and Caribbean Supreme Audit Institutions. (2010). *Declaración de Asunción. Principios sobre Rendición de cuentas*. Retrieved from http://www.olacefs.com/declaracion-de-asuncion-principios-sobre-rendicion-de-cuentas

OROC. (2013). *Continuidade: Estudo de um caso*. Newsletter abril/junho.

OROC. (2016). *Estatuto dos Revisores Oficiais de Contas*. Lisboa: Ordem dos Revisores Oficiais de Contas.

Ortiz, J., Benito, J., & Galende, J. (2006). Total quality management as a forerunner of business innovation capability. *Technovation*, *26*(10), 1170–1185. doi:10.1016/j.technovation.2005.09.008

Otalor, J., & Okafor, C. (2013). Imperatives of bridging the audit expectation gap and enhancing the credibility of corporate financial information. *International Journal of Business and Social Research*, *3*(5), 125–138.

Othman, A., Mansor, N., & Kari, F. (2014). Assessing the performance of co-operatives in Malaysia: An analysis of co-operative groups using a data envelopment analysis approach. *Asia Pacific Business Review*, *20*(3), 484–505. doi:10.1080/13602381.2014.933065

Owens-Jackson, L. A., Robinson, D., & Shelton, S. W. (2009). The Association Between Audit Committee Characteristics, the Contracting Process and Fraudulent Financial Reporting. *American Journal of Business*, *24*(1), 57–66. doi:10.1108/19355181200900005

Özdoğan, B. (2017). *The Future of Accounting Profession in an Era of Start-Ups*. Accounting and Corporate Reporting - Today and Tomorrow. doi:10.5772/intechopen.69264

Özsoylu, F. A. (2017). Industry 4.0. *Cukurova University Faculty of Economics and Administrative Sciences*, *1*, 41–64.

Paino, H., Razali, F., & Jabar, F. (2015). The Influence of External Auditor's Working Style, Communication Barriers and Enterprise Risk Management toward Reliance on Internal Auditor's Work. *Procedia Economics and Finance*, *28*(April), 151–155. doi:10.1016/S2212-5671(15)01094-1

Pallant, J. (2005). *SPSS survival manual*. Allen & Unwin.

Palmrose, Z.-V. (1986). Audit Fees and Auditor Size: Further Evidence. *Journal of Accounting Research*, *24*(1), 97–110. doi:10.2307/2490806

Pamuk, N. S., & Soysal, M. (2018). A research on new industrial revolution industry 4.0. *Verimlilik Dergisi*, *1*, 41–66.

Panigrahi, S., Sural, S., & Majumdar, A. K. (2009). *Detection of Intrusive Activity in Databases by Combining Multiple Evidences and Belief Update*. Paper presented at 2009 IEEE Symposium on Computational Intelligence in Cyber Security. 10.1109/CICYBS.2009.4925094

Park, H. M. (2008). *Univariate analysis and normality test using SAS, Stata, and SPSS* (Technical Working Paper). The University Information Technology Services (UITS) Center for Statistical and Mathematical Computing, Indiana University.

Pasquier, T., Singh, J., Powles, J., Eyers, D., Seltzer, M., & Bacon, J. (2017). *Data provenance to audit compliance with privacy policy in the Internet of Things*. Springer Personal and Ubiquitous Computing. Retrieved April 15, 2018, from https://scholar.harvard.edu/files/tfjmp/files/main.pdf

Pathak, J., Chaouch, B., & Sriram, R. S. (2005). Minimizing cost of continuous audit: Counting and time dependent strategies. *Journal of Accounting and Public Policy*, *24*(1), 61–75. doi:10.1016/j.jaccpubpol.2004.12.004

Pazowski, P., & Pastuszak, Z. (2013). Cloud Computing: A Case Study for the New Idea of the IS/IT Implementation. *Management, Knowledge and Learning International Conference 2013*, 855–862. Retrieved from http://www.toknowpress.net/ISBN/978-961-6914-02-4/papers/ML13-332.pdf

Pedrosa, I., & Costa, C. J. (2012b). Financial Auditing and Surveys : how are financial auditors using information technology? An approach using Expert Interviews. In *ISDOC '12 Proceedings of the Workshop on Information Systems and Design of Communication, June 11, 2012, Lisbon, Portugal* (pp. 37–43). Academic Press.

Pedrosa, I., Costa, C. J., & Laureano, R. M. S. (2015). Motivations and limitations on the use of Information Technology on statutory auditors' work: an exploratory study. In CISTI 2015 Proceedings, 2015 (pp. 1132–1137). Aveiro, Portugal: Academic Press.

Pedrosa, I., Laureano, R. M. S., & Costa, C. J. (2015). Motivações dos auditores para o uso das Tecnologias da Informação na sua profissão: aplicação aos Revisores Oficiais de Contas. *Revista Ibérica de Sistemas E Tecologias de Informação, 15*, 101–118.

Pedrosa, I., & Costa, C. J. (2012a). Computer Assisted Audit Tools and Techniques in Real World: CAATT's Applications and Approaches in Context. *International Journal of Computer Information Systems and Industrial Management Applications*, *4*, 161–168.

Pesaran, H., & Shuermann, T. (2006). Macroeconomic dynamics and credit risk: Global perspective. *Journal of Money, Credit and Banking*, *38*(5), 1211–1261. doi:10.1353/mcb.2006.0074

Pestana, M., & Gageiro, J. (2003). *Análise de dados para Ciências Sociais – a complementaridade do SPSS*. Lisboa: Edições Sílabo.

Peters, G., Abbott, L., & Parker, S. (2001). *Voluntary disclosures and auditor specialization: the case of commodity derivative disclosures*. Paper presented at the Western Regional Accounting Association Meeting, San Jose, CA.

Petersn, B. K., & Gibson, T. H. (2003). Student health services: A case of employee fraud. *Journal of Accounting Education*, *21*(1), 61–73. doi:10.1016/S0748-5751(02)00016-7

Petrascu, D., & Tieanu, A. (2014). The Role of Internal Audit in Fraud Prevention and Detection. *Procedia Economics and Finance*, *16*(May), 489–497. doi:10.1016/S2212-5671(14)00829-6

Pettersen, I. J., & Solstad, E. (2007). The role of accounting information in a reforming area: A study of higher education institutions. *Financial Accountability & Management*, *23*(2), 133–154. doi:10.1111/j.1468-0408.2007.00423.x

Pham, N., Duong, H., Pham, T., & Ho, N. (2017). Audit firm size, audit fee, audit reputation and audit quality: The case of listed companies in Vietnam. *Asian Journal of Finance & Accounting*, *9*(1), 429–447. doi:10.5296/ajfa.v9i1.10074

Pierce, B., & Kilcommins, M. (1996). The audit expectation gap: the role of auditing education. *Dublin City University Business School Research Papers,* (13), 1995-1996.

Piot, C. (2001). Agency costs and audit quality: Evidence from France. *European Accounting Review, 10*(3), 461–499. doi:10.1080/713764630

Pizzini, M., Lin, S., & Ziegenfuss, D. E. (2015). The Impact of Internal Audit Function Quality and Contribution on Audit Delay. *Auditing, 34*(1), 25–58. doi:10.2308/ajpt-50848

Power, D. J., Sharda, R., & Burstein, F. (2015). Decision support systems. In *Wiley Encyclopedia of Management* (pp. 1–4). Chichester, UK: John Wiley & Sons, Ltd.

Prawitt, D. F., Sharp, N. Y., & Wood, D. A. (2011). Reconciling Archival and Experimental Research. *Does Internal Audit Contribution Affect the External Audit Fee, 23*(2), 187–206. doi:10.2308/bria-10065

Premuroso, R. F., & Houmes, R. (2012). Financial statement risk assessment following the COSO framework: An instructional case study. *International Journal of Accounting and Information Management, 20*(1), 26–37. doi:10.1108/18347641211201063

Press, G. (2013). $16.1 Billion Big Data Market Predictions From IDC And IIA. *Forbes.*

Protiviti. (2012). *Top priorities for internal audit in technology | Protiviti - Canada.* Retrieved February 26, 2018, from https://www.protiviti.com/CA-en/insights/top-priorities-internal-audit-technology

Protiviti. (2013). *Executive perspectives on top risks for 2013.* Retrieved from https://www.protiviti.com/sites/default/files/united_states/insights/nc-state-protiviti-survey-top-risks-2013.pdf

Protiviti. (2013). *The updated COSO internal control framework. Frequently asked questions* (3rd ed.). Retrieved from https://www.protiviti.com/sites/default/files/united_states/insights/updated-coso-internal-control-framework-faqs-third-edition-protiviti.pdf

Puron-Cid, G., & Rodríguez-Bolívar, M. P. (2018). The effects of contextual factors into different features of financial transparency at the municipal level. *Government Information Quarterly, 35*(1), 135–150. doi:10.1016/j.giq.2017.10.005

PwC. (2012). *A study examining the future of internal auditing and the potential decline of a controls-centric approach.* Retrieved from https://www.pwc.com/sg/en/advisory/assets/publication-internal-audit-2012.pdf

PwC. (2014). *2014 state of the internal audit profession study. Higher performance by design: A blueprint for change.* Retrieved from https://www.iia.nl/SiteFiles/Nieuws/PPPPpwc-state-of-internal-audit-profession-study-2014-03-en.pdf

Quivy, R., & Campenhout, L. V. (2005). *Manual de investigação em ciências sociais* [Manual of research in social sciences] (4th ed.). Lisboa: Gradiva.

Rae, K., & Subramaniam, N. (2008). Quality of internal control procedures: Antecedents and moderating on organizational justice and employee fraud. *Managerial Auditing Journal, 23*(2), 104–124. doi:10.1108/02686900810839820

Rafal, D., Jan, S., & Wojciech, F. (2012). System supporting money laundering detection. *Digital Investigation, Elsevier, 9*(1), 8–21. doi:10.1016/j.diin.2012.04.003

Raghavan, S. (2013). Digital forensic research: Current state of the art. *CSI Transactions on ICT, 1*(1), 91–114. doi:10.100740012-012-0008-7

Rahimi, M. R., Ren, J., Liu, C. H., Vasilakos, A. V., & Venkatasubramanian, N. (2014). Mobile cloud computing: A survey, state of art and future directions. *Mobile Networks and Applications, 19*(2), 133–143. doi:10.100711036-013-0477-4

Raja, J., & Ramakrishnan, M. (2017). Implementing continuous auditing and compression technique in log auditing. In *2016 Eighth International Conference on Advanced Computing (ICoAC)* (pp. 196–200). IEEE. 10.1109/ICoAC.2017.7951769

Rasheed, H. (2014). Data and infrastructure security auditing in cloud computing environments. *International Journal of Information Management*, *34*(3), 364–368. doi:10.1016/j.ijinfomgt.2013.11.002

Raymond, E. S. (1999). *The Cathedral & the Bazaar: Musings on linux and open source by an accidental revolutionary*. O'Reilly Media. doi:10.100712130-999-1026-0

Razaque, A., & Rizvi, S. S. (2017). Privacy preserving model: A new scheme for auditing cloud stakeholders. *Journal of Cloud Computing*, *6*(1), 1–17. doi:10.118613677-017-0076-1

Razek, M. A. (2014). The Association between Internal Auditing Function Quality and External Audit Costs- Evidence from Egypt. *Research Journal of Finance and Accounting*, *5*(20), 104–110.

RBI. (2016). *Master Direction - Know Your Customer (KYC) Direction*. Retrieved on May 29, 2018 from https://rbi.org.in/scripts/NotificationUser.aspx?Mode=0&Id=10292

Reads, C. (2015). *Financial Audit in Cloud Computing: State of the Art Review*. Academic Press.

Rehana, F. (2010). *An empirical study on audit expectation gap: role of auditing education on Bangladesh*. Stamford University Bangladesh.

Reheul, A., Van Caneghem, T., Van den Bogaerd, M., & Verbruggen, S. (2017). Auditor gender, experience and reporting in nonprofit organizations. *Managerial Auditing Journal*, *32*(6), 550–577. doi:10.1108/MAJ-01-2016-1296

Renard, J. (2002). *Teoria si practica auditului intern. Editia a IV-a*. Bucuresti: Ministerul Finantelor Publice.

Ren, Y., Shen, J., Wang, J., Han, J., & Lee, S. (2015). Mutual verifiable provable data auditing in public cloud storage. *Journal of Internet Technology*, *16*(2), 317–323. doi:10.6138/JIT.2015.16.2.20140918

Repenning, N. P., & Sterman, J. D. (2002). Nobody ever gets credit for fixing problems that never happened: Creating and sustaining process improvement. *IEEE Engineering Management Review*, *30*(4), 64. doi:10.1109/EMR.2002.1167285

Reynolds, J., & Francis, J. (2001). Does size matter? The influence of large clients on office-level auditor reporting decisions. *Journal of Accounting and Economics*, *30*(3), 375–400. doi:10.1016/S0165-4101(01)00010-6

Rezaee, Z. (2004). Restoring public trust in the accounting profession by developing anti-fraud education, programs, and auditing. *Managerial Auditing Journal*, *19*(1), 134–148. doi:10.1108/02686900410509857

Rezaee, Z., Elam, R., & Sharbatoghlie, A. (2001). Continuous auditing: The audit of future. *Managerial Auditing Journal*, *16*(3), 150–158. doi:10.1108/02686900110385605

Rezaee, Z., Sharbatoghlie, A., Elam, R., & McMickle, P. L. (2002). Continuous auditing: Building automated auditing capability. *Auditing*, *21*(1), 147–163. doi:10.2308/aud.2002.21.1.147

Rezarta, S., & Muça, E. (2014). An analysis of cloud computing and its role in accounting industry in Albania. *Journal of Information Systems & Operations Management*, 1–12. Retrieved from http://ezproxy.aut.ac.nz/login?url=http://search.proquest.com/docview/1646125309?accountid=8440

Ribeiro, V. P., Aibar-Guzmán, C., Aibar-Guzman, B., & Monteiro, S. M. (2016). Determinants of environmental accounting and reporting practices in Portuguese local entities. *Corporate Communications*, *21*(3), 352–370. doi:10.1108/CCIJ-11-2015-0071

Rijwani, P., & Rajpurohit, P. (2017). Assessment of audit quality: An investigation into proxies. *Asian Journal of Management, 8*(2), 262–266. doi:10.5958/2321-5763.2017.00040.3

Rikhardsson, P., & Dull, R. (2016). An exploratory study of the adoption, application and impacts of continuous auditing technologies in small businesses. *International Journal of Accounting Information Systems, 20*, 26–37. doi:10.1016/j.accinf.2016.01.003

Ríos, A. M., Bastida, F., & Benito, B. (2017). Budget transparency and legislative budgetary oversight: An international approach. *American Review of Public Administration, 46*(5), 546–568. doi:10.1177/0275074014565020

Rios, A. M., Benito, B., & Bastida, F. (2013). Determinants of central government budget disclosure: An international comparative analysis. *Journal of Comparative Policy Analysis, 15*(3), 235–254. doi:10.1080/13876988.2013.798449

Rioux, G. (2012). Board Directors and Corporate Social Responsibility. In S. Boubaker & D. K. Nguyen (Eds.), New York: Palgrave Macmillan.

Rittenberg, L. E., Martens, F., & Landes, C. E. (2007, March). Internal control guidance – not just a small matter. *Journal of Accountancy*, 46–50.

Rocha, J. A. O. (1997). Esboço dum modelo de análise dos municípios. *Cadernos de Estudos Municipais, 8*, 1–25.

Rodríguez Bolívar, M. P., Alcaide Muñoz, L., & López Hernández, A. M. (2013). Determinants of financial transparency in government organizations: A meta-analytic study. *International Public Management Journal, 16*(4), 557–602. doi:10.1080/10967494.2013.849169

Rollins, T., & Bremser, W. (1997). The SEC's enforcement actions against auditors: An auditor reputation and institutional theory perspective. *Critical Perspectives on Accounting, 8*(3), 191–206. doi:10.1006/cpac.1996.0106

Rose, J. (2015). Mapping your career: Competencies necessary for internal audit excellence. *IIA Common Body of Knowledge.* Retrieved August 3, 2018 from http://contentz.mkt5790.com/lp/2842/197389/IIARF%20CBOK%20Mapping%20Your%20Career%20Dec%202015_1.pdf

Roshan, A. H. V., Prashanth, B., & Vineet, K. N. (2017). *Creating Secure Clouds by Continuous Auditing*. Academic Press.

Rus, I. (2015). Technologies and Methods for Auditing Databases. *Procedia Economics and Finance, 26*(15), 991–999. doi:10.1016/S2212-5671(15)00921-1

Saidin, S. Z. (2014). Does reliance on internal auditors ' work reduced the external audit cost and external audit work? *Procedia: Social and Behavioral Sciences, 164*(August), 641–646. doi:10.1016/j.sbspro.2014.11.158

Salazar, D. (2015). *Cloud Security Framework Audit Methods.* The SANS Institute.

Salehi, M. (2016). Quantifying Audit Expectation Gap: A new approach to Measuring Expectation Gap. *Zagreb International Review of Economics & Business, 19*(1), 25–44. doi:10.1515/zireb-2016-0002

Salman, S. (2015). *Auditing the internet of things.* Retrieved April 15, 2018, from https://iaonline.theiia.org/2015/auditing-the-internet-of-things

Sanaei, Z., Abolfazli, S., Gani, A., & Buyya, R. (2013). Heterogeneity in Mobile Cloud Computing:Taxonomy and Open Challenges. *IEEE Communications Surveys and Tutorials*, 1–24. doi:10.1109/SURV.2013.050113.00090

Sánchez, I.-M. G., Frias-Aceituno, J. V., & Garcia-Rubio, R. (2012). Determining Factors of Audit Committee Attributes: Evidence from Spain. *International Journal of Auditing, 16*(2), 184–213. doi:10.1111/j.1099-1123.2012.00451.x

Santos, C., Sousa, P., Ferreira, C., & Tribolet, J. (2008). Conceptual Model for Continuous Organizational Auditing with Real Time Analysis and Modern Control Theory+. *Journal of Emerging Technologies in Accounting*, *5*(1), 37–63. doi:10.2308/jeta.2008.5.1.37

Sarbanes Oxley Act. (2002). Retrieved August 3, 2018 from http://www.soxlaw.com/

Saxena, R., & Dey, S. (2016). Cloud audit: A data integrity verification approach for cloud computing. *Procedia Computer Science*, *89*, 142–151. doi:10.1016/j.procs.2016.06.024

Scheider, A. (2009). The nature, impact and facilitation of external auditor reliance on internal auditing. *Academy of Accounting and Financial Studies Journal*, *13*(4), 40–53.

Schein, E. (1999). *The corporate culture survival guide. Sense and nonsense about culture change* (1st ed.). San Francisco: Jossey-Bass.

Schmidt, P. J., Wood, J. T., & Grabski, S. V. (2016). Business in the Cloud: Research Questions on Governance, Audit, and Assurance. *Journal of Information Systems*, *30*(3), 173–189. doi:10.2308/isys-51494

Schneider, A. (2009). The Nature, Impact and Facilitation of External Auditor Reliance on Internal Auditing. *Academy of Accounting and Financial Studies Journal*, *13*(4), 41–53.

Schwarcz, S. L. (2009). The "principles" paradox. *European Business Organization Law Review*, *10*(02), 175–184. doi:10.1017/S156675290900175X

Searson, E. M., & Johnson, M. A. (2010). Transparency laws and interactive public relations: An analysis of Latin American government web sites. *Public Relations Review*, *36*(2), 120–126. doi:10.1016/j.pubrev.2010.03.003

Securities Exchange Commission. (2013). *The laws that govern the securities industry*. Retrieved August 3, 2018 from https://www.sec.gov/answers/about-lawsshtml.html

Sekaran, U. (2003). *Research Methods for Business*. New York: John Wiley & Sons, Inc.

Sekaran, U., & Bougie, R. (2011). *Research methods for business: A skill-building approach*. New York: John Wiley and Sons, Inc.

Semiz, Y. (2017). *3D yazıcı (printer) nedir? nasıl çalışır? neler yapılabilir?* Retrieved April 15, 2018, from http://maker.robotistan.com/3d-yazici-printer/

Sengupta, P. (1998). Corporate disclosure quality and the cost of debt. *The Accounting Review*, *73*(4), 459–474.

Sentz, K., & Ferson, S. (2002). *Combination of Evidence in Dempster–Shafer Theory*. Sandia National Laboratories. doi:10.2172/800792

Serra, S. (2013). *A relevância do relatório de auditoria para os investidores institucionais, analistas financeiros e analistas de crédito* (Unpublished doctoral dissertation). Universidade do Minho, Braga.

Serrano Cinca, C., Rueda Tomas, M., & Portillo Tarragona, P. (2009). Factors influencing e-disclosure in local public administrations. *Environment and Planning. C, Government & Policy*, *27*(2), 355–378. doi:10.1068/c07116r

Shaikh, J., & Talha, M. (2003). Credibility and expectation gap in reporting on uncertainties. *Managerial Auditing Journal*, *18*(6/7), 517–529. doi:10.1108/02686900310482650

Shanmugam, J.K., Haat, M.H.C., & Ali, A. (n.d.). An exploratory study of internal control and fraud prevention measures in SMEs. *International Journal of Business Research and Management*, *3*(2), 90–99.

Sharbatoghlie, A., Professor, A., Sepehri, M., & Professor, A. (2015). An integrated continuous auditing project management model (CAPM). In *6th International Management Conference* (pp. 1–11). Academic Press.

Shette, R., & Kuntluru, S. (2014). Rounding-up in reported income numbers: Evidence from Indian companies. *Review of Accounting and Finance*, *13*(2), 156–170. doi:10.1108/RAF-04-2013-0042

Shockley, R., & Holt, R. (1983). A behavioral investigation of supplier differentiation in the market for audit services. *Journal of Accounting Research*, *21*(2), 545–564. doi:10.2307/2490790

Shun, T. (2011, May 1). *The great Malaysian cooperative scam.* Retrieved from http://www.freemalaysiatoday.com/category/opinion/2011/11/24/the-great-malaysian-cooperative-scam/

Siemens. (2018). *Endüstri 4.0 yolunda.* Retrieved April 15, 2018, from http://siemens.e-dergi.com/pubs/Endustri40/Endustri40/#p=13

Sikka, P., Filling, S., & Liew, P. (2009). The audit crunch: Reforming auditing. *Managerial Auditing Journal*, *24*(2), 135–155. doi:10.1108/02686900910924554

Simunic, D. A. (1980). The Pricing of Audit Services: Theory and Evidence. *Journal of Accounting Research*, *18*(1), 161. doi:10.2307/2490397

Singh, H., & Newby, R. (2010). Internal audit and audit fees: Further evidence. *Managerial Auditing Journal*, *25*(4), 309–327. doi:10.1108/02686901011034153

Singh, K., Best, P. J., Bojilov, M., & Blunt, C. (2014). Continuous Auditing and Continuous Monitoring in ERP Environments: Case Studies of Application Implementations. *Journal of Information Systems*, *28*(1), 287–310. doi:10.2308/isys-50679

Skousen, C., Guan, L., & Wetzel, T. (2004). Anomalies and unusual patterns in reported earnings: Japanese managers round earnings. *Journal of International Financial Management & Accounting*, *15*(3), 212–234. doi:10.1111/j.1467-646X.2004.00108.x

Sookhak, M., Gani, A., Talebian, H., Akhunzada, A., Khan, S. U., Buyya, R., & Zomaya, A. Y. (2015). Remote Data Auditing in Cloud Computing Environments: A Survey, Taxonomy, and Open Issues. *ACM Computing Surveys*, *47*(4), 65:1--65:34. doi:10.1145/2764465

Sookhak, M., Gani, A., Khan, M. K., & Buyya, R. (2017). Dynamic remote data auditing for securing big data storage in cloud computing. *Information Sciences*, *380*, 101–116. doi:10.1016/j.ins.2015.09.004

Sookhak, M., Talebian, H., Ahmed, E., Gani, A., & Khan, M. K. (2014). A review on remote data auditing in single cloud server: Taxonomy and open issues. *Journal of Network and Computer Applications*, *43*, 121–141. doi:10.1016/j.jnca.2014.04.011

SOX. (n.d.). *Sarbanes Oxley Audit Requirements.* Retrieved on May 29, 2018, from http://www.sarbanes-oxley-101.com/sarbanes-oxley-audits.htm

Spatacean, I. O. (2012). Addressing fraud risk by testing the effectiveness of internal control over financial reporting – case of Romanian financial investment companies. *Procedia Economics and Finance*, *3*, 230–235. doi:10.1016/S2212-5671(12)00145-1

Spathis, T. C. (2002). Detecting false financial statements using published data: Some evidence from Greece. *Managerial Auditing Journal*, *17*(4), 179–191. doi:10.1108/02686900210424321

Spira, L. F., & Page, M. (2003). Risk management: The reinvention of internal control and the changing role of internal audit. *Accounting, Auditing & Accountability Journal, 16*(4), 640–661. doi:10.1108/09513570310492335

Srinivasan, S., & Raja, K. (2014). Dynamic Group Audit Control Mechanism for Cloud Computing Using k-means Inter-Batch Cluster Method Dynamic Group Audit Control Mechanism for Cloud Computing Using k- means Inter-Batch Cluster. *International Journal of Applied Engineering Research, 9*, 16821–16835.

Stamford, C. (2013). *Gartner says the internet of things installed base will grow to 26 billion units by 2020.* Retrieved April 15, 2018, from https://www.gartner.com/newsroom/id/2636073

Sucher, P., Moizer, P., & Zarova, M. (1999). The images of the Big Six audit firms in the Czech Republic. *European Accounting Review, 8*(3), 499–521. doi:10.1080/096381899335916

Sun, T., Alles, M., & Vasarhelyi, M. A. (2015). Adopting continuous auditing : A cross-sectional comparison between China and the United States (Kaynakçasına ileride bakmayı UNUTMA!!!). *Managerial Auditing Journal, 30*(2), 176–204. doi:10.1108/MAJ-08-2014-1080

Suwaidan, M. S., & Qasim, A. (2010). External auditors' reliance on internal auditors and its impact on audit fees: An empirical investigation. *Managerial Auditing Journal, 25*(6), 509–525. doi:10.1108/02686901011054845

Svanberg, J., & Öhman, P. (2016). Does Ethical Culture in Audit Firms Support Auditor Objectivity? *Accounting in Europe, 13*(1), 65–79. doi:10.1080/17449480.2016.1164324

Sweeney, B. (1997). Bridging the expectations gap – on shaky foundations. *Accountancy Ireland, 29*, 18–20.

Taborda, D. (2015). *Auditoria: Revisão legal das contas e outras funções do revisor oficial de contas.* Lisboa: Sílabo.

Tabuena, J. (2016). *Internet of things' role in internal audit & compliance.* Retrieved April 15, 2018, from https://www.complianceweek.com/blogs/jose-tabuena/internet-of-things-role-in-internal-audit-compliance#.WvsGVYiFMdU

Tambingon, H., Yadiati, W., & Kewo, C. (2018). Determinant factors influencing the quality of financial reporting local government in Indonesia. *International Journal of Economics and Financial Issues, 8*(2), 262–268.

Tarjo, N. H. (2015). Application of Beneish M-Score Models and Data Mining to Detect Financial Fraud. *2nd Global Conference on Business and Social Science-2015, GCBSS-2015.* 10.1016/j.sbspro.2015.11.122

Taylor, M., & Carolina, U. S. (2000). The effects of industry specialization on auditors' inherent risk assessments and confidence judgments. *Contemporary Accounting Research, 17*(4), 693–712. doi:10.1506/3LDH-AV52-0F4W-H4BB

The Institute of Internal Auditors. (2017). *International standards for the professional practice of internal auditing (standards).* Retrieved from https://na.theiia.org/standards-guidance/Public Documents/IPPF-Standards-2017.pdf

Thi, N., & Hong, P. (2017). The Determinants of Audit Fees for Companies in Vietnam. *Journal of Economic Development, 19*(2), 68–88.

Thiprungsri, S., & Vasarhelyi, M. (2011). Cluster analysis for anomaly detection in accounting. *The International Journal of Digital Accounting Research, 11*, 69–84.

Thomas, J. (1989). Unusual patterns in reported earnings. *The Accounting Review, 64*(4), 773–787.

Tolbert, C. J., Mossberger, K., & McNeal, R. (2008). Institutions, policy and egovernment in the American states. *Public Administration Review, 68*(3), 549–563. doi:10.1111/j.1540-6210.2008.00890.x

Tornatzky, L. G., Fleischer, M., & Chakrabarti, A. K. (1990). *The processes of technological innovation.* Lexington Books.

Toshiba at a Glance. (2018). Retrieved from https://www.toshiba.co.jp/about/ir/en/overview/index.htm

Trezentos, P., Dicosmo, R., Laurière, S., Morgado, M., Abecasis, J., Mancinelli, F., & Oliveira, A. (2007). New Generation of Linux Meta-installers. In Research Track of FOSDEM (pp. 1–8). Academic Press.

Two charged. (2018). *Two charged with stealing S$5m from Stat Boards co-op*. Retrieved from https://www.todayonline.com/singapore/two-former-co-op-employees-charged-s5m-fraud

Tysiac, K. (2012). Internal control, revisited. *Journal of Accountancy*, *213*(3), 24–29.

Tysiac, K. (2015). Data analytics helps auditors gain deep insight. *Journal of Accountancy*, *219*(4), 52.

Ul Haq, A., & Leghari, M. K. (2015). Determinants of Audit Fee in Pakistan. *Research Journal of Finance and Accounting*, *6*(9), 176–189.

Underwood, M. (2017). Big data complex event processing for internet of things provenance: Benefits for audit, forensics, and safety. In Cyber-Assurance for the Internet of Things (pp. 209-223). John Wiley & Sons, Inc.

Urhoghide, R. O., & Izedonmi, F. O. (2015). An Empirical Investigation of Audit Fee Determinants in Nigeria. *International Journal of Business and Social Research*, *5*(8), 48–58.

US Embassy in Nicaragua. (2018). *Foreign account tax compliance act (FATCA) – April 15th is tax day*. Retrieved August 3, 2018 from https://ni.usembassy.gov/foreign-account-tax-compliance-act-fatca-april-15th-tax-day/

Vafeas, N., & Waegelein, J. F. (2007). The association between audit committees, compensation incentives, and corporate audit fees. *Review of Quantitative Finance and Accounting*, *28*(3), 241–255. doi:10.100711156-006-0012-9

van Hillo, R., & Weigand, H. (2016). Continuous auditing & continuous monitoring: Continuous value? In *2016 IEEE Tenth International Conference on Research Challenges in Information Science (RCIS)* (pp. 1–11). IEEE.

Vardaman, J. M., Gondo, M. B., & Allen, D. G. (2014). Ethical climate and pro-social rule breaking in the workplace. *Human Resource Management Review*, *24*(1), 108–118. doi:10.1016/j.hrmr.2012.05.001

Vasarhelyi, M. A., Halper, F. B., & Ezawa, K. J. (1991). The Continuous Process Audit System: a UNIX-based auditing tool. *EDP Auditor Journal,* 85-91.

Vasarhelyi, M. A., Alles, M., Kuenkaikaew, S., & Littley, J. (2012). The acceptance and adoption of continuous auditing by internal auditors: A micro analysis. *International Journal of Accounting Information Systems*, *13*(3), 267–281. doi:10.1016/j.accinf.2012.06.011

Vasarhelyi, M. A., Kogan, A., & Tuttle, B. M. (2015). Big data in accounting: An overview. *Accounting Horizons*, *29*(2), 381–396. doi:10.2308/acch-51071

Vasarhelyi, M. A., Warren, J. D., Teeter, R. A., & Titera, W. R. (2014). Embracing the Automated Audit. *Journal of Accountancy*, *217*(4), 34–37.

Vasarhelyi, M., Vasarhelyi, M. A., Alles, M. G., & Kogan, A. (2004). Principles of analytic monitoring for continuous assurance. *Journal of Emerging Technologies in Accounting*, *1*(1), 1–21. doi:10.2308/jeta.2004.1.1.1

Verbruggen, S., & Christiaens, J. (2012). Do non-profit organizations manage earnings toward zero profit and does governmental financing play a role? *Canadian Journal of Administrative Sciences*, *29*(3), 205–217. doi:10.1002/cjas.1219

Vinnari, E., & Skærbæk, P. (2014). The uncertainties of risk management. *Accounting, Auditing & Accountability Journal*, *27*(3), 489–526. doi:10.1108/AAAJ-09-2012-1106

Wæraas, A. (2010). Communicating identity. the use of core value statements in regulative institutions. *Administration & Society*, *42*(5), 526–549. doi:10.1177/0095399710377435

Walker, P. L., & Casterella, J. R. (2000). The Role of Auditee Profitability in Pricing New Audit Engagements. *Auditing, 19*(1), 157–167. doi:10.2308/aud.2000.19.1.157

Wallace, W. (2002). Assessing the quality of data used for benchmarking and decision-making. *Journal of Government Financial Management, 51*(3), 16–22.

Wang, T., & Cuthbertson, R. (2015). Eight Issues on Audit Data Analytics We Would Like Researched. *Journal of Information Systems, 29*(1), 155–162. doi:10.2308/isys-50955

Wang, Y., & Kleiner, B. H. (2005). Defining employee dishonesty. *Management Research News, 28*(2/3), 11–22. doi:10.1108/01409170510785057

Warren, J. D. Jr, Moffitt, K. C., & Byrnes, P. (2015). How big data will change accounting. *Accounting Horizons, 29*(2), 397–407. doi:10.2308/acch-51069

Warshavsky, M. (2012). Analyzing Earnings Quality as a Financial Forensic Tool. *Financial Valuation and Litigation Expert Journal, 39*, 16–20.

Watts, R., & Zimmerman, J. (1978). Towards a positive theory of the determination of accounting standards. *The Accounting Review, 53*(1), 112–134.

Webster, J., & Watson, R. T. (2002). Analyzing the past to prepare for the future: Writing a literature review. *Management Information Systems Quarterly, 26*(2).

Wei, Z., & Yang, W. (2017). Research on building of cloud accounting financial sharing management model based on analysis in the era of big data. *Revista de la Facultad de Ingeniería, 32*(14), 34–40.

Whitehouse, T. (2014). Auditing in the era of big data. *Compliance Week.* Retrieved April 15, 2018, from http://www.acl.com/pdfs/CW_AuditingintheEraofBigData.pdf

Whittington, A., & Winters, J. (1990). Considering the Work of an Internal Auditor. *The CPA Journal, 60*(4), 28–34.

Williams, P. (2017). Accounting scandals are back in the big time. *ACCA Global.* Available at https://www.accaglobal.com/an/en/member/member/accounting-business/2017/03/in-focus/accounting-scandals.html

Wilson, A. C., & Key, K. G. (2012). Enron: A Case of Deception and Unethical Behavior. *Feature Edition, 1*, 88–97.

Wolf, F., Tackett, J., & Claypool, G. (1999). Audit disaster futures: Antidotes for the expectation gap? *Managerial Auditing Journal, 14*(9), 468–478. doi:10.1108/02686909910301556

Wood, D. A. (2004). *Increasing Value Through Internal and External Auditor Coordination.* The Institute of Internal Auditors Research Foundation.

Wyslocka, E., & Jelonek, D. (2015). *Accounting in the Cloud Computing.* Academic Press.

Xia, M., Gong, L., Lyu, Y., Qi, Z., & Liu, X. (2015). Effective real-time android application auditing. *Proceedings - IEEE Symposium on Security and Privacy,* 899–914. 10.1109/SP.2015.60

Xie, B., Davidson, W. N. III, & DaDalt, P. J. (2003). Earnings management and corporate governance: The role of the board and the audit committee. *Journal of Corporate Finance, 9*(3), 295–316. doi:10.1016/S0929-1199(02)00006-8

Yang, K., & Jia, X. (2012). Data storage auditing service in cloud computing: Challenges, methods and opportunities. *World Wide Web (Bussum), 15*(4), 409–428. doi:10.100711280-011-0138-0

Yang, K., & Jia, X. (2014). An Efficient and Secure Dynamic Auditing Protocol for Data Storage in Cloud Computing. *IEEE Transactions on Parallel and Distributed Systems, I*(9), 2–5. doi:10.1109/ICS.2016.137

Yatim, P., Kent, P., & Clarkson, P. (2006). Governance structures, ethnicity, and audit fees of Malaysian listed firms. *Managerial Auditing Journal, 21*(7), 757–782. doi:10.1108/02686900610680530

Yazıcı, E., & Düzkaya, H. (2016). Endüstri devriminde dördüncü dalga ve eğitim: Türkiye dördüncü dalga endüstri devrimine hazır mı? *Journal of Education and Humanities: Theory and Practice*, 7(13), 49–88.

Yong, H., Chalmers, K., & Faff, R. (2005). Asia Pacific banks' derivative and risk management disclosures. *Asian Review of Accounting, 13*(1), 15–44. doi:10.1108/eb060781

Yoon, K., Hoogduin, L., & Zhang, L. (2015). Big data as complementary audit evidence. *Accounting Horizons, 29*(2), 431–438. doi:10.2308/acch-51076

Zahirul, H. (2003). Total Quality Management and the balanced scorecard approach: A critical analysis of their potential relationships and directions for research. *Critical Perspectives on Accounting, 14*(5), 553–566. doi:10.1016/S1045-2354(02)00160-0

Zahmatkesh, S. & Rezazadeh, J. (2017). The effect of auditor features on audit quality. *TÉKHNE - Review of Applied Management Studies, 15*(2), 79-87.

Zain, M. M., Zaman, M., & Mohamed, Z. (2015). The Effect of Internal Audit Function Quality and Internal Audit Contribution to External Audit on Audit Fees. *The International Journal of Accounting, 19*(3), 134–147. doi:10.1111/ijau.12043

Zaman, M., Hudaib, M., & Haniffa, R. (2011). Corporate Governance Quality, Audit Fees and Non-Audit Services Fees. *Journal of Business Finance & Accounting, 38*(1-2), 165–197. doi:10.1111/j.1468-5957.2010.02224.x

Zarefar, A., & Zarefar, A. (2016). The influence of ethics, experience, and competency toward the quality of auditing with professional auditor skepticism as a moderating variable. *Procedia: Social and Behavioral Sciences, 219*, 828–832. doi:10.1016/j.sbspro.2016.05.074

Zgela, M., & Dobsä, J. (2011). Analysis of Top 500 Central and East European Companies Net Income Using Benford's Law. *Journal of Information and Organizational Sciences, 35*(2), 214–228.

Zhang, J., Yang, X., & Appelbaum, D. (2015). Toward effective big data analysis in continuous auditing. *Accounting Horizons, 29*(2), 469–476. doi:10.2308/acch-51070

Zheng, H. (2006). Interaction of credit and liquidity risks: Modeling and valuation. *Journal of Banking & Finance, 30*(2), 391–407. doi:10.1016/j.jbankfin.2005.04.026

Zuiderwijk, A., Janssen, M., Zhang, J., Puron-Cid, G., & GilGarcia, J. R. (2015). Towards decision support for disclosing data: Closed or open data? *Information Polity, 20*(2-3), 103–117.

About the Contributors

Rui Pedro Marques received the PhD degree in Computer Science in 2014 from the universities of Minho, Aveiro and Porto, three of the top universities in the north of Portugal. In 2008 he concluded his Masters degree in Electronics and Telecommunications Engineering, at the University of Aveiro, and in 2005 he graduated in the same area, also from the University of Aveiro. His main research interests are related to the integration of Information Systems into organizational topics, contributing with solutions to improve the risk management and the organizational efficiency. He is Professor of Information Systems and Technology since 2007 at the Higher Institute of Accounting and Administration, University of Aveiro, Portugal.

Carlos Santos completed his first degree in Electrical Engineering ate the University of Coimbra he got his masters degree in Electrical Engineering Sciences and he holds a PhD in Information Systems and Computer Engineering from the Instituto Superior Técnico (Technical University of Lisbon). Currently he teaches Computer Sciences within the area of scientific computing at Higher Institute for Accountancy and Administration of Aveiro (Aveiro University) and he is interested in researching information systems auditing, accounting information systems and XBRL language. He is a member of the Center of Research in Accounting and Taxation (CICF).

Helena Inacio has a PhD in Accounting and Management from the University Autonoma the Madrid, a MSc in Economy by the University of Coimbra and a degree in Accounting and Audit by the University of Aveiro. She teaches since 1988 Accounting and Auditing at Higher Institute for Accountancy and Administration of Aveiro University. She has a book of Internal Control, communications and publications in audit area. She is a member of the research unit on Competitiveness, Governance and Public Policies (GOVCOPP).

* * *

Dattatraya Adane did his M.Tech in Computer Science and Engineering from IIT Guwahati and PhD in Computer Science and Engineering from Visvesvaraya National Institute of Technology, Nagpur, India. He is working as professor in Information Technology department, Shri Ramdeobaba College of Engineering, Nagpur. He has over 24 years of experience in teaching and research. His research areas are Distributed and Mobile Computing, Mobile Agents, Wireless Sensor Networks and Network Security. He is Life Member of ISTE and Member of Institution of Engineers India (MIE).

Laura Alcaide-Muñoz is Associate Professor in Accounting and Finance in the Department of Financial Economy and Accounting at the University of Granada. She is interested in new technologies and internet favour the evolution and improvement the citizens' quality of life in Smart Cities. Also, she is interested in financial sustainability in local governments. She has been author of articles published in Administration & Society, International Journal of Information Management, International Public Management Journal, American Review of Public Administration, Information Technology for Development, Local Government Studies, Government Information Quarterly, Internet Research, among others, and has written book chapters in prestigious editorials like IGI Global, Palgrave Macmillan, Springer and Routledge-Taylor & Francis.

Rashid Ameer holds the position of Assistant Dean of the postgraduate programmes and responsible for a range of administrative services to the Faculty of International Studies at IPU New Zealand. Dr. Ameer is highly regarded for his research expertise in corporate finance, corporate governance, corporate social responsibility, and sustainability. His research in these areas has been published in the leading international journals such as the Journal of Business Ethics, Journal of Multinational Management, Managerial Finance, Asian Economic Journal, and Journal of Asian Economics. He received from the Emerald publishing the outstanding reviewer award in 2016 and the highly commended award for two papers published in 2013.

Lale Aslan was born in Istanbul on January 22nd, 1983. She graduated from Private Kalamis High School in 2000 with a degree of 5th, where she earned a 50% scholarship. She graduated from Environmental Engineering of Faculty of Engineering of the University of Istanbul in 2004. She completed the MBA program at Yildiz Technical University in 2007. She worked in finance sector between 2006 - 2016 as auditor and head of compliance in top international companies such as KPMG, Credit Agricole Cheuvreux and Yapi Kredi (Unicredit affiliate). She completed her Ph.D. degree in Accounting and Finance from Yeditepe University in January 2014 as the top of the class, while she was working in the finance sector. She has been teaching accounting, finance and other relevant business courses in Turkish-German University and Istanbul Yeni Yuzyil University since. She has Level 3 and Derivates Licenses of Capital Markets Board of Turkey and CRMA (Certificate of Risk Management) of the IIA (Institute of Internal Auditors). Her academic work focuses on intermediary institutions and financial markets. She is a member of fo-der (an NGO on promoting financial literacy) and enjoys yoga and pilates workouts.

Alp Aytaç was born in İzmir on 1 May 1989. He finished his bachelor and Master's degree in business administration from Uludağ University in Turkey. He has been working as a Research Assistant at Uludağ University since 2013. His work of field is Auditing, Internal Control, Financial Auditing, and Continuous Auditing.

Amidel Barros is a student of the Master's Degree in Auditing from the School of Management of the Polytechnic Institute of Cávado and Ave.

Adem Çabuk is a professor at Uludağ University on Accounting and Finance Division. He finished his bachelor and Ph.D. degree at İstanbul University Faculty of Economics. He has many publications on Accounting, Auditing and Budgeting.

Ángel Carrasco-Núñez is a System Administrator in Audit Office of Andalusia, Spain. He has an extensive professional experience in cybersecurity, networks and open systems. His interests are focused on IT audit, cybersecurity and, specially, security management. He has published in journals such as, Public Administration, Linux Actual and Mundo Linux. He has lectured on IT audit and security in forums such as EURORAI and Spanish audit congresses. He collaborates with ASOCEX that develops IAS application guides.

Hugo Cipriano is a student who is currently finishing his master's degree in Computer Science focused on Information Systems and working on his master thesis in the Continuous Auditing area. He currently works in Internal Audit. Started using computers early in his youth playing online videogames competitively which helped developing rational, logical, fast and critical thinking; teamwork capabilities; leadership; pressure handling and problem-solving skills. Hungry for knowledge, fast learner, problem solver and eager for challenges is what best defines him. Recently he has been delving into Data Science and Machine Learning.

Tânia Correia was born in 1989, in the town of Óbidos in the district of Leiria. Graduated in Accounting and Finance from the School of Technology and Management of Leiria (ESTG), where she established her interest on the area of Auditing. Tânia has a Master in Business and Public Auditing at the Coimbra Business School - Institute of Accounting and Administration of Coimbra (ISCAC). She currently works in accounting. Her first article "Open Source Software in Audit" was published in 2018 at The 13th Iberian Conference on Information Systems and Technologies (CISTI 2018).

Carlos Costa is Associate Professor at ISEG (Lisbon School of Econonics and Management), University of Lisbon. He is researcher at Advance and associate researcher at ISTAR-IUL. Previously he was in the School of Technology and Architecture of ISCTE-IUL. He was director of Adetti-IUL research center (2013-2014). He also taught in the Portuguese Catholic University and Portuguese Open University. He worked in a IT consulting firm and an Investment Bank. He is member of the board of EuroSIGDOC/ACM chapter and director of Project Management Pos-Graduation Program. He holds a Ph.D. in Information Science and Technology (Information Systems and Data Bases) from ISCTE, a MSc in Corporate Strategy also from ISCTE and a Bachelor degree (Licenciatura) from UCP (Lisbon), 1990. Research topics: web engeneering, web development, open source software, gamification.

Jesús Flórez-Parra holds a PhD in Economics and Business Sciences at the University of Granada. Teacher Special Associate of the Faculty of Economic and Administrative Sciences of the ECCI University. Researcher of corporate governance in the public sector and systems of financial information for management, administration and control of public and private organizations. He has published in journals such as Higher Education Research and Development, Journal International Review of Administrative Sciences, Journal of Education and Innovar Journal.

Patrícia Gomes is Professor at the Management School of the Polytechnic Institute of Cávado and Ave (IPCA). She holds a PhD in Accounting and is member of the Center for Research in Accounting and Taxation of IPCA. Her research interests are in the area of Public Sector Accounting, Management Accounting, Control management in public sector and Public Sector Performance. She is responsible for several scientific projects and projects applied in the community with external funding. She coordinated of the disciplinary area of Public Accounting in the Department of Accounting and Taxation. She is editor-in chief of the scientific journal Tékhne - Review of Applied Management Studies.

Harmeet Khanuja is currently a Researcher in the area of Database Forensics. She is working as Assistant Professor in the Department of Computer Engineering at Marathwada Mitra Mandal's College of Engineering. Pune, India. She is a life member of ISTE. She has presented and published papers in several International Conferences and Journals. Her areas of interest are Information security Applications, Digital Forensics and Mobile Computing.

Fawzi Laswad is Professor of Accounting and Head of School of Accountancy at Massey University, New Zealand, a FCA and a FCPA.

Kátia Lemos holds a PhD in Accounting by Santiago de Compostela University. The line of research is the financial accounting. Professor at the High School of Management, IPCA where teaches curricular units of Financial Accounting. Director the Department of Accounting and Taxation. Member of the Center for Research in Accounting and Taxation of IPCA.

Antonio López-Hernández is a Professor of Financial Economics and Accounting at the University of Granada. He teaches public sector management and control. His research focuses on E-Government, Corporate Social Responsibility, Management, Information and Control Systems of organizations. He has published in journals such as, Public Administration, International Public Management Journal, Government Information Quarterly, International Review of Administrative Science, American Review of Public Administration, Administration & Society, Urban Studies and Information Technology for Development.

Madalena Magalhaes has a Master Degree in Audit Working in the Municipality of Maia in Quality Management and Risk Management.

Norfaizah Manjah received her Bachelor Degree from the University Malaysia Sabah, Kota Kinabalu, Sabah dan Master Degree from University Teknologi MARA, Shah Alam, Selangor. She is currently holding the position as a Senior Assistant Director for SKM Academy, Malaysian Co-operative Societies Commission (MCSC) since joining the department in 2008. Her prior position was as an Assistant Director in MCSC training centre in Sabah. Her responsibilities include administration, human resources and facilities management. She has also been assigned to teach basic accounting to the co-operative members in Sabah and Sarawak.

Antonio Minguillón-Roy is an Auditor at the Audit Office of the Autonomous Community of Valencia, since 2008 Director of the Technical Department, with responsibilities in general planning, development of methodology and in the area of information systems audit. Coordinator of the Technical Committee of organs of external Control (OCEX). He has published in journals such as, Revista de Auditoría Pública and Revista Española de Control Externo.

Miguel Mira da Silva obtained the BSc and MSc degrees in Electrical Engineering at the Instituto Superior Técnico in Lisbon, a PhD in Computing Science from the University of Glasgow in Scotland, and a MSc degree in management titled "Sloan Fellowship" from the London Business School. He is currently Associate Professor of Information Systems at Instituto Superior Técnico, leader of the research group "Digital Transformation" at INOV, coordinator of the MISE online MSc degree, and consultant to several private companies and public institutes including the Ministry of Finance. During the almost 30 years of professional activity as a consultant, researcher, and professor, he created five companies, published four books and 165 articles in scientific journals and conferences, managed dozens of research and consulting projects, graduated 5 PhDs and 128 MSc students, and created a MOOC about digital transformation. His current interests include digital transformation, IT governance, and online learning.

David Ortiz-Rodríguez is Associate Professor in Accounting and Finance in the Department of Financial Economy and Accounting at the University of Granada. He teaches Public Sector Management and control. His research interests are focused on Public Government Management, mainly in matters such as Information and Control Systems of organizations, Public Social Responsability or e-government. He has published in journals such as Public Management Review, Journal of Cleaner Production, Government Information Quarterly, International Review of Administrative Sciences, International Public Management Journal, Administration & Society or Public Administration and Development, among other.

Radiah Othman is currently a Senior Lecturer with Massey University, New Zealand. Her Masters in Accountancy (with distinction) is from Curtin University of Technology (Australia), and PhD from Aston University (UK). She is an active researcher and has published papers in the area of public sector auditing, public sector information system, not-for-profit accounting and accountability in reputable journals such as Journal of Business Ethics, International Journal of Public Sector Management, International Journal of Public Information System, Accountancy, Business and Public Interest, International Journal of Voluntary and Non-profit Organisations. She received a Special Award for Corporate Social Responsibility (CSR) at the Malaysian Outstanding Research Paper Awards (2011), Pearson Best Author Award (2013) and Highly Commended Award Winner at the Literari Network Awards for Excellence from Emerald (2013).

Mahmut Sami Ozturk graduated from Business Administration in English Language of Istanbul University School of Business. Also as part of double major undergraduate program; he graduated from Industrial Engineering of Istanbul University Faculty of Engineering. He got his masters degree and PhD in Business Administration Department in Suleyman Demirel University. He is working as Assistant Professor in Suleyman Demirel University. He works on accounting and auditing in his academic studies.

Isabel Pedrosa has a Ph.D. degree in Information Science and Technology from the ISCTE- Instituto Universitário de Lisboa (2015). She is CIDA, Certified IDEA Data Analyst (2017). Works as Adjunct Professor at Coimbra Business School (since 2015). Previously, she was a lecturer at Coimbra Business School (2000-2015) and at College of Education (1998-2000) both at the Polytechnic Institute of Coimbra, Portugal. Isabel has a degree in Informatics Engineering (1994), a masters' degree in Systems and Informatics (2006), both from the University of Coimbra. Her main research interests are computer-assisted audit tools and techniques, business intelligence and data analytics in fraud detection. She has authored or co-authored more than 40 papers. She has been a session chair and Programme Committee member in several conferences. Isabel is Vice-Coordinator of Coimbra Business School Advanced Programmes (2010-2013 and since 2016) and was Vice-Coordinator of the International Relations Office (2015-2018). Isabel is Academic Advocate Program Member of ISACA (since 2013) as a "Silver Member" and senior member of Ordem dos Engenheiros - Computer Science College (since 2009).

Ruben Pereira is an Assistant Professor at ISCTE. He has a PhD in Information Systems at Instituto Superior Técnico where he also graduated as a Master in Computer Engineering and Computer Science. He has been a consultant in several industries, such as: services, banking, telecommunications, Ecommerce, among others. He is the author of several scientific papers in the area of Information Technology Services Management and Information Technology Governance, covering the most adopted IT Frameworks like ITIL and COBIT. Its areas of scientific interest extend to: Information Technology Risk Management, Business Process Management, continuous improvement and innovation, process optimization, among others.

Rui Robalo holds a PhD in Business Sciences by Faculty of Economics, University of Porto (Portugal). He is Associate Professor of the School of Management and Technology of the Polytechnic Institute of Santarém (Portugal). His teaching covers various accounting topics, in different cycles of studies. He has published research in relevant accounting journals and books.

Sara Serra holds a PhD in Accounting with doctoral thesis about audit reports. The line of research is the financial auditing. Professor at the High School of Management, IPCA where teaches curricular units of Auditing. Director of the Master's degree in Auditing and coordinator of the disciplinary area of Auditing in the Department of Accounting and Taxation. Member of the Center for Research in Accounting and Taxation of IPCA.

Sérgio Silva holds a master's degree in Accounting and Finance by School of Management of the Polytechnic Institute of Santarém (Portugal). Since 1996, he has been a Tax Inspector in the Finance Department of Faro, a member of the Tax and Customs Authority, under the supervision of the Portuguese Ministry of Finance. In his functions, he performs inspection, auditing, prevention, verification and tax verification procedures for all types of taxpayers, within the framework of taxes that are part of the Portuguese tax system.

Elisabete Vieira is Coordinator Professor, ISCA-UA, University of Aveiro. She is researcher at the Research Unit on Governance, Competitiveness and Public Policies (GOVCOPP), being Vice Coordinator of the Competitiveness, Innovation and Sustainability (CIS) Research Group. She has a Ph.D. in Finance from the ISCTE, Lisbon. Her research topics include corporate finance, corporate behavior finance, and corporate governance.

Haslinda Yusoff received her PhD from the University of South Australia, Adelaide, Australia and her Masters in Accountancy (with distinction) from Curtin University of Technology, Australia. She is currently an Associate Professor at the Faculty of Accountancy, Universiti Teknologi MARA (UiTM), Malaysia as well as the Head of Academic Operation Management at the Academic Affairs Division of the University. Active in research, she the responsibility as the Deputy Head of the Asia-Pacific Center for Sustainability (APCeS), a joint project initiated by the Accounting Research Institute (ARI), Faculty of Accountancy, UiTM with ACCA Malaysia. Her research interests are in areas relating to CSR reporting, corporate governance and sustainability management and practice. She has published research papers in scientific and high impact journals both nationally and internationally, which include Business Strategy and the Environment Journal, International Journal of Green Economics, International Journal of Business Governance and Ethics, Research in International Business and Finance, Journal of Applied Business Research, Journal of Sustainability Science and Management, Asian Review of Accounting, International Journal of Business and Globalisation and others.

Index

A

B

C

D

E

F

G

H

I

L

M

O

P

Q

R

www.ingramcontent.com/pod-product-compliance
Lightning Source LLC
LaVergne TN
LVHW062114300926
849161LV00010B/2459
* 9 7 8 1 5 2 2 5 7 3 5 6 2 *